# OPERATIONS STRATEGY

# OPERATIONS STRATEGY

## Fourth Edition

**Nigel Slack**

**Michael Lewis**

**PEARSON**

Harlow, England • London • New York • Boston • San Francisco • Toronto • Sydney
Auckland • Singapore • Hong Kong • Tokyo • Seoul • Taipei • New Delhi
Cape Town • São Paulo • Mexico City • Madrid • Amsterdam • Munich • Paris • Milan

**Pearson Education Limited**
Edinburgh Gate
Harlow CM20 2JE
United Kingdom
Tel: +44 (0)1279 623623
Web: www.pearson.com/uk

First published 2002 (print)
Second edition published 2008 (print)
Third edition published 2011 (print and electronic)
This edition published 2015 (print and electronic)

ISBN: 978-1-292-01779-2 (print)
     978-1-292-01782-2 (PDF)
     978-1-292-01780-8 (eText)

**British Library Cataloguing-in-Publication Data**
A catalogue record for the print edition is available from the British Library

**Library of Congress Cataloging-in-Publication Data**
Slack, Nigel.
  Operations strategy / Nigel Slack, Michael Lewis. – Fourth edition.
    pages cm
  Includes bibliographical references and index.
  ISBN 978-1-292-01779-2 (paperback) – ISBN 978-1-292-01782-2 (PDF – ISBN 978-1-292-01780-8 (eText)
  1. Production management. I. Lewis, Michael, 1969- II. Title.
  TS155.S563 2015
  658.5–dc23
                   2014036012

ARP impression 98

Print edition typeset in 9.5/12 and Stone Serif ITC Pro by 73
Printed by Ashford Colour Press Ltd

NOTE THAT ANY PAGE CROSS REFERENCES REFER TO THE PRINT EDITION

# Brief Contents

# Contents

## Supporting resources

Visit **www.pearsoned.co.uk/slack** to find valuable online resources

**For instructors**
- Complete downloadable Instructor's Manual
- PowerPoint slides that can be downloaded and used for presentations

For more information please contact your local Pearson Education sales representative or visit **www.pearsoned.co.uk/slack**

# List of figures, tables and exhibits from case studies

## Tables

## Exhibits from case studies

# Preface

Operations strategy is a major source of competitive advantage in for-profit businesses and the route to achieving social welfare in not-for-profit enterprises. No matter what sector, it can have a huge impact – not just in the short term, but also on an enduring basis. Just look at those companies that have transformed their prospects through the way they manage their operations resources strategically: Amazon, Apple, Dyson, Holcim, IKEA, Intel, Rolls Royce, Singapore Airlines, Tesco, ARM, Toyota, Wipro, Zara and many more, all have developed their strategic operations capabilities to the point where they represent a formidable asset. (And all are amongst the many examples to be found in this book.) These firms have found that it is the way they manage their operations, and their resources in general, that sets them apart from, and above, their competitors.

The dilemma is that when we talk about 'operations', we must include the majority of the firm's resources, because contributing to creating the firm's services and products is such an all-consuming task. And when something is all around us, like operations resources are, it can be difficult to see them in their entirety. This is the paradox of operations strategy. It lies at the heart of how organisations manage their strategic intent in practice and is vitally important for long-term success. Yet it is also so all-embracing that it becomes easy to underestimate the significance of the subject.

If you doubt the importance of the subject, the following are just some of the decisions with which operations strategy is concerned.

- How should the organisation satisfy the requirements of its customers?
- How should each function within the organisation satisfy the requirements of its *internal* customers?
- What intrinsic capabilities should the organisation try and develop as the foundation for its long-term success?
- How specialised should the organisation's activities become?
- Should the organisation sacrifice some of its objectives in order to excel at others?
- How big should the organisation be?
- Where should the organisation locate its resources?
- When should it expand or contract, and by how much?
- What should it do itself and what should it contract out to other businesses?
- How should it develop relationships with other organisations?
- What type of technology should it invest in?
- How should it organise the way it develops new products and services?
- How should it bind together its resources into an organisational structure?
- How should the organisation's resources and processes be improved and developed over time?
- What guiding principles should shape the way any organisation formulates its operations strategies?

All these questions are not merely important – they are fundamental. No organisation, whether large or small, for-profit or not-for-profit, in the services or manufacturing sector, international or local, can ignore such questions. Operations strategy is central, ubiquitous and vital to any organisation's sustained success.

## New to this edition

The success of the previous three editions was helped by the many suggestions we received from fellow teachers and students of operations strategy. They have been kind enough to provide further feedback that has informed the changes we have made for the fourth edition. These changes include the following:

- An approach that highlights some of the developments in operations strategy, especially how its concepts are having wider application.
- Many new and updated examples, which cover the topical issues in operations strategy. Two thirds of the examples used are new or updated for this edition.
- The inclusion of some new material relating to such issues as the links between operations management and strategy, triadic supply relationships, knowledge management and organisational ambidexterity.
- Introducing some new longer cases, but retaining those that proved popular from the previous edition. These cases can still be used to form the basis of a whole course in operations strategy.

## The aim of this book

The aim of this book is to provide a treatment of operations strategy that is clear, well-structured and interesting. It seeks to apply some of the ideas of operations strategy to a variety of businesses and organisations. The text provides a logical path through the key activities and decisions of operations strategy, as well as covering the broad principles that underpin the subject and the way in which operations strategies are put together in practice.

More specifically, the text aims to be:

- Balanced in its treatment of the subject. In addition to taking the orthodox 'market-led' approach to operations strategy, the book also provides an alternative but complementary 'resource-based' perspective.
- Conceptual in the way it treats the decisions, activities and processes that together form an organisation's operations strategy. Although some examples are quantified, the overall treatment in the book is managerial and practical.
- Comprehensive in its coverage of the more important ideas and issues, which are relevant to most types of business. In any book covering such a broad area as operations strategy, one cannot cover everything. However, we believe that the more important issues are all addressed.
- Grounded in the various bodies of knowledge that underpin operations strategy. Theory is included in most chapters, which introduces concepts and principles, often from other academic disciplines, and which illuminates the particular operations strategy issue being discussed.

- International in the examples it uses to describe practical operations strategy issues.

## Who should use this book?

This book is intended to provide a broad introduction to operations strategy for all students who wish to understand the strategic importance and scope of the operations function. For example:

- MBA students, who should find that it both links and integrates their experience and study of operations management with their core studies in business strategy.
- Higher-level undergraduates studying business or technical subjects, although we assume a prior knowledge of the basics of operations management.
- Postgraduate students on other specialised Masters degrees, who should find that it provides them with a well-grounded approach to the subject.
- Executives, who will also be able to relate the practical and pragmatic structure of the book to the more conceptual and theoretical issues discussed within the structure.

## Distinctive features

### Clear structure

The book employs coherent models of the subject that run through each part of the text and explain how the chapters fit into the overall subject. Key questions set the scene at the beginning of each chapter and also provide a structure for the summary at the end of each chapter.

### Illustration-based

The study of operations, even at a strategic level, is essentially a practical subject and cannot be taught in a purely theoretical manner. Because of this we have used both abstracted examples and 'boxed' examples, which explain some issues faced by real operations.

### Theory

Operations strategy is a practical subject that is driven by theoretical ideas. Most chapters contain one or more theories that explain the underpinning ideas that have contributed to our understanding of the issues being discussed.

### Case studies

The book includes a number of case studies suitable for class discussion. The cases are long enough to provide depth and serve as illustrations, which can be used to supplement class sessions.

## Selected further reading

Every chapter ends with a list of further reading, which takes the topic covered in the chapter further or treats some important related issues.

## Website

A website is available that helps students to develop a firm understanding of each issue covered in the book and provides lecturers with pedagogical assistance. There is also a teacher's manual available.

## Chapters

Chapter 1 defines operations strategy in terms of the reconciliation between market requirements and operations resources.

Chapter 2 looks at three interrelated issues that affect reconciliation – how operations change over time, how operations deal with trade-offs and how trade-offs can be used to understand 'targeted', or focused, operations.

Chapter 3 examines some of the popular approaches to improving operations performance. These are total quality management (TQM), lean operations, business process reengineering (BPR) and Six Sigma. Although they are not strategies as such, implementing any of them is a strategic decision.

Chapter 4 examines those decisions that shape the overall capacity of the operations resources, particularly the level of capacity and where the capacity should be located, and deals with the dynamics of the capacity decision by examining how capacity is changed over time.

Chapter 5 looks at supply networks – in particular, the nature of the relationships that develop between the various operations in a network, the advantages of taking a total network perspective and how networks behave in a dynamic sense.

Chapter 6 characterises the various types of process technology that are at the heart of many operations; it looks at the effects of some newer types of technology on operations capabilities and proposes some ideas that help operations to choose between different technologies and implement them once chosen.

Chapter 7 examines the way operations resources can be developed and improved within the organisation, especially how capabilities can be directed, developed and deployed in a cycle of improvement.

Chapter 8 applies some of the issues covered in the previous chapters to the activities associated with product and service development and organisation.

Chapter 9 is concerned with 'how' to reconcile market requirements with operations resources over the long term. In particular it looks at the first two of the four stages of the process of operations strategy, namely formulation and implementation.

Chapter 10 looks at the final two stages of the four stages of the process of operations strategy, namely monitoring and control.

# Acknowledgements

Again we have been fortunate enough to receive advice on this and earlier editions from a number of leading academics and industrialists. In particular: Pär Åhlström of Chalmers University, David Barnes of the Open University, Ruth Boaden of Manchester Business school, Mike Bourne of Cranfield University, Raffaella Cagliano of Politecnico di Milano, Dan Chicksand of Aston University, Ben Clegg of Aston University, Paul Coghlan of Trinity College Dublin, Henrique Correa of Rollins College, Pamela Danese of the University of Padova, Roland van Dierdonck of the University of Ghent, Kasra Ferdows of Georgetown University, Janet Godsell of Warwick University, Mike Gregory of Cambridge University, Linda Hendry of Lancaster University, Christer Karlsson of Copenhagen Business School, Bart McCarthy of Nottingham University, Samuel B. Larsen of IHK (Copenhagen University College of Engineering), Arunkumar Madapusi of Drexel University, Andy Neely of Cambridge University, Phil Morgan of Oxford Brooks University, Andy Neely of Cranfield University, Jan Olhager of Lund University, Ken Platts of Cambridge University, Dan Paulin of Chalmers University, Giovanni Perrone of the University of Palermo, Zoran Perunovic of Danish Technical University, Gerald Reiner of Université de Neuchâtel, Sofia Salgado Pinto of·Universidade Católica Portuguesa, Rui Sousa of Universidade Católica Portuguesa, Martin Spring of Lancaster University, Ann Vereecke of the University of Ghent, Helen Walker of Cardiff University and Gera Welker of The University of Groningen.

Our academic colleagues at Warwick and Bath Universities also helped us, both by contributing ideas and by creating a lively and stimulating work environment. At Warwick our thanks go to Nicola Burgess, Mehmet Chakkol, Emily Jamieson, Mark Johnson, Pietro Micheli, Nigel Pye, Ross Ritchie, Duncan Shaw, Mike Shulver, Rhian Silvestro and Chris Voss. At Bath our thanks go to Chris Archer-Brown, Alistair Brandon-Jones, Paul Goodwin, Emma Brandon-Jones, Jie Chen, Melanie Kreye and Jens Roehrich, Brian Squire and Baris Yalabik.

We are also grateful to many friends, colleagues and company contacts. In particular, thanks go to John Palmer of the Welsh NHS, Nigel Hayter of DS Smith, Steen Karstensen, Henrik Larsen and Morten Bo Christiansen of AP Moller-Maersk, Kevin Doolan, Partner at Moller PSF Group Cambridge and Gerard Chick of Optimum Procurement Group, Peter Norris of the Royal Bank of Scotland, Hans Mayer of Nestlé, Dr Andrew Court of QinetiQ, Tony Solomons, Chris Spencer and Maurice Dunster of Waitrose, Nathan Travis of Gloucestershire Fire and Rescue, John Richardson of Elizabeth Shaw and Dr Hanno Kirner of Rolls Royce Motors.

The team from Pearson Education provided their usual highly professional support. Particular thanks to Kate Brewin, Caitlin Lisle, Sarah Turpie, Dhanya Ramesh and Paul Kirkham.

Finally, and most importantly, we would like to thank our wives, Angela and Helen, for their forbearance and their unwavering support.

*Nigel Slack*
*Michael Lewis*

# Publisher's acknowledgements

We are grateful to the following for permission to reproduce copyright material:

## Figures

Figure 5.5 from The 50,000 mile journey of Wimbledon's tennis balls, *WBS News*, 02/07/2014 © Warwick Business School 2014; Figure 5.8 adapted from What Is The Right Outsourcing Strategy For Your Process?, *European Management Journal*, 26 (1), pp. 24–34 (McIvor, R. 2008), Copyright 2008, with permission from Elsevier; Figure 5.15 adapted from What is the right supply chain for your product?, *Harvard Business Review*, March–April, pp. 105–16 (Fischer, M.C. 1997); Figure 7.11 from *The Knowledge Creating Company*, New York: Oxford University Press (Nonaka, I. and Takeuchi, H. 1995), republished with permission of Oxford University Press, permission conveyed through Copyright Clearance Center, Inc.; Figure 10.3 after Management Control of Public and Not-For-Profit Activities, *Accounting, Organizations and Society*, 6 (3), pp. 193–211 (Hofstede, G.), Copyright 1981, with permission from Elsevier; Figure 10.12 adapted from *The Innovator's Dilemma*, Harvard Business School Press (Christenson, C.M. 1997), p. xvi.

## Tables

Table 5.4 adapted from The Bullwhip Effect in Supply Chains, *Sloan Management Review*, Spring (Lee, H.L., Padmanabhan, V. and Whang, S. 1997), © 1994 from MIT Sloan Management Review/Massachusetts Institute of Technology. All rights reserved. Distributed by Tribune Content Agency; Table 7.4 adapted from Measuring and managing technical knowledge, *Sloan Management Review*, Fall (Bohn, R.E. 1994), © 1994 from MIT Sloan Management Review/Massachusetts Institute of Technology. All rights reserved. Distributed by Tribune Content Agency.

## Text

Case Study 3 from Verweire, K. and Buekens, W., 17/03/2014, Vlerick Business School, http://www.vlerick.com/en/research-and-faculty/knowledge-items/knowledge/carglass-building-and-sustaining-a-customer-centric-organisation; Case Study 4 from Micheli, P. and Beer, H., Warwick Business School, University of Warwick, http://www.wbs.ac.uk/; Case Study 5 from Ocado Versus Tesco, *IMD*, 3-0323 (Keller-Birrer, V. and Tsikriktsis, N.), © 2010 by IMD International Institute for Management Development, Lausanne, Switzerland. Not to be used or reproduced without prior written permission directly from IMD; Case Study 9 from *IDEO: Service Design (A)*, 606-012-1 (2008), this case was written by Ritesh Bhavnani, Research Associate and INSEAD

MBA (July 2004), and Manuel Sosa, Assistant Professor of Technology and Operations Management at INSEAD, as basis for class discussion rather than to illustrate either effective or ineffective handling of an administrative situation. The information in this case has been obtained from both public sources and company interviews. © 2006 INSEAD; Example on pp. 288–9 with permission from Toyota (GB) PLC, solely for education purposes.

In some instances we have been unable to trace the owners of copyright material, and we would appreciate any information that would enable us to do so.

# 1 Operations strategy – developing resources and processes for strategic impact

## Introduction

For some business managers, the very idea of an 'operations strategy' is a contradiction in terms. After all, to be involved in the strategy process is the complete opposite of those detailed and day-to-day tasks and activities that are associated with being an operations manager. Yet at the same time we know that operations can have a real strategic impact. For many *enduringly* remarkable enterprises, from Amazon to IKEA and from Apple to Zara, the way they manage their operations resources and processes is central to long-term strategic success. This is why it is the prime purpose of this book to demonstrate how managing operations strategically can make all types of firm better, or different, or both, from their competitors. But just as revealing is that when companies do stumble, it is often because they have either taken their eye off the operations ball, or failed to appreciate its importance in the first place. More generally, all enterprises, *and all parts of the enterprise*, need to prevent strategic decisions being frustrated by poor operational implementation. And this idea leads us to the second purpose of this book. It is to show that the principles of operations strategy can be deployed in *all* parts of the business, *all* functions of the business, and *all* its extended supply network – and that, by using these principles, any type of enterprise will benefit. This is the first chapter of the book, and we look at both these meanings of operations strategy and how all parts of the business can use four perspectives on operations strategy to establish a connection between strategy and operational process and resources.

## KEY QUESTIONS

- *Why is operations excellence fundamental to strategic success?*
- *What is strategy?*
- *What is operations strategy and how is it different from operations management?*
- *How should operations strategy reflect overall strategy?*
- *How can operations strategy learn from operational experience?*
- *How do the requirements of the market influence operations strategy?*
- *How can the intrinsic capabilities of an operation's resources influence operations strategy?*
- *What is the 'content' of operations strategy?*
- *What is the 'process' of operations strategy?*
- *How is operations strategy developing?*

## Why is operations excellence fundamental to strategic success?

'Operations' is the part of the organisation that creates and/or delivers its products and services. Every organisation, whether a hotel, hospital consultancy, supermarket, games developer, government department, in fact any type of organisation, has an operations function, even if it is not called that.[1] This is because every organisation tries to add value by producing some mix of products and services for external or internal customers. It does so by transforming inputs into outputs that satisfy some customer need. This idea is called the 'input-transformation-output' model of operations. Some inputs are actually changed or 'transformed' (usually some combination of physical materials, information and customers). So, predominantly, a television factory processes materials, a firm of accountants processes information, while a theatre processes customers. Other resource inputs do the transforming. These are usually classified into the physical facilities (buildings, machines, equipment, computers, etc.) and the people, with their skills, knowledge and experience. Transforming resources are allocated to various activities in various parts of the operation. Transformed resources move through these activities until they are transformed into some mix of products and services. The arrangement of transforming resources and the way in which transformed resources move through them, are called 'processes' (see Figure 1.1). So operations managers are responsible for managing two interacting sets of issues:

- Resources – what type of materials, information, people (as customers or staff), technology, buildings and so on, are appropriate to best fulfil the organisation's objectives.

- Processes – how resources are organised to best create the required mix of products and services.

Or, to put it more succinctly, do we have the right resources and are we using them appropriately?

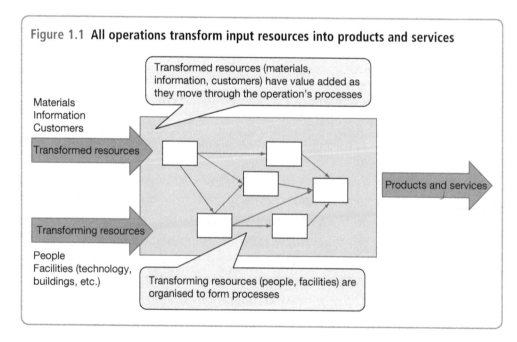

Figure 1.1 **All operations transform input resources into products and services**

Note that most operations produce both products *and* services. But some, such as an aluminium smelter, mainly produce products with only a peripheral service element. Others, such as a psychotherapy clinic, produce almost pure services. Yet the idea of the transformation model applies to all types of operation, manufacturing and service, for-profit and not-for-profit, those with external customers and those with internal customers. Hotels produce accommodation services, financial services invest, store, move or sell us money and investment opportunities, and manufacturing businesses physically change the shape and the nature of materials to produce products. Although these businesses are from different sectors (hospitality, banking, manufacturing, etc.), they share a very similar set of issues and problems. In fact, there are often bigger differences *within* economic sectors than *between* them. Note also that the transformation model describes functions other than the operations function. Marketing, finance, information systems and HRM all transform inputs into outputs (usually services) to satisfy customer needs. Sometimes these customers are external, sometimes internal. But the principle holds true: all parts of the business and all functions of the business are, in a sense, 'operations'.

## Operations, networks and 'levels of analysis'

In Figure 1.1 we illustrated 'processes' within a transformation system as a network of transforming resources. By a 'network' we simply mean a group of two or more sets of resources linked together.

The idea of the network is fundamental to operations because *all* operations are formed of networks: networks of individual staff with their technology (computers, for example), through which information flows; networks of work centres or departments moving physical products between them; and networks of businesses trading a complex mix of services. Networks can describe operations activity of many different types at many different levels of analysis. At a detailed micro level, networks of individual units of resource (technology and people) form processes. At a slightly higher 'level of analysis', these processes themselves are linked together to form larger organisational units that, again, are the elements of what is generally called 'the operation'. And many processes in this internal network will be in the other functions of the business. Thus, sales, marketing, HRM, finance and all the other functions' processes will form part of (and hopefully be integrated with) this internal process network. At an even higher level of analysis, any operation can also be viewed as part of a greater network of operations. It will have operations that supply it with the input products and services it needs to make its own products and services. And unless it deals directly with the end consumer, it will supply customers who themselves may go on to supply their own customers. Moreover, any operation could have several suppliers, several customers and may be in competition with other operations producing similar services to those it produces itself. This collection of operations is called the 'supply network'.

The important point here is that at each level of analysis, operations managers must understand the capabilities of the resources that form each element of their network, and how effectively they are linked together as networks. This idea is illustrated in Figure 1.2, which shows three levels of analysis: the level of the process (a network of individual units of resource), the level of the 'operation' (a network of processes) and the level of the supply network (a network of operations). This idea is called the 'hierarchy of operations'. In the study of operations strategy we shall largely (but not exclusively) focus on the higher levels of analysis.

**Figure 1.2 The hierarchy of operations describes networks at different levels of analysis. Three are illustrated here: the supply network, the operation and the process**

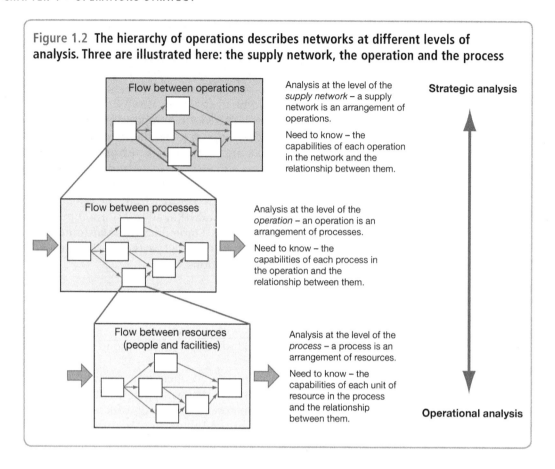

## All operations are not the same

All operations and processes differ in some way and so will need managing differently. Some differences are 'technical' in the sense that different products and services require different skills and technologies to produce them. However, processes also differ in terms of the nature of demand for their products or services. Four characteristics of demand, sometimes called the 'Four Vs', have a significant effect on how processes need to be managed:

1 **Volume** – A high volume of output means a high degree of repeatability, making a high degree of specialisation both feasible and economic. This allows the systemisation of activities and specialised technology that gives higher processing efficiencies. By contrast, low-volume processes with less repetition cannot specialise to the same degree. Staff perform a wider range of tasks that are less open to systemisation. Nor is it likely that efficient, high-throughput technology could be used. The implication of this is that high volume results in lower unit costs than low volume. So, for example, the volume and standardisation of large fast-food restaurant chains, such as McDonald's or KFC, enables them to produce with greater efficiency than a small, local cafeteria or diner.

2 **Variety** – Producing a high variety of products and services must involve a wide range of different activities, changing relatively frequently between each activity. It must also contain a wide range of skills and technology that is sufficiently 'general purpose' to cope with the range of activities and sufficiently flexible to change between them. High variety may also imply a relatively wide range of inputs and the additional complexity of matching customer requirements to appropriate products or services. Thus, high variety generally means higher costs than low variety. For example, a taxi company is usually prepared to pick up and drive customers almost anywhere (at a price). There are an infinite number of potential routes (products) that it offers. But, its cost per kilometre travelled will be higher than a less customised form of transport, such as a bus service.

3 **Variation** – Processes are generally easier to manage when they only have to cope with predictably constant demand. Resources can be geared to a level that is just capable of meeting demand. All activities can be planned in advance. By contrast, when demand is variable and/or unpredictable, resources will have to be adjusted over time. Worse still, when demand is unpredictable, extra resources will have to be designed into the process to provide a 'capacity cushion' that can absorb unexpected demand. For example, manufacturers of high-fashion garments have to cope with both seasonality and the uncertainty of whether particular styles may prove popular. Producing conventional business suits, by contrast, will be both less seasonal and more predictable. Because processes with lower variation do not need any extra safety capacity and can be planned in advance, they will generally have lower costs than those with higher variation.

4 **Visibility** – Process visibility is a slightly more difficult concept to envisage. It indicates how much of the value added by the operation is 'experienced' directly by customers, or how much it is 'exposed' to its customers. Generally, processes that act directly on customers (such as retail processes or health care processes) will have higher visibility than those that act on materials and information. However, even material- and information-transforming processes may provide a degree of visibility to the customers. For example, parcel distribution operations provide internet-based 'track and trace' facilities to enable their customers to have visibility of where their packages are at any time. In low-visibility operations the time lag between customer request and response could be measured in days rather than the near-immediate response expected from high-visibility ones. This lag allows the activities to be performed when it is convenient to the operation, thus achieving higher utilisation. Also, staff in high-visibility operations will need customer-contact skills. For all these reasons, high visibility tends to result in higher costs than low visibility.

## The implications of the Four Vs of processes

The importance of the Four Vs is that they are the result of strategic decisions that have been taken by an operation. The types of products and services it chooses to develop, and the type of markets that it chooses to enter, will define the volume, variety, variation and visibility with which the operation has to cope. At the same time, all four Vs will affect the way that the operation's processes are managed. The Four Vs act as a link between the strategic and operational aspects of operations management. The most obvious implication of an operation's positioning on the Four Vs is on processing costs. Put simply, high volume, low variety, low variation and

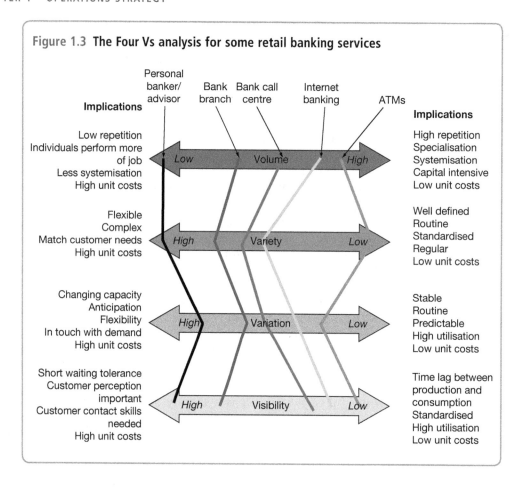

**Figure 1.3 The Four Vs analysis for some retail banking services**

low visibility all help to keep processing costs down. Conversely, low volume, high variety, high variation and high customer contact generally carry some kind of cost penalty for the process. This is why the volume dimension is often drawn with its 'low' end at the left, unlike the other dimensions, to keep all the 'low cost' implications on the right. Figure 1.3 summarises the implications of such positioning and illustrates the different positions on the Four Vs for some retail banking processes. Note that the personal banking/advice service is positioned at the high-cost end of the Four Vs, which is why it is generally offered to customers that represent high profit opportunities. Other, more automated services, such as ATMs and internet banking, have far lower costs.

**Example**  **Online versus supermarket grocery retailing[2]**

The retail industry is huge; we all shop – some more than others. For example, in the UK, wholesale and retail activity contributes almost 12 per cent of total Gross Value Added, and this is typical of developed economies. The retail industry, however, has been changing. In particular, more shopping takes place online. But for a time there was one exception – groceries. It is the biggest category in retailing but has been relatively impervious to the encroachment of online shopping. There are good reasons for this. First, established retailers worry that online shopping will simply reduce sales at their shops without reducing the costs of doing business. Second, many grocery items have relatively low value (and profit margins). Third, different items need to be stored at different temperatures. Fourth, delivery costs can be expensive – usually more than customers are willing to pay. Finally, many customers want to inspect fresh produce before they buy it. In addition, the early history of online grocery retailing was not encouraging. One of the first, California's Webvan, expanded fast but collapsed when its revenues could not match its costs.

In the UK, online grocery sales have made more of an impact than most of the world, partly because it is a small, relatively populous country. One of its largest online grocers is Ocado, which has built large, super-efficient warehouses (which require considerable investment). But the advantage of large 'fulfilment centres' such as Ocado's can be understood by looking at its Four Vs (see Figure 1.4 below). Each fulfilment centre serves a large geographic area that has a high volume of demand. Although it confines itself to grocery items, unlike some larger supermarkets that stock hardware and larger items, its variety is still relatively wide. Again, because of its scale, the variation in demand will be proportionally less than a conventional supermarket. Finally, the picking and packing is done centrally away from the customer, who will only have 'visibility' of Ocado though the website and at the time of delivery. Notice how the Ocado-style operation is positioned on the Four Vs towards the lower-cost end compared to a conventional supermarket. The question for online grocery retailers is whether these operational efficiencies will pay for the extra costs of delivery and the investment in fulfilment centres.

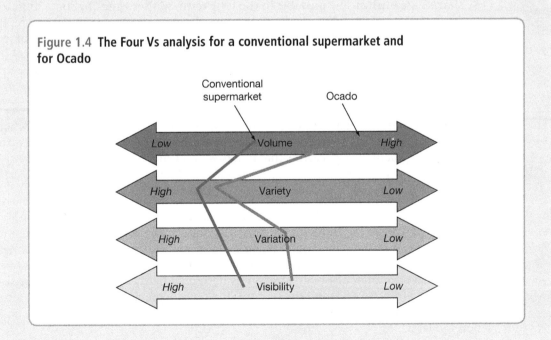

Figure 1.4 **The Four Vs analysis for a conventional supermarket and for Ocado**

## What is strategy?

We have used the word 'strategy' several times. But what exactly is strategy? Surprisingly, it is not easy to answer what seems like a straightforward question. Linguistically, the word derives from the Greek word *strategos*, meaning 'leading an army'. And although there is no direct historical link between Greek military practice and modern ideas of strategy, the military metaphor is powerful. Both military and business strategy can be described in similar ways, and include some of the following.

- Setting broad objectives that direct an enterprise towards its overall goal.
- Planning the path (in general rather than specific terms) that will achieve these goals.
- Stressing long-term rather than short-term objectives.
- Dealing with the total picture rather than stressing individual activities.
- Being detached from, and above, the confusion and distractions of day-to-day activities.

Later views of strategy have introduced some of the practical realities of business, based on observations of how organisations really do go about making (or not making) strategic decisions. These include the following.

- Business objectives may not ever become 'clear'. In fact, most organisations will have multiple objectives that may themselves conflict. For example, an outsourcing decision may improve profitability but could involve a firm in long-term reputational risk.
- Markets are intrinsically unstable in the long term, so there must be some limit to the usefulness of regarding strategy as simply planning what to do in the future. It may be more important to keep close to what is actually happening in the market and adapt to whatever circumstances develop.
- Many decisions are far less formal than the simple planning model assumes. In fact, many strategic decisions 'emerge' over time rather than derive from any single, formal senior management decision.
- Organisations do not always do in practice what they say they'll do, or even what they want to do. The only way to deduce the effect strategy of an organisation is to observe the pattern of decisions that it makes over time.

In this book we recognise the problematic nature of strategy. Nevertheless, we do offer some models and approaches that implicitly assume that managers can have some influence over the strategic direction of their organisation – even if this influence may, at times, be limited. So, notwithstanding the uncertainties and complexities of real strategy making, it is our belief that some kind of structure, model or plan can help most managers to understand what they believe they should be doing. Also note that, although strategy is described here as being an 'enterprise-level' issue, almost everything that is contained in the previous discussion can also apply to an individual function or subset of an enterprise. This is an area we shall develop later.

**Example** | Sometimes any plan is better than no plan

There is a famous story that illustrates the importance of having some kind of plan, even if hindsight proves it to be the wrong plan.[3] During manoeuvres in the Alps, a detachment of Hungarian soldiers got lost. The weather was severe and the snow was deep. In these freezing conditions, after two days of wandering, the soldiers gave up hope and became reconciled to a frozen death on the mountains. Then, to their delight, one of the soldiers discovered a map in his pocket. Much cheered by this discovery, the soldiers were able to escape from the mountains. When they were safe back at their headquarters, they discovered that the map was not of the Alps at all, but of the Pyrenees. The moral of the story? A plan (or a map) may not be perfect but it gives a sense of purpose and a sense of direction. If the soldiers had waited for the right map they would have frozen to death. Yet their renewed confidence motivated them to get up and create opportunities.

## What is operations strategy and how is it different from operations management?

One of the biggest mistakes a business can make is to confuse 'operations' with 'operational'. The meaning of 'operational' is the opposite of strategic; it means detailed, localised, short term and day to day. And operations *management* is very much like this. Yet 'managing the resources and processes that produce and deliver goods and services' should also be seen as a long-term and strategic issue. More importantly, it should be seen as one that can have a significant strategic impact. So, in answer to the question 'What is the difference between operations strategy and operations management?', at a superficial level, the answer is: 'It's a strategic perspective on how operations resources and processes are managed'. Yet this overlooks some important implications.

- **Operations strategy is longer term.** Operations management is largely concerned with short to medium time-scales while operations strategy is concerned with more long-term issues.

- **Operations strategy is concerned with a higher level of analysis.** Operations management is largely concerned with managing resources within and between smaller operations (departments, work units, etc.) whereas operations strategy is more concerned with decisions affecting a wider set of the organisation's resources and the supply network of which they are a part.

- **Operations strategy involves a greater level of aggregation.** Operations management is concerned with the details of how products and services are produced. Individual sets of resources are treated separately, as the component parts of the operation. Operations strategy, on the other hand, brings together and consolidates such details into broader issues.

- **Operations strategy uses a higher level of abstraction.** Operations management is concerned largely with what is immediately recognisable and tangible. Operations strategy often deals with more abstract, less directly observable, issues.

See Table 1.1 for some examples of operations management and operations strategy questions.

Table 1.1 **Examples of operations management and operations strategy questions**

| Difference | Operations management example | Operations strategy example |
|---|---|---|
| **Longer time-scale** | 'What demand fluctuations do we have to deal with over the next few months?' | 'When should we plan to add further capacity so that we can meet rising forecast demand?' |
| **Higher level of analysis** | 'Where should we position each product category within our department store?' | 'How many stores should we have, where should we locate them and how should we supply them?' |
| **Higher level of aggregation** | 'How do we provide tax advice to the small business sector in Antwerp?' | 'What is our overall business advice capability compared with our other European activities?' |
| **Higher level of abstraction** | 'How do we improve our purchasing procedures?' | 'Should we develop strategic alliances with selected medical products suppliers?' |

Nor is operations strategy simply a blend of the subjects of operations management and strategic management. It is an operations-based subject that is concerned with operations issues.

Its feet are firmly in the operations 'camp', even if its direction and purpose are strategic. Perhaps more significantly, it believes that many of the businesses that seem to be especially competitively successful, and who appear to be sustaining their success into the longer term, have a clear (and often innovative) operations strategy. Just look at some of the high-profile companies quoted in this book, or that feature in the business press. From Tesco to Ikea, from Ryanair to Singapore Airlines, it is not just that their operations strategy provides these companies with adequate support; it is their operations strategy that is the pivotal reason for their competitive superiority. Even businesses, such as Coca-Cola or Heinz, that are more marketing and brand-driven need a strong operations strategy. Their brand position may be shaped in the consumers' mind by their promotional activities, but it would soon erode if they could not deliver products on time, or if their quality was sub-standard, or if they could not introduce new products in response to market trends. So, for example, a 'fast-moving consumer goods' (FMCG) company that has operations that are capable of mastering new process technologies, or flexing their capacity, or running agile yet efficient supply chains, or continually cutting cost out of the business through its improvement programme, will have a huge advantage over less capable rivals.

## Four perspectives on operations strategy

Just as there is no overall agreement about what 'strategy' means, there is no universal agreement on how 'operations strategy' should be described. Different authors have slightly different views and definitions of the subject. Between them, four 'perspectives' on the subject emerge.

1 Operation strategy is a **'top-down'** reflection of what the whole group or business wants to do.

2 Operations strategy is a **'bottom-up'** activity where operations improvements cumulatively build strategy.

Figure 1.5 **Four perspectives on operations strategy: top-down, bottom-up, market requirements and operations resources**

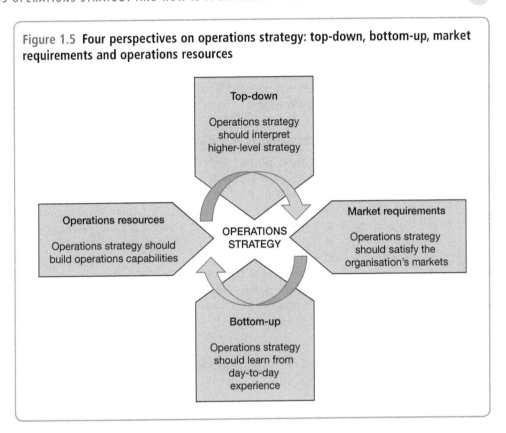

3 Operations strategy involves translating '**market requirements**' into operations decisions.

4 Operations strategy involves exploiting the capabilities of '**operations resources**' in chosen markets.

None of these four perspectives alone gives the full picture of what operations strategy is. But together they provide some idea of the pressures that go to form the content of operations strategy. We will treat each in turn (see Figure 1.5).

## How should operations strategy reflect higher-level strategy? The top-down perspective

An operations strategy must reflect the decisions taken at the top of the organisation, which set the overall strategic direction of the organisation. This is called a 'top-down' approach to operations strategy. So, if the organisation is a large, diversified corporation, its corporate strategy will consist of decisions about what types of business the group wants to be in, in what parts of the world it wants to operate, what businesses to acquire and what to divest, how to allocate its cash between its various businesses, and so on. Within the corporate group, each business unit will also need to put together its own business strategy, which sets out its individual mission and objectives, as well as defining how it intends to compete in its markets. Similarly, within the business each function will need to consider what part it should play in contributing to the strategic and/or competitive objectives of the business by developing a functional strategy that guides its actions within the business. So, in the 'top-down' view, these three levels of strategy – corporate, business and functional – form a hierarchy, with business strategy forming the context of functional strategies and corporate strategy forming the context of business strategies.

### A metrology instruments company example

For example, a manufacturer of metrology instruments is part of a group that contains several high-tech companies. It has decided to compete by being the first in the market with every available new product innovation. Its operations function, therefore, needs to be capable of coping with the changes that constant innovation will bring. It must develop processes that are flexible enough to manufacture novel parts and products. It must organise and train its staff to understand the way products are developing so that they can put in place the necessary changes to the operation. It must develop relationships with its suppliers that will help them to respond quickly when supplying new parts. Everything about the operation – its technology, its staff and its systems and procedures – must, in the short term, do nothing to inhibit the company's competitive strategy.

## How can operations strategy learn from day-to-day experience? The bottom-up perspective

In reality, the relationship between the levels in the strategy hierarchy is more complex than the top-down perspective implies and certainly does not represent the way strategies are always formulated. Businesses, when reviewing their strategies, will (hopefully) consult the individual functions within the business. In doing so they may also incorporate the ideas that come from each function's day-to-day experience. Therefore, an alternative view to the top-down perspective is that many strategic ideas emerge over time from actual experiences. Sometimes companies move in a particular strategic direction because the ongoing experience of providing products and services to customers at an operational level convinces them that it is the right thing to do. There may be no high-level decisions examining alternative strategic options and choosing the one that provides the best way forward. Instead, a general consensus emerges, often from the operational level of the organisation. The 'high-level' strategic decision making, if it occurs at all, may confirm the consensus and provide the resources to make it happen effectively. This idea of strategy being shaped by experience over time is sometimes called the concept of emergent strategies.[4] Strategy gradually becomes clearer over time and is based on real-life experience rather than theoretical positioning. Indeed, strategies are often formed in a relatively unstructured and fragmented manner to reflect the fact that the future is at least partially unknown and unpredictable. This may seem not to be a particularly useful guide for specific decision making. Yet, while emergent strategies are less easy to categorise, the principle governing a bottom-up perspective is clear: 'shape the operation's objectives and action, at least partly, by the knowledge it gains from its day-to-day activities'. The key virtues required for doing this are an ability to learn from experience and a philosophy of continual and incremental improvement that is built into the strategy-making process.

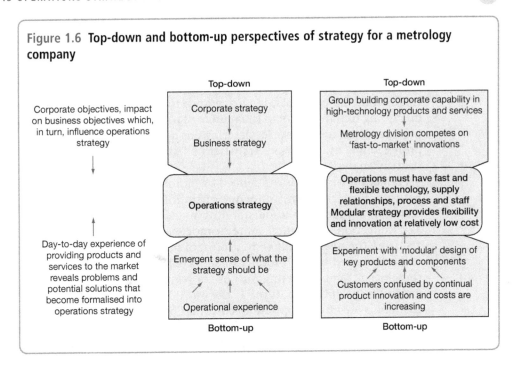

Figure 1.6 **Top-down and bottom-up perspectives of strategy for a metrology company**

*A metrology instruments company example (continued)*

For example, the manufacturer of metrology instruments, described earlier, discovers that continual product innovation both increases its costs and confuses its customers. The company's designers therefore work out a way of 'modularising' their product designs so that one part of the product can be updated without interfering with the design of the main body of the product. This approach becomes standard design practice within the company. Note that this strategy has emerged from the company's experience. No top-level board decision was probably ever taken to confirm this practice, but nevertheless it emerges as the way in which the company organises its designs. Figure 1.6 illustrates both the top-down and bottom-up for this example.

## How do the requirements of the market influence operations strategy? The market requirements perspective

Operations exist to serve markets. Indeed, a sensible starting point for any operations strategy is to look to its markets and ask the simple but important question, 'How can operations help the organisation to compete in its market place?' Remember, though, that the organisation itself usually has some influence over what its markets demand, if for no other reason than that it has chosen to be in some markets rather than others. Therefore, by choosing to inhabit a particular market position, the organisation is, to some extent, influencing how easy it is for the operations function to support the market position. This opens up the possibility that, in some circumstances, it may be sensible to shift the markets in which the organisation is trying to compete in order to reflect what its operation is good (or bad) at. We shall discuss this in more detail later; for now we return to the important point that operations strategy must reflect the organisation's market position. And the starting point for this is to develop an understanding of what is required from the operation in order to support the market position. One problem with this is that the concepts, language and, to some extent, philosophy used by the marketing function to help them understand markets are not always useful in guiding operations activities. So, descriptions of market needs developed by marketing professionals usually need 'translating' before they can be used in an operations strategy analysis.

Market positioning is influenced by (amongst other things) customers and competitors. Both, in turn, influence operations strategy. Market segmentation is a common approach to understanding markets by viewing heterogeneous markets as a collection of smaller, more homogeneous, markets. Usually this is done by assessing the needs of different groups of potential users in terms of the needs that will be satisfied by the product or service. Segmentation variables help to classify these needs. The marketing purpose of segmentation is to ensure that the product or service specification, its price, the way it is promoted and how it is channelled to customers are all appropriate to customer needs. However, market segmentation is also important in shaping operations strategy. The same needs that define markets will shape the objectives for operations' attempt to satisfy those needs. Similarly, how an organisation chooses to position itself in its market will depend on how it feels it can achieve some kind of advantage over its competitors. This, of course, will depend on how its competitors have positioned themselves. Although one particular segment of a market may look attractive, the number of other companies competing in it could deter any new entrants. However, if a company sees itself as having the operations capability of servicing that market better, even in the face of the competition from other firms, it may be worth entering the market. So, both customer and competitor analysis is a prerequisite to developing an effective operations strategy.

### A theatre lighting example

The original business of a medium-sized theatre lighting company was devoted to designing the lighting arrangements and hiring the necessary equipment for theatrical and entertainment events, exhibitions and conferences. The company could supply any specialist lighting equipment, partly because it held a wide range and partly because it had developed close relationships with other equipment hire firms. It also focused on the 'top end' of the lighting market, targeting customers who were less price-conscious. This was becoming a problem in the theatre lighting and exhibition markets because competition was forcing margins lower as competitors undercut prices. Soon they realised that the greatest potential for profitable growth lay in the conference market, where competition was not yet as fierce and where its high (but expensive) service levels, ability to give presentation advice and innovation were valued. The right-hand side of Figure 1.7 illustrates how this analysis of the company's customers and competitors sets the performance objectives for its operations strategy.

**Figure 1.7 The 'market requirements' and 'operations resources' analysis of a theatre lighting company**

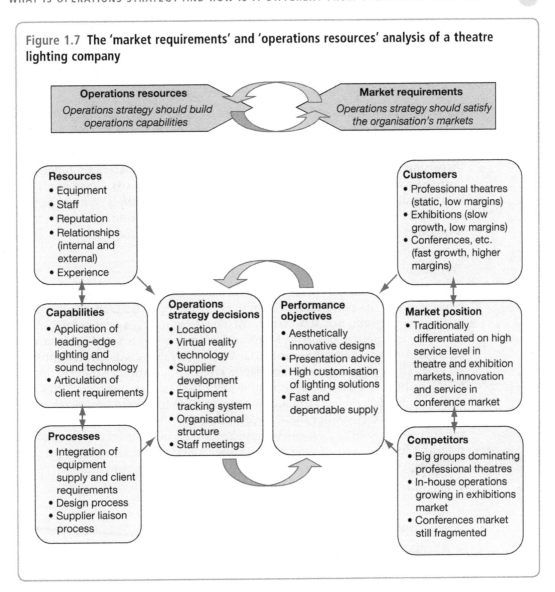

In this case the 'translation' logic goes something like the following:

(a) There are several segments in the lighting design and supply market, but the fastest-growing segment is the conference market.

(b) Competition is getting tougher in the theatre market because the large international lighting groups are able to provide lower-cost lighting solutions. Also, exhibition venues are increasingly developing in-house operations and encouraging exhibitors to use the in-house service. Margins are being squeezed in both markets.

(c) The company has therefore chosen to target the broad conference market, where margins and growth are higher.

(d) They believe they can differentiate themselves from competitors by their aesthetically innovative designs, ability to give good presentation advice, high customisation of lighting solutions and fast and reliable supply.

(e) Operations, therefore, needs to prioritise high-quality technical and aesthetic consultancy advice, customisation, fast response and dependability.

Although these are somewhat simplified statements, they demonstrate a path of increasing specificity, with increasing meaning to the operations function of the business. Not all businesses work through this logic in such a systematic way, nor is it intended to be a prescription as such, but it is an example of how the market to operations *translation* process can work. This perspective on operations strategy is sometimes called the 'outside-in' perspective.

### Performance objectives

The last stage of analysis described above needs more explanation. This is the stage that identifies the performance objectives for the operation; that is, the aspects of operations performance that satisfy market requirements and therefore that the operation is expected to pursue. Many authors on operations strategy have their own set of performance objectives, and no overall agreement exists on terminology. They are referred to variously as 'performance criteria', operations 'strategic dimensions', 'performance dimensions', 'competitive priorities' and 'strategic priorities'. Here, we will be using the term 'performance to objectives'. While there are differences between authors as to exactly what these performance dimensions are, there are some commonly used categories. Here, we will use a set of five performance objectives that have meaning for any type of operation (though obviously their relative priorities will differ). Within these five we will subsume the other dimensions.

- Quality
- Speed
- Dependability
- Flexibility
- Cost

Performance objectives, and the issue of performance in general, will be examined in more detail in the following chapter.

## How can the intrinsic capabilities of an operation's resources influence operations strategy? The operations resource perspective

The resources and processes within an operation are not simply passive elements; they have an existence and a role that should be part of any operations strategy. No surprise, then, that the long-term management of resources and processes is often regarded as the underlying rationale for operations strategy (although, generally, we drop the 'processes' bit and just call this perspective the 'operations resource' perspective). The problem again is one of translation because the approach and terminology that are useful for understanding a firm's resources are not necessarily appropriate to clarify the nature of the decisions that shape those resources. A useful starting point is to understand 'what we have' – that is, the totality of the resources owned by, or available to, the operation. Next, one needs to link the broad understanding of resources and processes with the specific operations strategy decisions: 'what actions we are going to take'. To achieve this linkage we need a concept to bridge the gap between the sometimes fuzzy understanding of 'what is there' and the necessarily more specific 'what should we do?' stages. In the operations resource perspective we use the concept of operations capabilities.

### Operations resources, processes, routines and capabilities

Listing its resources provides a first step in understanding an operation, but this is rather like describing an automobile by listing its component parts. To understand how an operation works we need to examine the interaction between its resources. For example, how different resources, such as processing centres, are positioned relative to each other, how staff are organised into units and so on. These arrangements of resources constitute the processes of the operation that describe the way things happen in the operation. To return to the automobile analogy, processes are the mechanisms that power, steer and control its performance. Yet even this technical explanation of an automobile's mechanisms does not convey either the full extent of how it performs on the road or its style, feel and 'personality'. Similarly, any view of an operation that limits itself to a description of its obvious tangible resources and processes fails to move our knowledge of the operation beyond the most basic level. Any audit of a company's resources and processes needs to include the organisation's intangible resources. These are the factors that may not be directly observable but are nonetheless significant in enabling any company to function. They include such things as:

- supplier relationships, contracts and mutual understanding of how suppliers are managed;
- knowledge of, and experience in, dealing with technology sources and labour markets;
- process knowledge relating to the day-to-day production of products and services;
- new product and service development skills and procedures;
- contacts and relationships in the market that enable an understanding of market trends and more specific customer needs.

Notice how many of the issues concerning intangible assets involve not so much what an operation has, but what it does. All operations have documented procedures to formalise their regular activities, such as 'generating orders', 'fulfilling orders', 'developing new products and services' and so on. But they also have ways of getting things done that are less formally documented. The effectiveness of these informal practices depends on the relationships between individual staff, their shared values and understandings of overall objectives, the tacit (non-articulated) knowledge accumulated by individuals, an understanding of 'who knows what' and 'who can get things done' and so on. It is these informal arrangements of a company's resources that go a long way to explaining the effectiveness of its operations. Not that the formal processes are unimportant. It is the combination of formal and informal processes, explicit and tacit knowledge, the intrinsic attributes of the company's resources and the way in which these resources are deployed that describes an operation's abilities. The collective term for both formal and informal processes is the 'routines' of the firm. Accountants have considerable trouble when dealing with intangible resources (or invisible assets as they are sometimes called). Yet intangible assets are often the reason for a firm's success. Bill Gates, who guided Microsoft in its most successful years, pointed out that '... *our primary assets, which are our software and software development skills, do not show up in the balance sheet at all'.*[5]

---

**Example** | **Amazon develops its operations capabilities**[6]

A firm's competencies are not always immediately apparent – they develop, sometimes to take a firm in surprising directions. To most of us, Amazon is generally seen as an online retailer that started selling books and now provides the biggest internet 'shop front' for all types of consumer products. Yet, over time, Jeff Bezos, Amazon's founder, has turned the company into a provider of infrastructure and services to many other firms, including many of its retail rivals. Amazon's store front is just the tip of an iceberg that touches so many people's lives that, according to some commentators, 'they're becoming as important as utilities'. As Jeff Bezos puts it: '*We are creating powerful self-service platforms that allow thousands of people to boldly experiment and accomplish things that would otherwise be impossible or impractical.*' In other words, the firm's resources and processes (customer information, cloud computing server space, high technology warehouse facilities, data mining expertise and so on) allow other companies to 'outsource' even their core processes to Amazon. In effect, Amazon can offer services that run marketing, customer relationships, payments, computing, logistics and distribution for any company wanting to sell its goods and services to the public.

It may not be glamorous, but Amazon has focused on what have been called 'the dull-but-difficult tasks' such as tracking products, managing suppliers, storing inventory and delivering boxes. Fulfilment by Amazon allows other companies to use Amazon's logistics capability, including the handling of returned items, and access to Amazon's 'back-end' technology.

Amazon Web Services, its cloud computing business, provides the computing power for small and larger high-profile customers, such as Spotify's digital music service and Netflix's video streaming service. But why should any business want to allow Amazon to have such control over its activities? Mainly because it allows entrepreneurs to create start-ups and established companies to expand their activities without the huge investment they would need to build appropriate infrastructure themselves. Amazon's large and efficient operations are also better value than smaller companies could achieve. On the other hand, it does mean that businesses using Amazon's services do lose some autonomy – Amazon can be both a rival retailer and a service provider. Amazon is also able to see some of their critical business details, such as sales and inventory levels. And what's in it for Amazon? Well, profit – generally, the service fees it charges companies are more profitable than buying and selling the products itself.

At first, some observers criticised Amazon's apparent redefinition of its strategy. 'Why not', they said, 'stick to what you know, focus on your core competence of internet retailing?' Bezos's response was clear: '*We are sticking to our core competence... The only thing that's changed is that we are exposing it for (the benefit of) others.*'

## The resource-based view of the firm

The concepts of intangible (or invisible) resources and of routines are central to what is sometimes called the 'resource-based view' (or RBV) of strategic management. The resource-based view is based on the notion that most companies consider themselves to be particularly good at some specific activities, but try to avoid head-to-head competition in others. It has its origins in early economic theory. Some of the initial works in strategic management also included consideration of the firm's internal resources.[7] The 'SWOT' (strengths/weaknesses/opportunities/threats) approach saw competitive advantage as exploiting the opportunities raised in the competitive environment using the firm's strengths, while neutralising external threats and avoiding being trapped by internal weaknesses. While one school of thought, the 'environmental' school, focused on a firm's opportunities and threats, the other, the 'resource-based', focused on a firm's strengths.[8] The two schools of thought differ in the way they explain why some companies outperform others over time – what strategists call a 'sustainable competitive advantage' (SCA). Through the 1970s and '80s, the dominant school, the environmental school, saw a firm's performance as being closely related to the industrial structure of its markets. In this view, key strategic tasks centred on how a firm positioned itself within its market. It should analyse the forces present within the environment in order to assess the profit potential of the industry, and then design a strategy that aligns the firm to the environment. By contrast, the 'resource-based' explanation of why some companies manage to gain sustainable competitive advantage focuses on the role of the resources that are (largely) internal to the company's operations. Put simply, 'above-average' performance is more likely to be the result of the core capabilities (or competences) inherent in a firm's resources than its competitive positioning in its industry.

The RBV also differs in its approach to how firms protect any competitive advantage they may have. The environmental view sees companies as seeking to protect their competitive advantage through their control of the market – for example, by creating barriers to entry through product or service differentiation. By contrast, the RBV sees firms being able to protect their competitive advantage by building up 'difficult-to-imitate' resources. So the resources that a firm possesses are closely linked to its ability to outperform competitors. Certain of these resources are particularly important, and can be classified as 'strategic' if they exhibit the following properties.[9]

- **They are scarce**. Unequal access to (or information about) resources can lead to their uneven distribution amongst competing firms. In this way, scarce resources such as specialised production facilities, experienced engineers, proprietary software, etc. can underpin competitive advantage.

- **They are imperfectly mobile**. Some resources are difficult to move out of a firm. For example, resources that were developed in-house, or are based on the experience of the company's staff, cannot be traded easily. As a result, the advantages that they create are more likely to be retained over time.

- **They are imperfectly imitable and imperfectly substitutable**. These critical dimensions help define the overall sustainability of a resource-based advantage. It is not enough only to have resources that are unique and immobile. If a competitor can copy these resources or, less predictably, replace them with alternative resources, then their value will quickly deteriorate. Again, the more the resources are connected with tacit knowledge and routines embedded within the firm, the more difficult they are for competitors to understand and to copy.

### Extended resource-based theory (ERBT)[10]

In recent years, resource-based theory (RBT) has been developed by some theorists to include the influence of the wider supply network of which the firm is a part. This idea is termed the 'extended' RBT (ERBT). It assumes that even strategic resources that are outside the boundaries of the firm can still be used to generate strategic advantage for the firm. Of course, this assumes that these strategic resources beyond the boundaries of the firm can be readily accessed. In other words, the relationships between operations within a supply network are suitably strong and/or collaborative, and the synergy between resources within each firm sufficiently close, to make access to another firm's resources valuable.

### A theatre lighting example (continued)

As an example of the operations resource perspective, we return to the lighting business described earlier. Its market requirements analysis had indicated a shift towards targeting commercial companies who needed lighting designs (and often specialised equipment) for sales promotion events, conferences, displays and exhibitions. An analysis of the firm's resources, processes and capabilities revealed that the company's history and experience of advising theatrical producers was a valuable asset, particularly in the conference market. It allowed them to excel at understanding how to translate someone else's vision into theatrical reality. Furthermore, their lighting and sound technicians were experienced at reprogramming equipment and configuring equipment to fit almost any concept their clients wanted. These skills, combined with an intimate network of contracts with equipment and software suppliers, enabled the company to outperform competitors and eventually dominate this (for them) new market. In order to maintain its competitive advantage it opened new sites in a number of locations where existing and potential customers were located, all of which had a resident lighting and sound design expert. The company also developed a virtual reality simulation, which helped demonstrate to potential customers how a set might look. This simulation was developed in consultation with key equipment suppliers, to utilise their expertise. In order to make all equipment readily available at all sites, it installed a computer-based equipment tracking and scheduling system that was integrated across all sites. The company also organised periodic 'state-of-play' conferences, where all staff discussed their experiences of serving clients. Some suppliers and customers were invited to these meetings.

Consider this example and how its resources have helped it to compete so effectively. Figure 1.7 illustrates how the firm has 'translated' an understanding of its resources to a set of operations strategy decisions. The translation logic goes something like this:

(a) We have a set of equipment that is sophisticated and useful in the theatre lighting business; we also have some staff that have sound and lighting design expertise.

(b) As a company we have developed a reputation for being able to take a theatre director's 'vision' for a production, and use our knowledge to make it reality – even improving the original vision.

(c) What allows us to do this so well is the way we have 'grown up together' and are able to understand all the stages of satisfying customers, from an understanding of what equipment is available right through to managing the design, installation, operating and dismantling of the production.

(d) These capabilities are particularly attractive in the commercial conference market, which is now our target market.

(e) In order to consolidate and sustain this competitive position, we must make a number of resource decisions as to how our capabilities can be preserved, developed and deployed – for example, concerning location, virtual reality technology, supplier development, tracking systems and organisational structure.

---

**Example**     **Thrift is at the core of IKEA's culture[11]**

Core competencies can be strongly linked to a firm's origins and history. And there are few better examples than IKEA – a firm that owes many aspects of how it operates to its origins in Sweden.

The flat-pack specialist is the world's largest furniture chain, with over 300 outlets around the world. *'Thrift is the core of IKEA's corporate culture',* says Mikael Ohlsson, IKEA's Chief Executive, who traces the thrift culture back to the company's origins in Smaland – a poor region in southern Sweden whose inhabitants, he says, are *'stubborn, cost-conscious and ingenious at making a living with very little'.* Ever since Ingvar Kamprad founded IKEA more than 70 years ago, the company has endeavoured to allow *'people with limited means to furnish their houses like rich people'.* Even those people who dislike queuing in its huge warehouse-like stores, or assembling its flat-pack furniture at home, acknowledge that IKEA's products are both stylish and remarkably cheap. *'We hate waste',* says Mikael Ohlsson. As an example, he points to one of their popular three-seater sofas. IKEA's designers developed a new packing method that squeezed twice the amount of sofa into the same space. This trimmed €100 from the price and reduced the carbon-dioxide emissions from transporting it.

But culture can work in less positive ways. IKEA has been accused of being instinctively secretive and, according to some, rigidly hierarchical. Certainly the firm's ownership structure is not straightforward.

A private Dutch-registered company is IKEA's parent, which, in turn, belongs entirely to a tax-exempt Dutch-registered entity – Foundation. A five-person executive committee runs Foundation. Separately, another private Dutch company, whose parent company is registered in Luxembourg, owns the IKEA trademark and concept. And, although the owners of this company remain hidden from view and IKEA refuses to identify them, they have been traced to a Liechtenstein foundation controlled by the Kamprad family, which earns its money from franchise agreements with IKEA stores. Mr. Kamprad has been reported as saying that, *'tax efficiency was a natural part of the company's low-cost culture'.*

## So, what *is* operations strategy?

The four perspectives on operations strategy that we have outlined are not 'alternative' views of what is operations strategy. Operations managers can (and should) hold all four views simultaneously. They simply represent alternative starting points for understanding the nature, scope and rationale of operations strategy. Bringing all four views together can even expose the dilemmas inherent within an operations strategy. In fact, operations strategy can be seen as the attempt to reconcile all four perspectives: the top-down with the bottom-up view, and the market requirements with the operations resource view. But there can be tensions between the perspectives.

The tension between the market requirements perspective and the operations resource perspective is central to the decisions that make up an operations strategy.

Operations managers must obviously satisfy the requirements of the market if their enterprise is to survive in the long term. Yet simply following a market is unlikely to provide long-term competitive advantage. After all, competitors will themselves be attempting to do the same thing. To escape from being permanently 'jerked around' by the dynamics of the market, operations should also be attempting to develop the long-term capabilities that competitors will find difficult to imitate. This is why our definition of operations strategy, and the main theme throughout this book, encompasses the reconciliation of market requirements with operations resources.

This is actually a very complex interaction. Sometimes the complexity lies in the difficulty most organisations have in clarifying either the nature of market requirements or the characteristics of their operations resources. Sometimes this is simply because not enough effort is put into clarifying their intended markets. Some operations strategies are formulated without the context of a well-understood market and/or business strategy. But, even in better-managed companies, market requirements may be unclear. For example, a company may compete in many different markets that exhibit sometimes subtle, but nevertheless important, differences in their requirements. Furthermore, markets are dynamic. Neither customers nor competitors are totally predictable. Customer behaviour may change for reasons that become clear only after the event. Competitor reaction, likewise, can be unpredictable and sometimes irrational. The links between customers, competitors and market positioning are not always obvious. Market positioning is not an exact science, and the strategic reconciliation process of operations strategy may have to take place under conditions of both uncertainty and ambiguity. The operations resources side of the equation may be equally unclear. Businesses do not always know the value, abilities or performance of their own resources and processes. Notwithstanding the popularity of the 'core competence' concept, organisations frequently find difficulty in identifying what are, could be, or should be their core competences. More significantly, the resources and processes within the operation are not deterministically connected, like some machine where adjustments to levers of control lead inexorably to a predictable and precise change in the behaviour of the operation. The cause–effect mechanisms for most operations are, at best, only partially understood.

A company may find that its intended market position is matched exactly by the capabilities of its operations resources, the strategic decisions made by its operations managers having, over time, generated precisely the right balance of performance objectives to achieve a sustainable competitive advantage in its markets. Then again, it may not. In fact, even where it is understood, the capabilities of its operations resources are unlikely to be in perfect alignment with the requirements of its markets. The objective of operations strategy is to attempt this alignment over time without undue risk to the organisation. Operations managers must attempt to do this through the process of reconciliation, a process that is ongoing and iterative. We can include this concept of 'reconciliation' into our definition of operations strategy.

> Operations strategy is the total pattern of decisions that shape the long-term capabilities of any type of operation and their contribution to overall strategy, through the reconciliation of market requirements with operations resources.

Similarly, there will usually be tension between the top-down and bottom-up perspectives. The top-down perspective is the most common view of what strategy is. Strategy is broad, long term, 'making the big decisions', 'steering the enterprise towards its ultimate objectives', and so on. Furthermore, strategy is in the hands of the senior people (because strategic decisions are, by their nature, important) who can view the, sometimes competing, needs of each part of the enterprise. It is they who tell the rest of the enterprise what to do and, hopefully, why. The bottom-up, 'emergent' perspective is very different. It is founded on the direct experience of those people who actually 'do' stuff. And these people tend to be more numerous and lower in the organisation. The bottom-up perspective is based on how we all learn from experience. Arguably, it places a greater emphasis on 'what is' rather than 'what should be'.

## 'Content' and 'process'

These two sets of tensions between the four perspectives of operations strategy are closely aligned with what is sometimes called the distinction between the 'content' and 'process' of operations strategy. 'Content' means the collection of decisions that are made (deliberately or by default) within the operations strategy domain. Content is concerned with the strategic decisions that shape and develop the long-term direction of the operation. It is the outcome of the reconciliation of market requirements and operations resource capabilities. The 'process' of operations strategy means the way in which operations strategies are (or can be) formulated. It is a reflection both of what operations managers should do and what they actually do in practice. It is the reconciliation of top-down and bottom-up perspectives. The distinction between content and process is illustrated in terms of the four perspectives in Figure 1.8.

However, this division between content and process, between the four perspectives is, to some extent, a simplification. The reality is that all decisions are partly a function

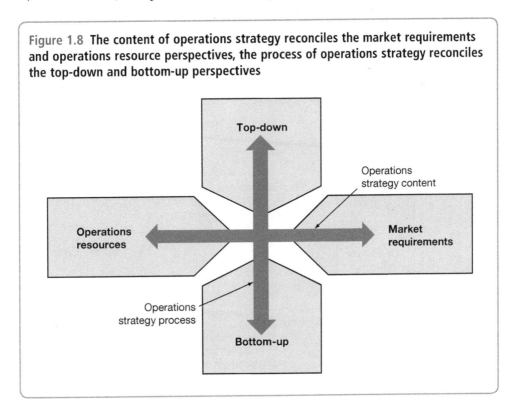

**Figure 1.8** **The content of operations strategy reconciles the market requirements and operations resource perspectives, the process of operations strategy reconciles the top-down and bottom-up perspectives**

of how they are made. But distinguishing between content and process does allow us to examine the set of issues associated with each in a logical manner. Chapters 2 to 8 of this book are concerned with issues concerning the *content* of operations strategy, while chapters 9 and 10 are concerned with the operations strategy *process*.

## What is the 'content' of operations strategy?

Operations strategy is concerned with the reconciliation of market requirements and operations resources. It attempts to influence the way it satisfies market requirements by setting appropriate performance objectives. It attempts to influence the capabilities of its operations resources through the decisions it takes in how those resources are deployed. So, the content of operations strategy is the interaction between the operation's performance objectives and the decisions that it takes concerning resource deployment. Figure 1.9 illustrates this idea. It particularly highlights the importance of:

• understanding the relative importance of the operation's performance objectives; and

• understanding the influence on them of the decision areas that determine resource deployment.

### Operations strategy performance objectives

In Figure 1.9 the market requirements perspective on operations strategy was summarised in terms of five generic performance objectives: quality, speed, dependability, flexibility and cost. Their purpose is to articulate market requirements in a way that

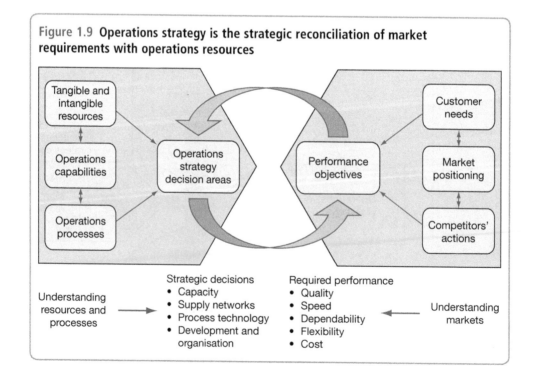

Figure 1.9 **Operations strategy is the strategic reconciliation of market requirements with operations resources**

will be useful to operations. However, before we can pursue the idea of performance objectives further, we must take a step back in order to consider market positioning and how competitive factors are used to describe positioning.

A company may try to articulate its position in the market in a number of ways. It might compare itself with a competitor; for example, *'We wish to offer a wider range of products than Gap, but not be as expensive as Donna Karen'*. Alternatively, they might associate themselves with the needs of a particular customer group. For example, *'We wish to provide a level of service and attention that discerning business people expect when they stay at our hotels'*. Either way, they finish up defining market position in terms of a number of dimensions – for example, range, price, quality of service, etc. These dimensions on which a company wishes to compete are called 'competitive factors'. Different words will be used for different types of operation and their relative importance will change depending on how the company wishes to compete. Nevertheless, their common characteristic is that they describe the things that a customer can see or experience. Table 1.2 illustrates this idea for two contrasting operations. This clusters

**Table 1.2 Competitive factors for three operations grouped under their generic performance objectives**

| Performance objective | Mortgage services – associated competitive factors include … | Steel plant – associated competitive factors include … | Finance function – associated competitive factors include … |
|---|---|---|---|
| Quality | Professionalism of staff<br>Friendliness of staff<br>Accuracy of information<br>Ability to change details in future | Percentage of products conforming to their specification<br>Absolute specification or products<br>Usefulness of technical advice | Accuracy of work<br>Insightfulness of financial advice<br>Trust and relationship with other functions |
| Speed | Time for call centre to respond<br>Prompt advice response<br>Fast loan decisions<br>Fast availability of funds | Lead time from enquiry to quotation<br>Lead time from order to delivery<br>Lead time for technical advice | Responsiveness to other functions' requests<br>Time between need for financial information and issuing it |
| Dependability | Reliability of original promise date<br>Customers kept informed | Percentage of deliveries 'on time, in full'<br>Customers kept informed of delivery dates | Financial information reliably available when needed; for example, in time for meetings |
| Flexibility | Customisation of terms, such as duration/life of offer<br>Cope with changes in circumstances, such as level of demand | Range of possible sizes, gauges, coatings, etc.<br>Rate of new product introduction<br>Ability to change quantity, composition and timing of an order | Customisation of financial reports<br>Ability to adjust volume of work to meet deadlines |
| Cost | Interest rate charged<br>Arrangement charges<br>Insurance charges | Price of products<br>Price of technical advice<br>Discounts available<br>Payment terms | Cost per transaction completed<br>Headcount (number and cost of finance staff)<br>Facilities (office space, IT, etc.) |

the competitive factors for each operation into the five generic performance objectives that they represent.

Note that the three operations we have used as examples in Table 1.2 have a different view of each of the performance objectives. So, for example, the mortgage service sees quality as being at least as much about the manner in which its customers relate to its service as it does about the absence of technical errors. The steel plant, on the other hand, while not ignoring quality of service, primarily emphasises product-related technical issues. The finance function, while valuing accuracy, also includes softer 'trust' and 'relationship' factors. Different operations will see quality (or any other performance objective) in different ways, and emphasise different aspects. Broadly speaking, though, they are selecting from the same pool of factors that together constitute the generic performance objective – in this case, 'quality'. So, each of the performance objectives represents a cluster of competitive factors grouped together for convenience. Sometimes operations may choose to rebundle, using slightly different headings. For example, it is not uncommon in some service operations to refer to 'quality of service' as representing all the competitive factors we have listed under quality and speed and dependability. In practice, the issue is not so much one of universal definition but rather consistency within one operation, or a group of operations. At the very least it is important that individual companies have it clear in their own minds what list of generic performance objectives is appropriate to their business, what competitive factors each represents and how each competitive factor is to be defined. However, note that cost is different from the other performance objectives. While most competitive factors are clear manifestations of their performance objectives, the competitive factors of 'price' are related to the cost performance objective. So, an improvement in cost performance does not necessarily mean a reduction in the price charged to customers. Firms who achieve lower costs may choose to take some, or all, of the improvement in higher margins rather than reduce prices.

## Decision areas

Also, in Figure 1.9 is a set of 'decision areas'. These are the sets of decisions needed to manage the resources of the operation. Again, different writers on operations strategy use slightly different groupings and refer to them collectively in slightly different ways, such as 'operations policy areas', 'sub-strategies' or 'operations tasks'. We shall refer to them throughout this book as 'operations strategy decisions' or 'decision areas', and the groupings of decision areas that we shall use are as follows.

- **Capacity strategy**: this concerns how capacity and facilities in general should be configured. It includes questions such as 'What should be the overall level of capacity?', 'How many sites should the capacity be distributed across, and what size should they be?', 'Should each site be engaged in a broad mixture of activities, or should they specialise in one or two?', 'Exactly where should each site be located?', 'When should changes be made to overall capacity levels?', 'How big should each change in capacity be?' and 'How fast should capacity expansion or reduction be pursued?' Chapter 4 will deal with the decisions concerning capacity strategy.

- **Supply network strategy** (including purchasing and logistics): this concerns how operations relate to the interconnected network of other operations, including customers, customers' customers, suppliers, suppliers' suppliers, and so on. All operations need to consider their position in this network, both to understand how the dynamic forces within the network will affect them, and to decide what role they wish to play in the network. Decisions here include such things as 'How much of the network do we wish to own?', 'How can we gain an understanding of our competitive position by placing it in a network context?', 'How do we predict and cope with dynamic disturbances and fluctuations within the network?', 'Should we attempt to manage the network in different ways depending on the types of market we are serving?', 'How many suppliers should we have?', 'What should be the nature of our relationship with our suppliers, purely market-based or long-term partnerships?' and 'What are the appropriate ways of managing different types of supplier relationships?' Chapter 5 deals with supply network strategy.

- **Process technology strategy**: this concerns the choice and development of the systems, machines and processes that act directly or indirectly on transformed resources to convert them into finished products and services. Decisions here include such things as 'How should we characterise alternative process technology?' and 'How should we assess the consequences of choosing a particular process technology?' Chapter 6 will deal with process technology decisions.

- **Development and organisation**: this concerns the set of broad and long-term decisions governing how the operation is run on a continuing basis. Decisions here include such things as 'How do we enhance and improve the processes within the operation over time?', 'How should resources be clustered together within the business?', 'How should reporting relationships be organised between these resources?' and 'How should new product and service development be organised?' We devote two chapters to these areas. Chapter 7 will deal with the strategic improvement, and Chapter 8 with product and service development.

### Why these decision areas?

All these decision areas will be familiar to managers in a wide variety of operations. However, it is possible to support this intuitive list of decision areas with a slightly more rigorous approach. To do this let us indulge in some simple ratio analysis.

Essentially, ratio analysis is an attempt to decompose a fundamental ratio of some element of performance into other ratios by inserting the same measure on the top and bottom of the resulting ratios. The idea is to split the fundamental ratio into other measures so that we can understand how it is built up. The best-known examples of this occur in financial accounting. Here we will do it in a slightly different way by inserting measures that have some meaning in an operations context. We are not proposing this ratio analysis as a practical analysis tool. Rather, it is intended to provide some underpinning for each decision area. Figure 1.10 shows how we can do this for the fundamental ratio of profit divided by total assets, or return on assets (ROA).[12]

The simple ROA ratio, profit over total assets, is broken down into 'profit/output' and 'output/total assets'. This first ratio (in effect, average profit) can be further broken down into average revenue minus average cost. Operations affect the former through the ability to deliver superior levels of competitive performance (better quality, speed, dependability and flexibility). They affect the latter through the more productive use of resources (lower costs). These are the two measures that have been seen as the great

**Figure 1.10 Decomposing the ratio profit/total assets to derive the four strategic decision areas of operations strategy**

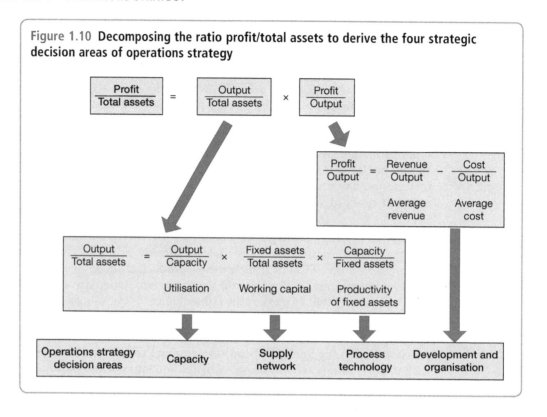

operations balancing act – keeping revenue high through standards of service and competitive pricing while keeping costs low. Both are a function of an organisation's success in achieving an effective and efficient operation through its development and organisation decisions. These decisions attempt to ensure that improvement and learning continually reduce costs, while the performance of products and services and its level of service to customers are continually increased.

The other part of the decomposed ROA ratio – output/total assets – represents the output being produced for the investment being put into the operation. It is shown in Figure 1.10 broken down into three ratios: 'output/capacity', 'fixed assets/total assets' and 'capacity/fixed assets'.

'Output/capacity', or the utilisation of the operation, is determined by the balance of demand on the operation and its long-term ability to meet that demand. To improve ROA, utilisation needs to be as close to 1 as possible. To do this, either demand must be generated to match capacity, or the operation must develop an ability to adjust its capacity to match demand. This ratio is largely a function of an organisation's capacity decisions. Has it managed to balance the provision of capacity with demand (output) and can it change its capacity to meet changing levels of demand?

'Fixed assets/total assets' is a ratio partially governed by the working capital requirements of the business. The smaller the working capital required by the operation, the closer fixed assets is to total assets. For the operations function, working capital minimisation is often a matter of reducing the inventories in its supply network, a function of an organisation's supply network decisions. Can the supply network maintain appropriate delivery of its products and services without carrying excessive levels of inventory?

'Capacity/fixed assets' is sometimes called the productivity of fixed assets. It is a measure of how much the operation has had to spend in order to acquire, or develop, its capacity. To some extent this is determined by the skill of the operation's designers and technologists. An operation that achieves the required capacity levels without needing large amounts of capital expenditure will have a better ratio than the operation that has 'thrown money at the problem'. This ratio is largely a function of an organisation's process technology decisions. Has it invested wisely in appropriate process technologies, which can create a sufficient volume of appropriate products and/or services, without excessive capital expenditure?

Obviously this is not a totally clean categorisation. In some way, all the decision areas will have some impact on all the ratios. For example, a company's development and organisation strategy includes such issues as how improvement is encouraged, how the organisation's structure works and how performance is measured. This will affect many of these ratios. Its main focus, however, is likely to be on improving average profit, by reducing costs through operations efficiency and increasing revenue through improved operations effectiveness at delivering its products and services.

Table 1.3 sets out some typical decisions that need to be taken in two very different types of operation, clustered under the four areas.

**Table 1.3 Some decisions in each decision area for a hotel chain and an automobile manufacturer**

| Hotel chain | Decision area | Automobile manufacturer |
|---|---|---|
| How many rooms and other facilities should each hotel have? Should each hotel have the same set of facilities? Where should our hotels be located? How do we manage the long-term expansion or contraction of capacity in each region? | Capacity | How big should each plant be? Should we focus all production on one model on a single site? Where should each site be located? How do we manage the long-term expansion or contraction of overall capacity? |
| What activities should we be performing in-house and what should we buy in? Do we develop franchise opportunities on our sites? Should we form alliances with other vacation or travel companies? | Supply networks | What parts should we be making in-house and what should we buy in? How do we coordinate deliveries from our suppliers? Should we form long-term supply alliances? How many 'first-tier' suppliers should we have? |
| To what extent should we be investing in multi-functional information systems? Should all information systems be linked to a central system? | Process technology | What processes should be receiving investment for automation? How can investment in technology increase our flexibility while keeping costs low? Should our process technologies be integrated? |

▶

Table 1.3 **Some decisions in each decision area for a hotel chain and an automobile manufacturer** (*Continued*)

| Hotel chain | Decision area | Automobile manufacturer |
|---|---|---|
| How can we integrate new services features smoothly into our existing operation?<br>What should be the reporting responsibility relationships within and between hotels?<br>Should we promote company-wide improvement initiatives?<br>How do we make sure sites learn from each other? | Development and organisation | How can we bring new products to market quickly?<br>Should we develop products on common platforms?<br>How do we manage product variety?<br>What should be the reporting responsibility relationships within and between sites?<br>Should we promote company-wide improvement initiatives?<br>How do we make sure sites learn from each other? |

## Structural and infrastructural decisions

A distinction is often drawn in operations strategy between the strategic decisions that determine an operation's structure, and those that determine its infrastructure. Structural issues primarily influence the physical arrangement and configuration of the operation's resources. Infrastructural strategy areas influence the activities that take place within the operation's structure. This distinction in operations strategy has been compared to that between 'hardware' and 'software' in a computer system. The hardware of a computer sets limits to what it can do. Some computers, because of their technology and their architecture, are capable of higher performance than others, although those computers with high performance are often more expensive. In a similar way, investing in advanced process technology and building more or better facilities can raise the potential of any type of operation. But the most powerful computer can only work to its full potential if its software is capable of exploiting the potential embedded in its hardware. The same principle applies with operations. The best and most costly facilities and technology will only be effective if the operation also has an appropriate infrastructure that governs the way it will work on a day-to-day basis.

However, it is a mistake to categorise decision areas as being either entirely structural or entirely infrastructural. In reality, all the decision areas have both structural and infrastructural implications. Capacity strategy, since it is concerned with the physical size and location of operations, is mainly a structural issue, but can also affect the organisation's reporting relationships systems and procedures. Similarly, supply network decisions have much to do with whether the organisation chooses to perform in-house and what it chooses to buy in, but this needs infrastructural support for communications and the development of relationships. Process technology, likewise, has its structural aspects that will partly determine the physical form of the operation, but much of an operation's process technology will be devoted to driving the systems, procedures and monitoring systems that form its infrastructure. Even decisions within the development and organisation category, while primarily being concerned with infrastructure, can have structural elements. A set of reporting relationships embedded within an organisational structure may reflect different locations and different process technologies. It is best to consider a spectrum withal.

## The operations strategy matrix

We can now bring together the two perspectives of market requirements and operations resources to form the dimensions of a matrix. This 'operations strategy matrix', shown in Figure 1.11, describes operations strategy as the intersection of a company's performance objectives with its decision areas. It emphasises the intersections between what is required from the operations function (the relative priority given to each performance objective), and how the operation tries to achieve this through the set of choices made (and the capabilities that have been developed) in each decision area.

Although sometimes complex, the matrix can, at the very least, be considered a checklist of the issues that are required to be addressed. Any operation that claims to have an operations strategy will presumably be able to have some kind of story to tell for each of the intersections. It should be able to explain exactly how capacity strategy is going to affect quality, speed, dependability, flexibility or cost. It should be able to explain exactly how flexibility is influenced by capacity, supply network, process technology and development and organisation decisions, and so on. In other words, the matrix helps operations strategies to be comprehensive. Also, it is unlikely that all the intersections on the matrix will necessarily be of equal importance. Some intersections will be more critical than others. Which intersections are critical will, of course, depend on the company and the nature of its operations, but they are likely to reflect the relative priority of performance objectives and those decisions areas that affect, or are affected by, the company's strategic resources. The example of Pret A Manger illustrates how the matrix can be used to describe a company's operations strategy.

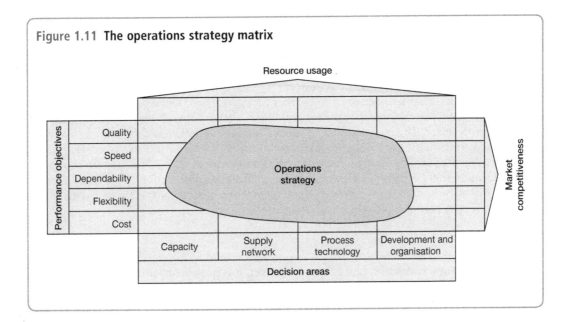

**Figure 1.11  The operations strategy matrix**

**Pret A Manger**[13]

When college friends Sinclair and Julian opened their first store in London in 1986, they wanted to '*make proper sandwiches avoiding the obscure chemicals, additives and preservatives common to so much of the "prepared" and "fast" food on the market*'. They created the sort of food they themselves craved but couldn't find anywhere else. Now there are over 300 Pret shops worldwide, most of them in the UK. The company are particularly proud of their customer service. '*We'd like to think we react to our customers' feelings (the good, the bad, the ugly) with haste and absolute sincerity*', they say. '*Pret customers have the right to be heard. Do call or email. Our UK Managing Director is available if you would like to discuss Pret with him. Alternatively, our CEO hasn't got much to do; hassle him!*'

It's a bold approach to customer service, but Pret has always been innovative. Described by the press as having 'revolutionised the concept of sandwich making and eating', Pret A Manger opened its first shop in London and now has over 260 shops in the UK, New York, Hong Kong and Tokyo. The founders say that their secret is to focus continually on the quality of the food and the service. They avoid the chemicals and preservatives common in most 'fast' food. '*Many food retailers focus on extending the shelf life of their food, but that's of no interest to us. We sell food that can't be beaten for freshness. At the end of the day, we give whatever we haven't sold to charity to help feed those who would otherwise go hungry. Pret A Manger shops have their own kitchen where fresh ingredients are delivered every morning, with food prepared throughout the day. The team members serving on the tills at lunchtime will have been making sandwiches in the kitchen that morning. We are determined never to forget that our hardworking people make all the difference. They are our heart and soul. When they care, our business is sound. If they cease to care, our business goes down the drain. In a retail sector where high staff turnover is normal, we're pleased to say our people are much more likely to stay around! We work hard at building great teams. We take our reward schemes and career opportunities very seriously. We don't work nights (generally), we wear jeans, we party!*' Customer feedback is regarded as being particularly important at Pret. Examining customers' comments for improvement ideas is a key part of weekly management meetings, and of the daily team briefs in each shop. Moreover, staff at Pret are rewarded in cash for being nice to customers; they collect bonuses for delivering outstanding customer service. Every week, a secret shopper who scores the shop on such performance measures as speed of service, product availability and cleanliness visits each Pret outlet. In addition, the mystery shopper rates the 'engagement level' of the staff; questions include, 'Did servers connect with eye contact, a smile and some polite remarks?' Assessors score out of 50. If the store gets 43 points or more every team member receives an extra payment for every hour worked; and if an individual is mentioned by the mystery shopper for providing outstanding service they get an additional payment. '*The emphasis on jollity and friendliness has been a winner*', said James Murphy – a management consultant for Future Foundation. '*In the highly competitive sandwich market, that's been a big contributor to their success.*' But not everyone agrees with using mystery shoppers. '*It is the equivalent of asking one customer in a shop what they thought at that exact moment, and then planning an entire store-improvement strategy around the one piece of feedback*', says Jeremy Michael of the Service Management Group, another consultancy.

For a company such as Pret A Manger, it is possible to find some kind of relationship between each performance objective and every decision area. However, in Figure 1.12 we have confined ourselves to some of the critical issues described in the example.[14] As in most analyses of this type, it is the interrelationship between the intersections (cells) of the matrix that are as important to understand as the intersections themselves.

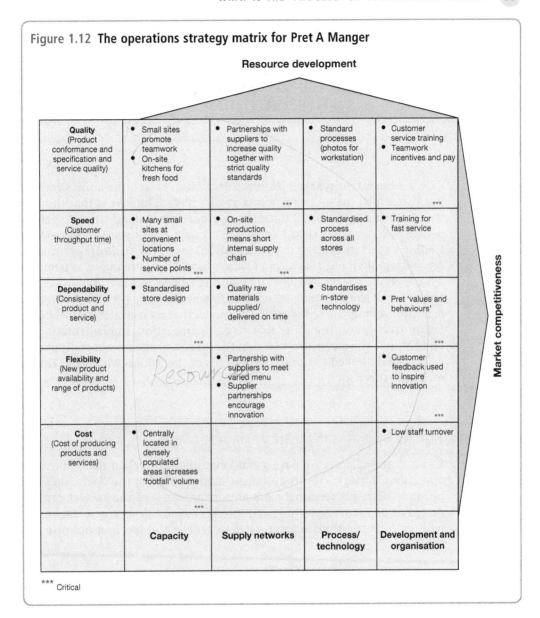

Figure 1.12 **The operations strategy matrix for Pret A Manger**

| | Capacity | Supply networks | Process/technology | Development and organisation |
|---|---|---|---|---|
| **Quality** (Product conformance and specification and service quality) | • Small sites promote teamwork<br>• On-site kitchens for fresh food | • Partnerships with suppliers to increase quality together with strict quality standards ✱✱✱ | • Standard processes (photos for workstation) | • Customer service training<br>• Teamwork incentives and pay ✱✱✱ |
| **Speed** (Customer throughput time) | • Many small sites at convenient locations<br>• Number of service points ✱✱✱ | • On-site production means short internal supply chain ✱✱✱ | • Standardised process across all stores | • Training for fast service |
| **Dependability** (Consistency of product and service) | • Standardised store design ✱✱✱ | • Quality raw materials supplied/delivered on time | • Standardises in-store technology | • Pret 'values and behaviours' ✱✱✱ |
| **Flexibility** (New product availability and range of products) | | • Partnership with suppliers to meet varied menu<br>• Supplier partnerships encourage innovation | | • Customer feedback used to inspire innovation ✱✱✱ |
| **Cost** (Cost of producing products and services) | • Centrally located in densely populated areas increases 'footfall' volume ✱✱✱ | | | • Low staff turnover |

_Resource development_ (top)

_Market competitiveness_ (right)

✱✱✱ Critical

## What is the 'process' of operations strategy?

The 'process' of operations strategy are the procedures that are, or can be, used to formulate operations strategy. 'Process' determines how an operation pursues the reconciliation between its market requirements and operations resources in practice. However, there are significant overlaps between content and process. For example, part of the 'content' of operations strategy is concerned with the organisational structure and responsibility relationships within the operations function. Yet these issues have a direct impact on the 'process' of how the organisation formulates its own operations strategies. Nevertheless, despite the overlap, it is conventional to treat content and process separately.

Figure 1.13 **The stages of the process of operations strategy**

Operations strategy formulation → Operations strategy implementation → Operations strategy monitoring → Operations strategy control

To a large extent we shall leave the discussion of 'process' until Chapters 9 and 10. But it is worth making two points at this stage. The first is that the practical reality of putting operations strategies together and making them happen in practice is extremely complex (and a subject in its own right). As Dr Andrew MacLennan, a leading expert in strategy implementation, says: *'The challenge of implementing strategy successfully is one that faces managers across the globe and in organizations of every kind. However, few organizations have discovered how to make strategy work reliably – the failure rate of planned strategies remains remarkably high. We use a simplified stage model to identify some of the key issues.'*[15] The model that we use later in the book is shown in Figure 1.13 and distinguishes four stages: formulation, implementation, monitoring and control. The second point is that the success of effective operations strategy 'process' is closely linked to the style and skills of the leaders who do it. The next section examines this issue.

## How is operations strategy developing?

So far in this chapter we have given what might be called the 'mainstream' view of operations strategy – it is the strategic management of the operation's resources and processes. Yet this seemingly straightforward view of the subject can still be interpreted in different ways, and each interpretation brings a new dimension to, and a new use for, operations strategy. Here we will look at just four new(ish) angles on the subject:

- Operations strategy as 'supply strategy'
- Operations strategy as 'functional strategy'
- Operations strategy as the firm's 'operating model'
- Operations strategy as 'strategy execution'

### Operations strategy as 'supply strategy'

Earlier in this chapter we described how all operations could be viewed as a network. Processes are a network of interconnected individual resources. Operations are a network of interconnected processes. And, at a strategic level of analysis, supply networks are an interconnected network of operations. So, if the natural context of all individual operations is as part of a supply network (and, indeed, all operations are part of a supply network – no operation does everything itself), then at a strategic level, what is the difference between operations strategy and supply (network) strategy? Surely, it is argued, the responsibility of operations is to supply its customers by reconciling market requirements (what customers want) with operations resources (what the operation can do). This is our definition of operations strategy. So, if we include in our definition of an operation's resources the whole network of its suppliers and their suppliers, as well as customers and their customers, and so on, operations strategy is indistinguishable from supply strategy.

However, some authorities would argue that there is more than a semantic difference between operations and supply strategy. The term 'supply strategy', they would argue, emphasises the responsibility that all operations have to take some accountability for the contribution of the supply network of which they are a part. To quote two well-used sayings of supply network practitioners: 'individual operations don't compete, supply chains (or networks – we shall explain the difference in Chapter 5) compete', and 'your customer doesn't care if your supplier let you down, it was you who failed to deliver'. No operations strategy should ignore the configuration and management of the supply network of which it is part, and no supply strategy should ignore the individual capabilities of the operations that constitute the network. In this book, we treat supply network strategy (or, more accurately, purchasing and supply strategy) as one of operations strategy's decision areas in Chapter 5, but we could just as easily have used 'supply strategy' as the over-arching framework for the whole book.

## Operations strategy as 'functional strategy'

Earlier we established that the transformation model, on which operations activities are based, not only applies to all types of business, but also describes functions other than the operations function, such as marketing, finance, information systems and HRM. So, it follows that if it is helpful to take a strategic view of the 'operations' transformation process, it should also be worthwhile doing the same for any other organisational function. In other words, operations strategy, its frameworks, concepts, models and tools, can form the basis of *any* functional strategy. Or, put another way, all functions deliver service externally or internally using their resources and processes, and just like the operations function, every function has a responsibility to make sure that the way they develop their resources and processes contributes to overall strategy. Therefore, the application of operations strategy should be central to senior managers in any function.

This is where we need to distinguish between the different components of expertise necessary to lead a function. There is a strong case for an appreciation of operations strategy being accepted as an essential part of chief officers' expertise. By 'chief officers' we mean the managers who often carry titles such as Chief Finance Officer (CFO), Chief Information Officer (CIO), Chief Operations Officer (COO), and so on. These people are often called 'C suite' managers. Everyone assumes that, to reach the top of their function, such people will have acquired a reasonable competence in their area of 'technical' expertise (finance, information, marketing, human resources, etc.). And that is a necessary, but nowhere near-sufficient, condition for being an effective functional chief.

We can now combine two ideas. The first is that all functions have processes and resources that are (or should be) integrated with the total internal network of processes within the enterprise. The second is that all functions need to develop their processes strategically over the longer term. This has an important implication for how we think about operations strategy. Its basic principles, concepts and tools can be used to help develop the strategy of any function of any type of organisation. Keep this in mind when you work through each chapter. The ideas may need adapting slightly and a different terminology may be more conventional, but, essentially the operations strategy approach holds true irrespective of functional responsibilities.

### Internal customers and the 'market requirements' perspective

For functional strategy, some 'customers' will be internal customers. By internal customers we mean the individuals or parts of the business to which the function provides internal service, as opposed to external customers that actually buy the businesses products or services. Yet there is clearly a difference between internal and external customers. At a fundamental level, the only real customer is the one that actually pays for products and services and provides revenues. Internal customers and the internal service providers that serve them are not 'stand alone' businesses, nor would many want them to be. The obvious difference between internal and external customers is that there are no effective 'competitors', at least in the short term. The idea of markets and market positioning is simply inappropriate when considering functional strategy for internal service providers. More dangerously, treating internal relationships as pseudo-commercial can promote competition between supplier and customer and general lack of internal alignment. However, the customer perspective is still important for shaping functional strategy. Internal customers have needs, and functional strategy must reflect these needs. Accepting that it is important to understand internal customer requirements is a starting point; understanding that internal customers (like external customers) may not always have fully articulated requirements is also imperative, as is to recognise that internal customer requirements and the top-down requirements of the business may not always align.

## Operations strategy as the firm's 'operating model'

Two concepts have emerged over the last few years that are relevant to operations strategy (or at least the terms are new – one could argue that the ideas are far older). These are the concepts of the 'business model' and the 'operating model'. Put simply, a 'business model' is the plan that is implemented by a company to generate revenue and make a profit. It includes the various parts and organisational functions of the business, as well as the revenues it generates and the expenses it incurs; in other words, what a company does and how they make money from doing it. More formally, it is... *'A conceptual tool that contains a big set of elements and their relationships and allows* [the expression of] *the business logic of a specific firm. It is a description of the value a company offers to one or several segments of customers and of the architecture of the firm and its network of partners for creating, marketing, and delivering this value and relationship capital, to generate profitable and sustainable revenue streams.'*[16]

One synthesis of literature[17] shows that business models have a number of common elements:

1 The **value proposition** of what is offered to the market.

2 The **target customer segments** addressed by the value proposition.

3 The communication and **distribution channels** to reach customers and offer the value proposition.

4 The *relationships* established with customers.

5 The *core capabilities* needed to make the business model possible.

6 The *configuration of activities* to implement the business model.

7 The *partners* and their motivations of coming together to make a business model happen.

8 The *revenue streams* generated by the business model constituting the revenue model.

9 The *cost structure* resulting from the business model.

One can see that this idea of the business model is broadly analogous to the idea of a 'business strategy', but implies more of an emphasis on *how* to achieve an intended strategy as well as exactly *what* that strategy should be.

An 'operating model' is a *'high-level design of the organisation that defines the structure and style which enables it to meet its business objectives'*. It should provide a clear, 'big-picture' description of what the organisation does, across both business and technology domains. It provides a way to examine the business in terms of the key relationships between business functions, processes and structures that are required for the organisation to fulfil its mission. Unlike the concept of a business model, which usually assumes a profit motive, the operating model philosophy can be applied to organisations of all types – including large corporations, not-for-profit organisations and the public sector.[18]

An operating model would normally include most or all of the following elements:

- Key performance indicators (KPIs) – with an indication of the relative importance of performance objectives.
- Core financial structure – P&L, new investments and cash flow.
- The nature of accountabilities for products, geographies, assets etc.
- The structure of the organisation – often expressed as capability areas rather than functional roles.
- Systems and technologies.
- Processes responsibilities and interactions.
- Key knowledge and competence.

Note two important characteristics of an operating model. First, it does not respect conventional functional boundaries as such. In some ways, the concept of the operating model reflects the idea that we proposed earlier in the chapter: namely that all managers are operations managers and all functions can be considered as operations because they comprise processes that deliver some kind of service. An operating model is like an operations strategy, but applied across all functions and domains of the organisation. Second, there are clear overlaps between the 'business model' and the 'operating model', but the main difference is that an operating model focuses more on how an overall business strategy is to be achieved. Operating models have an element of implied change or transformation of the organisation's resources and processes. Often, the term 'target operating model' is used to describe the way the organisation should operate in the future if it is going to achieve its objectives and make a success of its business model. Figure 1.14 illustrates the relationship between business and operating models.

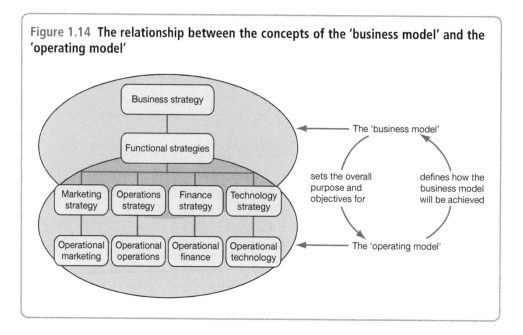

Figure 1.14 **The relationship between the concepts of the 'business model' and the 'operating model'**

## Operations strategy as 'strategy execution'

Writers on strategy sometimes distinguish between strategy formulation and strategy execution. To put it simply, strategy formulation is 'deciding what to do' and strategy execution is 'deciding how to do it'. And, while strategy formulation has been the subject of attention for literally thousands of academics and practitioners, strategy execution has been relatively neglected. Formally '... *strategy execution is the action that moves the organisation along its choice of route towards its goal – the fulfilment of its mission, the achievement of its mission ... strategy execution is the realisation of intentions*'.[19] Or, to put it in a way that better illustrates the closeness between strategy execution and operations strategy '... *strategy execution is the process of indirectly manipulating the pattern of resource and market interactions an organisation has with its environment in order to achieve its overall objective*'.[20]

Note how this last definition includes two ideas that bring strategy execution close to our view of operations strategy. First, it is defined as a 'process', in a similar way to how we have distinguished between content and process earlier. In fact, the terms 'strategy execution' and 'strategy implementation' (the latter a key stage in operations strategy process) are often used interchangeably. Second, the twin idea of 'manipulating' resources and market interactions is very similar to our idea of 'reconciling' operations resources and market requirements. And, at a common sense level, strategy execution must be concerned with making changes to the way things are done currently. Presumably this will involve changing some combination of the organisation's capacity, supply arrangements, technology, new product and service development and so on. Which is exactly what operations strategy does. So, the decision areas of operations strategy can be seen as a 'checklist' for the practical changes that executing any strategy implies. After all, any topic that deals with operations, whether at an operational or strategic level, must be concerned with practical issues. Operations is about doing stuff, getting things done, making things happen. It is about how we deal with the reality of creating services and products. It is about execution.

## SUMMARY ANSWERS TO KEY QUESTIONS

### Why is operations excellence fundamental to strategic success?

'Operations' is the activity of managing the resources and processes that produce and deliver goods and services. All operations transform resource inputs into outputs of products and services and can be analysed at three levels: that of the business itself; as part of a greater network of operations; and at the level of individual processes within the operation. Operations management contributes to the success of any organisation by reducing costs, by increasing revenue by reducing capital employed, and by providing the basis for future innovation.

### What is strategy?

Strategic decisions are those that set broad objectives that direct an enterprise towards its overall goal, plan the path that will achieve these goals, stress long-term rather than short-term objectives, deal with total picture rather than with individual activities, and are often seen as above or detached from routine day-to-day activities. However, it is not easy to totally characterise strategy or strategic decisions. Some organisations make no explicit strategic decisions, as such. Rather, they develop over time, often with strategies that 'emerge' from their ongoing experience of doing business. Furthermore, the strategy that is espoused by an organisation may not always be reflected in what it actually does. This is why strategy is often taken to be the 'pattern of decisions' that indicate the company's overall path.

### What is operations strategy?

Operations strategy is the total pattern of decisions that shape the long-term capabilities of any kind of operation and their contribution to overall strategy, through the ongoing reconciliation of market requirements and operation resources. All businesses have markets, all businesses own or deploy resources; therefore, all businesses are concerned with the reconciliation of markets and resources.

### How should operations reflect overall strategy?

An operations strategy will be one of several functional strategies that are governed by the decisions that set the overall strategic direction of the organisation. This is called the 'top-down' approach. So, corporate strategy should be reflected in the strategies of each business unit, which should, in turn, inform the strategy of each business function.

### How can operations strategy learn from operational experience?

An alternative view to the top-down perspective (one that is based on observing how strategy happens in practice) is the bottom-up perspective, which stresses how strategic ideas emerge over time from actual experiences. Companies adopt strategies partly because of their ongoing experience, sometimes with no high-level decision making involved. The idea of strategy being shaped by experience over time is also called the concept of emergent strategies. Shaping strategy from the bottom up requires an ability to learn from experience and a philosophy of continual and incremental improvement. ▶

*How do the requirements of the market influence operations strategy?*

Two important elements within markets are customers and competitors. The concept of market segmentation is used to identify target markets that have a clear set of requirements and where a company can differentiate itself from current, or potential, competitors. On the basis of this, the company takes up a market position. This market position can be characterised in terms of how the company wishes to compete for customers' business. By grouping competitive factors into clusters under the heading of generic performance objectives (quality, speed, dependability, flexibility and cost), market requirements are translated into a form useful for the development of the operation.

*How can the intrinsic capabilities of an operation's resources influence operations strategy?*

Over time, an operation may acquire distinctive capabilities, or competences, on the basis of the accumulation of its experiences. These capabilities may be embedded within a company's intangible resources and its operating 'routines'. So, they concern both what the operation has and what it does. Operations shapes these capabilities (consciously or unconsciously) through the way it makes a whole series of decisions over time. These decisions can be grouped under the headings of capacity, supply network, process technology and development and organisation.

*What is the 'content' of operations strategy?*

The 'content' of operations strategy is the building blocks from which any operations strategy will be formed. This includes the definition attached to individual performance objectives, together with a prioritisation of those performance objectives. It also includes an understanding of the structure and options available in the four decision areas of capacity, supply networks, process technology and development and organisation. Performance objectives and decisions areas interact in a way that can be described by the operations strategy matrix. When devising an operations strategy it is important to ensure that, in terms of the matrix, the strategy is comprehensive (all obvious aspects are at least considered) and has the critical intersections identified.

*What is the 'process' of operations strategy?*

The 'process' of operations strategy are the procedures that are, or can be, used to formulate operations strategy. It determines how an operation pursues the reconciliation between its market requirements and operations resources in practice. The practical reality of putting operations strategies together and making them happen in practice is complex, but, at a simple level, has four stages: formulation, implementation, monitoring and control. The success of effective operations strategy process is also closely linked to the style and skills of the leaders who do it.

*How is operations strategy developing?*

Although the 'mainstream' view of operations strategy is straightforwardly the strategic management of the operation's resources and processes, the subject can still be interpreted in different ways. For example, operations strategy can be interpreted as being equivalent to 'supply strategy', or 'functional strategy', or as the firm's 'operating model', and as 'strategy execution'.

## Further reading

Beckman, S.L. and Rosenfield, D.R. (2007) *Operations Strategy: Competing in the 21st Century (Operations Series)*. New York: McGraw-Hill.

Bettley, A., Mayle, D. and Tantoush, T. (eds) (2005) *Operations Management: A Strategic Approach*. London: Sage Publications.

Fitzsimmons, J.A. and Fitzsimmons, M.J. (2010) *Service Management: Operations, Strategy, Information Technology*. New York: McGraw-Hill Higher Education.

Hayes, R.H. Pisano, G.P., Upton, D.M. and Wheelwright, S.C. (2004) *Operations, Strategy, and Technology: Pursuing the Competitive Edge*. New York: Wiley.

Hayes, R.H. Pisano, G.P., Upton, D.M. and Wheelwright, S.C. (1996) *Strategic Operations: Competing Through Capabilities: Text and Cases*. Cambridge: The Free Press.

Hill, A. and Hill, T. (2009) *Manufacturing Operations Strategy: Texts and Cases*. Basingstoke: Palgrave Macmillan.

Kaplan, R.S. and Norton, D.P. (2004) *Strategy Maps: Converting Intangible Assets into Tangible Outcomes*. Cambridge, MA: Harvard Business School Publishing.

MacLennan, A. (2010) *Strategy Execution: Translating Strategy into Action in Complex Organisations*. London: Routledge.

Mintzberg, H., Ahlstrand, B. and Lampel, J.B. (2008) *Strategy Safari: The Complete Guide Through the Wilds of Strategic Management*. Harlow, UK: Financial Times/Prentice Hall.

Skinner, W. (1978) *Manufacturing in the Corporate Strategy*. New York: Wiley.

Slack, N., Brandon-Jones, A., Johnston, R. and Betts, A. (2015) *Operations and Process Management: Principles and Practice for Strategic Impact*, 4th edn. Harlow, UK: Pearson Education.

Wernerfelt, B. (1984) 'A resource-based theory of the firm', *Strategic Management Journal*, (5), pp. 272–280.

## Notes on the chapter

1 Operations managers are called by many names: the 'fleet manager' in a distribution company, or the 'administrative manager' in a hospital, or the 'store manager' in a supermarket.

2 Sources include: Rhodes, C. (2013) *The Retail Industry*. House of Commons Library Standard Note SN06186, 29 April 2013; 'Online Food Retailing – The raw and the clicked', *The Economist*, 30 November 2013; Ocado (2010) 'Ocado wins World Etailer Of The Year: Online supermarket scoops award at World Retail Awards in Berlin', Ocado press release; Davey, J. (2007) 'Ocado finally delivers the goods', *Sunday Times*, 25 November.

3 Weick, K.E. (1990) 'Cartographic myths in organizations', in A. Huff (ed) *Managing Strategic Thought*. London: Wiley.

4 Mintzberg, H. and Quinn, J. (1990) *The Strategy Process: Concepts Context and Cases*. Harlow, UK: Prentice Hall.

5 *Source*: Microsoft website (2007).

6 Sources include: Jopson, B. (2012) 'Amazon: From warehouse to powerhouse', *Financial Times*, 8 July; 'Lifting the bonnet', *The Economist*, 7 October 2006.

7 Learned, E.C., Christensen, C., Andrews, K. and Guth, W. (1969) *Business Policy: Text and Cases*. Homewood, IL: Irwin.

8 Penrose, E. (1959) *The Theory of the Growth of the Firm*. Oxford: Blackwell.

9 Barney, J. (1991) 'The resource-based model of the firm: Origins, implications and prospects; and firm resources and competitive advantage', *Journal of Management*, 17(1).

10 For example see, Dyer, J.H. and Nobeoka, K. (2000), 'Creating and managing a high performance knowledge-sharing network: The Toyota Case', *Strategic Management Journal*, 21, ▶

pp. 345–367. Granovetter, M.S. (1973) 'The strength of weak ties', *American Journal of Sociology* 78, pp. 1360–1380. Ireland, R.D., Hitt, M.A. and Vaidyanath, D. (2002) 'Alliance management as a source of competitive advantage', *Journal of Management*, 8(3), pp. 413–466. Madhok, A. and Taliman, S.B. (1998) 'Resources, transactions and rents: Managing value through interfirm collaborative relationships', *Organization Science* 9, pp. 326–339. Matthews, J.A. (2003) 'Competititve Dynamics and economic learning: An extended resource-based view', *Industrial and Corporate Change*, 12(1), pp. 115–145. Matthews, J.A. (2003) 'Strategizing by firms in the presence of markets for resources', *Industrial and Corporate Change*, 12(6), pp. 1157–1193. Szulanski, G. (2000) 'The process of knowledge transfer: A diachronic analysis of stickiness', *Organisational Behaviour and Human Decision Processes*, 82, pp. 9–27.

11  Sources include: BBC News (2014) 'Ikea sees record profit in 2013 as market share grows', 28 January; *The Economist* (2012) 'The secret of IKEA's success: Lean operations, shrewd tax planning and tight control', 24 February.

12  An idea put forward by Eilan, S. and Gold, B. (1978) *Productivity Measurement*. Oxford, UK: Pergamon Press.

13  Sources include: Goodman, M. (2011) 'Pret Smile, it will pay for everyone', *Sunday Times*, 6 March; Pret A Manger website, http://www.pret.com/

14  This is our analysis of the likely issues faced by Pret A Manger, it does not necessarily reflect the company's view.

15  MacLennon, A. (2010) *Strategy Execution: Translating Strategy into Action in Complex Organisations*. London: Routledge.

16  Osterwalder, A., Pigneur, Y. and Tucci, C. (2005) 'Clarifying Business Models: Origins, present and Future of the Concept', *CAIS*, Vol. 15, pp. 751–775.

17  Osterwalder, A. (2005) 'What is a business model?', http://business-model-design.blogspot .com/2005/11/what-is-business-model.html

18  Based on the definitions developed by Cap Gemini.

19  Eccles, T. (1994) *Succeeding with Change: Implementing Action-Driven Strategies*. London: McGraw-Hill.

20  MacLennan, A. (2011) *Strategy Execution: Translating Strategy into Action in Complex Organisations*. London: Routledge.

# 2 Operations performance

## Introduction

Operations 'performance' means the extent to which an operation accomplishes its objectives. In this chapter we look at how we judge the performance of operations, primarily in terms of the five performance objectives: quality, speed, dependability, flexibility and cost. We then look at three related aspects of performance that are fundamental to understanding operations strategy. First, we examine how the relative importance of different aspects of performance changes over time. This is because the relative importance of the market requirements and operations resource perspectives does not stay constant over time. Sometimes market requirements dominate and operations resources must be made to fit whatever the market dictates. At other times the capabilities and constraints of operations resources will place restrictions on the organisation's choice of its market positioning. Second, we look at how performance objectives trade off against each other. Operations are often called on to enhance some specific aspects of their performance. The key issue is, do improvements in some aspects of performance necessarily mean a reduction in the performance of others? Third, we examine how exceptional performance levels can be reached by focusing on a limited set of objectives and exploiting the trade-offs between objectives (see Figure 2.1).

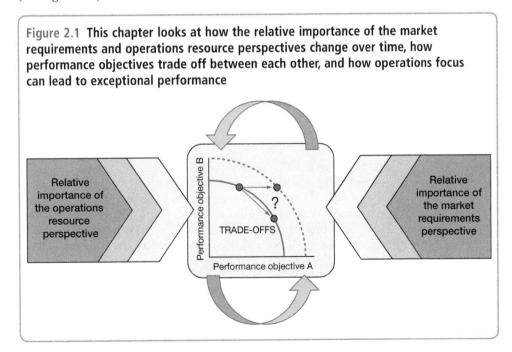

**Figure 2.1 This chapter looks at how the relative importance of the market requirements and operations resource perspectives change over time, how performance objectives trade off between each other, and how operations focus can lead to exceptional performance**

---

**KEY QUESTIONS**

- *How can operations performance 'make or break' the organisation?*
- *What are operations performance objectives?*
- *Do the role and key performance objectives of operations stay constant, or vary over time?*
- *Are trade-offs between operations performance objectives inevitable, or can they be overcome?*
- *What are the advantages and disadvantages of focused operations?*

---

## Operations performance can make or break any organisation

Operations strategy, and the resulting performance that it brings, can either 'make' or 'break' any business. Not just because the operations function is large and, in most businesses, represents the bulk of its assets and the majority of its people, but because the operations function gives the ability to compete by providing the ability to respond to customers and by developing the capabilities that will keep it ahead of its competitors in the future. For example, the performance of their operations functions proved hugely important in the Heathrow T5 and Dubai T3 launches (see the example box below). It was a basic failure to understand the importance of operations that (temporarily) damaged British Airways' reputation. It was Dubai's thorough operational preparation that avoided similar problems. However, assessing the performance of anything at any time is hardly ever straightforward. Perceived performance is a function of, amongst other things, who you are (customer, employee, stockholder, etc.), your objectives (often disputed), timescale (what is judged as good now may not be appropriate next year), measurability (how you measure trust, relationship, security, etc.), and how comprehensive you want to be (do you really want to measure everything every customer may find important?). Nor is operations-driven performance improvement always guaranteed. The example shown below on vehicle recalls ('Better operations performance equals better customer satisfaction – or does it?') shows that sometimes other factors can outweigh operations excellence.

---

**Example** | **A tale of two terminals**[1]

Terminal 5 at London's Heathrow Airport is now one of the best in the world, with awards for customer service and efficient operations. But when the terminal first opened in 2008 it was a disaster, culminating in two of British Airways' (BA) most senior executives, its director of operations and its director of customer services, leaving the company. They were paying the price for the ruinous opening of the new terminal that gave BA some of its worst headlines ever. The opening of the £4.3bn terminal, said BA's boss Willie Walsh with magnificent understatement, *'was not the company's finest hour'.* The chaos at the terminal on its opening days made news around the world and was seen by many as one of the most public failures of basic operations management in the modern history of aviation. *'It's a terrible, terrible PR nightmare to have hanging over you'*, said David Learmount, an aviation expert. *'Somebody who may have been a faithful customer and still not have their luggage after three weeks is not good for their [BA's] image. The one thing that's worse than having a stack of 15,000 bags is adding 5,000 a day to that heap.'* According to a BA spokeswoman, it needed an extra 400 volunteer staff and courier companies to wade through the backlog of late baggage. So the new terminal that had opened on 27 March could not even cope with BA's full short-haul service until 8 April (two hundred flights in and out of T5 were cancelled in its first three days). This delayed moving its long-haul operations to the new building from Terminal 4 as scheduled on 30 April, which, in turn, disrupted the operations of other airlines, many of whom were scheduled to move into Terminal 4 once BA had moved its long-haul flights from there. Sharing the blame with BA was the British Airports Authority (BAA), which was already suffering criticism from passenger groups, airlines and businesses for allegedly poor performance. BAA's non-executive chairman, Sir Nigel Rudd, said he was *'bitterly disappointed'* about the opening of the terminal. *'It was clearly a huge embarrassment to the company, me personally, and the board. Nothing can take away that failure. We had all believed genuinely that it would be a great opening, which clearly it wasn't.'*

Yet it all should have been so different. T5 took more than six years and around 60,000 workers to build. And it's an impressive building. It is Europe's largest free-standing structure. It was also keenly anticipated by travellers and BA alike. Willie Walsh had said that the terminal *'will completely change his passengers' experience'*. He was right, but not in the way he imagined! So what went wrong? As is often the case with major operations failures, it was not one thing but several interrelated problems (all of which could have been avoided). Press reports initially blamed glitches with the state-of-the-art baggage handling system that consisted of 18km of conveyor belts and was (theoretically) capable of transporting 12,000 bags per hour. And, indeed, the baggage handling system did experience problems that had not been exposed in testing. But BAA, the airport operator, doubted that the main problem was the baggage system itself. The system had worked until it became clogged with bags that were overwhelming BA's handlers loading them onto the aircraft. Partly this may have been because staff were not sufficiently familiar with the new system and its operating processes, but handling staff had also suffered delays getting to their new (and unfamiliar) work areas, negotiating (new) security checks and finding (again, new) car parking spaces. Also, once staff were airside they had problems logging-in. The cumulative effect of these problems meant that the airline was unable to get ground handling staff to the correct locations for loading and unloading bags from the aircraft, so baggage could not be loaded onto aircraft fast enough, so baggage backed up – clogging the baggage handling system, which, in turn, meant closing baggage check-in and baggage drops, leading eventually to baggage check-in being halted.

However, not every airline underestimates the operational complexity of airport processes. During the same year that Terminal 5 at Heathrow was suffering queues, lost bags and bad publicity, Dubai International Airport's Terminal 3 opened quietly with little publicity and fewer problems. Like T5, it is also huge and designed to impress. Its new shimmering facilities are solely dedicated to Emirates airline. Largely built underground (20 metres beneath the taxiway area) the multi-level environment reduces passenger walking by using 157 elevators, 97 escalators and 82 moving walkways. Its underground baggage handling system is the deepest and the largest of its kind in the world, with 90 km of baggage belts handling around 15,000 items per hour, with 800 RFID (see Chapter 8) read/write stations for 100% accurate tracking. Also, like T5, it handles about 30 million passengers a year.

▶

But one difference between the two terminals was that Dubai's T3 could observe and learn lessons from the botched opening of Heathrow's Terminal 5. Paul Griffiths, the former head of London's Gatwick Airport, who is now Dubai Airport's chief executive, insisted that his own new terminal should not be publicly shamed in the same way. '*There was a lot of arrogance and hubris around the opening of T5, with all the … publicity that BA generated*', Mr Griffiths says. '*The first rule of customer service is under-promise and over-deliver because that way you get their loyalty. BA was telling people that they were getting a glimpse of the future with T5, which created expectation and increased the chances of disappointment. Having watched the development of T5, it was clear that we had to make sure that everyone was on-message. We just had to bang heads together so that people realised what was at stake. We knew the world would be watching and waiting after T5 to see whether T3 was the next big terminal fiasco. We worked very hard to make sure that didn't happen.*'

Paul Griffiths was also convinced that Terminal 3 should undergo a phased programme, with flights added progressively, rather than a 'big bang' approach where the terminal opened for business on one day. '*We exhaustively tested the terminal systems throughout the summer … We continue to make sure we're putting large loads on it, week by week, improving reliability. We put a few flights in bit by bit, in waves rather than a big bang.*' Prior to the opening he also said that Dubai Airport would never reveal a single opening date for its new Terminal 3 until all pre-opening test programmes had been completed. '*T3 opened so quietly*', said one journalist, '*that passengers would have known that the terminal was new only if they had touched the still-drying paint.*'

## The 'stakeholder' perspective on operations performance

For operations strategy to be effective, performance must be assessed in some way – and an obvious starting point is to consider the operation's range of stakeholders. All operations have stakeholders. Stakeholders are the people and groups who have a legitimate interest in the operation's strategy. Some are internal – for example, the operation's employees; others are external – for example, customers, society or community groups and a company's shareholders. External stakeholders may have a direct commercial relationship with the organisation, such as suppliers and customers; others may not – for example, industry regulators. In not-for-profit operations, these stakeholder groups can overlap. So, voluntary workers in a charity may be employees, shareholders and customers all at once. However, in any kind of organisation, it is a responsibility of the operations function to understand the (sometimes conflicting) objectives of its stakeholders and set its objectives accordingly.

Example | **Better operations performance equals better customer satisfaction – or does it?[2]**

One of the best-known examples of positive change in operations performance is how cost and quality no longer seem to be inversely related, at least as far as conformance quality is concerned. This is certainly true for the automobile industry. Just because we buy a 'budget' (i.e. cheap) car doesn't mean that we expect it to fall to bits after a couple of years. Compared with some years ago, automobile manufacturers (with only a few exceptions) can turn out quality cars at levels of efficiency that keep costs relatively low. So why is it that motor vehicle recalls, where a manufacturer requests owners to return cars to a dealer to be modified, have not fallen significantly? In fact, in some markets (for example, the USA) recalls have risen. One estimate is that one in four vehicles suffers at least one recall during its life, and some will be recalled a number of times. It certainly is not that manufacturers make recall decisions lightly. Recalling a vehicle can be a costly business for carmakers, suppliers and dealers, both financially and in terms of reputational damage. The answers tell us a lot about how the link between operations performance and customer perception is not always straightforward.

In fact, there are several reasons that explain the high levels of recalls. First, almost all auto makes have made the same improvements in cost and quality, so it's not particularly a case of differential performance. Customers now expect low cost and good quality and they have many and various channels to make any dissatisfaction known if they don't get it. Social media and comparison websites, as well as more conventional complaints procedures, can all impact carmakers' reputations. Second, and partly because of the first point, the manufacturers are increasingly aware that delaying a recall, especially if it's a safety issue, can result in a public relations disaster. Manufacturers may be more fearful of litigation than they used to be, and this has increased their propensity to recall. Third, many national regulators are getting tougher as lawmakers attempt to protect citizens. Fourth, cars are getting more complex; an average car has 15,000 components. There is simply more to go wrong. Finally, the automobile industry is generally better at tracking part failures that may go on to produce safety problems. So detecting and diagnosing specific problems is a more accurate process, and ignoring problems is increasingly indefensible. But don't think that the message here is either that operations improvement is not important or that it has little effect on strategic success. On the contrary, without making such improvements to cost and quality performance any individual company would struggle to compete. However, improvements in operations performance can be influenced by the behaviour of competitors, the changing expectations of customers, increased sophistication of products and services, technological innovation and regulatory shifts.

Figure 2.2 illustrates some main stakeholder groups for a parcel delivery company, together with some of the aspects of operations performance in which they may be interested. The company is clearly concerned to satisfy its customers' requirements for fast and dependable services at reasonable prices, as well as helping and improving its own suppliers (a whole range of organisations, from those who print packets to those who clean the offices). Similarly, it is concerned to ensure the long-term economic value delivered to its stockholders. But the company also has a responsibility to ensure that its own employees are well treated and that society at large is not negatively affected by the operation's activities – the company must minimise vehicle pollution, minimise wastage of materials or energy, ensure that its operations do not disrupt the life and well-being of those who live nearby, and so on. But although each of these groups, to different extents, will be interested in operations performance, they are likely to have very different views of which aspect of performance is important. Table 2.1 identifies typical stakeholder requirements. But stakeholder relationships are not just one-way. It is also useful to consider what an individual organisation or business wants of the stakeholder groups themselves. Some of these requirements are also illustrated in Table 2.1.

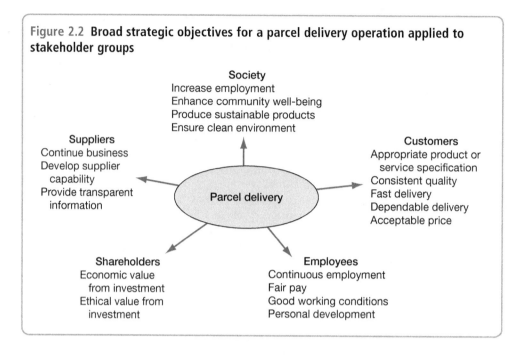

**Figure 2.2 Broad strategic objectives for a parcel delivery operation applied to stakeholder groups**

## Table 2.1 Typical stakeholders' performance objectives

| Stakeholder | What stakeholders want from the operation | What the operation wants from stakeholders |
|---|---|---|
| Shareholders | Return on investment (ROI)<br>Stability of earnings<br>Liquidity of investment | Investment capital<br>Long-term commitment |
| Directors/top management | Low/acceptable operating costs<br>Secure revenue<br>Well-targeted investment<br>Low risk of failure<br>Future innovation | Coherent, consistent, clear and achievable strategies<br>Appropriate investment |
| Staff | Fair wages<br>Good working conditions<br>Safe work environment<br>Personal and career development | Attendance<br>Diligence/best efforts<br>Honesty<br>Engagement |
| Staff representative bodies (e.g. trade unions) | Conformance with national agreements<br>Consultation | Understanding<br>Fairness<br>Assistance in problem solving |
| Suppliers (of materials, services, equipment, etc.) | Early notice of requirements<br>Long-term orders<br>Fair price<br>On-time payment | Integrity of delivery, quality and volume<br>Innovation<br>Responsiveness<br>Progressive price reductions |

▶

| Regulators (e.g. financial regulators) | Conformance to regulations<br>Feedback on effectiveness of regulations | Consistency of regulation<br>Consistency of application of regulations<br>Responsiveness to industry concerns |
|---|---|---|
| Government (local, national, regional) | Conformance to legal requirements<br>Contribution to (local/national/regional) economy | Low/simple taxation<br>Representation of local concerns<br>Appropriate infrastructure |
| Lobby groups (e.g. environmental lobby groups) | Alignment of the organisation's activities with whatever the group are promoting | No unfair targeting<br>Practical help in achieving aims (if the organisation wants to achieve them) |
| Society | Minimise negative effects from the operation (noise, traffic, etc.) and maximise positive effects (jobs, local sponsorship, etc.) | Support for organisation's plans |

The dilemma with using this wide range of stakeholders to judge performance is that organisations, particularly commercial companies, have to cope with the conflicting pressures of maximising profitability on one hand with the expectation that they will manage in the interests of (all or part of) society in general with accountability and transparency. Even if a business wanted to reflect aspects of performance beyond its own immediate interests, how is it to do it? According to Michael Jensen of Harvard Business School, *'At the economy-wide or social level, the issue is this: If we could dictate the criterion or objective function to be maximized by firms (and thus the performance criterion by which corporate executives choose among alternative policy options), what would it be? Or, to put the issue even more simply: How do we want the firms in our economy to measure their own performance? How do we want them to determine what is better versus worse?'* He also holds that using stakeholder perspectives gives undue weight to narrow special interests who want to use the organisation's resources for their own ends. The stakeholder perspective gives them a spurious legitimacy which *'undermines the foundations of value-seeking behaviour'.* The stakeholder perspective is also covered in Chapter 10, when we discuss the monitoring and control of operations strategy implementation.

## Corporate social responsibility (CSR)

Strongly related to the stakeholder perspective of operations performance is that of corporate social responsibility (generally known as CSR). According to the UK Government's definition: *'CSR is essentially about how business takes account of its economic, social and environmental impacts in the way it operates – maximizing the benefits and minimizing the downsides... Specifically, we see CSR as the voluntary actions that business can take, over and above compliance with minimum legal requirements, to address both its own competitive interests and the interests of wider society.'* A more direct link with the stakeholder concept is to be found in the definition used by Marks and Spencer, the

UK-based retailer: *'Corporate Social Responsibility ... is listening and responding to the needs of a company's stakeholders. This includes the requirements of sustainable development. We believe that building good relationships with employees, suppliers and wider society is the best guarantee of long-term success. This is the backbone of our approach to CSR.'*

The issue of how broader social performance objectives can be included in operations management's activities is of increasing importance, both from an ethical and a commercial point of view. It is treated again at various points throughout this book.

---

**Example**  **Holcim works with the 'triple bottom line'[3]**

Holcim is a global company, based in Switzerland, employing around 80,000 people, with production sites in around 70 countries. It is one of the world's leading manufacturers and distributors of cement and aggregates (for example, crushed stone, gravel and sand). It also supplies ready-mix concrete and asphalt, as well as offering consulting, research, trading, engineering and other services. But, along with other companies in this sector, Holcim faces some considerable challenges in pursuing its CSR objectives. After all, cement manufacture is an activity that has a significant impact on almost every aspect of sustainability and social responsibility. Concrete is the second-most used resource in the world after water. As the chief ingredient in concrete, cement is therefore a key requirement of modern society, but its manufacture is a resource- and energy-intensive process. This possibly explains why Holcim put so much effort into its sustainable development strategies. It aspires, it says, *'to be the world's most respected and attractive company in our industry, creating value for all our stakeholders; by placing sustainable development at the core of our business strategy aims to enhance this value, safeguards our reputation and contributes to continued success'*. Holcim's strategy and their approach to value creation attempts to integrate economic, environmental and social impacts. These are the three elements of what has become known as the 'triple bottom line'.

Triple bottom line accounting for company performance first came to prominence in John Elkington's book, *Cannibals with Forks: the Triple Bottom Line of 21st Century Business*. It advocated expanding the conventional financial reporting conventions to include ecological (sustainability) and social performance in addition to financial performance. To achieve its triple bottom line business goals, Holcim has established a set of group-wide performance targets. But, before targets are met the company aims to understand its current performance. It does this by establishing consistent measurement and reporting techniques, as well as implementing management systems to monitor progress toward its goals. Yet CSR-related performance measurement systems should not, say Holcim, be separate from the more conventional business systems. To work effectively, CSR performance systems are integrated into overall business processes and supported by appropriate training.

---

## The five generic performance objectives

Understanding broad stakeholder objectives is important, mainly because different or conflicting priorities between stakeholder groups often provide the backdrop to operations strategy decision making. But, in practical terms, an operation requires a more tightly defined set of objectives. These are the five generic 'performance objectives' that were briefly introduced in the previous chapter and that apply to all types of operation. It is worth examining each of them in a little more detail, not to present any precise definitions but rather to illustrate how the terms quality, speed, dependability, flexibility and cost may be used to mean slightly different things depending on how they are interpreted in different operations. This is not to imply that broad stakeholder objectives are irrelevant to operations strategy, far from it. But the five generic performance objectives have meaning for all types of operation and relate specifically to operations' basic task of satisfying customer requirements.

## Quality

Many definitions of quality refer to the 'specification' of a product or service, usually meaning high specification – as in 'the Mercedes-Benz S Class is at the quality end of the market'. Quality can also mean appropriate specification, meaning that the products and services are 'fit for purpose'; they do what they are supposed to do. 'Fit-for-purpose' quality includes two concepts that are far more useful treated separately. One is the level of the product or services specification; the other is whether the operation achieves conformance to that specification.

Specification quality is also a multidimensional issue. We needed to use several aspects of specification in the automobile example above, even to reach a crude indication of what type of car is being produced. So any product or service needs to use several dimensions of specification to define its nature. These dimensions can be separated into 'hard' and 'soft' aspects of specification quality. Hard dimensions are those concerned with the evident and largely objective aspects of the product or service. Soft dimensions are associated with aspects of personal interaction between customers and the product or (more usually) service. Table 2.2 identifies some hard and soft dimensions of specification quality, though each list will change depending on the type of product or service being considered.[4]

Conformance quality is more a concern of the operation itself. It refers to the operation's ability to produce goods and services to their defined specification reliably and consistently. This is not always a simple matter of yes it can, or no it cannot. Rather, the issue is often a matter of how closely the operation can achieve the product or service specification consistently. Here there is a difference between hard and soft dimensions of specification. Generally the conformance to soft dimensions of quality is more difficult to measure and more difficult to achieve. This is largely because soft dimensions, being related to interpersonal interaction, depend on the response of individual customers relating with individual staff.

Table 2.2 **Examples of 'hard' and 'soft' dimensions of specification quality**

| *'Hard' dimensions of specification quality* | *'Soft' dimensions of specification quality* |
|---|---|
| e.g. | e.g. |
| Features | Helpfulness |
| Performance | Attentiveness |
| Reliability | Communication |
| Aesthetics | Friendliness |
| Security/safety | Courtesy |
| Integrity | Etc. |
| Etc. | |

## Speed

At its most basic, speed indicates the time between the beginning of an operations process and its end. It is an elapsed time. This may relate to externally obvious events; for example, from the time when the customer requests a product or service, to the time when the customer receives it. Or it may be used internally in the operation; for example, the time between when material enters an operation and when it leaves fully processed. As far as operations strategy is concerned, we are usually interested in the former. Part of this elapsed time may be the actual time to 'produce the product or service' (the 'core' processing time). It may also include the time to clarify a customer's exact needs (for example, designing a product or service), the 'queuing' times before operations resources become available and, after the core processing, the time to deliver, transport and/or install the product or service. Figure 2.3 illustrates some of the significant 'process' times that signify the steps in customer response for two operations – a hospital and a software producer. One issue for these organisations' operations is how to define the speed of delivery. Clearly, limiting it to the elapsed

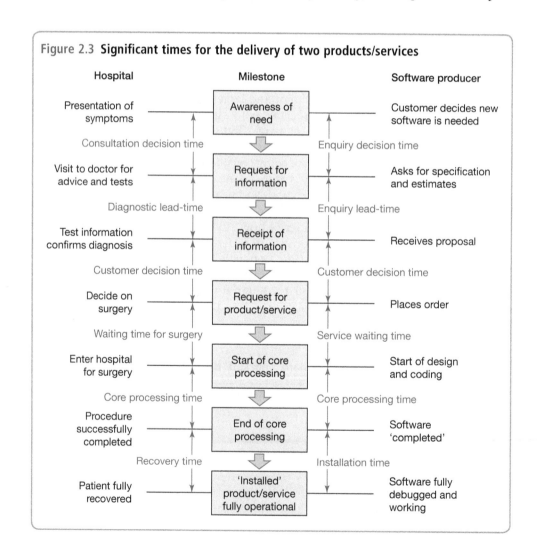

Figure 2.3 **Significant times for the delivery of two products/services**

time taken by the core process (though this is the part they can most directly control) is inadequate. From the customers' view, the total process starts when they become aware that they may need the product or service and ends when they are completely satisfied with its 'installation'. Some may even argue that, given the need continually to engage the customer in other revenue-generating activities such as maintenance or improvement, the process never ends.

## Dependability

The term 'dependability' is here used to mean keeping delivery promises – honouring the delivery time given to the customer. It is the other half of total delivery performance, along with delivery speed. The two performance objectives are often linked in some way. For example, theoretically, one could achieve high dependability merely by quoting long delivery times. In which case the difference between the expected delivery time and the time quoted to the customer is being used as an insurance against lack of dependability within the operation. However, companies that try to absorb poor dependability inside long lead-times can finish up being poor at both. There are two reasons for this. First, delivery times tend to expand to fill the time available. Attempting to discipline an operation to achieve delivery in two weeks when three are available is unambitious and allows the operation to relax its efforts to use all the available time. Second, long delivery times are often a result of slow internal response, high work-in-progress, and large amounts of non-value-added time. All of these can cause confusion, complexity and lack of control, which are the root causes of poor dependability. Good dependability can often be helped by fast throughput, rather than hindered by it. In principle, dependability is a straightforward concept:

$$\text{Dependability} = \text{due delivery time} - \text{actual delivery time}.$$

When delivery is on time, the equation should equal zero. Positive means it is early and negative means it is late. What, though, is the meaning of 'due time'? It could be the time originally requested by the customer or the time quoted by the operation. Also, there can be a difference between the delivery time scheduled by operations and that promised to the customer. Delivery times can also be changed – sometimes by customers, but more often by the operation. If the customer wants a new delivery time, should that be used to calculate delivery performance? Or, if the operation has to reschedule delivery, should the changed delivery time be used? It is not uncommon in some circumstances to find four or five arguable due times for each order. Nor is the actual delivery time without its complications. When, for example, should the product or service be considered to have been delivered? Here we are facing a similar issue to that posed when considering speed. Delivery could be when the product or service is produced, when the customer receives it, when it is working, or when they are fully comfortable with it. Then there is the problem of what is late. Should delivery to the promised minute, hour, day, week or even month be counted as on time?

## Flexibility

The word 'flexibility' means two different things. One dictionary definition has flexibility meaning the 'ability to be bent'. It is a useful concept, which translates into operational terms as the ability to adopt different states – take up different positions or do different things. So one operation is more flexible than another if it can do more things – exhibit a wide range of abilities. For example, it might be able to produce a greater variety of products or services, or operate at different output levels. Yet the range of things an operation can do does not totally describe its flexibility. The same word is also used to mean the ease with which it can move between its possible states. An operation that moves quickly, smoothly and cheaply from doing one thing to doing another should be considered more flexible than one that can only achieve the same change at greater cost and/or organisational disruption. Both the cost and time of making a change are the 'friction' elements of flexibility. They define the response of the system – the condition of making the change. In fact, for most types of flexibility, time is a good indicator of cost and disruption, so response flexibility can usually be measured in terms of time. So the first distinction to make is between range flexibility (how much the operation can be changed) and response flexibility (how fast the operation can be changed).

The next distinction is between the way we describe the flexibility of a whole operation and the flexibility of the individual resources that, together, make up the system. Total operations flexibility is best visualised by treating the operation as a 'black box' and considering the types of flexibility that would contribute to its competitiveness. For example:

- **product or service flexibility** – the ability to introduce and produce novel products or services or to modify existing ones;
- **mix flexibility** – the ability to change the variety of products or services being produced by the operation within a given time period;
- **volume flexibility** – the ability to change the level of the operation's aggregated output;
- **delivery flexibility** – the ability to change planned or assumed delivery dates.

Each of these types of total operations flexibility has its range and response components, as described in Table 2.3.

Table 2.3 **The range and response dimensions of the four types of total operations flexibility**

| Total operations flexibility | Range flexibility | Response flexibility |
|---|---|---|
| Product/service flexibility | The range of products and services that the company has the design, purchasing and operations capability to produce. | The time necessary to develop or modify the products or services and processes that produce them, to the point where regular production can start. |
| Mix flexibility | The range of products and services that the company produces within a given time period. | The time necessary to adjust the mix of products and services being produced. |
| Volume flexibility | The absolute level of aggregated output that the company can achieve for a given product or service mix. | The time taken to change the aggregated level of output. |
| Delivery flexibility | The extent to which delivery dates can be brought forward. | The time taken to reorganise the operation so as to replan for the new delivery date. |

## Cost

Cost is here treated last, not because it is the least important performance objective, but because it is the most important. To companies that compete directly on price, cost clearly will be their major performance objective. The lower the cost of producing their products and services, the lower can be the price to their customers. Yet even companies that compete on things other than price will be interested in keeping their costs low. Other things being equal, every euro, dollar or yen removed from an operation's cost base is a further euro, dollar or yen added to its profits. Not surprisingly, low cost is a universally attractive objective.

Here we are taking a broad definition of 'cost' as it applies in operations strategy. In this broad definition, cost is any financial input to the operation that enables it to produce its products and services. Conventionally, these financial inputs can be divided into three categories:

- **Operating expenditure** – the financial inputs to the operation needed to fund the ongoing production of products and services. It includes expenditure on labour, materials, rent, energy, etc. Usually the sum of all these expenditures is divided by the output from the operation (number of units produced, customers served, packages carried, etc.) to give the operation's 'unit cost'.

- **Capital expenditure** – the financial inputs to the operation that fund the acquisition of the 'facilities' that produce its products and services. It includes the money invested in land, buildings, machinery, vehicles, etc. Usually the funding for facilities is in the form of a lump sum 'outflow' investment, followed by a series of smaller inflows of finance in the form of either additional revenue or cost savings. Most methods of investment analysis are based on some form of comparison between the size, timing and risks associated with the outflow and its consequent inflows of cash.

- **Working capital** – the financial inputs needed to fund the time difference between regular outflows and inflows of cash. In most operations, payments must be made on the various types of operating expenditure that are necessary to produce goods and services before payment can be obtained from customers. Thus, funds are needed to bridge the time difference between payment out and payment received. The length of this time difference, and therefore the extent of the money required to fund it, is largely influenced by two processes – the process that handles the day-to-day financial transactions of the business and the operations process itself, which produces the goods and services. The faster the financial process can get payment from customers and the more it can negotiate credit delays to its suppliers, the shorter the gap between money going out and money coming in, and the less working capital is required. Similarly, the faster the operations process can move materials through the operation, the shorter the gap between obtaining the materials and having products and services ready for sale. This argument may also apply to information processing or even customer processing operations if operating expenditure is associated with the information or customers entering and progressing through the operation process.

**The reputational risk of cost cutting**

There is a good reason why most electronic components are made in China. It's cheap. Companies such as Taiwan's Foxconn, who produce many of the world's computer, consumer electronics and communications products for customers such as Apple, Dell, Nokia, and Sony, have perfected the art and science of squeezing cost out of their operations processes. But, although Foxconn is known for having an obsession with cutting its costs and has moved much of its manufacturing into China and other low-cost areas with plants in South-East Asia, Eastern Europe, and Latin America, it has been criticised for pushing its workers too far. In 2010 there was a cluster of suicides at its factories, with 18 workers throwing themselves from the tops of the company's buildings; 14 people died. The firm operates a huge industrial park, which it calls Foxconn City, in Shenzhen, just across the border from Hong Kong, with 15 multi-storey manufacturing buildings, each devoted to one customer. This is where the suicides took place. It prompted Foxconn to install safety nets in some of its factories and to hire counsellors to help its workers.

However, Boy Lüthje of the Institute of Social Research in Frankfurt says that conditions at the firm are actually not that bad when compared with many others. Food and lodging are free, as are extensive recreational facilities. But workers routinely put in overtime in excess of the 36 hours a month permitted under Chinese law and plenty of people seek jobs with the company. Moreover, the suicide rate at the company is lower than that among the general population in China. Yet the deaths raised questions about working conditions in electronics manufacturing in general, and in particular at Foxconn. Nor was this the last time concern was raised over working conditions. In 2012, around 150 workers at Wuhan threatened to commit suicide by leaping from their factory roof in protest at their working conditions. They were eventually coaxed down by managers after two days on top of the three-floor plant. '*We were put to work without any training, and paid piecemeal*', said one of the protesting workers. '*The assembly line ran very fast and after just one morning we all had blisters and the skin on our hand was black. The factory was also really choked with dust and no one could bear it.*' Some reports indicate that Foxconn is more advanced in designing its processes than many of its competitors, but it is run in a regimented fashion that is not always popular with workers.

## The internal and external effects of the performance objectives

The whole idea of generic performance objectives is that they can be clearly related to some aspects of external market positioning, and can be clearly connected to the internal decisions that are made concerning the operations resources. Because of this, it is worthwhile examining each of the performance objectives in terms of how they affect market position outside the operation and operations resources inside the operation. Table 2.4 identifies some of these effects. What is interesting is that whereas the consequences of excellent performance outside the operation are specific and direct, the consequences inside the operation are more interdependent. So, for example, a high performance in terms of speed of delivery outside the operation gives clear benefits to customers who value short delivery times for products or queuing times for services. If an operation competes on speed of delivery, then it will need to develop the speed objective inside its operations. Internally, fast throughput time will presumably help it to achieve short delivery times to its external customers. However, there are other benefits that may come through fast throughput times inside the operation. Materials, information or customers moving rapidly through an operation can mean less queuing, lower inventory levels, a lower need for materials, information

Table 2.4 **Internal and external benefits of excelling at each performance objective**

| Operations resources – potential internal benefits include … | Performance objective | Market requirements – potential external benefits include … |
|---|---|---|
| Error-free processes<br>Less disruption and complexity<br>More internal reliability<br>Lower processing costs | Quality | High-specification products and services<br>Error-free products and services<br>Reliable products and services |
| Faster throughput times<br>Less queuing and/or inventory<br>Lower overheads<br>Lower processing costs | Speed | Short delivery/queuing times<br>Fast response to requests |
| Higher confidence in the operation<br>Fewer contingencies needed<br>More internal stability<br>Lower processing costs | Dependability | On-time delivery/arrival of products and services<br>Knowledge of delivery times |
| Better response to unpredicted events<br>Better response to variety of activities<br>Lower processing costs | Flexibility | Frequent new products and services<br>Wide range of products and services<br>Volume adjustments<br>Delivery adjustments |
| Productive processes<br>Higher margins | Cost | Low prices |

or customers to be organised and tracked through the process. All this adds up to lower processing costs in general. This gives operations strategy one of its more intriguing paradoxes. Even if a performance objective has little value externally in terms of helping the company to achieve its desired market position, the operation may still value high performance in that objective because of the internal benefits it brings.

## The relative priority of performance objectives differs between businesses

Not every operation will apply the same priorities to its performance objectives. Businesses that compete in different ways should want different things from their operations functions. So, a business that competes primarily on low prices and 'value for money' should be placing emphasis on operations objectives such as cost, productivity and efficiency; one that competes on a high degree of customisation of its services or products should be placing an emphasis on flexibility, and so on. Many successful companies understand the importance of making this connection between their message to customers and the operations performance objectives that they emphasise. For example,[5]

> 'Our management principle is the commitment to quality and reliability... to deliver safe and innovative products and services... and to improve the quality and reliability of our businesses' (Komatsu).
> 'The management team will... develop high quality, strongly differentiated consumer brands and service standards... use the benefits of the global nature and scale economies of the business to operate a highly efficient support infrastructure (with)... high quality and service standards which deliver an excellent guest experience...' (InterContinental Hotels Group).

*'A level of quality durability and value that's truly superior in the market place... the principle that what is best for the customer is also best for the company... (our)... customers have learnt to expect a high level of service at all times – from initiating the order, to receiving help and advice, to speedy shipping and further follow-up where necessary... (our)... employees "go that extra mile"'* (Lands' End).

## The relative priority of performance objectives differs between different products and services within the same businesses

If, as is likely, an operation produces goods or services for more than one customer group, it will need to determine a separate set of competitive factors and, therefore, different priorities for the performance objectives for each group. For example, one of the most obvious differences to be found within an airline's activities is that between the operations supporting business and first-class travellers on one hand, and those supporting economy-class travellers on the other. This is shown in Figure 2.4.

Figure 2.4 **Different product groups require different performance objectives**

|  | First/Business Class | Economy Class |
|---|---|---|
| Services | First/Business Class cabin, airport lounges, pick-up service | Economy cabin |
| Customers | Wealthy people, business people, VIPs | Travellers (friends and family), holiday makers, cost-sensitive business travellers |
| Service range | Wide range, may need to be customised | Standardised |
| Rate of service innovation | Relatively high | Relatively low |
| Volume of activity | Relatively low volume | Relatively high volume |
| Profit margins | Medium to high | Low to medium |
| Main competitive factors | Customisation, extra service, comfort features, convenience | Price, acceptable service |
| Performance objectives | Quality (specification and conformance), flexibility, speed | Cost, quality (conformance) |

## The polar representation of performance objectives

A useful way of representing the relative importance of performance objectives is shown in Figure 2.5(a). This is called the polar representation because the scales that represent the importance of each performance objective have the same origin. A line describes the relative importance of each performance objective. The closer the line is to the common origin, the less important is the performance objective to the operation. Two services are shown – a newspaper collection (NC) recycling service and general recycling (GR) service. Each essentially provides a similar type of service, but for different markets and therefore different objectives. Of course, the polar diagram can be adapted to accommodate any number of different performance objectives. For example, Figure 2.5(b) shows a proposal for using a polar diagram to assess the relative performance of different police forces in the UK. Note that this proposal uses three measures of quality (reassurance, crime reduction and crime detection), one measure of cost (economic efficiency) and one measure of how the police force develops its relationship with 'internal' customers (the criminal justice agencies). Note also that actual performance as well as required performance is also marked on the diagram.

### Order-winning and qualifying competitive factors

One way of determining the relative importance, or at least the different nature, of competitive factors is to distinguish between what are sometimes called 'order-winning' and 'qualifying' factors.[6] Although not a new idea, it is a particularly useful one. Different authors use different terms, so order-winners can also be called 'competitive edge factors', 'critical' or 'primary factors', 'motivating factors', 'enhancing factors', and so on. Qualifiers sometimes go under the names 'hygiene factors' or 'failure preventors'.

Order-winning factors are things that directly and significantly contribute to winning business. Customers regard them as key reasons for purchasing the product or service. They are, therefore, the most important aspects of the way a company defines its competitive stance. Raising performance in an order-winning factor will either result in more business or improve the chances of gaining more business. Of course,

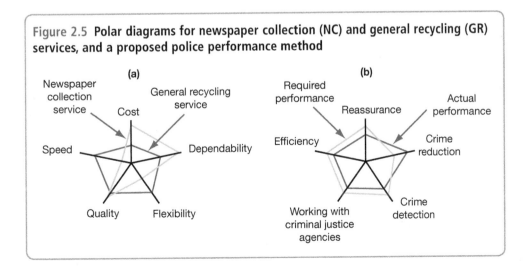

Figure 2.5 **Polar diagrams for newspaper collection (NC) and general recycling (GR) services, and a proposed police performance method**

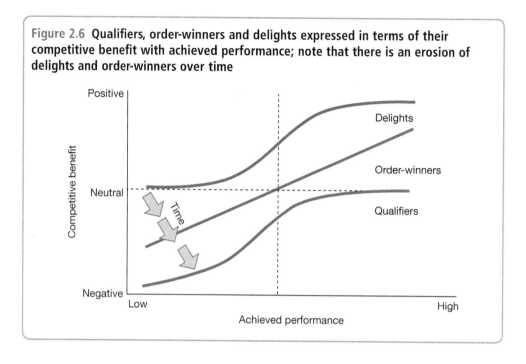

**Figure 2.6** Qualifiers, order-winners and delights expressed in terms of their competitive benefit with achieved performance; note that there is an erosion of delights and order-winners over time

some order-winning factors are more important than others. In Figure 2.6 the slope of the line indicates how sensitive competitive benefit is to an operation's achieved performance in the factor.

Qualifying factors may not be the major competitive determinants of success, but are important in another way. They are those aspects of competitiveness where the operation's performance has to be above a particular level just to be considered by the customer. Below this 'qualifying' level of performance many customers probably won't even consider the company. Above the 'qualifying' level it will be considered, but mainly in terms of its performance in the order-winning factors. Any further improvement in qualifying factors above the qualifying level is unlikely to gain much competitive benefit.

### Delights

In addition to order-winners and qualifiers, some authorities add a third category, generally known as 'delights'. Notwithstanding its rather off-putting name, 'delights' are aspects of performance that customers have not yet been made aware of, or that are so novel that no one else is aware of them. If an organisation presents a customer with a 'delight', the implication is that because the customer is unaware of it, no competitor has offered it to them. For example, health care companies that supply products and services to clinics and hospitals have always been aware that they need to supply their customers in a fast and efficient manner. Factors such as the range of products supplied and the dependability of supply would be regarded as qualifiers, with speed of supply and cost regarded as order winners. Thus, the basis of competition was relatively clear. Then, one or two companies started to offer a much more comprehensive service that included, in effect, taking over the whole supply responsibility for individual customers. A hospital could not just buy products from a company, it could hand over total responsibility for forecasting demand, purchasing, delivery and storage of its supplies. This was a 'delight' to the hospitals that were able to effectively outsource the supply of these items, enabling them to concentrate on their core task of curing and caring for the sick.

### The benefits from order-winners and qualifiers

The distinction between qualifiers, order-winners and delights does illustrate the important point that competitive factors differ – not only in their relative importance, but also in their nature. This is best thought of as how the competitive benefit (which is derived from a competitive factor) varies with how well an operation performs in delivering that competitive benefit. In other words, it is an indication of the benefits an operation gains by being good at different aspects of performance. Figure 2.6 shows the benefits from qualifiers, order-winners and delights as performance levels vary. No matter how well an organisation performs at its qualifiers, it is not going to achieve high levels of competitive benefits. The best that it can usually hope for is neutrality. After all, customers expect these things, and are not going to applaud too loudly when they receive them. They are the givens. However, if the organisation does not achieve satisfactory performance with its qualifiers, it is likely to result in considerable dissatisfaction amongst customers – what in Figure 2.6 is termed as 'negative competitive benefit'. In effect, there is a discontinuity in the benefit function. This is different from an order-winner, which can achieve negative or positive competitive benefit, depending on performance, and whose benefit function is far more linear. The advantage of order-winners (and why they are called order-winners) is that high levels of performance can provide positive competitive benefit, and hence more orders.

The benefits to be derived from 'delights' are also shown in Figure 2.6. The absence of delights (that is, very low achieved performance) will not upset customers because they didn't expect them anyway. However, as the operation starts to perform successfully in terms of its 'delights', the potential for customer satisfaction and therefore positive competitive benefit could be very significant. Note that for something to be classed as a 'delight' it must be both novel (and therefore unexpected) and genuinely add value for customers. The idea is that the combination of added value together with their unexpected nature will make delights, when delivered effectively, particularly attractive. But because they are unexpected, the competitive benefit will not become negative for the very reason that customers are not aware of the delights.

Two points should be made about 'delights'. The first is that the curves in Figure 2.6 are conceptual; they are there to illustrate an idea rather than to be drawn with any degree of precision. (Nevertheless, the theory of delights is closely associated with what some people know as the 'Kano model', which product designers can use in a more quantitative manner.[7]) The other point to make is that delights apply only at one point in time. By definition, because delights rely on their novelty, when offered in the market they will no longer be novel. This means that competitors can attempt to imitate them. So, in the example of the health care companies discussed previously, when they introduced their enhanced service it provided considerable competitive advantage for the few companies that could satisfactorily deliver the service. Since that time many more companies have introduced similar services. Therefore, what was once a delight became an order-winner, with customers choosing supplies on the basis of the effectiveness of their supply chain management service. In time, it may even become a qualifier, where all companies who wish to compete in the market for health care supplies are expected to offer this service. So, what were once delights will, over time, erode as competitors achieve high levels of performance in the same competitive factors.

This prompts an interesting debate for any organisation. How sustainable are the order-winners and delights on which your business depends? Figure 2.7 illustrates a matrix that will allow for this kind of analysis. For any particular product or service it is important first to understand which competitive factors are order-winners, which

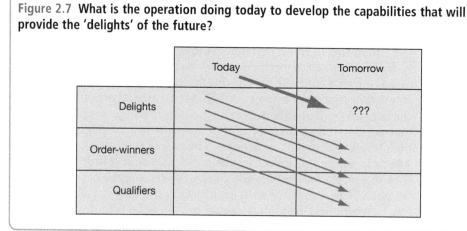

**Figure 2.7 What is the operation doing today to develop the capabilities that will provide the 'delights' of the future?**

are qualifiers, and which (if any) are delights. But, because delights and order-winners can both erode over time, in the future what will happen is that some (if not all) delights will become order-winners and some (if not all) order-winners will become qualifiers. There is a general drift downwards (as shown by the arrows in the figure) as competitors catch up or exceed the level of performance. Usually the cell in the matrix that is the most problematic is that marked as 'tomorrow's delights'. This prompts the intriguing question of 'What is the organisation doing today in order to develop the things that will delight its customers tomorrow?'

### Criticisms of the order-winning and qualifying concepts

Not everyone agrees with the idea of categorising competitive factors as order-winners or qualifiers. There are two major criticisms.[8] The first is that order-winners and qualifiers are based on how potential purchasers of services and products behave when considering a single transaction. Increasingly though, purchasers of both consumer and 'industrial' services and goods do not consider a single transaction but rather think in terms of longer-term relationships. Some purchasers may be willing to accept occasional lapses in performance in either order-winners or qualifiers because they wish to preserve the long-term relationship with their supplier. So, the relationship both transcends the idea of order-winners and qualifiers and becomes the major order-winning competitive factor itself. Second, the original interpretation of the order-winner/qualifier concept is based on considering past sales data, including the reaction of individual customers for individual orders. A more traditional, market-based approach would treat far larger groups of customers in its segmentation procedures.

## The relative importance of performance objectives changes over time

In addition to the 'erosion' effect mentioned previously, there are more generic changes caused by the way markets change over time and operations resource capabilities develop over time. Not surprising, then, that the nature of the reconciliation process, and therefore the role of operations strategy, changes over time – though the stimulus for change may vary. At some times markets change fast: competitors may be particularly aggressive, or novel products or services may redefine customer expectations. If so, the competitive agenda for the business will be influenced largely by how the organisation positions itself in its markets.

## Changes in the firm's markets – the product/service life cycle influence on performance

One way of generalising the market requirements that operations need to fulfil is to link them to the life cycle of the products or services that the operation is producing. The exact form of product/service life cycles will vary, but generally they are shown as the sales volume passing through four stages – introduction, growth, maturity and decline. The important implication of this for operations management is that products and services will require operations strategies in each stage of their life cycle (see Figure 2.8).

### Introduction stage

When a product or service is first introduced, it is likely to be offering something new in terms of its design or performance. Few competitors will be offering the same product or service, and because the needs of customers are not perfectly understood, the design of the product or service could frequently change. Given the market uncertainty, the operations management of the company needs to develop the flexibility to cope with these changes and the quality to maintain product/service performance.

**Figure 2.8 The effects of the product/service life cycle on operations performance objectives**

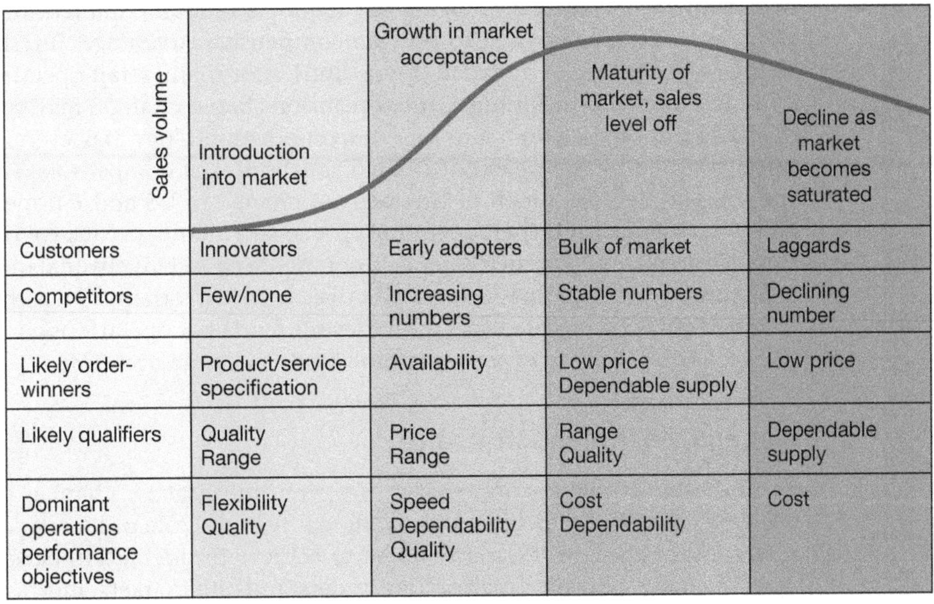

| | Introduction into market | Growth in market acceptance | Maturity of market, sales level off | Decline as market becomes saturated |
|---|---|---|---|---|
| Customers | Innovators | Early adopters | Bulk of market | Laggards |
| Competitors | Few/none | Increasing numbers | Stable numbers | Declining number |
| Likely order-winners | Product/service specification | Availability | Low price Dependable supply | Low price |
| Likely qualifiers | Quality Range | Price Range | Range Quality | Dependable supply |
| Dominant operations performance objectives | Flexibility Quality | Speed Dependability Quality | Cost Dependability | Cost |

### Growth stage

As the volume of products or services grows, competitors start to develop their own products and services. In the growing market, standardised designs emerge. Standardisation is helpful in that it allows the operation to supply the rapidly growing market. Keeping up with demand could prove to be the main operations preoccupation. Rapid and dependable response to demand will help to keep demand buoyant while ensuring that the company keeps its share of the market as competition starts to increase. Also, increasing competition means that quality levels must be maintained.

### Maturity stage

Eventually, demand starts to level off. Some early competitors will have left the market and the industry will probably be dominated by a few larger companies. The designs of the products or services will be standardised and competition will probably emphasise price or value for money, although individual companies might try to prevent this by attempting to differentiate themselves in some way. So operations will be expected to get the costs down in order to maintain profits or to allow price cutting, or both. Because of this, cost and productivity issues, together with dependable supply, are likely to be the operation's main concerns.

### Decline stage

After time, sales will decline and competitors will start dropping out of the market. To the companies left there might be a residual market, but if capacity in the industry lags demand, the market will continue to be dominated by price competition. Operations objectives will therefore still be dominated by cost.

## Changes in the firm's resource base

At other times the focus for change may be within the resources and processes of the operation itself. New technologies may require a fundamental rethink of how operations resources can be used to provide competitive advantage. Internet-based technologies, for example, provided opportunities for many retail operations to shift, or enhance, market positioning. Other operations-based changes may be necessary, not to change, but merely to maintain a market position. They may even reflect opportunities revealed by the operations-based capabilities of competitors. For example, for the last two decades much of the focus of change in US and European automotive companies was within their operations processes, mainly because of the lower operations costs realised by their Japanese competitors. Again, this balance may change as niche markets become more distinctive. But this is the point: although different industries may have a predisposition towards market or operations concerns, the relative balance is likely to experience some kind of change over time.

## Mapping operations strategies

To understand how an organisation's operations strategy changes over time is to understand how it views its markets, how it sees the role of its operations resources and, most of all, how it has attempted to achieve reconciliation between the two. It also illustrates how an organisation understands its markets and how its resources evolve, often reacting to external pressures and internal possibilities. Of course, the minutiae of the thousands of decisions that constitute the mechanics of the reconciliation process over time are the key to understanding how the balance between markets and resources moves. Ideally, we need to map the pattern and flow of each of these decisions, but this would be an immense task if our historical perspective is to be longer than a few years. Often, though, it is at the nature of an organisation's products or services that one looks to see how the internal reconciliation process resolved itself. Products and services are, after all, the outward manifestation of the reconciliation process. Within their design they embody the characteristics that the company hopes will satisfy the market and, at the same time, exploit its resource capabilities. The following example illustrates this.

**Example**   **VW: The first seventy years[9]**

For years, Ferdinand Porsche had dreamt of designing a 'peoples' car'. Presenting his ideas to the Reich government in 1934, he found enthusiastic support for the idea. By 1939 the factory was completed, although the Second World War meant that it was almost immediately turned over to the production of war vehicles. By the end of the war, two-thirds of the factory had been destroyed, the local infrastructure was in ruins and both material and labour were in desperately short supply. Although attempts were made to sell the plant, no one seemed to want a ruined plant. In 1948, the occupying authorities appointed Heinrich Nordhoff to run the business. Nordhoff had faith in the basic concept of Porsche's design but added an emphasis on quality and engineering excellence. Throughout the 1950s the company overcame the difficulties of manufacturing in a recovering economy, and expanded both its manufacturing and its sales operations. The car itself, however, hardly changed at all. In fact, Nordhoff actively suppressed any change to the design. Nothing would be allowed to interfere with the core values of a simple, cheap, robust and standardised people's car. Yet the world was changing. Local economies were recovering fast and customers were demanding more choice and touches of luxury in their motor vehicles. Eventually Volkswagen was forced to introduce a new model (the 1500). In all essentials, however, the company strategy was unchanged. During the early part of the 1960s, the 1500 model helped to take some of the pressure off the company. But consumer tastes were still moving faster than the company's response. Although sales held up, increased costs, together with stiff price competition, were having a severe effect on the company's profitability. By the end of the 1960s profits were declining and, in an attempt to find a new way forward, Volkswagen introduced several new products and acquired some smaller companies – most notably Auto Union GmbH from Daimler Benz, which later would form the nucleus Audi.

Out of this somewhat rudderless period (Nordhoff had died in 1968), the company eventually started to find a coherent strategy, with new models formed around the designs emerging from Audi. More in tune with modern tastes, they were front wheel drive, water-cooled and more stylish than the old VW Beetle. Also the company started to rationalise its operations to ensure commonality between models and bring enhanced organisation to its global manufacturing operations, and the company resumed profitable growth in 1975. During the remainder of the 1970s and through the 1980s, Volkswagen continued to produce its successful Polo, Golf and Passat models. Production facilities continued to expand around the world, but never again, Volkswagen vowed, would they be left behind consumer tastes. Design and product performance moved to the front of VW's strategy and all models were updated at regular intervals. The next big challenge for the company came not from the inadequacy of its models, but from its manufacturing facilities.

In the early 1990s Volkswagen's models were still highly regarded and commercially success-ful, but costs were significantly above both its local European rivals and its Japanese competi-tors. And, although by now it was by far the largest auto-maker in Europe, the prospects for VW looked bleak. Management structures were bureaucratic, labour costs in Germany were significantly higher than other European and US levels, and one estimate had Volkswagen needing to operate at 95 per cent of capacity just to cover its costs. The break-even points of its rivals were significantly lower, at around 70 per cent. A fundamental cost-cutting exercise was seen by many commentators as the only thing that would save the company.

By the late 1990s, once again things were looking brighter in most of the company's mar-kets. It had negotiated pay and flexibility deals with its employees, successfully cut the costs of buying parts from its supply base (at one point hiring the controversial José Ignacio López from General Motors) and was continuing to introduce its new models. The most eye-catching of these was the new Beetle – a design based on the old Beetle but with thoroughly modern parts under its skin. Just as significantly, the company worked on the commonality of its designs. Within the VW group several models, although looking different on the surface, were based on the same basic platform. Yet the company found that there were limits to how far one could sell essentially the same car as different brands at different prices, and it eventually devised a less obvious modular design strategy. Throughout the 2000s there was continued cost pressure from (mainly Japanese and Korean) competitors and a severe recession at the end of the decade. In response, VWs production shifted increasingly to lower-cost locations such as East Europe and China. At the same time it started to seriously adopt lean principles in all its operations. Yet some markets defied the Group's overall success. Although, by 2012, VW had become the biggest auto-maker in China and Europe, the group had been losing money in the United States for years. So much so that in 2014 VW's works council chief labelled the car-maker's US operations a 'disaster' and called for more models and swift decisions to revive the German group's declining fortunes in the world's second-largest auto market.

### *Understanding VW's operations strategy over time*[10]

Like any company, VW's strategy has changed over time and, in turn, so has its operations strategy. The requirements of the market have changed as world markets have grown, matured and become increasingly sophisticated over time, but also in response to how VW's competitors have behaved. Thus, VW markets that were small, local and disrupted at the beginning of the period became increasingly large, interna-tional and differentiated over time. Also, competitive pressure counted for little at the beginning of the period, but by the 2000s automobile markets had become fiercely competitive. Likewise, the nature of VW's operations resources has changed, starting with a desperate effort merely to satisfy even the most primitive of markets. Then, at various times through the next fifty years, VW's operations resources became more systematised, considerably larger and far more complex, involving an interconnected network of internationally located operations.

Figure 2.9 shows the relative significance of market requirements and operations resources over time. This gives an indication of the relative degree of strategic activity within the firm's operations over time. It also gives us a clue as to the *role* of operations strategy over time. At some stages the role of operations strategy is relatively minor, often confined merely to implementing the company's market strategy. So, during the period 1959 to 1964 the firm's strategy was driven largely by a desire to change its market posi-tion slightly through the introduction of the 1500 model. The firm's operations strat-egy was limited to ensuring that the new model could be manufactured satisfactorily.

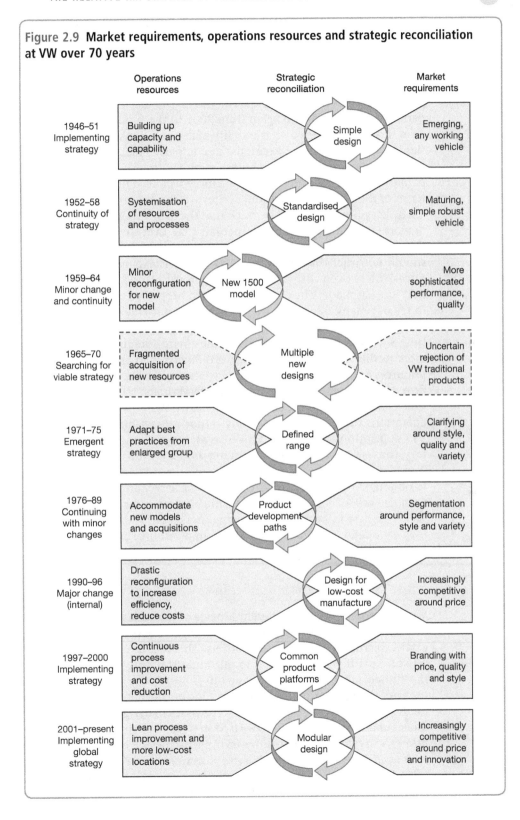

Figure 2.9 Market requirements, operations resources and strategic reconciliation at VW over 70 years

Similarly, in the period 1976 to 1989, the firm's focus was mainly on how its markets could be segmented in order to achieve successful differentiation of its various products. At other times the strategy of the company not only relies on its operations capabilities but could be described as being driven by them. So, in the period 1946 to 1951, the company's strategy was dictated largely by the ability of its operations resources to produce the cars in sufficient quantity to satisfy its emerging market. Similarly, in the period 1990 to 1996, and again from 2001 to the present, the firm's profitability, and even survival, depended on the ability of its operations resources to reduce its cost base significantly. In both these periods the company's market activity was, to some extent, driven by its operations capabilities (or lack of them). At other times the relative roles of market and operations strategy are more balanced (even if they are balanced only in terms of their mutual confusion, as they were in the 1965 to 1970 period).

The key point here is not so much that the firm's operations strategy is at times better or worse than at other times. Rather it is that, over the long term, any firm can expect the role of its operations strategy to change as its circumstances change. However, one should not infer that the role of operations is exclusively driven by environmental forces. Interwoven with environmental pressures are a whole set of significant choices that VW has made. The company chose to suppress new designs in the 1950s, it chose to try out many designs in the late 1960s and it chose to develop its common products platform strategy in the late 1990s. The development of operations strategy over time is a combination of uncontrollable environmental forces and factors that can be more readily influenced. Above all, it is determined by choices about how operations resources are developed and the role we expect of the operations function within the firm. Notice how the two major crises for VW, in its loss of strategic direction in the late 1960s and its loss of cost control in the early 1990s, were preceded by a period where operations strategy had a relatively minor role within the company. Note also how VW's operations objectives changed as market circumstances changed. In its early history, the very basic objective of making products available (a combination of *speed* and *dependability*) was pre-eminent in an environment where basic resources were difficult to obtain. Latterly, the company, by now far larger and more complex, was struggling with the task of reducing its *costs* while maintaining its performance in other areas. The issue here is, because of changing market requirements, *not all performance objectives are equally important.* But also, from a resource perspective, *operations cannot be exceptionally good at every single aspect of performance at the same time.*

## Trade-offs – are they inevitable?

Volkswagen emphasised different aspects of performance at different points in time. And, in order to excel in some particular aspects of performance, they would, to some extent, sacrifice performance in others. This idea is usually referred to as the 'trade-off concept'. It is fundamental to our understanding of operations strategy. Perhaps most importantly, the idea of trade-offs is also at the heart of how operations seek to improve their performance over time. One of the many questions central to improvement efforts is, 'What do we want to be particularly good at?' Is there one particular aspect of performance that we wish to stress above everything else (*'with us it is quality first, second and third'*), or are we trying to achieve a balance between objectives (*'we wish to offer the customer a wide range of services but not to the extent that costs get out of control'*)? In order to answer these questions we need to understand the way performance objectives relate to each other. This is where trade-offs come in.

## What is a trade-off?

All of us are familiar with the simple idea that (much as we would like) we cannot have everything. Most of us want some combination of health, wealth and happiness. But we also know that sometimes we must sacrifice one to get the others. Driving ourselves too hard at work may give us wealth but can have negative effects on both health and happiness. Of course we cannot let the wealth objective decrease too far or our poverty will undermine happiness and even health. We all instinctively understand that (a) the three objectives are related, (b) because some resource is finite (time, ability, etc.) we must, to some extent, trade off each objective against the others, (c) the trade-off relationship is not simple and linear (we do not decrease, or increase, our health by a fixed amount for every €1,000 earned), (d) the nature of the relationship will differ for each individual (some of us can derive great happiness *and* wellbeing from the process of making money) and, perhaps most importantly, (e) none of us is always totally certain just how our own trade-offs operate (although some of us are better at knowing ourselves than others).

That these ideas also apply to operations was first articulated by Professor Wickham Skinner at Harvard University. As ever, in those days he was speaking of manufacturing operations, but broadly the same principles apply. He said:

> 'Few executives realise the existence of trade-offs. Yet most managers will readily admit that there are compromises or trade-offs to be made in designing an airplane or a truck. In the case of an airplane, trade-offs would involve matters such as cruising speed, take-off and landing distances, initial costs, maintenance, fuel consumption, passenger comfort, and cargo or passenger capacity. A given stage of technology defines limits of what can be accomplished in these respects. For instance, no one today can design a 500-passenger plane that can land on a carrier and also break the sonic barrier. Much the same thing is true of manufacturing. The variables of cost, time, quality, technological constraints, and customer satisfaction place limits on what management can do, force compromises, and demand an explicit recognition of a multitude of trade-offs and choices.'[11]

## Why are trade-offs important?

We judge the effectiveness of any operation by how well it performs. The call centre that can respond to our call and solve our problems within seconds, any time of the day or night, is superior to one that takes several minutes to answer our call and does not operate through the night. The plant that can deliver products in 24 hours is judged superior to one that takes 3 days; plants turning over their stock 25 times a year are superior to one that, operating under similar conditions, only manages to turn over stock 7 times a year, and so on. Yet in making our judgement we recognise two important characteristics of operations performance. The first is that all measures of performance will not have equal importance for an individual operation. Certain aspects of performance will outweigh others – their relative importance being determined by both the competitive characteristics of the market in which the operation is competing and, more importantly, the way in which the company chooses to position itself within that market. The second characteristic of performance that will shape our view of the operation is that we recognise that aspects of performance will, to some extent, trade off against each other. So, for example, we are less impressed with the call centre that answers our calls quickly at all times of the day or night if its costs of running the operation make it necessary to charge us higher fees, or if the plant that delivers within 24 hours is achieving this only by investing in high levels of finished goods inventory. Though maybe we will be more indulgent towards the operation if we discover it has deliberately positioned itself in the market to compete primarily on instant response or fast delivery. Then the cost implications of high finished goods inventory may not matter so much. The operations have chosen to 'trade off' higher costs or high inventory to achieve fast response and fast delivery. However, we would be even more impressed with the call centre if it had 'overcome' the trade-off and was achieving both fast and 24-hour response *and* low cost levels; similarly, with the manufacturing plant, if it was achieving both fast delivery *and* low inventories. In both these examples we are using a broad understanding of the relationship between different performance objectives to judge the effectiveness of their operations management. But we are also implying that, in order to improve, these operations must overcome the trade-offs by changing the nature of the relationship between performance objectives.

## Are trade-offs real or imagined?

Skinner's original idea of trade-offs was both straightforward and intuitively attractive. Essentially it formalised the notion that there is no such thing as a free lunch. Any operation, like any machine, is 'technologically constrained'.[12] It therefore cannot provide all things to all people. The trade-off relationships between competitive objectives (cost, quality, delivery, variety, inventory, capital investment, etc.) mean that excellence in one objective usually means poor performance in some or all of the others. Operations that attempt to be good at everything finish up by being mediocre at everything. Therefore the key issue of operations strategy is to *position* the competitive objectives of the operation to reflect the company's overall competitive strategy. Although Skinner has subsequently modified his original ideas, he maintains their essential validity: *'trade-offs ... are as real as ever but they are alive and dynamic'*.[13]

The counter-view came from a new breed of more evangelical academics and consultants inspired by the perceived success of some (mainly Japanese) companies in overcoming at least some trade-offs – most notably that between cost and quality. They embraced the 'bottom-up' improvement techniques of 'world class' operations. Both trade-offs and positioning, they claimed, are illusions. Trade-offs are not real – therefore positioning is not necessary. Citing the success of many companies that achieved improvements in several aspects of performance *simultaneously*, they dismiss trade-offs as distractions to what should be the real imperative of operations – namely, improvement. Making choices between alternative aspects of performance leads to 'merely good', as opposed to 'outstanding', achievements. This is what some called *'the tyranny of either/or'*. Rather than accepting the either/or approach, they recommend the more positive 'and/also' approach, which works towards 'having it all'. New forms of operations organisation and practice could overcome the 'technical constraints' of any operation, this being especially true if they are applied with a radical creativity hitherto unexpected in operations managers.

In spite of the appealing positive approach of this school, it could not fully explain away the intuitive appeal of the trade-off concept, and several attempts at an inclusive compromise that brings the two schools together were proposed. For example, it was suggested that some trade-offs did still, and would always, exist, while others had, for all practical purposes, been overcome by the new technologies and methodologies of manufacturing. Others suggested that while all trade-offs were real in the very short term, they could all be overcome in the long term. Most recent authors hold that 'trading off' and 'overcoming trade-offs' are in fact distinct strategies, either of which may be adopted at different times by organisations. Neither are they mutually exclusive; operations may choose to trade off by repositioning the balance of their performance, both as a response to changes in competitive strategy and to provide a better starting point for improvement. And key to overcoming trade-off constraints is the building of appropriate operating capabilities. Thus, operations performance improvement is achieved by overcoming trade-offs, which, in turn, is achieved through enhanced operations capabilities.

The position taken in this book is close to the last school of thought. That is, that while there is a clear requirement for operations managers to position their operation such that they achieve the balance between performance objectives that is most appropriate for competitive advantage, there is also a longer-term imperative that involves finding ways of overcoming the intrinsic trade-offs caused by the constraints imposed by the operation's resources.

## Trade-offs and the efficient frontier

Figure 2.10(a) shows the relative performance of several companies in the same industry in terms of their cost efficiency and the variety of products or services that they offer to their customers. Presumably all the operations would ideally like to be able to offer very high variety while still having very high levels of cost efficiency. However, the increased complexity that a high variety of product or service offerings brings will generally reduce the operation's ability to operate efficiently. Conversely, one way of improving cost efficiency is to severely limit the variety on offer to customers. The spread of results in Figure 2.10(a) is typical of an exercise such as this. Operations A, B, C and D all have chosen a different balance between variety and cost efficiency. But none is dominated by any other operation in the sense that another operation necessarily has 'superior' performance. Operation X, however, has an inferior performance

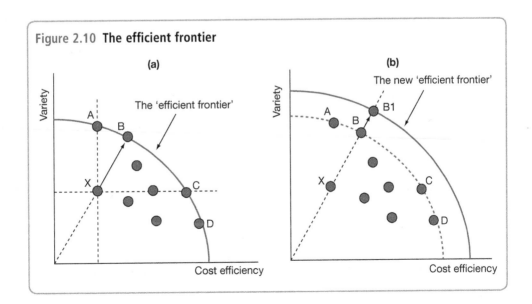

Figure 2.10 **The efficient frontier**

because operation A is able to offer higher variety at the same level of cost efficiency, and operation C offers the same variety but with better cost efficiency. The convex line on which operations A, B, C and D lie is known as the 'efficient frontier'. They may choose to position themselves differently (presumably because of different market strategies) but they cannot be criticised for being ineffective. Of course, any of these operations that lie on the efficient frontier may come to believe that the balance they have chosen between variety and cost efficiency is inappropriate. In these circumstances they may choose to reposition themselves at some other point along the efficient frontier. By contrast, operation X has also chosen to balance variety and cost efficiency in a particular way but is not doing so effectively. Operation B has the same ratio between the two performance objectives but is achieving them more effectively. Operation X will generally have a strategy that emphasises increasing its effectiveness before considering any repositioning.

However, a strategy that emphasises increasing effectiveness is not confined to those operations that are dominated, such as operation X. Those with a position on the efficient frontier will generally also want to improve their operations effectiveness by overcoming the trade-off that is implicit in the efficient frontier curve. For example, suppose operation B in Figure 2.10(b) is the metrology systems company described in Chapter 1. By adopting a modular product design strategy it improved both its variety and its cost efficiency simultaneously (and moved to position B1). What has happened is that operation B has adopted a particular operations practice (modular design) that has pushed out the efficient frontier. This distinction between positioning on the efficient frontier and increasing operations effectiveness to reach the frontier is an important one. Any operations strategy must make clear the extent to which it is expecting the operation to reposition itself in terms of its performance objectives and the extent to which it is expecting the operation to improve its effectiveness.

## Improving operations effectiveness by using trade-offs

Improving the effectiveness of an operation by pushing out the efficient frontier requires different approaches depending on the original position of the operation on the frontier. For example, in Figure 2.11 operation P has an original position that offers a high level of variety at the expense of low-cost efficiency. It has probably reached this position by adopting a series of operations practices that enable it to offer the variety even if these practices are intrinsically expensive. For example, it may have invested in general purpose technology and recruited employees with a wide range of skills. Improving variety even further may mean adopting even more extreme operations practices that emphasise variety. For example, it may reorganise its processes so that each of its larger customers has a dedicated set of resources that understands the specific requirements of that customer and can organise itself to totally customise every product and service it produces. This will probably mean a further sacrifice of cost efficiency, but it allows an ever greater variety of products or services to be produced (P1). Similarly, operation Q may increase the effectiveness of its cost efficiency by becoming even less able to offer any kind of variety (Q1). For both operations, P and Q effectiveness is being improved through increasing the focus of the operation on one performance objective (or a very narrow set of them), and accepting an even further reduction in other aspects of performance.

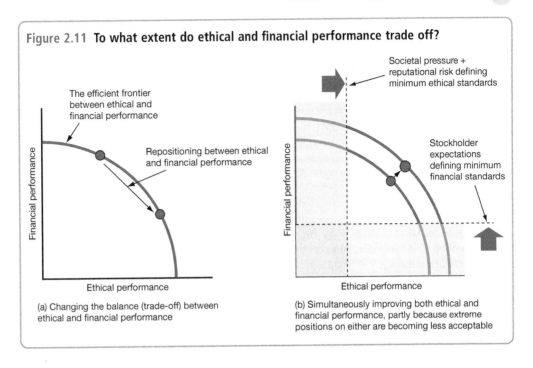

Figure 2.11 **To what extent do ethical and financial performance trade off?**

The efficient frontier between ethical and financial performance

Repositioning between ethical and financial performance

Societal pressure + reputational risk defining minimum ethical standards

Stockholder expectations defining minimum financial standards

Financial performance

Ethical performance

(a) Changing the balance (trade-off) between ethical and financial performance

Financial performance

Ethical performance

(b) Simultaneously improving both ethical and financial performance, partly because extreme positions on either are becoming less acceptable

For example, if an audit firm designed an operation to carry out *only* simple standard audits on small to medium-sized engineering manufacturing companies, it could develop processes and procedures specifically to meet the needs of such clients. It could devise expert systems to automate much of its decision making and it could train its staff with only the knowledge to carry out such audits. Focused and efficient, the operation could achieve exceptional productivity, provided the demand could keep it fully employed. However, such an operation is something of a one-trick pony. Ask it to do anything else and it would have considerable difficulty. Increasing the variety placed on the operation outside its design specification would have an immediate and significant impact on its costs. In effect, designing the operation this way has made the relationship curve between variety and cost concave rather than convex. Asking the operation to move away from the performance objectives for which it was specifically designed brings an immediate penalty. Asking it to move even further away from its design specification also brings a cost, but not one to match that initial penalty.

**Example** Flat beds trade off utilisation for comfort

At one time most airlines operated a 'twin class' system – First Class and Economy Class. Then came Business Class, with service standards placed between First and Economy. Ideally designed for the burgeoning business travel market, it attracted customers from both the First and Economy Classes. British Airways' strategy was typical: on most non-European sectors, BA offered all three levels of cabin service to their customers, with First and Business Classes particularly popular on long-haul flights – the transatlantic route being the single biggest market. By the mid-1990s the First Class market seemed to be in terminal decline, with many airlines

▶

pulling out of the First Class product entirely and, instead, concentrating on offering superior service in Business Class.

British Airways took a different view. They believed that the whole concept of First Class travel needed to be redefined, and in early 1994 they decided to refurbish their First Class cabins. Existing First Class cabins had 18 passenger seats, each with a 62-inch seat pitch, serviced by four cabin crew. BA's research, using passenger focus groups, showed that the most important factors associated with First Class travel were, in fact, space-related. The main challenge was to create maximum passenger space within the existing area and simultaneously boost revenues from this segment. Their answer was a new design for their First Class cabins – the 'Bed in the Sky': a private, first-class seat encased in a shell that could transform itself into a completely horizontal bed. With the help of in-cabin technology, all control facilities were accessible within an arm's length of the passenger seat – audio/video, light switches, call buttons, etc. However, the more spacious seats meant that cabin size, in terms of seating, was reduced to 14 passenger seats. BA was also able to complement the new cabin designs with improved standards of cabin service and cuisine.

Refitting all their long-haul aircraft in this way succeeded in repositioning BA's First Class product so it had a unique First Class offering with no comparable competition. But it also had spent money to have fewer seats. Service quality was improved, but its costs per passenger were higher. This meant that BA had to increase its seat utilisation (the proportion of seats actually filled with paying passengers) in order to generate higher revenues from its improved service. In fact, BA were able to arrest the decline in First Class travel, and increase its market share and revenues in the segment (revenues exceeded the business plan proposals by over 10 per cent). BA had traded off cost efficiency (it went down) for service quality (it went up). This paid off because of the extra revenue it brought. So successful was this exercise that BA repeated the strategy in its Business Class products. But now many other airlines have implemented a similar strategy, so the concept of 'erosion of delights' applies. Flat beds have become an 'order-winner', even in Business Class.

## Trade-offs, operations strategy and CSR

The idea of trade-offs and the 'efficient frontier' can also help with an understanding of how corporate social responsibility (CSR) fits into operations strategy. Many advocates of 'green' operations talk about how being environmentally sustainable is also economically efficient. If Marks and Spencer (the UK-based retailer) make their trucks more aerodynamic then they save fuel and save costs; if a firm reduces its travel budgets and increases use of teleconferencing, they save money and reduce carbon footprint, etc. Yet within these dimensions of sustainability, it seems clear that there can also be trade-offs. For example, in choosing between local suppliers and those in developing countries whose activities promote economic self-sufficiency, there may well be a higher total carbon footprint associated with the transaction. Others are less obvious but equally challenging. For example, doing things voluntarily is often presented as an important principle of corporate social responsibility and yet subsequent regulatory changes – such as a universally accepted price for carbon – may require an organisation to make further adaptations.

In fact, there are several 'dimensions' of CSR, some of which are briefly described in Table 2.5. And even at this simple level one can see that CSR is a very broad term, encompassing a range of potentially complementary, but also potentially contradictory, objectives.

Table 2.5  **Multiple dimensions of sustainability**

| Type | Definition |
| --- | --- |
| Environmental | The impact of operations on the natural environment (e.g. pollution) and, in particular, carbon footprint. |
| Social | The relationship between business and society in general; considering all stakeholders or stakeholder groups. |
| Economic | The contribution made to economic development – in particular in areas/countries with relative economic disadvantage. |
| Voluntariness | Undertaking actions not prescribed by law. Doing more than you have to. |

Figure 2.11 illustrates the idea of trade-offs between the financial and the ethical performance of any operations. The first point to make is that there are relatively extreme positions on both financial and ethical performance. On the side of those who believe that CSR is essentially a distraction for business, the most famous quote comes from Milton Freeman, the famous economist, who said, '*The business of business is business. A society that puts equality before freedom will get neither. A society that puts freedom before equality will get a high degree of both.*' In the opposite corner, representing those who believe that business should exist only in the context of a broader set of social responsibilities, is the founder of Body Shop – Anita Roddick. She said, '*In terms of power and influence there is no more powerful institution in society than business ... The business of business should not be about money, it should be about responsibility. It should be about public good, not private greed.*'

In between these two positions, most businesses try and reach some degree of compromise. In this sense they are 'repositioning' themselves on an efficient frontier, as in Figure 2.11(a). As pointed out earlier, repositioning an operation on the efficient frontier is sometimes necessary as the demands of the market (or environment) change. In this case, it is increasingly difficult to focus exclusively on either financial or ethical performance. Societal pressure and issues of reputational risk are defining minimum ethical standards, while tough market conditions and stockholder expectations are defining minimum financial standards. Thus, exercising improvement creativity to try and become better at financial and ethical performance simultaneously could be argued to be the only realistic option for most businesses (see Figure 2.11(b)).

## Targeting and operations focus

The idea of repositioning the trade-off balance between conflicting performance objectives underpins one of the most effective 'types' of operations strategy – *focused operations*. This concept of focus is both powerful and proven because at its heart lies a very simple notion – that many operations are carrying out too many (often conflicting) tasks. The obvious result is that they are unable to perform them all with any real degree of success, whereas concentrating on one or two specific objectives, even at the expense of adopting a vulnerable 'concave' trade-off curve as discussed previously, can lead to substantially superior performance in those few objectives. It means redeploying operations resources to the needs of only a very specific part of the market.

## The concept of focus

Most of the early work on what was then called the 'focused factory' concept was carried out by Wickham Skinner of Harvard Business School. Based on his ideas of how trade-offs dominated operations decision making, he argued that one way of achieving an effective operations strategy is through the concept of factory focus. This meant that first a business should establish a consistent set of policies for the various elements of its operations, which will support not only each other but also marketing requirements. Second, because of the inherent trade-offs, one operation cannot provide peak performance in all performance objectives at the same time. In his article 'The Focused Factory',[14] Skinner based these arguments on his observations of a variety of US industries in the early 1970s. He found that most factories were trying to tackle too many tasks and therefore trying to achieve too many objectives. Because of this they were failing to perform well in any single objective. He concluded that a factory that was focused on a narrow range of products, and aimed at satisfying a particular section of the market, would outperform a plant that was attempting to satisfy a broader set of objectives. The equipment, systems and procedures that are necessary to achieve a more limited range of tasks for a smaller set of customers could also result in lower (especially overhead) costs. Focus, according to Skinner, can be expressed as dedicating each operation to a limited, concise, manageable set of products, technologies, volumes and markets, then structuring policies and support services so they focus on one *explicit* task, rather than on a variety of inconsistent, conflicting, *implicit* tasks.

### Focus as operations segmentation

In Chapter 1 we briefly described how marketing managers attempt to understand their markets through the process of segmentation. Market segmentation breaks heterogeneous markets down into smaller, more homogeneous markets. Within operations resources, what we have called 'focus' is very similar to the process of segmentation. In fact it can be regarded as operations segmentation. Operations, like markets, are complex. A whole range of different skills, process technologies, flow sequences, knowledge applications, individual decisions and so on, come together to create a range of different products and/or services. Operations managers spend much of their time attempting to split up the tasks of managing these resources in order to simplify them and thereby manage them more effectively. In effect, they are segmenting their operations resources. And, just as in marketing there are continual debates around the best way to segment markets, so in operations there are similar debates as to the most sensible way to segment resources. Ideally, operations segmentation and market segmentation should correspond; that is, separate clusters of resources clearly and distinctively serve individual market segments. The major problem with the whole idea of focus, however, is that what is a sensible basis for segmenting markets does not always map onto the ideal basis for segmenting operations resources. For example, an advertising agency may segment its market by the size of the promotional accounts of its clients. Ideally, it may wish to have different service offerings for large, medium and small accounts. Each of these offerings would have different mixes of services specialising in different types of communication, such as TV, posters, radio, press, etc. In this way they can position themselves as 'one-stop shops' that will produce entire marketing campaigns seamlessly for each market segment. However, from an operations viewpoint, the company's creative staff (its main resource) may retain their creativity more effectively if they work in teams focused on specific media – for example, one team specialising in TV advertising, another in press campaigns, and so on. So, what is ideal for the market (one-stop shops by size of promotional spend) does not match the ideal way of organising resources to maintain or improve their effectiveness (in this case, creativity).

### The 'operation-within-an-operation' concept

Any decision to focus an operation might appear to carry with it the need to set up completely new operations if further products/services are added to the range, and it is true that in some cases a failure to do this has undermined successful operations. However, it is not always feasible, necessary or desirable to do this and the 'operation-within-an-operation' (or 'plant-within-a-plant', or 'shop-within-a-shop') concept is a practical response that allows an organisation to accrue the benefits of focus without the considerable expense of setting up independent operations. A portion of the operation is partitioned off and dedicated to the manufacture of a particular product/ delivery of a particular service. The physical separation of products/services will allow the introduction of independent workforces, control systems, quality standards, etc. In addition, this approach allows for easier supervision, motivation and accounting.

**Example** **Did Ryanair go too far in cost cutting?**[15]

Ryanair is arguably the best-known budget airline in Europe, but it was not the first to focus its operations strategy on very low operating costs. The idea was born when Southwest Airlines in the USA organised its airline operations ruthlessly around providing a low-cost 'no frills' service. It could both grow its customer base and do so profitably. Around the world, Southwest's example inspired a number of imitators, who likewise focused on focus. In Europe, the European Airlines Deregulation Act prompted the emergence of several low-cost airlines (LCAs). The larger airlines had been drawn towards longer-haul routes where their interconnecting network of services and their extended levels of service were a major attraction. So, even in Europe, which has a viable and popular rail network, several companies saw the opportunity to offer low-cost, short-haul services. Companies such as Ryanair adopted similar strategies for keeping costs down. To some extent these strategies included trading off levels of service for reduced costs. So complimentary in-flight services were kept to a minimum, secondary and sometimes less convenient airports were used, and one standard class of travel was offered. In other ways these companies attempted to overcome trade-offs by focusing their operations. For example, they focused on a standardised fleet of aircraft, thus keeping maintenance costs down. They focused on their key processes, such as passenger handling, while outsourcing more peripheral processes. They focused on direct sales to their customers, often pioneering low-cost channels such as the internet. They also focused on those elements of the process that hinder the effective utilisation of their expensive resources, such as reducing aircraft turn-around time at the airports.

To keep focused, however, requires clarity of vision. The policy of Ryanair's boss, Michael O'Leary, on customer service is also clear: *'Our customer service', he says, 'is about the most well defined in the world. We guarantee to give you the lowest air fare. You get a safe flight. You get a normally on-time flight. That's the package. We don't, and won't, give you anything more. Are we going to say sorry for our lack of customer service? Absolutely not. If a plane is cancelled, will we put you up in a hotel overnight? Absolutely not. If a plane is delayed, will we give you a voucher for a restaurant? Absolutely not.'*

One attempt by Ryanair to cut costs prompted a backlash when it was accused of being 'puerile and childish' by the UK's Office of Fair Trading (OFT). John Fingleton, the OFT's boss, criticised the company for adding extra fees when customers use anything but a MasterCard prepaid card to pay for flights, using, he said, a legal loophole to justify charging the extra fee. Mr Fingleton was reported as saying that, *'Ryanair has this funny game where they have found some very low frequency payment mechanism and say: "Well because you can pay with that". It's almost like taunting consumers and pointing out: "Oh well, we know this is completely outside the spirit of the law, but we think it's within the narrow letter of the law".'* Stephen McNamara, Ryanair's Head of Communications, retorted that, *'Ryanair is not for the overpaid John Fingletons of this world but for the everyday Joe Bloggs who opt for Ryanair's guaranteed lowest fares. What the OFT must realise is that passengers prefer Ryanair's model as it allows them to avoid costs, such as baggage charges, which are still included in the high fares of high cost, fuel surcharging... airlines.'* But the backlash against Ryanair's policy continued, perhaps encouraged by the airline's reluctance to apologise, or sometimes even comment. Ryanair was even voted the worst of Britain's 100 biggest brands by readers of the consumer magazine *Which?*. Then, after a drop in their hitherto rapid profit growth and shareholder concern, Ryanair announced that it was to reform its 'abrupt culture, and try to eliminate things that unnecessarily annoy customers'. Included in these annoying practices were fines for small luggage size transgressions and an unpopular €70 fee for issuing boarding passes at the airport rather than printing them out at home (it was lowered to €10). Yet Ryanair insisted that such charges were not money-spinning schemes, but were designed to encourage operational efficiency that kept fairs low; in fact, fewer than ten passengers a day had to pay for forgotten boarding passes.

## Types of focus

Just as there are many ways of segmenting markets, so there are several approaches to focusing operations. The organisation of process technologies staff and processes can be based on several criteria. Table 2.6 illustrates some of the more common approaches to focus. These can be placed on a spectrum from those that take market-related factors as being an appropriate way to segment operations resources, through to those that allow the resource characteristics themselves to dictate how operations are split up.

- *Performance objective focus* – The operation is set up solely to satisfy the performance requirements of a particular market or market segment. All products or services produced in an operation have very similar characteristics in terms of generic performance objectives.

- *Product/service specification focus* – The operation is set up for a clearly defined product or service, or range of products or services, the implication being that each defined range of products or services is targeted at a clearly defined market segment.

- *Geographic focus* – Sometimes operations can be segmented in terms of the geographic market they serve. This may be because the characteristics of a company's different market segments are largely defined by their geographic location. Alternatively, it may mean that the nature of the service offered by an operation is geographically limited. Most high-contact operations, such as fast-food restaurants, would fall into this category.

- *Variety focus* – A company may wish to segment its operations in terms of the number of different activities (usually dictated by the number of different products

Table 2.6 **Firms can use various criteria to 'focus' their operations**

| | Focus criteria | Ideal operations resource conditions | Ideal market requirements conditions |
|---|---|---|---|
| *Operations segmentation based on market criteria* | **Performance objectives** Cluster products/services by market requirements | Products and services with similar market requirements have similar processing requirements | Market segmentation is based clearly on customer requirements |
| | **Product/service specification** Limit number of products/services in each part of the operation | Similar products and services require similar technologies, skills and processes | Products and services are targeted on specific market segments |
| | **Geography** Cluster products/services by the geographic market they serve | The geographic area where products and services are created has a significant impact on operations performance | Market segmentation can be based on geographic regions |
| | **Variety** Separately cluster high-variety products/services and low-variety products/services together | The nature of technology, skills and processes is primarily determined by the variety with which products/services are created | Market segmentation can be based on the degree of product/service choice required by customers |
| | **Volume** Separately cluster high-volume products/services and low-volume products/services together | The nature of technology, skills and processes is primarily determined by the volume at which products/services are created | Market segmentation can be summarised as 'mass markets' versus more 'specialised markets' |
| *Operations segmentation based on resource criteria* | **Process requirements** Cluster products/services with similar process requirements together | The process requirements (types of technology, skills, knowledge, etc.) of products/services can be clearly distinguished | Products and services with similar processing requirements are targeted on specific market segments |

or services) it is engaged in. So, for example, one site may concentrate on relatively low variety or standardised products and services while another concentrates on high variety or customised products and services.

● *Volume focus* – High-volume operations, with their emphasis on standardisation and repetition, are likely to need different process technologies, labour skills and planning and control systems from those with lower volume. Volume focus extends this thinking to the creation of separate operations for different volume requirements.

- *Process requirements focus* – Here, a particular technology is the point of focus for the operation. This allows the organisation to concentrate on extending its knowledge and expertise about the process. Over the life cycle of a production/service system, the likely advantage to be gained from a process focus will change. As an operation starts up and moves into the growth phase, building process capability will be critical; however, as volumes stabilise, the process itself will become more stable. A process focus can also become very significant as volumes decline and the organisation seeks to redirect its operations. However, many firms choose to close an operation rather than redirect it.

**Example**  **Burning your bridges (or boats)[16]**

The nature of focus is that it is not ambiguous. Opting for excellence in a narrow set of objectives at the expense of the ability to be excellent at the others calls for a significant level of commitment to the objectives that have been chosen. The idea of commitment to a strategy has long been debated in business strategy and, before that, in military strategy.

A classic military illustration of commitment is shown in Figure 2.12. Two armies want to occupy an island, though neither is particularly keen to fight the other for it. Suppose Army 1 occupies the island pre-emptively and burns the bridge behind it. Army 2 is likely to cede the island because it realises that Army 1 has no option other than to fight if Army 2 attacks. By restricting its own flexibility (to retreat) and ensuring its commitment, Army 1 has won the island without having to fight.

An example of this is the action taken by the Spanish Conquistador Hernán Cortés. In 1518 he landed his twelve ships on the coast of Mexico and soon determined to strike inland to the Aztec capital to defeat the Emperor Montezuma. However, Montezuma's troops had such a fearsome reputation that Cortés' men were somewhat reluctant to face the far larger Aztec army, especially since they knew that capture would mean a horrible death. Discontent reached such a pitch that one group of men planned to steal a ship and sail back to their homes. Cortés' solution to this was to execute the chief conspirators and beach nine of his twelve ships. In the face of such focused commitment, his men had little option but to follow him.

**Figure 2.12  Burning bridges behind you increases commitment but reduces flexibility**

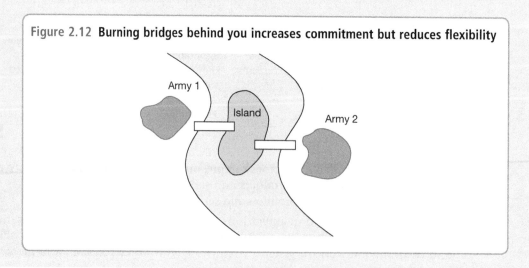

## Benefits and risks in focus

Different kinds of focus criteria carry different kinds of benefits and risk. However, usually the benefits and risks of focus can be summarised as follows.

Benefits include:

- *Clarity of performance objectives* – Clearly targeted markets imply at least some degree of discrimination between market segments. This, in turn, makes easier the task of prioritising those few performance objectives that are important for that market. This allows operations managers to be set relatively unambiguous and non-conflicting objectives to pursue in their day-to-day management of resources.

- *Developing appropriate resources* – A narrow set of focused resources allows those resources to be developed specifically to meet the relatively narrow set of performance objectives required by the market. Process technologies, skills and infrastructural resources can all be organised so as to trade off unimportant aspects of performance for those valued by the target market.

- *Enhanced learning and improvement* – A combination of clear objectives, together with resources organised to meet those objectives, can enhance an operation's ability to manage its learning and improvement of its processes. Certainly the opposite holds true. Broad and/or confused objectives, together with complex resource structures, make it difficult to build process knowledge, learn how to extend the capabilities of processes or thereby improve their performance.

The risks involved in focus include:

- *Significant shifts in the marketplace* – Although less common than 'scare stories' often suggest, it is clear that a dramatic shift in the overall competitive environment can undermine the effectiveness of a focus strategy. For example, in turn-of-the-twentieth-century New England, one firm dominated the market for domestic and commercial ice throughout North America. They had established an immensely successful and highly focused production and distribution system but they were powerless when a technical innovation – the domestic refrigerator – effectively removed their market.

- *Few economies of scale* – Within an operation, focusing often involves separating out resources that were once bundled together. This allows these resources to be developed appropriately for the market they serve but, because they no longer form part of a larger whole, they may not be able to achieve the same economies of scale as before. For example, a corporate purchasing department, buying goods and services for a whole corporation, may achieve economies of scale in the use of its resources and in its purchasing power. Splitting up such a department between businesses may allow them to enhance their capabilities in the type of purchasing necessary for each individual business but this may be gained at the expense of buying power and efficiency.

- *Structural vulnerability* – Combine the two risks above and any focused set of resources may be structurally vulnerable. Relatively minor changes in market requirements may destroy the benefits of being close to a market while, at the same time, there are few economies of scale to protect their viability.

## Drifting out of focus

Even when operations are set up to focus on one clearly specified set of objectives, they can, over time, drift out of focus. In fact, some authorities would argue[17] that unfocused operations are often a result of a gradual, but insidious drift away from a clear strategy. There can be several reasons for this.

- *New products and services* – Many companies, after developing new products or services, look to their existing operations to produce/deliver them. There is clearly a temptation to do this without examining the specific requirements of that particular product/service and evaluating the merits (and costs) of developing a new operation. Problematically, it is the firm's most successful operations that are perceived as being most able to cope with new products/services – even if their success is built upon focus.
- *Strategy drift* – In the absence of a clear competitive direction, managers often attempt to perform equally well against all of the many operations performance measures that exist. This (as discussed earlier) can lead to the dilution of the overall strategic impact of the firm.
- *Control by specialist* – Specialists in areas such as process technology, computer systems, inventory control, etc. will tend, in the absence of a more explicit operations strategy, to develop their own 'systems', which protect their own organisational position or optimise their local objectives, at the expense of greater strategic objectives.
- *Company-wide solutions* – This involves looking for panaceas in the belief that one solution can cure all the problems of every operation, without sufficient regard for the need to tailor solutions to suit particular circumstances.
- *Business growth* – When operations have to stretch or be reconfigured to deal with larger volumes, this often leads to a loss of focus.

## SUMMARY ANSWERS TO KEY QUESTIONS

### How can operations performance 'make or break' an organisation?

The way that an organisation's operations strategy is fashioned and implemented determines how its resources are used and, because the operations function is large and, in most businesses, represents the bulk of its assets and the majority of its people, this has a profound impact on the organisation's performance. But it is not only the size of the operations function that determines operations strategy's centrality to competitiveness, it is also its ability to develop the capabilities that will keep it ahead of competitors in the future. And for operations strategy to be effective, its performance must be assessed in terms of all its stakeholders. All operations have stakeholders; they are the people and groups who have a legitimate interest in the operation's strategy. Strongly related to the stakeholder perspective of operations performance is that of corporate social responsibility (generally known as CSR).

### What are operations performance objectives?

Operations strategy must include a relatively wide range of objectives that take into account the needs and aspirations of its stakeholders. However, because operations strategy is always concerned with addressing customers' needs, in this book we focus primarily on the five generic performance objectives of quality, speed, dependability, flexibility and cost. Each of these performance objectives has both internal and external effects. Externally their relative importance will differ depending on the nature of the markets served by the operation and/or its products and services. Internally these objectives can be mutually dependent. One way of distinguishing between the relative importance of each performance objective is by classifying them as order-winners and qualifiers, and, more recently, as 'delights'.

### Do the role and key performance objectives of operations stay constant or vary over time?

Both is true. Markets change, and the capabilities of operations resources develop over time. Therefore, not only does operations strategy change, the relative importance of its performance objectives will change. In fact, over the long term, the operations strategies of most enterprises can be seen to vary, either in response to deliberate attempts to change overall strategic direction or in a more emergent sense, where a consensus of the most appropriate strategic direction forms through accumulated operational experience.

### Are trade-offs between operations performance objectives inevitable, or can they be overcome?

Again, both is true. Yes, trade-offs are always, to some extent, inevitable in that pushing an operation to extremes in one aspect of performance will inevitably mean some sacrifice in other aspects of performance. Yet trade-offs can, at the margin, be overcome. In fact, the whole concept of operations performance improvement is, in effect, an attempt to overcome trade-offs. It is therefore the responsibility of all operations managers to seek ways of overcoming trade-offs. This also holds true when broader trade-offs are being considered, such as those between corporate social responsibility (CSR) performance and more obviously commercial aspects of performance.

### What are the advantages and disadvantages of focused operations?

The benefits of focus include achieving a *clarity* of performance objectives, which aids day-to-day decision making, developing resources in a manner *appropriate* to achieve a narrow set of objectives, and the enhanced *learning* and improvement that derives from concentrating on a narrow set of tasks. On the other hand, the problems with focus include the dangers inherent if there are significant *shifts in the marketplace*, which may leave the operation 'stranded' with an inappropriate performance mix, the reduction in opportunities for *economies of scale* as operations are segmented internally, and some *structural vulnerability* because of the first two issues.

## Further reading

Boyer, K.K. and Lewis, M.W. (2002) 'Competitive priorities: Investigating the need for trade-offs in operations strategy', *Production and Operations Management,* 11(1), pp. 241–250

Hayes, R. and Pisano, G.P. (1996) 'Manufacturing strategy: at the intersection of two paradigm shifts', *Production and Operations Management,* 5(1).

Hayes, R., Pisano, G., Upton, D. and Wheelwright, S. (2005) *Pursuing the competitive edge.* New York: Wiley.

Menda, R. and Dilts, D. (1997) 'The manufacturing strategy formulation process: linking multifunctional viewpoints', *Journal of Operations Management,* 15(4), pp. 223–241.

▶

Merchant, K. and Van der Stede, W. (2012) *Management Control Systems: Performance Measurement, Evaluation and Incentives*. Harlow, UK: Financial Times (Prentice Hall).

Neely, A. (ed.) (2012) *Business Performance Measurement: Unifying Theory and Integrating Practice*. Cambridge, UK: Cambridge University Press.

Neely, A. (2005) *Measuring business performance*. London: Economist Books.

Parmenter, D. (2007) *Key performance indicators (KPI): Developing, implementing and using winning KPIs*. New York: Wiley.

Savitz, A.W. and Weber, K. (2006) *The Triple Bottom Line: How Today's Best-run Companies Are Achieving Economic, Social and Environmental Success – And How You Can Too*. San Francisco: Jossey Bass.

## Notes on the chapter

1 Sources include: BBC website (2008) 'BA managers leave after T5 fiasco', 15 April; Browning, A. (2008) 'How do you clear a bags backlog?', BBC website, 19 April; Fran Yeoman and Nico Hines (2008) 'Heathrow T5 disruption to continue over weekend', *Times Online*, 28 March; Kevin Done (2008) 'BA to cancel hundreds more flights from T5', *Financial Times*, 30 March; Kevin Done (2008) 'Long haul to restore BA's reputation', *Financial Times*, 28 March; David Robertson (2008) 'Why Heathrow's T5 disaster provided a lesson for Dubai's T3', *The Times*, 29 November.

2 Sources include: Nelson, G. and Beene, R. (2013) 'Despite quality improvements, costly safety issues continue to dog automakers', *Automotive News*, 28 October; Bates, H., Holweg, M., Oliver, N. and Lewis, M. (2004) 'Motor vehicle recalls: Trends, patterns and emerging issues', ESRC Centre for Business Research, University of Cambridge Working Paper No. 295.

3 Elkington, J. (1998) *Cannibals with Forks: the Triple Bottom Line of 21st Century Business*. Canada: New Society Publishers.

4 Driver, C. and Johnston, R. (2000) 'Understanding Service Customers: the value of hard and soft attributes', Warwick University Working Paper.

5 All quotes taken from company websites.

6 Hill, T. (1993) *Manufacturing Strategy*, London: MacMillan.

7 Kano, S.T., Seraku, N. and Takahashi, F. (1984) 'Attractive quality and must-be quality', *Journal of the Society of Quality Control*, 14(2).

8 Spring, M. and Bowden, R. (1997) 'One more time: how do you win orders: a critical appraisal of the Hill manufacturing strategy framework', *International Journal of Operations and Production Management*, 17(8).

9 Based partly on information provided by Volkswagen Kommunikations (2007) and *The Economist* (2005) 'Dark days for Volkswagen', 16 July.

10 Mintzberg, in his classic paper, Mintzberg, H. (1978) 'Patterns of strategy formulation', *Management Science*, 24(9), carried out an analysis of VW on which the first part of this analysis is based.

11 Skinner, W. (1969) 'Manufacturing – missing link in corporate strategy', *Harvard Business Review*, May–June, p. 136.

12 Ibid.

13 Skinner, W. (1992) 'Missing the links in manufacturing strategy', in Voss, C.A., *Manufacturing Strategy – Process and Content*. London: Chapman & Hall.

14 Skinner, W. (1974) 'The focused factory', *Harvard Business Review*, May–June, p. 113.

15 Sources include: *The Economist* (2013) 'Ryanair's future - Oh really, O'Leary?', *The Economist Print Edition*, 19 October; BBC News site (2010) 'OFT watchdog says Ryanair payment policy is "puerile"', 3 January.

16 For further discussion see Ghemawat, P. and del Sol, P. (1998) 'Commitment versus flexibility?', *California Management Review*, 40(4).

17 Hill, T. (1993) *Manufacturing Strategy*. London: Macmillan.

# 3  Substitutes for strategy

## Introduction

Most chief operating officers (or whoever is in charge of the operations function) like to think that they have an important impact on their organisation's success (which they do) and that they have an operations strategy that ensures this (which they may not). Some will not even know what is meant by 'operations strategy', some will have a clearly worked out and thought through articulation of how they reconcile market requirements with operations resource capabilities. But there are also some who are likely to mention one of the 'new approaches' to operations that they have picked up, or been sold by consultants, or have judged to be particularly appropriate in improving their operations performance. Such responses might include, 'We are trying to make our operations as lean as possible' or 'We are reengineering our operations to avoid organisational silos'. But are these approaches to operations strategy as such, or are they merely substitutes for strategy? In this chapter we will examine some of these approaches and the extent to which they can be seen as 'strategic', as well as discussing how they fit into operations strategy implementation (see Figure 3.1).

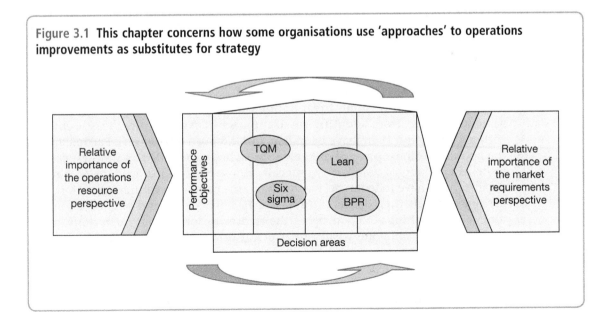

Figure 3.1 **This chapter concerns how some organisations use 'approaches' to operations improvements as substitutes for strategy**

> ### KEY QUESTIONS
>
> - *How does total quality management fit into operations strategy?*
> - *How do lean operations fit into operations strategy?*
> - *How does business process reengineering fit into operations strategy?*
> - *How does Six Sigma fit into operations strategy?*
> - *What place do these new approaches have in operations strategy?*

## Fads, fashion and the 'new' approaches to operations

One of the defining characteristics of business over the last two or three decades has been the number of 'new approaches' to the management of operations. Many of these new approaches have captured popular management imagination, at least for a short while. This is why many managers will say that their operations strategy is to implement 'lean operations principles', or 'total quality management', or 'business process reengineering', or 'enterprise resource planning', or 'Six Sigma'. What such responses indicate is that the company has opted to use a pre-packaged approach to improve its operations performance. And it is an increasingly common response. This is because either (a) these approaches are an easily understood and relatively simply way to tackle the complexities of modern operations, or (b) they seem to have worked in other organisations, or (c) they sound as if they are new and by implication therefore must be better than what went before, or (d) they have been sold the idea by a consultant (or read about it in a book) and it's worth trying something new because many other things have failed to bring improvements. So, are these approaches really strategic? Or are they simply a way of avoiding the difficult process of reconciling market requirements and operations resource capabilities?

The answer is probably that they are a bit of both. Why one adopts a particular approach and how it is implemented is at least as important as which approach is adopted. Certainly some organisations have gained significant operations-based advantages from adopting these approaches. None of the ideas is entirely without merit, and there have been many well reported triumphs. Particularly in the popular business press, these new approaches were hailed as almost a prerequisite to any kind of competitive success. However, it is also evident that many organisations have failed to derive much, if any, benefit from their adoption, and partly as a result there has come a backlash. This is a natural phenomenon. No sooner is something set up as being the answer to sorting out operations' many problems, than someone wishes to knock it down again. There is always mileage for journalists and academics in 'smashing the myth', 'exposing the truth', etc. Yet, amidst these predictable reactions, there were several studies that called into serious question the universal applicability and universal success of the new approaches. Although these studies do vary, many indicate that (at the most) only around one third of all initiatives involving these new approaches are deemed successful.

One study[1] examined the huge volume of management literature that deals with all the various 'new' approaches and plotted how interest in them grows and (often) falls over time. The study identified eight common characteristics or warning signs that most of the short-lived fads had, but the more enduring did not.

1 *Fads tend to be simple* – The ideas are straightforward, easy to communicate, easy to understand and reduced to a small number of factors or characteristics. Clear-cut distinctions are made; perfect and ideal types are proposed. Simple solutions are suggested.

2 *Fads promise results* – Fads have no false humility. They promise outcomes such as greater control and efficiency, more motivated and productive workers, more satisfied customers, or some other desired consequence.

3 *Fads are universal* – Fads propose solutions that work for all types of operation, function, task and culture. They claim universal relevance.

4 *Fads have 'step-down capability'* – Fads can be implemented in straightforward ways, often without having much effect on existing organisational practices. Large expenditures on resources or substantial redistributions of power can be avoided.

5 *Fads are in tune with the* Zeitgeist – Fads are in tune with the major trends or business problems of the day. They respond to challenges that are broadly felt and openly discussed.

6 *Fads are novel, but not necessarily radical* – Fads may question existing assumptions, criticise widespread practices and point to fresh new ways of doing things. However, this novelty is often the repackaging of older ideas or approaches.

7 *Fads gain legitimacy via gurus and well-known examples* – Fads are supported by high-profile publicity from gurus and success stories from excellent companies rather than by solid empirical evidence.

8 *Fads are lively and entertaining* – Fads are almost always presented in a way that can be described as concrete, articulate, bold, memorable and upbeat. They make use of catchphrases, lists and acronyms, anecdotes and corporate 'war stories'. Descriptions are vivid and extreme, making fads fun to read about and listen to.

Before anyone can judge whether any of these new approaches is right for them (whether they class as 'fads' or not), they must understand what they are, their underlying philosophy and how they differ from each other. In this chapter we look at four of the most commonly adopted of these solutions. They are as follows:

- total quality management;
- lean operations;
- business process reengineering;
- Six Sigma.

## Total quality management (TQM)

Total quality management was one of the earliest management 'fashions'. Its peak of popularity was in the late 1980s and early 1990s. As such, it has suffered from something of a backlash in recent years. Yet the general precepts and principles that constitute TQM are still huge. Few, if any, managers have not heard of TQM and its impact on improvement. Indeed, TQM has come to be seen as an approach to the way operations and processes should be managed and improved, generally.

## What is TQM?

A.V. Feigenbaum, generally held to be the originator of the term, defines TQM as: '*an effective system for integrating the quality development, quality maintenance and quality improvement efforts of the various groups in an organization so as to enable production and service at the most economical levels which allow for full customer satisfaction*'.[2] However, it was the Japanese who first made the concept work on a wide scale and subsequently popularised the approach and the term 'TQM'. It was then developed further by several so-called 'quality gurus'. Each 'guru' stressed a different set of issues, from which emerged the TQM approach to operations improvement (although they rarely used the term 'TQM'). For example, W.E. Deming (considered in Japan to be the father of quality control) asserted that quality starts with top management and is a strategic activity.[3] Deming's basic philosophy is that quality and productivity increase as 'process variability' (the unpredictability of the process) decreases. He emphasises the need for statistical control methods, participation, education, openness and purposeful improvement.

## The elements of TQM

TQM is best thought of as a philosophy of how to approach the organisation of quality improvement. This philosophy, above everything, stresses the 'total' of TQM. It is an approach that puts quality (and indeed improvement generally) at the heart of everything that is done by an operation. This totality can be summarised by the way TQM lays particular stress on the following elements.

### *Meeting the needs and expectations of customers*

TQM was one of the first of the 'customer-centric' approaches. In the TQM approach, meeting the expectations of customers means more than simply meeting customer requirements. It involves the whole organisation in understanding the central importance of customers to its success and even to its survival. Customers are seen not as being external to the organisation but as the most important part of it.

### *Covering all parts of the organisation*

One of the most significant elements of TQM is the concept of the internal customer and internal supplier. This means that everyone is a customer within the organisation and consumes goods or services provided by other internal suppliers, and everyone is also an internal supplier of goods and services for other internal customers. The assumption is that errors in the service provided within an organisation will eventually affect the external customer. TQM utilises this concept by stressing that each process in an operation has a responsibility to manage these internal customer–supplier relationships.

### Including every person in the organisation

TQM uses the phrase 'quality at source' – stressing the impact that each individual has on quality. The contribution of all individuals in the organisation is expected to go beyond 'not make mistakes'. Individuals are expected to bring something positive to improving the way they perform their jobs. The principles of 'empowerment' are frequently cited as supporting this aspect of TQM, an idea that seemed radical when it first began to migrate from Japan in the late 1970s. Some Japanese industrialists even thought (mistakenly) that companies in Western economies would never manage to change. Take, for example, a statement by Konosuke Matsushito, which, at the time, attracted considerable publicity:

> 'We are going to win and the industrial West is going to lose out – there is nothing much you can do about it, because the reasons for your failure are within yourselves. For you, the essence of management is getting the ideas out of the heads of bosses into the hands of labour. For us, the core of management is precisely the art of mobilizing and pulling together the intellectual resources of all employees in the service of the firm. Only by drawing on the combined brainpower of all its employees can a firm face up to the turbulence and constraints of today's environment. That is why our large companies give their employees three to four times more training than yours. This is why they foster within the firm such intensive exchange and communication. This is why they seek constantly everybody's suggestions and why they demand from the educational system increasing numbers of graduates as well as bright and well-educated generalists, because these people are the lifeblood of industry.'[4]

### Examining all costs that are related to quality, especially failure costs

The costs of quality are usually categorised as prevention costs (identifying and preventing potential problems, improving the design of products and services and processes to reduce quality problems, training and development, process control, etc.), appraisal costs (the costs of controlling quality to check to see if problems or errors have occurred during and after production), internal failure costs (costs associated with errors that are dealt with inside the operation, scrap, rework, lost production time, failure-related disruption, etc.) and external failure costs (the loss of customer goodwill, litigation, guarantee and warranty costs, etc.). TQM holds that increasing the costs associated with prevention will bring even greater reductions in the other cost categories.

### Getting things 'right first time', i.e. designing-in quality rather than inspecting it in

TQM shifts the emphasis from reactive (waiting for something to happen) to proactive (doing something before anything happens). This change in the view of quality costs has come about with a movement from an inspect-in (appraisal-driven) approach to a design-in (getting-it-right-first-time) approach.

### Developing the systems and procedures that support improvement

Typical of these is the ISO 9000 series – a set of worldwide standards that establishes requirements for companies' quality management systems. It is different from, but closely associated with, TQM. ISO 9000 registration requires a third-party assessment of a company's quality standards and procedures, and regular audits are made to ensure that the systems do not deteriorate.

Example **The Swiss Army knife: 'Our best means of protection is quality'[5]**

It is known all over the world for its usefulness, and its quality. The famous Swiss Army knife, which traces its history back to 1891, is made by the Victorinox Company in its factory in the small Swiss town of Ibach, Canton Schwyz. The company has numerous letters from its customers testifying to its product's quality and durability. The following story from one engineer is typical:

> 'I was installing a new piece of equipment in a sewage treatment plant. One morning, as I was crossing the bridge over the aeration tank of the treatment plant, I saw that the setting on one of the instruments was incorrect. I took out my Swiss Army knife to make the necessary adjustment. The knife slipped out of my hand and fell into the aeration tank whose function is to oxidise organic waste – the oxidising environment which is extremely corrosive to metals. Four years later, I received a small parcel with a note from the supervisor of the plant. They had emptied the aeration tank and found my knife at the bottom. The parcel contained the knife, which was in astonishingly good condition. The plastic casing and cover had only suffered very minor damage. I can assure you that very few products could have survived treatment like this, the components would have dissolved or simply disappeared.'

Today, the Victorinox factory assembles 27,000 knives a day (plus nearly 100,000 other items). More than 450 steps are required in the knife's manufacture. But times have not been easy for the Victorinox Company. Airport security restrictions after 9/11 hit sales of the knife. 'Our sales plummeted almost overnight', says Carl Elsener, the company's CEO and the great-grandson of its founder. 'All airport shops were suddenly banned from selling knives and we lost 30 per cent of our income that came from spontaneous airport purchases.' But rather than shut down some of its production lines and get rid of a considerable chunk of its workforce to cut costs (the factory hasn't fired a single person for economic reasons in all of the 125 years of its existence), Victorinox developed new products including laser-fronted ballpoint pens, bladeless 'in-flight' knives and Swiss Memory and Swiss Flash foldable USB drives. Another major threat to sales that has been growing is the appearance on the market of fake 'Swiss Army' knives, made mostly in China. Many of them look similar to the original; they even have the familiar Swiss cross on the handle.

So what is their defence against these fakes? 'Quality', says Carl Elsener. 'We have exhausted all legal means for the brand protection of our popular products. Our best means of protection is quality, which remains unsurpassed and speaks louder than words.' And the three components of the 'Victorinox total quality management system' is at the heart of this quality defence. First, incoming materials are checked to conform to quality specifications. Nonconforming products are identified, evaluated and reviewed according to set procedures. Only steel and plastic that comply with Victorinox's rigorous quality standards are used in the manufacturing of the products. Second, process control is employed at all stages of the production process. Third, the Final Inspection Department employs 50–60 people who are responsible for ensuring that all products conform to requirements. Any nonconforming products are isolated and identified. Nonconforming parts are repaired or replaced at the repair department.

## Criticisms of TQM

Many of the criticisms of TQM tend to fall into two slightly conflicting categories. The first is that, historically, many TQM initiatives fail – or at least are not entirely successful. The second is that, even if TQM is not the label given to improvement initiatives, many of the elements of TQM, such as continuous improvement, have now become routine.

As far as the first criticism is concerned, not all TQM initiatives that are launched, often with high expectations, will go on to have a major impact on performance. Companies who were in the vanguard of the TQM movement, such as Hewlett-Packard, admit that at one time they pushed quality for its own sake, and have shifted too much responsibility down to the shop floor. Similarly *The Economist* magazine, reporting on some companies' disillusionment with their experiences, quoted from several surveys.[6] For example:

- 'Of 500 US manufacturing and service companies, only a third felt their Total Quality programmes had significant impact on their competitiveness.'

- 'Only a fifth of the 100 British firms surveyed believed their quality programmes had achieved tangible results.'

- 'Of those quality programmes that have been in place for more than two years, two-thirds simply grind to a halt because of their failure to produce hoped-for results.'

Also, the excessive 'quality bureaucracy' associated with TQM – in particular, the continued use of standards and procedures – encourages 'management by manual' and over-systematised decision making, and is expensive and time-consuming. Furthermore, it is too formulaic, encouraging operations to substitute a 'recipe' for a more customised and creative approach to managing operations improvement.

As far as the second criticism ('we have incorporated much of TQM anyway') is concerned, it is undoubtedly true that some of the fundamentals of TQM have entered the vernacular of operations improvement. The idea of continuous improvement is perhaps the most obvious example. However, other elements such as the internal customer concept including service level agreements (SLAs), the idea of internal and external failure-related costs, and many aspects of individual staff empowerment, have all become widespread. Yet this is not really a criticism of TQM as such. Rather, it is a criticism of the practice of 'packaging' individual improvement elements under a single improvement 'brand'. It is an issue that we shall return to later in this chapter.

## Lessons from TQM

The core concept of a 'total, or holistic, view' of any issue is both powerful and attractive. At its simplest, it provides on outline 'checklist' of how to go about operations improvement. It is also capable of being developed into a more prescriptive form. The best example of this is the EFQM Excellence Model, developed by the European Foundation for Quality Management (EFQM). Originally the European Quality Award (EQA), awarded to the most successful exponent of total quality management in Europe each year, the model was modified and renamed the 'EFQM Excellence Model' or 'Business Excellence Model'. The EFQM Excellence Model is shown in Figure 3.2. The five 'enablers' are concerned with how results are being achieved, while the four 'results' are concerned with what the company has achieved and is achieving. The main advantage of using such models for self-assessment seems to be that companies find it easier to understand some of the more philosophical concepts of TQM when they are translated into specific areas, questions and percentages. Self-assessment also allows organisations to measure their progress in changing their organisation and in

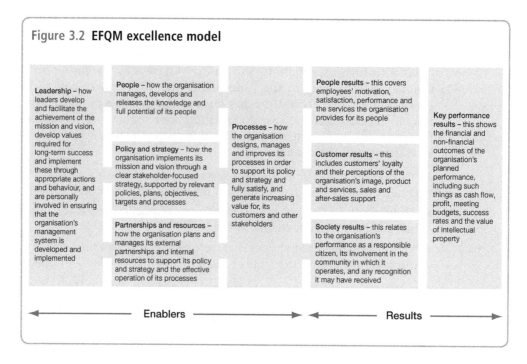

Figure 3.2 **EFQM excellence model**

achieving the benefits of TQM. An important aspect of self-assessment is an organisation's ability to judge the relative importance of the assessment categories to its own circumstances.

## Where does TQM fit into operations strategy?

Various authors have put forward prescriptions on how to integrate TQM into a business strategy. Many of these prescriptions stress that operations quality programmes should be both strategic and comprehensive. In other words, if one applied the operations strategy matrix to such an initiative, we would expect to see a spread of activities (albeit of differing priority) at the intersections with each of the decision areas. To test this assertion out, look at Deming's (one of the quality 'gurus') 14 points.[7] These are, in many ways, a summary of his and other authorities' ideas on quality. In order to translate these different elements onto the operations strategy matrix, we have listed each of Deming's 14 points followed by the operations strategy decision areas to which they relate:

1 Plan for a long-term commitment to quality (development and organisation).

2 Quality must be built into the processes at every stage (process technology, supply network, development and organisation).

3 Cease mass inspection (process technology, supply network, development and organisation).

4 Do not make purchase decisions on price alone (supply network, development and organisation).

5 Identify problems and work continuously to improve the system (supply network, development and organisation).

6 Implement SPC and quality training (process technology, development and organisation).

7 Institute leadership and a human-centred approach to supervision (development and organisation).

8 Eliminate fear (supply network, development and organisation).

9 Break down barriers between departments (supply network, development and organisation).

10 Stop demanding higher productivity without the methods to achieve it (capacity strategy, process technology, supply network, development and organisation).

11 Eliminate performance standards based solely on output (capacity strategy, process technology, supply network, development and organisation).

12 Remove barriers to pride in workmanship (development and organisation).

13 Institute education and self-improvement programmes (development and organisation).

14 Create a top management structure that emphasises the above 13 points every day (development and organisation).

The matrix in Figure 3.3 summarises Deming's points in each decision area and illustrates that the Deming points are comprehensive, though heavily emphasising the infrastructural aspects of operational change. However, changing behaviours and beliefs is not easy and requires constant emphasis over an extended period of time.

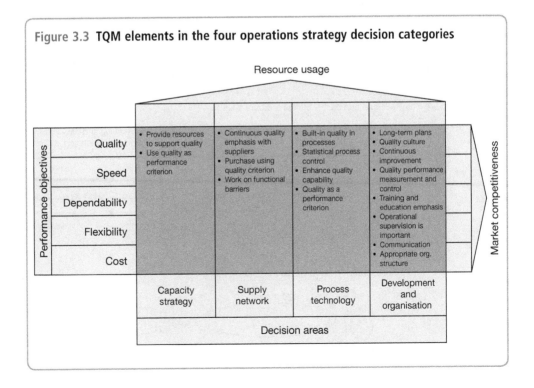

**Figure 3.3 TQM elements in the four operations strategy decision categories**

## Lean operations

The idea of lean operations (also known as 'just-in-time', 'lean synchronisation' and 'continuous flow operations') spread beyond its Japanese roots and became fashionable in the West at about the same time as TQM. And although its popularity has not declined to the same extent as TQM, over 25 years of experience (at least in manufacturing) have diminished the excitement once associated with the approach. But, unlike TQM, it was seen initially as an approach to be used exclusively in manufacturing. Now, lean has become newly fashionable as an approach that can be applied in service operations.

### What is 'lean'?

The lean approach aims to meet demand instantaneously, with perfect quality and no waste. Put another way, it means that the flow of products and services always delivers exactly what customers want (perfect quality), in exact quantities (neither too much nor too little), exactly when needed (not too early or too late), exactly where required (not to the wrong location) and at the lowest possible cost. It results in items flowing rapidly and smoothly through processes, operations and supply networks. It is best illustrated with an example. Figure 3.4(a) shows a simple three-stage process. The traditional approach assumes that each stage in a process or supply network will be 'buffered' from the next stage downstream. These buffers 'insulate' each stage from its neighbours, making each stage relatively independent so that if one stage stops operating for some reason, the next stage can continue, at least for a time. The larger the buffer inventory, the greater the degree of insulation between the stages, but throughput times will be slow because items will spend time waiting in the inventories. The main argument against this

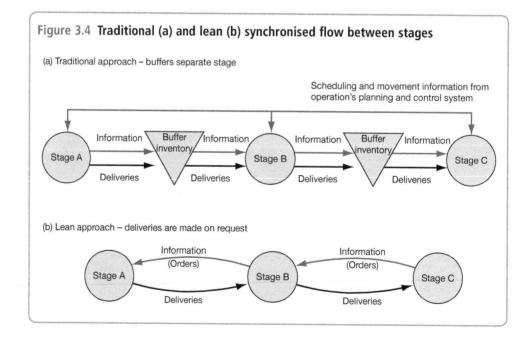

**Figure 3.4 Traditional (a) and lean (b) synchronised flow between stages**

(a) Traditional approach – buffers separate stage

Scheduling and movement information from operation's planning and control system

Stage A — Information → Buffer inventory — Information → Stage B — Information → Buffer inventory — Information → Stage C

Deliveries — Deliveries — Deliveries — Deliveries

(b) Lean approach – deliveries are made on request

Stage A ← Information (Orders) — Stage B ← Information (Orders) — Stage C

Deliveries — Deliveries

traditional approach is that when a problem occurs at one stage it will not imme-diately be apparent elsewhere in the system, so the responsibility for solving the problem will be centred largely on the people within that stage. By contrast, with a pure lean process, as shown in Figure 3.4(b), items will flow from one to another only when the subsequent stage requests them. This means that problems at any stage are quickly exposed. The responsibility for solving the problem is now shared and is more likely to be solved. By preventing items accumulating between stages, the operation has increased the chances of the intrinsic efficiency of the process being improved. The lean approach exposes the process (although not suddenly) to problems, both to make them more evident and to change the motivation towards solving the problems.

## The elements of lean

Return to our simple example illustrated in Figure 3.4(b). Note how the trigger for any activity is the direct request of the internal customer; this reflects the emphasis that lean places on meeting the needs of customers exactly. Second, note how, in the absence of inventories, items flow in a smooth and synchronous manner. In fact the term 'lean synchronisation' is perhaps a more accurate name for what we are here calling the 'lean approach'. Third, note how the synchronisation leads to fewer inventories in the process, which, in turn, leads to a change in peoples' behaviour and involvement in and motivation for improvement. Finally, note how this motivation to improve reinforces the quest for seeking out and eliminat-ing waste within processes. It is these four elements of customer-based demand triggers, synchronised flow, enhanced improvement behaviour and waste elimin-ation that mesh together to form the lean approach. We will briefly examine each in turn.

### Customer-based demand triggers

In the lean approach, demand is to be met exactly when it is needed, no more no less, not early not late, and always to exact levels of quality. This is obviously easier when demand is predictable and, preferably, relatively steady. The implica-tion of this is that the ability to implement lean principles are much enhanced when an organisation understands (and to some extent controls) the nature and level of the demands on its resources. The most common approach to achieving customer-based triggering is by utilising 'pull control' as opposed to 'push control'. Push control was illustrated in Figure 3.4(a) when any items that are processed by a stage are immediately pushed forward to the next stage, irrespective of whether that customer stage actually requires them at that time. Pull control is implicit in Figure 3.4(b), where items are 'pulled' forward only in response to a specific customer request.

### Synchronised flow

Synchronised flow means that items in a process, operation or supply network flow smoothly and with even velocity from start to finish. This is a function of how inven-tory accumulates within the operation. Whether inventory is accumulated in order to smooth differences between demand and supply, or as a contingency against unexpected delays, or simply to batch for purposes of processing or movement, it all means that flow becomes asynchronous – it waits as inventory rather than progressing smoothly on. Of course, once this state of perfect synchronisation of flow has been achieved, it becomes easier to expose any irregularities of flow that may be the symptoms of more deep-rooted, underlying problems.

### Enhanced improvement behaviour

Like TQM, the lean approach has always stressed the importance of staff involvement. However, the way in which this was expressed, often using terms such as 'respect for humans' and 'enlightened vision', did not always resonate with Western perspectives on organisational behaviour. Indeed, the lean approach often seemed naïve, patronising, or worse to liberal Western eyes. Yet, return to the fundamental idea as illustrated in our simple example and we have something that is not fundamentally countercultural: namely, that smooth flow and the absence of inventory motivates individuals to help their colleagues improve the whole process rather than focusing exclusively on their own area of direct responsibility. So, behaviour is partly a function of synchronous flow that is itself a function of customer-based triggering of demand. Furthermore, it is these changes in motivation and behaviour that in turn leads on to the fourth element – waste elimination.

### Waste elimination

This is arguably the most significant part of the lean philosophy: the elimination of all forms of waste, where waste is any activity that does not add value. Identifying waste is the first step towards eliminating it. The car manufacturer Toyota has described seven types. Here we consolidate these into four broad categories of waste that apply in many different types of operation:

- *Waste from irregular flow* – Perfect synchronisation means smooth and even flow through processes, operations and supply networks.
- *Waste from inexact supply* – Perfect synchronisation is supplying exactly what is wanted, exactly when it is needed. Any under or over supply and any early or late delivery will result in waste.
- *Waste from inflexible response* – Customer needs can vary, in terms of what they want, how much they want and when they want it. But unless an operation is flexible, it can make change only infrequently. This mismatch is the cause of much inventory – for example, because machines make a large batch of similar products together.
- *Waste from variability* – Synchronisation implies exact levels of quality. If there is variability in quality levels then customers will not consider themselves as being adequately supplied. Variability therefore is an important barrier to achieving synchronised supply.

Some organisations, especially now that lean is being applied more widely in service operations, view waste elimination as the most important of all the elements of the lean approach. In fact, they sometimes see the lean approach as consisting almost exclusively of waste elimination. What they fail to realise is that effective waste elimination is best achieved through changes in behaviour. It is the behavioural change brought about through synchronised flow and customer triggering that provides the window onto exposing and eliminating waste.

*Capacity utilisation may be sacrificed in the short term*

A paradox in the lean concept is that it may mean some sacrifice of capacity utilisation. In organisations that place a high value on the utilisation of capacity this can prove particularly difficult to accept. It occurs because, when stoppages occur in the traditional system, the buffers allow each stage to continue working and thus achieve high-capacity utilisation. The high utilisation does not necessarily make the system as a whole produce more because the extra production goes into the large buffer inventories. In a lean process, stoppages will affect the rest of the operation. This will lead to lower-capacity utilisation, at least in the short term. However, there is no point in producing output just for it to increase inventory. In fact, producing just to keep utilisation high is not only pointless, it is counter-productive, because the extra inventory produced merely serves to make improvements less likely.

## Criticisms of lean

The lean approach to people management can be viewed as, at best, patronising. It may be less autocratic than some earlier Japanese management practices, but it is not always in line with 'Western' job design philosophies. Even in Japan, the JIT (just-in-time) approach is not without its critics. S. Kamata wrote an autobiographical description of life as an employee at a Toyota plant called *Japan in the Passing Lane*.[8] His account speaks of 'the inhumanity and the unquestioning adherence' of working under such a system. Similar criticisms have been supported in some studies that point out some of the negative effects of the flexibility principles within the lean approach.[9]

Lean principles can also be taken to an extreme. When lean ideas first started to have an impact on operations practice in the West, some authorities advocated the reduction of between-process inventories to zero. While in the long term this provides the ultimate in motivation for operations managers to ensure the efficiency and reliability of each process stage, it does not admit the possibility of some processes always being intrinsically less than totally reliable. An alternative view is to allow inventories around process stages with higher-than-average uncertainty. This at least allows some protection for the rest of the system. The same ideas apply to just-in-time delivery between factories. The Toyota Motor Corp., often seen as the epitome of lean, has suffered from its low inter-plant inventory policies. Both the Kobe earthquake and fires in supplier plants have caused production at Toyota's main factories to close down for several days because of a shortage of key parts. Even in the best-regulated manufacturing networks, one cannot always account for such events.

Arguably, the major weakness of lean principles is that they can break down when fluctuations in supply or demand become extreme, especially when they are also unpredictable. The pull control of hamburgers in a fast-food restaurant works perfectly well when demand stays within predictable limits. However, when subjected to an unexpected, large influx of customers, it leaves most of those customers waiting for their meal. Similarly, in very complex and interrelated processes, lean principles are sometimes difficult to apply.

## Lessons from lean

Looking back to when the lean approach was first introduced into Western manufacturing, it is easy to forget just how radical and, more importantly, counter-intuitive it seemed. Although ideas of continuous improvement were starting to be accepted, the idea that inventories were generally a bad thing, and that throughput time was more important than capacity utilisation, seemed to border on the insane to the more traditionally minded. So, as lean ideas have been gradually accepted, we have likewise come to be far more tolerant of ideas that are radical and/or counter-intuitive. This is an important legacy because it opened up the debate on operations practice and broadened the scope of what are regarded as acceptable approaches.

Similarly, the idea that protecting parts of the operation (by buffering them with inventory) is not sensible in the long term has also had profound effects. Opening up an operation's resources to its external customers is now seen as promoting the same behavioural change as reducing inventory between the stages of a process. It exposes the operation to the realities of the market and forces it to adapt to what the market really wants, often by increasing the flexibility of its resources.

A further legacy that the absorption of lean ideas has brought operations in general concerns the interdependence of a number of important ideas. Before the lean approach there was relatively little understanding of how inventory, throughput time, value-added and waste elimination, utilisation and flexibility all related to each other. Although the way in which lean philosophy integrated these ideas was novel, it was at least coherent. In fact, it legitimised the whole idea of a philosophy of operations. Prior to lean, operations was a relatively loose collection of ideas from the scientific management era of the early twentieth century, some elegant but relatively naïve mathematical modelling and simple practical ideas based on pragmatic operations practice.

It is also worth remembering that when Taiichi Ohno wrote his seminal book on lean (called *Toyota Production System: Beyond Large-Scale Production*, and after retiring from Toyota in 1978) he was able to portray Toyota's manufacturing plants as embodying a coherent production approach. However, this encouraged observers to focus in on the specific techniques of lean production and de-emphasised the importance of 30 years of 'trial and error'. The success of Toyota has much to do with the process of fit (see Chapter 8). Staff at Toyota worked over decades to ensure alignment between their intended market position and their operations resources. Maybe the real achievement of Toyota was not so much what they did but how long they stuck at it.

---

**Example** | **Lean health care[10]**

Health-care funding varies significantly around the world. It is also an emotional and deeply political issue. In many European countries (the UK, for example) some people shudder at the thought of private companies profiting from providing health care. However, some claim that private health-care companies can have advantages. First, they are more likely to make services provision more efficient because they benefit directly from the savings. Second, they are better at persuading their staff to embrace innovation. Third, it is in their interests to spread the adoption of new ideas. One health-care operation that is cited as demonstrating these advantages is Stockholm's Saint Goran's Hospital, which is run by a private company, Capio. Yet, for the patient, St Goran's is the same as any other Swedish public hospital. St Goran's gets nearly all its money from the state and treatment is free, apart from the small charge that is charged at all Swedish hospitals.

This is the setting for one of the more successful examples of lean management in health-care services. Britta Wallgren, the hospital's chief executive and an anaesthetist by training, admits that she never heard the term 'lean' when she was at medical school, yet now it is the central philosophy driving St Goran's approach to organising its medical care. The hospital's lean concept is based on the two lean principles of 'flow' and 'quality'. It has reduced waiting times by increasing throughput. Everything is done to try to 'maximise throughput', so as to minimise cost and 'give taxpayers value for money'. Nor should hospitals be in the hotel business, they say. So, to minimise the time patients spend in hospital, they invest in preparing patients for admission and providing support after they are released. Before the adoption of lean principles, doctors and nurses used to 'work in parallel'; now they work together in teams. No longer do staff concentrate exclusively on their field of medical expertise, they are also responsible for suggesting operational improvements. The drive to save costs also runs to how patients are treated. The hospital has been called the medical equivalent of a budget airline. There are four to six patients to a room and the décor is 'institutional' rather than opulent. Similarly, staff are included in establishing improved working practices, many of which are relatively 'low tech'. For example, staff used to waste valuable time looking for equipment such as defibrillators. Then someone suggested marking a reserved space on the floor with yellow tape and insisting that the machines were always kept there.

Of course, none of these ideas is new. Even in health care there are several examples of lean principles being used to increase throughput, reduce waste and keep costs down while maintaining (or improving) quality. The question here is whether the strategic funding decisions made by the Swedish government are, at least partly, responsible for its successful deployment. Sweden has gone further than other European countries in using state funding to buy public services from whichever providers, public or private, offer the best combination of price and quality. Yet there are plenty of examples of publicly funded providers who have adopted lean. And that is the point. The argument is not so much about the effectiveness of lean as an operating philosophy. Rather, it is about the relationship between how a health-care system is organised strategically, and the system's ability to effectively use important, but essentially operational, ideas such as lean.

## Where does lean fit into operations strategy?

Figure 3.5 summarises some of the elements of the lean approach, again using the four decision categories in the operations strategy matrix. This shows that the core principles of the lean approach are contained largely within the supply network and development and organisation decision areas. This is not surprising given the emphasis on flow (which is what supply network strategy is partly about) and improvement through waste elimination (an important part of development and organisation strategy). The role of process technology strategy is largely to ensure that technology choices support the core elements of lean through flexibility, reliability and reduced variability. Although there is only one entry under the category of capacity strategy, it is none the less important. If lean principles are to be adopted through the supply chain, then to maintain synchronous flow it will be necessary to tolerate reduced capacity utilisation. Or putting it the other way round, one cannot allow capacity bottlenecks to disturb smooth and synchronous flow through the chain. The implication is that, under a lean approach, more capacity may have to be provided than under a more traditional approach to managing supply chain throughput.

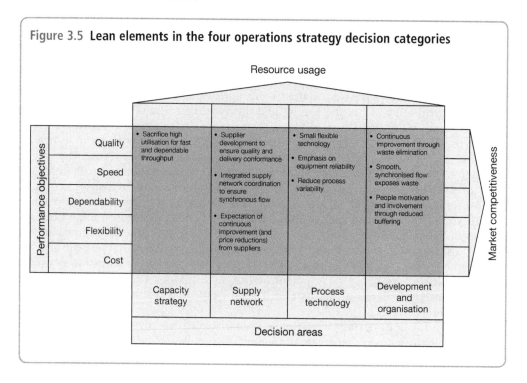

Figure 3.5 **Lean elements in the four operations strategy decision categories**

## Business process reengineering (BPR)

Business process reengineering (BPR) originated in the early 1990s when Michael Hammer proposed that rather than using technology to automate work, it would be better applied to doing away with the need for the work in the first place ('don't automate, obliterate'). In doing this he was warning against establishing non-value added work within an information technology system where it would be even more difficult to identify and eliminate. All work, he said, should be examined for whether it adds value for the customer and, if not, processes should be redesigned to eliminate it. In doing this, BPR was echoing similar objectives in both scientific management and, more recently, lean approaches. But BPR, unlike those two earlier approaches, advocated radical changes rather than incremental changes to processes. Shortly after Hammer's article, other authors developed the ideas – again the majority of them stressing the importance of a radical approach. This radicalism was summarised by Davenport who, when discussing the difference between BPR and continuous improvement, held that, *'Today's firms must seek not fractional, but multiplicative levels of improvement – ten times rather than ten per cent.'*[11]

### What is BPR?

BPR has been defined as:

> '...the fundamental rethinking and radical redesign of business processes to achieve dramatic improvements in critical, contemporary measures of performance, such as cost, quality, service and speed.'[12]

But there is far more to it than that. In fact, BPR was a blend of a number of ideas that had been current in operations management for some time. Lean concepts, process flow charting, critical examination in method study, operations network management and customer-focused operations all contribute to the BPR concept. It was the potential of information technologies to enable the fundamental redesign of processes, however, which acted as the catalyst in bringing these ideas together. It was the information technology that allowed radical process redesign, even if many of the methods used to achieve the redesign had been explored before. For example, 'Business Process Reengineering, although a close relative, seeks radical rather than merely continuous improvement. It escalates the effort of ... (lean) ... and TQM to make process orientation a strategic tool and a core competence of the organization. BPR concentrates on core business processes, and uses the specific techniques within the ... (lean) ... and TQM tool boxes as enablers, while broadening the process vision.'[13]

## The elements of BPR

The main principles of BPR can be summarised in the following points.

### Rethink business processes

Rethink business processes in a cross-functional manner that organises work around the natural flow of information (or materials or customers). This means organising around outcomes of a process, rather than the tasks that go into it. Underlying the BPR approach is the belief that operations should be organised around the total process, which adds value for customers, rather than the functions or activities that perform the various stages of the value-adding activity. The core of BPR is a redefinition of the processes within an operation, to reflect the business processes that satisfy customer needs. Figure 3.6 illustrates this idea.

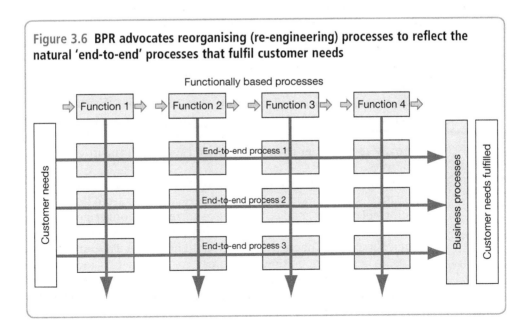

Figure 3.6 **BPR advocates reorganising (re-engineering) processes to reflect the natural 'end-to-end' processes that fulfil customer needs**

### Strive for dramatic improvements

Strive for dramatic improvements in performance by radically rethinking and redesigning the process. It was this radical approach that generated much of the publicity surrounding BPR when it was first proposed. But many would argue that it is inevitable that a BPR 'solution' will be radical when it seeks to redesign processes on an end-to-end basis, as described above. Traditional organisational and functional boundaries will have to be reconfigured and individuals' jobs and responsibilities redefined. Furthermore, the use of new information technologies is likely to promote previously unexplored process designs. In fact, Hammer and Champy discussed the role of what they termed 'disruptive technologies' that would directly challenge the orthodoxy of process design.[14]

### Have those who use the output from a process, perform the process

Check to see if all internal customers can be their own supplier, rather than depending on another function in the business to supply them (which takes longer and separates out the stages in the process). In process design this idea is sometimes referred to as a 'short fat' process, as opposed to the more conventional, multi-stage, 'long thin' process.

### Put decision points where the work is performed

Do not separate those who do the work from those who control and manage the work. Control and action are just one more type of supplier–customer relationship that can be merged.

## Criticisms of BPR

BPR has aroused considerable controversy, mainly because BPR sometimes looks only at work activities rather than at the people who perform the work. Because of this, people become 'cogs in a machine'. Many of these critics equate BPR with the much earlier principles of scientific management, pejoratively known as 'Taylorism'. Generally, these critics mean that, like some forms of early scientific management, BPR is overly harsh in the way it views human resources. Certainly, there is evidence that BPR is often accompanied by a significant reduction in staff. Studies at the time when BPR was at its peak often revealed that the majority of BPR projects could reduce staff levels by over 20 per cent.[15] Often, BPR was viewed as merely an excuse for getting rid of staff. Companies that wished to 'downsize' were using BPR as the pretext, putting the short-term interests of the shareholders of the company above either their longer-term interests or the interests of the company's employees.

   The real danger is that a combination of radical redesign together with downsizing could mean that the essential core of experience is lost from the operation. This leaves it vulnerable to any market turbulence since it no longer possesses the knowledge and experience of how to cope with unexpected changes. This is a similar criticism to what we describ in Chapter 8 as overly 'tight fit' between resources and market requirements. When the operation's resources are designed to focus exclusively on one narrowly defined set of market requirements, it is vulnerable to any changes either in market requirements or its own resource capabilities. In this sense the outcome of a BPR project, even when implemented effectively, could be seen as carrying the same combination of advantages and disadvantages as the focus strategy described in Chapter 2: namely, exceptional performance under a defined set of circumstances but excess risk when these circumstances no longer apply.

## Lessons from BPR

Although one of the later of the new approaches to operations, BPR is already suffering from a backlash. Perhaps this is not surprising given its radical nature. The greater the deviation from orthodoxy, the greater the level of criticism. Nevertheless, even with a relatively short experience of using BPR principles, certain lessons emerge.

- Don't dismiss radical approaches to reconfiguring operations resources. A radical reconfiguration may carry a higher risk but it is a legitimate alternative to incremental development. Although, like many of these new approaches, there are examples where expectations have not been met, there are also examples where radical redesign has brought significant benefits. General Motors, South West Airlines, Hewlett Packard and many other high-profile companies all claim to have experienced some significant success with BPR.

- New process technology, especially information technology, needs to be fully incorporated into process redesign. These new technologies often have much more potential than simply speeding up, or doing better, what was done before. They both have capabilities (often associated with flexibility) that could be exploited in new ways and they may need new infrastructural support to develop their potential.

- Beware of the publicity that comes when a new approach is branded in a particular way. Very soon after its introduction, BPR had polarised expectations. Labour representatives assumed that it would always be used as a heartless exercise for 'employment bloodshed'. Business leaders, looking forward to often over-inflated estimates of the saving that could be achieved, became disenchanted when these expectations were not met immediately.

- Many of the ideas generated by BPR and the debate it provoked were already commonplace in manufacturing processes. BPR succeeded in moving the arena of this debate from manufacturing to direct service processes and even to non-operations processes. In that sense BPR helped to establish the idea that processes are ubiquitous in business, and the same ideas and principles that shape process design within the operations function can also be used outside it.

- Beware of any approach that dismisses the contribution played by people in operations or processes. Even the originators of BPR later admitted that they had paid insufficient attention to human resources within process. Because of this, the initial impression (that BPR inevitably meant trampling over human aspirations and potential) became difficult to reverse.

## Where does BPR fit into operations strategy?

Figure 3.7 places some of the elements of BPR into our strategic decision areas. Again, note how most of the elements lie within the infrastructural area of development and organisation. Organisationally, BPR's recommendations regarding where decisions should be made and how processes should be conceptualised do much to

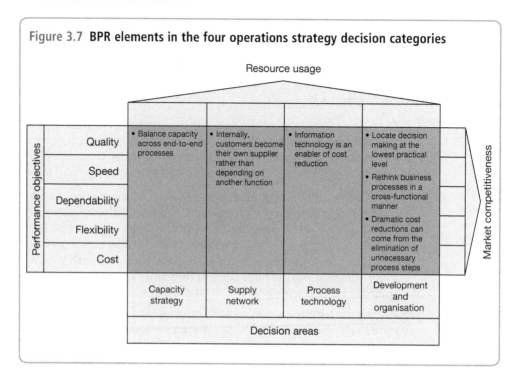

Figure 3.7 **BPR elements in the four operations strategy decision categories**

shape the underlying philosophy of an operation's organisational design. Similarly, the idea that dramatic reductions in cost can be gained from eliminating unnecessary process steps is as much a state of mind as it is any change in the business's structural resources. Where structural resources are affected it is to emphasise the potential of process technology in facilitating cost reduction, recommend merging stages in the internal supply chain in order to simplify processes and imply that capacity should be balanced along end-to-end process lines, rather than between functions.

## Six Sigma

Motorola, the electronics and communications systems company, first popularised the 'Six Sigma' approach. When it set its quality objective as 'total customer satisfaction' in the 1980s, it started to explore what the slogan would mean to its operations processes. They decided that true customer satisfaction would only be achieved when its products were delivered when promised, with no defects, with no early-life failures and when the product did not fail excessively in service. To achieve this, Motorola focused initially on removing manufacturing defects. However, it soon came to realise that many problems were caused by latent defects, hidden within the design of its products. These may not show initially but eventually could cause failure in the field. The only way to eliminate these defects was to make sure that design specifications were tight (i.e. narrow tolerances) and its processes very capable (exhibited little variability relative to design tolerances).

## What is Six Sigma?

Motorola's Six Sigma quality concept was so named because it required that the natural variation of processes (±3 standard deviations) should be half their specification range. In other words, the specification range of any part of a product or service should be ±6 the standard deviation of the process. The Greek letter sigma ($\sigma$) is often used to indicate the standard deviation of a process, hence the 'Six Sigma' label. Now the definition of Six Sigma has widened to well beyond this rather narrow statistical perspective. General Electric (GE), who were probably the best known of the early adopters of Six Sigma, defined it as, '*A disciplined methodology of defining, measuring, analysing, improving, and controlling the quality in every one of the company's products, processes, and transactions – with the ultimate goal of virtually eliminating all defects.*' So now, Six Sigma should be seen as a broad improvement concept rather than a simple examination of process variation, even though this is still an important part of process control, learning and improvement.

## The elements of Six Sigma

Although the scope of Six Sigma is disputed, the following elements are frequently associated with the process.

### Customer-driven objectives

Six Sigma is sometimes defined as:

'the process of comparing process outputs against customer requirements'.

In taking on this definition, Six Sigma is conforming to what almost all of the new approaches to operations do – namely, starting by emphasising the importance of understanding customers and customer requirements. The idea of comparing what processes can do against what customers want can be seen as an operational-level articulation of the definition of operations strategy used in this book – reconciling market requirements against operations resource capabilities. Although the Six Sigma approach is inevitably narrower, it uses a number of measures to assess the performance of operations processes. In particular, it expresses performance in terms of defects per million opportunities (DPMO). This is exactly what it says: the number of defects that the process will produce if there were one million opportunities to do so. This is then related to the 'Sigma measurement' of a process and is the number of standard deviations of the process variability that will fit within the customer specification limits.

### Use of evidence

Although Six Sigma is not the first of the new approaches to operations to use statistical methods (some of the TQM gurus promoted statistical process control, for example), it has done a lot to emphasise the use of quantitative evidence. In fact, much of the considerable training required by Six Sigma consultants is devoted to mastering quantitative analytical techniques. However, the statistical methods used in Six Sigma do not always reflect conventional academic statistical knowledge, as such. Six Sigma emphasises observational methods of collecting data and the use of experimentation to examine hypothesis. Techniques include graphical methods, analysis of variance and two-level factorial experiment design. Underlying the use of these techniques is an emphasis on the scientific method – responding only to hard evidence and using statistical software to facilitate analysis.

### Structured improvement cycle

The structured improvement cycle used in Six Sigma is called the DMAIC (pronounced De-Make) cycle (see Figure 3.8). The DMAIC cycle starts with defining the problem, or problems, partly to understand the scope of what needs to be done and partly to define exactly the requirements of the process improvement. Often, at this stage, a formal goal or target for the improvement is set. After definition comes the measurement stage. This is an important point in the cycle, and the Six Sigma approach generally, which emphasises the importance of working with hard evidence rather than opinion. This stage involves validating the problem to make sure that it really is a problem worth solving, using data to refine the problem and measuring exactly what is happening. Once these measurements have been established, they can be analysed. The analysis stage is sometimes seen as an opportunity to develop hypotheses as to what the root causes of the problem really are. Such hypotheses are validated (or not) by the analysis and the main root causes of the problem identified. Once the causes of the problem are identified, work can begin on improving the process. Ideas are developed to remove the root causes of problems, solutions are tested and those solutions that seem to work are implemented, formalised and the results measured. The improved process needs then to be continually monitored and controlled to check that the improved level of performance is sustaining. After this point the cycle starts again and defines the problems that are preventing further improvement. Remember, though, it is the last point about both cycles that is the most important – the cycle starts again. It is only by accepting that in a continuous improvement philosophy these cycles quite literally never stop that improvement becomes part of every person's job.

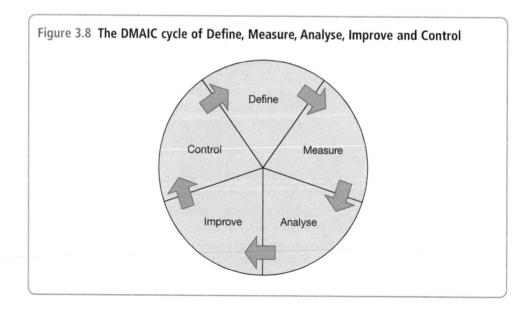

Figure 3.8 **The DMAIC cycle of Define, Measure, Analyse, Improve and Control**

## Structured training and organisation of improvement

The Six Sigma approach holds that improvement initiatives can only be successful if significant resources and training are devoted to their management. It recommends a specially trained cadre of practitioners, many of whom should be dedicated full time to improving processes as internal consultants. The terms that have become associated with this group of experts (and denote their level of expertise) are 'Master Black Belt', 'Black Belt' and 'Green Belt'. Master Black Belts are experts in the use of Six Sigma tools and techniques, as well as how such techniques can be used and implemented. Primarily, Master Black Belts are seen as teachers who can not only guide improvement projects, but also coach and mentor Black Belts and Green Belts who are closer to the day-to-day improvement activity. They are expected to have the quantitative analytical skills to help with Six Sigma techniques and also the organisational and interpersonal skills to teach and mentor. Given their responsibilities, it is expected that Master Black Belts are employed full time on their improvement activities. Black Belts can take a direct hand in organising improvement teams. Like Master Black Belts, Black Belts are expected to develop their quantitative analytical skills and also act as coaches for Green Belts. Black Belts are dedicated full time to improvement, and although opinions vary on how many Black Belts should be employed in an operation, some organisations recommend one Black Belt for every hundred employees. Green Belts work within improvement teams, possibly as team leaders. They have significant amounts of training, although less than Black Belts. Green Belts are not full-time positions; they have normal day-to-day process responsibilities but are expected to spend at least 20 per cent of their time on improvement projects.

## Process capability and control

Not surprisingly, given its origins, process capability and control is important within the Six Sigma approach. Processes change over time, as does their performance. Some aspect of process performance (usually an important one) is measured periodically (either as a single measurement or as a small sample of measurements). These are then plotted on a simple time-scale. This has a number of advantages. The first is to check that the performance of the process is, in itself, acceptable (capable). They can also be used to check if process performance is changing over time, and to check on the extent of the variation in process performance.

## Process design

Latterly, Six Sigma proponents also include process design into the collection of elements that define the Six Sigma approach. This is somewhat surprising because process design (or rather, redesign) is implicit in the DMAIC cycle. Presumably, by formally including this element, practitioners are emphasising the need to improve whole processes rather than individual elements of a process.

## Process improvement

Some of the ideas of continuous improvement are also now formally included in Six Sigma, but it does not confine itself to continuous improvement only. In fact, Six Sigma projects may often be relatively wide in scope and aim to achieve relatively large improvements.

## Criticisms of Six Sigma

One common criticism of Six Sigma is that it does not offer anything that was not available before the term was used. Its emphasis on improvement cycles comes from TQM, its emphasis on reducing variability comes from statistical process control, its use of experimentation and data analysis is simply good quantitative analysis. The only contribution that Six Sigma has made, argue its critics, is using the rather gimmicky martial arts analogy of Black Belt, etc. to indicate a level of expertise in Six Sigma methods. All Six Sigma has done is package pre-existing elements together in order for consultants to be able to sell it to gullible chief executives. In fact, it's difficult to deny some of these points. Maybe the real issue is whether it is really a criticism. If bringing these elements together really does form an effective problem-solving approach, why is this is a problem? Six Sigma is also accused of being too hierarchical in the way it structures its various levels of involvement in the improvement activity (as well as the dubious use of martial arts-derived names such as Black Belt). It is also expensive. Devoting such large amounts of training and time to improvement is a significant investment, especially for small companies. Nevertheless, Six Sigma proponents argue that the improvement activity is generally neglected in most operations and, if it is to be taken seriously, it deserves the significant investment implied by the Six Sigma approach. Furthermore, they argue, if operated well, Six Sigma improvement projects run by experienced practitioners can save far more than they cost.

There are also technical criticisms of Six Sigma, most notably that in purely statistical terms the normal distribution that is used extensively in Six Sigma analysis does not actually represent most process behaviour. Other technical criticisms (that are not really the subject of this book) imply that aiming for the very low levels of defects per million opportunities, as recommended by Six Sigma proponents, is far too onerous.

## Lessons from Six Sigma

If one were cynical one would argue that the real lesson from Six Sigma is that with a scientific-sounding title and a set of common sense analytical tools, consultants can sell anything. But whether one accepts that or not, one cannot deny the success of how Six Sigma has been sold. So, maybe a more charitable view is that there is a genuine hunger for, and appreciation of, evidence-based improvement tools. Certainly, one can argue that before Six Sigma there was too little emphasis on evidence-based and statistical analysis. Softer and more cultural and behaviour-based approaches are useful, but they must be balanced with more rigorous quantitative perspectives.

## Where does Six Sigma fit into operations strategy?

Figure 3.9 categorises some of the elements of Six Sigma in the four operations strategy decision areas. It shows that Six Sigma is very much biased towards infrastructural decision making. One could argue that Six Sigma's emphasis on process control is a function of how process technology is managed, but it is very much towards the infrastructural end of process technology strategy. All the other elements of Six Sigma are firmly in the development and organisation category. In other words, Six Sigma is more about how the systems, procedures, organisational structure and routines of the business are shaped, rather than how its physical presence is configured.

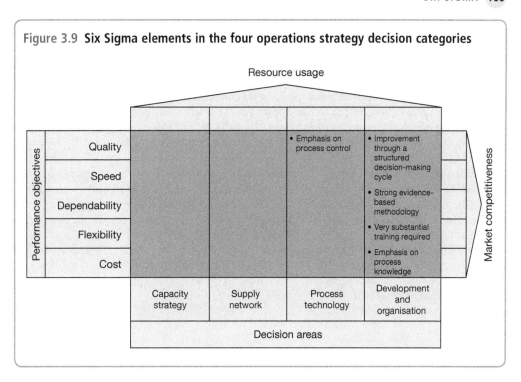

Figure 3.9 **Six Sigma elements in the four operations strategy decision categories**

**Six Sigma at Wipro[16]**

There are many companies that have benefited from Six Sigma-based improvement, but few have gone on to be able to sell the expertise that they gathered from applying it to themselves. Wipro is one of these few. Wipro is a global information technology, consulting and out-sourcing company, with 145,000 employees serving over 900 clients in 60 countries. It pro-vides a range of business services from 'business process outsourcing' (processing for other firms) to 'software development', and from 'information technology consulting' to 'cloud computing'. (Surprisingly, for a global IT services giant, Wipro was actually started in 1945 in India as a vegetable oil company.) Wipro also has one of the most developed Six Sigma pro-grammes in the IT and consulting industries, especially in its software development activities, where key challenges include reducing the data transfer time within the process, reducing the risk of failures and errors and avoiding interruption due to network downtime. For Wipro, Six Sigma simply means a measure of quality that strives for near-perfection. It means:

● having products and services that meet global standards;

● ensuring robust processes within the organisation;

● consistently meeting and exceeding customer expectations;

● establishing a quality culture throughout the business.

Individual Six Sigma projects are selected on the basis of their probability of success and are completed relatively quickly. This gives Wipro the opportunity to assess the success and learn from any problems that have occurred. Projects are identified on the basis of the prob-lem areas under each of the critical business processes that could adversely impact business

▶

performance. Because Wipro takes a customer-focused definition of quality, Six Sigma implementation is measured in terms of progress towards what the customer finds important (and what the customer pays for). This involves improving performance through a precise quantitative understanding of the customer's requirements. Wipro says that its adoption of Six Sigma has been an unquestionable success, whether in terms of customer satisfaction, improvement in internal performance, or in the improvement of shareowner value.

However, as the pioneers of Six Sigma in India, Wipro's implementation of the process has not been without difficulties – and, they stress, opportunities for learning from these difficulties. To begin with, it has taken time to build the required support from the higher-level managers, and to restructure the organisation to provide the infrastructure and training to establish confidence in the process. In particular, the first year of deployment was extremely difficult. Resourcing the stream of Six Sigma projects was problematic, partly because each project required different levels and types of resource. Also, the company learned not to underestimate the amount of training that would be required. To build a team of professionals and train them for various stages of Six Sigma was a difficult job. (In fact, this motivated Wipro to start its own consultancy that could train its own people.) Nevertheless, regular and timely reviews of each project proved particularly important in ensuring the success of a project and Wipro had to develop a team of experts for this purpose.

## Some common threads

Before adapting any of the 'approaches to operations' that we have covered in this chapter, it is worth considering the extent to which one should be influenced by the experiences of other organisations, especially when packaged as 'best practice'. It may be that operations that rely on others to define what is 'best practice' are always limiting themselves to currently accepted methods of operating, or currently accepted limits to performance. 'Best practice' is not 'best' in the sense that it cannot be bettered, it is only 'best' in the sense that it is the best that one can currently find. Accepting this may prevent operations from ever making the radical breakthrough or improvement that takes the concept of 'best' to a new and fundamentally improved level. Furthermore, because one operation has a set of successful practices in the way it manages its operations does not mean that adopting those same practices in another context will prove equally successful. It is possible that subtle differences in the resources within a process (such as staff skills or technical capabilities), or the strategic context of an operation (for example, the relative priorities of performance objectives), will be sufficiently different to make the adoption of seemingly successful practices inappropriate. But, even if one accepts 'best practice' as distilled into the new approaches that we have reviewed, there are some important points to consider.

### Senior managers sometimes use these new approaches without fully understanding them

In this chapter we have chosen to explain very briefly six of the approaches sometimes referred to as 'operations strategies'. One could easily have extended this list of four to include several others, such as total preventive maintenance (TPM), lean Sigma (a combination of lean and Six Sigma) and so on. But these four, in our view, constitute a representative sample of the most commonly used approaches. Nor do we have the space to describe them fully. Each of the approaches is the subject of several books that describe them in great detail. There is no shortage of advice from consultants and academics as to how they should be used. Yet it is not difficult to find examples of where senior management have embarked on a programme of using one or more of these approaches without fully understanding them. And if senior management do not understand these approaches, how can the rest of the organisation take them seriously? The details of Six Sigma or lean, for example, are not simply technical matters; they are fundamental to how appropriate the approach could be in different contexts. Not every approach fits every set of circumstances. So, understanding in detail what each approach means must be the first step in deciding whether it is appropriate.

### All these approaches are different

There are clearly some common elements between some of these approaches. The most obvious element, for example, is the idea of a 'customer-centric' perspective. Furthermore, as these approaches develop over time, they may acquire elements from elsewhere. Look how Six Sigma has developed beyond its process control roots to encompass many other elements. Yet there are also differences between them, and these differences need to be understood. For example, one important difference relates to whether the approaches emphasise a gradual, continuous approach to change, or whether they recommend a more radical 'breakthrough' change. Another difference concerns the aim of the approach. What is the balance between whether the approach emphasises *what* changes should be made or *how* changes should be made? Some approaches have a firm view of what is the best way to organise the operation's processes and resources. Other approaches hold no particular view on what an operation should do but rather concentrate on how the management of an operation should decide what to do. Put in operations strategy terms, this distinction is similar to that between the content and process of operations strategy. Figure 3.10 places each of the six approaches on these two dimensions.

Just as different authors have differing views as to the exact nature of some of these approaches, one could position them on the two dimensions shown in Figure 3.10 in slightly different ways. Nevertheless, there are some important differences between the approaches that should be recognised. First, they differ in the extent that they prescribe appropriate operations practice. BPR, for example, is relatively clear in what it is recommending. It has a definite list of things that operations resources should or should not be – processes should be end-to-end, non-value added work should be eliminated, inventory should be reduced, technology should be flexible, and so on. Contrast this with both Six Sigma and TQM, which focus to a far greater extent on how operations should be improved. Six Sigma, in particular, has relatively little to say about what is good or bad in the way operations resources are organised (with the possible exception of it emphasising the negative effects of process variation). Its concern is largely the way improvements should be made: using evidence, using quantitative analysis, using the DMAIC cycle, and so on. They also differ in terms of whether they emphasise gradual or rapid change. BPR is explicit in its radical nature; it implicitly assumes a fairly dramatic change. By contrast, TQM and lean both incorporate ideas of continuous improvement. Six Sigma is relatively neutral on this issue and can be used for small or very large changes.

**Figure 3.10 Each of the 'new approaches' positioned in terms of its emphasis on what changes to make or how to make changes, and whether it emphasises rapid or gradual change**

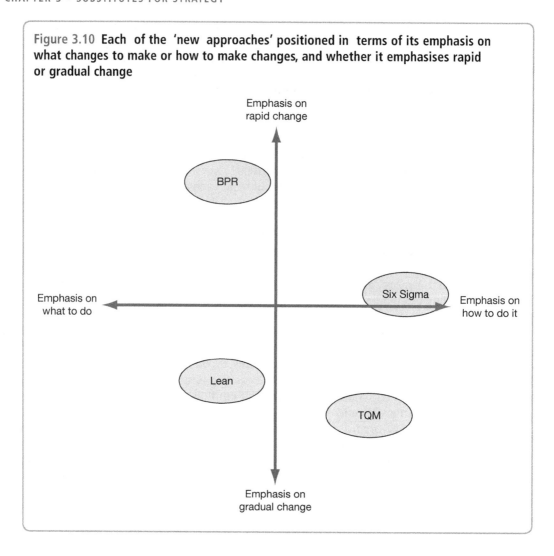

### These approaches are not strategies but they are strategic decisions

So, can any of the approaches that we have described in this chapter be described as operations strategies? Remember that our definition of operations strategy is the reconciliation of market requirements and operations resource capabilities. Implicit in this definition, and indeed in everything we have discussed in this book, is the idea that an individual enterprise's market requirements and their operations resource capabilities are, to some extent, unique to that enterprise. Even companies competing in ostensibly the same market for the same customers will generally have to position themselves slightly differently. Certainly, given that there are an infinite number of ways that they can organise their resources, they are likely to have different operations resource capabilities. The essence of an operations strategy is that it is individual and specific to one organisation at one point in time. By contrast, the approaches we have described in this chapter are generic in nature. That is, after all, why they are attractive: they offer generic advice that is broadly applicable across a range of businesses.

That is also why they are not strategies. And that is why senior managers who adopt them as operations strategies are deluding themselves.

Nevertheless, none of them is incompatible with a sensible operations strategy. They can all be considered as part of a strategy, either in terms of its content or its process. In fact the choice of which, if any, approach to adopt is an important strategic decision. Before adopting any of the approaches, at least some of the following issues should be considered.

- Does the approach have the potential to add value in terms of the requirements of our customers?
- Do we have the resources (expertise, capacity, budget) to adopt the approach?
- Have similar organisations to ours adopted this approach and what is their experience of using it?
- Is this approach compatible with other strategic decisions that we have made?
- Are we capable of communicating the ideas behind the approach and carrying out the necessary training and development to ensure that all staff understand how it fits into the company's strategy?

### Avoid becoming a victim of improvement 'fashion'

Finally, remember that operations improvement has, to some extent, become a fashion industry, with new ideas and concepts continually being introduced as offering a novel way to improve business performance. There is nothing intrinsically wrong with this. Fashion stimulates and refreshes through introducing novel ideas. Without it, things would stagnate. The problem lies not with new improvement ideas, but rather with some managers becoming victims of the process, where some new idea will entirely displace whatever went before. Most new ideas have something to say, but jumping from one fad to another will not only generate a backlash against any new idea, but also destroy the ability to accumulate the experience that comes from experimenting with each one. Avoiding becoming an improvement fashion victim is not easy. It requires that those directing the strategy process take responsibility for a number of issues.

(a) They must take responsibility for improvement as an ongoing activity, rather than becoming champions for only one specific improvement initiative.

(b) They must take responsibility for understanding the underlying ideas behind each new concept. Improvement is not 'following a recipe' or 'painting by numbers'. Unless one understands *why* improvement ideas are supposed to work, it is difficult to understand *how* they can be made to work properly.

(c) They must take responsibility for understanding the antecedents to a 'new' improvement idea, because it helps to understand it better and to judge how appropriate it may be for one's own operation.

(d) They must be prepared to adapt new ideas so that they make sense within the context of their own operation; 'one size' rarely fits all.

(e) They must take responsibility for the (often significant) education and learning effort that will be needed if new ideas are to be intelligently exploited.

(f) Above all, they must avoid the over-exaggeration and hype that many new ideas attract. Although it is sometimes tempting to exploit the motivational 'pull' of new ideas through slogans, posters and exhortations, carefully thought out plans will always be superior in the long run, and will help avoid the inevitable backlash that follows 'over-selling' a single approach.

## SUMMARY ANSWERS TO KEY QUESTIONS

### How does total quality management fit into operations strategy?

TQM is a philosophy of how to approach the organisation of quality improvement that stresses the 'total' of TQM. It puts quality and improvement generally at the heart of everything that is done by an operation. It provides a checklist of how to organise operations improvement. It has also been developed into a more prescriptive form, as in the EFQM Excellence Model, developed by the European Foundation for Quality Management (EFQM).

### How do lean operations fit into operations strategy?

The lean approach aims to meet demand instantaneously, with perfect quality and no waste. It can be seen as having four elements: customer-based demand triggers, synchronised flow, enhanced improvement behaviour and waste elimination. However, the lean concept implies some sacrifice of capacity utilisation. It occurs because when stoppages occur in the traditional system, buffers allow each stage to continue working and thus achieve high-capacity utilisation. There is far less buffering in lean processes.

### How does business process reengineering fit into operations strategy?

BPR is the fundamental rethinking and radical redesign of business processes to achieve dramatic improvements in critical, contemporary measures of performance, such as cost, quality, service and speed. The approach strives for dramatic improvements in performance by radically rethinking and redesigning the process using 'end-to-end' processes and by exploiting the power of IT to integrate processes.

### How does Six Sigma fit into operations strategy?

Six Sigma is a disciplined methodology of defining, measuring, analysing, improving and controlling the quality in every one of the company's products, processes and transactions – with the ultimate goal of virtually eliminating all defects. Although it started as a statistical process control-based concept, it is now a broad improvement concept rather than a simple examination of process variation. It stresses the use of (preferably quantitative) evidence in decision making, systematic problem solving and the use of improvement specialists called Black Belts, Green Belts, etc.

### What place do these new approaches have in operations strategy?

These approaches are not strategies in themselves (operations strategy specific to one organisation at one point in time), they are generic in nature, but they are strategic decisions. Although none of them is incompatible with operations strategy, they can all be considered as part of a strategy. It is also important to understand fully any approach before it is adopted, because all the approaches are different. Some emphasise gradual change, others more radical change. Some hold a view of the best way to organise resources, others concentrate on how to decide what to do. So, the focus of BPR is what should happen rather than how it should happen, and lean is similar. But both Six Sigma and TQM focus more on how operations should be improved. BPR is explicit in its advocacy of radical and dramatic change. TQM and lean, on the other hand, both incorporate ideas of continuous improvement, whereas Six Sigma can be used for small or very large changes.

## Further reading

Bicheno, J. and Holweg, M. (2009) *The Lean Toolbox: The Essential Guide to Lean Transformation*. Buckingham, UK: PICSIE Books.

Dale, B.D., van der Wiele, T. and van Iwaarden, J. (2007) *Managing Quality*, 5th Edition. New Jersey: Wiley-Blackwell.

George, M.L., Rowlands, D. and Kastle, B. (2003) *What Is Lean Six Sigma?* New York: McGraw-Hill Publishing Co.

George, M.L., Maxey, J., Rowlands, D.T. and Upton, M. (2005) *The Lean Six Sigma Pocket Toolbook: A Quick Reference Guide to 70 Tools for Improving Quality and Speed*. New York: McGraw-Hill Publishing Co.

Jeston, J. and Nelis, J. (2008) *Business Process Management: Practical Guidelines to Successful Implementations*, 2nd edition. Oxford, UK: Butterworth-Heinemann.

Liker, J. (2003) *The Toyota Way: 14 Management Principles from the World's Greatest Manufacturer*. New York: McGraw-Hill Education.

Modig, N. and Ahlstrom, P. (2012) *This is Lean: Resolving the Efficiency Paradox*. Stockholm, Sweden: Rheologica Publishing.

Oakland J.S. (2014) *Total Quality Management and Operational Excellence: Text with Cases*. London: Routledge.

Pande, P.S., Neuman, R.P. and Cavanagh, R. (2002) *Six Sigma Way Team Field Book: An implementation guide for project improvement teams*. New York: McGraw Hill.

Womack, J.P. and Jones, D.T. (2003) *Lean Thinking: Banish Waste and Create Wealth in Your Corporation*. New York: Simon and Schuster.

## Notes on the chapter

1 Miller, D., Hartwick, J. and Le Breton-Miller, I. (2004) 'How to detect a management fad – and distinguish it from a classic', *Business Horizons*, 47/4, July–August (7–16).

2 Feigenbaum, A.V. (1986) *Total Quality Control*. New York: McGraw Hill.

3 Deming, W.E. (1986) 'Out of Crisis', MIT Centre for Advanced Engineering Study, Cambridge, Boston.

4 Matsushito, K. (1985) 'Why the West Will Lose', *Industrial Participation*, Spring.

5 Sources include: Vitaliev, V. (2009) 'The much-loved knife', *Engineering and Technology Magazine*, 21 July; Victorinox website (2012) 'The Victorinox Quality System'.

6 The *Economist* (2000) 'Was It All Worth It?', 24 April.

7 Deming, W.E. (1986) 'Out of Crisis', MIT Centre for Advanced Engineering Study, Cambridge, Boston.

8 Kamata, S. (1983) *Japan in the Passing Lane: An insider's account of life in a Japanese auto factory*. London: Allen and Unwin.

9 Schultz, K., McCain, J. and Thomas, L.J. (2003) 'Overcoming the dark side of worker flexibility', *Journal of Operations Management*, Vol. 21, pp. 81–92.

▶

10 Sources include: *The Economist* (2013) 'Schumpeter, Sweden is leading the world in allowing private companies to run public institutions', 18 May.

11 Davenport, T. (1995) 'Reengineering – The fad that forgot people', *Fast Company*, November.

12 Hammer, M. and Champy, J. (1993) *Reengineering the Corporation: A manifesto for business revolution*. New York: Harper Business.

13 Johansson, H.J. (1993) *Business Process Reengineering: Break point strategies for market dominance*. New York: Wiley.

14 Hammer, M. and Champy, J. (1993) *Reengineering the Corporation: A manifesto for business revolution*. New York: Harper Business.

15 For example, Davenport, T. (1995) op.cit.

16 Sources include: Sharma, M., Pandla, K. and Gupta, P. (2014) 'A Case Study On Six Sigma at Wipro Technologies: Thrust on Quality', Working Paper, The Jaipuria Institute of Management; Wipro website, www.wipro.com.

# Capacity strategy

## Introduction

Capacity is a fundamental decision in operations. That is why it is the first of the operations strategy decision areas to be treated. After all, the purpose of operations strategy is to provide and manage the ability to supply demand, and capacity is a vital part of that ability. Also, capacity strategy decisions affect a large part of the business (indeed capacity decisions can create a large part of the business), and the consequences of getting them wrong are almost always serious and sometimes fatal to a firm's competitive abilities. Too much capacity under-utilises resources and drives costs up. Too little capacity limits the operation's ability to serve customers and therefore earn revenues. The risks inherent in getting capacity wrong lie both in having an inappropriately configured set of resources and in mismanaging the process of changing capacity over time. This chapter will look at the principles behind how operations configure, and reconfigure, their capacity.

### KEY QUESTIONS

- *What is capacity strategy?*
- *How much capacity should an operation have?*
- *How many separate sites should an operation have?*
- *What issues are important when changing capacity levels?*
- *Where should capacity be located?*

Figure 4.1 **This chapter looks at capacity strategy**

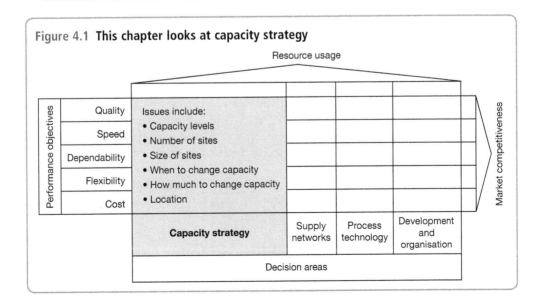

## What is capacity strategy?

An operation's capacity dictates its potential level of productive activity. It is '*the maximum level of value-added activity over a period of time that the operation can achieve under normal conditions*'. Operations strategy is the set of decisions concerned with how operations configure and change their overall capacity in order to achieve a particular level of output potential. Note that capacity is not the same as output. Demand may not be sufficient to warrant an operation producing at full capacity, and in many high customer-contact operations, such as theatres, 'output' (i.e. the number of customers entertained) cannot normally exceed demand.

The capacity strategy of an operation defines its overall scale, the number and size of different sites between which its capacity is distributed, the specific activities allocated to each site and the location of each site. All these decisions are related. For example, an air conditioning servicing operation will have sites with relatively small individual capacity if it chooses to have many sites located no more than 30 minutes' travelling time from any customer. If it relaxed this 'response time' to 60 minutes, it could have fewer, larger sites. Together these decisions determine the configuration of an operation's capacity, its overall shape, size and deployment. An appropriate configuration of capacity for one set of products or services, and pattern of demand, will not necessarily be appropriate for another. So when the nature of competition shifts in some way, companies often need to reconfigure their capacity. This process of changing (or reconfiguring) capacity is also part of capacity strategy. It usually involves deciding when capacity levels should be changed (up or down), how big each change step should be and overall how fast capacity levels should change.

### Capacity at three levels

The provision of capacity is not just a strategic issue. It takes place in all operations minute by minute, day by day and month on month. Every time an operations manager moves a staff member from one part of the operation to another, he or she is adjusting capacity within the operation. Similarly, when setting shift patterns to determine working hours, effective capacity is being set. Neither of these decisions is strategic – they do not necessarily impact directly on the long-term physical scale of the operation. But shift patterns will be set within the constraints of the physical limits of the operation, and the minute-by-minute deployment of staff will take place within the constraints of the number and skills of the people present within the operation at any time. Thus, although capacity decisions are taken for different time-scales and spanning different areas of the operation, each level of capacity decision is made with the constraints of a higher level.

Table 4.1 illustrates this idea. Note, though, that the three levels of capacity decision used here are, to some extent, arbitrary and there is, in practice, overlap between the levels. Also, the actual time-scales of the three levels will vary between industries.

Table 4.1  **Three levels of capacity decision**

| Level | Time-scale | Decisions concern provision of... | Span of decisions | Starting point of decision | Key questions |
|---|---|---|---|---|---|
| Strategic capacity decisions | Years–Months | Buildings and facilities<br>Process technology | All parts of the business | Probable markets to be served in the future<br>Current capacity configuration | How much capacity do we need in total?<br>How should the capacity be distributed?<br>Where should the capacity be located? |
| Medium-term capacity decisions | Months–Weeks | Aggregate number of people<br>Degree of subcontracted resources | Business – site | Market forecasts<br>Physical capacity constraints | To what extent do we keep capacity level or fluctuate capacity levels?<br>Should we change staffing levels as demand changes?<br>Should we subcontract or off-load demand? |
| Short-term capacity decisions | Weeks–hours–minutes | Individual staff within the operation<br>Loading of individual facilities | Site<br>Department | Current demand<br>Current available capacity | Which resources are to be allocated to what tasks?<br>When should activities be loaded on individual resources? |

## The overall level of operations capacity

The first capacity-related decision faced by any operation is 'How much capacity should we have?' or, put simply, 'How big should we be?' It sounds a straightforward question, but is in fact influenced by several factors particular to each operation and its competitive position. Each of the main factors that will influence the overall level of capacity will be discussed in this section. Figure 4.2 illustrates them. As usual, some of the factors are related primarily to the requirements of the market, while others are largely concerned with the nature of the operation's resources.

### Forecast demand

Only rarely will a business decide to invest in a level of capacity that is exactly equal to its expectation of future demand. However, it is a starting point in trying to understand why operations finish up the size they are. So, for example, if a leisure business

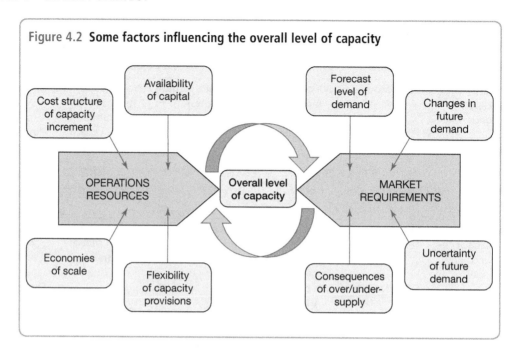

Figure 4.2 **Some factors influencing the overall level of capacity**

believes there is likely to be a demand for 500 rooms per night at a newly developed resort location, then it may build a 500-roomed hotel. If an insurance company's call centre is forecast to handle 500,000 calls per week and one operator can handle a call every 3 minutes, then it may build a 625-station call centre (operators have $40 \times 60$ minutes a week, so can receive 2,400/3 = 800 calls a week, so 500,000/800 = 625 operators are needed). But capacity decisions are not always as simple as this. Although a 'single point' forecast of future demand for an operation's products and services will have a major influence on how big its operations will be, other considerations will affect the decision. It is these other factors, acting to modify a simple demand forecast, that reveal much about the strategic context of operations decisions.

## Example    Economies of scale in heart surgery and shipping[1]

Don't think that the idea of economies of scale only applies to manufacturing operations. It's a universal concept. Here are just two examples.

In the 1,000-bed Narayana Hrudayalaya hospital, in Bangalore, India, Dr Devi Shetty (who has been called the 'Henry Ford' of heart surgery) has created what, according to *Forbes* magazine, is the world's largest heart factory. It is a radical new approach, he says, and proves that economies of scale can transform the cost of cardiology. Dr Shetty calls his approach the 'Wal-Martisation' of surgery – referring to the high-volume approach of the world's largest supermarket chain – Wal-Mart. The hospital has 42 surgeons who perform 6,000 heart operations each year, including 3,000 on children. This makes the hospital the busiest facility of its type in the world. And it's needed; it is estimated that India requires 2.5 million heart operations every year yet only 90,000 are performed. *'It's a numbers game'*, said Dr Shetty, who has performed 15,000 heart operations. *'Surgeons are technicians. The more practice they get, the more specialised they become and the better the results.'* The result is that costs are slashed and the hospital can be profitable, even though many patients are poor. The hospital's charges for open-heart surgery are, on average, a tenth of the cost of the cheapest procedures in the United States. But, even then, treatment is too expensive for many, so wealthier patients are charged more to subsidise the poorest.

The Maersk Triple-E class ships are owned by Maersk Lines, the world's biggest container-shipping company. They are among the biggest ships ever built: almost 400 metres long (the length of four football pitches), 59 metres wide and 73 metres high. The 20 new vessels will be deployed on the vital Asia to Europe trade route. According to Maersk, the Triple-E is about more than size, though. In fact, the name refers to the three main purposes behind the creation – economy of scale, energy efficiency and environmentally improved. The ships will emit 20 per cent less $CO_2$ per container moved compared to the Emma Maersk, currently the world's largest container vessel, and 50 per cent less than the industry average on the Asia–Europe trade lane. They will be equipped with a waste heat recovery system, saving up to 10 per cent of main engine power. This equals the average annual electricity consumption of 5,000 European households. Triple-E vessels travel 184 kilometres, using 1 kWh of energy per ton of cargo, whereas a jumbo jet travels half a kilometre using the same amount of energy per ton of cargo. They are also powerful, with the largest internal-combustion engines ever built – as powerful as 1,000 family cars, which enables them to move all their cargo from China to Europe in just over three weeks. Yet the ships are so automated that they require only 13 people to crew them. It is these economies of scale that allow a T-shirt made in China to be sent to The Netherlands for just 2.5 cents.

## Uncertainty of future demand

Even when the demand for an operation's products or services can be reasonably well forecast, the uncertainty inherent in all estimates of future demand may inhibit the operation from investing to meet the most likely level of demand. The economics of the operation may mean that, should the lower level of demand occur, the financial consequences would be unacceptable to the company. There are also other consequences of over- and under-supply. For example, the availability of excess capacity may give an operation the flexibility to respond to short-term surges in demand. This could be especially valuable when either demand needs to be satisfied in the short term, or when satisfying short-term demand can have long-term implications, so immediately after the introduction of a new product or service, especially when there are several competitors, is a bad time not to be able to satisfy demand. Market share lost at this point may never be regained. Paradoxically, though, in some circumstances, under-supplying a market may increase the value (and therefore price) of an operation's goods or services. Such a scarcity-based strategy, however, does rely on an appropriate market positioning and a confidence in the lack of competitor activity.

## Changes in demand – long-term or short-term demand?

In addition to any uncertainty surrounding future demand, there is also the question of the time-scale over which demand is being forecast. For example, short-term expected demand may be higher than expected long-term sustainable demand. In which case, does an organisation plan to provide capacity to meet the short-term peak or, alternatively, plan to satisfy only longer-term sustainable levels of demand? Conversely, short-term demand may be relatively low compared to longer-term demand. Again, there is the same dilemma. Should the operation build capacity for the short or long term? Like many capacity strategy decisions, this is related to the economies of scale of individual operations and the ease with which they can add or subtract increments of capacity. The dynamics of changing capacity levels will be discussed later in the chapter. Here we are concerned with the decision of where initially to pitch capacity levels.

### Long-term demand lower than short-term demand

Suppose a confectionery company is launching a new product aimed at the children's market. From previous experience it realises that it must make an initial impact in the market with many sales based on the novelty of the product, in order to reach a lower but sustainable level of demand. It estimates that initial demand for the product will be around 500 tons per month. However, longer-term demand is more likely to settle down to a reasonably steady level of 300 tons per month.

A key issue here is whether the higher level of demand will sustain for long enough to recoup the extra capital cost of providing capacity to meet that high level. Furthermore, even if this is the case, can an operation with a nominal capacity of 500 tons per month operate sufficiently profitably when it is only producing 300 tons per month? If the answer to either of these questions is 'No', then a capacity-based analysis would tend to discourage investment at the higher level of capacity. The main problem with this approach is that it may prove to be self-fulfilling. Under-supplying the market may depress demand that would otherwise have grown to justify the 500-tons-per-month capacity level. More likely, competitors will take advantage of the company's inability to supply to increase their own share of the market. Of course, the company may wish to counteract any under-supply by adopting pricing and promotion strategies that minimise the effects of, or even exploit, product shortage. The lesson here is that setting the initial capacity level cannot be done in isolation from the company's market positioning strategy.

### Short-term demand lower than long-term demand

Again, the issues here are partly concerned with economies of scale versus the costs of operating at levels below the operation's capacity. If the economies of scale of providing capacity at the higher level of demand mean that the profits generated in the long term are worth the costs associated with under-utilisation of capacity in the short term, then building capacity at the higher level may be justified. Once more, though, the relationship between capacity provision, costs and market positioning needs to be explored. Initial over-capacity may be exploited by producing at higher volume, and therefore lower costs, and pricing in order to take market share or even stimulate the total market. Indeed, over-capacity may be deliberately provided in order to allow such aggressive market strategies.

## The availability of capital

One obvious constraint on whether operations choose to meet demand fully is their ability to afford the capacity with which to do it. So, for example, a company may have developed a new product or service that they are convinced will be highly attractive in the marketplace. Sales forecasts are extremely bullish, with potential revenues being two or three times higher than the company's present revenue. Competitors will take some time to catch up with the company's technological lead and so they have the market to themselves for at least the next two years. All of this sounds very positive for the company: its products and services are innovative, the market appears to want them, forecasts are as firm as forecasts can be and the company is in a position to make very healthy profits for at least the next two years. But consider what the company will have to do to its resource base. Irrespective of how novel or technologically difficult the new processing requirements are, there will certainly be a lot more of them. The company will need to increase its operations resources by two or three hundred per cent. The question must arise of whether it can afford to do this or, more accurately, whether it is prepared to face the consequences of doing this? Borrowing enough cash to double or triple the worth of the company may not be possible from conventional sources of lending. The owners may not wish to float the company at this stage. Other sources of finance, such as venture capitalists, may demand an equity stake. Under these circumstances the company may forego the opportunity to meet forecast demand fully. Even though in pure accounting terms the return on any investment in operating capacity may be perfectly acceptable, the consequence in terms of ownership or vulnerability of the company to being taken over may not be worth risking. An alternative for the company may be to increase capacity only as fast as their currently feasible borrowing capability will allow. The risk, then, is that competitor companies will have the time to enter the market and reduce its longer-term potential for the company.

## The cost structure of capacity increments – break-even points

One of the most basic, and yet most important, issues in capacity strategy is concerned with the relationship between the capacity of an operation, the volume of output that it is actually processing and its profitability. Simple break-even analysis can illustrate the basics of this. Each additional unit of capacity results in a fixed-cost break. The fixed costs of a unit of capacity are those expenditures that have to be incurred irrespective of how much the capacity is actually being used. The variable costs of operating the capacity are those expenditures that rise proportionally to output. As volume increases for one operation, the additional capacity required can move an operation through its 'break-even' point from profitability to loss. Further additions to the capacity of the operation will be needed to cope with increased demand. Each addition brings a new set of fixed costs. Fixed-cost breaks may mean that there are levels of output within which a company might not wish to operate. This issue is particularly important when the fixed costs of operation are high compared with the variable costs.

Figure 4.3 shows how this might be in one operation. Each unit of capacity can process 4,000 units of output per month. The fixed costs of operating this capacity are $2,000 per month and the variable costs $0.25 per unit. The revenue from each unit processed to the operation is $0.9 per unit. Demand is forecast to be steady at around 9,000 units per month. To meet this demand fully, three units of capacity would be needed, though the third unit would be much under-utilised. As Figure 4.3 shows, meeting demand fully the company's total costs are higher than its total revenue. It would therefore be operating at a loss. Under these circumstances, the company

Figure 4.3 **Cost, volume, profit illustration**

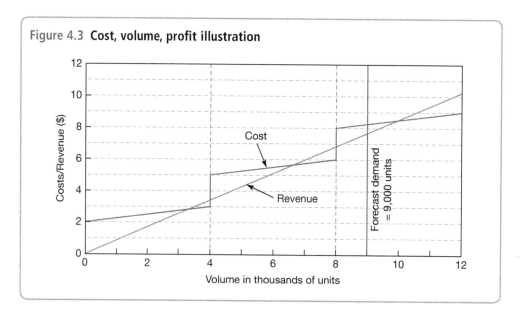

might very well choose to process only 8,000 units per month – not meeting demand but operating more profitably than if they were meeting demand.

## Economies of scale

If the total cost of the output from an operation is its fixed costs plus its output multiplied by its variable costs per unit, then we can calculate the average cost per unit of output simply by dividing total costs by the output level. So, for example, Figure 4.4(a) shows the unit cost for an increment of capacity of the operation described earlier. In reality, though, the real average cost curve may be different from that shown in Figure 4.4(a) for a number of reasons.

Figure 4.4 **Unit cost curves**

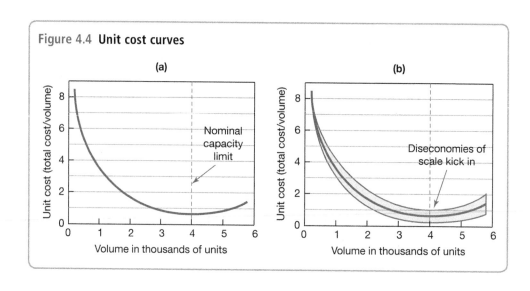

The real maximum capacity may be larger than the theoretical maximum capacity. For example, the theoretical capacity in Figure 4.4(a) was based on an assumption that the operation would be working 112 hours a week (14 shifts a week out of a possible 21 shifts a week), whereas the operation is theoretically available 168 hours a week. Utilising some of this unused time for production will help to spread further the fixed costs of the operation but could also incur extra costs. For example, overtime payments and shift premiums, together with incrementally higher energy bills, may be incurred after a certain level of output.

There may also be less obvious costs of operating above nominal capacity levels. Long periods of overtime may reduce productivity levels, reduced or delayed maintenance time may increase the chances of breakdown and operating facilities and equipment at a higher rate or for longer periods may also expose problems which hitherto lay dormant. These 'diseconomies' of over-using capacity can have the effect of increasing unit costs above a certain level of output.

However, all the fixed costs are not usually incurred at one time at the start of operations. Rather, they occur at many points as volume increases. Furthermore, operations managers often have some discretion as to where these fixed-cost breaks will occur. So, for example, the manager of a delivery operation may know that at the level of demand forecast for next month a new delivery vehicle should be purchased. This extra vehicle (together with the extra fixed cost it brings) could be purchased now in order to improve service delivery next month, when it is technically needed, or delayed beyond next month. This last option may involve taking the risk that any vehicle breakdown would leave the operation dangerously short of capacity but may yet be preferred if the operations manager has little faith in next month's level of demand being sustained.

All these points taken together mean that, as is illustrated in Figure 4.4(b), in practice, unit cost curves:

- are capable of being extended beyond nominal capacity;
- often show increases in cost beyond a certain level of volume;
- are best represented by a band within which the true cost will lie, rather than a smooth, clean line.

The factors that go together to reduce costs as volume increases are often called 'economies of scale'. Those that work to increase unit costs for increased output beyond a certain volume are called 'diseconomies of scale'. What we have described above are the economies and diseconomies of scale for a single increment of capacity within an operation. Yet the same logic can be applied for the whole operation. As more units of capacity are added, the total fixed costs per unit of potential output tend to decrease. So, for example, the number of people staffing support services such as maintenance, supervision, warehousing, etc. is unlikely to double when the capacity of the whole operation doubles.

| Example | Big auto[2] |

Scale is important in car making, so when Toyota became the first member of the 'ten million club' (a total volume of output in excess of 10 million when all its brands including its affiliates, Daihatsu and Subaru, were taken into account), the industry knew that a significant milestone

▶

had been passed. Not every automobile company relies on scale of course. Manufacturers of expensive up-market brands, such as BMW, may sell far fewer cars and yet are successful because their technical excellence and market desirability command relatively high margins. But for less expensive cars with lower profit margins, scale is increasingly important. Straightforward production economies of scale are important, but so are other advantages that volume brings. Distribution and sales operations also benefit from economies of scale, as do research, design and other functions. Suppliers respect the bargaining power that scale brings, not just by reducing the cost of supply, but also to invest in developing new technologies. Similarly, the car companies themselves will generally be more willing to invest in new technologies if the (often huge) cost can be spread over more output. High volume also makes it easier to exploit the flexibility of production lines to offer customers a wider product range. So what do mid-scale car makers do? They do not have the volume of Toyota; neither do they necessarily command the high margins of luxury brands. Some merge to form a bigger combined group; in 2014 Fiat bought the 41 per cent of Chrysler that they did not already own. Others do not go all the way to a full merger but form close partnerships. The French firm Renault and Japan's Nissan have a long-standing partnership, even though they have remained separate businesses (but they do share some platforms and parts). And if a broad partnership is not attractive, otherwise-competing car makers may collaborate on specific projects or technologies.

As the size of the operation increases it becomes possible eventually to replace the capacity that has been built up incrementally over time with new, larger and more integrated units. This may allow two further economies of scale. The first comes through the increases in operations efficiency that can be gained by integrating, or combining, the processes established separately over time. So, for example, each increase of capacity may have included a particular kind of machine that could be replaced by a larger, more efficient machine once total capacity exceeds a certain level. Second, the capital costs of building operations do not increase proportionally to their capacity. The reason for this is that whereas the capacities of many types of facilities and equipment that go into an operation are related to their volume (a cubic function), the capital cost of the facilities and equipment are related to its surface area (a square function). Generally, the cost ($C_y$) of providing capacity in one increment of size y is given as follows:[3]

$$C_y = Ky^k$$

where $K$ is a constant scale factor and $k$ is a factor that indicates the degree of economies of scale for the technology involved (usually between 0.5 and 1.0).

There may, however, be significant diseconomies of scale as the size of one site increases. The most significant of these are related to the complexity inherent in a large operation. As organisations grow larger they may become more unwieldy and need a greater degree of planning and coordination. More activities are needed just to keep the organisation operating, and more staff are needed to manage the extra support processes. All this not only adds cost, it can make the whole operation incapable of responding to changes in customer demands. Very large operations find it difficult to be flexible because even if they can sense changes in the markets, they may not be able to respond to them. As operations grow, communication also becomes more complex, which in turn provides more opportunities for mis-communication and errors.

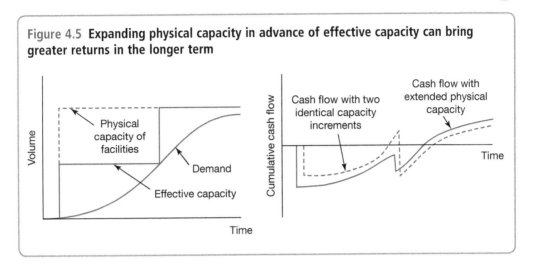

Figure 4.5 **Expanding physical capacity in advance of effective capacity can bring greater returns in the longer term**

## Flexibility of capacity provision

Committing to an investment in a particular level of capacity may be managed in such a way as to facilitate later expansion. Effective capacity requires all the required resources and processes to be in place in order to produce goods and services. This may not necessarily imply that all resources and processes are put in place at the same time. It may be possible, for example, to construct the physical outer shell of an operation without investing in the direct and indirect process technologies that will convert it into productive capacity. There may be capital expenditure efficiencies to be gained by constructing a larger building than is strictly necessary in the medium term, which can be fitted out with equipment when demand justifies it in the future. Clearly there is some risk involved in committing even part of the capital expenditure necessary before demand is certain. However, such a strategy is frequently employed in growing markets. Figure 4.5 shows alternative capacity strategies, and the resultant cash flow profiles, for an operation that is planning to expand its capacity to meet the forecast demand. One option involves building the whole physical facility (with a larger net cash outflow) but only equipping it to half its potential physical capacity. Only when demand justifies it would expenditure be made to fully exploit this capacity. The alternative is to build a fully equipped facility of half the capacity. A further identical capacity increment would then be added as required. Although this latter strategy requires a lower initial cash outflow, it shows a lower cumulative cash flow in the longer term.

## The number and size of sites

The decision of how many separate operational sites to have is concerned with where a business wants to be on the spectrum between many small sites on the one hand and few large sites on the other. Once again, we can think of this decision as the reconciliation of market factors and resource factors. This is illustrated in Figure 4.6. Separating capacity into several small units may be necessary if demand

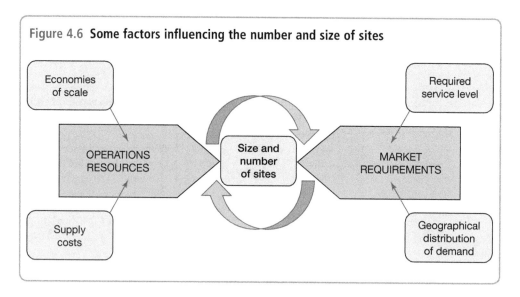

Figure 4.6 **Some factors influencing the number and size of sites**

for a business's products or services is widely distributed. This will be especially true if customers demand high absolute levels, or immediate service. Of course, dividing capacity into small units may also increase costs because of the difficulty of exploiting the economies of scale possible in larger units. A small number of larger units may also be less costly to supply with their input resources. There again, in material transformation operations, a single large unit will bear extra transportation costs in supplying its distributed market.

### Example | Distribution operation

Suppose a company that stores and distributes books to book shops is considering its capacity strategy. Currently, in its European market, it has three distribution centres – one in the UK, one in France and one in Germany. The UK depot looks after the UK and Ireland, the French depot looks after France, Spain, Portugal and Belgium, and the German depot looks after the rest of Europe. The company is facing conflicting pressures. On one hand it wants to minimise the total operations cost of its distribution services; on the other hand it wishes to improve its level of service to its customers. In order to explore alternatives to its existing depots it engages a firm of consultants to evaluate two alternative proposals, which had been discussed within the company. Option 1 would require the company to concentrate its operations in one central depot that would serve the whole of Europe. It is likely that this would be in The Netherlands, probably in Rotterdam. Option 2 would require the company to move in the opposite direction, in the sense that it envisages a depot to be located in each of its six sales regions in Western Europe. These regions are the Iberian Peninsula, the UK, France and the Benelux countries, Italy, Germany and Scandinavia. The consultants decide to simulate the alternative operations in order to estimate (a) the cost of running the depots (this includes fixed costs such as rent and local taxes, heating, wages, security and working capital charges for the inventory, etc.),

Table 4.2 **Analysis of existing operation and two options**

| Capacity configuration | Depot costs | Transport costs | Average delivery time (working days) |
|---|---|---|---|
| Current three sites<br>• Toulouse<br>• Birmingham<br>• Hamburg | €55.3m | €15.6m | 6.3 |
| One large site<br>• Rotterdam | €41.1m | €20.7m | 7.7 |
| Six smaller sites<br>• Madrid<br>• Paris<br>• Stockholm<br>• Milan<br>• Berlin<br>• Birmingham | €68.8m | €11.4m | 3.8 |

(b) transportation costs of delivering the books to customers and (c) the average delivery time in working days between customers requesting books and them being delivered. Table 4.2 shows the results of this simulation.

From Table 4.2 one can see that concentrating on one large site gives substantial economies of scale in terms of the costs of running the depot but increases transportation costs, and (because there is further, on average, to travel) increases the average delivery time. Conversely, moving to several smaller sites increases depot costs but reduces transportation costs as well as improving the average delivery time. The company is faced with a dilemma. By moving to one large site it can save €9.1 million per year (the savings on depot costs easily outweighing the increase in transportation costs). Yet delivery times will increase on average by 1.4 days. Alternatively, moving to six smaller sites would increase costs by €9.3 million per year, yet gives what looks like a significant improvement in delivery time of 2.5 days. In theory, the financial consequences of the different delivery times could be calculated, combined with the capital costs of each option, and a financial return derived for each option. In practice, however, the decision is probably more sensibly approached by presenting a number of questions to the company's managers.

- Is an increase in average delivery time from 6.3 to 7.7 days likely to result in losses of business greater than the €9.1 million savings in moving to a large site?
- Is the increase in business that may be gained from a reduction in delivery time from 6.3 days to 3.8 days likely to compensate for the €9.3 million extra cost of moving to six smaller sites?
- Are either of these alternative positions likely to be superior to its existing profitability?

One final point: in evaluating the sizes and number of sites in any operation it is not just the increase in profitability that may result from a change in configuration that needs to be considered, it is whether that increase in profitability is worth the costs of making the change. Presumably, either option will involve this company in not only capital expenditure, but a great deal of management effort and disruption to its existing business. It may be that these costs and risks outweigh any increase in profitability.

## Capacity change

Planning changes in capacity levels would be easy if it were not for two characteristics of capacity – lead time and economies of scale. If capacity could be introduced (or deleted) with zero delay between the decision to expand (or contract) and the capacity coming on- (or off-) stream, an operation could wait until demand clearly warranted the change. The fact that changing capacity takes time means that decisions need to be made before demand levels are known for sure. So, deciding to change capacity inevitably involves some degree of risk, but so does delaying the decision, because delay may still mean that capacity is not appropriate to demand. And all this is made even more problematic because of economies of scale (the tendency for both capital and operating costs to reduce as the increment of capacity increases). This means that, when changing capacity levels, there is pressure to make the change big enough to exploit scale economies. Again, though, this carries risks that demand will not be sufficient for the capacity to be utilised sufficiently for the scale economies to be realised. Conversely, changing capacity by too little may mean opportunity risks of tying the operation in to small, non-economic units of capacity. Put both long lead times and significant economies of scale together and capacity change decisions become particularly risky.

### Timing of capacity change

The first decision in changing capacity levels is when to make the change. As with so many capacity decisions, the forecast level of future demand will be a major influence on the timing of capacity change. Capacity will be increased, or decreased, when forecasts indicate that extra capacity is needed, or current capacity not needed. Forecasting, though, especially with the long-term planning horizons necessary for capacity planning, is a very uncertain process. Therefore, the degree of confidence an operation has in its forecasts will likewise influence the timing decision. So will the response of the market to under- or over-capacity. If competitive conditions dictate fast response times, then an operation might err on the side of timing capacity change to ensure over-capacity. Conversely, if customers are willing to wait, or if alternative supplies can be arranged, then there are fewer risks in under-capacity. Nor is the timing decision exclusively dictated by customers. Competitor activities and responses may also prompt capacity change. An operation may choose to invest in capacity even before demand warrants it, just to pre-empt a competitor getting in first. The economics of the investment may even mean that whoever expands their capacity first renders capacity expansion by any other operation uneconomic. Figure 4.7 illustrates the factors that influence the timing decision.

### Generic timing strategies

There are three generic strategies for timing capacity change:

- *Capacity leads demand* – timing the introduction of capacity in such a way that there is always sufficient capacity to meet forecast demand.
- *Capacity lags demand* – timing the introduction of capacity so that demand is always equal to or greater than capacity.

**Figure 4.7 Some factors influencing the timing of capacity change**

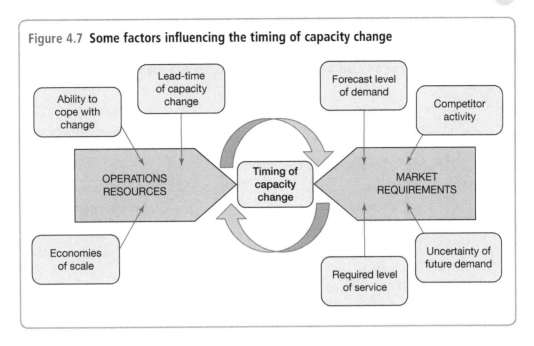

- *Smoothing with inventories* – timing the introduction of capacity so that current capacity plus accumulated inventory can always supply demand.

For example, Figure 4.8 shows the forecast demand for an air conditioning company that has decided to build 400-unit/week capacity plants to meet the growth in demand. Figure 4.8(a) illustrates capacity leading and lagging strategies, while Figure 4.8(b) illustrates the 'smoothing with inventories' strategy. Each strategy has its own advantages and disadvantages. These are shown in Table 4.3. The actual approach taken by any company will depend on how it views these advantages and disadvantages. For example, if the company's access to funds for capital expenditure is limited, it is likely to find the delayed capital expenditure requirement of the capacity-lagging strategy relatively attractive.

Pure leading and pure lagging strategies can be implemented so that no inventories are accumulated. All demand in one period is satisfied (or not) by the activity of the operation in the same period. For a customer-processing operation there is no alternative to this. A hotel cannot satisfy demand in one year by using rooms that were vacant the previous year. For some materials- and information-processing operations, however, the output from the operation that is not required in one period can be stored for use in the next period. Inventories can be used to obtain the advantages of both capacity-leading and capacity-lagging. In Figure 4.8(b) plants have been introduced such that over-capacity in one period is used to make air conditioning units for the following or subsequent periods. This may seem like an ideal state. Demand is always met and so revenue is maximised. Capacity is usually fully utilised and so costs are minimised. The profitability of the operation is therefore likely to be high. There is a price to pay, however, and that is the cost of carrying the inventories. Not only will these have to be funded, but also the risks of obsolescence and deterioration of stock are introduced.

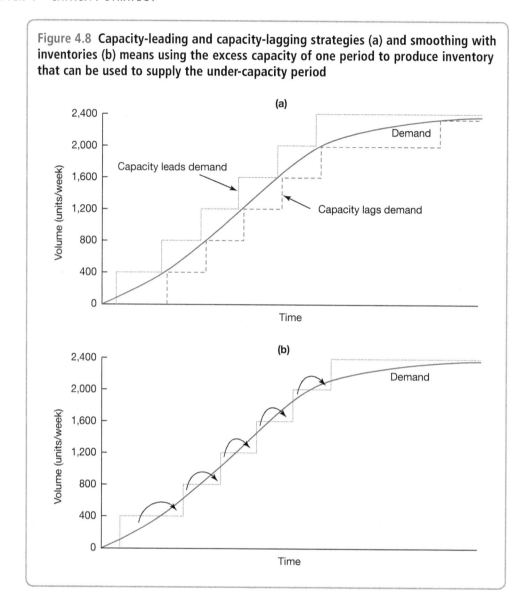

Figure 4.8 **Capacity-leading and capacity-lagging strategies (a) and smoothing with inventories (b) means using the excess capacity of one period to produce inventory that can be used to supply the under-capacity period**

*Leading, lagging or smoothing*

Which of these strategies is used and at what time is partly a matter of the company's competitive objectives at any point in time. Just as significant, though, is the effect these strategies have on the financial performance of the organisation. Both the capacity-leading strategy and the smoothing-with-stocks strategy will tend to increase the cash requirements of the company through earlier capital expenditure and higher working capital respectively. Sometimes companies may wish to time capacity introduction in order to have a particular effect on the balance of cash requirement and profitability. It may be that some strategies of capacity change improve profitability at the expense of long-term cash requirements, while others minimise longer-term cash requirements but do not yield as high a level of short-term profitability. Thus, capacity

Table 4.3 **The advantages and disadvantages of pure leading, pure lagging and smoothing-with-inventories strategies of capacity timing**

|  | Advantages | Disadvantages |
|---|---|---|
| Capacity-leading strategy | Always sufficient capacity to meet demand, therefore revenue is maximised and customers satisfied. Most of the time there is a 'capacity cushion', which can absorb extra demand if forecasts are pessimistic. Any critical start-up problems with new plants are less likely to affect supply to customers. | Utilisation of the plants is always relatively high. Risks of even greater (or even permanent) over-capacity if demand does not reach forecast levels. Capital spending on plant early. |
| Capacity-lagging strategy | Always sufficient demand to keep the plants working at full capacity, therefore unit costs are minimised. Over-capacity problems are minimised if forecasts are optimistic. Capital spending on the plants is delayed. | Insufficient capacity to meet demand fully, therefore reduced revenue and dissatisfied customers. No ability to exploit short-term increases in demand. Under-supply position even worse if there are start-up problems with the new plants. |
| Smoothing-with-inventories strategy | All demand is satisfied, therefore customers are satisfied and revenue maximised. Utilisation of capacity is high and therefore costs are low. Very short-term surges in demand can be met from inventories. | The cost of inventories in terms of working capital requirement can be high. This is especially serious at a time when the company requires funds for its capital expansion. Risks of product deterioration and obsolescence. |

strategy may be influenced by the required financial performance of the organisation, which in turn may be a function of where the company is raising its finance, on the equity markets or from long-term loans.

## The magnitude of capacity change

Earlier we examined some of the advantages of large capacity increments (economies of scale, category killer effects, etc.). Large units of capacity also have some disadvantages when the capacity of the operation is being changed to match changing demand. If an operation where forecast demand is increasing seeks to satisfy all demand by increasing capacity using large capacity increments, it will have substantial amounts of over-capacity for much of the period when demand is increasing, which results in higher unit costs. However, if the company uses smaller increments, although there will still be some over-capacity it will be less than that using large capacity increments. This results in higher-capacity utilisation and therefore lower costs. Remember, though, that the larger increments of capacity can be intrinsically more efficient (because of economies of scale) when they are well utilised. For example, suppose that the air conditioning unit manufacturer

**Figure 4.9** Capacity plans for meeting demand using either 800- or 400-unit capacity plants (a); smaller-scale capacity increments (b) allow the capacity plan to be adjusted to accommodate changes in demand

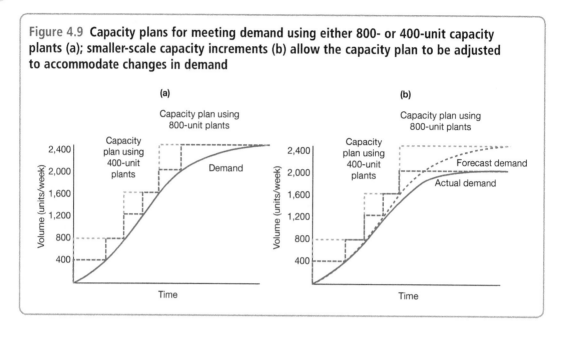

forecasts demand increase over the next three years, as shown in Figure 4.9(a), to level off at around 2,400 units a week. If the company seeks to satisfy all demand by building three plants, each of 800 units' capacity, the company will have substantial amounts of over-capacity for much of the period when demand is increasing. Over-capacity means low-capacity utilisation, which in turn means higher unit costs. If the company builds smaller plants, say 400-unit plants, there will still be over-capacity but to a lesser extent, which means higher-capacity utilisation and possible lower costs.

### Risks of over-capacity with large capacity increments

The inherent risks of changing capacity using large increments can also be high. For example, if the rate-of-change-demand unexpectedly slows, the capacity will be only partly utilised. However, if smaller units of capacity are used the likelihood is that the forecast error would have been detected in time to delay or cancel the capacity adjustment, leaving demand and capacity in balance. For example, if demand does not reach 2,400 units a week but levels off at 2,000 units a week, the final 800-unit plant will only be 50-per-cent utilised. However, if 400-unit plants are used the likelihood is that the over-optimistic forecast would have been detected in time. Figure 4.9(b) shows the consequences of adopting each of the two strategies in this case.

---

Example | **Why industries have more capacity than they need[4]**

There are few industries where the total demand for products and services matches the cumulative capacity of all the firms in the industry. In many industries, capacity far exceeds demand. The automotive, computer chips, steel, chemicals, oil and hotel industries all have significant over-capacity because of over-investment and/or a collapse in demand. Take the automobile industry, for example. One estimate claimed that the industry worldwide was wasting $70 billion a year because of over-capacity. By the year 2000 around 30 per cent of all car-making capacity was unused. The lost profit amounted to around $2,000 per car, which is more than the combined industry profits worldwide. This is partly bad news for those firms with the higher level of over-capacity because most car plants can only make significant profits when operating at over 80 per cent of capacity. However, over-capacity may not be viewed with too much alarm. Many of the well-known Western hotel chains in Asia, such as Westin and Sheraton, do not own the properties but confine themselves to managing them. The owners may be local property developers or business people who invested for prestige or tax purposes. Many of the management contracts of this type, put together in the boom times, included fees based on a percentage of total revenue as well as a percentage of gross operating profits. So, even with no profit, the management company could make healthy returns. By contrast, other hotel chains, such as Shangri-La Asia, Mandarin-Oriental and Peninsular Hotels, both owned and managed their hotels. Because of this they were far more exposed to the consequences of over-capacity because it hit profits directly.

So why do companies invest, even when there is a high risk of industry over-capacity and thus under-utilised operations? One reason, of course, is optimistic forecasting. The risks of mis-forecasting are high, especially when there is a long gap between deciding to build extra capacity and the capacity coming on-stream. A second reason is that all capacity is not the same. Newer operations are generally more efficient and may have other operations advantages compared to older operations using less state-of-the-art technologies. Thus, there is always the chance that a new operation coming on-stream will attract business at the expense of older capacity. A third reason is that individual firms usually make investment decisions, whereas industry over-capacity is a result of all their decisions taken together. So a firm might be able to reduce its costs by investing in new capacity but the prices it receives for its products and services are partly determined by the cumulative decisions of its competitors. This also explains why it is not always easy to reduce over-capacity in an industry. Often it is in nobody's interest to be the first mover to shut down capacity. Its owner pays the costs of closing down capacity. The benefits, however, in terms of higher prices and margins, are spread across the industry as a whole. So every firm wants capacity to be reduced as long as it is not its own capacity.

### Balancing capacity change

During 2006 the price of oil (and therefore gasoline) shot up to unprecedented levels (in dollar terms). Why was this? Well, there was uncertainty in the supply of crude oil and demand from developing economies was growing, but the reason that these elements of supply and market uncertainty had such a dramatic effect was because there was a shortage of refining capacity. The oil companies had failed to plan for sufficient refinery capacity and the bottleneck in the supply chain had increased the fear of shortages. So, planning for capacity change must take into account that the lowest capacity, or 'bottleneck', part of the chain will limit the capacity of a whole chain of operations. For example, if the 800-unit capacity air conditioning plant, introduced earlier, not only assembles products but also manufactures the parts from which they are made, then any change in the assembly plant must be matched by changes in the ability to supply it with parts. Similarly, further down the chain, operations such as warehousing and distribution may also have to change their capacity. For the chain to operate efficiently, all its stages must have more or less the same capacity. This is not too much of an issue if the economic increment of capacity is roughly the same for

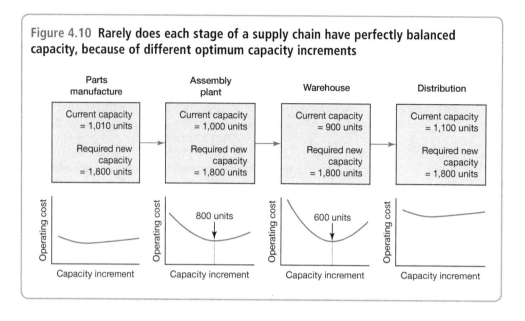

Figure 4.10 **Rarely does each stage of a supply chain have perfectly balanced capacity, because of different optimum capacity increments**

each stage in the chain. However, if the most cost-effective increment in each stage is very different, changing the capacity of one stage may have a significant effect on the economics of operation of the others. Figure 4.10 illustrates the air conditioning plant example. Currently, the capacity of each stage is not balanced. This could be the result of many different factors involving historical demand and capacity changes. The bottleneck stage is the warehouse, which has a weekly capacity of 900 units. If the company wants to increase output from its total operations to 1,800 units a week, all four stages will require extra capacity. The economy of scale graphs for each stage are illustrated. They indicate that for the parts manufacturing plant and the distribution operation, operating cost is relatively invariant to the size of capacity increment chosen. Presumably this is because individual trucks and/or machines can be added within the existing infrastructure. However, for both the assembly plant and the warehouse, operating costs will be dependent on the size of capacity increment chosen. In the case of the assembly plant the decision is relatively straightforward. A single addition to the operation of 800 units will both minimise its individual operating costs and achieve the required new capacity. The warehouse has more of a problem. It requires an additional capacity of 900 units. This would involve either building units of sub-optimum capacity or building two units of optimal capacity and under-utilising them with its own cost penalties.

The same issues apply on a wider scale when independent operations are affected by imbalance in the whole chain. Air travel is a classic example of this. Three of the most important elements in the chain of operations that provides air travel are the terminals that provide passenger facilities at airports, the runways from which aircraft take off and land and the aircraft themselves operating on all the various sectors, which include the airport. Each of these stages, in planning their capacity, is subject to different pressures. Building new terminals is not only expensive in terms of the capital required, but also subject to environmental considerations and other issues of public concern. The individual aircraft that use these facilities are both far smaller units of capacity in themselves and form an element in the capacity chain that is subject to normal business commercial pressures. Different sizes of aircraft will be used for different routes depending on the 'density' (volume of demand) of the route. Because they represent relatively small units of capacity, the number of aircraft using an airport can change relatively smoothly over time. Runways and terminals, however, represent large increments of capacity and therefore change less frequently. Also, within each part of the chain the effective capacity may improve because of technical changes. Terminals are becoming more efficient in the way they can handle large amounts of baggage, or even tag customers with micro-chipped tickets so that they can be traced and organised more effectively. All of which can, to some extent, increase the capacity of a terminal without making it any larger. Likewise, runways can accommodate more aircraft landing by providing more 'turn-offs', which allow aircraft to clear the main runway very soon after landing in order to let the next aircraft land. On high-density routes the aircraft themselves are getting larger. When the number of slots available to an airline is limited, and if route density warrants it, very large aircraft can increase the number of passengers carried per landing or take-off slot. However, these changes in effective capacity at each stage in the chain may affect the other stages. For example, very large aircraft have to be designed so as to keep the air turbulence they cause to a minimum so that it does not affect the time between landing slots. Also, very large aircraft may need different terminal equipment such as the air bridges that load and unload passengers.

## Location of capacity

Often, the reason why operations are where they are is not always obvious. Sometimes historical reasons have dictated the location. Such operations are 'there because they're there'. Even more recent location decisions are not always logical. Entrepreneurial whim or lifestyle preference may overcome seeming locational disadvantages. In other cases, the location decision is only reached after extensive thought and analysis.

### The importance of location

The location decision is rarely unimportant, but sometimes can be very important to the long-term health of an organisation. This is because the location decision can have a significant impact on both the investment in the operation's resources and in the market impact of the operation's resources. For example, locating a fire service station in the wrong place can both slow down the average time for the fire crew to respond to the call or increase the required investment to build the station, or both. Similarly, locating a manufacturing plant where it is difficult to attract labour with appropriate skills may affect the quality of its products (hence revenues), or the wages it has to pay to attract appropriate labour (hence costs).

**Example** | **Rolls-Royce opens up in Singapore[5]**

The Rolls-Royce Trent family of aircraft engines is an impressive and successful example of aerospace engineering. The Trent 900 is used on the four-engine Airbus A380 'superjumbo' and the Trent 1000 powers Boeing's 787 Dreamliner. And, by any standards, the technology is impressive. '*Do you know that one of these Trent engines is powerful enough to light up a town of*

▶

*100,000 people; that the fan blades rotate at 1,200mph, faster than the speed of sound; and that one of the internal blades heats up to 200C higher than its melting point but, thanks to our cooling system, still does not melt? These engines are the most technically difficult things in the world to make. They keep 400,000 people up in the air, safely, at any hour of the day or night'*, says Jonathan Asherson, the South East Asia Director of Rolls-Royce.

It is this technical sophistication that limits where the engines can be made. Any location must have the access to the skills and infrastructure to support technically complex manufacturing. Which is why Rolls-Royce chose Seletar in Singapore to host its almost £400-million Asian expansion. But the company is no stranger to the region; it already serviced Singapore Airlines' engines at a special plant near Changi airport. Yet Rolls-Royce already has an established factory at Derby in the UK, where all its engines were developed, so why not simply expand that plant to cope with the increased demand? Partly it is because Asia is where the demand is. The world's fastest-growing airlines are in China, Singapore, Indonesia, India and in the Gulf. More than half of new orders for Trent engines come from airlines in the region. *'It's good to be near the market, [but] this is not about transplanting activity from one place to another'*, says Asherson. By 2020 the company plan to double its output, with production split 50:50 between Singapore and Derby. Also, the generous tax incentives offered by the Singaporean government played a part, as did the construction of a road from Seletar to Changi airport so that engines can be loaded on to the cargo planes that fly them to Rolls-Royce's customers in Toulouse and Seattle. Yet, says the company, although important, these incentives were not as important as the 'soft' factors that make Singapore so attractive. In particular, the city state's universities and colleges, which produce the highly skilled scientists, engineers and staff who are vital to producing products that cannot be allowed to fail. Says Jonathan Asherson:

> *'We think that the focus in Asia, from an education and training perspective, will continue to be in areas of technology and engineering. The talent pipeline that we need as an industry and company will remain solid. That will influence the thinking around our investments. You need to develop technologies and business models that adapt to increasing pressure on costs, increasing pressure on reliability and the environment. We've worked with government agencies around developing work skills, qualifications, and developing curricula for the polytechnics and universities, where we work with them to predict the requirement and work on how that pipeline of talent can be built. Singapore is quite flexible and nimble where they see the high multiplier effect of, for example, high-value-added manufacturing.'*

The costs of physically moving the operation's resources may be high, but the risks involved may be even more important. Complex arrangements involving changes to many parts of the operation's resources invariably increase the risk of something going wrong with the move. Delays can mean inconvenience to customers, interruption of supply and increased costs. All this adds inertia to the location decision. Once made, a location decision is difficult to change, which is why few operations want to move frequently. But organisations do move their location, and it is usually for one of two reasons. Either:

● there are changes in the demand for its goods and services; or
● there are changes in the supply of its input resources to the operation.

Where the stimulus for relocation is a change in demand, it may be because of a change in the aggregated volume of demand. For example, if the demand for a clothing manufacturer's products is increasing beyond its capacity, the company could either expand at its existing site or, alternatively, if the site is not large enough it could move to a larger site in another location. A third option would be to keep its existing site and find a second location for an additional plant. Two of these options involve a location decision. Similarly, a reduction in the aggregate volume of demand may mean the company under-utilising its site, selling or leasing part of the site, or moving to a smaller new site.

Some high-customer-contact operations do not have the choice of expanding on the same site to meet rising demand. For example, a fast-food restaurant chain competes, at least partially, by having locations close to its customers. As demand increases, it may well respond by investing in more locations. There will come a time, however, when locating a new restaurant in between the areas covered by two existing ones will, to some extent, cannibalise demand. The other reason for relocation is some kind of change in the cost or availability of its supply of inputs. An oil company, for example, will need to relocate as the oil it is extracting becomes depleted. A manufacturing company might choose to relocate its operations to a part of the world where labour costs are low. In other words, the labour costs differential, in the context of its competitive position, has changed. Similarly, the value of the land it has occupied compared with an alternative location may become too great to forego the opportunity of releasing the value of the land.

### Spatially variable factors

A prerequisite to effective location decisions is to understand the spatial characteristics of costs, revenues and investment. 'Spatial characteristics' are those whose value changes with geographical location. In not-for-profit organisations, where revenue may not be a relevant objective, customer service may be used as a substitute. So, for example, the fire service may use average (or maximum) response time as its 'market phasing' objective. Figure 4.11 identifies some of the spatially variable factors that organisations may use in location decisions.

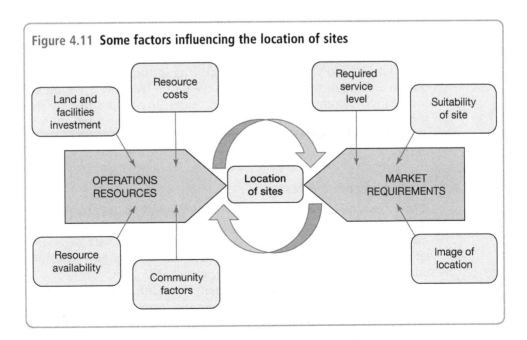

Figure 4.11 **Some factors influencing the location of sites**

### The suitability of the site itself

The intrinsic characteristic of a location may affect an operation's ability to serve its customers and generate revenue. For example, locating a luxury business hotel in a high-prestige site close to the business district may be appropriate for the hotel's customers. Move it one or two kilometres away where it is surrounded by warehouses and it rapidly loses its attraction.

### The image of the location

Some locations are firmly associated in customers' minds with a particular image. Suits made and sold in Savile Row, which is the centre of the up-market bespoke tailoring district in London, may be little better than high-quality suits made elsewhere. However, a location there will establish a tailor's reputation and possibly its revenue. The availability of appropriate local skills can also have an impact on how customers see the nature of an operation's products or services. For example, science parks are located close to universities because they hope to attract companies interested in using the skills available there. An entertainment production company may locate in Hollywood, partly, at least, because of the pool of talent on which it can draw to produce high-quality (or at least high-revenue-earning) projects.

### Service level

For many operations this is by far the most important demand-side factor. Locating a general hospital, for example, in the middle of the countryside may have many advantages for its staff and even maybe for its costs, but clearly would be very inconvenient for its customers. Not only would those visiting the hospital need to travel long distances, but those being attended to in an emergency would have to wait longer than necessary to be brought in for admission. Because of this, hospitals are located close to centres of demand. Similarly, with other public services location has a significant effect on the ability of an operation to serve its customers effectively. Likewise, other high-customer-contact operations, such as restaurants, stores, banks, etc., have revenues that are directly affected by how easily customers can access the service. Also, speed and dependability issues are becoming more important in many parts of manufacturing industry. Locating close to customers can be a competitive advantage, or even a prerequisite for some customers. It is increasingly common for large manufacturers to demand that their suppliers build local plants, so as to ensure regular, fast and dependable supply. These may even be physically adjoining, so that a supplier is able to deliver products through a 'hole in the wall' to its customers.

### Land and facilities investment

If the operation is considering purchasing the land for its site, this may be an important factor. If the operation is leasing the land then it is usually regarded as a supply-side cost factor. Certainly both land and rental costs vary between countries and cities. Companies sometimes locate where they already have available land, or even unused buildings, in order to avoid the investment costs.

In some location decisions, investment in the infrastructure needed to support the main operations facility can be as significant, if not more so, than the investment in the operation itself. At a simple level, infrastructural investment may include such things as building access roads, improving waste disposal, or building power generation support. At a more extensive level, a company locating in an under-developed part of the world may need to invest in road, or even rail, links. It may even be necessary to invest significantly in the local supply industry, either providing sites for suppliers or encouraging such things as producer cooperatives. Indeed, part of the deal that may be struck with the local government of the site may include a commitment to develop infrastructures.

---

**Example** | **Counting clusters[6]**

Similar companies with similar needs often cluster together in the same geographical area. Why? For a number of reasons. Michael Porter of Harvard Business School, the famous strategy professor and an authority on industrial clusters, says that firms' geographical proximity helps to promote economies of scale, learning and productivity, as well as boosting innovation and encouraging the growth of new supplier firms. This is a winning combination, according to Professor Porter, and accounts for the existence of such clusters around the world. Here are just a few examples.

**Financial services** are clustered in a relatively few centres globally. Even after the turbulence of recent years, London, New York, Hong Kong, Singapore, Tokyo, Chicago and Zurich dominate the industry. According to Deutsche Bank, 'Big is beautiful – and will remain so.' It is far easier to build on existing market strength than start afresh. Banks have to trade with each other, and even in an increasingly globalised world being close helps. Combine this with good regulation and free markets and it becomes a significant competitive advantage.

**High-tech industries** provide one of the most famous location clusters in the area south of San Francisco, know as Silicon Valley – probably the most important intellectual and commercial hub of technological innovation. Yet other locations are developing. For example, Bangalore in India is fast becoming a cluster for the computer industry because of the ready availability of well-educated, low-cost, English-speaking software technicians; it has now attracted more and more sophisticated business. Something similar is happening in Shanghai in China. *'Over the next ten years, China will become a ferociously formidable competitor for companies that run the entire length of the technology food chain',* says Michael J. Moritz, a Californian venture-capital firm. Even in higher-cost countries, new clusters are growing. One is around 'silicon roundabout', in East London, where old Victorian warehouses are home to a growing number of Web and technology start-ups, working on everything from online game design to streaming music services and general Web services (Google has offices there). The history of start-ups in the area stretches back a couple of decades because of relatively low office rents, a creative atmosphere generated by an influx of artists and designers, London's world-class universities, art galleries and the kind of cafés, bars, shops and clubs that help attract creative staff. So, again, the cluster developed for clear reasons then grew because size and focus attracts other companies.

**Racing cars** are mostly made in Britain – in particular in the area around Oxfordshire or Northamptonshire. Most Formula 1 teams are based in Britain, as are many Indy Car teams. Even those who are not are likely to use British services. Motorsport is a flourishing cluster, with around 4,500 firms working at building, maintaining, modifying and restoring cars, making engines and components and providing technical and management services. Almost everything a racing team needs can be found without leaving the area.

### Resource costs – labour

Although wages and the other costs of employing people can vary between different areas in any country, it is more likely to be a significant factor when international comparisons are made. Here, wage costs mean those costs to the organisation of paying wages directly to individual employees. Non-wage costs are the employment taxes, social security costs, holiday payments, and other welfare provisions that the organisation has to make in order to employ people. However, such labour costs should be treated with some caution. Two factors can influence them. The first is the productivity of labour. On an international level this is often inversely related to labour costs. This means that, generally, the average amount produced by each individual employed in a given unit of time is greater in countries with higher labour costs. This is, at least partly, because in countries with high labour costs there is more incentive to invest in productivity-enhancing technology. This effect goes some way to offsetting the large international variations in labour costs. The second factor is the rate of exchange of countries' currencies that may swing considerably over time. This, in turn, changes relative labour costs. Yet, in spite of these adjustments to the real value of relative labour costs, they may exert a major influence on the location decision, especially in industries such as clothing, where labour costs are a high proportion of total costs.

### Resource costs – energy

Those operations that use large amounts of energy – for example, aluminium smelting – may be influenced in their location decisions by the availability of relatively inexpensive energy. Low-cost energy sources may be direct, as in the availability of hydro-electric generation in an area, or indirect, for example a low-cost coal area that can be used to generate inexpensive electricity.

### Resource costs – transportation

Transportation costs are clearly spatially variable because the operation's resources need to be transported (or transport themselves) from their point of origin to the operation itself. In many operations, also, goods and services (or the people who perform the services) need to be transported from the operation to customers. Of course, not all goods and services are transported to customers. In operations such as hotels, retailers and hospitals, customers visit the operation to receive their services. In these cases we treat the ease with which customers access such services as a demand-side or revenue-influencing factor (or customer service factor in not-for-profit operations).

Proximity to sources of supply dominates location decisions where the cost of transporting input materials is high. So, for example, food processing or other agriculturally based activities are often located close to growing areas. Similarly, forestry and mining operations could only be located close to their sources of supply. Proximity to customers dominates location decisions where the transportation of products and services to customers is expensive or impossible. So, for example, many civil engineering projects are constructed where they are needed; similarly, accountancy audits take place at customers' own facilities because that is where the information resides.

## Community factors

The general category of community factors is those influences on an operation's costs that derive from the social, political and economic environment of its location. These include:

- government financial or planning assistance;
- local tax rates;
- capital movement restrictions;
- political stability;
- language;
- local amenities (schools, theatres, shops, etc.);
- history of labour relations, absenteeism, productivity, etc.;
- environmental restrictions and waste disposal.

Community factors can be particularly influential on the location decision. Some issues obviously affect the profitability of the operation, such as local tax rates, which can clearly affect the viability of a new location. Others are less obvious. For example, the European country that has had the most inward investment from Japanese companies is the UK. Some investments, especially the early ones, were influenced by the UK Government's generous financial support and tax concessions. Other factors included a relatively cheap but well-educated workforce. Yet a less obvious, but equally important, factor was language. Many Japanese companies were accustomed to trading and producing in the USA. The English language is the first foreign language for most Japanese business people. Drawings of products and processes, for example, together with instruction sheets, computer programs, etc., were often immediately available for use without further translation for the UK. This means a lower risk of misunderstandings and mistranslation, thus smoothing communications between the new location and its Japanese head office.

## Offshoring' and 're-shoring'[7]

Over the last two or three decades 'offshoring' has been one of the major phenomena of global operations strategy. Firms that were once seen as firmly located in their home markets have 'offshored' at least some of their activities to other locations. Lower labour costs were almost always the chief motivation for offshoring. Operating capacity was shut down in the USA and Europe and new factories were opened in China, Mexico, Taiwan, and Vietnam – in fact, wherever costs were low and capabilities adequate. And, although the anxiety over lost jobs in the rich world caused some opposition, the economic benefits of offshoring have been huge. Workers in low-cost countries have gained jobs and secured rising standards of living. Rich-world companies gained lower labour costs and higher profits. Customers secured access to products at far lower prices than if production had stayed at home. Later, increasing numbers of service jobs followed as firms exploited the internet to offshore IT development and back-office work to places such as India and the Philippines. Business process outsourcers (BPOs), such as India's Wipro and Tata, grew dramatically on the back of this trend.

But is the offshoring trend now going into reverse? Some see signs that it may be. For example, after decades of decline a new production line making laptop computers opened up in Whitsett, North Carolina. And which company was it that chose the USA rather than China, where almost all such products are made? It was one of the world's largest PC makers, Lenovo – the successful Chinese technology group. Nor is Lenovo alone. Jeff Immelt, the CEO of General Electric (GE), calls outsourcing 'yesterday's model' and has returned the production of some of its domestic appliances from China back to Kentucky. This so-called 're-shoring' is not confined to manufacturing. GE has also moved back much of its IT development work from abroad to a new centre in Michigan. (Ironically GE was one of the earliest and most enthusiastic offshoring companies, starting back in the 1980s.)

So what has prompted re-shoring to seemingly 'high-cost' locations? Some observers argue that firms that once were enthusiastic offshorers now have realised the hidden costs and impact on revenue of moving activities a long way from home. Partly, it is the cost equation that has changed. For example, wages in many Chinese factories are increasing by around 20 per cent a year – faster than their productivity is growing. Added to this is a stronger Chinese currency that has closed the gap between Chinese and Western labour costs. And, anyway, labour costs are accounting for a smaller proportion of total manufacturing costs as processes become more automated. Of course, there are still regions where labour costs are significantly below those in Western economies. For some types of job, countries such as Vietnam and Bangladesh can still provide low-cost labour. However, they struggle to emulate China's broad yet large-scale supply base. Nor is distance between offshored suppliers and developed world customers cost-free. Companies must factor in the rising cost of ocean transportation as well as the chance that supply chains could be disrupted by environmental disasters or geopolitical events. Also, goods can spend weeks in transit, slowing down the whole supply chain and reducing the chance of responding flexibly to changing market demand. Innovation is also an issue. Although the technological support available in China and India is increasingly sophisticated, some firms are discovering that innovation is smoother when manufacturing is in the same place as research. Of course, firms could move their research out to the 'offshored' location, but that may increase the risk of intellectual property 'leakage' to suppliers.

Perhaps more fundamentally, offshoring was often predicated on the idea that the 'non-core' activities that were offshored were not vital to a firm's success – an assumption that is being reevaluated. Surely, it is increasingly argued, activities such as developing new IT applications and providing high-quality customer care are in fact a 'core' part of any business. Certainly, customer frustration at dealing with Indian contact centres, whether justified or not, is contributing to the return of customer interaction jobs.

### The nature of location decisions

Although all location decisions will involve some, or all, of the market requirement and operations resource factors outlined above, the nature of the decision itself can vary significantly. Locating new fast-food restaurant franchises is a very different type of decision from locating a new electronics factory, for example. The differences between these two location decisions (or indeed any other location decisions) can be characterised on two dimensions: the objectives of the location decision and the number of location options available. In many high-contact operations, such as fast-food restaurants, retail shops and hotels, both costs and revenue are spatially variable. In other words, both the market and resource sides of the reconciliation process are significant. So, for example, locating a fast-food restaurant in an out-of-the-way location may allow it to operate with very low costs but its ability to attract customers (and therefore revenue) will be, likewise, very low. A more attractive location will undoubtedly be more expensive but would also attract higher custom. Most low-contact operations have revenues that are relatively invariant to location. Costs, however, will vary with location. Thus, location is largely one of cost-minimisation, this being an approximation for profit-maximisation.

The other major dimension of the location decision is concerned with the number of options between which a choice will be made. The electronics manufacturer may first decide on a relatively large geographic region, such as 'Hungary'. Once that broad decision is made, the number of possible sites is very large indeed – in fact, for all practical purposes, infinite. The decision process involves narrowing the number of options down to a smaller representative number that can be systematically evaluated against a common set of criteria. Many high-contact operations, however, are not located in this way. More likely, a company will first of all decide on a relatively limited area. For example, 'We wish to locate one of our franchises in Budapest.' Once this decision is made the search begins for a suitable site. The choice then is between any site that may be immediately available or, alternatively, waiting until a more attractive site becomes available. Each decision is, in effect, a yes/no decision of accepting a site or, alternatively, deferring a decision in the hope that a better one will become available.

## SUMMARY ANSWERS TO KEY QUESTIONS

### What is capacity strategy?

Capacity-related decisions are conventionally divided into three time horizons – long-term strategic, medium-term and short-term. Strategic decisions are those concerned with the provision of buildings, facilities and process technology, in all parts of the business, for at least months and probably years into the future. Capacity strategy includes a number of interrelated decisions, that include defining the overall scale of the operation, the number and size of the sites between which capacity is distributed, the specific activities allocated to each site, when capacity levels should be changed, how big each step change should be and the location of each site.

### How much capacity should an operation have?

The starting point in determining overall capacity level will be the demand forecast. However, actual capacity may not be the same as forecast demand. It may be modified to account for the relative certainty, or uncertainty, of demand, long-term changes in expected demand level, the availability of capital needed, the ratio of fixed to variable costs and general economies of scale. Also, a company may choose to provide more of one kind of resource (for example, the size of the physical building) before demand warrants it, in order to save capital costs in the long run.

▶

### How many separate sites should an operation have?

The decision here concerns the choice between many small sites on the one hand, or fewer larger sites on the other. The geographical distribution of demand, together with customers' required service level, will influence this decision, as will the economies of scale of the operation and the costs associated with supply. If demand is widely distributed between customers demanding high levels of service, and if there are no significant economies of scale or costs of supply, then the business is more likely to operate with many small sites.

### What issues are important when changing capacity levels?

Capacity can be introduced to either lead or lag demand. Lead-demand strategies involve early capital expenditure and under-utilisation of capacity but ensure that the operation is likely to be able to meet demand. Lagging capacity strategies involve later capital expenditure and full utilisation of the capacity but fail to fulfil forecast demand. If inventories are carried over so as to smooth the effects of introducing capacity increments, it may be possible to achieve both high sales and high utilisation of resources, and therefore low costs. However, working capital requirements will be higher because the inventory needs to be funded. Changing capacity in large increments can minimise the costs of changing capacity (closure costs if demand is decreasing and capital expenditure if demand is increasing), but can also mean a significant mismatch between capacity and demand at many points in time. Conversely, changing by using small increments of capacity will match demand and capacity more exactly but require more frequent changes. Especially when increasing capacity, these changes can be expensive in capital cost and disruption terms. Often it is the risks of making too large a change in capacity that weigh heavily with operations, especially when forecasts of future demand are uncertain. Generally, the more uncertain is future demand, the more likely operations are to choose relatively small increments of capacity change. Notwithstanding this, there is a general pressure in many industries towards building new capacity, even when over-capacity exists in the industry.

### Where should capacity be located?

Required service levels from customers will influence this decision. Fast and regular supply implies location close to customer locations. Other market-related factors include the suitability of the site and the general image of its location. As far as operations resources are concerned, significant factors include the resource costs associated with the site, such as land and energy costs, the investment needed in land and facilities, the availability of any specialist resources required and general community factors.

### Further reading

DeToni, A., Filippini, R. and Forza, C. (1992) 'Manufacturing strategy in global market: an operations management model', *International Journal of Operations and Production Management*, 12(4).

DuBois, F.L., Toyne, B. and Oliff, M.D. (1993) 'International manufacturing strategies of US multinationals: a conceptual framework based on a four industry study', *Journal of International Business Studies*, 24(2).

Evans, P. and Wurster, T.S. (2000) *Blown to Bits: How the new economics of information trans-forms strategy*. Boston: Harvard Business School Press.

Gunther, N.J. (2006) *Guerrilla Capacity Planning: A Tactical Approach to Planning for Highly Scalable Applications and Services*. Berlin and Heidelberg: Springer-Verlag.

Hill, C.W.L. (2012) *International Business: Competing in the Global Market Place*. New York: McGraw-Hill.

Küpper, A. (2005) *Location-Based Services: Fundamentals and Operation: Fundamentals and Application*. Oxford: Wiley-Blackwell.

Tombak, M.M. (1995) 'Multinational plant location as a game of timing', *European Journal of Operational Research*, 86(4).

Wolfe, D. and Lucas, M. (eds) (2005) *Global Networks and Local Linkages: The Paradox of Cluster Development in an Open Economy*. School of Policy Studies, Queen's University.

## Notes on the chapter

1   Sources include: Blakely, R. (2010) 'Britain can learn from India's assembly-line heart opera-tions, says doctor', *The Times*, 14 May; *The Economist* (2011) 'Economies of scale made steel – The economics of very big ships', 12 November; Maersk website: www.maersk.com/innovation

2   Sources include: *The Economist* (2014) 'Big carmakers, Kings of the road, Size is not every-thing for mass-market carmakers. But it helps', 11 January.

3   Hayes, R.H. and Wheelwright, S.C. (1984) *Restoring Our Competitive Edge*. New York: Wiley.

4   Sources include: Liu, H.C.K. (2005) 'Scarcity economics and overcapacity', *Asia Times online*, 28 July; *The Economist* (1999) 'Double parked', 9 January.

5   Sources include: Arlidge, J. (2013) 'Rolls finds its Derby in the east', *Sunday Times*, 27 October; Raghuvanshi, G. (2013) 'Rolls-Royce Pushes Focus on Singapore', *Wall Street Journal*, 15 September; Syed, S. (2013) 'Rolls-Royce gears up for Singapore production', *BBC News website*, 21 February.

6   Sources include: *The Economist* (2011) 'Clusters flustered – Global competition seems to be weakening the benefits of being in a cluster', 14 April; Deutsche Bank Research (2010) 'Global financial centres after the crisis', 2 August; *The Economist* (2009) 'Britain and Formula 1 – Cluster champs', 22 October; Wendling, M. (2011) 'Can "Silicon Roundabout" challenge Silicon Valley?', *BBC News* website, 8 September.

7   Sources include: The Economist (2013) 'Welcome home; the outsourcing of jobs to faraway places is on the wane. But this will not solve the West's employment woes', 19 January; Booth, T. (2013) 'Here, there and everywhere', The Economist special report on outsourcing and offshoring, 19 January.

# 5 Purchasing and supply strategy

## Introduction

No operation works in isolation – it is always, directly or indirectly, part of a larger value network. It follows that no operations *strategy* can work in isolation – it must always consider the role of the operation in its supply network. Some would argue that, in today's globalised and technology-enabled economy, purchasing and supply decisions are often the *most critical* set of operations strategy decisions. Think about Apple's phenomenally successful iPhone. The firm has world-class operations – it designed the phone, created the operating software, runs the Apps (applications) store, and so on. But it is Apple's suppliers that undertake almost everything else. Firms, large and small, from around the world provide a range of, often extremely sophisticated, inputs into the product. So, Apple's phenomenal recent success has been built as much on the back of its purchasing and supply strategy as its research and development. In fact, when the consultancy AMR generates its annual list of the world's best supply chain players it is no surprise to discover that Apple has been consistently rated very highly (this in spite of having not been in the top 25 in 2005). In other words, underlying performance is increasingly determined through those decisions relating not only to what an organisation does by itself, but also what it purchases, where it buys from and how it manages these crucial external connections. Figure 5.1 illustrates the coverage of this chapter.

### KEY QUESTIONS

- *What is purchasing and supply strategy?*
- *What should we do and what should we buy?*
- *How do we buy; what is the role of contracts and/or relationships?*
- *How do we manage supply dynamics?*
- *How do we manage suppliers over time?*
- *How do we manage supply chain risks?*

## What is purchasing and supply strategy?

At the heart of purchasing and supply strategy is the deceptively simple concept of buyer–supplier interaction. Buying and selling is not new, of course, but in recent years shifts in the business environment have led to an increased strategic emphasis

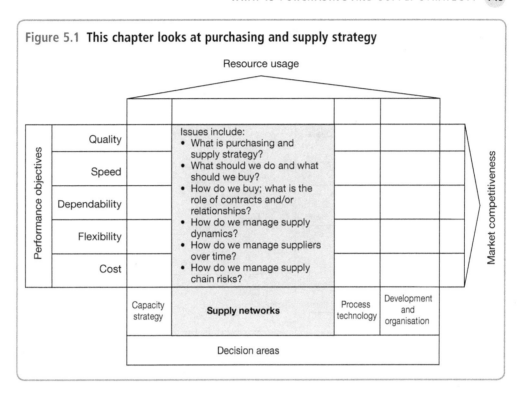

Figure 5.1 **This chapter looks at purchasing and supply strategy**

on more complex value-creating supply networks. Here we define value-creating supply networks as:

*'a set of interconnected organizations whose different processes and activities together produce value.'*

Figure 5.2 illustrates a supply network, with three main companies (A, B and C) at the centre of the network, Company A is called the 'focal' company of the network and, together with companies B and C, forms the 'focal level' of the network. In other words, the network is drawn from company A's perspective. Company A's suppliers, together with its suppliers' suppliers and so on, form the upstream or supply side of the network, while its customers and customers' customers, etc. form the downstream or demand side of the network. The various processes within company A form the *internal* supply network. Outside its boundaries, company A will have direct contact with a number of suppliers and a number of customers; this forms the *immediate* supply network. The linkages of suppliers to company A's suppliers, and customers to company A's customers, form its *total* supply network. Companies that are predominantly part of the focal level's immediate supply network are called first-tier suppliers or first-tier customers. Those who are one level beyond this are called second-tier suppliers and customers, and so on. The relationships between companies within the network are not always exclusive. Company A may purchase exactly the same products or services from a number of different suppliers, who in turn may 'multi-source' from several second-tier suppliers. Also, the focal company's networks all involve several parallel relationships, each having several first-tier suppliers and several first-tier customers, which themselves may have more than one second-tier supplier or customer.

Figure 5.2 **Supply networks are the interconnections of relationships between operations**

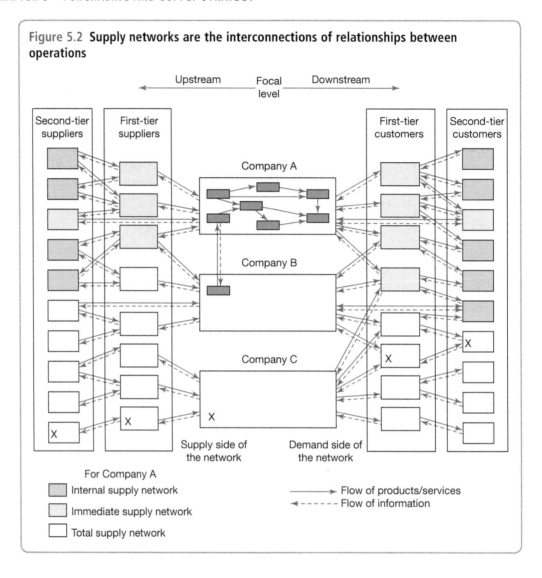

But within these parallel relationships there are several supply chains. These are the sequential linkages of operations that intersect at the focal company. So, for example, the operations marked with an *X* form one of the supply chains passing through company C.

## Describing supply networks – dyads and triads

Figure 5.2, and all diagrams that try to describe supply networks, can be complex. There are many operations, all interacting in different ways, to produce end products and services. Because of this, and to understand them better, supply network academics and professionals often choose to focus on the individual interaction between two specific operations in the network. This is called a 'dyadic' (simply meaning 'two') interaction, or dyadic relationship, and the two operations are referred to as a 'dyad'.

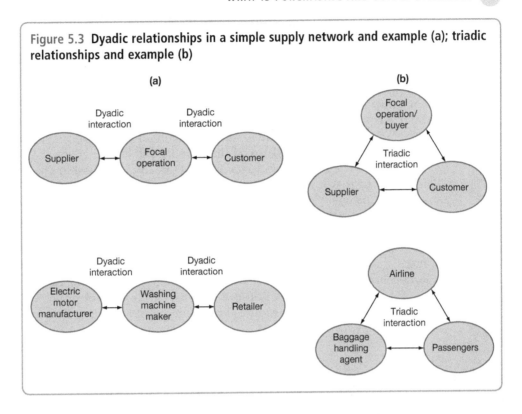

**Figure 5.3 Dyadic relationships in a simple supply network and example (a); triadic relationships and example (b)**

So, if one wanted to examine the interactions that a focal operation had with one of its suppliers and one of its customers, one would examine the two dyads of 'supplier–focal operation', and 'focal operation–customer' (see Figure 5.3(a)). For many years, most discussion (and research) on supply networks was based on dyadic relationships. This is not surprising as all relationships in a network are based on the simple dyad. However, more recently, and certainly when examining service supply networks, many authorities make the point that dyads do not reflect the real essence of a supply network. Rather, they say, it is triads, not dyads, that are the basic elements of a supply network (see Figure 5.3(b)). No matter how complex a network, it can be broken down into a collection of triadic interactions. The idea of triads is especially relevant in service supply networks. Operations are increasingly outsourcing the delivery of some aspects of their service to specialist providers, who deal directly with customers on behalf of the focal (more usually called the 'buying operation', or just 'buyer' in this context). For example, Figure 5.3(b) illustrates the common example of an airline contracting a specialist baggage handling company to provide services to its customers on its behalf. Similarly, internal services are increasingly outsourced to form internal triadic relationships. For example, if a company outsources its IT operations, it is forming a triad between whoever is purchasing the service on behalf of the company, the IT service provider and the employees who use the IT services.

Thinking about supply networks as a collection of triads rather than dyads is strategically important. First, it emphasises the dependence that organisations are placing on their suppliers' performance when they outsource service delivery. A supplier's service performance makes up an important part of how the buyer's performance is viewed. Second, the control that the buyer of the service has over service delivery to its customer is diminished in a triadic relationship. In a conventional supply chain, with a series of dyadic relationships, there is the opportunity to intervene before the customer receives the product or service. However, products, or services in triadic relationships bypass the buying organisation and go directly from provider to customer. Third, and partially as a consequence of the previous point, in triadic relationships the direct link between service provider and customer can result in power gradually transferring over time from the buying organisation to the supplier that provides the service. Fourth, it becomes increasingly difficult for the buying organisation to understand what is happening between the supplier and customer at a day-to-day level. It may not even be in the supplier's interests to be totally honest in giving performance feedback to the buyer. Finally, this closeness between supplier and customer, if it excludes the buyer, could prevent the buyer from building important knowledge. For example, suppose a specialist equipment manufacturer has outsourced the maintenance of its equipment to a specialist provider of maintenance services. The ability of the equipment manufacturer to understand how its customers are using the equipment, how the equipment was performing under various conditions, how customers would like to see the equipment improved, and so on is impaired. The equipment manufacturer may have outsourced the cost and trouble of providing maintenance services, but it has also outsourced the benefits and learning that come from direct interaction with customers.

---

**Example** **What's the nationality of your car?[1]**

On average, car companies source around three quarters of their parts externally. This means that although an automobile company may be thought of as German or Italian or British, many (if not most) of its components may have been sourced abroad, and it may also have been assembled abroad. This can give some problems to cars whose brand is associated with a particular nationality, or whose core markets are particularly 'patriotic'. Italians may prefer to buy Fiat cars because Fiat is an Italian company, even though in reality many Fiats are now produced in Turkey and Poland. More than half of German buyers choose cars produced by German-owned companies. Yet there is a good chance that the car has been made in Poland or Slovakia. Even the most nationally conservative French buyers will buy 'French' cars, even though Citroën and Peugeot have plants in Slovakia. Buy an Audi TT in the UK and it was probably made in Hungary. Mercedes' ML-Class is built in the United States, as is BMW's X5. Porsche builds the Boxter sports car in Finland. Even the Aston Martin, beloved by James Bond fans for its Britishness, has its front seats, automatic transmission, steering components, crankshafts, stability control and even its engine made in Germany. Even stranger, buy a Nissan Micra in Europe and you will find that it was designed in London, engineered in Bedfordshire and manufactured in Sunderland. It's more British than the Aston Martin.

## Why adopt a network perspective?

A key insight derived from adopting a network perspective is the recognition that different organisations in a network relate to each other in a range of different ways. These include 'classic' interactions, such as upstream and downstream market linkages (i.e. buying and selling from each other), and competition (i.e. ultimately, a whole range of performance attributes – such as price – will be driven, even if indirectly, by competitor offerings). But a broader network perspective also reveals that organisations, many of them direct competitors, frequently collaborate; it is increasingly common, for instance, for groups of organisations to combine together into consortia when buying goods and services, or to work together on 'pre-competitive' research and development. Moreover, many organisations' value propositions are also dependent on complementors – other businesses providing complementary services and products.

### A network perspective enhances understanding of competitive and cooperative forces

When a business sees itself in the context of the whole network it may help it to understand why its customers and suppliers act as they do. Any operation has only two options if it wants to understand its ultimate customers at the end of the network. It can rely on all the intermediate customers and customers' customers, etc., which form the links in the network between the company and its end customers, to transmit the end-customer needs efficiently back up the network, or it can take the responsibility on itself for understanding how customer–supplier relationships transmit competitive requirements through the network. Increasingly, organisations are taking the latter course. Relying exclusively on one's immediate network is seen as putting too much faith in someone else's judgement of things that are central to an organisation's own competitive health. There is also a further category of companies in the supply network – 'complementors'. Most businesses would find their lives more difficult if it were not for 'complementors' – other businesses providing complementary services and products (for example, internet retailers depend on 'order fulfilment' delivery companies). Figure 5.4 illustrates the 'value net' for a company. It sees any company as being surrounded by four types of players: suppliers, customers, competitors and complementors.[2]

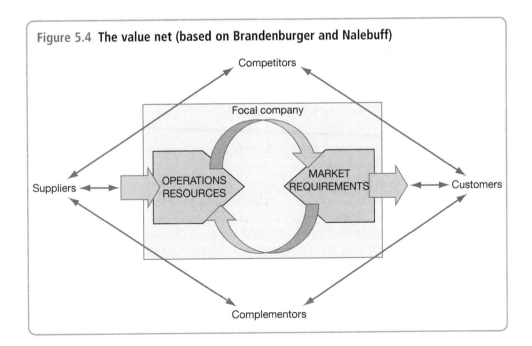

Figure 5.4 **The value net (based on Brandenburger and Nalebuff)**

Complementors enable customers to value your product or service more when they also have the complementor's product and service, as opposed to when they have yours alone. Competitors are the opposite: they make customers value your product or service less when they can have the competitor's product or service, rather than yours. However, competitors can be complementors, and vice versa. For example, adjacent restaurants may see themselves as competitors for customers' business. A customer standing outside and wanting a meal will choose between the two of them. Yet in another way they are complementors. Would that customer have come to this part of town unless there was more than one restaurant for him or her to choose between? Restaurants, theatres, art galleries and tourist attractions generally all cluster together in a form of cooperation to increase the total size of their joint market. It is important to distinguish between the way companies cooperate in increasing the total size of a market and the way in which they then compete for a share of that market. Historically, insufficient emphasis has been put on the role of the supplier. Harnessing the value of suppliers is just as important as listening to the needs of customers. Destroying value in a supplier in order to create it in a customer does not increase the value of the network as a whole. For example, pressurising suppliers because customers are pressurising you will not add long-term value. In the long term it creates value for the total network to find ways of increasing value for suppliers as well as customers. All the players in the network, whether they be customers, suppliers, competitors or complementors, can be both friends and enemies at different times. This is not 'unusual' or 'aberrant' behaviour. It is the way things are. The term used to capture this idea is 'co-opetition'.

### A network perspective confronts the operation with its strategic resource options

A supply network perspective illustrates to any operation exactly where it is positioned in its network. It also, therefore, highlights where it is not. That is, it clearly delineates between the activities that are being performed by itself and those that are being performed by other operations in the network. This prompts the question of why the operations boundaries are exactly where they are. Should the operation extend its direct control over a greater part of the network through vertical integration? Alternatively, should it outsource some of its activities to specialist suppliers? Furthermore, should it encourage particular patterns of relationships in other parts of the network? Again, it is the network perspective that raises the questions – and sometimes helps to answer them.

### A network perspective highlights the 'operation-to-operation' nature of business relationships

This may be the most far-reaching implication of a supply network perspective. It concerns the nature of the relationships between the various businesses in the network. Traditionally, these relationships have been seen as 'customer–supplier' relationships. What is new in the way supply networks are now treated is that rather than conceptualising the relationship as 'doing business' with customers and suppliers, we are concerned with the 'flow of goods and services' between operations. Look at any supply network and the vast majority of businesses represented in it have other businesses as their customers rather than end customers. Not that the end customer is unimportant. But behind each business serving the end customer is a whole network of other businesses. To the end customer, it is the chain of operations lying behind the one they can see that is important. For that chain of operations the important questions are not 'How can I sell to my customer?' and 'How can I get supplies from my supplier?' Rather, the questions should be 'How can my operation help my customer's operation to be more effective?' and 'How can my supplier's operation help my operation to be more effective?'

## Globalisation and sourcing

Globalisation is the more or less simultaneous marketing and sale of identical goods and services around the world. So widespread, says *The Economist* newspaper, has the phenomenon become over the past two decades that no one is surprised any more to find Coca-Cola in rural Vietnam, Accenture in Tashkent and Nike shoes in Nigeria.[3] It has made supply network strategy into a global issue. Global sourcing means identifying, evaluating, negotiating and configuring supply across multiple geographies. Traditionally, even companies who exported their goods and services still sourced the majority of their supplies locally. Companies are now increasingly willing to look further afield for their supplies, and for very good reasons. Most companies report a 10–35 per cent cost saving by sourcing from low-cost-country suppliers.[4] Also, there are other factors promoting global sourcing. The formation of trading blocks in different parts of the world, such as the European Union (EU), the North American Free Trade Agreement (NAFTA) and the South American Trade Group (MERCOSUR), has lowered tariff barriers within those blocks. Transportation infrastructures are considerably more sophisticated and cheaper than they once were. Super-efficient port operations in Rotterdam and Singapore, for example, integrated road–rail systems, jointly developed auto route systems and cheaper air freight have all reduced some of the cost barriers to international trade. But, most significantly, far tougher world competition has forced companies to look to reducing their total costs.

---

**Example**    The 80,000-kilometre journey of Wimbledon's tennis balls[5]

The Wimbledon 'Grand Slam' tennis tournament is a quintessentially British occasion, and Slazenger (a UK sports equipment manufacturer) has been the official ball supplier for Wimbledon since 1902. Yet those balls used at Wimbledon, and the materials from which they are made, will have travelled 81,385 kilometres between 11 countries and across four continents before they reach Centre Court. Dr Mark Johnson, of Warwick Business School, said:

*'It is one of the longest journeys I have seen for a product. On the face of it, travelling more than 80,000 kilometres to make a tennis ball does seem fairly ludicrous, but it just shows the global nature of production, and in the end, this will be the most cost-effective way of making tennis balls. Slazenger are locating production near the primary source of their materials in Bataan in the Philippines, where labour is also relatively low cost.'*

The complex supply chain is illustrated in Figure 5.5. It sees clay shipped from South Carolina in the USA, silica from Greece, magnesium carbonate from Japan, zinc oxide from Thailand, sulphur from South Korea and rubber from Malaysia to Bataan, where the rubber is vulcanised – a chemical process for making the rubber more durable. Wool is then shipped from New Zealand to Stroud in the UK, where it is weaved into felt and then flown back to Bataan in the Philippines. Meanwhile, petroleum naphthalene from Zibo in China and glue from Basilan in the Philippines are brought to Bataan, where Slazenger manufacture the ball. Finally, the tins that contain the balls are shipped in from Indonesia and, once the balls have been packaged, they are sent to Wimbledon. *'Slazenger shut down the factory in the UK years ago and moved the equipment to Bataan in the Philippines'*, says Mark Johnson. *'They still get the felt from Stroud, as it requires a bit more technical expertise. Shipping wool from New Zealand to Stroud and then sending the felt back to the Philippines adds a lot of miles, but they obviously want to use the best wool for the Wimbledon balls.'*

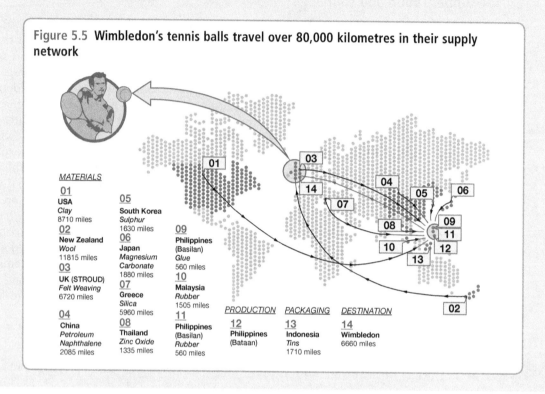

**Figure 5.5** Wimbledon's tennis balls travel over 80,000 kilometres in their supply network

*MATERIALS*

**01**
USA
*Clay*
8710 miles

**02**
New Zealand
*Wool*
11815 miles

**03**
UK (STROUD)
*Felt Weaving*
6720 miles

**04**
China
*Petroleum Naphthalene*
2085 miles

**05**
South Korea
*Sulphur*
1630 miles

**06**
Japan
*Magnesium Carbonate*
1880 miles

**07**
Greece
*Silica*
5960 miles

**08**
Thailand
*Zinc Oxide*
1335 miles

**09**
Philippines (Basilan)
*Glue*
560 miles

**10**
Malaysia
*Rubber*
1505 miles

**11**
Philippines (Basilan)
*Rubber*
560 miles

*PRODUCTION*

**12**
Philippines (Bataan)

*PACKAGING*

**13**
Indonesia
*Tins*
1710 miles

*DESTINATION*

**14**
Wimbledon
6660 miles

There are, of course, problems with global sourcing. The risks of increased complexity and increased distance need managing. The risks of delays and hold-ups can be far greater than when sourcing locally. Also, negotiating with suppliers whose native language is different from one's own makes communication more difficult and can lead to misunderstandings over contract terms. Therefore, global sourcing decisions require businesses to balance cost, performance, service and risk factors, not all of which are obvious. These factors are important in global sourcing because of non-price or 'hidden' cost factors, such as cross-border freight and handling fees, complex inventory stocking and handling requirements, even more complex administrative, documentation and regulatory requirements and issues of social responsibility.

### Global sourcing and corporate social responsibility (CSR)

This last point, that global sourcing requires extra attention to be placed on social responsibility, has significant risk implications. Although the responsibility of operations to ensure that they deal only with ethical suppliers has always been important, the expansion of global sourcing has brought the issue into sharper focus. Local suppliers can (to some extent) be monitored relatively easily. However, when suppliers are located around the world, often in countries with different traditions and ethical standards, monitoring becomes more difficult. Not only that, but there may be genuinely different views of what is regarded as ethical practice. Social, cultural, and religious differences can easily make for mutual incomprehension regarding each other's ethical perspective. This is why many companies are putting significant effort into articulating and clarifying their supplier selection policies.

**Example** **Disaster at Rana Plaza[6]**

It was a disaster that grabbed the attention of the world: on 24 April 2013 the Rana Plaza clothing factory near Dhaka in Bangladesh collapsed, killing at least 1,100 people. Many well-known clothing brands were sourcing products, either directly or indirectly, from the factory. It was claimed that local police and an industry association issued a warning that the building was unsafe, but the owners had responded by threatening to fire people who refused to carry on working as usual. Understandably there was an immediate call for tighter regulation and oversight by the Bangladesh authorities and for the predominantly Western retailers who sourced from the Rana Plaza, and similar unsafe factories, to accept some of the responsibility for the disaster and change their buying policies. Campaigning organisations including 'Labour Behind the Label', 'War on Want' and 'Made in Europe', urged retailers to be more transparent about their supply chains. They also called for compensation to be paid. But a year after the tragedy, the compensation initiative that intended to raise $40m had raised only $15m, despite being backed by the UN's International Labour Organization. Less than half the brands linked to clothes-making at the building had made donations. Benetton and Matalan said they preferred to support other funds that assisted victims, while the French retailer Auchan claimed that they had no official production taking place in the building when it collapsed so they did not need to contribute towards compensation. Other contributions were relatively small. Walmart, the largest retailer in the world, offered to contribute about $1m compared to more than $8m from the far smaller Primark. The Bangladeshi authorities also came in for international criticism. For years they had made only relatively weak attempts to enforce national building regulations, especially if the landlords involved were politically well-connected. After the disaster, they promised to apply the laws more rigorously, but such promises had been made before.

So, what are the options for Western retailers? One option is to carry on as before and simply source garments from wherever is cheapest. Doing so would obviously be ethically questionable, but would it also carry a reputational cost, or would consumers not enquire too deeply about where garments came from if they were cheap enough? Alternatively, retailers could quit sourcing from Bangladesh until they improve. But that may be difficult to enforce unless they took on the responsibility to police the whole supply chain, right back to the cotton growers. It would also damage all Bangladesh firms – even those who try to abide by safety rules. This, in turn, could be damaging to the retailers' reputations. The third option is to stay and try to change how things are done in the country. Even before the Rana Plaza disaster, retailers had met with some interested parties and governments to develop a strategy to improve safety in Bangladesh's 5,000 factories. Also, some individual retailers had launched initiatives. Walmart had launched a fire-safety training academy and Gap had announced a plan to help factory owners upgrade their plants. However, individual initiatives are no substitute for properly coordinated safety improvements. And anyway, some claim, what right have Western companies to impose their rules on another sovereign state?

## Inter-operations arrangements in supply networks

Writers on supply network management have offered several ways of categorising the arrangements between players in supply networks, and again we distinguish between the market and resource perspectives of relationship.[7] In terms of the resources with suppliers, what is the degree and importance of the activities that are performed in-house – from doing everything in-house, through doing the most important things in-house, to totally outsourcing all activities? In terms of the market relationship, what is the number of separate supply arrangements and how close are they – from using many suppliers with little closeness in the arrangements, through to a few close (or even one very close) supplier?

Figure 5.6 illustrates this. Different types of supply network arrangement can be positioned in terms of their implied resource scope and market relationships. At an extreme on both dimensions is the vertically integrated operation. This type of operation performs everything (or almost everything) within the organisation's boundaries. Unless the organisation has chosen to perform the same activity in many different parts of its operations, there will be few (probably one) internal suppliers. This allows the potential for very close arrangements. At the other extreme, an operation may choose to do nothing in-house and buy in all its requirements – the so-called 'virtual company' that retains relatively few physical resources. Its network is one of information and contacts with other players in the network who can supply all it requires to satisfy its own customers. When the nature of these supply arrangements is

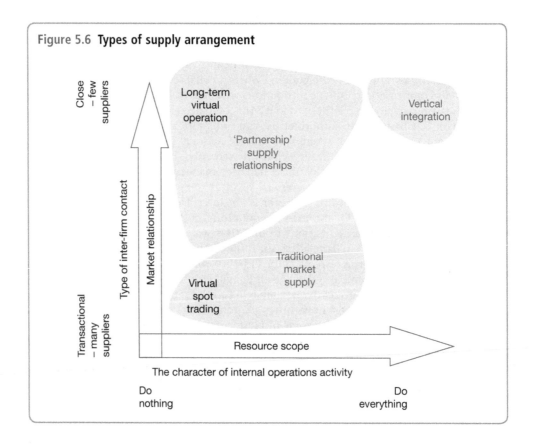

Figure 5.6 **Types of supply arrangement**

temporary and market-based, it is called 'virtual spot trading'. Spot trading means that at any point in time an organisation looks at the spot price, or spot terms of supply, and makes a choice independently of what its previous or future choices might be. But not all virtual operations need be based on transactional market arrangements. When almost all its activities are outsourced, an organisation may seek to compensate for its lack of control by attempting to build long-term and close arrangements with relatively few suppliers. This is the long-term virtual operation.

## Do or buy? The vertical integration decision

The decision whether to *do* (i.e. create, deliver, design, etc.) something within the organisation ('in-house'), or *buy* it from external suppliers (outsource it) is the most fundamental purchasing and supply strategy issue. Too often the decision is made on narrow, short-term cost savings, with firms who are struggling to be price competitive and searching for ways to shift their cost base – often by using global suppliers. Whilst efficiency maximisation should be a central feature of any 'do/buy' analysis, it is a profoundly strategic decision and its results will affect the operations performance objectives in a number of complicated ways (see Table 5.1).

Table 5.1 **How in-house and outsourced supply may affect an operation's performance objectives**

| Performance objective | 'Do it yourself' in-house supply | 'Buy it in' outsourced supply |
|---|---|---|
| Quality | The origins of any quality problems are usually easier to trace in-house and improvement can be more immediate, but can be some risk of complacency. | Supplier may have specialised knowledge and more experience, also may be motivated through market pressures, but communication of quality problems more difficult. |
| Speed | Can mean closer synchronisation of schedules, which speeds up the throughput of materials and information, but if the operation also has external customers, internal customers may receive low priority. | Speed of response can be built into the supply contract where commercial pressures will encourage good performance, but there may be significant transport/delivery delays. |
| Dependability | Easier communications internally can help dependable delivery, which also may help when internal customers need to be informed of potential delays; but, as with speed, if the operation also has external customers, internal customers may receive low priority. | Late delivery penalties in the supply contract can encourage good delivery performance, but distance and organisational barriers may inhibit communication. |
| Flexibility | Closeness to the real needs of a business can alert the in-house operation that some kind of change is required in its operations, but the ability to respond may be limited by the scale and scope of internal operations. | Outsource suppliers are likely to be larger and have wider capabilities than in-house suppliers; this gives them more ability to respond to changes, but they can only respond when asked to do so by the customer and they may have to balance the conflicting needs of different customers. |

▶

Cost

| | |
|---|---|
| In-house operations give the potential for sharing some costs, such as research and development or logistics; more significantly, in-house operations do not have to make the margin required by outside suppliers so the business can capture the profits that would otherwise be given to the supplier. Relatively low volumes may mean that it is difficult to gain economies of scale or the benefits of process innovation. | Probably the main reason why outsourcing is so popular. Outsourced companies can achieve economies of scale and they are motivated to reduce their own costs because it directly impacts on their profits, but extra costs of communication and coordination with an external supplier need to be taken into account. |

The outsourcing debate is just part of a far larger issue that will shape the fundamental nature of any business. Namely, what should the scope of the business be? In other words, what should it do itself and what should it buy in? This is often referred to as the 'do or buy decision' when individual components or activities are being considered, or 'vertical integration' when it is the ownership of whole operations that is being decided. Vertical integration is the extent to which an organisation owns the network of which it is a part. It usually involves an organisation assessing the wisdom of acquiring suppliers or customers. Vertical integration can be defined in terms of three factors.

1 *The direction of vertical integration* – should an operation expand by buying one of its suppliers or by buying one of its customers? The strategy of expanding on the supply side of the network is sometimes called backward or upstream vertical integration, and expanding on the demand side is sometimes called forward or downstream vertical integration.

2 *The extent of vertical integration* – how far should an operation take the extent of its vertical integration? Some organisations deliberately choose not to integrate far, if at all, from their original part of the network. Alternatively, some organisations choose to become very vertically integrated.

3 *The balance among stages* – is not strictly about the ownership of the network, but rather the exclusivity of the relationship between operations. A totally balanced network arrangement is one where one operation produces only for the next stage in the network and totally satisfies its requirements. Less than full balance allows each operation to sell its output to other companies or to buy in some of its supplies from other companies. Fully balanced networks have the virtue of simplicity and also allow each operation to focus on the requirements of the next stage along in the network. Having to supply other organisations, perhaps with slightly different requirements, might serve to distract from what is needed by their (owned) primary customer. However, a totally self-sufficient network is sometimes not feasible, nor is it necessarily desirable.

**Example**    **Contrasting vertical integration strategies: ARM versus Intel[8]**

Nothing better illustrates the idea that there is more than one approach to competing in the same market than the contrasting business models of ARM and Intel in the microchip business. At one point in 2014 ARM's chip designs were to be found in almost 99 per cent of mobile devices in the world, while Intel dominates the PC and server markets. Yet ARM and Intel are very different companies, with different approaches to vertical integration and, some claim, very different prospects for their future. They are certainly of a different size. In revenue terms Intel is around 50 times bigger than ARM. More interestingly, Intel is vertically integrated, both designing and manufacturing its own chips, while ARM is essentially a chip designer, developing intellectual property. It then licenses its processor designs to manufacturers such as Samsung, who in turn rely on subcontracting 'chip foundry' companies to do the actual manufacturing (including Intel, ironically).

Intel's vertically integrated supply network monitors and controls all stages of production, from the original design concept right through to manufacturing. Keeping on top of fast-changing (and hugely expensive – it can cost around $5 billion to build a new chip-making plant) operations requires very large investments. It is Intel's near-monopoly (therefore high volume) of the server and PC markets that helps it to keep its unit prices high, which in turn gives it the ability to finance the construction of the latest semiconductor manufacturing equipment before its competitors. And, having the latest manufacturing technology is important – it can mean faster, smaller and cheaper chips with lower power consumption. As one industry source put it, '*Intel is one of the few companies left with the financial resources to invest in state-of-the-art manufacturing R&D. Everyone else – including all the ARM licensees – have to make do with shared manufacturing, mainstream technology, and less-aggressive physics.*' By contrast, ARM's supply network strategy was a direct result of its early lack of cash. It did not have the money to invest in in its own manufacturing facilities (or to take the risk of subcontracting manufacturing), so it focused on licensing its 'reference designs'. Reference designs provide the 'technical blueprint' of a microprocessor that third parties can enhance or modify as required. This means that partners can take ARM reference designs and integrate them flexibly to produce different final designs. And, over the years, a whole 'eco-system' of tools has emerged to help developers build applications around the ARM design architecture. The importance of ARM's supply 'eco-system' should not be underestimated. It is an approach that allows ARM's partners to be part of the ARM's success, rather than cutting them out of the revenue opportunities.

## The process of do/buy analysis

In addition to the effect on the operation's performance objectives, there are other issues when deciding if outsourcing is a sensible option. If an activity has long-term strategic importance to a company, it is unlikely to outsource it. For example, a retailer might choose to keep the design and development of its website in-house, even though specialists could perform the activity at less cost, because it plans to move into web-based retailing at some point in the future. Nor would a company usually outsource an activity where it had specialised skills or knowledge. For example, a company making laser printers may have built up specialised knowledge in the production of sophisticated laser drives. This capability may allow it to introduce product or process innovations in the future. It would be foolish to 'give away' such capability. After these two more strategic factors have been considered, the company's operations performance can be taken into account. Obviously, if its operation's performance is already too superior to any potential supplier, it would be unlikely to outsource the activity. But also, even if its performance was currently below that of potential suppliers, it may not outsource the activity if it feels that it could significantly improve its performance. Figure 5.7 illustrates this decision logic.

A strategic approach to do/buy decisions requires the firm to reflect on its own relative capabilities and their contribution to competitive advantage. Insights from the

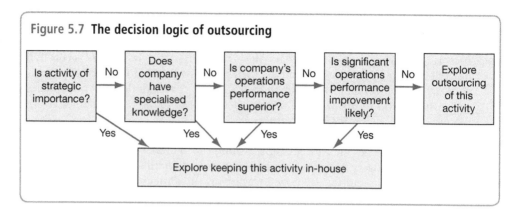

Figure 5.7 **The decision logic of outsourcing**

resource-based view of the firm (see discussion in Chapter 1) are potentially valuable here. Having identified those operations in which the firm has neither any meaningful competitive advantage nor critical strategic need, the analysis also has to look for the most effective sourcing arrangement. In determining what is effective, the firm must pay full attention to the possibility of opportunistic supplier behaviour. Insights from transaction cost economics (see below) are extremely valuable here.

## Transaction cost economics (TCE)

This hugely influential theory, most closely associated with the work of economists Oliver Williamson and, before him, Ronald Coase, attempts to explain the particular structure of firms or, more specifically, why managers choose to undertake certain transactions within the firm as opposed to letting them take place in supply markets. Addressing as it does the fundamental 'do and/or buy' question, it has become a core theory for understanding purchasing and supply behaviour. TCE assumes that most people can't remember everything and often can't figure out what to do with the information they do have (i.e. they exhibit bounded rationality), and exchange partners aren't always completely honest about their intentions (i.e. they may act opportunistically); as a result, transaction costs emerge. For example, in any real buying activity, lack of information about alternative suppliers often leads firms to pay too high a price for something they purchase. The most pragmatic contribution of the theory comes from the dimensions that are used to characterise the nature of different transactions:

- *Frequency.* Why would a firm choose to bring 'in-house' the provision of a good or service that is very rarely used? For example, most firms don't have their own legal department because this is a highly specialised and infrequently used resource.

- *Asset specificity.* In general terms, when transactions involve highly specific assets, such as dedicated production facilities, transaction costs are likely to be higher in a market exchange.

- *Uncertainty.* The greater the duration of a transaction (e.g. contract period) the more difficult it is to envisage all potential eventualities that might occur during the course of the transaction. For example, if entering into a long-term arrangement with a supplier – how do you know if it will still be in business?

**Figure 5.8 Generic sourcing strategies**

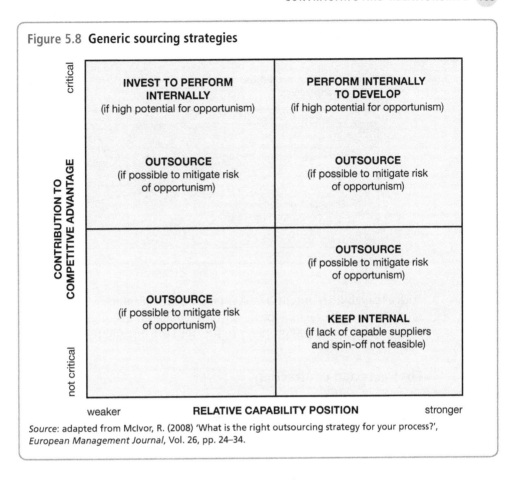

Source: adapted from McIvor, R. (2008) 'What is the right outsourcing strategy for your process?', *European Management Journal*, Vol. 26, pp. 24–34.

Finally, although TCE is very useful it does have limitations. For example, it is often very difficult to measure transaction costs in practice. Equally, although TCE assumes bounded rationality, it doesn't consider other factors such as power, reputation and trust, which affect supply-related decision making. The interaction of these two dimensions suggests a range of generic outsourcing options (see Figure 5.8).

## Contracting and relationships

There are two basic ingredients of any supply arrangement: they are 'contracts' and 'relationships'. Whatever arrangement with its suppliers a firm chooses to take, it could be described by the balance between contracts and relationships (see Figure 5.9). They are strongly complementary and, in the same way that separating marketing and operations decisions can cause major supply dysfunction, a lack of alignment between contracting activity (negotiating, legal procedures, etc.) and relationship strategy can cause significant damage. Moreover, what is clear from the do/buy typology is that effective supply management – effective in the sense that it maximises the benefits to the buyer whilst protecting against opportunism – will require a range of different approaches in different capability and market contexts. If a very strong trusting relationship can be built with a supplier, then the risk of outsourcing even very

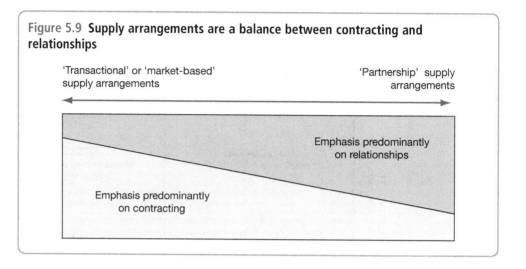

Figure 5.9 **Supply arrangements are a balance between contracting and relationships**

critical capabilities might be acceptable. In the absence of this trust, even the most sophisticated contractual form may be felt to afford insufficient protection – for example, against intellectual property rights (IPR) infringements.

## Contracts and contracting

Contracts are those explicit (usually written, often detailed) and formal documents that specify the legally binding obligations and roles of both parties in a relationship. Using the logic of transaction cost economics (TCE), contracts are intended to both reduce uncertainty (e.g. by providing a clear specification of what is and what is not allowed within a relationship) and minimise the risk of opportunism (e.g. by enforcing legal rules, standards and other remedies implied in law). There are lots of different contract types, usually categorised according to the type of payment.

For a buyer to be able to achieve effective control of its supply by using contracts, three underlining conditions need to be fulfilled.

- *Codification.* Formal contracts are reliant on tasks working broadly to plan and the 'up front' measurability of outcomes.
- *Monitoring.* Formal contracts require monitoring to determine supplier behaviour with regards to the rules set out in the contract.
- *Safeguards.* For effective control there need to be structures in place to enforce the contract – it has to be worth the paper it's written on!

Although the 'best' contract is generally assumed to be the most 'complete' one (the one that covers the greatest number of contingencies), all organisations entering into a contractual exchange face information asymmetry – that is, imperfect and incomplete information about their suppliers' preferences and characteristics. Table 5.2 summarises the problems that can arise as a result of this asymmetric information.

So, whatever the specific cause, in most exchanges one party has an unavoidable informational advantage over another. And, in purely contractual terms, it could potentially be exploited to the benefit of that party at the expense of the partner. This reinforces the tendency to incur additional contract-related costs such as up-front

Table 5.2 **A summary of some problems that can arise from asymmetric information**

| Risk | *'Adverse selection'* | *'Moral hazard'* | *'Hold up'* |
|------|----------------------|------------------|-------------|
| *Timing* | ***Ex ante*** (before signing contract) | ***Ex post*** (after signing a contract) | ***Ex post*** (after signing a contract) |
| *Illustration* | Cannot accurately judge supplier 'quality' as determined by soft skills, education, etc. Cannot judge the future plans of the supplier. | Cannot completely control supplier activities (even if the buyer can fully monitor actions) but observes that supplier maximising own profit instead of realising the buyer's objectives. | Regardless of performance, buyer further employs a particular supplier because of irreversible invest-ments ('sunk costs'). |

supplier search and selection costs (adverse selection risk) and on-going monitoring and enforcement costs (moral hazard and hold-up risks).

## Partnership supply relationships

Partnership supply relationships, sometimes called just 'relationships', are those inter-organisational mechanisms that are not part of formal contractual positions but emerge from ongoing interactions (for example, regular calls to enquire 'how is it going?'). Partnership supply relationships can be based, at least partly, on social processes such as personal bonding. Because of this they tend to be 'emergent' arrangements, developing over time, that are not readily accessible through written documents and often cannot be directly observed. Their development between customers and suppliers in supply networks is sometimes seen as a compromise between the 'extremes' of vertical integration and contractual market trading. It attempts to achieve some of the closeness and coordination efficiencies of vertical integration without the necessity to own the assets, and it attempts to achieve the sharpness of service and the incentive to continually improve, which is often seen as the benefit of traditional market trading. Yet partnership is more than a mixture of vertical integration and market trading; it is an approach to how relationships in supply networks can be formed with a degree of trust that effectively substitutes for the ownership of assets. Partnership relationships can be viewed as strategic alliances that have been defined as:

> 'relatively enduring inter-firm cooperative arrangements, involving flows and linkages that use resources and/or governance structures from autonomous organisations, for the joint accomplishment of individual goals linked to the corporate mission of each sponsoring firm'.[9]

In such an alliance, partners are expected to cooperate – even to the extent of sharing skills and resources – to achieve joint benefits beyond those they could achieve by acting alone. Figure 5.10 identifies some of the major elements that contribute to the closeness that is necessary for partnership and divides them into those that are primarily related to the attitude with which the customer and supplier approach the relationship, and those that relate to the actions undertaken by both parties.

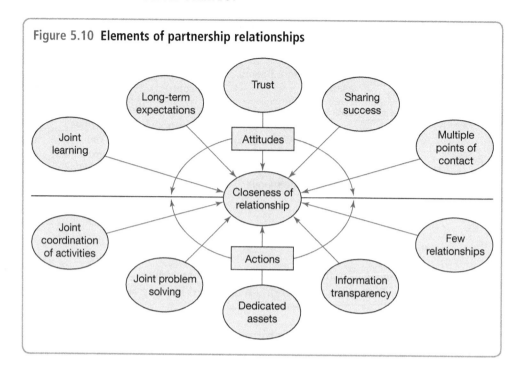

Figure 5.10 **Elements of partnership relationships**

## Closeness

Closeness is the degree of intimacy, understanding and mutual support that exists between partners and reflects the degree of interdependence of the partners. An analogy is often drawn between the concept of closeness in business relations and how the word is used in personal relations. Interpersonal intimacy relies on the attitude with which individuals approach the relationship with their partner/friend, and is also affected by an accumulation of individual actions. Both are important. Intimacy relies on each partner's belief in the other's attitude and motivation in maintaining the relationship. It is that belief that helps dispel any doubt that we can rely on supportive actions from our partner. But it is also those actions that, over time, deepen and enhance the positive beliefs and attitudes concerning the relationship itself. In this way, closeness can be seen as the result of, and the objective of, the interplay between attitudes towards the relationship and the ongoing activities that are the day-to-day manifestations of the relationship.

## Trust

In this context, trust means:

> 'the willingness of one party to relate with another in the belief that the other's actions will be beneficial rather than detrimental to the first party, even though this cannot be guaranteed.'[10]

The greater the degree of trust, the greater is the willingness to make oneself vulnerable to the actions of the other, even though this vulnerability is not as keenly felt because of the existence of trust. If there were no risk involved in a relationship there would be no need for trust, and without some degree of trust there is little justification for taking risks with a partner. Although most organisations are aware of different degrees of trust in their relationships with suppliers or customers, they do not always see trust as an issue to be managed explicitly. Sometimes this is the result of a broad philosophical view of the issue (*'in the end suppliers will always look after their interests, it's foolish to believe otherwise'*). At other times it may be that managers do not believe that such a nebulous concept can be either analysed or indeed managed (*'trust is one of those things which is either there or it isn't, you can't account for it like profit and loss'*). However, almost all research in the area of supplier–customer relationships highlights the role of trust in determining the scope and limits to the relationship. Furthermore, it is at the heart of any understanding of partnership relationships. It is useful to think of trust in three stages.[11] Progression through these states of trust is often associated with time and the accumulation of positive, relationship-building experiences.

- *Calculative trust* is the most basic level of trust that arises because one of the parties calculates that trusting the partner is likely to lead to a better outcome than not trusting them. Underlying this is often the belief that the benefits from maintaining trust are greater than those from breaking it.

- *Cognitive trust* is based on a sharing of each partner's cognitions or understandings of aspects concerned with the relationship. By knowing how each other sees the world, each partner is able to predict how the other will react. In other words, the other partner's behaviour can be anticipated; it therefore comes as no surprise and, therefore, will not threaten the relationship.

- *Bonding trust* is deeper. It is based on partners holding common values, moral codes and a sense of what obligations are due to each other. The partners identify with each other at an emotional level beyond the mere mechanics of the day-to-day transactions that occur. Trust is based on the belief that each party feels, as well as thinks, the same.

### Sharing success

An attitude of shared success means that both partners recognise that they have more to gain through the success of the other partner than they have individually, or by exploiting the other partner. Both customers and suppliers are less interested in manoeuvring in order to get a bigger slice of the pie and are more interested in increasing the size of the pie. It is this belief that helps to prevent individual partners from acting against the interests of the other in order to gain immediate advantage – what economists call opportunistic behaviour. However, it must be clear that the size of pie will indeed be larger if both partners are to cooperate. It also is important to have an agreement as to how the larger pie will be divided up.

### Long-term expectations

Partnership relationships imply relatively long-term relationships between suppliers and customers. The deeper levels of trust require time to develop. Furthermore, there is no need to incur the transaction costs of frequent changes of partner, always assuming that the partner behaves in the best interests of the other. All of which points to long-term relationships – but not necessarily permanent ones. At the heart of the partnership concept is that either party could end the partnership. That is (partly) what keeps each motivated to do the best for the other. Maintaining the relationship is an affirmation that each partner has more to gain from the relationship than from ending it.

### Multiple points of contact

Multiple points of contact means that communication between partners involves many links between many individuals in both organisations. Although this sounds like an action rather than an attitude, it is best thought of as an attitude that allows, and indeed encourages, multiple person-to-person relationships. It implies that both partners are sufficiently relaxed in their mutual dealings not to feel they have to control every discussion and development. Over time, this may lead to a complex web of agreements and understandings being formed, perhaps not in the legal contractual sense of a single 'all-embracing' agreement, but as a multi-stranded, intertwined 'velcro-connected' binding of the two partners.

### Joint learning

Again, this sounds like an action but, in reality, is more of an attitude that encourages approaching the relationship in a sense of mutual learning. Presumably, a partner has been selected on the basis that the partner has something to contribute beyond what the customer can do for themselves. While the customer would not necessarily wish to gain technical knowledge of these core processes (they have, after all, decided not to do these things themselves), it may be able to learn much about the application of whatever is supplied.

### Few relationships

Partnership relationships do not necessarily imply single sourcing by customers, nor does it imply exclusivity by suppliers. However, even if the relationships are not monogamous, they are not promiscuous. Partnerships inevitably involve a limit on the number of other partnerships, if for no other reason than a single organisation cannot maintain intimacy in a large number of relationships. Furthermore, it also implies that the other partner has some say in the others' relationships. Generally, partners agree the extent to which they might form other relationships, which may involve some longer-term threat to their partner.

### Joint coordination of activities

Partly because there are fewer individual partners with whom to coordinate, the quantity, type and timing of product and service deliveries are usually subject to a greater degree of mutual agreement in a partnership relationship. However, notwithstanding the mutuality of interest, it is usually the customer side of a partnership that has a far greater say in the coordination of activities than the supplier. Customers, after all, are closer to the demand-driven end of a supply chain and thus subject to a greater degree of demand-pull. A customer's increased involvement in a supplier's day-to-day planning and control (combined with a degree of trust) allows inventory to be reduced.

### Information transparency

Open and efficient information exchange is a key element in partnership, as well as the natural consequence of the various attitudinal factors discussed earlier. It means that each partner is open, honest and timely in the way they communicate with each other. As a way of encouraging appropriate decisions to be made by each party, and as a way of preventing misunderstanding between the parties, efficient information exchange and dissemination is vital. But, the nature of the information exchanged by the partners may become increasingly sensitive; meaning that it would be embarrassing if one party leaked it. And, if the information is commercially valuable, leakage could mean one partner being placed at a commercial and/or strategic disadvantage.

### Joint problem solving

Partnerships do not always run smoothly. In fact, the degree of closeness between partners would be severely limited if they did. When problems arise, either minor problems concerned with the day-to-day flow of products and services, or more fundamental issues concerned with the nature of the relationship itself, they will need to be addressed by one or both partners. The way in which such problems are addressed is widely seen as being central to how the partnership itself develops. In fact, it can be argued that it is only when problems arise that the opportunity exists to explore fully many of the issues we have been discussing regarding trust, shared success, long-term expectations and so on.

### Dedicated assets

One of the more evident ways of demonstrating a commitment to partnership, and one of the most risky, is by one partner (usually the supplier) investing in resources that will be dedicated to a single customer. A company will only do this if it is convinced that the partnership will be long term, that advantages can be gained by both parties and that the customer will not exploit the investment in order to bargain the price down below what was originally agreed.

## Limitations of partnership relationships

It is important to point out that trust *'not only binds, but also blinds'* buyers and suppliers.[12] Long-standing relationships can result in a sub-optimal information search. That is, organisations become 'locked-into' those relationships and thereby neglect to obtain other relevant information from the market. Such information may, for instance, prove vital for spotting shifting market trends or emerging innovative technology. In summary, as with contracting, relationships (with trust as their key component) are equally unreliable as a stand-alone supply management mechanism and therefore some form of formal control is still needed to reduce the hazards of opportunism. In other words, we need to proactively develop both contracting and relationship-building capabilities.

## E-procurement

By making it easier to search for alternative suppliers, the internet has changed the economics of the search process and offers the potential for wider searches. It has also changed the economics of scale in purchasing. Purchasers requiring relatively low volumes find it easier to group together in order to create orders of sufficient size to warrant lower prices. E-procurement is the generic term used to describe the use of electronic methods in every stage of the purchasing process, from identification of requirement through to payment, and potentially to contract management. Many of the large automotive, engineering and petrochemical companies, for example, have adopted such an approach. Typical of these companies' motives are those put forward by Shell Services International, part of the petrochemical giant:

> *'Procurement is an obvious first step in e-commerce. First, buying through the web is so slick and cheap compared to doing it almost any other way. Second, it allows you to aggregate, spend and ask: Why am I spending this money, or shouldn't I be getting a bigger discount? Third, it encourages new services like credit, insurance and accreditation to be built around it.'*

Generally, the benefits of e-procurement are taken to include the following:

- it promotes efficiency improvements (the way people work) in purchasing processes;
- it improves commercial arrangements with suppliers;
- it reduces the transaction costs of doing business for suppliers;
- it opens up the marketplace to increased competition and therefore keeps prices competitive;
- it improves a businesses' ability to manage their supply chain more efficiently.

The cost savings from purchased goods may be the most visible advantages of e-procurement, but some managers say that it is just the tip of the iceberg. It can also be far more efficient because purchasing staff are no longer chasing purchase orders and performing routine administrative tasks. Much of the advantage and time savings comes from more effective transactions. Purchasing staff can negotiate with vendors faster and more effectively. Online auctions can compress negotiations from months to one or two hours, or even minutes.

### Electronic marketplaces

E-procurement has grown, largely because of the development over the last ten years of electronic marketplaces offering services to both buyers and sellers. They are information systems that allow buyers and sellers to exchange information about prices and product and service offerings, and the firm operating the electronic marketplace acts as an intermediary. These firms can be categorised as consortium, private, or third party.

- *A private e-marketplace* is where buyers or sellers conduct business in the market only with its partners and suppliers by previous arrangement.
- *The consortium e-marketplace* is where several large businesses combine to create an e-marketplace controlled by the consortium.
- *A third-party e-marketplace* is where an independent party creates an unbiased, market-driven e-marketplace for buyers and sellers in an industry.

The internet is also an important source of purchasing information, even if the purchase is actually made by using more traditional methods. Also, even because many businesses have gained advantages by using e-procurement, it does not mean that everything should be bought electronically. When businesses purchase very large amounts of strategically important products or services, they will negotiate multimillion-euro deals, which involve months of discussion, arranging for deliveries up to a year ahead. In such environments, e-procurement adds little value. Deciding whether to invest in e-procurement applications (which can be expensive) depends, say some authorities, on what is being bought. For example, simple office supplies such as pens, paper clips and copier paper may be appropriate for e-procurement, but complex, made-to-order engineered components are not. Four questions seem to influence whether e-procurement will be appropriate.

1 *Is the value of spending high or low?* – High spending on purchased products and services gives more potential for savings from e-procurement.

2 *Is the product or commodity highly substitutable or not?* – When products and services are 'substitutable' (there are alternatives), e-procurement can identify and find lower cost alternatives.

3 *Is there a lot of competition or a little?* – When several suppliers are competing, e-procurement can manage the process of choosing a preferred supplier more effectively and with more transparency.

4 *How efficient are your internal processes?* – When purchasing processes are relatively inefficient, e-procurement's potential to reduce processing costs can be realised.

## First-, second-, third- and fourth-party logistics

An important decision for companies dealing in physical products (such as manufacturers) is how much of the logistical process of organising the movement of goods to trust to outside service providers. The extent and integration of this type of service provision is often referred to as first-, second-, third- or fourth-party logistics (or 1PL, 2PL, 3PL, 4PL for short). However, the distinction between the PL classifications can sometimes be blurred, with different firms using slightly different definitions.

- *First-party logistics* (1PL) – is when, rather than outsourcing the activity, the owner of whatever is being transported organises and performs product movements themselves. For example, a manufacturing firm will deliver directly, or a retailer such as a supermarket will collect products from a supplier. The logistics activity is an entirely internal process.

- *Second-party logistics* (2PL) – is when a firm decides to outsource or subcontract logistics services over a specific segment of a supply chain. It could involve a road, rail, air, or maritime shipping company being hired to transport and, if necessary, store products from a specific collection point to a specific destination.

- *Third-party logistics* (3PL) – is when a firm contracts a logistics company to work with other transport companies to manage its logistics operations. It is a broader concept than 2PL and can involve transportation, warehousing, inventory management and even packaging or re-packaging products. Generally, 3PL involves services that are scaled and customised to a customer's specific needs.

- *Fourth-party logistics* (4PL) – is a yet broader idea than 3PL. Accenture, the consulting group, originally used the term '4PL'. Their definition of 4PL is:

'*A 4PL is an integrator that assembles the resources, capabilities, and technology of its own organization and other organizations to design, build and run comprehensive supply chain solutions.*'

4PL service suppliers pool transport capabilities, processes, technology support and coordination activities to provide customised supply chain services for part or all of a client's supply chain. 4PL firms can manage all aspects of a client's supply chain. They may act as a single interface between the client and multiple logistics service providers, and are often separate organisational entities founded on a long-term basis or as a joint venture between a client and one or more partners. (See the example below on Cooper Bikes.)

- *5PL?* – you guessed it: almost inevitably, some firms are selling themselves as fifth-party logistics provides, mainly by defining themselves as broadening the scope further to e-business.

**Example** **4PL at Cooper Bikes[13]**

Utilising the engineering and technical know-how that has been synonymous with the Cooper Car Company for 50 years, Cooper Bikes, the bicycle division of the company, first launched its new range in 2009. Mike Cooper commented: *'The Cooper Car Company has always had a passion for bicycles and we had been thinking about diversifying the business for a while. We wanted to turn our engineering know-how to making bicycles that offered the best possible components for the best possible price.'*

The bicycle industry in the UK is mostly artisan based, small scale and uses a mixture of UK-manufactured and imported components. Generally, volumes are insufficient to finance large-scale bike manufacturing. By contrast, the recognised centre of mass bike building is in Taiwan, whose exports alone are around 4.5 million bicycles every year. Not surprising, then, that Cooper bikes are mostly made in Taiwan. However, as well as keeping economically viable, Cooper wanted to leverage the appeal of the Cooper brand from the heritage of John Cooper's racing days through the original Mini Cooper to the John Cooper Works partnership with BMW. Accordingly, their designs feature British brands such as Reynolds tubing, Brooks saddles and Sturmey-Archer chain sets – all well-known British names in the cycle world. Of course, Cooper design the bikes and specify the materials and components from their London base.

In order to manage its operations effectively, Cooper decided to use a fourth-party logistics (4PL) service provider to source the completed bike. The outline of the supply chain is shown in Figure 5.11. The 4PL agent, Action Trading International Ltd (ATI), initially sought a frame builder and checked them for quality control, including sending samples to Cooper for approval. Once the frame builder (Maxway) was approved, ATI contracted an assembly company (Sanfa) that would receive the frame from Maxway and build the complete bike ready for shipping to Cooper's distribution centre (DC). Again, completed samples were sent to Cooper for approval. These samples, once approved, were used to attain orders from

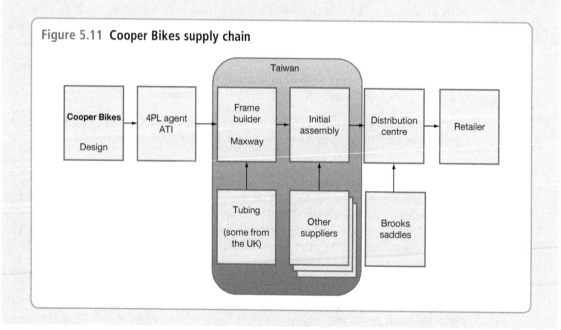

Figure 5.11 **Cooper Bikes supply chain**

retailers. Based on retailer orders, Cooper ordered about 2,000 bikes a year from ATI. ATI manage the procurement and ordering of the parts that are delivered to Sanfa. 'Reynolds 520' tubing is made under licence in Taiwan, but other, more advanced Reynolds tubing is sourced from the UK. Sturmey-Archer was originally a UK brand, but the parts are now made in Taiwan. ATI arranges for the assembled bikes to be delivered to the distribution centre that is based in Munich and is run by Cooper Distribution GmBH – a firm that Cooper Bikes co-own with a German partner. At this point the bikes do not have saddles and the brake levers and bar tape are not fitted, nor are the cable clamps that clip the rear-brake cable to the top tube.

The Brooks Saddles are sent to the Munich DC for fitting (if fitted in Taiwan, they would attract an import tax). In addition to the postponed fitting of the saddles, the DC also fits the brake levers (because different markets have the brake levers on different sides), and since the cables for the levers run under the bar-tape this, too, has to be fitted at the DC once the final destination of the bike is known. The rear-brake cable clips are fitted at the retailer when the bike is put on display. This gives the paint on the frame the maximum drying time and so reduces the potential for damage to the paint. This is particularly important for these steel frames as they would be liable to rust were the paint damaged.

## Which type of arrangement?

There is no simple formula for choosing what form of arrangement to develop, but one can identify some of the more important factors that can sway the decision. Before doing so, however, it is worthwhile reminding ourselves that firms do not make an overall policy decision to adopt one of the three forms of arrangement we have described here. Most have a portfolio of widely differing arrangements, where a whole set of factors have been influential.

From a market perspective, the most obvious issue will be how the firm intends to differentiate itself through its market positioning. If a firm is competing primarily on price then the arrangement could be dictated by minimising transaction costs. If it is competing primarily on product or service innovation, then it may well wish to form a collaborative alliance with a partner with whom it can work closely. Unless, that is, the market from which innovations derive is turbulent and fast growing (as with many software and internet-based industries), in which case it might wish to retain the freedom to change partners quickly through the market mechanism. However, in such turbulent markets a firm might wish to develop arrangements that reduce its risks. One way to do this is to form relationships with many different potential long-term customers and suppliers, until the nature of the market stabilises. Opportunities to develop arrangements, however, may be limited by the structure of the market itself. If the number of potential suppliers, or customers, is small, then it may be sensible to attempt to develop a close relationship with at least one customer or supplier. Opportunities to play off customers and suppliers against each other may be limited. Firms will also be influenced by likely competitor behaviour. For example, close partnership, or even vertical integration, may be seen as a defensive move against a competitor acquiring a major supplier or customer. From an operations resource perspective, economies of scale are important if the total requirement for a given product or service falls below the optimum level of efficiency. Low volume is one of the main factors that prevents firms doing things in-house. The level of transaction costs also is important. Low transaction costs favour market-based arrangements, while the possibility of jointly reducing transaction costs makes partnership an attractive option. Partnership is also attractive when there is the potential for learning from a partner. An absence of any potential learning suggests a more market-based relationship. Finally, although obvious, it is worthwhile pointing out that any sort of outsourcing, whether partnership or market-based, may be as a response to some sort of resource deficiency. That is, a firm will go outside for products and services if it does not have the resources to create them itself.

## Supply network dynamics

Supply chains have their own dynamic behaviour patterns that tend to distort the smooth flow of information up the chain and product moving down the chain. Flow in supply chains can be turbulent, with the activity levels in each part of the chain differing significantly, even when demand at the end of the chain is relatively stable. Small changes in one part of the chain can cause seemingly erratic behaviour in other parts. This phenomenon is known as 'supply chain amplification', 'supply chain distortion', 'the Forrester effect'[14] (after the person who first modelled it) or, most descriptively, 'the bull whip effect'.[15]

For convenience, we shall examine the underlying causes of supply chain behaviour in terms of their:

● quantitative dynamics, and
● qualitative dynamics.

### Quantitative supply chain dynamics

Inventory in supply chains has an 'uncoupling' effect on the operations they connect, which has advantages for each operation's efficiency but it also introduces 'elasticity' into the chain, which limits its effectiveness. This is because of the errors and distortions that are introduced to decision making in the chain. Not that the managers of each individual operation are acting irrationally; on the contrary, it is a rational desire by the operations in the supply chain to manage their production rates and inventory levels sensibly. To demonstrate this, examine the production rate and stock levels for the supply chain shown in Figure 5.12. This is a four-stage supply chain, where an original equipment manufacturer (OEM) is served by three tiers of suppliers. The demand from the OEM's market has been running at a rate of 100 items per period, but in period 2 demand reduces to 95 items per period. All stages in the supply chain work on the principle that they will keep in stock one period's demand. This is a simplification but not a gross one. Many operations gear their inventory levels to their demand rate. The column headed 'stock' for each level of supply shows the starting stock at the beginning of the period and the finished stock at the end of the period. At the beginning of period 2 the OEM has 100 units in stock (that being the rate of demand up to period 2). Demand in period 2 is 95 and so the OEM knows that it would need to produce sufficient items to finish up at the end of the period with 95 in stock (this being the new demand rate). To do this it only needs

Figure 5.12 **Fluctuations of production levels along supply chain in response to small change in end-customer demand**

| Period | Third-tier supplier | | Second-tier supplier | | First-tier supplier | | Original equipment mfg. | | Demand |
|---|---|---|---|---|---|---|---|---|---|
| | Prodn. | Stock | Prodn. | Stock | Prodn. | Stock | Prodn. | Stock | |
| 1 | 100 | 100 100 | 100 | 100 100 | 100 | 100 100 | 100 | 100 100 | 100 |
| 2 | 20 | 100 60 | 60 | 100 80 | 80 | 100 90 | 90 | 100 95 | 95 |
| 3 | 180 | 60 120 | 120 | 80 100 | 100 | 90 95 | 95 | 95 95 | 95 |
| 4 | 60 | 120 90 | 90 | 100 95 | 95 | 95 95 | 95 | 95 95 | 95 |
| 5 | 100 | 90 95 | 95 | 95 95 | 95 | 95 95 | 95 | 95 95 | 95 |
| 6 | 95 | 95 95 | 95 | 95 95 | 95 | 95 95 | 95 | 95 95 | 95 |

Orders → 3 ← Items → 2 ← Items → 1 ← Items → OEM ← Items → Market

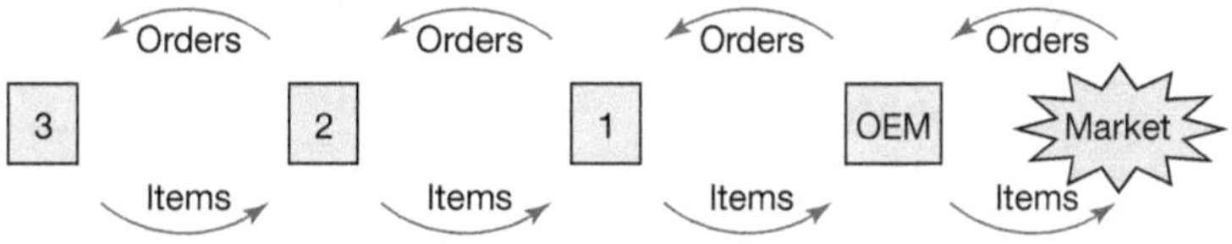

(Note – all operations keep one period's inventory)

*Source*: Slack et al. (2013) *Operations Management*, 7th edn. Harlow, UK: Pearson Education.

manufacture 90 items; this, together with five items taken out of the starting stock, will supply demand and leave a finished stock of 95 items. The beginning of period 3 finds the OEM with 95 items in stock. Demand is also 95 items and therefore its production rate to maintain a stock level of 95 will be 95 items per period. The OEM now operates at a steady rate of producing 95 items per period. Note, however, that a change in demand of only five items has produced a fluctuation of ten items in the OEM's production rate.

Now carry the same logic through to the first-tier supplier. At the beginning of period 2 the second-tier supplier has 100 items in stock. The demand that it has to supply in period 2 is derived from the production rate of the OEM. This has dropped down to 90 in period 2. The first-tier supplier, therefore, has to produce sufficient to supply the demand of 90 items (or the equivalent) and leave one month's demand (now 90 items) as its finished stock. A production rate of 80 items per month will achieve this. It will therefore start period 3 with an opening stock of 90 items but the demand from the OEM has now risen to 95 items. It therefore has to produce sufficient to fulfil this demand of 95 items and leave 95 items in stock. To do this it must produce 100 items in period 3, and so on. Note again, however, that the fluctuation has been even higher than that in the OEM's production rate, decreasing to 80 items per period, increasing to 100 items per period, and then achieving a steady rate of 95 items per period.

This logic can be extended right back to the third-tier supplier. If you do this you will notice that the further back up the supply chain an operation is placed the more drastic are the fluctuations caused by the relatively small change in demand from the final customer. In this simple case, the decision of how much to produce each month was governed by the following relationship:

Total available for sale in any period = Total required in the same period

Starting stock + production rate = Demand + closing stock

Starting stock + production rate = 2 × demand (because closing stock must be equal to demand)

Production rate = 2 × demand − starting stock

## Qualitative supply chain dynamics

Supply fluctuation is also caused because at each link in the chain there is the potential for misunderstandings and misinterpretation, both of what each operation wants and how each is seen to be performing. It may not be able to make the logical association between how it should be serving its customers and, therefore, what demands it should be placing on its own suppliers. There are three logical links that have to be correctly executed:

1 understanding customer's needs correctly;
2 understanding the association between what an operation's customers need and therefore what its suppliers should be providing;
3 ensuring that suppliers really do understand what is required.

These three links represent the information specifying market requirements flowing back up the supply chain. For the chain to be working effectively it is also necessary to ensure that the performance of each part of the chain is monitored. Again, any operation in the chain can identify three logical links that must be in place for effective supply chain performance monitoring:

1 suppliers understand how they are performing;
2 the operation itself understands the association between its supplier's performance and its ability to serve its own customers;
3 the operation is correctly interpreting its customer's view of its own performance.

A model that identifies four types of mismatch that occur between and within each stage in a supply chain is shown in Figure 5.13 and Table 5.3, which pursues the analysis from the viewpoint of operation B – the focal operation. It highlights some obvious questions with which an operation can assess its own supply chain performance. Here, it is enough to point out that, even in the simple three-stage supply chain shown in Figure 5.13, there are ample opportunities for gaps to exist between market requirements and operations performance within the chain.

**Figure 5.13 Potential perception mismatches in supply chains**

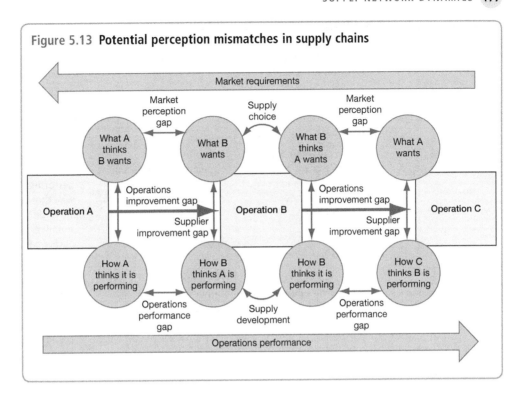

**Table 5.3 Understanding the qualitative dynamics of supply chains**

| Gaps | Definition | What it indicates | Questions to ask |
|---|---|---|---|
| Supply choice | The association between what an operation believes its customer wants and what it believes it needs from its supplier. | The significance of a supply arrangement for competitive success. | What are the key competitive factors for our customers? Which of these rely on our supplier's performance? |
| Supply development | The association between how an operation views its own performance and how it views the performance of its suppliers. | The effectiveness of a supplier arrangement on competitive success. | What have been our competitive successes and failures? To what extent were our competitive successes and failures the result of supplier performance? |
| The supplier improvement gap | The gap between our view of our own requirements and our view of our supplier's performance. | Prioritisation for supplier development. | What do we need from our suppliers? What are we getting from our suppliers? What are the main gaps? |

▶

| The market perception gap | The gap between what we believe we need from our suppliers and what they think we need. | The perceived differences in requirements between customers and suppliers. | Can we be sure that our assumptions concerning our customer's needs and priorities are correct? Can we be sure that our suppliers have the correct assumptions regarding our needs and priorities? |
|---|---|---|---|
| The operations performance gap | The gap between how we see our supplier's performance and how they see their own performance. | The differences in perception of operations performance between customers and suppliers (objective performance could be different from both). | Can we be sure that our customers see our performance in the same way that we do? Can we be sure that our suppliers judge their own performance in the same way that we do? |
| The operations improvement gap | The gap between our perception of what our customers want and our perception of our own performance. | The differences between an internal perception of performance and an internal perception of customer's requirements. | Even assuming our perception of customers' needs and their view of our performance are correct, are we meeting our customers' requirements? |

## Supply chain instability

Put together both qualitative and quantitative dynamics and it is easy to understand why supply chains are rarely stable. Figure 5.14 shows the fluctuations in orders over time in a typical consumer goods chain. One can see that fluctuations in order levels (the demand at the preceding operation) increase in scale and unpredictability the further back an operation is in the chain, with relatively small changes in consumer demand causing wild and disruptive activity swings at the first-tier, and subsequent suppliers. Four major causes of this type of supply chain behaviour can be identified.[16]

- *Demand forecast updating* – this was the cause of the dynamics that were illustrated in Figure 5.10. The order sent to the previous operation in the chain is a function of the demand it receives from its own customers, plus the amount needed to replenish its inventory levels. In effect, the view an operation holds about future demand is being changed every decision period.

- *Order batching* – every time a supermarket sells a box of breakfast cereal it does not order a replacement from its suppliers. Rather, it waits until it needs to order a sufficient quantity to make the order administration, transport, etc. economic. This batching effect may be exaggerated further when many customers batch their orders simultaneously.

- *Price fluctuation* – businesses often use the price mechanism in the short term to increase sales. The result of price promotions is that customers place orders for quantities of goods that do not correspond to their immediate needs, inducing distortions into the supply chain. Promotions have been called the 'dumbest marketing ploy ever' in a now-famous *Fortune* magazine article.[17]

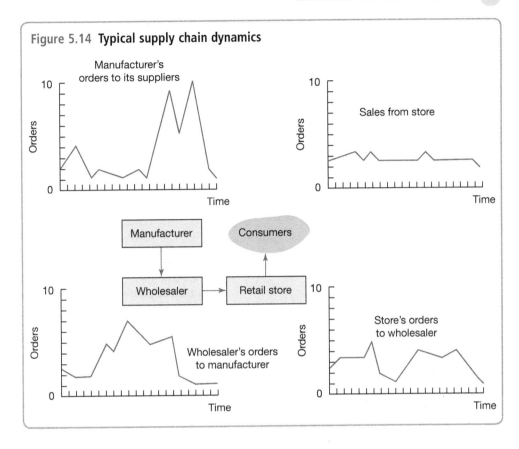

Figure 5.14 **Typical supply chain dynamics**

- *Rationing and shortage gaming* – this cause of supply chain distortion occurs when a supplier rations supplies to its customers. If the customers are aware this is happening, it is in their interests to place a larger order in the hope that they will still get what they need, even after the order has been rationed down.

## Managing suppliers over time

Operations spend most of their supply chain effort in trying to overcome the worst effects of supply chain dynamics. While the first step in doing this is clearly to understand the nature of these dynamics, there are several, more proactive actions that operations take. These include: coordination activities, differentiation activities and reconfiguration activities.

### Coordination

Efforts to coordinate supply chain activity have been described as falling into three categories, as illustrated in Table 5.4.[18]

1 *Information sharing* – demand information, not just from immediate customers, is transmitted up the chain so that all the operations can monitor true demand, free of the normal distortions. Information regarding supply problems, or shortages,

**Table 5.4 Coordinating mechanisms for reducing supply chain dynamic instability**

| Causes of supply chain instability | Supply chain coordination activities | | |
| --- | --- | --- | --- |
| | Information sharing | Channel alignment | Operational efficiency |
| Demand forecast update | Understanding system dynamics <br> Use of point-of-sale (POS) data <br> Electronic data interchange (EDI) <br> Internet <br> Computer-assisted ordering (CAO) | Vendor-managed inventory (VMI) <br> Discount for information sharing <br> Consumer direct | Lead-time reduction <br> Echelon-based inventory control |
| Order batching | EDI <br> Internet ordering | Discount for truck-load assortment <br> Delivery appointments <br> Consolidation <br> Logistics outsourcing | Reduction in fixed cost of ordering by EDI or electronic commerce <br> CAO |
| Price fluctuations | | Continuous replenishment programme (CPR) <br> Everyday low cost (EDLC) | Everyday low price (EDLP) <br> Activity-based costing (ABC) |
| Shortage gaming | Sharing sales, capacity and inventory data | Allocation based on past sales | |

*Source*: adapted from Lee, H.L. et al. (1997) 'The Bullwhip Effect in Supply Chains', *Sloan Management Review*, Spring.

may also be transmitted down the line so that downstream customers can modify their schedules and sales plans accordingly.

2 *Channel alignment* – this is the adjustment of scheduling, material movements, pricing and other sales strategies and stock levels, to bring them into line with each other.

3 *Operational efficiency* – each operation in the chain can reduce the complexity of its operations, reduce costs and increase throughput time. The cumulative effect of these individual activities is to simplify throughput in the whole chain.

## Differentiation – matching supply network strategy to market requirements

Supply networks should differentiate between different market requirements. Supply chains, just like operations, need to ask, 'How do we compete?' If the answer turns out to be, 'We compete in different ways in different parts of the market', then the supply chains serving those markets need to be organised in different ways. If a supply chain is organised in a standardised manner, notwithstanding the different market needs it is serving, it results in the supply distortions described previously. Here we will take an approach articulated by Marshall Fisher of Wharton Business School,[19] who makes a connection between different types of market requirements and different objectives for operations resources.

### Different market requirements

Operations producing one set of products and services may still be serving markets with different needs. For example, Volvo Heavy Truck Corporation, selling spare parts, found itself with a combination of poor service levels at the same time as its inventory levels were growing at an unacceptable rate. Market analysis revealed that spare parts were being used in two very different situations. Scheduled maintenance was predictable, with spare parts ordered well ahead of time. Emergency repairs, however, needed instant availability and were far more difficult to predict. The fact that the parts are identical is irrelevant – they are serving two different markets with different characteristics. It is a simple idea and it applies in many industries. Chocolate manufacturers have their stable lines but also produce 'media-related' specials, which may last only a matter of months. Garment manufacturers produce classics, which change little over the years, as well as fashions that last only one season.

### Different resource objectives

The design and management of supply chains involves attempting to satisfy two broad objectives – speed and cost. Speed means being responsive to customer demand within the chain. Its virtue lies in the ability it gives the chain to keep customer service high, even under conditions of fluctuating or unpredictable demand. Speed can also keep costs down. Fast throughput in the supply chain means that products do not hang around in stock and, therefore, the chain consumes little working capital. Other contributors to keeping costs down include keeping the processes, especially manufacturing processes, well utilised.

### Achieving fit between market requirements and supply chain resource policies

Professor Marshall Fisher's advice to companies reviewing their own supply chain policies is: first, to determine whether their products are functional or innovative; second, to decide whether their supply chain is efficient or responsive; and third, to plot the position of the nature of their demand and their supply chain priorities on a matrix similar to that shown in Figure 5.15.

## Reconfiguration

The most fundamental approach to managing network behaviour is to reconfigure the network so as to change the scope of the activities performed in each operation and the nature of the relationships between them. This could mean changing the trading relationships between operations in the network, or merging the activities currently performed in two or more separate operations into a single operation, or bypassing a stage in a current supply network. When one or more operations are bypassed in a supply chain, the rather clumsy term 'disintermediation' is used. This need not mean that those bypassed operations become totally redundant; it just means that for some final customers they are not used. So, for example, when internet retailers started selling goods to consumers through their websites, it 'disintermediated' retail stores. Yet retail stores still exist; indeed, the internet has become an alternative channel for providing service to customers.

Disintermediation is becoming a particularly significant issue because of the potential of technology to bypass traditional elements in supply chains. For example, originally, corporate banks serving large business clients borrowed money on the

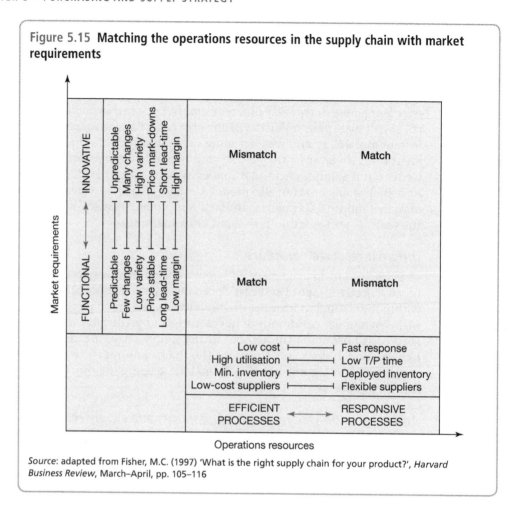

Figure 5.15 Matching the operations resources in the supply chain with market requirements

Source: adapted from Fisher, M.C. (1997) 'What is the right supply chain for your product?', *Harvard Business Review*, March–April, pp. 105–116

capital markets at one rate of interest and lent it to their corporate clients at a higher rate of interest. This 'spread' between the two interest rates was how they earned their revenue. Other services that may have been provided to clients were used to justify, or even increase, this spread. Now large corporations have direct access to those same capital markets, partly because information technology makes it easy for them to do so. Corporate banking now makes its revenue by guiding and facilitating this process, advising clients on the best way to exploit capital markets. Corporate banks charge fees for these services. Disintermediation has caused the whole business model of corporate banking to change.

## Purchasing and supply chain risk

The increased significance of purchasing and supply strategies reflects the growing importance of outsourcing and the reliance on global supply networks. We have already discussed the numerous significant benefits associated with these trends (i.e. efficiency, improved business focus, reduced capital investment, etc.) but, inevitably, increased dependency on suppliers increases exposure to suppliers' risk profiles.

Consider the attractions of building a strong relationship with a single source of supply. This might offer the buyer significant benefits – extra leverage in terms of volume discounts, easy sharing of market and operational data, etc. – but for all the additional capability that such an arrangement provides it also, as per our previous discussion of transaction cost economics, creates extra rigidity and risk. More obviously, since the publication of the first edition of this book, numerous events have had a major impact on global supply networks. But regardless of whether we are discussing the September 11 terrorist attacks, the Severe Acute Respiratory Syndrome (SARS) pandemic in 2002–2003, the Banking Crisis and subsequent economic recession, or the Icelandic Eyjafjallajokull volcano that grounded flights across Europe for a week in 2010 – all of these events produced significant disruptions for supply chains and produced major losses for many companies involved. Even less severe events can trigger significant supply chain problems and have a corresponding impact on financial performance: stock market reactions to announcements of supply disruptions have resulted in market capitalisation declines of as much as 10 per cent.[20]

**Example** **Tsunami disrupts Japan's global supply chains[21]**

The volcanic ash from Iceland that disrupted air transport across Europe provided a preview of how natural disasters could throw global supply chains into disarray – especially those that had adopted the lean, low-inventory, just-in-time philosophy. That was in 2010. Yet the following year an even more severe disaster caused chaos in all supply chains with a Japanese connection, and that is a lot of supply chains. It was a quadruple disaster: an earthquake off Japan's eastern coast, one of the largest ever recorded, caused a tsunami that killed thousands of people and caused a meltdown at a nearby nuclear power plant, which necessitated huge evacuations and nationwide power shortages. The effect on global supply networks was immediate and drastic. Sony Corporation shut down some of its operations in Japan because of the ongoing power shortages and announced that it was giving its staff time off during the summer (when air conditioning needs are high) to save energy. Japanese automobile companies' production was among the worst affected. Toyota suspended production at most of its Japanese plants and reduced and then suspended output from its North American and European operations. Nissan said it would be suspending its UK production for three days at the end of the month due to a shortfall of parts from Japan. Honda announced that it was halving production at its factory in Swindon in the south of England. However, the disruption was not as severe as it might have been. Honda said that the vast majority of the parts used in Swindon are made in Europe, and added that its flexible working policy would allow it to make up for the lost production later in the year. '*Thanks to a working-time agreement, there will be no loss of earnings for the workforce while the company cuts production*', said Jim D'Avila, regional officer for the Unite union.

In the longer term, the disruption caused a debate amongst practitioners about how supply chains could be made more robust. Hans-Paul Bürkner, chief of the Boston Consulting Group, said, '*It is very important now to think the extreme. You have to have some buffers.*' Some commentators even drew parallels with financial meltdowns, claiming that just as some financial institutions proved 'too big to fail', some Japanese suppliers may be too crucial to do without. For example, at the time of the disruption, two companies, Mitsubishi Gas

▶

Chemical and Hitachi Chemical, controlled about 90 per cent of the market for a specialty resin used to make the microchips that go into smartphones and other devices. Both firms' plants were damaged and the effect was felt around the world. So maybe suppliers who have near-monopolies on vital components should spread their production facilities geographically. Similarly, businesses that rely on single suppliers may be more willing to split their orders between two or more suppliers.

## Categories of purchasing and supply risks

So what are the key purchasing supply chain-related risks? Some fall into the category discussed above – major disruptions that become headlines across the world, but others are less public but still potentially devastating in terms of their consequences. Table 5.5 offers a helpful starting point for considering these different risk categories and then, more importantly, deciding what needs to be done to avoid and/or mitigate their impact.

Table 5.5 **Indicative purchasing and supply-related risks**

| Category of risk | Typical drivers of risk |
|---|---|
| Supply disruptions | Natural disaster (e.g volcano) |
| | Industrial dispute (e.g. postal strike) |
| | Supplier bankruptcy |
| | War and terrorism |
| Supply delays | High-capacity utilisation at supply source |
| | Inflexibility of supply source |
| | Poor quality or yield at supply source |
| | International travel (including customs, etc.) |
| Systems breakdown | Upgrading information infrastructure |
| | Web 'attack' on e-commerce |
| Forecast inaccuracy | Long lead times, seasonality, product variety, short life cycles, small customer base |
| | 'Bullwhip effect' caused by sales promotions, incentives, lack of visibility and demand exaggeration |
| Loss of intellectual property | Global outsourcing/overlapping supply base |
| | Weaker IP enforcement regimes |
| Procurement problems | Exchange rate risk |
| | Raw material price increases |
| | Industry-wide capacity utilisation |
| | Weak contracting capability |
| Inventory costs | Rate of product obsolescence |
| | Inventory holding cost |
| | Demand and supply uncertainty |

*Source*: adapted from Chopra, S. and Sodhi, M.S. (2004) 'Managing Risk To Avoid Supply-Chain Breakdown', *MIT Sloan Management Review*, Fall, 46(1).

All these risks identified in Table 5.5 can be managed – not necessarily avoided, but certainly managed. A firm can always avoid single-source supply arrangements, always purchase more capacity than necessary, pay to hedge exchange rate and raw material price risks, never source in countries with weak intellectual property regimes, and so on. The problem is that the 'resilient enterprise' comes at a cost. Yet a firm may be able to find a strategic option that *both* reduces risk and increases profit. For example, when Apple moved in to its digital music delivery model, it could deliver music while eliminating the need for physical inventory, thus reducing holding costs and increasing margins. If no such option can be found, the question is often how much is a firm willing or able to pay in order to manage supply-chain risks. Professors Chopra and Sodhi argue that *'the manager's role here is similar to that of a stock portfolio manager: achieve the highest possible profits for varying levels of risk and do so efficiently'*.

## SUMMARY ANSWERS TO KEY QUESTIONS

### What is purchasing and supply strategy?

A supply network is an interconnection of organisations that relate to each other through upstream and downstream linkages between the different processes and activities that produce value in the form of products and services to the ultimate consumer. Purchasing and supply strategy is the strategic direction of an organisation's relationships with suppliers, customers, suppliers' suppliers, customers' customers, etc. It includes understanding the supply network context, determining supply network relationships and understanding the dynamics of the supply network.

### What should we 'do' and what should we 'buy'?

Deciding on the extent of outsourcing (or lack of vertical integration) involves an operation in drawing the boundaries of its organisation in terms of the direction of integration, the extent, or span, of integration, and the balance between its vertically integrated stages. In doing so, an organisation is primarily trying to leverage the advantages of coordination, and cost reduction, as well as trying to secure product and process learning. However, the disadvantages of vertical integration can be significant. The internal monopoly effect is often held to inhibit improvement. In addition, vertical integration is said to limit economies of scale, reduce flexibility, insulate a firm from innovation and be distracting from what should be the core activities of the firm. In determining what is effective, the firm must pay full attention to the possibility of opportunistic supplier behaviour. Insights from transaction cost economics can be used to help make these types of decision.

### How do we buy; what is the role of contracts and/or relationships?

Contracts are those explicit (usually written, often detailed) and formal documents that specify the legally binding obligations and roles of both parties in a relationship. Contracts and relationships are the basic ingredients of any supply arrangement. Market-based supply depends on contracts, while 'partnerships' are built on relationships. The issue of trust is important in partnerships; strong trusting relationships can facilitate outsourcing even critical activities. Long-term partnerships with a relatively small number of strategic partners have been put forward as a way of maintaining ▶

the coordination and low transaction-cost effects of vertical integration, while at the same time avoiding the internal monopoly effect on operations improvement. The major problem with partnerships, however, is the difficulty of maintaining the attitudes and activities that bolster the high degree of trust that is necessary for them to work effectively.

### How do we manage supply dynamics?

Because supply networks are interrelationships of independent operations, the way in which each operation relates to the others in the network provides an opportunity for supply network distortions. These distortions can be considered in both a quantitative and a qualitative sense. Quantitative distortions are caused by the necessity to manage the inventories between operations in the supply network. This can lead to short-term imbalance between supply and demand, the overall effect of which is to amplify the level of activity fluctuations back up the supply chain. So, relatively small changes in ultimate demand can cause very large changes in the output levels of operations upstream in the supply chain. Qualitative distortions can occur through misperceptions in the way market requirements are transmitted up a supply chain and the way in which operations performance is viewed down the supply chain. It can also be caused by mismatches between what is perceived as required by customers and suppliers and the performance that is perceived as being given to customers.

### How do we manage suppliers over time?

Operations attempt to overcome the worst effects of distortions in the supply chain, usually by one of three methods: coordination, differentiation and reconfiguration. Coordination attempts to line up the activities of operations in a supply chain through information sharing, channel alignment and changes in operational efficiency. Differentiation involves adopting different supply chain management strategies for different types of market. Reconfiguration involves changing the scope and shape of a supply chain. This may mean attempting to merge or reorder the activities in a supply chain, so as to reduce complexity or response times in the network. Increasingly, technology is having the effect of disintermediating operations in supply chains.

### How do we manage supply chain risks?

Increased dependency on suppliers increases exposure to risk. Social, political, geographic and many other factors all produce significant disruptions for supply chains and can produce major losses for companies. There are several categories of purchasing and supply risks, such as supply disruptions, supply delays, systems breakdown, forecast inaccuracy, procurement problems and so on. Supply risk management uses three dynamic dimensions: robustness (reducing the likelihood of risks having an impact), reduction and rapidity (reducing the recovery time).

## Further reading

Barney, J.B. (1999) 'How a firm's capabilities affect its boundary decisions', *Sloan Management Review*, Spring.

Brandenburger, A.M. and Nalebuff, B.J. (1996) *Co-opetition*. New York: Doubleday.

Caplan, S. and Sawhney, M. (2000) 'E-hubs: the new B2B market places', *Harvard Business Review*, May–June.

Chopra, S. and Meindl, P. (2009) *Supply Chain Management*, 4th edition. Harlow, UK: Pearson Education.

Christopher, M., (2011) *Logistics and Supply Chain Management: Creating Value – Adding Networks*, 4th Edition. Harlow, UK: Financial Times/Prentice Hall.

Cohen, S. and Roussel, J. (2004) *Strategic Supply Chain: The Five Disciplines for Top Performance*. New York: McGraw-Hill.

Farrington, B. and Lysons, K. (2005) *Purchasing and Supply Chain Management*, 7th edition. Harlow, UK: Financial Times/Prentice Hall.

Friedman, T. (2006) *The World is Flat: A Brief History of the Globalised World in the Twenty-first Century*. London: Penguin.

Handley, S.M. and Benton Jr, W.C. (2009) 'Unlocking the business outsourcing process model', *Journal of Operations Management*, Vol. 27, pp. 344–361.

Harvard Business School (2006) *Harvard Business Review on Supply Chain Management*. Boston, MA: Harvard Business School Press.

Hines, T. (2013) *Supply Chain Strategies: Demand Driven and Customer Focused*. London: Routledge.

Lysons, K. and Farrington, B. (2005) *Purchasing and Supply Chain Management*, 7th edition. Harlow, UK: Financial Times/Prentice Hall.

Oliveira, A. and Gimeno, A. (2014) 'Supply Chain Management Strategy: Using SCM to Create Greater Corporate Efficiency and Profits', FT Press Operations Management.

Van Weele, A. (2009) *Purchasing and Supply Chain Management: Analysis, Strategy, Planning and Practice*, 5th edition. Boston, MA: Cengage Learning.

## Notes on the chapter

1 *Source:* Sunday Times (2006) 'How British is that car?', 21 May.

2 Brandenburger, A.M. and Nalebuff, B.J. (1996) *Co-opetition*. New York: Doubleday.

3 *The Economist* (2009) 'Globalisation', Economist.com, 20 July.

4 Minahan, T. (2003) 'Global sourcing: What you need to know to make it work', CIO.com, 11 August.

5 We are grateful to our friend and colleague, Dr. Mark Johnson, for this example.

6 *Sources* include: Butler, S. (2014) 'Rana Plaza disaster marked by Oxford Street demonstration', *The Guardian*, Thursday, 24 April; *The Economist* (2013) 'Disaster at Rana Plaza – A gruesome accident should make all bosses think harder about what behaving responsibly means', 4 May; *The Economist* (2013) 'Bangladesh's clothing industry – Bursting at the seams', 26 October.

7 For example, see Ford, D.L. (1998) *Managing Business Relationships*. New York: Wiley.

8 *Sources* include: Burton, G. (2013) 'ARM vs Intel: a battle of business models', *Computing*, 29 May; Turley, J. (2014) 'Intel vs. ARM: Two titans' tangled fate', InfoWorld.com, created 27 February.

9 Parkhe, A. (1993) 'Strategic Alliance Structuring: a game theoretic and transaction cost examination of interfirm co-operation', *Academy of Management Journal*, Vol. 36, pp. 794–829.

10 Child, J. and Faulkner, D. (1998) *Strategies of co-operation: Managing alliances, networks and joint ventures*. Oxford: Oxford University Press.

11 Lane, C. and Backmann, R. (eds) (1998) *Trust Within and Between Organisations*. Oxford: Oxford University Press.

12 Poppo, L., Zheng Zhou, K. and Ryu, S. (2008) 'Alternative origins to interorganizational trust: an interdependence perspective on the shadow of the past and the shadow of the future', *Organization Science*, 19(1), pp. 39–55.

13 This example kindly supplied by Nigel Pye, Assistant Dean, Warwick Business School. With thanks to Cooper Bikes for their cooperation.

▶

14  Forrester, J.W. (1961) *Industrial Dynamics*. Boston. MA: MIT Press.

15  Lee, H.L., Padmanebhan, V. and Wang, S. (1997) 'The Bullwhip effect in supply chains', *Sloan Management Review*, Spring.

16  Ibid., pp. 93–102.

17  Sellers, P. (1992) 'The dumbest marketing ploy', *Fortune*, 126(5), pp. 88–93.

18  Lee, H.L. *et al.*, op. cit.

19  Fisher, M.L. (1997) 'What is the right supply chain for your product?', *Harvard Business Review*, March–April, pp. 105–116.

20  Hendricks, K. and Singhal, V.R. (2005) 'The effect of supply chain disruptions on long-term shareholder value, profitability, and share price volatility', *Production and Operations Management*, 14(1), pp. 35–52.

21  *Sources* include: *The Economist* (2011) 'Broken links - The disruption to manufacturers worldwide from Japan's disasters will force a rethink of how they manage production', Economist Print Edition, 31 March; BBC (2011) 'Sony considers two-week shutdown due to power shortages – Production at some of Japan's biggest companies has been affected by power shortages', BBC News Website, 11 April; BBC (2011) 'Toyota motors has suspended production at most of its plants in Japan and also reduced output at its North American and European factories', BBC News Website, 11 April.

# Process technology strategy

## Introduction

Technology has always had a profound impact on all operations, and with the emergence of powerful new technologies this impact is becoming even more significant. These new technologies can emerge because of the 'push' or 'supply' of new knowledge, or the 'pull' from the 'demand' from market opportunities. Yet, despite a widespread acceptance of its significance, strategic analysis too often treats it as a 'black box' – fit only for technical experts. However, all operations need to understand the analytical dimensions for identifying the technical, managerial and 'operations strategy' characteristics of technology. This is an essential prerequisite for deciding 'what' technological options to explore. Operations managers need to clarify 'what' technology options exist, 'why' potential investments in process technology investments can give strategic advantage, and explore 'how' managers can make such investments work in practice. The risks associated with implementation are particularly important given the number of high-profile failures and claims of waste that seem to go hand-in-hand with such investments.

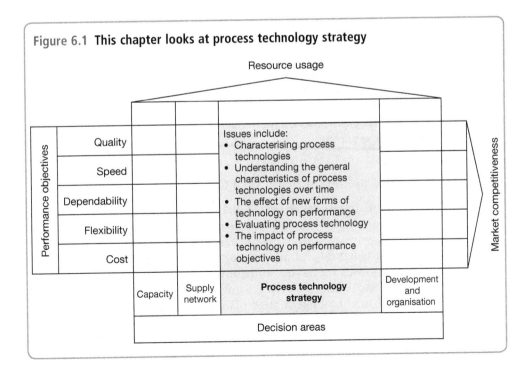

Figure 6.1 **This chapter looks at process technology strategy**

## KEY QUESTIONS

- *What is process technology strategy?*
- *What are suitable dimensions for characterising process technology?*
- *How do market volume and variety influence process technology?*
- *What are some of the challenges of information technology?*
- *How can process technology be evaluated strategically?*

## What is process technology strategy?

Although the word 'technology' is frequently used in managerial conversation, what does this term actually mean? The Oxford Dictionary defines it as: 'The application of scientific knowledge for practical purposes, especially in industry.' We employ a similar generic definition for technology used as a corporate slogan by white goods manufacturer Zanussi. In its advertisements it talked about its products being the result of *the appliance of science*. In this chapter we shall be examining how process technologies add value in the creation of products and services. Therefore, combining the Zanussi slogan with our transformation process view of operations, we can say that process technology is the *'appliance of science to any operations process'*. Note the 'process' in this definition. In this chapter we shall focus upon *process* technology as distinct from *product or service* technology. In manufacturing operations, it is a relatively simple matter to separate the two. For example, the product technology of a computer is embodied in its hardware and software. But the process technology that manufactured the computer is the technology that assembled all the different components. In service operations it can be far more difficult to distinguish process from product/service technology. For example, theme parks such as Disney World use flight simulator technologies in some of their rides. These are large rooms mounted on a moveable hydraulic platform that, when combined with wide-screen projection, give a realistic experience of, say, space flight. But is it product/service or process technology? It clearly processes Disney's customers, yet the technology is also part of the product – the customers' experience. Product/service and process technologies are, in effect, the same thing.

### Direct or indirect process technology

A common misapprehension is that the term 'process technology' describes only technology that acts directly on resource inputs to operations. Yet both manufacturing and service operations are increasingly reliant upon less 'direct' forms of technology. Infrastructural and information technologies that help control and coordinate direct processes are having a major impact on operations. In mass services, such as retailing, stock control systems link specific customer requirements into complex supply chains. Intelligent yield planning and pricing systems provide airlines with the cornerstone of their competitive strategies. Many professional service firms (consultants, accountants, engineers, etc.) utilise information databases in order to retain knowledge and experience. But the distinction between direct and indirect process technology is not always clear. For example, the 'direct' functional capabilities of an insurance company's IT system will define the types of product that the firm can offer. Yet the same IT system's 'indirect' capability to forecast demand, schedule call centre staff to meet demand and issue billing details will be of equal importance.

## Material, information and customer processing

In Chapter 1 we distinguished between operations that predominantly processed materials, information or customers. Process technologies can be similarly classified; Table 6.1 shows some common process technologies of each type. Note that some of these technologies may have secondary, though important, elements in other categories. For example, many material processing technologies used in manufacturing may also be processing information relating to the physical dimensions, or some other property, of what is being processed. A machine, while processing materials, may also be deciding whether tooling needs changing, whether to slow the rate of processing because of rising temperature, noting small variations in physical dimensions to plot on process control charts, and so on. In effect, an important aspect of the technology's capability is to integrate materials and information processing. Similarly, internet-based technologies used by online retailers may be handling specific order information but are also integrating this information with characteristics of your previous orders, in order to suggest further purchases. Sometimes technologies integrate across all three types of technology. The systems used at the check-in gate of airports is integrating the processing of airline passengers (customers), details of their flight, destination and seating preference (information) and the number and nature of their items of luggage (materials). Technologies are increasingly 'overlapping' to become integrating technologies.

## Process technology strategy

We define process technology strategy as:

*'the set of decisions that define the strategic role that direct and indirect process technology can play in the overall operations strategy of the organisation and sets out the general characteristics that help to evaluate alternative technologies'.*

**Table 6.1 Some process technologies classified by their primary inputs**

| Material processing technologies | Information processing technologies | Customer processing technologies |
|---|---|---|
| Flexible manufacturing systems (FMS) | Optical character-recognition machines | Surgical equipment |
| Weaving machines | Management information systems | Milking machines |
| Baking ovens | Global positioning systems | Medical diagnostic equipment |
| Automatic vending machines | Search engines on the internet | Body scanners |
| Container handling equipment | Online financial information systems | Aircraft |
| Trucks | Telecommunication technologies | Mass Rapid Transit (MRT) systems |
| Automated guided vehicles (AGVs) | Archive storage systems | Renal dialysis systems |
| Automatic warehouse facilities | | Cinema digital projection |
| Low-temperature warehouses | | Computer games |
| | | Theme park rides |

Operations managers cannot avoid involvement with process technologies. They work with them on a day-by-day basis and should also be able to articulate how technology can improve operational effectiveness. Other functional areas will, of course, also be involved, such as engineering/technical, accountancy and human resources. Yet it is operations that must act as 'impresario' for other functional areas' contributions, and that is likely to take responsibility for implementation. And to carry out their 'impresario role', operations should have a grasp of the technical nature of process technologies. This does not necessarily mean that operations managers need to be experts in engineering, computing, biology, electronics, or whatever is the core science behind the technology, but they need to know enough about the technology to be comfortable in evaluating technical information, and be able to ask relevant questions of the technical experts. These questions include the following.

- What does the technology do that is different from other similar technologies?
- How does it do it?
- What constraint does using the technology place on the operation?
- What skills will be required from the operations staff in order to install, operate and maintain the technology?
- What capacity does each unit of technology have?
- What is the expected useful lifetime of the technology?

## Technology planning – technology roadmapping

However operations managers are involved with the strategic development of process technologies, it is likely to be in consultation and collaboration with other parts of the firm. It is also likely to be in the context of some kind of formal planning process such as technology roadmapping. A technology roadmap (TRM) is an approach that provides a structure that attempts to assure the alignment of developments (and investments) in technology, possible future market needs and the new development of associated operations capabilities. Motorola originally developed the approach in the 1970s so that it could support the development of its products and their supporting technologies. Bob Galvin, then Motorola's CEO, defined a TRM as: '*an extended look at the future of a chosen field of inquiry composed from the collective knowledge and imagination of the brightest drivers of change in that field*'. A TRM is essentially a process that supports technology development by facilitating collaboration between the various activities that contribute to technology strategy. It allows technology managers to define their firm's technological evolution in advance by planning the timing and relationships between the various elements that are involved in technology planning. For example, these 'elements' could include the business goals of the company, market developments or specific events, the component products and services that constitute related offerings, product/service and process technologies, the underlying capabilities that these technologies represent, and so on. Figure 6.2 shows the generic form of technology roadmaps, while Figure 6.3 shows an example of a technology roadmap for the development of products/services, technologies and processes for a facilities management service.

The benefits of TRMs are mainly associated with the way they bring together the significant stakeholders involved on technology strategy and the various (and often differing) perspectives that they have. The approach forms a basis for communication,

Figure 6.2 **The generic form of technology roadmaps (TRM)**

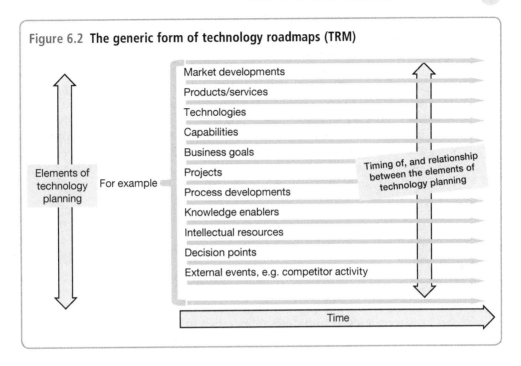

Figure 6.3 **Simplified example of a technology roadmap for the development of products/services, technologies and processes for a facilities management service**

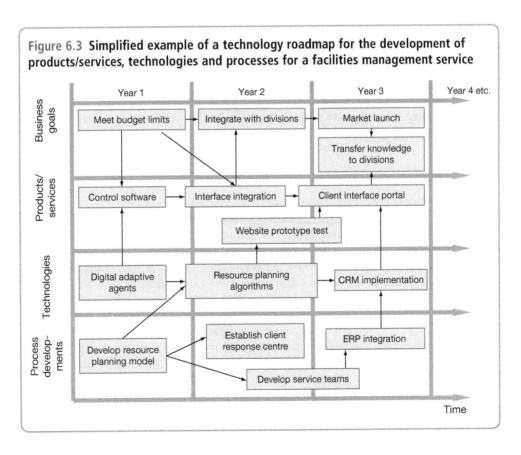

and possibly consensus. After all, it does tackle some fundamental questions that concern any technology strategy. Why do we need to develop our technology? Where do we want to go with our technological capabilities? How far away are we from that objective? How can we get to where we want to be? In what order should we do things? By when should development goals be reached? Yet TRMs do not offer any solutions to any firm's technological strategic options; in fact they need not offer options or alternative technology trajectories. They are essentially a narrative description of how a set of interrelated developments should (rather than will) progress. Because of this they have been criticised as encouraging over-optimistic projections of the future. Nevertheless, they do provide, at the very least, a plan against which technology strategy can be assessed.

## Process technology should reflect volume and variety

Although process technologies vary between different types of operation, there are some underlying characteristics that can be used to distinguish between them. These characteristics are strongly related to volume and variety, with different process technologies appropriate for different parts of the volume–variety continuum. High variety–low volume processes generally require process technology that is *general purpose,* because it can perform the wide range of processing activities that high variety demands. High volume–low variety processes can use technology that is more *dedicated* to its narrower range of processing requirements. Within the spectrum from general purpose to dedicated process technologies three characteristics in particular tend to vary with volume and variety. The first is the extent to which the process technology carries out activities or makes decisions for itself – that is, its degree of 'automation'. The second is the capacity of the technology to process work – that is, its 'scale' or 'scaleability'. The third is the extent to which it is integrated with other technologies – that is, its degree of 'coupling' or 'connectivity'. We shall look at each of these characteristics.

### Scale/scalability – the capacity of each unit of technology

Scale is an important issue in almost all process technologies and is closely related to the discussion in Chapter 4 dealing with capacity strategy. Here we delve inside 'capacity' to explore how individual units of process technology go to make up the overall capacity of an operation. For example, consider a small regional airline serving just one main route between two cities. It has an overall capacity of 2,000 seats per day in either direction on its route. This capacity is 'defined' by its two 200-seater aircraft making five return journeys each day between the two cities. An alternative plan would be to replace its two identical 200-seat aircraft with one 250-seater and one 150-seater. This gives the company more flexibility in how it can meet varying demand levels throughout the day. It also may give more options in how its aircraft are deployed should it take on another route and buy additional aircraft. Of course, costs will be affected by the company's mix of aircraft. Generally, at full utilisation larger aircraft offer superior cost performance per passenger-mile than smaller aircraft. The important point here is that by adopting units of process technology (aircraft) with different scale characteristics, the airline could significantly affect its operation's performance. Factors influencing the desirability of large-scale technology include the following.

- *What is the capital cost of the technology?* Broadly speaking, the larger the unit of technology the more its capital cost but the less its capital cost per unit of capacity. Similarly, the costs of installing and supporting the technology are likely to be lower per unit of output. Likewise, operating (as opposed to capital) costs per unit are often lower on larger machines, the fixed costs of operating the plant being spread over a higher volume.

- *Can the process technology match demand over time?* As discussed in Chapter 4, there is a traditional trade-off between large increments of capacity exploiting economies of scale but potentially resulting in a mismatch between capacity and demand, and smaller increments of capacity with a closer match between capacity and demand but fewer economies of scale. The same argument clearly applies to the units of process technology that make up that capacity. Also, larger increments of capacity (and therefore large units of process technology) are difficult to stream on and off if demand is uncertain or dynamic. Small units of process technology with the same or similar processing costs as larger pieces of equipment would reduce the potential risks of investing in the process technology. This is why efficient but smaller-scale technologies are being developed in many industries. Even in industries where received wisdom has always been that large scale is economic (i.e. the steel and electricity generation), smaller, more flexible operations are increasingly amongst the most profitable.

- *How vulnerable is the operation?* Building an operation around a single large machine introduces greater exposure to the risk of failure. Suppose that the choice is between setting up a mail sorting operation with ten smaller or one very large machine. If there is a single machine failure, then the operation with ten machines is more robust, as 90 per cent of the mail can still be sorted. In the large-scale machine operation, no mail can be sorted.

- *What scope exists for exploiting new technological developments?* Many forms of process technology are advancing at a rapid rate. This poses a threat to the useful life of large units of technology. If an operation commits substantial investment to a few large pieces of equipment, it changes them only infrequently and the opportunities for trying out new ideas are somewhat limited. Having a broader range of different technological options (albeit each of a smaller scale) makes it easier to take advantage of new developments – providing the operation can cope with potential inconsistencies.

### From 'scale' to 'scalability'

Information processing technologies are an important exception to some of the issues discussed above. Information is transmitted far more easily between units of technology than between either materials or customers. Information technology also has the capability of overcoming traditional links between volume and variety. Both of these factors mean that information technology processes can be linked relatively easily to combine their total processing capacity. Because of this, in many new technologies the dynamic capacity challenges relate less to absolute scale and more to scalability. By scalability we mean the ability to shift to a different level of useful capacity quickly, cost-effectively and flexibly. Yet one of the key challenges for information processing technology is still to judge how much computing capacity is required. This is especially true if the process technology is customer-facing and in a dynamic marketplace (such as e-commerce), where demand uncertainty and variability are common. As many business-to-consumer internet-based businesses have discovered, too little capacity means that the technology (website server, etc.) can quickly become swamped and lead to extreme customer dissatisfaction. (It is worth reflecting at this point on your own experience of trying to connect to and use a very busy website.) Conversely, too much technology means excess invested capital to service too few customers.

Scalability, however, does depend on the ability of IT systems to work together. Upgrading the functionality (what it can do) of an IT system is usually a matter of evolution rather than revolution. Sometimes totally separate and only partially connected systems are installed alongside existing ones. So, some IT systems finish up with patched and inconsistent system architectures. This does not mean that they are in themselves inefficient. However, it does make them difficult to scale up because they do not fit conveniently with other units of technology. Thus, the underlying consistency and stability of an IT platform's architecture is an important determinant of its scalability. Also, a more stable platform often will have support staff who have developed a greater depth of expertise. Similarly, if IT is stable and standardised, one of the possible reasons for changing a process is removed. It is partly because of these issues that many organisations have adopted 'off-the-shelf' internal business process management systems, such as enterprise resource planning (ERP). Indeed, many adopters of ERP systems have chosen to change their business processes to match the IT, rather than the other way around.

## Degree of automation/'analytical content' – what can each unit of technology do?

Very few technologies operate continually, totally and completely in isolation, without ever needing some degree of human intervention. The degree of human intervention varies from almost continual (the driver's control over a bus) to the very occasional (an engineer's control in an automated pharmaceutical plant). This relative balance between human and technological effort is usually referred to as the capital intensity or degree of automation of the technology. Early applications of automation to material transformation processes revolved around relatively simple and regularly repeated tasks because technology is 'dumber' than humans; it cannot match people in many delicate tasks or those requiring complex (and especially intuitive) thought processes. But low automation often means higher direct costs – a requirement for control skills and human creativity – whereas automated technology can repeat tasks endlessly and is capable of repeating these tasks with precision, speed and power. However, in many cases there have not been overall savings associated with automation, especially if a complex system requires regular and expensive maintenance. It is common for a shift towards greater capital intensity to necessitate the employment (either directly or contractually) of more engineers, programmers, etc. who normally come with a much higher price tag than the direct labour that was replaced. Other potential downsides of automated technology include possible decreases in flexibility (labour-intensive technologies can usually be changed more readily than capital-intensive technologies) and dependability (highly automated technology can be less robust than a more basic 'tried and tested' technology).

### From 'automation' to 'analytical content'

Again, information-processing technologies are, to some extent, an exception. Even when considering automation of the most sophisticated forms of material and customer processing technology there is usually an underlying strategic choice to be made about the balance between people and technology. The choice is often between emphasising the power, speed and general physical abilities of automation against the flexible, intuitive and analytical abilities of human beings. However, an increasing number of purely information transformation processes are entirely automated (including most processing technology in the financial services sector, for instance). We need a different metric to differentiate between different information processing technologies that are 100 per cent 'automated', or very close to it.

Consider the range of new information-based technologies. Sophisticated data management and decision-making systems are being used to enhance existing processes. These might include the use of expert systems to help authorise financial transactions or adding automatic measurement and process control to manufacturing technology. Two drivers influence the analytical content of the technology. The first is the amount of parallel processing required. One of the real operational attractions of IT is that it can transform sequential tasks into ones that can be carried out in parallel. This parallel processing could be in a complex multinational design process, such as that used by Ford for their global product development platform, or more simply in IT 'work-flow' applications for compiling an insurance policy. In order to do this, and regardless of the precise tasks, the IT requires internal scheduling and data management protocols that are inherently more analytical than those employed in a straightforward sequential process. The second is the level of customer interaction. The greater the degree of customer interaction that is required, the greater is the information 'richness' that must be inputted, processed and outputted. This can be directly related to the underlying task complexity with which the technology has to cope. Although using your mobile phone to order cinema seats with a credit card is a valuable automated and interactive service, such a system is really only a virtual vending machine. The system has a finite (and relatively small) number of options (just like the limited range of snack foods in a vending machine). The analytical content of the system, such as checking seat availability and verifying the credit card, is relatively low (using the vending machine analogy again, it is like checking if a particular candy bar has run out and then verifying that coins are correct).

## Degree of coupling/connectivity – how much is joined together?

Process technologies are increasingly coupled together. Many newer advanced manufacturing technologies derive their competitive cost and quality advantages from the 'coupling' or integration of activities that were previously separated. Coupling could consist of physical links between pieces of equipment – for example, a robot removing a piece of plastic from an injection moulding machine and locating it in a machine tool for finishing, or it could mean merging the formerly managerial tasks of scheduling and controlling these machines with their physical activities to form a synchronised whole. Many of the direct benefits associated with increased coupling echo those described with respect to automation and scale. For example: the integration of separate processes often involves high capital costs; increasing coupling removes much of the fragmentation caused by physical or organisational separation (what is called 'straight through processing' in financial services); closer coupling can lead to a greater degree of synchronisation, thereby reducing work-in-process and costs; and closer integration can increase exposure (with positive and negative effects) if there is a failure at any stage.

### From 'coupling' to 'connectivity'

Coupling in information processing technology once meant physically 'hard-wiring' together disparate process elements and, as a result, was economically viable only at higher volumes and lacked the flexibility to cope with very high variety. However, more recently, information processing has moved towards platform independence, allowing communication between computing devices regardless of their specification, and increasingly organisational boundaries. For example, supermarkets have dramatically altered the way they manage their buying process. Connected IT systems allow many suppliers access to a common data portal that gives real-time information about how products are selling in all stores. Such systems enable the supply companies to modify their production schedules in order to meet demand more precisely and ensure fewer stock-outs. Here the defining technological characteristic associated with platform independence is not coupling in the classic sense of integration, but rather a greater degree of connectivity.

The issues connected with connectivity are similar to those concerned with scalability and analytical content. Low connectivity is often associated with idiosyncratically designed, bespoke and 'legacy' IT systems. Often such systems come with restricted opportunities for the access that is a prerequisite to connectivity. High-connectivity technologies, on the other hand, are usually based on the platform independence discussed above and have the bandwidth capacity to enable rich communications. Sometimes, however, their very openness and easy access can give security concerns. Much new technology, although offering wonderful levels of connectivity, creates new opportunities for fraud, 'denial of service' attacks and so on. Two key drivers have allowed 'connectivity' to develop at such a phenomenal rate.

1 *Hardware development* – Client/server systems (initially promoted as a less costly replacement for mainframe technology) have permitted the separation of user interfaces, processing applications and data sources. This has encouraged the development of interconnection technology, including software protocols and connection technology (such as bandwidth enhancement).

2 *Software development* – Arguably, the distinguishing feature of the development of the World Wide Web has been the adoption of a universal browser interface, which has considerably expanded the potential for connectivity.

---

**Example** | **Technology or people? The future of jobs[1]**

In his book, *The Power of Habit*, Charles Duhigg relates a story to demonstrate that human beings are more predictable than we sometimes like to think. A man walked into a supermarket to complain to the manager. They had been sending direct mail to the man's daughter containing discount vouchers for baby clothes and equipment. 'She is only in high school', the father protested. The manager apologised profusely. 'It's the fault of a new programme that predicted pregnancy based on the buying behaviour of our customers', he said. It was, obviously, a mistake and he was very sorry. A few days later, the man again visited the supermarket and said that it was his turn to apologise. His daughter was indeed pregnant and due to give birth in a few months' time. The point of the story is that technology is increasing in sophistication to the extent that it is now capable of performing tasks that previously required skilled people making judgments based on insight and experience. Moreover, technology can often do those tasks better. A piece of software has replaced the marketing team trying to guess who to sell baby clothes to. So, technology is not only replacing people, but it is also 'climbing the skills ladder all the time'.

Of course, technological advances have always had an impact on the type of jobs that are in demand by businesses and, by extension, the type of jobs that are eliminated. So, much of the highly routine work of some mass manufacturing, or the type of standardised accounting processes that pay invoices, have been overtaken by 'the robot and the spreadsheet'. Yet the type of work that is more difficult to break down into a set of standardised elements is less prone to being displaced by technology. The obvious examples of work that is difficult to automate are the type of management tasks that involve decision making based on judgment and insight – teaching small children, diagnosing complex medical conditions, and so on. However, the future may hold a less certain future for such jobs. As the convenience of data collection and analysis becomes more sophisticated, and process knowledge increases, it becomes easier to break more types of work down into routine constituents, which allows them to be automated. Carl Benedikt Frey and Michael Osborne, of the University of Oxford, maintain that the range of jobs that are likely to be automated is far higher than many assume, especially traditionally white-collar jobs such as accountancy, legal work, technical writing and (even) teaching. It is not simply that technology is getting cleverer; in addition it can exploit the capability to access far more data. Medical samples can be analysed cheaper and faster by image-processing software than by laboratory technicians, case precedents can be sourced by 'text-mining' programs more extensively than by para-legals, and computers can even turn out new stories based on sports results or financial data. Frey and Osborne go so far as to estimate the probability that technology will mean job losses for certain jobs in the next two decades (bravely, because such forecasting is notoriously difficult). Amongst jobs most at risk are telemarketers (0.99, where 1.0 = certainty), accountants and auditors (0.94), retail salespersons (0.92), technical writers (0.89) and retail estate agents (0.86). Those jobs least likely to be replaced include actors (0.37), firefighters (0.17), editors (0.06), chemical engineers (0.02), athletic trainers (0.007) and dentists (0.004).

## The product–process matrix

Generally, the characteristics of process technology affect cost and flexibility, as shown in Figure 6.4. All of the three technology dimensions described above are strongly related. For example, the larger the unit of capacity, the more likely it is to be capital- rather than labour-intensive; this gives more opportunity for high coupling between its various parts. Conversely, small-scale technologies, combined with highly skilled staff, tend to be more flexible than large-scale, capital-intensive, closely coupled systems. As a result, these systems can cope with a high degree of product variety or service customisation ('boutique' strategy consulting firms are an example of this). Conversely, where flexibility is of little importance (with standardised, low-cost products such as industrial fastenings, or a mass transaction service

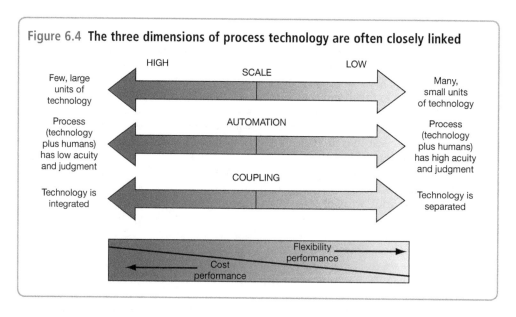

Figure 6.4 **The three dimensions of process technology are often closely linked**

such as letter sorting) but achieving dependable high volumes and low unit costs is critical, these inflexible systems come into their own. In IT-rich technologies, scalability generally depends upon connectivity (hence the emphasis upon standardisation in systems architecture and underlying operating processes). The analytical functionality that is so central to complex task automation normally requires different applications and data sources, so the greater the connectivity, the greater the analytical power, and so on. Remember, though, although the three dimensions of process technology do often go together in this way, they do not always match perfectly.

Several authors have also made a further link to the volume and variety requirements of the market. The logic goes something like this: companies serving high-volume, and therefore usually low-variety, markets usually have a competitive position that values low prices, therefore low-cost operations are important and process technologies need to be large, automated and integrated. Conversely, low-volume, high-variety operations need the flexibility that comes with small-scale, loosely coupled technologies with significant human intervention. This idea is incorporated in the product–process matrix, which was first described by Professors Robert Hayes and Stephen Wheelwright (both of Harvard Business School). Although they used it to link the volume and variety requirements of the market with process design in general, here we use it to draw a link between volume and variety on the one hand and the three dimensions of process technology on the other. This is shown in Figure 6.5. The relationship between the volume/variety and process technology dimensions suggests that there is a 'natural' diagonal fit, and that deviating from the 'diagonal' will therefore have predictable consequences for the operation.

Operations to the right of the diagonal have more capability to deal with their requisite variety than is necessary. Such surplus capability will normally be associated with excess operating costs. Similarly, operations to the left of the diagonal have insufficient flexibility to cope with their requisite variety. This may result in substantial opportunity costs (being unable to fulfil orders economically), not to mention

## Figure 6.5 **The product–process matrix and the technology dimensions**

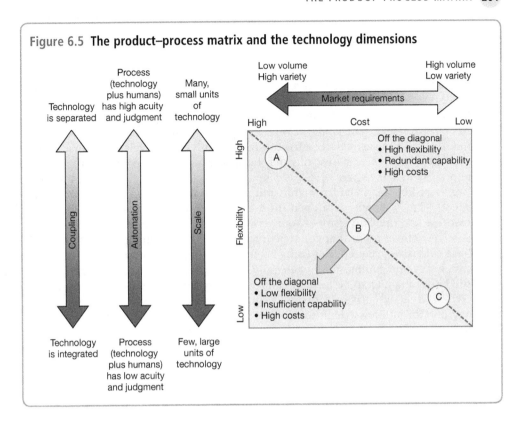

the competitive impact of having insufficient capability. Remember, though, that the matrix cannot prescribe the 'correct' process technology. It can, however, give a general idea of how an operation's process technology profile will need to be adapted as its market context changes.

### Moving down the diagonal

Operations will change their position in the matrix. For example, a 'home-made' luxury ice-cream product, selling a few litres in a farm shop, might begin life by being manufactured in a farmer's own kitchen using domestic equipment (position A in Figure 6.5). Growth in sales (and health and safety legislation) would necessitate investment in a small production facility, although, because of the different varieties, the production unit will still need some flexibility (position B in Figure 6.5). Ultimately, if projected demand for some flavours and sizes reaches mass-market levels, major continuous-flow process investment will be necessary (position C in Figure 6.5). Equally, at this stage the product might become attractive to a large established manufacturer because the volume and variety of demand would match its existing integrated production facilities.

The natural trajectory of movement 'down' the product/process matrix can be observed in many different operational contexts. Many financial service firms, for instance, have been able to make major reductions in their back-office operations by reducing clerical and administrative staffing and cost levels through investment in large-scale, integrated, automated process technology.

**Universal Robots[2]**

Just because a job can be automated does not mean that it necessarily will be; the economics have to justify the investment. For example, Toyota, Nissan and other Japanese car producers rely heavily on robot technology when making cars in Japan. However, in their Indian factories they are far more likely to use labour that is relatively cheap and plentiful. In countries such as Denmark, where employee-related costs are particularly expensive, robotics can be a particularly attractive investment, even for relatively small companies. The productivity gains from investing in robotic technology could help to stop some companies relocating to somewhere with less expensive labour costs. This is one of the factors driving Universal Robots, a Danish manufacturer of robotic arms aimed at small manufacturing clients. The company developed from a group of engineers at the Danish Technological Institute and the University of Southern Denmark. Its founders wanted to produce a light, relatively cheap robot that could be installed and programmed by customers who did not have extensive experience of using robotics. At the time, competitors' robots were expensive, heavy and cumbersome – generally unsuitable for shorter, more agile tasks. 'SMEs will still be our main focus because we can really make a big difference to them', says Enrico Krog Iversen, chief executive of Universal. 'But we also see that large companies like our technology because it allows them to robotise a number of applications using their traditional, industrial models.'

### Market pressures on the flexibility/cost trade-off?

The traditional flexibility/cost trade-off inherent in the scale, automation and integration dimensions of process technology (and the product/process matrix for that matter) is coming under increasing pressure from more challenging and demanding markets. In many sectors, increased market fragmentation and the demand for more customisation is reducing absolute volumes of any one type of product or service. Simultaneously, shortening product/service life cycles can mean periodic step changes in the requirements placed on an operation and its process technology. This can severely reduce the potential for applying large-scale and relatively inflexible, though traditionally low-cost, technologies. Yet, at the same time, there is increasing pressure to compete on cost, which is driving ongoing reductions in direct labour and placing increased emphasis on automation. In fact, for many traditionally labour-intensive sectors such as the banking industry referred to earlier, absence of sufficient technological investment (and the corresponding presence of 'too many staff') has a significant impact on analyst and shareholder confidence and therefore share price. Both these pressures are placing conventional process technology solutions under strain (see Figure 6.6). Of course, this competitive challenge has proved to be simply too much for many operations but, interestingly, many of those that have survived and prospered have not abandoned technology in their operations strategies. Rather, many operations have more fully embraced process technology, albeit in new IT-rich forms. Indeed it is increasingly difficult to overstate the impact that information technology is having upon organisational life. There is almost no sphere of operations where computing technology in one form or another has not had a substantial impact.

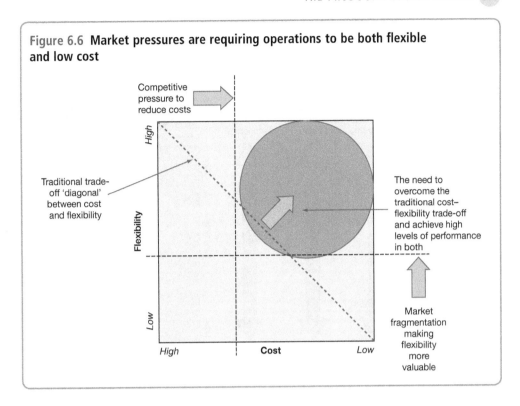

**Figure 6.6 Market pressures are requiring operations to be both flexible and low cost**

## Process technology trends

So, markets seem to be demanding both greater flexibility and lower costs simultaneously from process technology. To the traditional mind-set, which we illustrated in Figure 6.5, this seems to be difficult, bordering on impossible. Yet, remember our discussions on trade-offs between performance objectives back in Chapter 2? There we saw the development and improvement of operations (including process technology) as being a process of overcoming trade-offs. Now we must include developments in information technology, especially their effect of shifting traditional balances and trade-offs. In effect, we have argued that emerging scalability, analytical content and connectivity characteristics have enabled process technologies to enhance their flexibility while still retaining reasonable efficiency and vice versa. In other words, these trends in process technology are having the net effect of overcoming some of the traditional trade-offs inherent within the dimensions of process technology. This has, for some industries, changed the nature of the product–process matrix, which we discussed earlier. Figure 6.7 shows how three separate but connected ideas have come together.

- The three dimensions of process technology – scale, automation and coupling – are related to the volume/variety characteristics of the market. In traditional process technologies, especially those with relatively little IT element, large, automated and tightly coupled technologies were capable of processing at low cost but had relatively little flexibility. This made them suitable for high-volume, low-variety processes. If process requirements were for high variety but low volume, process technology is likely to consist of smaller separated units with relatively little automation.

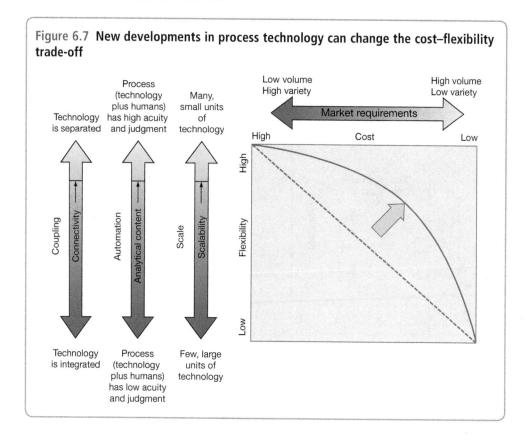

**Figure 6.7** New developments in process technology can change the cost–flexibility trade-off

- Trends in the development of each dimension of process technology, especially those related to their increasing richness in information processing, are overcoming some of the traditional trade-offs within each dimension. In particular, technology with high levels of scalability can give the advantages of flexible, small-scale technology and yet be quickly expanded if demand warranted it. Similarly, even high-volume information processing technology can still display the relatively high analytical content at one time reserved for more manual processes. Finally, technology with high connectivity can integrate processes without the rigidity once associated with high coupling.

- Market trends are themselves calling for simultaneously high performance in both cost and flexibility. No longer is it acceptable to suffer high costs if flexibility is demanded by the market, nor operations rigidity if costs need to be kept low. As far as market requirements are concerned, the ideal area in the traditional product–process matrix is one that delivers both low cost and high flexibility.

This is why information processing technology has had such an impact in so many industries. In effect it has partially overcome some of the traditional trade-offs in choosing process technology. But note the words 'partially' and 'some'. There are still trade-offs within technology choice, even if they are not as obvious as they were once. Moreover, information processing and computing power has undoubtedly had a major impact on almost all technologies but there are still limits to what computers can do.

## The challenges of information technology (IT)

As we saw in the previous discussion of the three 'dimensions' of process technology, the dominance of information technology (IT) has caused a profound rethink of the issues connected with technology in an operations strategy context. Surprisingly, given the ubiquity of IT, the cost effectiveness of investment in IT is not altogether straightforward. Generally, research recognises a plain and positive connection between investment in IT and operations productivity growth, even if the returns can vary widely. As one authority put it, *'there's no bank where companies can deposit IT investment and withdraw an "average" return ... [A] strategy of blindly investing in IT and expecting productivity to automatically rise is sure to fail.'*[3] Moreover, there is a high failure rate for IT projects (often cited as between 35 and 75 per cent, although the definition of 'failure' is debated). Yet there is extensive agreement that the most common reasons for failure are connected in some way with managerial, implementation or organisational factors. And of these managerial, implementation or organisational factors, one of the main issues was the degree of alignment and integration between IT strategy and the general strategy of the firm. This is a particularly important point for operations strategy. It reinforces the idea that IT strategy must be regarded as an integral part of overall operations strategy.

Of course, different kinds of IT pose different kinds of challenge. The impact of some IT is limited to a defined and (relatively) limited part of the operation. This type of IT is sometimes called 'function IT' because it facilitates a single function or task.[4] Examples include computer-aided design (CAD), spreadsheets and simple decision support systems. The organisational challenges for this type of technology can usually be treated separately from the technology itself. Put another way, function IT can be adopted with or without any changes to other organisational structures. Yet this does not mean that no organisational, cultural or development challenges will be faced. Often, the effectiveness of the technology can be enhanced by appropriate changes to other aspects of the operation. By contrast, 'enterprise IT' extends across much of, or even the entire, organisation; because of which, enterprise IT will need potentially extensive changes to the organisation. The most common (and problematic) enterprise IT is an enterprise resource planning (ERP) system. Because of the importance of ERP to operations strategy we will describe it in some detail in the next section. The third IT category is network IT. Network IT facilitates exchanges between people and groups inside and/or outside the organisation. However, it does not necessarily predefine how these exchanges should work. For example, email is a network IT. It has brought significant changes to how operations and supply networks function, but the changes are not imposed by the technology itself; rather they emerge over time as people gain experience of using the technology. The challenge with this type of technology is to learn how to exploit its emergent potential.

### Enterprise resource planning (ERP)

As information technology established itself within most businesses, the various functions within the business developed appropriate systems and databases to meet their own needs. Enterprise resource planning (ERP) systems attempt to integrate all these various systems. This allows changes made in one part of the business to be reflected immediately in information held for the benefit of other parts of the business, thereby improving both the communication and the effectiveness of the systems as a whole. However, this obvious and seemingly straightforward idea is, in practice, hugely complex and expensive to adopt. And that is what ERP has become known for: its high cost and difficult implementation. Some large corporations are reported as having spent 100s of millions of Euros on their ERP systems. Even medium-sized companies can easily spend 100s of thousands of Euros. And although some authorities claim that even successfully implemented ERP systems will never offer any significant return on their investment, others argue that ERP was simply one of those things that any large company had to invest in simply to keep pace with its customers, suppliers and competitors.[5]

### What is ERP?

One of the most important issues in resource planning and control is managing the, sometimes vast, amounts of information generated from all functions of the business. So, unless all relevant information is brought together and integrated it is difficult to make informed planning and control decisions. This is what enterprise resource planning (ERP) is about. It is often described as a complete enterprise-wide business solution that integrates the planning, resource allocation and control activities of all parts of the business. The intent is that all transaction information is entered into the system at its source and done only once. Consider, for instance, a manufacturing firm receiving an order for a product. The transaction is entered into the system and the data is then sent to the master database, which accesses and updates the other business processes. For example, the finance process is instructed to raise an invoice, the sales and marketing processes are advised of sales and customer information and the production process triggers the manufacturing, etc. If the system does not have its own scheduling software, it can (to varying degrees) be integrated with pre-existing packages (see Figure 6.8).

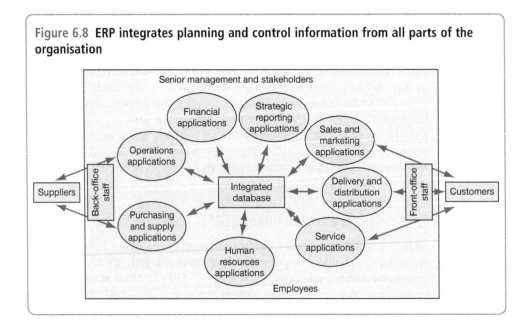

Figure 6.8 **ERP integrates planning and control information from all parts of the organisation**

Arguably the most significant issue in many company's decision to buy an off-the-shelf ERP system is that of its compatibility with the company's current business processes and practices. Experience of ERP installation suggests that it is extremely important to make sure that the current way of doing business will fit (or can be changed to fit) with a standard ERP package. If a business's current processes do not fit, they can either change their processes to fit the ERP package, or modify the software within the ERP package to fit their processes. However, both of these options involve costs and risks. Changing business practices that are working well will involve reorganisation costs as well introducing the potential for errors to creep into the processes. Adapting the software will both slow down the project and introduce potentially dangerous software 'bugs' into the system. It would also make it difficult to upgrade the software later on.

### Supply network ERP

The step beyond integrating internal ERP systems with immediate customers and suppliers is to integrate it with the systems of other businesses throughout the supply network. This is often exceptionally complicated. Not only do different ERP systems have to communicate together, they have to integrate with other types of system. For example, sales and marketing functions often use systems such as customer relationship management (CRM) systems that manage the complexities of customer requirements, promises and transactions. Getting ERP and CRM systems to work together is itself often difficult. Nevertheless, such web-integrated ERP applications are emerging. Although a formidable task, the benefits are potentially great. Transaction costs between supply network partners could be dramatically reduced and the potential for avoiding errors is significant. Yet such transparency also brings risks. If the ERP system of one operation within a supply chain fails for some reason, it may block the effective operation of the whole integrated information system throughout the network.

### Criticisms of ERP

Attempting to get new systems and databases to talk to old legacy systems can be very problematic. Not surprisingly, many companies choose to replace most, if not all, of their existing systems simultaneously. New common systems and relational databases help to ensure the smooth transfer of data between different parts of the organisation. Therefore, ERP installation can be particularly expensive. In addition, there are also considerable 'adjustment costs' associated with many of the implementations. ERP implementations have developed a reputation for exceeding their budgets, with 200/300 per cent cost and time overruns being commonly cited for reasonably sized installations. Yet, given that such systems are predicated on both substantial IT development and process redesign work, it should not be surprising that costs and timeframes proved to be larger and longer than predicted.

In addition to the obvious investment of time and effort, there is also the cost of providing training in new ways of working. Given that old systems, procedures and routines are being replaced in an ERP implementation, this retraining cost can be very significant. During the retraining period there may also be an increased chance of staff error that, combined with the novelty of the system, could cause further failures.

By definition, ERP systems are 'enterprise wide'. This means that all parts of the enterprise must agree on a shared way of working (that coincides with the ERP system's underlying structure) and uniformly implement the system in the same way. There are two important implications of this. First, getting all parts of the enterprise to agree on a common business model is rarely straightforward, even supposing that the ERP system's business model is appropriate for the way the enterprise prefers to operate. Second, because all parts of the enterprise are linked together, the whole business could be held back by the 'weakest link'. That is, inefficiency or incompetence in one part of the enterprise may hold back the whole business.

Note that these disadvantages of ERP are not so much concerned with the fundamental logic of integrating enterprise-wide information systems. Rather, they are concerned with the sheer difficulty of making it happen. This leads some authorities to argue that the disadvantages of ERP systems are not really disadvantages. The question is really whether any individual firm has the money, time, and talent to exploit the advantages of ERP.

### Lessons from ERP

When ERP is implemented successfully it has the potential to significantly improve performance. This is partly because of the, very much enhanced, visibility that information integration gives, but it is also a function of the discipline that ERP demands. Yet this discipline is itself a 'double-edged sword'. On one hand it 'sharpens up' the management of every process within an organisation, allowing best practice (or at least common practice) to be implemented uniformly through the business. No longer will individual idiosyncratic behaviour by one part of a company's operations cause disruption to all other processes. On the other hand, it is the rigidity of this discipline that is both difficult to achieve and (arguably) inappropriate for all parts of the business. Nevertheless, the generally accepted benefits of ERP are as follows:

● greater visibility of what is happening in all parts of the business;

● forcing the business process-based changes that potentially make all parts of the business more efficient;

● improved control of operations that encourages continuous improvement (albeit within the confines of the common process structures);

● more sophisticated communication with customers, suppliers and other business partners, often giving more accurate and timely information;

● integrating whole supply chains, including suppliers' suppliers and customers' customers.

An important justification for embarking on ERP is the potential it gives to link up with the outside world. For example, it is much easier for an operation to move into internet-based trading if it can integrate its external internet systems into its internal ERP systems. However, as has been pointed out by some critics of the ERP software companies, ERP vendors were not prepared for the impact of e-commerce and had not made sufficient allowance in their products for the need to interface with internet-based communication channels. The result of this has been that whereas the internal complexity of ERP systems was designed only to be intelligible to systems experts, the internet has meant that customers and suppliers (who are non-experts) are demanding access to the same information.

## Evaluating process technology

Evaluating process technology quite literally means determining its value or worth. It involves exploring, understanding and describing the strategic consequences of adopting alternatives. Although there can be no 'all-purpose' list of attributes to be evaluated, indeed the precise nature of the attributes to be included in any evaluation should depend on the nature of the technology itself, it is useful to consider three generic classes of evaluation criteria (Figure 6.9):

- the feasibility of the process technology – that is, the degree of difficulty in adopting it, and the investment of time, effort and money that will be needed;
- the acceptability of the process technology – that is, how much it takes a firm towards its strategic objectives, or the return the firm gets for choosing it;
- the vulnerability associated with the process technology – that is, the extent to which the firm is exposed if things go wrong and the risk that is run by choosing the technology.

### Evaluating feasibility

All process technology decisions have resource implications – even the decision to do nothing liberates resources that would otherwise be used. In this context we are not just talking about financial resources, which, although critical, are no help if, say, the technical skills necessary to design and implement a technology are not available. Therefore, if the resources required to implement technology are greater than those that are either available or can be obtained, the technology is not feasible. So, evaluating the feasibility of an option means finding out how the various types of resource that the option might need match up to what is available. Four broad questions are applicable.

*What technical or human skills are required to implement the technology?* Every process technology will need a set of skills to be present within the organisation, so that it can be successfully implemented. If new technology is very similar to that existing in the organisation, it is likely that the necessary skills will already be present. If, however, the technology is completely novel, it is necessary to identify the required skills and to match these against those existing in the organisation.

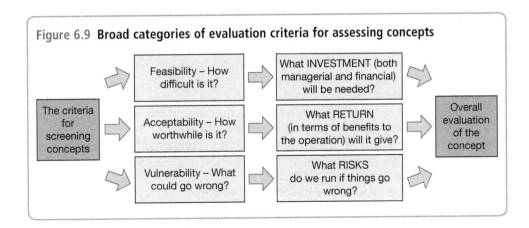

Figure 6.9 **Broad categories of evaluation criteria for assessing concepts**

*What 'quantity' or 'amount' of resources is required to implement the technology?* Determining the quantity of resources (people, facilities, space, time, etc.) required for the implementation of a technology is an important stage in assessing feasibility because it is time-dependent. Rarely will a lack of sufficient process engineers, for example, rule out a particular process technology, but it could restrict when it is adopted. So, a firm may deliberately choose to delay some of its process technology decisions because it knows that its current commitments will not allow it. In order to assess this type of feasibility a company may compare the aggregate workload associated with its implementation over time with its existing capacity.

*What are the funding or cash requirements?* The previous two questions can be difficult to answer in a meaningful way, but this does not diminish their significance. However, in any real investment evaluation, one 'feasibility' factor will inevitably come to dominate all other considerations – do we have enough money? Because of this significance we will spend a little more time reviewing some of the many approaches that have been developed to aid managers in their analysis of cash flow and funding requirements over the lifetime of an investment project.

*Can the operation cope with the degree of change in resource requirements?* Even if all these resource requirements can quite feasibly be obtained individually by the organisation, the degree of change in the total resource position of the company might itself be regarded as infeasible. Consider, for instance, a bespoke manufacturer of road-racing bicycles being encouraged to leverage its reputation for high quality into the 'top end' of the mass cycle market (i.e. much higher volumes). This would require the firm to make substantial investment in automated tube welding equipment. The firm is confident that it will be able to obtain all the different categories of resource required for the project. It believes that it can recruit the appropriate expertise in sufficient quantity from the labour market. Furthermore, it believes that it could fund the project until it broke even. Yet, in the final analysis, the company regards the investment as infeasible. It decides that absorbing such a radical new process technology in a relatively short time-frame would put too great a strain on its own capacity for self-organisation. Thus, sometimes it is not the absolute level but rather the rate of change in resource requirements that renders a project infeasible.

## Assessing financial requirements

In most process technology decisions the most important feasibility question is, 'How much financial investment will the technology require, and can we afford it?' At its simplest, this could mean simply examining the one-off cost of the purchase price of the technology. Usually, though, an examination of the effect of the cash requirements on the whole organisation is necessary. If so, it is often necessary to simulate the organisation's cash flow over a period of time. Computing the total inflow of cash over time as it occurs, and subtracting from it the total outflow of cash as it occurs, leaves the net funding requirement for the option. For example, Figure 6.10 shows the net cash inflows likely to be earned if a proposed technology is adopted and the cash outflows associated with its purchase and implementation. The resulting cash requirements show that a maximum funding requirement of €1,050,000 occurs within the first eight months of the project, and diminishes only slowly for two years. After that, the project enjoys a large net inflow of cash. Of course, this analysis does not include the effects of interest payments on cash borrowed. When it is decided how the cash

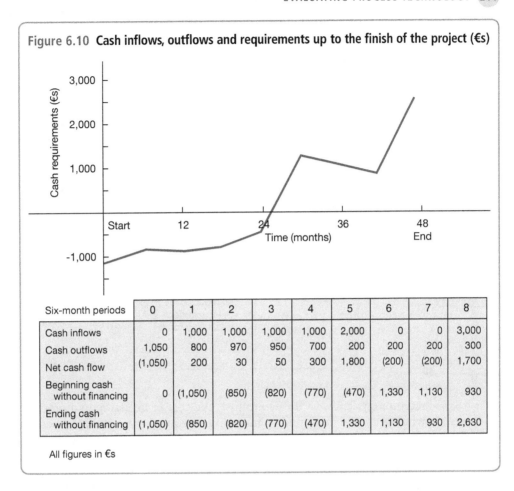

Figure 6.10 **Cash inflows, outflows and requirements up to the finish of the project (€s)**

| Six-month periods | 0 | 1 | 2 | 3 | 4 | 5 | 6 | 7 | 8 |
|---|---|---|---|---|---|---|---|---|---|
| Cash inflows | 0 | 1,000 | 1,000 | 1,000 | 1,000 | 2,000 | 0 | 0 | 3,000 |
| Cash outflows | 1,050 | 800 | 970 | 950 | 700 | 200 | 200 | 200 | 300 |
| Net cash flow | (1,050) | 200 | 30 | 50 | 300 | 1,800 | (200) | (200) | 1,700 |
| Beginning cash without financing | 0 | (1,050) | (850) | (820) | (770) | (470) | 1,330 | 1,130 | 930 |
| Ending cash without financing | (1,050) | (850) | (820) | (770) | (470) | 1,330 | 1,130 | 930 | 2,630 |

All figures in €s

is to be raised (i.e. borrowed from a bank or private investor or raised from the equity markets), this can be included.

## Evaluating acceptability

Evaluating acceptability can be done from many technical and managerial perspectives. Here we limit our discussion to cover the financial perspective on evaluation and the 'market requirements' and 'operations resource' perspectives. Figure 6.11 summarises the different elements of our analysis.

### Acceptability in financial terms

Financial evaluation involves predicting and analysing the financial costs to which an option would commit the organisation, and the financial benefits that might accrue from acquiring the process technology. However, 'cost' is not always a straightforward concept. An accountant has a different view of 'cost' to that of an economist. The accountant's view is that the cost of something is whatever you had to pay to acquire it originally. The economist, on the other hand, is more likely to define costs in terms of the benefits forgone by not investing elsewhere: that is, the opportunity cost of the

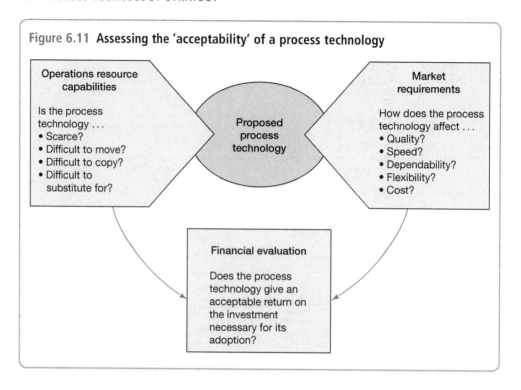

Figure 6.11 **Assessing the 'acceptability' of a process technology**

technology. Thus, to the economist, the cost of investing in a process technology is whatever could be gained by investing an equivalent sum in the best feasible alternative investment. While opportunity costing has obvious intuitive attractions, and is particularly useful in process technology investments where alternative technologies may bring very different benefits, it does depend on what we define as the best feasible alternative use of our resources. The accountant's model of acquisition cost is at least stable – if we paid €1,000 for something, then its value is €1,000, irrespective of whatever alternative use we might dream up for the money.

### The life cycle cost

The concept of life cycle costing is useful in process technology evaluation. It involves accounting for all costs over the life of the investment that is influenced directly by the decision. For example, suppose a company is evaluating alternative integrated warehousing systems. One system is significantly less expensive and seems at first sight to be the least costly. But what other costs should the company consider apart from the acquisition cost? Each system would require some initial development to remedy outstanding technical problems before installation. The systems would also have to be 'debugged' before operation, but, more importantly, during its years of life the plant will incur operation and maintenance costs that will, in part, be determined by the original choice of system. Finally, if the company wants to look so far ahead, the disposal value of the plant could also be significant. In fact, total life cycle costing is impossible in any absolute sense. The effects of any significant investment ripple out like waves in a pond, impinging on and influencing many other decisions. Yet it is sensible to include more than the immediate and obvious costs involved in a decision, and a life cycle approach proves a useful reminder of this.

## The time value of money: net present value (NPV)

One of the most important questions to be answered in establishing the 'real' value of either costs or benefits is determining when they are incurred or realised. This dynamic is important, because money in your hand today is worth more to you than the same money would be worth in a year's time. Conversely, paying out a sum in one year's time is preferable to paying it out now. The reason for this has to do with the opportunity cost of money. If we receive money now and invest it (in a bank account or in another project giving a positive return), then in one year's time we will have our original investment plus whatever interest has been paid for the year. Thus, to compare the alternative merits of receiving €100 now and receiving €100 in one year's time, we should compare €100 with €100 plus one year's interest. Alternatively, we can reverse the process and ask ourselves how much would have to be invested now, in order for that investment to pay €100 in one year's time. This amount (lower than €100) is called the present value of receiving €100 in one year's time.

For example, suppose current interest rates are 10 per cent per annum. The amount we would have to invest to receive €100 in one years' time is:

$$€100 \times \frac{1}{1.10} = €90.91$$

$$€100 \times \frac{1}{(1.10)} \frac{1}{(1.10)} = €100 \times \frac{1}{(1.10)^2} = €82.65$$

The rate of interest assumed (10 per cent in our case) is known as the discount rate. More generally, the present value of €$x$ in $n$ years' time, at a discount rate of $r$ per cent is:

$$\frac{x}{(1 + r/100)^n}$$

## Limitations of conventional financial evaluation

Conventional financial evaluation has come under criticism for its inability to include enough relevant factors to give a true picture of complex investments. Nowhere is this more evident than in the case of justifying investment in process technologies comprising a significant IT element. Here costs and benefits are uncertain, intangible and often dispersed throughout an organisation. Indeed, with all the talk about there being a 'new economy', the myriad discussions about computers removing cost (labour) from operational processes, or the impact of the creation of knowledge and information-based markets, you could be forgiven for thinking that the computer age was an unambiguously positive thing for business. Until recently, however, there has been little actual evidence that, for all the IT investment that firms have made, there has been any real impact upon overall productivity.

## Acceptability in terms of impact on market requirements

Extending the idea of considering all competitive benefits from an investment, we have argued elsewhere in this chapter that process technology can impact all of the generic operational performance objectives: quality, speed, dependability, flexibility and cost. The questions listed in Table 6.2 can help provide a framework for assessing the impact of any proposed investment on each of them. In order to illustrate this we have applied them to a generic analysis of the effect of process technology on the airline industry.

Table 6.2 **Evaluating the acceptability of process technology investment on market criteria**

|  | Generic questions | Example |
|---|---|---|
| Quality | Does the process technology improve the specification of the product or service? That is, does it provide something better or different that customers value? Does the process technology reduce unwanted variability within the operation? Even if absolute specification quality is unaffected by process technology, it may contribute to conformance quality by reducing variability. | An airline investing in in-flight entertainment technology to enhance the specification of its flight services. An airline investing in maintenance equipment that keeps the performance of its aircraft and ancillary systems within very tight tolerances. This reduces the risk of failure in equipment, as well as increasing the internal predictability of the airline's processes. |
| Speed | Does the process technology enable a faster response to customers? Does it shorten the time between a customer making a request and having it confirmed (or a product delivered, etc.)? Does the process technology speed the throughput of internal processes? Even if customers do not benefit directly from faster process throughput within an operation, technology increasing 'clock speed' can benefit the operation by, for instance, reducing costs. | The check-in technology used by airlines at airport gates and lounges in effect allows customers' requests for seating or dietary requirements to be explored quickly and, if possible, confirmed. The technology that allows the fast loading of customers' bags and in-flight catering supplies, allows fuel to be loaded and engines to be checked, etc. all reduces the time the aircraft spends on the ground. This allows the aircraft to be used more intensively. |
| Dependability | Does the process technology enable products and/or services to be delivered more dependably? Although many of the causes of poor dependability may appear to be outside the control of an operation, technology may help to bring some of the factors within its control. Does the process technology enhance the dependability of processes within the operation? Again, even when customers see no direct result of more dependable technology, it can provide benefits for the operation itself. | Specialist navigation equipment installed in aircraft can allow them to land in conditions of poor visibility, thus reducing the possibility of delays due to bad weather. Customers benefit directly from such an increase in dependability. Airlines invest in advanced aircraft communications technology. Efficient communication between aircraft and control centres reduces the possibility of miscommunication, which, even when presenting no danger, can waste time and cause confusion. Indeed, an oft-cited concern of many airlines is that airports around the world do not always match their investment in communications technology – preventing maximum productivity gains from their equipment. |
| Flexibility | Does the process technology allow the operation to change in response to changes in customer demand? Such changes may be in either the level or nature of demand. Does the process technology allow for adjustments to the internal workings of the operations processes? | When an airline considers the mix of aircraft types to include in its fleet, it does so partly to retain sufficient flexibility to respond to such things as timetable changes or unexpected demand. Some aircraft (notably the Boeing 777) permit the precise configuration of cabins and seating to be changed. While this may not happen very frequently, it offers airlines the flexibility to provide a different mix of services without having different types of aircraft. |

▶

| | | |
|---|---|---|
| Cost | Does the process technology process materials, information or customers more efficiently? As we mentioned previously, this is by far the most common basis for justifying new process technology, even if it is not always the most important. It is never unimportant, however. | A major driver for airlines to invest in new aircraft is the greater efficiency (€/passenger mile flown) of each new generation of aircraft that derives from the overall design of the aircraft and, most especially, the engines powering them. |
| | Does the process technology enable a greater effectiveness of the operations processes? Even if straightforward efficiency is unaffected, process technology can aid the deployment of the operations capabilities to increase profitability or general effectiveness. | The 'yield management' decision support systems used by airlines enable them to maximise the revenue from flights by adjusting capacity and pricing strategies to match demand patterns. |

Although the examples in Table 6.2 were set in the airline industry, we could have done the same for any industry. The most important point to emerge from any similar analysis in any sector is that the market opportunities associated with process technology are far greater than the traditional narrow focus on cost reduction. Any sensible evaluation of process technology must include all the effects impacting on quality, speed, dependability, flexibility and cost. As we stressed in Chapter 2, the generic performance objectives are very rarely equally important for all types of operation. Their relative importance will reflect the actual and intended market position of the organisation. The implication of this for evaluating process technology is straightforward: any evaluation must reflect the impact of process technology on each performance objective relative to their importance to achieving a particular market position. Often there will be trade-offs involved in adopting a new process technology. Reverting to our airline examples earlier, one advantage of having a fleet of mixed aircraft is the flexibility it provides to match aircraft to routes as the demand on different routes changes. Yet different types of aircraft require different spare parts, different maintenance procedures and different interfaces with ground technology and so on. This may add more cost and complexity to the total airline operations than is gained through the benefits of flexibility. For example, Airbus, the European airline consortium and great rival to the US aerospace giant Boeing, claims that its strategy of common cockpit and flight control systems across its range of planes saves considerable cost. Commonality in such systems allows pilots and ground crews to deal with similar systems with 120-seater to 400-seater aircraft.

### Acceptability in terms of impact on operational resources

Using the generic performance objectives can help us to characterise the potential contribution that process technology can make to market requirements. At the same time, however, it is important to build up a picture of the contribution that process technology can make to the longer-term capability 'endowment' of the operation. We can use the dimensions described in Chapter 1 as being 'strategic' according to the resource-based view of the firm. As a reminder, these four dimensions are:

- the scarcity of resources;
- how difficult the resources are to move;

- how difficult the resources are to copy;
- how difficult the resources are to substitute.

These four dimensions provide us with a 'first cut' mechanism for assessing the impact that a specific technological resource will have upon sustainable competitive advantage. Table 6.3 develops these four dimensions with examples.

**Table 6.3 The four dimensions of 'strategic' operations resources**

|  | *Generic questions* | *Example* |
|---|---|---|
| Scarcity | Does the technology represent any kind of first-mover advantage? In other words, how much of the developed technology (or perhaps its underlying R&D) is not possessed by competitors? Does the technology help create or exploit proprietary product/service knowledge, perhaps in the tangible form of a database? | Such resources might include bespoke production facilities in industries such as petrochemicals and pharmaceuticals, where first-mover advantage often generates superior returns. Capturing customer data over time and then exploiting this information has long been a core element of airline competitive strategies – such information is extremely scarce. |
| Difficult to move | How much of the process technology was developed in-house? If a process technology is unique and, moreover, it was developed 'in-house', then such resources cannot easily be accessed without purchasing the firm. How many of the critical technological resources 'don't walk on legs'? In other words, highlight those resources that are more than contractually tied into the operation. | The value of resource immobility helps to explain the increased emphasis being placed upon infrastructure development in the management consulting sector – to facilitate the retention of skills, knowledge and experience. Mobility concerns in, say, the IT sector explain the emergence of more complicated contracts (constraining subsequent employment, etc.) and wage inflation for certain key staff. |
| Difficult to copy | How far down the 'learning curve' is the process technology? How strong is the legal protection? Patents offer some protection, even though the process is long, often expensive and may attract greater competitive risk than simply having better site security. | Experiences such as those documented in high-volume processes, such as Intel and semiconductors, can create competitive performance barriers. In the competitive confectionery market, for instance, there is almost pathological secrecy associated with proprietary production processes, but very little recourse to the filing of patents. |
| Difficult to create a substitute | What, if any, market mechanisms exist to prevent process technology simply becoming irrelevant through the introduction of a substitute? | Traditional EDI-type connections integrate supply chains but can also help to establish de-facto standards and introduce switching costs. They can therefore prevent rivals offering substitute services. |

## *Tangible and intangible resources*

It is important to recall that in our discussion in Chapter 1 on the importance of operations resources and process we were careful to distinguish between tangible and intangible resources. Tangible resources are the actual physical assets that the company possesses. In process technology terms these will be the machines, computers, materials handling equipment and so on, used within the operation. Intangible resources are not necessarily directly observable but nevertheless have value for the company. Things such as relationship and brand strength, supplier relationships, process knowledge and so on are all real but not always directly tangible. This concept of intangible resources is important when considering process technology. A unit of technology may not be any different physically from the technology used by competitors. However, its use may add to the company's reputation, skills, knowledge and experience. Thus, depending on how the process technology is used, the value of the intangible aspect of a process technology may be greater than its physical worth. If the usefulness of process technology also depends on the software it employs, then this also must be evaluated. Again, although software may be bought off the shelf and is therefore available to competitors, if it is deployed in imaginative and creative ways its real value can be enhanced.

## Evaluating market and resource acceptability

Consider, for instance, a Windows-based data management system for a police force to help manage their crime laboratory. The lab is where samples from a range of crime scenes are tested in a large variety of different processes (DNA testing, fingerprint analysis, etc.) that vary widely in their sophistication and complexity. Although speed is often of the essence in the lab, accuracy and dependability are equally critical, as is their legal requirement to store and access information over extended periods of time (for legal appeals, long-term investigations, etc.). While this operation does not have a market position as such, it still has a set of social and legal priorities that are its direct equivalent. Figure 6.12 illustrates this by adding a further line to the profile that indicates what the laboratory's performance targets are. Although the new process technology does not improve operations performance in all aspects of the crime lab's 'market' requirements, it does improve some specific areas of performance and does not appear to have any negative effects. However, it is when we turn our attention to the resource profile of the technology that the relevance for 'not-for-profit' operations of dimensions derived from a competitive marketplace needs to be more closely examined. Although we might see the usefulness of a unique and difficult-to-copy crime database in the 'war against crime', the positive advantage of having resources that rank highly on the RBV dimensions is not clear for an accountable public sector operation.

In other words, if a resource (such as knowledge or experience) is difficult to move or copy, this can contribute to sustainable advantage in a competitive marketplace. However, such characteristics can act against critical public sector objectives such as effective information transfer or even accountability over performance. In this type of application, therefore, it is necessary to see the resource characteristics as useful in a different way. So, for instance, imagine that the staff experience associated with analysing particular types of DNA evidence is crucial for the crime lab but very difficult to copy and therefore shared both within and between labs. The operations strategy response might therefore be to diminish (rather than embrace) this 'imitability' characteristic by developing systems and procedures that seek to codify (i.e. papers,

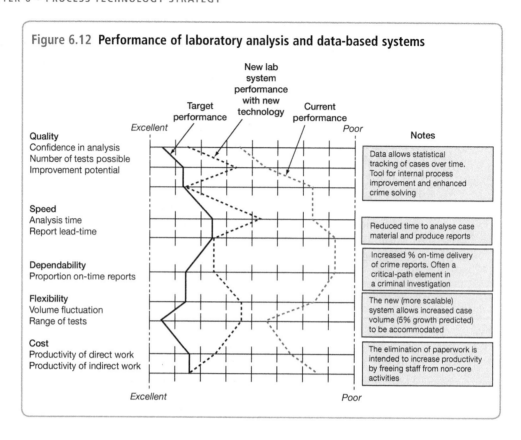

**Figure 6.12 Performance of laboratory analysis and data-based systems**

technical diaries, open databases) and encourage regular sharing of experiences (i.e. seminars, staff exchanges and apprenticeships).

## Evaluating vulnerability

There have been some spectacular and very public failures associated with the introduction of new process technology. Yet presumably all of these process technology 'failures' were at one time determined to be both feasible and acceptable to the operation. Their subsequent failure highlights one further important issue to explore – vulnerability. That is, what exposure is the firm accepting if something goes wrong with the technology once the decision to invest is made?

Evaluating the risks associated with new process technology can be based on a very similar type of analysis as we used for assessing acceptability; namely, by assessing risk in terms of market, resource and financial perspectives.

### *Market vulnerability*

Any investment in new technology needs to make an assumption concerning the market (and more generable environment) that will exist when the technology is 'up and running'. The possibility to which any technology is subject to, therefore, is that of market conditions being different from those envisaged when the technology was initially planned. This type of vulnerability is inherent in every process innovation.

Uncertainty results from the fact that, on the one hand, events in the future do not follow the course of past events and, on the other, knowing about the future is always incomplete. At its simplest, this could be that market demand is different, either larger or smaller to such an extent that the scale of the technology is inappropriate.

Six factors creating the uncertainty that leads to vulnerability in the innovation process can be identified.[6]

1 *Market vulnerability* – will the technology, when developed and implemented, meet the needs (real or perceived) of the market?

2 *Regulatory vulnerability* – will the technology conflict with any likely 'constraining regulations' related to the environment, health or market behaviour (a significant factor, for example in financial services)?

3 *Social and political vulnerability* – will the technology prove acceptable to all the organisation's stakeholders? Or will it expose a dysfunctional diversity of interests within the total stakeholder body? For example, certain legitimate oil and gas extraction technologies may provoke social opposition.

4 *Acceptance and legitimacy of vulnerability* – will groups or individuals who feel themselves affected by it accept the technology? Although rationally an improved technology, does it threaten existing jobs?

5 *Timing vulnerability* – will the technology be implemented either too early or too late with respect to parallel developments (for example, competitors' new technology)?

6 *Response vulnerability* – will the technology provoke hostile competitor innovations? Is a 'technology war' desirable?

---

**Example**   **Two technology failures[7]**

**Not enough people choose 'Choose and Book'**

It was a technology project that was ten years in the making. The 'Choose and Book' system should have transformed the way in which patients and their 'General Practitioner' (GP) physicians could select an outpatient hospital appointment at a convenient date and time in the UK's National Health Service (NHS). The aim was to speed up the process and cut out the need for costly paperwork. Yet in 2014 it was quietly dropped, despite costing £356m during the ten years that it been struggling to establish itself. It was taken as another example of the difficulties of introducing new technology systems into such a huge and complex organisation. An investigation by the UK's House of Commons' public accounts committee was told by NHS staff that, although some GPs liked the 'Choose and Book' system, many did not. Moreover, not all outpatient appointment slots were available on the system, which limited its usefulness. Many patients and doctors found 'Choose and Book' complicated and time-consuming. One GP, Sarah Wollaston, said, '*the system suits patients who were good with technology but not those who were less so. Doctors often did not have time to log on to it during appointments with their patients.*' A Member of Parliament said: '*It's another NHS cock up. A system designed for use by GPs but only used by half of them ... has been quietly dropped, so quietly that even most of the NHS seems unaware. In the middle of all of this are patients. Choose and Book was supposed to speed things up but the evidence we heard in committee showed this was not so in most cases.*' Despite the failure of 'Choose and Book' (or only partial success), the government department that oversees the NHS decided to replace it with a potentially even more expensive e-referral scheme, saying

▶

that the new e-referral system would use different technology and have additional features as well as being available on mobile apps. A spokesperson said, *'we are aiming to have 100 per cent electronic referrals within the next five years – sooner than that if we can make it. That will cut out a lot of these errors.'* It was also reported that the idea of making it compulsory for GPs to use the replacement system when it comes on-stream, with an inbuilt incentive and penalty scheme for doctors and hospitals, was being considered.

## The BBC's Digital Media Initiative

The BBC is one of the best-known broadcasters in the world, with an unrivalled reputation for the quality of some of its programmes. Sadly, its reputation for introducing new technology is less exemplary. Amongst its more spectacular failures was its Digital Media Initiative (DMI). The DMI was an endeavour by the BBC to dispense with videotapes and create a kind of 'internal YouTube' of archive content that staff could access, upload, edit and then air from their computers. When the project was originally envisaged, creating a single TV programme could involve 70 individual video-handling processes. DMI was meant to halve that. The project cost almost £100 million and lasted five years before it was scrapped. The flaws in the technology were exposed during the BBC's coverage of the State funeral of Margaret Thatcher, a well-known ex-Prime Minister. The DMI was supposed to create a production system linked to the BBC's huge broadcasting archive, but instead of streamlining access to old video footage, video editors were unable to access archive footage to use in news reports from their computers in central London. Instead, they had to transport videotapes there using taxis and the underground network from the archive storage facility in northwest London. Admitting that to continue with the project would be 'throwing good money after bad', the BBC suspended its chief technology officer. One BBC manager called the DMI project 'the axis of awful', while another said, 'The scale of the project was just too big, and it got out of hand.' Anthony Fry, a member of the BBC's governing body, said that the project had 'generated little or no assets' for the corporation. This is because much of the software and hardware that has been developed could only be used by the BBC if the project were completed, which, due to technological difficulties and changes to business needs was not possible. Tony Hall, the BBC's Director General, said that off-the-shelf tools 'that simply didn't exist five years ago' had now become available, and they could do the same job as some elements of the DMI. Professors Elizabeth Daniel of the Open University Business School and John Ward of Cranfield School of Management, commenting on the BBC DMI case, said, *'it is not the biggest or the worst IT project failure in the public or private sectors and, without organisations' implementing measures to guard against them, it will almost certainly not be the last'*. While at first glance, they say, it seems the BBC's Digital Media Initiative project suffered from the challenges encountered in many other large IT projects, there are some aspects of the BBC operation and culture that may have exacerbated them. The organisation appears to have reacted slowly to concerns raised at senior level; there was an inability to identify that things were going wrong and to then act impartially. The failure of the DMI was regarded as an IT failure, not of the BBC, and, most worrying, there was a culture that apparently did not allow staff involved to be given a voice. So, unable to feed their concerns about projects into review processes, they were instead reduced to privately voicing them.

### Resource vulnerability

All process technologies depend, for their effective operation, on support services. Specific skills are needed if the technology is to be installed, maintained, upgraded and controlled effectively. In other words, the technology has a set of 'resource dependencies'.

Changing to a different process technology often means changing this set of resource dependencies. This may have a positive aspect. The skills, knowledge and experience necessary to implement and operate the technology can be scarce and difficult to copy and hence provide a platform for sustainable advantage. But there can also be a downside to a changed set of resources dependencies. For example, the specific skills needed to implement or operate a new process technology, because they are scarce, could become particularly valuable in the labour market. The company is vulnerable to the risk of the staff that have these skills leaving in order to leverage their value.

Issues of trust and power also influence the vulnerability created by dependence upon external organisations, such as suppliers and customers. If there is a high degree of trust between a firm and its technology supplier, it can be entirely appropriate to become dependent for the installation, maintenance and upgrading of process technology upon a particular external provider. Dependence can also work the other way. Customers may ask for a particular piece of technology to be dedicated to their business. Again, this can be entirely legitimate if the operation trusts its customer to continue generating work for them over a suitable period. However, such exclusive relationships inevitably introduce vulnerabilities. For example, suppose an operation is choosing between alternative suppliers of software. One supplier seems to be particularly price-competitive, very service-oriented and has developed a particularly effective leading-edge application. Unfortunately, this supplier is also smaller than the alternative suppliers. Although its products and service may be superior, it is itself more vulnerable to business pressures. If it went out of business the company would be left with unsupported infrastructure. Under these circumstances the company may decide that choosing this supplier would expose it to unacceptable levels of vulnerability.

### Financial vulnerability

By 'financial vulnerability, we mean the financial exposure that adopting a new technology poses to the adopting organisation. Of course, financial vulnerability can result from market and/or resource vulnerability. Unexpected market conditions or failure of the technology to perform as expected can both seriously impact the financial consequences of investing in new process technology. Revenues, running costs, capital requirements and the resulting cash flows will all be affected by market and resource vulnerabilities. At the very least, one would expect any firm to explore the sensitivity of financial outcomes to possible deviations from expected market and resource-based conditions. But it is also important to recognise that, even if market and resource conditions are exactly as expected, other conditions that impact on financial outcomes could be unexpected. For example, the availability of credit, interest rates, stock market sentiment and currency exchange rates can all affect the financial outcome of a project.

## SUMMARY ANSWERS TO KEY QUESTIONS

### What is process technology strategy?

Here, technology is defined as the practical 'appliance of science', and 'process technology' is technology as applied to operational processes (as opposed to product/service technology). This distinction is inevitably less clear in many service operations where the product is the process. We can further classify two types of process technology: the first is that contributing 'directly' to the production of goods and services; ▶

the second type is the 'indirect' or 'infrastructure' technology that acts to support core transformation processes. Process technology strategy is the set of decisions that define the strategic role that direct and indirect process technology can play in the overall operations strategy of the organisation, and sets out the general characteristics that help to evaluate alternative technologies. Any technology strategy is likely to be planned in consultation with other parts of the firm, maybe using some kind of formal planning process such as technology roadmapping. A technology roadmap (TRM) is an approach that provides a structure that attempts to assure the alignment of developments (and investments) in technology, possible future market needs and the new development of associated operations capabilities.

### What are suitable dimensions for characterising process technology?

Although generic dimensions will always fail to capture completely the rich detail of any individual piece of process technology, it is normally useful to describe scale (capacity of each technology unit), automation (what the machine can do) and coupling (how much is or can be joined together) characteristics. Although these three dimensions are unlikely to be equally relevant for all types of technology, they do offer a useful categorisation for comparing a range of process technology options.

We can modify our original dimensions (scale, automation and integration) to more accurately reflect the characteristics of IT-rich process technology. More suitable characteristics are therefore scalability, analytical content and connectivity. We argued that these new characteristics were overcoming the traditional flexibility/cost trade-off, and that new process technologies were able to enhance operational flexibility while still retaining reasonable underlying efficiency, and vice versa.

### How do market volume and variety influence process technology?

There is often a 'natural' diagonal-fit relationship between the volume/variety and process technology dimensions. For example, the larger the unit of capacity, the more likely that it is capital- rather than labour-intensive, which gives more opportunity for high coupling between its various parts. Where flexibility is unimportant but achieving dependable high volumes and low unit costs is critical, such inflexible systems come into their own. Conversely, small-scale technologies, combined with skilled staff, tend to be more flexible than large-scale, capital-intensive, closely coupled systems. As a result, these systems can cope with a high degree of variety.

### What are some of the challenges of information technology?

The dominance of information technology (IT) has caused a rethink of how technology fits into operations strategy. Although there is a positive connection between adopting IT and productivity growth, it is not guaranteed. But where failure occurs it is usually caused by managerial, implementation or organisational factors. Moreover, different kinds of IT pose different kinds of challenge. Limited 'function IT', such as CAD, facilitates a single function or task. Enterprise IT extends across the entire organisation. Because of this it will need potentially extensive changes to the organisation. Network IT facilitates exchanges between people and groups inside and/or outside the organisation. However, it does not necessarily pre-define how these exchanges should work. Enterprise resource planning (ERP) is an example of enterprise IT. It integrates the planning, resource allocation and control activities of all parts of the business – the better to make informed planning and control decisions. However, the practical implementation of this idea has proved to be very complex and expensive. If a business's current processes do not fit with the structure of whatever ERP package is purchased, they can either change their processes to fit the ERP package, or modify the software within the ERP package to fit their processes. But both of these options involve costs and risks.

### How can process technology be evaluated strategically?

Evaluating process technology quite literally means determining its value or worth. It involves exploring, understanding and describing the strategic consequences of adopting alternatives. We outlined three possible dimensions: (1) the 'feasibility' of technology indicates the degree of difficulty in adopting it, and should assess the investment of time, effort and money that will be needed; (2) the 'acceptability' of technology is how much it takes a firm towards its strategic objectives. This includes contribution in terms of cost, quality, speed, etc., as well as the development of strategic resources. In general terms it is about establishing the return (defined in a very broad manner) that the operation gets for choosing a process technology. And (3) the 'vulnerability' of technology indicates the extent to which the firm is exposed if things go wrong. It is the risks that are run by choosing that specific technology. The uncertainties that lead to vulnerability in the innovation process include:

- market vulnerability;
- regulatory;
- social and political vulnerability;
- acceptance and legitimacy of vulnerability;
- timing vulnerability;
- response vulnerability.

## Further reading

Arthur, W.B. (2009) *The Nature of Technology: What it is and How it Evolves*. London: Allen Lane.

Boardman, A., Greenberg, D., Vining, A. and Weimer, D. (2006) *Cost Benefit Analysis: Concepts and Practice*, 3rd edition. Harlow, UK: Prentice Hall. ,

Bocij, P., Greasley, A. and Hickie, S. (2008) *Business Information Systems: Technology, Development and Management for the E-Business*. Harlow, UK: Financial Times/Prentice Hall.

Brynjolfsson, E. and McAfee, A. (2014) *The Second Machine Age: Work, Progress, and Prosperity in a Time of Brilliant Technologies*. New York: W.W. Norton & Company.

Carlopio, J. (2003) *Changing Gears: The Strategic Implementation of Technology*. Basingstoke: Palgrave Macmillan.

Edgerton, D. (2006) *The Shock of the Old: Technology in Global History Since 1900*. London: Profile Books.

Hayes, R.H., Pisano, G.P., Upton, D.M. and Wheelwright, S.C. (2004) *Operations, Strategy, and Technology: Pursuing the Competitive Edge*. New York: Wiley.

McKeen, J.D. (2003) 'Making IT Happen: Critical Issues in Managing Information Technology', John Wiley Series in Information Systems.

Shane, S.A. (2013) *Technology Strategy for Managers and Entrepreneurs*. Harlow, UK: Pearson. ▶

## Notes on the chapter

1   *Sources* include: *The Economist* (2014) 'The future of jobs: Previous technological innovation has always delivered more long-run employment, not less. But things can change', 18 January; *The Economist* (2013) 'Schumpeter – The age of smart machines', 25 May; Finkelstein (2013) 'Machines are becoming cheaper than labour', *The Times*, 6 November; Groom, B. (2014) 'Automation and the threat to jobs', *Financial Times*, 26 January; Frey, B. and Osborne, M.A. (2013) 'The Future Of Employment: How Susceptible Are Jobs To Computerisation?', Oxford Martin School Working Paper, 17 September; Brynjolfsson, E. and McAfee, A. (2014) *The Second Machine Age: Work, Progress, and Prosperity in a Time of Brilliant Technologies*. New York: W.W. Norton & Company.

2   *Sources* include: Devi, S. (2014) 'Universal Robots are a big hit', *Financial Times*, 19 May.

3   Brynjolfsson, E. (1994) 'Technology's true payoff', *Information Week*, October.

4   This categorisation is described in McAffee, A. (2007) 'Managing in the Information Age', Harvard Business School, Teaching note 5-608-011.

5   Teach, E. (2004) 'Watch how you think', *CFO Magazine*, January.

6   This classification is based partly on: Jalonen, H. and Lehtonen, A. (2011) 'Uncertainty in the innovation process', Proceedings of the European Conference on Innovation and Entrepreneurship, 15–16 September, Aberdeen, Scotland, UK.

7   *Sources* include: Helm, T. and Campbell, D. (2014) 'NHS hit by new tech failure as it scraps patient booking system', *The Observer*, 10 May; Warwick Ashford, W. (2014) 'NHS to scrap £356m outpatient booking system', *Computer Weekly*, 12 May; Conlan, T. (2014) 'BBC considering keeping 40-year-old system after £100m DMI failure', www.theguardian.com, 5 February; Daniel, E. and Ward, J. (2014) 'BBC's DMI project failure is a warning to all organisations', www.computerweekly.com/; Conlan, T. and Arthur, C. (2013) 'BBC suspends technology officer after Digital Media Initiative failure', *The Guardian*, 24 May.

# Improvement strategy

## Introduction

All of operations strategy is concerned with improving operations. The whole purpose of taking a strategic view of operations resources and processes is to enhance their contribution to achieving a long-term advantage. Nevertheless, the study of improvement as a specific activity, and how it is managed strategically, has attracted significant attention from both academics and practitioners. Some of this attention focuses on specific techniques and prescriptions while some looks at the underlying philosophy of improvement. Our treatment of the other 'content' decision areas in operations strategy, such as capacity, supply networks and technology, is all based on the implicit assumption that we take decisions in these areas in order to improve the operation. However, most organisations review their overall operations strategy relatively infrequently, and the final three chapters will look at the operations strategy formulation process, which presumably is done to improve overall performance. Between these times they do not expect the operation to 'freeze itself' between each major strategic review. Rather, organisations aspire to develop and improve their operations on a more routine basis. This chapter deals with the more ongoing improvement activity. We are concerned not with strategy formulation on the grand scale, but with the more general issues of how companies can shape the routines that encourage the ongoing development of their operations (see Figure 7.1).

### KEY QUESTIONS

- *What are the differences between managing large 'breakthrough' improvements and managing continuous improvement?*
- *How do the needs of the market direct the ongoing development of operations processes?*
- *How can the ongoing management and control of operations be harnessed to develop their capabilities?*
- *What can operations do to deploy their capabilities into the market?*

## Operations improvement

In this chapter we examine the development of operations resources and processes – that is, the way in which operations build their capabilities and by doing so improve their performance. Many authorities stress the importance of how organisations

Figure 7.1 **This chapter looks at development and organisation (operations development and improvement)**

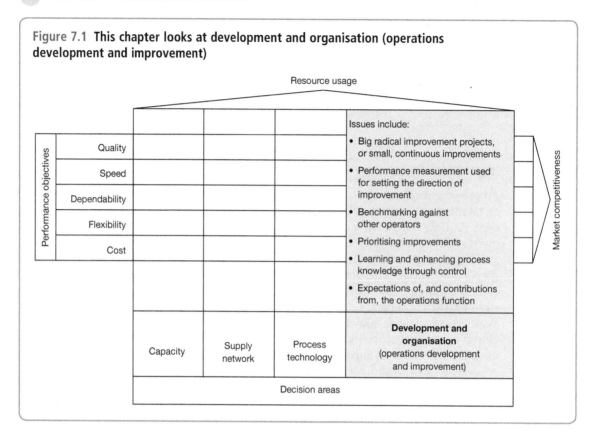

manage their development and improvement efforts. For example:

> '*The companies that are able to turn their…organisations into sources of competitive advantage are those that can harness various improvement programs…in the service of a broader [operations] strategy that emphasises the selection and growth of unique operating [capabilities].*'[1]

Yet we must accept some ambiguity as to the role of the development and improvement activity within operations strategy. On one hand it is a content decision area in the sense that there are decisions to be taken about how the operation thinks about and organises its own development. On the other hand, because we are dealing with the way in which improvement decisions are made, the topics covered in this chapter could also be considered part of the process of operations strategy formulation.

## Continuous and breakthrough improvement

We will start by revisiting a distinction that was described in Chapter 3 – one that represents different, and to some extent opposing, philosophies: 'continuous improvement' and 'breakthrough improvement'. One analogy, which helps us to understand the difference between breakthrough and continuous improvement, is that of the sprint and the marathon. Breakthrough improvement is a series of explosive and impressive sprints. Continuous improvement, like marathon running, does not require the expertise and prowess required for sprinting, but it does require that the runner (or operations manager) keeps on going.

Continuous improvement adopts an approach to improving performance that assumes more and smaller incremental improvement steps – for example, simplifying the question sequence when taking a hotel reservation. While there is no guarantee that other steps will follow such a small step towards better performance, the whole philosophy of continuous improvement attempts to ensure that there will be. Continuous improvement is not concerned with promoting small improvements *per se*, but it does see small improvements as having one significant advantage over large ones – they can be followed relatively painlessly by other small improvements. Thus, continuous improvement becomes embedded as the 'natural' way of working within the operation. So, in continuous improvement it is not the rate of improvement that is important, it is the momentum of improvement. It does not matter if successive improvements are small; what does matter is that every month (or week, or quarter, or whatever period is appropriate) some kind of improvement has actually taken place.

Breakthrough, or 'innovation'-based, improvement assumes that the main vehicle of improvement is a major and dramatic change in the way the operation works, such as the total redesign of a computer-based hotel reservation system, for example. The impact of these improvements is relatively sudden, abrupt and represents a step-change in practice (and hopefully performance). Such improvements are rarely inexpensive (usually calling for high investment), often disrupting the ongoing workings of the operation and frequently involving changes in the product/service or process technology. Moreover, a frequent criticism of the breakthrough approach to improvement is that such major improvements are, in practice, difficult to realise quickly.

## 'Exploitation' or 'exploration' improvement

A closely related distinction to that between continuous and breakthrough improvement is the one that management theorists draw between what they call 'exploitation' versus 'exploration'. Exploitation is the activity of enhancing processes (and products) that already exist within a firm. The focus of exploitation is on creating efficiencies rather than radically changing resources or processes. Its emphasis is on tight control of the improvement process, standardising processes, clear organisational structures and organisational stability. The benefits from exploitation tend to be relatively immediate, incremental and predictable. They also are likely to be better understood by the firm and fit into its existing strategic framework. Exploration, by contrast, is concerned with the exploration of new possibilities. It is associated with searching for and recognising new mind-sets and ways of doing things. It involves experimentation, taking risks, simulation of possible consequences, flexibility and innovation. The benefits from exploration are principally long term but can be relatively difficult to predict. Moreover, any benefits or discoveries that might come may be so different from what the firm is familiar with that it may not find it easy to take advantage of them.

### Organisational 'ambidexterity'

It is clear that the organisational skills and capabilities required to be successful at exploitation are likely to be very different from those that are needed for the radical exploration of new ideas. Indeed, the two views of improvement may actively conflict. A focus on thoroughly exploring for totally novel choices may consume managerial time, effort and the financial resources that would otherwise be used for refining existing ways of doing things, thus reducing the effectiveness of improving existing processes. Conversely, if existing processes are improved over time, there may be less motivation to experiment with new ideas. So, although both exploitation and exploration can be beneficial, they may compete both for resources and for management attention. This is where the concept of 'organisational ambidexterity' becomes important. Organisational ambidexterity means the ability of a firm to both exploit and explore as it seeks to improve; to be able to compete in mature markets where efficiency is important, by improving existing resources and processes, while also competing in new technologies and/or markets where novelty, innovation and experimentation are required.

In their classic *Harvard Business Review* paper, O'Reilly and Tushman[2] described the difficulties faced by any firm that attempted to thoroughly exploit existing capabilities while exploring new opportunities and called it 'one of the toughest mental balancing acts faced by managers', saying that 'it was unsurprising that companies in general do not do it well'. Those that did, tended to organise separate operations that had very different strategies, structures, processes and cultures and which focused on either efficiency or innovation. This approach to achieving organisational ambidexterity – putting in place 'dual structures' to focus on either exploitation or exploration – is often called 'structural ambidexterity' and is closely related to the concept of operations 'focus' discussed in Chapter 2. Of course, such separate focused units will need to be overseen at some higher level in an organisation. Even if units are structurally independent they must be integrated into the management hierarchy. So, at some level, managers will need to act in an 'ambidextrous' manner.

---

**Example** ┃ Anarchy at 6Wonderkinder[3]

It's a problem every creative firm faces – how do you organise yourself so you can keep some kind of control over what's happening in the firm while not inhibiting the creativity of the people that you are paying to be creative? When 6Wonderkinder, a Berlin-based developer of 'Wunderlist' (the task management tool), was founded in 2010 with only six people, it was relatively easy to foster a creative and innovative atmosphere. But by the time the company had grown tenfold, it was more difficult to preserve the 'start-up spirit'. Chad Fowler, the company's chief technology officer, understands the importance of keeping the innovative culture: '*Probably every single company wants to maintain the feeling of being in a start-up, no matter how big they get.*' As the company grew it used several mechanisms to preserve the 'start-up spirit', such as the yearly 'Wunderkamp', when all staff spend a week away in Bavarian forest cabins or on the Baltic coast, and 'Sexy Friday' when developers get a day a week to pursue their own passions – the aim being to challenge established patterns of working and encourage novel thinking. Christian Reber, the German chief executive and co-founder, says: '*On an assembly line you always get the work you expect. People do the stuff you tell them to do. What we, here, try to achieve is that we regularly get the "wow" factor ... if everyone acts like a CEO, they make the decisions, [if] they are responsible for their own projects, then it completely changes [the] dynamics.*' The relatively flat hierarchy is also an advantage in retaining skilled staff in a sector where the competition for the best developers can be fierce. '*The talent pool is extremely limited, people choose the workplace, especially developers, based more on the working atmosphere – the culture, rather than the salary*', says Christian Reber.

## Two types of improvement?

The two types of distinction discussed here – 'continuous' versus 'breakthrough' improvement and 'exploitation' versus 'exploration', are not quite the same, but they are very similar. Table 7.1 combines the two classifications and lists some of the differences between the two types of approach to improvement. But, notwithstanding the fundamental differences between the two approaches, the continuing challenge that is debated both by practitioners and academics is how to combine the two in order to achieve the ambidextrous organisation.

Although these polarised distinctions are useful to expose the range of what we imply by the seemingly simple idea of 'improvement', they clearly represent extremes. An alternative approach is to imagine the type (and scale) of improvement as a continuum. Such a scale, shown in Table 7.2, characterises process improvement as being, in order of increasing degree of change, concerned with 'modification', 'extension', 'development' and 'pioneer' levels of change. Table 7.2 also illustrates what these degrees of process change could mean in two types of process. Modifications to existing processes are relatively small changes, where the nature of the activities within a process remains largely the same even if there are some minor rearrangements in the details of the sequence or arrangement of the activities within the process. At the other extreme, 'pioneer' change implies adopting radically different, or at least novel to the operation, types of change both to what is done in the process and how it is done. What we have termed 'extension' and 'development' lie in between these extremes. Continuous improvement is usually taken to mean degrees of process change limited

Table 7.1 **Some features of continuous/exploitation improvement and breakthrough/exploration improvement**

| Characteristic | Continuous/exploitation | Breakthrough/exploration |
| --- | --- | --- |
| Strategic intention | Improve existing processes and resources | Innovate to change or introduce new processes, resources or ideas |
| Success measured by | Improved quality, speed, dependability, flexibility, cost | Rate of innovation, new services/ products, growth |
| Pace of improvement | Many gradual and constant continuous small steps | Fewer, abrupt, volatile and dramatic, large steps |
| Probability and time-scale of improvement | Relatively certain and short-term improvements | Risky, longer-term, radical improvements |
| Investment | Requires little investment but great effort to maintain it | Requires large investment but little effort to maintain it |
| Risks | Spread – many projects, but potential 'lost opportunity' risk | Concentrated – 'all (or most) eggs in one (or few) baskets' |
| Competencies | Operational | Strategic/entrepreneurial |
| Organisation | Formal, controlled, top-down, clear objectives | Adaptive, loose, networked, flexible, visionary |
| Culture | Efficient, low-risk, quality, customer-focused | Experimental, risk-taking, challenging |

**Table 7.2** The degree of process change can be characterised by changes in the arrangement and nature of process activities

| | Degree of process change | | | |
| --- | --- | --- | --- | --- |
| | Modification | Extension | Development | Pioneer |
| Arrangement of activities (what is done) | Minor rearrangement of activities | Redesign of sequence or routing between activities | Redefinition of purpose or role activities | Novel/radical change |
| Nature of activities (how it is done) | No or little change to nature of activities | Minor change in nature of activities | Some change in core methodology/ technology process | Novel/radical change |
| Example: thin film precision coating process | New reel-change unit, allows faster changeovers | Clean-room filtering technology introduced, which reduces contamination | High-energy drying allowing shorter drying path and energy savings | High-capacity machine with 'fluid electron' vacuum coating, which gives exceptional quality and low costs |
| Example: health monitoring/ diagnostics process | Patient completes pre-check-up questionnaire and brings it to regular check-up | Nurse performs initial checks at clinic, including new combined heart and respiration testing | Internet-based pre-visit routine allows test programme to be customised for each patient, plus after-visit monitoring of patient health routine | Total remote testing/ monitoring service using 'body shirts', which download via the internet |

to 'modification' or 'extension' changes to the process. Breakthrough improvement is usually assumed to mean what we have termed 'development' or 'pioneer' process change. For example, illustrations of business process re-engineering described in the press tend to be at this end of the scale, although some examples of BPR are relatively minor – what we have called 'extension' change. The most important issues here are, first, that the greater the degree of process change the more difficult that change is to manage successfully and, second, that many small changes need managing in a different way from few, relatively large changes.

## Improvement cycles

A recurring theme in operations process development is the idea that continuous improvement is cyclical in nature – a literally never-ending cycle of repeatedly questioning and adjusting the detailed workings of processes. There are many improvement cycles that attempt to provide a prescription for continuous improvement – some of them proposed by academics, others devised by consultancy firms. And although most of these cycles are not 'strategic', the concept of improvement as a cycle can be translated to mean an ongoing readjustment of strategic understandings, objectives and performance. In fact, the model of operations strategy and reconciliation between market requirements and operations resources itself implies ongoing cyclical readjustment. Market potential responds to the capabilities that the operations function is capable of deploying. Conversely, the operation adjusts its resources and processes in response to the direction set by the company's intended market position. Also, within the operations function, operations capabilities are continually developed or evolved by learning how to use operations resources and processes more effectively. Similarly, within the marketing function, the company's intended market position may be refined and adjusted at least partly by the potential market positioning made possible because of operations capabilities.

## Direct, develop and deploy

Figure 7.2 illustrates the strategic improvement cycle we shall use to structure this chapter. It employs the three 'operations strategy' elements of direct, develop and deploy described below, plus a market strategy element.

- *Direct* – A company's intended market position is a major influence on how the operations function builds up its resources and processes. Some authorities argue that the most important feature of any improvement path is that of selecting a direction. In other words, even micro-level, employee-driven improvement efforts must reflect the intended strategic direction of the firm.

- *Develop* – Within the operations function those resources and processes are increasingly understood and developed over time so as to establish the capabilities of the operation. Essentially this is a process of learning.

- *Deploy* – Operations capabilities need to be leveraged into the company's markets. These capabilities, in effect, define the range of potential market positions that the company may wish to adopt. But this will depend on how effectively operations capabilities are articulated and promoted within the organisation.

- *Market strategy* – The potential market positions that are made possible by an operation's capabilities are not always adopted. An important element in any company's market strategy is to decide which of many alternative market positions it wishes to adopt. Strictly, this lies outside the concerns of operations strategy. In this chapter we shall restrict ourselves to examining the direct, develop and deploy elements.

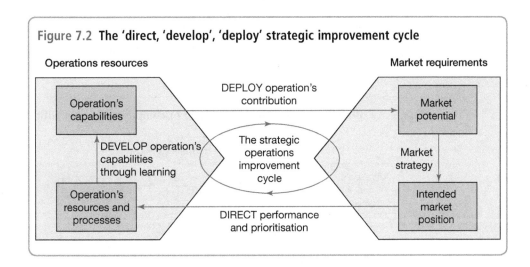

Figure 7.2 **The 'direct, 'develop', 'deploy' strategic improvement cycle**

In reality, the improvement process is never so straightforward, sequential or simple. This cyclical model is not prescriptive. Rather, it merely identifies the types of activity that together contribute to operations improvement at a strategic level. Moreover, no organisation would execute each link in the cycle in a rigorous sequential manner. The activities of directing the overall shape of the operations resources and processes, developing their capabilities through learning, deploying the operations contribution and deciding on market strategy all should occur continually and simultaneously.

## Setting the direction

An important element in the improvement process is the influence a company's intended market position has on the way it manages its resources and processes. In the view of many, it is the only important element. According to this view, operations improvement is a constant search for better ways of supporting the company's markets. And although the model of operations development used here (and our view of operations strategy generally) also takes into account the influence of operations capabilities on market position, the 'direction' to improvement provided by market requirements is clearly an important element. At its simplest, it involves translating the intended market position of the organisation into performance goals or targets for the operation. In fact, just as the whole improvement task can be seen as a cycle, so can each stage. In this case, the cycle involves the ongoing refinement of these targets. For example, a company may decide that its customers place reasonable importance on its products being delivered on time. It therefore sets a target on-time delivery performance of 99.5 per cent. However, it finds that some customer requirements are so complex that manufacturing time is difficult to forecast and therefore delivery dates cannot be met. Because of this, its overall delivery performance is only 97 per cent. However, it emerges during discussions with those customers that they understand the inherent difficulty in forecasting delivery times. What is important to them is not that the original delivery date is met, but that they are given at least two weeks' notice of what the delivery date will actually be. Thus the failure of the operation's performance to match its target prompts the targets to be changed to reflect customers' real requirements more exactly. It is the cycle of setting targets and attempting to meet them that can lead to a more accurate interpretation of the real requirements of the market. In this section of the chapter we will briefly examine three approaches to managing this cycle: performance measurement systems, benchmarking and 'importance–performance' comparisons (see Figure 7.3).

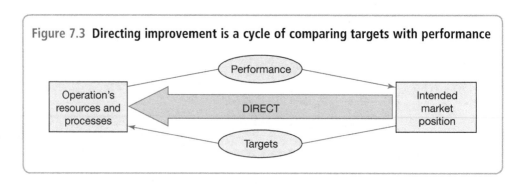

Figure 7.3 **Directing improvement is a cycle of comparing targets with performance**

# Performance measurement

At a day-to-day level, the direction of improvement will be determined partly by whether the current performance of an operation is judged to be good, bad or indifferent, so some kind of performance measurement is a prerequisite for directing improvement. Traditionally, performance measurement has been seen as a means of quantifying the efficiency and effectiveness of action.

Performance measurement, as we are treating it in this chapter, concerns four generic issues:

- what factors to include as performance targets;
- which are the most important;
- how to measure them;
- on what basis to compare actual against target performance.

## *What factors to include as performance targets*

In operations performance measurement there has been a steady broadening in the scope of what is measured. First, it was a matter of persuading the business that because the operations function was responsible for more than cost and productivity, it should therefore measure more than cost and productivity. For example:

> 'A ... major cause of companies getting into trouble with manufacturing is the tendency for many managements to accept simplistic notions in evaluating performance of their manufacturing facilities ... the general tendency in many companies is to evaluate manufacturing primarily on the basis of cost and efficiency. There are many more criteria to judge performance'.[4]

After this, it was a matter of broadening out the scope of measurement to include external as well as internal, long-term as well as short-term and 'soft' as well as 'hard' measures. The best-known manifestation of this trend is the 'Balanced Scorecard' approach taken by Kaplan and Norton.

## *The degree of aggregation of performance targets*

From an operations perspective, an obvious starting point for deciding which performance targets to adopt is to use the five generic performance objectives: quality, speed, dependability, flexibility and cost. Of course, these can be broken down further into more detailed performance targets since each performance objective, as we have mentioned before, is in reality a cluster of separate aspects of performance. Conversely, they can be aggregated with composite performance targets. Broad aspects of performance, such as 'customer satisfaction', 'operations agility' or 'productivity', can give a higher-level picture of both what is required by the market and what performance the operation is achieving. These broad targets may be further aggregated into even broader aims, such as 'achieve market objectives' or 'achieve financial objectives', or even 'achieve overall strategic objectives'. This idea is illustrated in Figure 7.4. The more aggregated performance targets have greater strategic relevance in so much as they help to draw a picture of the overall performance of the business, although by doing so they necessarily include many influences outside those that operations strategy would normally address. The more detailed performance targets are usually monitored more closely and more often, and although they provide only

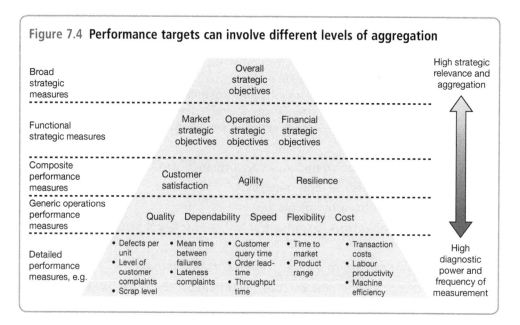

Figure 7.4 **Performance targets can involve different levels of aggregation**

a very limited view of an operation's performance, they provide, in many ways, a more descriptive and complete picture of what should be and what is happening within the operation. In practice, most organisations will choose to use performance targets from throughout the range.

## Which are the most important performance targets

One of the problems of devising a useful performance measurement system is trying to achieve some balance between having a few key measures on the one hand (straightforward and simple, but may not reflect the full range of organisational objectives), and, on the other, having many detailed measures (complex and difficult to manage, but capable of conveying many nuances of performance). Broadly, a compromise is reached by making sure that there is a clear link between competitive strategy, the key performance indicators (KPIs) that reflect the main performance objectives and the bundle of detailed measures that are used to 'flesh out' each key performance indicator. Obviously, unless competitive strategy is well defined (not only in terms of what the organisation intends to do but also in terms of what the organisation will not attempt to do), it is difficult to focus on a narrow range of key performance indicators. So, for example, an international company that responds to oil exploration companies' problems during drilling by offering technical expertise and advice might interpret the five operations performance objectives as follows:

● *Quality* – Operations quality is usually measured in terms of the environmental impact during the period when advice is being given (oil spillage etc.) and the long-term stability of any solution implemented.

● *Speed* – The speed of response is measured from the time the oil exploration company decide that they need help to the time when the drilling starts safely again.

● *Dependability* – This is largely a matter of keeping promises on delivering after-the-event checks and reports.

- *Flexibility* – This is a matter of being able to resource (sometimes several) jobs around the world simultaneously, i.e. volume flexibility.
- *Cost* – This is the total cost of keeping and using the resources (specialist labour and specialist equipment) to perform the emergency consultations.

The company's competitive strategy is clear: it intends to be the most responsive company at getting installations safely back to normal working conditions, while also providing long-term effectiveness of technical solutions offered with minimum environmental impact. It is not competing on cost. The company therefore decides that speed and quality are the two performance objectives key to competitive success. This it translates into three key performance indicators (KPIs):

1 the time from drilling stopping to it starting safely again;

2 the long-term stability of the technical solution offered;

3 the environmental impact of the technical solution offered.

From these KPIs several detailed performance measures were derived. For example, some of those that related to the first KPI (the time from drilling stopping to it starting again) were as follows:

- the time from drilling stopping to the company being formally notified that its services were needed;
- the time from formal notification to getting a team on site;
- on-site time to drilling-commence time;
- time between first arrival on customer's site to getting full technical resources on site.

### How to measure performance targets

The five performance objectives – quality, speed, dependability, flexibility and cost – are really composites of many smaller measures. For example, an operation's cost is derived from many factors, which could include the purchasing efficiency of the operation, the efficiency with which it converts materials, the productivity of its staff, the ratio of direct to indirect staff, and so on. All of these factors individually give a partial view of the operation's cost performance, and many of them overlap in terms of the information they include. Each of them does give a perspective on the cost performance of an operation, however, which could be useful – either to identify areas for improvement or to monitor the extent of improvement. If an organisation regards its 'cost' performance as unsatisfactory, therefore, disaggregating it into 'purchasing efficiency', 'operations efficiency', 'staff productivity', etc. might explain the root cause of the poor performance. Table 7.3 shows some of the partial measures that can be used to judge an operation's performance.

Table 7.3 **Some typical partial measures of performance**

| Performance objective | Some typical measures |
| --- | --- |
| Quality | Number of defects per unit |
| | Level of customer complaints |
| | Scrap level |
| | Warranty claims |
| | Mean time between failures |
| | Customer satisfaction score |

▶

| Speed | Customer query time |
| --- | --- |
| | Order lead time |
| | Frequency of delivery |
| | Actual versus theoretical throughput time |
| | Cycle time |
| Dependability | Percentage of orders delivered late |
| | Average lateness of orders |
| | Proportion of products in stock |
| | Mean deviation from promised arrival |
| | Schedule adherence |
| Flexibility | Time needed to develop new products/services |
| | Range of products/services |
| | Machine change-over time |
| | Average batch size |
| | Time to increase activity rate |
| | Average capacity/maximum capacity |
| | Time to change schedules |
| Cost | Minimum delivery time/average delivery time |
| | Variance against budget |
| | Utilisation of resources |
| | Labour productivity |
| | Added value |
| | Efficiency |
| | Cost per operation hour |

### On what basis to compare actual against target performance

Whatever the individual measures of performance that we extract from an operation, the meaning we derive from them will depend on how we compare them against some kind of standard. So, in Figure 7.5 for example, one of the company's performance measures is delivery performance (in this case defined as the proportion of orders delivered on time, where 'on time' means on the promised day). The actual figure this month has been measured at 83 per cent. However, by itself it does not mean much. Yet, as Figure 7.5 shows, any judgment regarding performance is very dependent on the basis of comparing performance against targets.

An obvious basis for comparison involves using an historical standard. The graph in Figure 7.5 shows that, when compared to last year's performance of 60 per cent, this month's performance of 83 per cent is good. But, there again, with an average performance last year of 69 per cent, the company is likely to have some kind of improvement goal in mind that represents what is regarded as a reasonable level of improvement. So, if the improvement goal was 95 per cent, the actual performance of 83 per cent looks decidedly poor. The company may also be concerned with how it performs against competitors' performance. If competitors are currently averaging delivery performances of around 75 per cent, the company's performance looks rather good. Finally, the more ambitious managers within the company may wish at least to try to seek perfection. Why not, they argue, use an absolute performance standard of 100 per cent delivery on time? Against this standard the company's actual 83 per cent again looks disappointing.

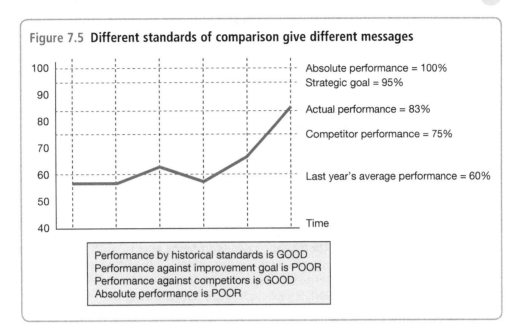

Figure 7.5 **Different standards of comparison give different messages**

Benchmarking

Another very popular, although less 'day-to-day', method for senior managers to drive organisational improvement is to establish operational benchmarks. By highlighting how key operational elements 'shape up' against 'best in class' competitors, key areas for focused improvement can be identified. Originally, the term 'benchmark' derives from land surveying, where a mark, cut in the rock, would act as a reference point. In 1979 the Xerox Corporation, the document and copying company, used the term 'competitive benchmarking' to describe a process 'used by the manufacturing function to revitalise itself by comparing the features, assemblies and components of its products with those of competitors'. Since that time, the term 'benchmarking' has widened to include all types of operation (service or manufacturing), is no longer practised only by experts and consultants but can involve all staff in the organisation, and the term 'competitive' has been widened to mean more than just the direct comparison with competitors. It is now taken to mean benchmarking to gain competitive advantage (perhaps by comparison with, and learning from, non-competitive organisations).

Types of benchmarking

According to the British Quality Foundation, who specialise in such things, there are several different types of benchmarking, including the following.

- *Strategic benchmarking* – that involves examining long-term strategies, core competencies, new product and service development, capabilities for dealing with change and other strategic issues.

- *Performance (or competitive) benchmarking* – that looks at performance characteristics in relation to key products and services in the same sector (often undertaken through trade associations or third parties in order to protect confidentiality).

- *Process benchmarking* – that focuses on improving critical processes and operations through comparison with best practice organisations performing similar work.

- *Functional benchmarking* – that compares a business with partners drawn from different sectors to find innovative ways of improving work processes.

- *Internal benchmarking* – that involves benchmarking businesses or operations from within the same organisation. Access to sensitive and/or standardised data is easier, usually less time and resources are needed and ultimately practices may be relatively easier to implement.

- *External benchmarking* – that analyses 'best in class' outside organisations, providing the opportunity to learn from those at the leading edge.

- *International benchmarking* – that identifies and analyses best practitioners elsewhere in the world, perhaps because there are too few benchmarking partners within the same country to produce valid results.

### The objectives and process of benchmarking

Benchmarking is partly concerned with being able to judge how well an operation is doing. It can be seen, therefore, as one approach to setting realistic performance standards. It is also concerned with searching out new ideas and practices that might be able to be copied or adapted. For example, a bank might learn some things from a supermarket about how it could cope with demand fluctuations during the day. The success of benchmarking, however, is largely due to more than its ability to set performance standards and enable organisations to copy one another. Benchmarking is essentially about stimulating creativity and providing a stimulus that enables operations better to understand how they should be serving their customers. Many organisations find that it is the process itself of looking at different parts of their own company, or looking at external companies, that allows them to understand the connection between the external market needs that an operation is trying to satisfy and the internal operations practices it is using to try to satisfy them. In other words, benchmarking can help to reinforce the idea of the direct contribution that an operation has to the competitiveness of its organisation.

There are many different approaches and 'stage models' that suggest the required steps for successful benchmarking, ranging from models of quality measurement to basic, pragmatic comparisons. Many consultants have their own processes, and larger firms may have an approach tailored to their own strategic goals and business needs. However, most processes are based on four steps:

1  gain a detailed understanding of existing business processes;
2  study the business processes of others;
3  compare steps 1 and 2 to find gaps between current and desired practice/performance;
4  implement whatever is necessary to close the gaps between current and desired practice/performance.

## Importance–performance mapping

Importance–performance mapping is a particularly useful approach to directing operations improvement because it explicitly includes both of the major influences on the generic performance objectives that define market requirements:

- the needs and importance preferences of customers, and
- the performance and activities of competitors.

Both importance and performance have to be brought together before any judgement can be made as to the relative priorities for improvement. Because something is particularly important to its customers does not mean that an operation should give it immediate priority for improvement. The operation may already be considerably better than its competitors in this respect. Similarly, because an operation is not very good at something when compared with its competitors' performance does not necessarily mean that it should be immediately improved. Customers may not particularly value this aspect of performance. Both importance and performance need to be viewed together to judge improvement priority.

Yet, although we have associated importance with the view of customers and performance with the activities of competitors, the approach may be adapted to deviate from this. For example, a company may choose to give importance to some aspect of operations activity even when customers do not find it important. If a company is working towards providing customised products or services in the near future, it may regard flexibility as being more important than do its customers, who are, as yet, unaware of the change in the company's market stance. Neither is performance always judged against competitors. Although it may be an obvious benchmark, it does presuppose the existence of competitors. Many not-for-profit organisations may not see themselves as having competitors as such. They could, however, assess their performance against other similar organisations. Alternatively, they could measure performance against customer perception or customer expectations.

## The importance–performance matrix

The priority for improvement that each competitive factor should be given can be assessed from a comparison of their importance and performance. This can be shown on an importance–performance matrix that, as its name implies, positions each competitive factor according to its score or ratings on these criteria. Figure 7.6 shows an importance–performance matrix where both importance and performance are judged using (in this case) a simple 9-point scale, and where the matrix is divided into zones of improvement priority.

The first zone boundary is the 'lower boundary of acceptability', shown as line AB in Figure 7.6. This is the boundary between acceptable and unacceptable performance. When a competitive factor is rated as relatively unimportant (8 or 9 on the importance scale) this boundary will, in practice, be low. Most operations are prepared to tolerate performance levels that are 'in the same ballpark' as their competitors (even at the bottom end of the rating) for unimportant competitive factors. They only become concerned when performance levels are clearly below those of their competitors. Conversely, when judging competitive factors that are rated highly (1 or 2 on the importance scale), they will be markedly less sanguine at poor or mediocre levels of performance. Minimum levels of acceptability for these competitive factors will usually be at the lower end of the 'better than competitors' class. Below this minimum bound of acceptability (AB) there is clearly a need for improvement; above this line there is no immediate urgency for any improvement. However, not all competitive factors falling below the minimum line will be seen as having the same degree of improvement priority. A boundary approximately represented by line CD represents a distinction between an urgent priority zone and a less urgent improvement zone. Similarly, above the line AB not all competitive

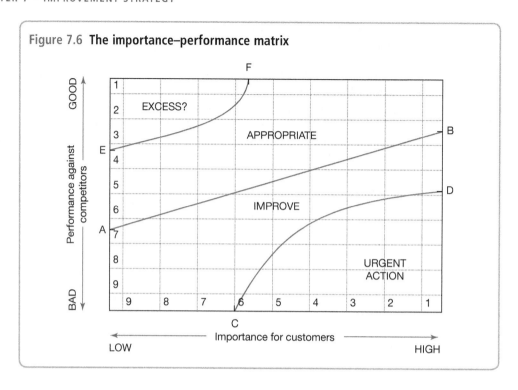

Figure 7.6 **The importance–performance matrix**

factors were regarded as having the same priority. The line EF can be seen as the approximate boundary between performance levels that were regarded as 'good' or 'appropriate' on one hand and those regarded as 'too good' or 'excess' on the other. Segregating the matrix in this way results in four zones that imply very different priorities:

- *The 'appropriate' zone* – This zone is bounded on its lower edge by the 'lower bound of acceptability' – that is, the level of performance below which the company, in the medium term, would not wish the operation to fall. Moving performance up to, or above, this boundary is likely to be the first-stage objective for any improvement programme. Competitive factors that fall in this area should be considered satisfactory, at least in the short to medium term. In the long term, however, most organisations will wish to edge performance towards the upper boundary of the zone.

- *The 'improve' zone* – Any competitive factor that lies below the lower bound of the 'appropriate' zone will be a candidate for improvement. Those lying either just below the bound or in the bottom left-hand corner of the matrix (where performance is poor but it matters less) are likely to be viewed as non-urgent cases. Certainly they need improving, but probably not as a first priority.

- *The 'urgent-action' zone* – More critical will be any competitive factor that lies in the 'urgent-action' zone. These are aspects of operations performance where achievement is so far below what it ought to be, given its importance to the customer, that business is probably being lost directly as a result. Short-term objectives must be, therefore, to raise the performance of any competitive factors lying in this zone at least up to the 'improve' zone. In the medium term they would need to be improved beyond the lower bound of the 'appropriate' zone.

- *The 'excess?' zone* – The question mark is important. If any competitive factors lie in this area their achieved performance is far better than would seem to be warranted. This does not necessarily mean that too many resources are being used to achieve such a level, but it may do. It is only sensible, therefore, to check if any resources that have been used to achieve such a performance could be diverted to a more needy factor – anything that falls in the 'urgent-action' area, for example.

**Example** | **TAG Transport**

TAG Transport is a successful logistics company that is reviewing one of its fastest-growing services – an overnight, temperature-controlled delivery service for chilled food. It is particularly keen to improve the level of service that it gives to its customers. As a first stage in the improvement process it has devised a list of the various aspects of its operations performance:

- Price/cost – the price (including discounts etc.) that it can realise from its customers and the real internal cost of providing the service.
- Distribution quality – the ability to deliver goods in an undamaged state and its customers' perceptions of the appearance of its vehicles and drivers.
- Order/dispatch quality – the courtesy and effectiveness of its customer-facing call centre staff.
- Enquiry lead-time – the elapsed time between an enquiry from a new customer and providing a fully specified proposal.
- Drop time – the earliest time each morning when delivery can be made.
- 'Window' quote – the guaranteed time window around the drop time within which delivery should be made.
- Delivery performance – the proportion of actual deliveries made within the quoted 'window'.
- Delivery flexibility – the ability to change delivery destination.
- Volume flexibility – the ability to provide extra capacity at short notice.
- Documentation service – the reliability of documents such as temperature control charts supplied with each delivery.

Based on its discussions with customers, the laboratory manages to assign a score to each of these factors on the 1 to 9 scale. A score of 1 for 'importance' means that the factor is extremely important to customers and 9 means that it has no importance. For performance, a score of 1 means that TAG is considerably and consistently better than any of its competitors; a score of 9 means that it is very much worse than any competitor. TAG plotted the importance and performance rating they had given to each aspect of performance on an importance–performance matrix. This is shown in Figure 7.7. It shows that the most important issue, delivery performance, is also where the company performs well against its competitors. Several issues need improving, however, and three urgently: enquiry lead-time, order/dispatch quality and delivery flexibility are all relatively important yet the company scores poorly against its competitors.

▶

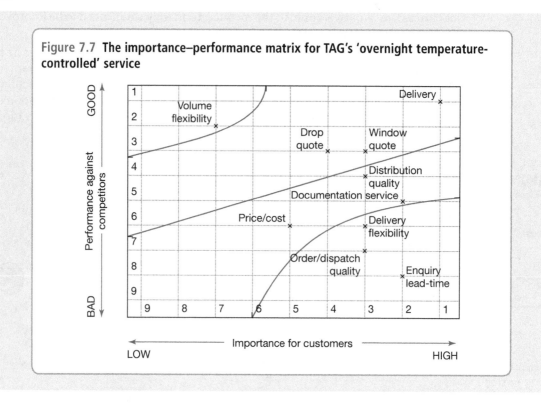

Figure 7.7 **The importance–performance matrix for TAG's 'overnight temperature-controlled' service**

## The sandcone theory

Techniques such as the importance–performance matrix assume that the improvement priority given to various aspects of operations performance is contingent upon the specific circumstances of an organisation's market position. But some authorities believe that there is also a generic 'best' sequence in which operations performance should be improved. The best-known theory of this type is sometimes called the 'sandcone theory'. Although there are slightly different versions of this, the best known is that originally proposed by Arnoud de Meyer and Kasra Ferdows.[5] In fact, the sandcone model incorporates two ideas. The first is that there is a best sequence in which to improve operations performance; the second is that effort expended in improving each aspect of performance must be cumulative. In other words, moving on to the second priority for improvement does not mean dropping the first, and so on.

According to the sandcone theory, the first priority should be quality, since this is a precondition to all lasting improvement. Only when the operation has reached a minimally acceptable level in quality should it then tackle the next issue – that of internal dependability. Importantly, though, moving on to include dependability in the improvement process should not stop the operation making further improvements in quality. Indeed, improvement in dependability will actually require further improvement in quality. Once a critical level of dependability is reached, enough to provide some stability to the operation, the next stage is to turn attention to the speed of internal throughput, but again only while continuing to improve quality and dependability further. Soon it will become evident that the most effective way

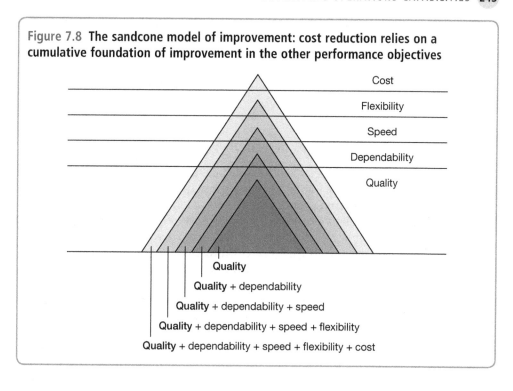

Figure 7.8 **The sandcone model of improvement: cost reduction relies on a cumulative foundation of improvement in the other performance objectives**

to improve speed is through improvements in response flexibility – that is, changing things within the operation faster; for example, reacting to new customer requirements quickly, changing production volumes rapidly and introducing new products faster. Again, including flexibility in the improvement process should not divert attention from continuing to work further on quality, dependability and speed. Only now, according to the sandcone theory, should cost be tackled head on.

The 'sandcone model' is so called because the sand is analogous to management effort and resources. To build a stable sandcone, a stable foundation of quality improvement must be created. Upon such a foundation one can build layers of dependability, speed, flexibility and cost – but only by widening up the lower parts of the sandcone as it is built up (see Figure 7.8). Building up improvement is thus a cumulative process, not a sequential one. Amongst those who have attempted to verify the sandcone theory there is not universal support. Some operations (manufacturing in most studies) appear to be following the sandcone sequence, and benefiting in terms of operational performance, while others do not.

## Developing operations capabilities

Underlying the whole concept of continuous improvement is a simple yet far-reaching idea – small changes, continuously applied, bring big benefits. Small changes are relatively minor adjustments to those resources and processes and the way they are used. In other words, it is the interaction between resources, processes and the staff who manage and operate them wherein lies the potential inherent in continuous improvement. It is the way in which humans learn to use and work with their operations resources and processes that is the basis of capability development. Learning, therefore, is a fundamental part of operations improvement. Here we examine two views of how operations learn. The first is the concept of the learning curve – a largely descriptive device that attempts to quantify the rate of operational improvement over time. Then we look at how operations' learning is driven by the cyclical relationship between process control and process knowledge.

## The learning/experience curve

The relationship between the time taken to perform a task and the accumulated learning or experience was first formulated in the aircraft production industry in the 1930s. The learning curve argues that the reduction in unit labour hours will be proportional to the cumulative number of units produced, and that every time the cumulative output doubles, the hours reduce by a fixed percentage. For example, in much labour-intensive manufacturing (e.g. clothing manufacture) a reduction in hours per unit of 20 per cent is found every time cumulative production has doubled. This is called an 80 per cent learning curve. When plotted on log-log paper, such a curve will appear as a straight line – making extrapolations (and strategic planning) more straightforward. Such 'learning' curves are still used in the aerospace, electronics and defence industries.

The patterns that exist in labour hours have also been found when costs are examined. They have been found not only in individual product costs but also in operation and industry-wide costs. When used to describe cost behaviour, the term 'experience curve' rather than learning curve is used. Where costs are not available, price has often been found to be a suitable proxy. An example of an experience curve is shown in Figure 7.9. It charts the progress of a 'voucher processing operation' in a bank. Voucher processing operations sort, read (using optical character recognition) and process the information from the paper documents generated by the branch operations of the bank. This figure shows how the average cost of processing a voucher reduced over time. To begin with, the operation had not used the type of large machines used in

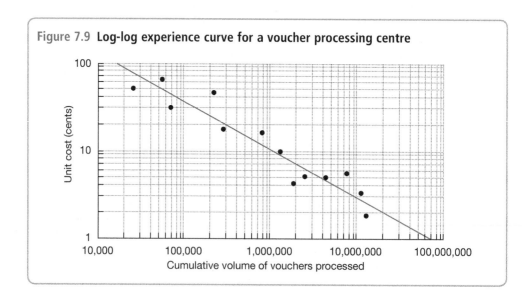

Figure 7.9 **Log-log experience curve for a voucher processing centre**

these processes, nor had it organised itself to receive the hundreds of thousands of vouchers from the branches it serviced. Over time it learned how to organise itself and to use the machines effectively. Although the data in Figure 7.9 stops at a point in time, future learning can be extrapolated from the operation's 'learning history'. This enabled the bank to establish its capacity requirements for the future, work out the cost savings from using such large processing operations and provide improvement targets for this and other similar operations.

## Limits to experience-curve-based strategies

There are clearly risks associated with any strategy that is based exclusively on one form of analysis. In this instance, basing the long-term competitive viability of a firm solely on the potential for ongoing cost reduction is open to a number of serious criticisms:

- Attributing specific costs is notoriously difficult and overhead costs are often arbitrarily allocated. In addition, units may perform poorly because they have the oldest capital equipment and their volume–variety mix may be inappropriate – factors that the experience may not capture.

- The product or service may be superseded. Innovation from within or, even less predictably, from outside of an industry can shift the competitive 'rules of the game'.

- Relentless pursuit of cost reduction (to the detriment of all the other key performance measures) can lead to operational inflexibility. Although traditional trade-off models are questioned in the 'world-class operations' paradigm, there remains an inevitable link between cost and flexibility.

- The control of cost is not the only way that an operation can contribute to the competitive position of the firm. Competing on quality, service, speed, etc. are all equally viable strategic options.

## Process knowledge

Central to developing operations capabilities is the concept of process knowledge. The more we understand the relationship between how we design and run processes and how they perform, the easier it is to improve them. No process will ever reach the point of absolutely perfect knowledge – but most processes can benefit from attempting to move towards it. Moreover, few if any processes operate under conditions of total ignorance. Most operations have at least some idea as to why the processes behave in a particular way. Between these two extremes lies the path of process improvement along which operations managers attempt to journey. It is useful to identify some of the points along this path. One approach to this has been put forward by Roger Bohn.[6] He described an eight-stage scale ranging from 'total ignorance' to 'complete knowledge' of the process (see Table 7.4).

- *Stage 1: Complete ignorance* – There is no knowledge of what is significant in processes. Outputs appear to be totally random and unconnected with any phenomena that can be recognised.

- *Stage 2: Awareness* – There is an awareness that certain phenomena exist and that they are probably relevant to the process, but there is no formal measurement or

Table 7.4 **Characteristics of Bohn's eight stages of process knowledge[7]**

| Stage Term | Indication | Operations activity | Process learning | Process knowledge | To maintain | To move up |
|---|---|---|---|---|---|---|
| 1 Complete ignorance | Pure chance | Expertise-based | Artistic | In people's heads | | Tinkering |
| 2 Awareness | Art | €€€ | | | Professionalism | Develop standards and systematic measures |
| 3 Measurement | Measure good output | | | | Preserve standards | Eliminate causes of large disturbance to process |
| 4 Control of mean | Mean made stable | | | | Observe and correct deviations from limits | Eliminate causes of important variance, identify new sources of variability |
| 5 Process capability | Transitions between products and processes are known | | Natural experiments | Written and oral | Eliminate new causes of variability | Stabilise process transitions and differences in process conditions for different parts |
| 6 Know how | Transitions between products and processes are known | | | | Monitor process parameters and transitions and eliminate causes of new variability | Scientific experimentation and theory building on important variables for new product introduction |
| 7 Know why | Science about all key variables | Procedure-based | Controlled experiments and simulations | Databases and software | Science enquiry and debate | Scientific experimentation and theory building on all variables |
| 8 Complete knowledge | Know all variables and relationships for products, now and in the future | | | | | |

understanding of how they affect the process. Managing the process is far more of an art than a science, and control relies on tacit knowledge (that is, unarticulated knowledge within the individuals managing the system).

- *Stage 3: Measurement* – There is an awareness of significant variables that seem to affect the process with some measurement, but the variables cannot be controlled as such. The best that managers could do would be to alter the process in response to changes in the variables.

- *Stage 4: Control of the mean* – There is some idea of how to control the significant variables that affect the process, even if the control is not precise. Managers can control the average level of variables in the process even if they cannot control the variation around the average. Once processes have reached this level of knowledge, managers can start to carry out experiments and quantify the impact of the variables on the process.

- *Stage 5: Process capability* – The knowledge exists to control both the average and the variation in significant process variables. This enables the way in which processes can be managed and controlled to be written down in some detail. This, in turn, means that managers do not have to 'reinvent the wheel' when repeating activities.

- *Stage 6: Know how* – By now the degree of control has enabled managers to know how the variables affect the output of the process. They can begin to fine-tune and optimise the process.

- *Stage 7: Know why* – The level of knowledge about the processes is now at the 'scientific' level, with a full model of the process predicting behaviour over a wide range of conditions. At this stage of knowledge, control can be performed automatically, probably by microprocessors. The model of the process allows the automatic control mechanisms to optimise processing across all previously experienced products and conditions.

- *Stage 8: Complete knowledge* – In practice, this stage is never reached because it means that the effects of every conceivable variable and condition are known and understood, even when those variables and conditions have not even been considered before. Stage 8 therefore might be best considered as moving towards this hypothetically complete knowledge.

## Example   The Checklist Manifesto[8]

Improvement methodologies are often associated with repetitive operations. Performing the same task repeatedly means that there are plenty of opportunities to 'get it right'. The whole idea behind continuous improvement (see Chapter 3) derives from this simple idea. By contrast, operations that have to perform more difficult activities, especially those that call for expert judgment and diagnostic ability, must call for equally complex improvement approaches – no? Well no, according to Atul Gawande, an oncologist at the prestigious Johns Hopkins Hospital. Gawande thinks that the very opposite is true. Although medicine is advancing at an astounding rate and medical journals produce learned papers adding the results of advanced research to an ever-expanding pool of knowledge, surgeons carry out over two hundred major operations a year and unfortunately not all of them are successful. The medical profession overall does not always have a reliable method for learning from its

▶

mistakes. Atul Gawande's idea is that his, and similar 'knowledge-based' professions, are in danger of sinking under the weight of facts. Scientists are accumulating more and more information and professions are fragmenting into ever-narrower specialisms.

Gawande tells the story of Peter Pronovost – a specialist in critical care at Johns Hopkins Hospital – who, in 2001, tried to reduce the number of patients who were becoming infected on account of the use of intravenous central lines. There are five steps that medical teams can take to reduce the chances of contracting such infections. Initially, Pronovost simply asked nurses to observe whether doctors took the five steps. What they found was that at least a third of the time they missed one or more of the steps. So nurses were authorised to stop doctors who had missed out any of the steps and, as a matter of course, ask whether existing intravenous central lines should be reviewed. As a result of applying these simple checklist-style rules, the ten-day line-infection rates went down from 11 per cent to zero. In one hospital it was calculated that, over a year, this simple method had prevented 43 infections, 8 deaths and saved about $2 million. Using the same checklist approach, the hospital identified and applied the method to other activities. For example, a check in which nurses asked patients about their pain levels led to untreated pain reducing from 41 per cent to 3 per cent. Similarly, the simple checklists method helped the average length of patient stay in intensive care to fall by half. When Pronovost's approach was adopted by other hospitals, within 18 months 1,500 lives and $175 million had been saved.

Gawande describes checklists used in this way as a 'cognitive net' – a mechanism that can help prevent experienced people from making errors due to flawed memory and attention, and ensure that teams work together. Simple checklists are common in other professions. Civil engineers use them to make certain that complicated structures are assembled on-schedule. Chefs use them to make sure that food is prepared exactly to the customers' taste. Airlines use them to make sure that pilots take off safely and also to learn from, now relatively rare, crashes. Indeed, Gawande is happy to acknowledge that checklists are not a new idea. He tells the story of the prototype of the Boeing B17 Flying Fortress that crashed after take-off on its trial flight in 1935. Most experts said that the bomber was 'too complex to fly'. Facing bankruptcy, Boeing investigated and discovered that, confronted with four engines rather than two, the pilot forgot to release a vital locking mechanism. But Boeing created a pilot's checklist, in which the fundamental actions for the stages of flying were made a mandated part of the pilot's job. In the following years, B17s flew almost two million miles without a single accident. According to Gawande, even for pilots (many of whom are rugged individualists) it is usually the application of routine procedures that saves planes when things go wrong, rather than the 'hero-pilotry' so fêted by the media. It is discipline rather than brilliance that preserves life. In fact, it is discipline that leaves room for brilliance to flourish.

## Knowledge management

Central to the idea of improvement is the importance of learning how to do things better. And central to learning how to do things better is the idea of 'knowledge', where knowledge is defined as:

> *'facts, information, and skills acquired through experience or education; the theoretical or practical understanding of a subject.'*[9]

Note how the definition stresses the source of knowledge, and distinguishes between two sources – experience (doing things) and education (explaining or describing what experience has taught you for the benefit of other people). Doing something may lead to you knowing more about it, but having to articulate it or explain it makes your knowledge more valuable because it can be shared with others. It is this process of formalising experience that distinguishes between what is often called 'tacit' knowledge and 'explicit' knowledge.

- Tacit knowledge is knowledge that is in people's heads rather than written or formally articulated or described. It is often based on nuanced information that is difficult to explain to another person by means of writing it down or expressing it verbally. An example of tacit knowledge that is often used is the knowledge of how to ride a bicycle. If you can do it, it is easy to understand, but explaining how to do it in precise terms is very difficult (or almost impossible without one-to-one demonstration, and difficult even then).

- Explicit knowledge, by contrast, is that which is set out in definite form. It can be transmitted in formal, organised language. It has been 'codified'. That is, it has been arranged into systematic language. It is probably included in manuals, records or process maps. Explicit knowledge can be relatively easily communicated between individuals formally and systematically.

The practice of improvement (at least as operations managers are concerned) relies on the continual transformation of experience (tacit knowledge) into a formal, recognised 'better way of doing things' (explicit knowledge). The activity of managing how knowledge is formalised in this way is called 'knowledge management' (often abbreviated to KM). It is an idea that became popular in the early 1990s[10] and means, *'the process of capturing, distributing, and effectively using knowledge'.*[11] It is an approach that tries to bring together the way information (both tacit and explicit) is recognised, recorded, evaluated, retrieved and shared. Amongst the first types of operation to formally use KM were professional services such as consultants. Intellectual capital (IC) is their principal resource, so they realised the potential of the internet for collecting knowledge and connecting together their, often geographically spread, staff.

In the early days of KM it was often seen as a way to improve the productivity of knowledge workers. Not having to 'reinvent the wheel' and building on the previous experience of colleagues would reduce the learning curve time and improve efficiency. More recently, KM has also been seen as a facilitator of product, service and process innovation because of its potential to combine ideas from all parts of an organisation and its external contacts. In addition, especially in regulated markets, KM can enhance compliance, particularly if KM is used to help monitor knowledge access and, as a result, minimise risk.

KM has two distinct, but connected, functions:

- It *collects* knowledge together, often codifying tacit into explicit knowledge. This involves recording knowledge gathered – sometimes directly from a specific experience, sometimes from individual staff's more general tacit knowledge. Collection and codification allows anyone with access to the knowledge base to search for, use (and reuse) the knowledge whenever and from wherever it is needed. This requires the building of large information repositories such as databases (both internal and external).

- It *connects* individual staff (who themselves are holders of tacit knowledge) with the formal codified knowledge that has been collected, and to each other. Connecting individuals together is particularly important because it is not always possible to completely codify tacit knowledge into explicit knowledge. People need to interact with the tacit knowledge that is embodied in the people who have the understanding derived from direct experience in order to gain the insights that may not be obvious in its formal codified form.

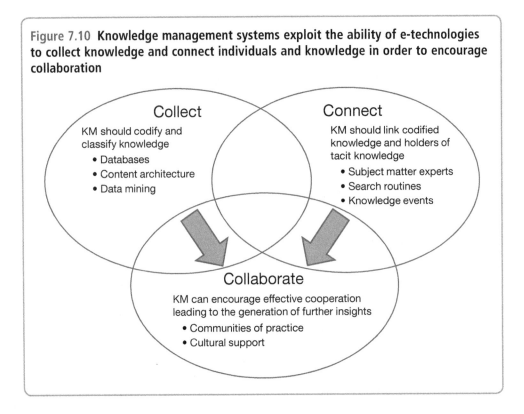

Figure 7.10 **Knowledge management systems exploit the ability of e-technologies to collect knowledge and connect individuals and knowledge in order to encourage collaboration**

These two components of KM have the obvious potential to prevent the underutilisation of an operation's fund of knowledge, but the combination of collection and connection can also have a further effect – it encourages the type of collaboration that can generate even more insights (see Figure 7.10). The idea is that individual staff with appropriate experience (who have been identified by the KM system) will share their understanding of a problem in the context of what is formally known about it (again, as recorded in the KM system), and through this discussion identify additional insights not typically stored in any explicit form.

Since the advent of user-generated and social media-type Web applications, the collaborative aspect of KM has been increasingly emphasised. Operations, even those with a large and geographically dispersed staff with diverse skills, have used KM to collaborate. Tools such as wikis, blogs and social intranet networking allow individuals or teams to facilitate collaboration, not only between internal employees but also with external partners and customers.

### Communities of practice (CoPs)

A community of practice (CoP) is a collection of people who engage on an ongoing basis in some common endeavour. Communities of practice emerge in response to a common interest or position, and play an important role in forming their members' participation in, and orientation to, the world around them.[12] In the context of KM, they are groups of individuals with common interests that 'meet' in person, or virtually, to share and discuss problems and opportunities, best practices and 'lessons learned'. These communities of practice emphasise the social nature of learning within or across organisations. Given KM's reliance on Web-based technologies, CoPs are normally assumed to mean electronically linked communities. However, even with such technologies, maintaining the effectiveness of CoPs is not straightforward. There are at least three key roles[13] to be filled, which have been described as manager, moderator and thought leader. They need not necessarily be three separate people, but in some cases they will need to be.

Well-organised CoPs have been credited with several benefits.[14]

- They help to drive strategy by facilitating the smooth implementation of strategic decisions.
- They can start new lines of business by exploring the application of knowledge to potential new products and services.
- They help to solve problems quickly because they link appropriate solutions with problem 'owners'.
- They transfer best practice by focusing on 'what really works' in practice.
- They develop professional skills because knowledge workers often prefer to learn from like-minded, and like-experienced, colleagues.
- They help to recruit and retain staff because CoPs help to identify professionally satisfying opportunities to practice their expertise.

However, the idea of CoPs is not uncontroversial, especially in academic circles. While many practitioners and consultants have adopted the concept in its entirety, critics point out that they tend to promote a set of general principles without due consideration of context. Also, the idea of 'community' can be problematic. CoP advocates often assume that members will, if provided with sufficient time and technological resources, be happy to cooperate with each other and, in effect, surrender their knowledge for the benefit of the community and the organisation. Yet, in any community there is an inherent tension between individual and group interests. Conventional CoP proponents, they argue, largely ignore issues such as resistance to change, conflict, status, struggle and power.

---

**Example** | **The Eureka knowledge management system at Schlumberger[15]**

Schlumberger is huge – a global company with a turnover of over $40 billion that employs 118,000 people, many of whom are highly qualified and experienced professionals working in the oilfield services industry supplying the latest technology to: *'optimize reservoir performance for customers working in the oil and gas industry'*. The company operates at the leading edge of exploration and extraction, using its expertise to help its clients (oil and gas exploration companies), often in difficult environments. So, managing its knowledge base is central to Schlumberger's continued success in providing innovative and high-quality products and services to its clients.

The company describes knowledge management (KM) as the:

*'development and deployment of processes and technology to improve organizational performance and reduce costs for Schlumberger and its customers by enabling individuals to capture, share and apply their overall knowledge – in real time'.*

▶

Or, as the company sometimes puts it more simply, '*apply everywhere what you learn anywhere*'. According to Susan Rosenbaum, Schlumberger's director of knowledge management, the founding Schlumberger brothers sowed the seeds of a knowledge culture back in the 1930s when they instituted a technical bulletin for the company's pioneering engineers.

> '*That mind-set has flourished. Knowledge is respected as an important asset at Schlumberger. We've had technological solutions internally to capture knowledge since before the term "knowledge management" entered the popular business lexicon. But, while such systems are essential, the key is in how we make use of these tools. It's the sustained interaction between our people that makes the difference.*'

As is normal in KM, technology is important. Schlumberger's proprietary InTouch system is central for knowledge capture and sharing at Schlumberger, which has a direct impact on its customers' experience. The InTouch database, which contains more than one million knowledge items and receives 8 million views per year, is typically the first recourse for field engineers experiencing a persistent technical problem. It also comprises a team of 125 dedicated InTouch engineers available to help solve field issues one on one. These specialists, who 'sleep with beepers and cell phones', have at least five years of field experience and are drawn from all of the company's product and domain segments. Their location within the company's research and technology centres gives them immediate access to the scientists and engineers involved in developing the products and services in the first place.

Schlumberger also supports internal Eureka technical bulletin boards, many of which log 20 or more discussion threads per week. '*You have field and InTouch engineers interacting through the InTouch system*', says Rosenbaum. '*But you also have field engineers helping other field engineers on the bulletin boards. InTouch engineers routinely scan these discussion threads to glean information and spot experienced contacts.*' Increasingly, the flow of knowledge is cyclical, making it more robust than ever. '*Field engineers can flag content on the InTouch database that they feel is outdated, to ensure it gets checked*', says Rosenbaum. '*We're using the power of the people to keep our information up to date.*'

Since it was started, the InTouch system has improved response time by 95 per cent for resolving technical queries, and by 75 per cent for deploying engineering modifications globally. These reductions translate directly into improved operational performance and service to Schlumberger's customers. '*We have a giant web of people helping people at Schlumberger*', says Rosenbaum. '*It's become an entrenched part of the company culture.*'

Some see the success of Schlumberger's KM efforts as being founded on three principles:

- freedom – staff are free to join any community they want to without registration and independent of experience, education or title;
- leadership – each community is managed and run by a leader (or two for a large community) who is democratically elected for one year by the community's members;
- flexibility – communities are not fixed, they change over time with new ones emerging and others disappearing.

## The Nonaka and Takeuchi knowledge model

One of the most influential theories about how knowledge is accumulated through learning is that propounded by Nonaka and Takeuchi.[16] It builds on the idea of the distinction between tacit and explicit knowledge. The model sees knowledge transfer as a spiral process, moving between tacit and explicit knowledge, and back again – both formally and informally. It is usually illustrated as a four-stage progression (see Figure 7.11), showing the transfer of tacit or explicit knowledge. Seen as a continuous learning process, the model shows a clockwise spiral, with organisational learning

**Figure 7.11 The Nonaka and Takeuchi knowledge model**

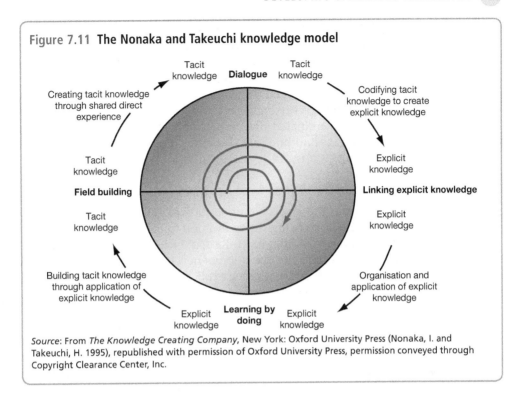

*Source*: From *The Knowledge Creating Company*, New York: Oxford University Press (Nonaka, I. and Takeuchi, H. 1995), republished with permission of Oxford University Press, permission conveyed through Copyright Clearance Center, Inc.

depending on starting, continuing and supporting the learning spiral. Nonaka and Takeuchi stress that the learning path is a spiral, not a cycle, because as one 'learns' around the cycle, understanding moves to progressively more profound levels. The four quadrants of the model are as follows.

### Socialisation (tacit-to-tacit knowledge)

Socialisation is the process of sharing tacit knowledge through social interactions. Although tacit knowledge is essentially personal (it resides in people's brains), it can be broadened and deepened by interacting with others who have similar or complementary tacit knowledge. Increased insights and understandings can come from sharing, discussing, comparing and challenging each other's mental models. It is largely an experiential, informal process, capturing knowledge by walking around and through direct interaction with internal colleagues and external customers and suppliers. And, even when the socialisation process involves structured experiences such as pre-arranged meetings, it is primarily a process between individuals.

### Externalisation (tacit-to-explicit knowledge)

Externalisation is the process of providing a visible form to tacit knowledge by converting it to explicit knowledge. Nonaka and Takeuchi define it as '*a quintessential knowledge creation process in that tacit knowledge becomes explicit, taking the shapes of metaphors, analogies, concepts, hypotheses, or models*'. In other words, individuals are able to articulate and reflect on their tacit knowledge and know-how and put it into a transferable form understandable to others. This stage is not applicable only to internal individuals. It can also include the conversion of external customers', suppliers' and external experts' tacit knowledge into explicit knowledge.

### Combination (explicit-to-explicit knowledge)

Combination is the process of organising individual pieces of explicit knowledge into a new form to make the knowledge more usable. This stage does not involve the creation of new knowledge as such. Rather it consolidates and synthesises existing knowledge by gathering, editing and diffusing existing knowledge. It is at this stage where information technology is most helpful. Explicit knowledge can be established in databases, disseminated through blogs, Web-based portals, emails, etc., as well as through meetings and briefings. It is the combination stage that allows knowledge transfer among groups and across organisations.

### Internalisation (explicit-to-tacit knowledge)

Internalisation is the process of understanding and absorbing explicit knowledge and then, through experiencing the application of the explicit knowledge, developing new insights and understandings in the form of tacit knowledge. It is the actual 'learning by doing' that encourages the formation of new tacit knowledge. The internalisation process transfers organisation and group explicit knowledge to the individual.

Central to this model is the assertion that organisations should not be viewed as simply information-processing entities, because this fails to capture the dynamic nature of how organisations interact with individual staff and their environment. Rather, they should be seen as knowledge-creating entities where various contradictions are synthesised through dynamic interactions among individuals, the organisation and the environment. Knowledge is created in the spiral by moving between seemingly opposing concepts such as order and chaos, micro and macro, part and whole, mind and body, tacit and explicit, self and other, deduction and induction and creativity and efficiency:

> 'the key to understanding the knowledge-creating process is dialectic thinking and acting, which transcends and synthesizes such contradictions. Synthesis is not compromise. Rather, it is the integration of opposing aspects through a dynamic process of dialogue and practice.'[17]

However, the theory is not without its critics – although most are academics with reservations either about the use (or not) of previous research, or the generalisability of the theory. Criticisms include, for example, that the model is based on Japanese management cultural practices that are not transferable to other contexts. Further, the theory does not fully discuss how knowledge can be built in an organisation that is culturally diverse, with staff from different world views, backgrounds, educations, occupations and speaking different languages.

## The strategic importance of operational knowledge

One of the most important sources of process knowledge is the routines of process control. Process control, and especially statistically based process control, is one of the foundations of the Six Sigma improvement approach, explained in Chapter 3. And while process control and process knowledge may seem surprisingly operational for a book about the more strategic aspects of managing operations, it is vital to establishing an operations-based strategic advantage. In reality, the strategic management of any operation cannot be separated from how resources and processes are managed at a detailed and day-to-day level. The process control cycle of capability development is one of the best illustrations of this. As an operation increases its process knowledge it has a better understanding of what its processes can do at the limits of their capability, even though

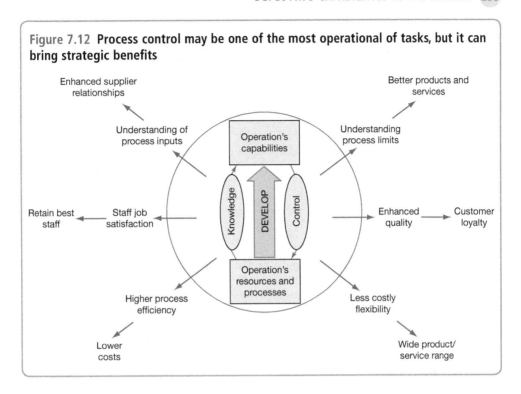

Figure 7.12 **Process control may be one of the most operational of tasks, but it can bring strategic benefits**

those limits are continually expanding. This allows them to develop better products and services not only because of the enhanced process capability but also because of the operation's confidence in that capability. Similarly, as process knowledge increases, some of the more obvious operations trade-offs can be overcome. Often, processes become more flexible in terms of widening their range of capabilities, without excessive additional cost. This, in turn, allows the operation to produce a wider range of products and services. At the same time, fewer process errors mean better conformance quality and (usually) happier customers. Most staff, too, will prefer to work in a process that is under control. Certainly, process uncertainty can undermine staff morale. Retaining good staff within chaotic processes is not easy in the long term. Well-controlled processes will also have fewer errors and waste, and therefore high efficiency and low cost. It can even affect the relationship with suppliers. High levels of process knowledge imply an understanding of how input will affect the process. Armed with this knowledge, relationships with suppliers can develop on a more professional basis. The important point here is that whereas grappling with the details of process control may seem operational, its benefits are not. The increased revenue opportunities of better products and services, a wide product range and customer loyalty, together with better supply relationships, good staff and lower costs, are unquestionably strategic (see Figure 7.12).

## Deploying capabilities in the market

Operations capabilities are of little benefit if not used. Indeed, it could be argued that operations capabilities do not really exist unless they are used; they remain nothing more than unrealised potential. A vital element in strategic operations improvement,

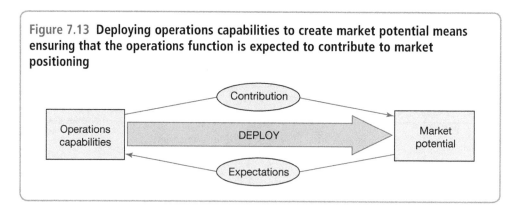

**Figure 7.13** Deploying operations capabilities to create market potential means ensuring that the operations function is expected to contribute to market positioning

therefore, is the ability to leverage developed operations capabilities into the market. Not that operations capability will necessarily exclusively define a company's market position. We are not suggesting that because a company's operations have a particular capability it should always attempt to exploit it in the market. But the deployment of capability does create potential in the market. How this potential is realised (or not) and how organisations target market segments is beyond the scope of this book. However, what is very much important to operations strategy is how the operation can deploy its capabilities to provide the potential for the organisation to inhabit profitable market segments.

Again, we use the idea of a cycle within the overall strategic improvement cycle. This is illustrated in Figure 7.13. Operations capabilities must provide a contribution to what the organisation regards as being its range of potential market positions, but how the operation can contribute to this potential is influenced strongly by the expectations that the rest of the organisation has for its operations. However, before exploring that idea, it is worth distinguishing improvement ideas that emerge internally, and those that are 'inspired' by external players.

## Deploying external ideas

Most of the literature that deals with improvement focuses on the generation, development and deployment of improvement ideas that originated within, rather from outside, the organisation. Yet to ignore the improvements that other companies are deploying is to ignore a potentially huge source of innovation. Whether they are competitors, suppliers, customers, or simply other firms with similar challenges, firms in the wider external business environment can provide solutions to internal problems. The discussion on benchmarking earlier in this chapter is clearly related to the idea of finding inspiration from outside the organisation. But some commentators on innovation go further and argue that (legally) 'copying' from outsiders can be an effective, if underused, approach to improvement. In his book, *Copycats: How Smart Companies Use Imitation to Gain a Strategic Edge*,[18] Oded Shenkar claims that although to argue *'imitation can be strategic seems almost blasphemous in the current scholarly climate'*, it can, *'be strategic and should be part of the strategic repertoire of any agile firm'*. In fact, *'imitation can be a differentiating factor and has the potential to deliver unique value'*. He cites Apple, making the point that the iPod was not the first digital-music player; nor was the iPhone the first smartphone or the iPad the first tablet. To some extent, Apple imitated ideas found in others' products but solved the technical problems, established an appropriate supply chain operating model and made the products far more appealing. Similarly, Ray Kroc, who took McDonald's to worldwide success, copied White Castle – inventor of the fast-food burger joint. And Ireland's Ryanair imitated the business model originally developed in the USA by Southwest Airlines.

Shenkar identifies three 'strategic types' of imitators:[19]

1 *The pioneer importer* – an imitator that is the pioneer in another place (another country, industry, or product market). This is what Ryanair did in Europe when it imported the Southwest model. Pioneer importer imitators may actually be able to move relatively slowly, especially if the original innovator, or other imitators, is unlikely to compete directly in the same market.

2 *The fast second* – a rapid mover arriving quickly after an innovator or pioneer, but before they have had an opportunity to establish an unassailable lead, and before other potentially rival imitators take a large share of the market. This strategy basically lets the pioneer take much of the risk of innovation in the hope that the follower can learn from the pioneer's experience.

3 *The come from behind* – a late entrant or adopter that has deliberately delayed adopting a new idea, maybe because of legal reasons, or because they want to be more certain that the idea will be acceptable. When they do adopt the idea, they may rely on differentiating themselves from the original pioneers. Samsung did this with its chip-making business, by using its manufacturing capability and knowledge to halve the time it takes to build a semiconductor plant. It then established a lead over competitors by exploiting its strengths in key technical, production and quality skills.

---

> **Example** | **Learning from Formula One[20]**
>
> As driving jobs go, there could be no bigger difference than between a Formula One racing driver weaving their way through some of the fastest competitors in the world and a Supermarket truck driver quietly delivering beans, beer and bacon to distribution centres and stores. But they have more in common than one would suspect. Both Formula One and truck drivers want to save fuel, either to reduce pit-stops (Formula One) or keep delivery costs down (heavy goods vehicles). And although grocery deliveries in the suburbs do not seem as thrilling as racing round the track at Monza, the computer-assisted simulation programs developed by the Williams Formula One team are being deployed to help the drivers for Sainsbury's (a British supermarket group) develop the driving skills that could potentially cut their fuel bill by up to 30 per cent. The simulator technology, which allows realistic advanced training to be conducted in a controlled environment, was developed originally for the advanced training of Formula One drivers and was developed and extended at the Williams Technology Centre in Qatar. It can now train drivers to a high level of professional driving skills and road safety applications.
>
> Williams chief executive, Alex Burns, commented:
>
> *'Formula One is well recognised as an excellent technology incubator. It makes perfect sense to embrace some of the new and emerging technologies that the Williams Technology Centre in Qatar is developing from this incubator to help Sainsbury's mission to reduce its energy consumption and enhance the skills and safety of those supporting its crucial logistics operation.'*

▶

Sainsbury's energy-related improvement programmes tackle energy supply (for example, wind, solar and geothermal energy) as well as energy consumption (for example, switching to LED lighting, $CO_2$ refrigeration, etc.). Learning from Formula One will help Sainsbury's to improve further in the field of energy efficiency. Roger Burnley, Sainsbury's retail and logistics director, said:

*'We are committed to reducing our environmental impact and, as a result, we are often at the very forefront of technological innovation. By partnering with Williams F1, we can take advantage of some of the world's most advanced automotive technology, making our operations even more efficient and taking us a step closer to meeting our $CO_2$-reduction targets.'*

## The four-stage model

The ability of any operation to contribute to opening up market potential for the organisation and the organisational aims, expectations and aspirations of the operations function has been captured in a model developed by Professors Hayes and Wheelwright of Harvard University.[21] With later contributions from Professor Chase of the University of Southern California,[22] they developed what they call the 'Four-Stage Model', which is ideal for evaluating the effectiveness of the contribution/expectation cycle. The model traces the progression of the operations function from what is the largely negative role of Stage 1 operations to it becoming the central element of competitive strategy in excellent Stage 4 operations.

### Stage 1 – internal neutrality

This is the very poorest level of contribution by the operations function. In a Stage 1 organisation, the operation is considered a 'necessary evil'. The other functions in the organisation regard it as holding them back from competing effectively. The operations function, they would say, is inward-looking and, at best, reactive. It certainly has very little that is positive to contribute towards competitive success. The best that can be expected from the operations function is to cure the most obvious problems. Certainly, the rest of the organisation would not look to operations as the source of any originality, flair or competitive drive. The expectations on it are to be 'internally neutral' – a position it attempts to achieve not by anything positive but by avoiding the bigger mistakes.

### Stage 2 – external neutrality

The first step of breaking out of Stage 1 is for the operations function to begin comparing itself with similar companies or organisations in the outside market. A Stage 2 operation has achieved a sufficient level of capability to cease holding the company back, even if it may not yet be particularly creative in its contribution to competitiveness. It is expected, at least, to adopt 'best practice' and the best ideas and norms of performance from the rest of its industry. It is expected to be 'externally neutral', with operations capabilities similar to its competitors. This may not give the organisation any competitive advantage but neither is operations the source of competitive disadvantage.

### Stage 3 – internally supportive

Stage 3 operations may not be better than their competitors on every aspect of operations performance but they are broadly up with the best. Nevertheless, good as they may be, Stage 3 operations aspire to be clearly and unambiguously the very best in the market. They try to achieve this level of contribution by a clear understanding of the company's competitive or strategic goals. Then they organise and develop their operations resources to excel in the things in which the company needs to compete effectively. The expectation on the operations function is to be 'internally supportive' by providing credible support to operations strategy.

## Stage 4 – externally supportive

At one time, Stage 3 was taken as the limit of the operations function's contribution. Yet Hayes and Wheelwright capture the emerging sense of the growing importance of operations management by suggesting a further stage – Stage 4. The difference between Stage 3 and Stage 4 is admitted by Hayes and Wheelwright to be subtle, but nevertheless important. A Stage 4 company is one that sees the operations function as providing the foundation for its future competitive success because it is able to deploy unique competencies that provide the company with the performance to compete in future market conditions. In effect, the contribution of the operations function becomes central to strategy making. Stage 4 operations are creative and proactive. They are likely to organise their resources in ways that are innovative and capable of adaptation as markets change. Essentially, they are expected to be 'one step ahead' of competitors – what Hayes and Wheelwright call being 'externally supportive'.

Figure 7.14 brings together the two concepts of role and the contribution of the operations function. Moving from Stage 1 to Stage 2 requires operations to overcome its problems of implementing existing strategies. The move from Stage 2 to Stage 3 requires

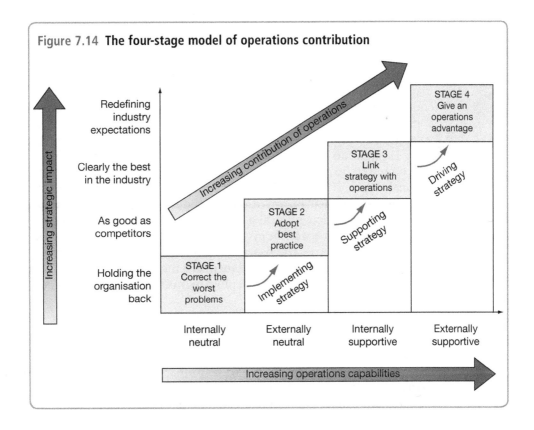

Figure 7.14 **The four-stage model of operations contribution**

operations actively to develop its resources so that they are appropriate for long-term strategy. Moving up to Stage 4 requires operations to be driving strategy through its contribution to competitive superiority. Notice also how moving up from Stage 1 to Stage 4 requires operations progressively to adapt the roles of the operations function discussed in the previous chapter – implementer, supporter and driver, as shown in Figure 7.14.

Two points are important in understanding the power of the four-stage 1 to 4 model. First, it is linked to the company's aspirations (at least its operations management aspirations). In other words, there is an active desire (some might say even an evangelical desire) to improve the operation. Second, it is the endpoint of progression that emphasises the increasing importance and centrality of operations strategy to overall competitive advantage. The idea of a proactive and inventive 'Stage 4' operations function, described by Hayes and Wheelwright, foreshadows the somewhat later concept of 'world-class operations'. That is, the idea that companies should aspire not only to have performance levels equal to, or better than, any other similar business in the world, but should achieve this superiority because of their operations ability.

## SUMMARY ANSWERS TO KEY QUESTIONS

### What are the differences between managing large 'breakthrough' improvements and managing continuous improvement?

Although it is common to distinguish between major 'leaps forward' in terms of operations improvement on the one hand, and more continuous incremental improvement on the other, these are really two points on a spectrum describing the degree of operations change. Major improvement initiatives (such as most business process re-engineering) are dramatic and radical changes in the way operations resources and processes are organised. Continuous improvement, on the other hand, is less dramatic and longer term, involving small incremental steps. Change is gradual and constant and involves most or all staff. Continuous improvement is often described as a 'never-ending cycle'. A closely related distinction is that between 'exploitation' and 'exploration'. Exploitation is the activity of enhancing existing processes (and products). Exploration is concerned with the exploration of new possibilities, recognising new mind-sets, experimentation, taking risks, flexibility and innovation. The organisational skills and capabilities needed for exploitation will be different from those for exploration. So-called 'organisational ambidexterity' is the ability to both exploit *and* explore, which is recognised as a particularly difficult 'mental balancing act faced by managers'. The concept of the cycle, commonly used to describe continuous/exploitation improvement, can also be used to put in place the routines and procedures that help to embed continuous improvement at a more strategic level. One such cycle uses the stages 'direct', 'develop' and 'deploy' to link market position to market potential.

### How do the needs of the market direct the ongoing development of operations processes?

Usually, market needs make their impact on how operations improve themselves through formal mechanisms such as performance measurement systems and benchmarking efforts, although these formal mechanisms are themselves cycles, in so much as they involve continually seeking gaps between the formal targets for the operation set by what the market requires and the actual performance of the operation. Designing performance measurement systems includes four generic issues. First, what factors to include as performance targets? It is likely that performance measures at different levels of aggregation will be needed. The second question is, what are the most important performance targets? These are the aspects of performance that reflect the particular market strategy adopted by an organisation. Often these are contained in a small number of key performance indicators (KPIs). The third question is, how to measure the performance targets? Usually a number of measures are needed to describe broader or more aggregated performance measures adequately. The final question concerns the basis on which to compare actual against target performance. Different bases of performance can affect how we judge performance. Typically, bases for comparison are against historical standards, against improvement goals, against competitors or against some idea of absolute perfection. Benchmarking is also used to direct improvement within operations. There are several different types of benchmarking, including strategic benchmarking, performance (or competitive) benchmarking, process benchmarking, functional benchmarking, internal benchmarking, external benchmarking and international benchmarking. One particular type of benchmarking is importance–performance mapping. This involves formally assessing the relative importance and performance of different aspects of the operation and plotting them on a matrix.

### How can the ongoing management and control of operations be harnessed to develop their capabilities?

As operations gain experience they improve. In some ways this improvement is predictable and can be plotted over time using learning or experience curves. Of more immediate concern in operations strategy, however, is how operations can improve by building their capabilities over time. An important mechanism of capability building is the way in which operations increase their knowledge of their processes through attempting to control them. And although such control may be very operational in nature, the results of the improvement it brings can result in important strategic benefits. Central to improvement is the idea of knowledge acquisition. The process of acquiring knowledge distinguishes between 'tacit' and 'explicit' knowledge. Tacit knowledge is knowledge that is in people's heads rather than written or formally articulated or described. Explicit knowledge is that which is set out in definite form. The activity of managing how knowledge is formalised is called 'knowledge management' (KM) and means, 'the process of capturing, distributing, and effectively using knowledge'. It has two distinct functions: it collects knowledge together, often codifying tacit into explicit knowledge, and it connects individual staff with formal codified knowledge and to each other. KM systems often use the idea of a 'community of practice' (CoP), which is a collection of people who engage on an ongoing basis in some common endeavour. An influential theory about how knowledge is accumulated through learning is the Nonaka and Takeuchi knowledge model that builds on the idea of the distinction between tacit and explicit knowledge. The model sees knowledge transfer as a spiral process, moving between tacit and explicit knowledge, and back again – both formally and informally.

### What can operations do to deploy their capabilities into the market?

Most improvement models focus on improvement ideas that originated within the organisation, but many ideas can originate externally from competitors, suppliers, customers, or other firms with similar challenges. Some commentators argue that ▶

copying ideas from outsiders is an underused approach to improvement. The extent to which an operation deploys its capabilities to create the potential for the organisation to operate in profitable parts of the market is shaped partly by the expectations placed on the operations function. The greater the expectations on the operations function, the more it will attempt to make a significant strategic contribution. The greater the contribution it makes, the higher the expectations of the rest of the organisation will be, and so on. One relatively well-known model for assessing contribution is the Hayes and Wheelwright four-stage model. This model traces the progression of the operations function from the largely negative role of stage 1, to becoming the central element in competitive strategy in so-called stage 4 operations.

## Further reading

Dale, B.D., van der Wiele, T. and van Iwaarden, J. (2007) *Managing Quality*, 5th edition. New York: Wiley-Blackwell.

Goldratt, E.M., Cox, J. and Whitford, J.C.D. (2004) *The Goal: A Process of Ongoing Improvement*, 3rd edition. Great Barrington, MA: North River Press.

Jeston, J. and Nelis, J. (2008) *Business Process Management: Practical Guidelines to Successful Implementations*, 2nd edition. Oxford: Butterworth-Heinemann.

Kaplan, R.S. and Norton, D.P. (2004) *Strategy Maps: Converting Intangible Assets into Tangible Outcomes*. Boston, MA: Harvard Business School Publishing.

Kaplan, R.S. and Norton, D.P. (2008) *Execution Premium. Linking Strategy to Operations for Competitive Advantage*. Boston, MA: Harvard Business School Press.

Leonard-Bart, D. (1995) *Wellsprings of Knowledge: Building and sustaining the sources of innovation*. Boston, MA: Harvard Business School Press.

Liker, J. and Franz, J.K. (2011) *The Toyota Way to Continuous Improvement: Linking Strategy and Operational Excellence to Achieve Superior Performance*. New York: McGraw-Hill Professional.

MacLennon, A. (2010) *Strategy Execution: Translating strategy into action in complex organisations*. London: Routledge

Neely, A. (ed.) (2007) *Business Performance Measurement: Unifying Theory and Integrating Practice*, 2nd edition. Cambridge, UK: Cambridge University Press

Upton, D. (1996) 'Mechanisms for building and sustaining operations improvement', *European Management Journal*, 14(3).

## Notes on the chapter

1 Hayes, R.H. and Pisano, G.P. (1996) 'Manufacturing strategy: at the intersection of two paradigm shifts', *Production and Operations Management*, 5(1).

2 O'Reilly, C.A., and Tushman, M.L. (2004) 'The ambidextrous organization', *Harvard Business Review*, 82(4), pp. 74–83.

3 Vasagar, J. (2014) 'Experiment with a bit of anarchy', *Financial Times*, 28 January.

4 Skinner, W. (1974) 'The focused factory', *Harvard Business Review*, May-June.

5 Ferdows, K. and de Meyer, A. (1990) 'Lasting Improvement in Manufacturing', *Journal of Operations Management*, 9(2).

6 Bohn, R.E. (1994) 'Measuring and managing technical knowledge', *Sloan Management Review*, Fall.

7 Adapted from Bohn (1994), ibid.

8 *Sources:* Gawande, A. (2010) 'The Checklist Manifesto: How to Get Things Right', *Metropolitan*; Aaronovitch, D. (2010) 'The Checklist Manifesto: Review', *The Times* (of London), 23 January.

9 *The New Oxford Dictionary of English*. Oxford: Oxford University Press.

10 Koenig, M.E.D. (2012) 'What is KM? Knowledge Management Explained', *Knowledge Management World*, 4 May, http://www.kmworld.com/

11 Davenport, T.H. (1994) 'Saving IT's Soul: Human Centered Information Management', *Harvard Business Review*, March-April, 72(2), pp. 119–131; Duhon, B. (1998) 'It's All in our Heads', *Inform*, September, 12(8).

12 Eckert, P. (2006) *Communities of Practice, Encyclopaedia of language and linguistics*. Amsterdam: Elsevier.

13 Durham, M. (2004) 'Three Critical Roles for Knowledge Management Workspaces', in M.E.D. Koenig and T.K. Srikantaiah (eds), *Knowledge Management: Lessons Learned: What Works and What Doesn't*. Medford, NJ: Information Today, for The American Society for Information Science and Technology, pp. 23–36.

14 Wenger, E.C. and Snyder, W.M. (2000) 'Communities of Practice: the organizational frontier', *Harvard Business Review*, Jan-Feb.

15 *Sources* include: Schlumberger Press Release (2010) 'Schlumberger Cited for Knowledge Management', Schlumberger Press Office Date: 03/12/2010; Francçois Deltour, F., Loïc Plé, L. and Roussel, C.S. (2013) 'Eureka! Developing Online Communities of Practice to Facilitate Knowledge Sharing At Schlumberger', IESEG School of Management, LEM, Case Study 313-122-1.

16 Nonaka, I. and Takeuchi (1995) *The Knowledge-creating Company*. New York: Oxford University Press.

17 Nonaka, I. and Toyama, R. (2003) 'The knowledge-creating theory revisited: knowledge creation as a synthesizing process', *Knowledge Management Research & Practice*, Vol 1, pp. 2–10.

18 Shenkar, O. (2010) *Copycats: How Smart Companies Use Imitation to Gain a Strategic Edge*. Boston, MA: Harvard Business School Press.

19 Shenkar, O. (2012) 'Just Imitate It! A Copycat Path To Strategic Agility', *Ivey Business Journal*, May–June.

20 *Sources* include: West, K. (2011) 'Formula One trains van drivers', *The Times*, 1 May; F1network.net: http://www.f1network.net/main/s107/st164086.htm

21 Hayes, R.J. and Wheelwright, S.C. (1984) *Restoring our Competitive Edge*. New York: Wiley.

22 Chase, R.B. and Hayes, R.J. (1991) 'Beefing up operations in service firms', *Sloan Management Review*, Fall, pp. 15–16.

# Product and service development and organisation

## Introduction

The products and services produced by an operation are its 'public face' in so much as they are what markets judge a company on: good products and services equals good company. Because of this, it has always made sense to devote time and effort to how new products and services are developed. Moreover, it has long been accepted that there is a connection between how companies go about developing products and services and how successful those products and services are in the marketplace. Now two things have changed: first, both the speed and scale of market and technology changes has increased; second, there is a greater understanding of how closely connected are the processes by which products and services are developed and the outcomes from those processes. Given that product and service development is a core issue for operations strategy, it is appropriate that it is treated here (see Figure 8.1). And, even though it is a subject in its own right, it can still benefit from an operations strategy analysis.

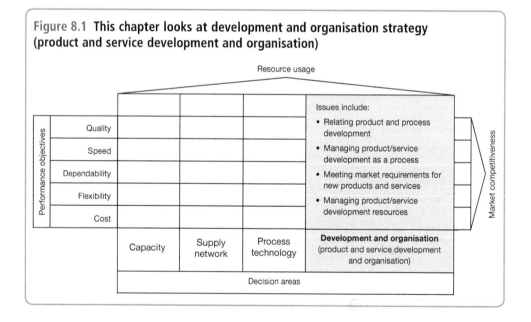

Figure 8.1 **This chapter looks at development and organisation strategy (product and service development and organisation)**

**KEY QUESTIONS**

- *Why is the way in which companies develop their products and services so important?*
- *What process do companies use to develop products and services?*
- *How should the effectiveness of the product and service development process be judged in terms of fulfilling market requirements?*
- *What operations resource-based decisions define a company's product and service development strategy?*

## The strategic importance of product and service development

Figure 8.2 illustrates some of the more significant reasons why product and service development is seen as increasingly strategically important. From a market perspective, international competition has become increasingly intense. In many markets there are a number of competitors bunched together in terms of their product and service performance. Even small advantages in product and service specifications can have a significant impact on competitiveness. This has made customers both more sophisticated in exercising their choice and often more demanding in terms of wanting products and services that fit their specific needs. Also, markets are becoming more fragmented. Unless companies choose to follow relatively narrow niche markets, they are faced with developing products and services capable of being adapted in different ways to different markets. If this were not enough,

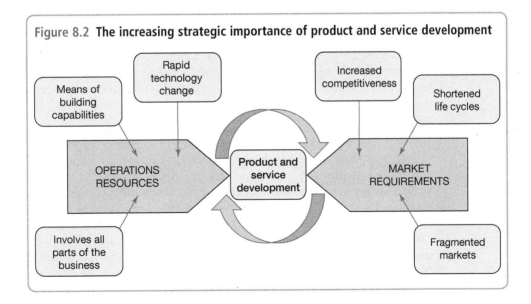

Figure 8.2 **The increasing strategic importance of product and service development**

product and service life cycles have become shorter. An obvious way to try to gain advantage over competitors is to introduce updated products and services. Competitors respond by doing the same and the situation escalates. While not every industry has such short life cycles as, say, the entertainment or fashion garment industry, the trend, even in industrial markets, is towards more frequent new product and service introductions.

A different, but equally important, set of pressures affect the operations resources that have to develop and deliver new products and services. Perhaps most importantly, rapid technology changes have affected most industries. For example, internet-based technologies have introduced startlingly new possibilities (and uncertainties) for almost all products and services in all industries. Partly because of the scale and pace of such technological developments, it has become increasingly obvious that effective product and service development places responsibilities on every part of the business. Marketing, purchasing, accounting, operations are all, like it or not, an integral part of any organisation's ability to develop products and services effectively and efficiently. Every part of the business is now faced with the question, 'How can we deploy our competencies and skills towards developing better or different products and services?' New product and service development is now seen as the mechanism by which all parts of the business, but especially operations, leverage their capabilities into the marketplace.

## Developing products and services and developing processes

For convenience and for ease of explanation we often treat the design of products and services on the one hand, and the design of the processes that produce them on the other, as though they were totally separate activities. In many organisations the two developments are organised separately. But this does not imply that they necessarily should be treated or organised separately, and they are clearly interrelated. It would be foolish to develop any product or service without taking into consideration the constraints and capabilities of the processes that will produce it. Similarly, developing processes to take advantage of new technologies or process methods will have implications for the development of products and services in the future. Successful developments often have a history of both product/service and process development.

### *The degree of product change is important*

Just as it was important in the previous chapter to understand the degree of process change expected of the development process, so here it is important to understand the degree of product or service change. Again, we can construct a conceptual scale that helps to give some degree of discrimination between different levels of change. Also again, we can calibrate this scale from relatively minor modifications to a product or service at one extreme, through to the novel and/or radical changes exhibited by a 'pioneer' product or service. In the previous chapter we distinguished between what is done in a process and how it is done. The equivalent here is the distinction between what is seen externally to have changed in the product or service and how the product or service performs its function through its internal mechanisms. Table 8.1 describes four levels of change, 'modification', 'extension', 'development' and 'pioneer', in terms of the product's or services' external and internal characteristics. It also shows two illustrative examples, one

Table 8.1 **The degree of product/service change can affect both its external appearance and its internal methodology/technology**

| | Degree of product/service change | | | |
| --- | --- | --- | --- | --- |
| | Modification | Extension | Development | Pioneer |
| External customer awareness (what is seen) | Little/none | More functionality | 'Next generation' progression | Novel/radical change |
| Internal methodology/ technology (how it is done) | Minor/isolated | Some changes to original methodology/ technology | Extensive redesign of original method/ technology | Novel/radical change |
| Example: exercise machines | Minor engineering change to component parts | Extra options on control/display of computer | Aesthetic redesign and changes to internal resistance mechanism | 'Total health monitoring' concept with intelligent machines' response to body monitoring and full automatic analysis |
| Example: bank card services | Minor changes to back-office procedures | Improvement of monthly statement with analysis of expenditure | Incorporation of smart-card technology | Ultimately flexible 'one card' concept with advanced smart-card capability and links with other financial services. |

based on a company that manufactures exercise machines, the other a financial service company that runs a bank card service. Remember, though, that the level of change implied by these categories of development to products and services is approximate. What is important is to recognise that the nature of the product and service development process is likely to be different depending on the degree of product/service change.

Relatively small 'modification' changes, such as those described in the two examples in Table 8.1, are likely to be relatively frequent and will probably be made using routine procedures. Most companies have standard procedures such as 'engineering change orders' (ECOs), where small changes are proposed in one part of the organisation and approved by other relevant departments. But although these small modifications may be incorporated into standard procedures, they may still require organisation-wide exposure, especially if the part of the product or service being modified has high 'connectivity'. Connectivity is the degree to which changes in one part of a product or service impact on other parts. It is a concept that can also apply at an organisational level and is important in understanding why, as the degree of product or service change moves thorough 'extension' and 'development' to 'pioneer', the changes become more difficult and more risky. Fundamental changes to products and services almost always involve the whole organisation. So, in addition to the obvious difficulties of market acceptability and resource capability inherent in high degrees of product and service change, the coordination between functional strategies must be well managed.

**Example** **The troubled history of the Airbus A380[1]**

If anyone doubted the importance of product/service development to strategic success (or failure), just look at the history of the Airbus A380. It is now a successful aircraft, but its long and incident-packed journey from drawing board to reality illustrates the dangers when the design activity goes wrong. This is the story in brief:

**1991** – Airbus consults with international airlines about their requirements for a super-large passenger aircraft.

**January 1993** – Airbus' rival, Boeing, says it has begun studies into 'very large' commercial aircraft.

**June 1993** – Boeing decides not to go for a super-large passenger aircraft, but instead to focus on designing smaller 'jumbos'. Airbus and its partners set up the A3XX team to start the 'super-jumbo' project.

**1996** – Airbus forms its 'Large Aircraft' division. Because of the size of the aircraft, it is decided to develop specially designed engines rather than adapt existing models.

**2000** – The commercial launch of the A3XX (later to be named the A380).

**2002** – Work starts on manufacturing the aircraft's key components.

**February 2004** – Rolls-Royce delivers the first Airbus engines to the assembly plant in Toulouse.

**April 2004** – The first Airbus wings are completed in the north Wales factory. London's Heathrow Airport starts to redevelop its facilities so that it can accommodate the new aircraft.

**May 2004** – Assembly begins in the Toulouse plant.

**December 2004** – EADS, the parent company of Airbus, reveals the project is €1.45billion over budget, and will now cost more than €12billion.

**January 2005** – Airbus unveils the A380 to the world's press and European leaders.

**27 April 2005** – The aircraft makes its maiden flight, taking off in Toulouse and circling the Bay of Biscay for four hours before returning to Toulouse. A year of flight-testing and certification work begins.

**June 2005** – Airbus announces that the plane's delivery schedule will slip by six months.

**March 2006** – The plane passes important safety tests, involving 850 passengers and 20 crew safely leaving the aircraft in less than 80 seconds with half the exits blocked.

**July 2006** – The A380 suffers another production delay. Airbus now predicts a delay of a further six to seven months. This causes turmoil in the boardrooms of both Airbus and EADS. The company's directors are accused of supressing the news for months before revealing it to shareholders. It leads to the resignations of Gustav Humbert, Airbus' chief executive, Noel Forgeard, EADS co-chief executive, and Charles Campion, the A380 programme manager.

**October 2006** – Airbus infuriates customers by announcing yet a further delay for the A380, this time of a whole year. The first plane is now forecast to enter commercial service around twenty months later than had been originally planned. The delays will cost Airbus another estimated €4.8billion over the next four years. The company announces a drastic cost-cutting plan to try to recoup some of the losses. The Power8 programme is intended to 'reduce costs, save cash and develop new products faster'. It wants to increase productivity by 20 per cent and reduce overheads by 30 per cent.

**October 2007** – The super-jumbo eventually takes off in full service as a commercial airliner for Singapore Airlines. It wins rave reviews from both airlines and passengers – even if it is two years late!

So what caused the delays? First, the A380 was the most complex passenger jet ever to be built. Second, the company was notorious for its internal rivalries, its constant need to balance work between its French and German plants so that no country had too obvious an advantage, constant political infighting, particularly by the French and German governments, and frequent changes of management. According to one insider, '*the underlying reason for the mess we were in was the hopeless lack of integration [between the French and German sides] within the company*'. Even before the problems became evident to outsiders, critics of Airbus claimed that its fragmented structure was highly inefficient and prevented it from competing effectively. Eventually it was this lack of integration between design and manufacturing processes that was the main reason for the delays to the aircraft's launch. During the early design stages the firm's French and German factories had used incompatible software to design the 500km of wiring that each plane needs. Eventually, to resolve the cabling problems, the company had to transfer 2,000 German staff from Hamburg to Toulouse. Processes that should have been streamlined had to be replaced by temporary and less efficient ones, described by one French Union official as a '*do-it-yourself system*'. Feelings ran high on the shop floor, with tension and arguments between French and German staff. '*The German staff will first have to succeed at doing the work they should have done in Germany*', said the same official. Electricians had to resolve the complex wiring problems, with the engineers having to adjust the computer blueprints as they modified them so they could be used on future aircraft. '*Normal installation time is two to three weeks*', said Sabine Klauke, a team leader. '*This way it is taking us four months.*' Mario Heinen, who ran the cabin and fuselage cross-border division, admitted the pressure to keep up with intense production schedules and the overcrowded conditions made things difficult. '*We have been working on these initial aircraft in a hand-made way. It is not a perfectly organised industrial process.*' But, he claimed, there was no choice. '*We have delivered five high-quality aircraft this way. If we had left the work in Hamburg, to wait for a new wiring design, we would not have delivered one by now.*' But the toll taken by these delays was high. The improvised wiring processes were far more expensive than the planned 'streamlined' processes, and the delay in launching the aircraft meant two years without the revenue that the company had expected.

But Airbus was not alone. At the same time, its great rival, Boeing, was also having problems. Engineers' strikes, supply chain problems and mistakes by its own design engineers had further delayed its '787 Dreamliner' aircraft. Specifically, fasteners used to attach the titanium floor grid to the composite 'barrel' of the fuselage had been wrongly located, resulting in 8,000 fasteners having to be replaced. The Boeing aircraft was also two years late.

## Product and process change should be considered together

We can put together the degree of process change scale from the previous chapter with the scale indicating the degree of product/service change described in Table 8.1. This is done in Figure 8.3. Advanced, or 'blue sky', research and development lies beyond both of these scales, but it is from this direction that most radical innovation emerges. The dotted lines indicate the degree of difficulty encountered in the development process. Put simply, product/service change is easier when the underlying processes that produce them are not being changed at the same time, and vice versa. Figure 8.3

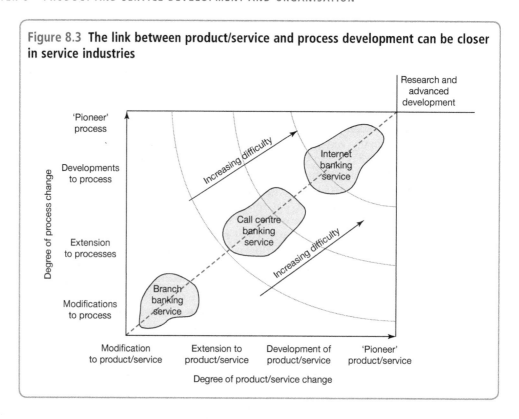

Figure 8.3 **The link between product/service and process development can be closer in service industries**

also shows three service/process developments at a bank. Making changes to the services offered in a bank branch involves relatively minor 'product' and process changes compared with the redesign of both product and process involved in a major new call centre. This, in turn, is less than the development of a totally new internet banking service.

### Managing the overlap between product and process development

Because it is often difficult to untangle a service 'product' from the process that produces it, operations developing new services know they have to develop new processes concurrently. But manufacturing operations are different. It is often possible to develop products independently of the processes that make them, and also common practice for many companies. Yet, because product development and process development are not the same thing, it does not mean that they should not overlap. In fact, one of the more important trends in product design has been the considerable effort that recently has been put into managing the overlap. There are probably two reasons for this. First, there is a growing recognition that the design of products has a major effect on the cost of making them. Many decisions taken during the development of products such as the choice of material, or the way components are fastened together, will define much of the cost of making the product. It clearly makes sense, therefore, to build into the development process the need to evaluate product design choices in terms of their effect on manufacturing processes, as well as the functionality of the product itself. Second, the way overlap is managed between product and process development has a significant effect on the effectiveness and efficiency of the development process itself. This is particularly true for the time between the initial product or service concept and its eventual delivery into the market, and the overall cost of the total development effort. We shall deal with this issue later in the chapter.

### Modular design and mass customisation

Two separate, but related, ideas – modularity in product and service design and mass customisation – have made an impact on product and service development. We will consider them separately and then bring the two ideas together.

*Modularity* – is a strategy for organising complex products (and services) and processes efficiently. A modular system is composed of units (or modules) that are designed independently but still function as an integrated whole.[2] So, rather than designing a product and service as a totally integrated and indivisible whole, the design is divided into modules that can be put together in various ways. Putting different modules together will result in products or services with different functionality. Yet because the modules themselves are standardised, they can be produced in a standardised low-cost manner. The most obvious examples of modular design are in the computer industry, where relatively complex products can be built up using smaller subsystems. Customers who have different requirements can simply choose which modules they require within the overall product. Provided the overall architecture of the design (the way modules fit together and the functions they perform) and the interfaces between the modules allow for easy connection and communication, then modularity can offer considerable advantages. For example, innovative ideas can be tried out in one module without it necessarily interfering with the design of the product or service as a whole. So, suppose a medical centre offers a range of different health check-up services. If it designs its processes and systems to separate its different clinical procedures, it could introduce new tests in one area while leaving the others undisturbed. Of course, it would have to ensure that the interfaces between the improved test area and the other parts of its services processes (records, diagnostics, follow-up appointments, and so on) could handle any new information generated.

*Mass customisation* – is the ability to provide customers with high levels of variety and customisation through flexible and responsive processes and flexible product and service designs.[3] The vision of mass customisation is to reduce radically the effect of the assumed trade-off between variety and cost. Some authorities see it as an inevitable successor to mass production, while others argue that there is little essentially new in the idea, rather it pushes existing ideas such as flexibility and agility to their logical conclusion.[4] The mass-customisation concept includes the ideas that, as far as market requirements are concerned, markets are becoming increasingly fragmented, while as far as operations resources are concerned, new forms of organisation and technology are allowing greater degrees of flexibility and responsiveness. Thus, it is possible to 'mass produce' a basic family of products or services that can still be customised to the needs of individual customers. The major management task, therefore, is to understand the implications of market and operations developments and harness them by embracing an attitude that stresses sensitivity to customers' individual needs and a willingness to supply them with customised offerings. This means changes in the way the operation produces its products and services and the way it markets them. But, of particular relevance here, it also implies a different approach to designing products and services. Predominantly, this involves the standardisation and modularisation of components (see above) to increase variety while reducing production costs.

One much-quoted example of how modular design contributed to mass customisation is the way Black and Decker, the hand-tool manufacturer, produced a wide range of well over 100 basic hand tools, each with their own variants, from a relatively small set of modular and standardised components. The first consequence of this modular approach was more effective and efficient design:

> 'Much of the work in design and tooling was eliminated because of the standardisation of motors, bearings, switches, ... etc. New designs could be developed using components already standardised for manufacturing ability. The product did not have to start with a blank sheet of paper and be designed from scratch'.[5]

The second was drastically reduced production costs because standardised parts enabled standardised production processes.

---

**Example** **The sad tale of Kodak and its digital camera[6]**

The once-mighty Eastman Kodak Company dominated the photographic and film markets for decades. But no longer. Thirty years ago it employed over 140,000 people and made substantial profits; by 2010 it had shrunk to around 19,000, with regular quarterly losses. This dramatic fall from grace is usually put down to the company's failure to see the approach of digital photography or fully appreciate how it would totally undermine Kodak's traditional products. Yet, ironically, Kodak was far more than ahead of its competitors than most people outside the company realised. It actually invented the digital camera. Sadly, though, it lacked the foresight to make the most of it. For years the company had, as one insider put it, '*too much technology in its labs rather than in the market*'.

It was back in 1975 when a newly hired scientist at Kodak, Steve Sasson, was given the task of researching how to build a camera using a comparatively new type of electronic sensor – the charged-couple device (CCD). He found little previous research so he used the lens from a Kodak motion-picture camera, an analogue-to-digital convertor, some CCD chips and some digital circuitry that he made himself. By December 1975 he had an operational prototype. Yet the advance was largely, although not completely, ignored inside the company. '*Some people talked about reasons it would never happen, while others looked at it and realised it was important*', he says. He also decided not to use the word 'digital' to describe his trial product. '*I proposed it as filmless photography, an electronic stills camera. Calling it "digital" would not have been an advantage. Back then "digital" was not a good term. It meant new, esoteric technology*.' Some resistance came from genuine, if mistaken, technical reservations. But others feared the magnitude of the changes that digital photography could bring. Objections ... '*were coming from the gut: a realisation that [digital] would change everything – and threaten the company's entire film-based business model*'. Some see Kodak's reluctance to abandon its traditional product range as understandable. It was making vast profits and as late as 1999 it was making over three billion dollars from film sales. Todd Gustavson, curator of technology at the George Eastman House Museum, says that, '*Kodak was almost recession-proof until the rise of digital. A film-coating machine was like a device that printed money.*' So Kodak's first digital camera, the Quicktake, was licensed to and sold by Apple in 1994.

In 2012 Kodak filed for Chapter 11 bankruptcy protection. It did emerge from bankruptcy the following year, but only having sold many of its businesses and patents (including its photography film business) for a fraction of what they were once worth.

## Product and service development as a process

There are two views of how to characterise product and service development. One sees it as essentially a creative process, where a technical understanding of the mechanisms involved in the service or product is brought together with ingenuity and flair. The emphasis should be on creativity, novelty and innovation. For all this to happen, the people involved must be given the space and time to be creative. Of course, the activity has to be managed but not to the point where it interferes with originality. Typically this view of product and service development sees the activity as a collection of, sometimes interdependent, projects. And although some aspects of project management may be relevant in guiding the activity, it cannot be regarded as a 'process'. Processes are what create products and services on a routine basis, whereas product and service development is the creation of original one-offs. Furthermore, the raw material of this knowledge is a substance that is difficult to define and even more difficult to identify. Product and service development, therefore, must focus on its outcome and not worry too much about how that outcome is achieved.

The counter-argument contends that, as with everything, output depends on process. Great ideas for products and services emerge from a process that makes them great. Therefore, of course, one should examine the process of product and service development. While no two development projects are exactly alike, there is sufficient commonality in all such projects to be able to model the process and work on improving its overall performance. The normal generic performance objectives that apply to any operations process – quality, speed, dependability, flexibility and cost – all have relevance to product and service development. Most companies would willingly adopt an approach that gave them higher-quality designs for new products and services, delivered faster and more dependably while maintaining sufficient flexibility to incorporate new ideas that are produced at lower cost. It makes sense, therefore, to apply similar approaches to improving product and service development processes as one would to any other process. Define the steps in the process, examine the characteristics of how prospective product and service designs flow through the resources that act upon them, look for bottlenecks and attempt to smooth them out, identify critical points in the flow and guard against quality failures at these points, and so on. This is the approach we shall take. Product and service development is a process, and needs to be managed strategically.

---

**Example**   Spangler, Hoover and Dyson[7]

In 1907 a janitor called Murray Spangler put together a pillowcase, a fan, an old biscuit tin and a broom handle. It was the world's first vacuum cleaner. One year later he sold his patented idea to William Hoover, whose company went on to dominate the vacuum cleaner market for decades, especially in its United States homeland. Yet between 2002 and 2005 Hoover's market share dropped from 36 per cent to 13.5 per cent. Why? Because a futuristic-looking and comparatively expensive rival product, the Dyson vacuum cleaner, had jumped from nothing to over 20 per cent of the market. In fact, the Dyson product dates back to 1978, when James Dyson noticed how the air filter in the spray-finishing room of a company where he had been working was constantly clogging with power particles (just like a vacuum cleaner bag clogs with dust). So he designed and built an industrial cyclone tower, which removed the

▶

powder particles by exerting centrifugal forces. The question intriguing him was, *'Could the same principle work in a domestic vacuum cleaner?'* Five years and five *thousand* prototypes later he had a working design, since praised for its 'uniqueness and functionality'. However, existing vacuum cleaner manufacturers were not as impressed – two rejected the design outright. So Dyson started making his new design himself. Within a few years Dyson cleaners were, in the UK, outselling the rivals who had once rejected them. The aesthetics and functionality of the design help to keep sales growing in spite of a higher retail price. To Dyson, good *'is about looking at everyday things with new eyes and working out how they can be made better. It's about challenging existing technology.'*

Dyson scientists were determined to challenge even their own technology and create vacuum cleaners with even higher suction. So they set to work developing an entirely new type of cyclone system. They discovered that a smaller-diameter cyclone gives greater centrifugal force. So they developed a way of getting 45 per cent more suction than a dual cyclone and removing more dust, by dividing the air into eight smaller cyclones. This advanced technology was then incorporated into their new products.

## Product/service development – an operations strategy analysis

Product and service development can be treated as a coherent operation in its own right. We include it here as a part of the development and organisation decision area because developing products and services is clearly vital to any organisation's strategic development. However, the topic could be treated as an entirely separate function (which it is in many organisations). Indeed, for professional design consultancies, for example, it is their whole reason for existing. We include the topic within operations strategy not because we believe product and service development should be always an integral part of the operations function organisationally. Rather, it is because of the difficulty in untangling the process of producing and delivering products and services and that of developing those products and services in the first place. Also, because we treat the topic as an integral part of operations strategy does not mean that no benefit can be derived from analysing product and service development as a distinct operations strategy in its own right.

For example, Figure 8.4 illustrates how an operations strategy matrix (discussed in Chapter 1) can be constructed for product and service development operations. The generic performance objectives of quality, speed, dependability, flexibility and cost can be used to describe the impact of new or modified products and services in the marketplace. In order to achieve competitive 'production' of product and service designs, the resources and processes that are used to develop them will themselves need organising along the lines of any other operation. The company's design capacity will have to be matched to the demand placed on it over time; relationships with an external supply network for design and development knowledge will have to be established; process technologies such as computer-aided design (CAD) systems, expert systems, simulations and so on may be needed; and also the resources technology and processes used to develop products and services will need organising and themselves developing over time. All decision areas are of some relevance to most companies' development efforts.

The remainder of this chapter will first examine the nature of the product and service development process and then use the operations strategy approach to illustrate the requirements of the market and the capabilities of development resources.

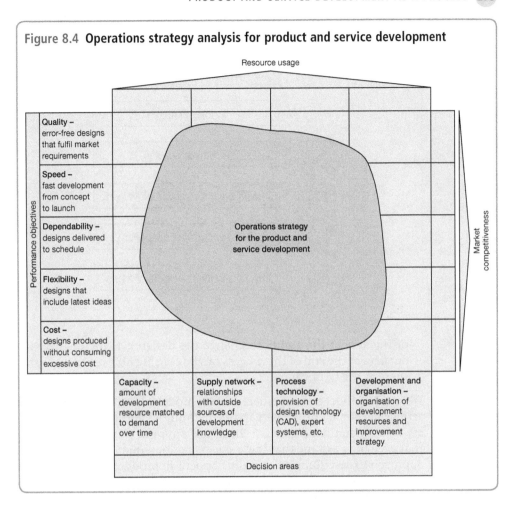

Figure 8.4 **Operations strategy analysis for product and service development**

## Stages of development

Describing the way in which organisations develop products and services is problematic because different organisations will adopt different processes. Furthermore, what companies specify as a formal product or service development procedure, and what happens in reality, can be very different things. Yet three ideas do seem to have found wide acceptance:

1  The development process moves through a series of stages, some of which may be missed out and sometimes the process recycles back through stages. Somewhere towards the beginning of the process, there are stages concerned with collecting ideas and generating product and service concepts, and towards the end of the process there are stages concerned with specifying the detail of the product or service.

2  As the development process moves through these stages, the number of alternative design options reduces until one final design remains. The process often includes decision points that screen out options deemed to be unsatisfactory.

3  As these possible design options are reduced, there is a move from a state of uncertainty regarding the final design to a state of increasing certainty. One consequence

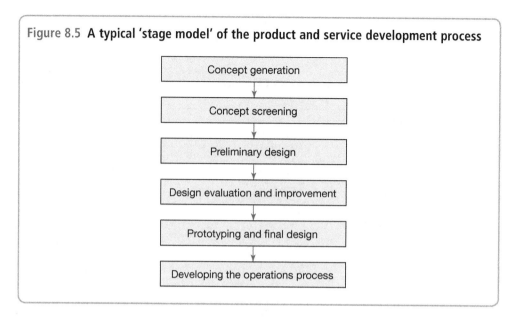

Figure 8.5 **A typical 'stage model' of the product and service development process**

of this is that the ability to change the design gets increasingly limited. Making changes at the end of the process can be considerably more expensive than making them at the beginning.

Different authors present different stage models that attempt to describe product and service development. These vary in the number and type of stages they include but are broadly similar. Figure 8.5 illustrates a typical stage model. Remember, though, that even if we assume that these stages are not sequential, it is a somewhat simplistic approach to describing what really happens in product and service development. The reality of bringing products and services from concept to market introduction is, in reality, both complex and messy.

### Concept generation

Ideas for new product or service concepts may be generated from sources outside the organisation, such as expressed customers' needs or competitor activity, or from sources within the organisation such as sales staff and front-of-house operations staff, or, more formally, from the R&D department. There are many market research tools for gathering data in a formal and structured way from customers, including questionnaires and interviews. These techniques, however, usually tend to be structured in such a way as only to test out ideas or check products or services against predetermined criteria.

### Concept screening

Not all concepts, or variants within a concept, have the potential to be developed through to market launch. The purpose of the concept-screening stage is to take the flow of concepts emerging from the development process and evaluate them. Concepts may have to pass through many different screens, and several functions might be involved – each using different criteria to screen the proposals. Screening may be divided into three sets of criteria related to market positioning, operations/ technical implications and financial evaluation:

- Does the proposed product or service occupy a market position that is both attractive in its own right and consistent with the organisation's overall marketing strategy?
- Does the proposed product or service exploit existing operations resource capabilities or help the operation to develop attractive new capabilities?
- Is the investment in the proposed product or service feasible, and is the return from this investment acceptable?

### Preliminary design

This stage represents the beginning of detailed work on the product or service design. It includes defining what will go into the product or service. This will require the collection of information about such things as the constituent component parts that make up the product or service package, the product/service structure – that is, the order in which the component parts of the package have to be put together, and the bill of materials (BOM) – that is, the quantities of each component part required to make up the total package. This stage also may include specifying how the various components are put together to create the final product or service.

### Design evaluation and improvement

This stage takes the preliminary design and attempts to improve it before the prototype product or services are tested in the market. There are a number of techniques that can be employed at this stage to evaluate and improve the preliminary design. Some of these techniques are concerned with costing the proposed product or service and identifying areas for cost improvement. Some are concerned with fully exploring the technical characteristics of the product or service in an effort to improve its overall value. Most are based on an approach that emphasises systematic questioning of exactly what each part of the product or service is intended to contribute to its overall value, why it is being done in a particular way and how it might be done differently. It is not the purpose of this book to explore any of these techniques in detail.

---

**Example**  **Apple nearly ditched the iPhone[8]**

There can be few more successful products launched in modern times – the iPhone has changed the way we look at smartphones and provided the benchmark for competitors' efforts. It has sold millions worldwide and helped to make Apple into the world's most valuable company. But few outside Apple know that the company considered abandoning the whole idea. Sir Jonathan Ive, senior vice-president of design at Apple, has admitted that Apple had worked on several 'incredibly compelling' products over the years, but decided to call a halt to their development because of what seemed to be insurmountable technical or sourcing problems. For example, one of the iPhone's fundamental innovations (at the time that it was being developed) was the touchscreen. And it was this component that proved so difficult that it brought the project to the brink of being aborted. *'There were multiple times when we*

▶

*nearly shelved it because there were fundamental problems that we couldn't solve'*, said Sir Jonathan. *'I would put the phone to my ear and my ear dialled a number. The challenge is that you have to then detect all sorts of ear shapes, chin shapes, skin colour and hairdos. We had to develop technology, basically a number of sensors, to inform the phone that "this is now going up to an ear, please deactivate the touchscreen".'*

The fact that the Apple designers overcame several technology and production bugs during its development is partly a testament to the design team's belief, both in their technological skills and in their understanding of what people will buy. Yet Apple avoids conducting market research when designing its products – a policy introduced by Steve Jobs, its late chief executive. *'We absolutely don't do focus groups'*, said Ive. *'That's designers and leaders abdicating responsibility. That's them looking for an insurance policy, so if something goes wrong, they can say, well this focus group says that only 30 per cent of people are offended by this and, look, 40 per cent think it's OK. What a focus group does is that it will guarantee mediocrity.'*

### Prototyping and final design

Often 'close-to-final' designs are 'prototyped'. Partly the next stage in the design activity is to turn the improved design into a prototype so that it can be tested. This may be to learn more about the nature of the proposed product or service but often it is also to reduce the risk inherent in going straight to market. Product prototypes may include clay models of car designs and computer simulations, for example. Computer simulations can be used as service prototypes but also can include the actual implementation of the service on a pilot basis. Many retailing organisations pilot new products and services in a small number of stores in order to test customers' reaction to them.

### Developing the operations process

Most models of product and service development assume that the final stage will involve developing the operations processes that will eventually produce the designed product or service. Although we dealt with process development in the previous chapter, it is important to stress again that, in practice, produce/service development on the one hand and process development on the other are inexorably linked. Placing this stage at the end of the development process, however, does reinforce the idea that, generally speaking, if the development process is intended to design products and services that will fulfil a market need, then process decisions can only take place after some product or service characteristics have been decided.

## Product and service development as a funnel

Although stage models, such as we illustrated in Figure 8.5, are useful in identifying the activities that must at some time take place within the overall development activity, they do not form a strict set of stages to which the development process must conform. In reality, stages may merge, the sequence of stages may vary and, almost always, the development process recycles back and forth between the stages. But the underlying ideas behind such stage models are widespread. For example, a common method of describing the product or service development process is to liken it to a funnel. The mouth of the funnel, being wide, can accommodate many alternative designs for the product or service. Indeed, theoretically, there will always be an infinite number of ways in which the benefits required from a product or service design can be delivered, even if some are only minor variants on each other. As the development process progresses, some design operations are discarded. There may be formal 'filters' at various points in the funnel whose sole purpose is to exclude some of the options. These filters often represent 'screens', which evaluate alternative designs against criteria of market acceptability, technical capability, financial return and so on. Eventually, only one design option remains, which is then developed into its final form. The whole process moves from a broad concept capable of infinite interpretation at one end of the funnel to a fully formed and specified design at the other.

Just as the stage model in Figure 8.5 was a simplification, so is the concept of the development funnel. Do not expect that all product and service development will conform to the obvious and regular funnel shape as shown in Figure 8.6(a). Most developments do not look like this and, more to the point, nor necessarily should they. Rather than see the funnel as a prescription for how development should be, it is better to see it as a metaphor for the design process that can be reshaped to reflect how the development process itself can be designed. The implication of this is that, even if an organisation does not want to progressively reduce its new product and service ideas using a perfectly smooth funnel, it certainly needs to understand what shape of funnel it really does want.

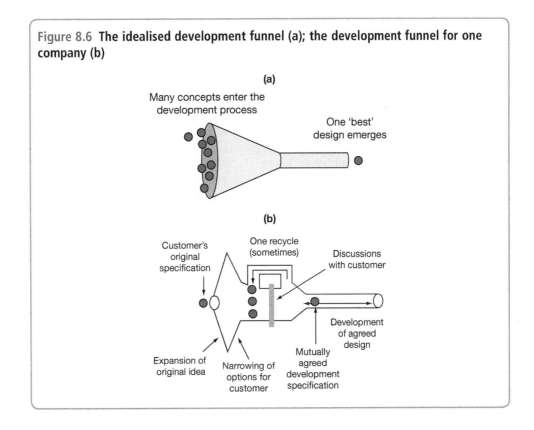

Figure 8.6 **The idealised development funnel (a); the development funnel for one company (b)**

Consider the following quote from the vice president in charge of product development in a company that makes advanced and customised electronic devices:

'*Our customers put business our way mainly because we are experts in taking their problems and solving them. They usually give us an initial specification, to which we design, then at some time in the future they approve the design and we start to manufacture for them. What we have learnt to do right at the start of the development process is deliberately expand the number and scope of ideas beyond that which the customer first gives us. This can often result in a more creative solution than the customer had originally envisaged. After all, they are not the experts in this technology, we are. The trick is to not let this period last too long before we start narrowing down to two or three options which we can present to the customer. It is important to get to this stage before the customer's own internal deadline. That gives us time to refine ideas after we have presented them. Some designs will be recycled at this point if the customer wants a further development, but we have a rule that we only ever recycle once. From experience, if the customer wants further substantial changes then they are not even sure in their own mind what they really want. After this stage we go into the final development of a single design tied to a very tight specification agreed between ourselves and the customer.*'

Figure 8.6(b) illustrates how this particular executive saw the development funnel in her company. It may not be the perfect funnel of the textbooks, but it is well-defined, well-understood in the company and can be easily communicated to the customer.

## Simultaneous development

Earlier we described the development process as a set of individual, predetermined stages. Sometimes one stage is completed before the next one commences. This step-by-step, or sequential, approach was traditionally the typical form of product/service development. It has some advantages: it is easy to manage and control development projects organised in this way because each stage is clearly defined. In addition, each stage is complete before the next stage is begun, so each stage can focus its skills and expertise on a limited set of tasks. The main problem of the sequential approach is that it is both time-consuming and costly. Any difficulties encountered during one stage might necessitate the design being halted while responsibility moves back to the previous stage. Yet often there is really little need to wait until the absolute finalisation of one stage before starting the next. Perhaps while generating the concept, the evaluation activity of screening and selection could be started. It would have to be a crude evaluation maybe, but nevertheless it is likely that some concepts could be judged as 'non-starters' relatively early on in the process of idea generation. Similarly, during the screening stage it is likely that some aspects of the developing product or service will become obvious before the phase is finally complete. The preliminary work on these parts of the design could be commenced before the end of the final screening and selection process. In other words, one stage commences before the previous one has finished, so there is simultaneous or concurrent work at the stages (see Figure 8.7).

We can link this idea with the idea of uncertainty reduction, discussed earlier. We made the point that uncertainty reduces as the design progresses. This also applies to each stage of the design, so uncertainty regarding the concept reduces through the concept generation stage, uncertainty about the preliminary design reduces through that phase and so on. If this is so, then there must be some degree of certainty as to which the next stage can take as its starting point prior to the end of the previous

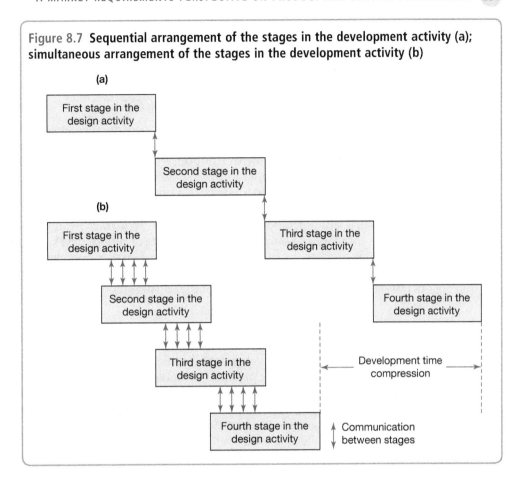

Figure 8.7 **Sequential arrangement of the stages in the development activity (a); simultaneous arrangement of the stages in the development activity (b)**

stage. In other words, designers can be continually reacting to a preceding stage. However, this can only work if there is effective communication between each part of the stages.

## A market requirements perspective on product and service development

Products and services are developed to satisfy market needs. It follows, then, that an important way of judging the effectiveness of the product and service development process is to judge how it performs in terms of quality, speed, dependability, flexibility and cost. These performance objectives have just as much relevance for the production of new product and service ideas or designs as they do for their ongoing production once they are introduced to the market. There is, however, a difference in judging how development processes satisfy market needs. When customers are both familiar and relatively satisfied with existing products and services they find it difficult to articulate their needs for novel products or services.[9] Customers often develop an enhanced understanding of their own needs only when they come into direct contact with the product or service and start to use it. Many software companies talk about the 'I don't know what I want but I'll know when I see it' syndrome, meaning that only when customers use the software are they in a position to articulate what they do or don't require.

## Quality of product and service development

In Chapter 1, when we were discussing generic performance objectives, quality was not easy to define precisely. It is no easier when we are looking at the quality of product and service development. However, it is possible to distinguish high-quality product and service development from low-quality product and service development (although this is easier to do in hindsight). A useful approach if we wish to judge ongoing product and service development is to use the distinction between market requirements quality and operations resource quality. By market requirements quality we mean the ability of the output from the product or service development process (its final design) to meet the requirements of the company's intended market position. Operations resource quality indicates the extent to which the final design of the product or service allows the exploitation of the capabilities of the company's processes.

## Speed of product and service development

Fast product and service development has become the norm in many industries. Sometimes this is because the pressures of market competition have forced companies to capture the markets' imagination with the frequent introduction of new offerings. Consumer electronics, for example, significantly increased the rate of new product introduction during the 1980s and 1990s. Sometimes it is the result of fast-changing consumer fashion. Getting to market quickly in order to capture a trend is important in many sectors of the garment and toy industries, for example. Sometimes, fast development is the result of a rapidly changing technology base. Personal computers need to be updated frequently because their underlying technology is constantly improving. Sometimes all of these pressures are evident, as in many internet-based services, for example. But no matter what pressures have motivated organisations to speed up their development processes, many have discovered that fast development brings a number of specific advantages:

- *Early market launch* – The most obvious advantage of an ability to develop products and services speedily is that they can be introduced to the market earlier and thus earn revenue for longer. Not only that, but if the product or service is the first of its type into the market, initially it has a 100 per cent of the market share, and customers may subsequently be reluctant to move to a competitor. Moreover, new offerings often can command price premiums.

- *Starting development late* – An alternative way of deploying a fast development advantage is by starting the development process late rather than introducing a product or service early. In some markets this has advantages, especially those where either the nature of customer demand or the availability of technology is uncertain and dynamic. In both cases, fast development allows design decisions to be made closer to the point at which they are introduced to the market.

- *Frequent market stimulation* – Short development times allow the introduction of new or updated products or services more frequently. With a given set of development resourcing, if it takes 12 months to develop a new product and service, a company can only introduce a new or updated offering every 12 months. A six-month development process doubles their potential for making an impact in the market.

- *More opportunities for innovation* – In markets where the underlying 'technology' base is moving fast, it may be important to have frequent opportunities to introduce these new technologies as often as possible. Short development time with frequent updates produces more windows of opportunity for this type of innovation.

## Dependability of product service development

Fast product and service development processes that cannot be relied on to deliver innovations dependably are, in reality, not fast at all. Development schedule slippage can extend development times, but worse, a lack of dependability adds to the uncertainty surrounding the development process. Conversely, processes that are dependable give stability and minimise development uncertainty. Yet this poses a problem for most development processes. Unexpected technical difficulties, innovations that do not work or have to be modified, suppliers who themselves do not deliver solutions on time, customers or markets that change during the development process itself, and so on, all contribute to an uncertain and sometimes ambiguous environment. Certainly professional project management of the development process can help to reduce uncertainty. At least, it should minimise the risk of internal disturbance to the development process if effective project management can prevent (or give early warning of) missed deadlines, detect bottlenecks and spot resource shortages. External disturbances to the process, however, will remain. Again, these may be minimised through close liaison with suppliers and effective market or environmental monitoring. Nevertheless, unexpected disruptions will always occur and the more innovative the development, the more likely they are to occur. This is why flexibility within the development process is one of the most important ways in which dependable delivery of new products and services can be ensured.

## Flexibility of product and service development

Flexibility in new product and service development is usually taken to mean the ability of the development process to cope with external or internal change. The most common reason for external change is because the market in general, or specific customers, change their requirements. This may be prompted by their own customers and markets changing, or because developments in competitors' products or services dictate a matching or leapfrogging move in specification. Internal changes could include the emergence of superior materials or technical solutions. One suggestion for measuring development flexibility is to compare the cost of modifying a product or service design in response to such changes against the consequences to profitability if no changes are made. The higher the cost of modifying a product or service in response to a given change, the lower is the development flexibility.[10]

Two trends in many markets make development flexibility particularly important. The first is the pace and magnitude of environmental change. Although flexibility may not be needed in relatively predictable environments, it is clearly valuable in more fast-moving and volatile environments. The second factor, however, which amplifies environmental volatility, is increasing complexity and interconnectedness of products and services. A bank, for example, may bundle together a number of separate services for one particular segment of its market. Privileged account holders may obtain special deposit rates, premium credit cards, insurance offers, travel facilities and so on together in the same 'product'. Changing one aspect of this bundle may require changes to be made in other elements. So, extending the credit card benefits to include extra travel insurance may also mean the redesign of the separate insurance element of the package.

One of the biggest benefits from development flexibility is that it can reduce development risk. Much development risk derives from the changes that occur during the development period. At the beginning of the development time, managers will presumably form a view concerning customer requirements, available technologies and specification of competitor products and services. During the development period any, or all, of these might change. Customers may change their mind, either because their needs have changed or because they did not understand their own needs in the first place. The boundary of what was technologically possible may change as new technologies come onto the market, and competitors introduce rival products and services with superior or different performance. Development flexibility can help to minimise the impact of such occurrences.

### The newspaper metaphor

Not all aspects of a development programme need to be flexible. Some aspects of a product or service may be judged unlikely to change over the development period, whereas others may be particularly difficult to forecast. It would seem sensible, therefore, to delay decisions regarding the uncertain elements until as late as possible in the process and build in sufficient flexibility in these elements rather than 'waste' it on the more stable elements. This is exactly how a daily newspaper designs its content. Special feature sections may be planned several weeks in advance and may even be printed well before their publication. Similarly, regular sections such as television times and advertisements are prepared several days before the newspaper is due to come out. On the day of publication, several stories may be vying for the front page. This is where flexibility is needed. The more flexible is the news desk in taking in new news and deciding the layout and priority of stories, the later the decision can be made and the more current the newspaper will be. Thus, in the development of any product or service, the more stable elements can be designed (in terms of making decisions around their form) well in advance, with their specification fixed early in the process. Other elements of the design can remain fluid so as to incorporate the latest thinking and then fixed only at the last moment.[11]

### Incremental commitment

One method of retaining some flexibility in development processes is to avoid yes/no decisions. Alternative and parallel options can be progressed in stages; so, for example, an idea might be given approval to move to the next stage with no implied commitment to develop that idea through to the end of the project. One often-quoted example concerns the development of the Boeing 777. Unusually for this type of product, the drawing that defined some parts had six or seven 'release levels'. This means that rather than confirming the final design of a part, it would be done in stages. So the design may be given approval for purposes of purchasing test materials but not for purposes of confirming tool design. This provided a more flexible way of delaying decisions until the last minute without holding up the whole development process.

## IKEA's slow development process[12]

Most companies are obsessed with reducing the time to market (TTM) of their design process. Short TTM means lower development costs and more opportunities to hit the market with new designs. Some automobile companies have reduced the design time for their products to less than three years, while a new smartphone (a far more dynamic market) can be developed in as little as six months. So why does IKEA, the most successful homeware retailer ever, take five years to design its kitchens? Because, with the huge volumes that IKEA sells, development costs are small compared with the savings that can result from product designs that bring down the final price in their stores.

'It's five years of work into finding ways to engineer cost out of the system, to improve the functionality', IKEA's new chief executive, Peter Agnefjäll, said of the company's 'Metod' kitchen (which means 'method' in English). Metod is a complex product: it has over 1,000 different components; and the kitchen is a product of IKEA's 'democratic design' process that ensures designs that will work in homes anywhere in the world – an important consideration when you sell about one million kitchens a year. Also, unlike some big-ticket purchases, consumer taste in home furnishing does not shift rapidly. 'We still hang paintings above the sofa and tend to have a TV in the corner', says IKEA's creative director, Mia Lundström. But even if trends do not materialise overnight, it is still important to spot emerging consumer preferences. A research team visits thousands of homes annually and compiles reports that look as far as a decade into the future. So without the imperative to change its product designs too frequently, product cost becomes a key driver. Rather than buy prefabricated components from outside sources, IKEA will develop its own if it keeps costs down. For example, IKEA's designers created their own LED lighting system to light one of the kitchen drawers.

## Cost of product and service development

The cost of developing products and services is conventionally analysed in a similar way to the ongoing cost of producing the goods and services. In other words, cost factors are split up into three categories: the cost of buying the inputs to the process, the cost of providing the labour in the process and the other general overhead costs of running the process. In most in-house development processes the latter two costs outweigh the former. As with day-to-day production of products and services, however, it is perhaps more revealing to consider how the other performance objectives drive cost:

- *Quality* – 'Error-free' processes reduce reworking concepts and designs.
- *Speed* – Fast development can use resources for shorter periods.
- *Dependability* – On-time development provides process stability, allows efficient resource planning and prevents expensive launch date slippage.
- *Flexibility* – The ability to delay design decisions can ensure the most appropriate options being chosen, preventing the costs of changing direction in the development.

One way of thinking about the effect of the other development performance objectives on cost is shown in Figure 8.8. Whether through quality errors, intrinsically slow development processes, a lack of project dependability, or delays caused through inflexible development processes, the end result is that the development is late. Delayed completion of the development results in both more expenditure on the development and delayed (and probably reduced) revenue. The combination of both

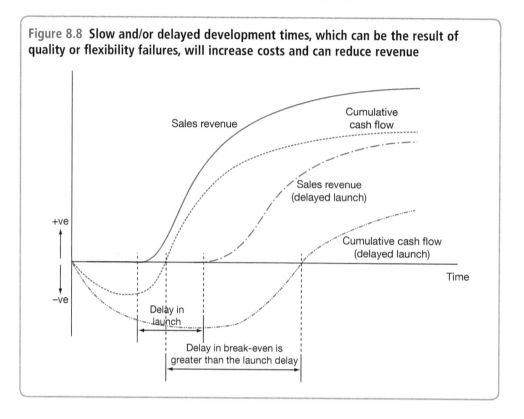

**Figure 8.8** Slow and/or delayed development times, which can be the result of quality or flexibility failures, will increase costs and can reduce revenue

these effects usually means that the financial breakeven point for a new product or service is delayed far more than the original delay in the product or service launch.

## An operations resources perspective on product and service development

An operations resources perspective on product and service development involves examining the decision areas that we would normally use but applying them specifically to the development process. This is not difficult since all the categories can be applied directly. The capacity of the organisation's development processes needs managing over the long term, choices need to be made about whether some activities are performed in-house or subcontracted, investments in process technology are becoming an increasingly important element in managing new product and service development, and the organisation of the development process has become an important factor in managing the development process. Furthermore, behind each of these decisions lies the general objective of nurturing and exploiting the organisation's capabilities.

### Product and service development capacity

As in any other process, the management of capacity involves deciding on the overall level of activity that an operation can support and also deciding how that level of support can be changed in order to respond to likely changes in demand. Essentially, all the issues discussed in Chapters 4 and 5, in the context of the whole operation, also apply to the product and service development process. However, remember that the development process is a service in that it creates and works with knowledge for the benefit of its (usually internal) customers. This means that such options as building up an 'inventory' of designs are not usually feasible, as such. Storing knowledge in a relatively developed form, however, may be possible. Indeed, in many ways, the whole development process can be characterised as building up and then deploying 'inventories' of design-based knowledge. Similarly, a 'capacity lagging' strategy (see Chapter 3) is not usually practical. The whole ethos of product and service development is one of broadly anticipating market requirements and attempting to bring ideas to market as early as possible. Deliberately planning to have a level of design capacity lower than the likely demand for such development rather implies extended time-to-market performance.

### Uneven demand for development

The central issue for managing product and service development in many organisations is that the internal 'demand' for such development is uneven. Even in very large companies, the rate of new service or product introduction is not constant. The need for product/service innovation is likely to be dictated by several complex and interrelated market factors. This may lead to several new offerings being introduced to the market close together, while at other times little development is needed – thus posing a resourcing problem. The capacity of a firm's development capability is often difficult to flex. The expertise necessary for development is embedded within designers, technologists, market analysts and so on. Some expertise may be able to be hired in as and when it is needed, but much development resource is, in effect, fixed. Such a combination of varying demand and relatively fixed development capacity leads some organisations to be reluctant to invest in development capacity because they see it as an under-utilised resource. This may lead to a vicious cycle in which, although there is a short-term need for development resources, companies fail to invest in those resources because many of them (such as skilled development staff) cannot be hired in the short term, which leads to development projects being under-resourced with an increased chance of project overrun or failure to deliver appropriate technical solutions. This, in turn, may lead to the company losing business or otherwise suffering in the marketplace, which makes the company even less willing to invest in development resources (see Figure 8.9).

## Product and service development networks

Most interest in supply networks has focused on the flow of parts, products and, occasionally, services. Recently, interest has also started to focus around the exchange of product and service development knowledge, and the integrating of suppliers into the innovation process. This network of knowledge exchange is sometimes called the 'design (or development) network', or 'design chain', and in many ways the operations strategy decisions concerning conventional supply networks are also reflected in development networks. Two decisions in particular do much to determine the effectiveness of development networks. The first is the extent of vertical integration – the decisions of how much development to do in-house and how much to subcontract. The second is how to manage the relationship between the 'players' (most notably, customers and suppliers) in the network.

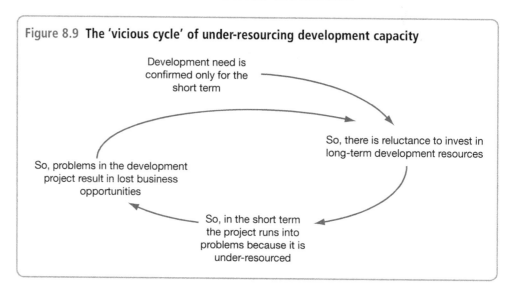

Figure 8.9 The 'vicious cycle' of under-resourcing development capacity

**Example** **Two development partnerships: BMW with Toyota and Suzuki with VW[13]**

Two years after announcing a technology development partnership for a variety of projects such as fuel cell systems, powertrain electrification and lightweight materials, Toyota and BMW unveiled plans for a joint sports car vehicle platform. It was the first publicly announced output from the collaboration that was set up to share the huge development costs needed to develop a new vehicle and to fill a hole in both companies' product line-ups. The collaborative undertaking was designed to bring together the development expertise, knowledge and financial resources of two of the most successful automobile companies in what they called '*a mid-to-long-term collaboration on next-generation environment-friendly technologies*'. BMW's chairman at the time, Norbert Reithofer, emphasised the strategic importance of the partnership: '*Toyota is the leading provider of environment-friendly technology in the volume segment and the BMW Group is the most innovative and sustainable manufacturer of premium automobiles. We are now joining forces to further develop environment-friendly technologies and to expand our innovation leadership in each of our segments.*' Akio Toyoda, president of Toyota, said the deal was '*a great joy and a thrill*' and that he looked forward to allying his company to one that '*makes cars that are fun to drive. Both companies will bring their wide-ranging knowledge, starting with that concerning environmental technologies, to the table and make ever-better cars.*' The new sports car was intended to bring together Toyota's world-class manufacturing expertise with its BMW partner's engineering talents and understanding of high-performance engines. '*We could do a sports car by ourselves. But if you look at the whole package ... it makes sense. Both companies can have benefits. Sports cars are all about volumes because they can be relatively small*', said Herbert Diess, BMW board member and head of development. The new model could be powered by hybrid engine technology similar to that established by Toyota in its Prius models.

Alliances and shared products are becoming increasingly common in the automobile industry, mainly to keep down escalating development costs and to share the, sometimes considerable, investment needed to meet new regulatory curbs on such things as carbon dioxide emissions and safety standards. Yet not all alliances have been successful. Two years before the announcement of the Toyota–BMW deal, a partnership between VW and Suzuki broke up acrimoniously. The original intention was for the largest European carmaker, VW, to share development of a small car with Suzuki – the fourth player in the Japanese market. The jointly developed model was supposed to be aimed at growing markets such as India through Suzuki's leading position in that country. However, the deal fell apart. There were claims that VW was not doing as much sharing of its technology as Suzuki had envisaged (VW denied the claims), while VW argued that a deal between Suzuki and Fiat for diesel engines was a contractual breach. Suzuki had formed an alliance with Fiat some years earlier to make diesel engines in Asia and then extended the deal by sourcing diesel engines from Fiat for cars built in Hungary (Suzuki denied that the deal broke the agreement). After the break-up, industry analysts said the partnership had failed to benefit either company. Part of the problem seemed to be a lack of strategic fit. Volkswagen was a very big company trying to become the world's biggest automobile company, while Suzuki was a relatively small company trying to focus on specific regional markets. But there were also different, and contrasting, corporate cultures that inhibited cooperation. Some saw Volkswagen as wanting to be the lead player in the partnership and Suzuki, with a reputation for valuing their independence, refusing to play the role of junior partner.

## In-house and subcontracted development

Companies position themselves on a continuum of varying degrees of design engagement with suppliers. At one extreme, a firm may retain all the necessary design capabilities in-house, while at the other end it outsources all its development work, acting only as a focal point for the coordination of the design process. Between these extremes there exist options with varying degrees of internal and external design capability. In general, though, few companies are at the extremes of this continuum since process development necessitates some kind of interaction.

Design resources will be easy to control if they are kept in-house because they are closely aligned with the company's normal organisational structures, but control should be relatively loose because of the extra trust present in working with familiar colleagues. Outsourced design requires greater control and, because it has to be applied at a distance, contracts – often with penalty clauses for delay – may be needed. However, penalty clauses and contracts do not help to build long-term partnership relationships. In-house design has an advantage here because of its strong familiarity with the rest of the company's product or service range, operations processes, materials and market requirements. In contrast, outsourcing design can mean a weaker understanding in the short term, though if long-term relationships do develop, product and service familiarity will become stronger. The underlying capabilities built up through the development activity are generally assumed to be highly accessible when the development is done in-house. It is more difficult to provide access to tacit knowledge when it is housed outside the organisation. One motive behind companies investing heavily in common computer-aided design systems with their design suppliers is to ensure better accessibility. The overall cost of in-house versus outsourced development will vary, depending on the firm and the development project. An important difference, however, is that external development tends to be regarded as a variable cost. The more external resources are used, the higher the cost will be. In-house development is more of a fixed cost. Indeed, a shift to outsourcing may occur because fixed development costs are viewed as too great. Paradoxically, though, as external sourcing of development becomes an integral part of a company's strategy and relationships become stable, costs tend to be more or less fixed. Finally, a major driver of this decision can be the risk of knowledge leakage. Firms become concerned that experience gained through collaboration with a supplier of development expertise may be transferred to competitors. Again, there is a paradox here. Companies usually outsource development primarily because of the supplier's capabilities that are themselves an accumulation of specialist knowledge from working with a variety of customers. Without such knowledge 'leakage', the benefits of the supplier's accumulated development capabilities would not even exist.

### Involving suppliers in development

The nature of the relationship with suppliers of product or service design services is not the same as when a supplier (even the same supplier) is providing product or services on an ongoing basis. For example, a component manufacturer, asked by a customer to design a new part, is providing a service rather than making a physical product. Even a supplier of services, in designing a new service for a customer, is engaged in a one-off (or at least relatively infrequent) exchange with its customer, in which its own knowledge is embedded in the design. In fact, a development relationship between customer and supplier is very similar to that between professional service firms, such as lawyers or consultants, and their clients. When choosing suppliers of design and development knowledge, companies often use criteria such as experience, trust, technical knowledge and 'relationship' – a very similar list to that used to select their accountancy firm and their legal representatives.[14]

Characterising development relationships as professional services has practical implications, especially for suppliers. First, it emphasises the importance of customer perception of the 'process' of development, as well as the final design that emerges from the process. Frequently demonstrating expertise during the development process allows suppliers to build their 'technical' reputation. Second, just as professional services, such as accountants, keep 'client files' that detail all contacts with individual clients, so design suppliers can use similar client knowledge management to manage the development of the relationship with customers. Third, it broadens the nature of contact with customers to include a more general responsibility for the development of relationships among other sources of expertise in the network. This has implications for the way suppliers might organise their design activity – for example, in the way they attempt to respond to change in client needs during the creation of the design service, or in the use of implicit 'service guarantees'.

### Involving customers in development

Few people know the merits and limitations of products and services better than the customers who use them. An obvious source, then, of feedback on product or service performance will be those who regularly use (or have ceased using) them. Different types of customer have the potential to provide different types of information. New users can pinpoint more attractive product and service features; those who have switched to a competitor offering can reveal its problems. A particularly interesting group of customers are the so-called 'lead users'.[15] Lead users have requirements of a product or service that will become more general in a market, but they are aware of these needs well ahead of the rest of the market. They are also users who will benefit significantly by finding a solution to their requirements. This may prompt them to develop or modify products or services themselves rather than wait for them to become commercially available. One reported example of lead-user research[16] concerns a new product development manager at Bose – the high-quality hi-fi and speaker company. On visiting his local music store, his professional ear noted the high quality of the background music being played. Investigating, he found that the store manager was using Bose speakers designed for home use but had attached metal strips around the speaker boxes so that they could be suspended close to the ceiling of the store. Inspired by this, Bose built prototypes of speakers that would satisfy the need for quality in-store speakers. These were taken back to the music store for further testing and eventually led to the company successfully entering the market for high-fidelity background music speakers.

## Product and service development technology

One of the more significant changes in product and service development has been the growing importance of 'process' technology within the development process. Until relatively recently, although product/service technology knowledge was an important input into the development activity, technology used to process this knowledge was relatively unusual. It was limited to testing and evaluation technologies such as the mechanical devices that would simulate the stresses of everyday use on products such as automobiles or sports shoes, often testing them to destruction. Now process technologies are much more common, especially those based on computing power. For example, simulation software is now common in the design of everything from transportation services through to chemical factories. This allows developers to make design decisions in advance of the actual product or service being created. The process technologies allow designers to work through the experience of using the service or product and learn more about how it might operate in practice. They can explore possibilities, gain insights and, most importantly, they can explore the consequences of their decisions. In that sense, simulation is often a predictive rather than an optimising technology.

### Knowledge management technologies

In many professional service firms, such as management consultancies, service development involves the evaluation of concepts and frameworks that can be used in client organisations to diagnose problems, analyse performance and construct possible solutions. They may include ideas of industry best practice, benchmarks of performance within an industry and ideas that can be transported across industry boundaries. However, the characteristics of management consulting firms are that they are geographically dispersed and rarely are staff at their offices. The consultants spend most of their time in client organisations acquiring knowledge day by day. Yet, at the same time, it is vital for such companies to avoid 'reinventing the wheel' continually. Any means of collectivising the cumulative knowledge and experience within the organisation must greatly assist the development of new concepts and frameworks. Most consultancy companies attempt to tackle this problem using knowledge management routines based on their intranet capabilities. See the section on knowledge management in the previous chapter. This allows consultants to put their experience into a common pool, contact other staff within the company who have skills relevant to a current assignment and identify previous similar assignments. In this way, information is integrated into the ongoing knowledge development process within the company and can be tapped by those charged with developing new products.[17]

The significance of most of these development technologies is that they help to reduce the impact both of uncertainty and complexity. Simulation technologies allow developers to reduce their own uncertainty of how products and services will work in practice. Similarly, knowledge management systems consolidate and juxtapose information on what is happening within the organisation, thus presenting a more comprehensive vision and reducing uncertainty. CAD systems also help to deal with complexity by storing data on component details as they develop through various interactions. The absolute size and interrelatedness of some large products requires sophisticated CAD systems if they are to be developed effectively. One of the most reported examples was the development of Boeing's 777 aircraft. The powerful CAD system used on this project was credited with Boeing's success in being able to involve its customers in the design process, allow more product configuration flexibility (such as the proportion of seats in each class, etc.) and still bring the huge project success-fully to completion.

## The organisation of product and service development

Amongst the criteria that are used to assess the effectiveness of different organisa-tional forms, two in particular are important to product and service development – specialisation and integration. Specialisation is important because it encourages the depth of knowledge and technical understanding that is required in a con-centrated form during the development process. Because of the (normally) finite time allowed for product and service development, technical knowledge needs to be deployed in a concentrated manner during limited windows of opportunity. Clustering resources around technical specialisms encourages the development of such concentrated knowledge. Integration is important because both product and services are composed of smaller components or subsystems. Coordinating the efforts of developers in different parts of a project and integrating their technical solutions in such a way as to reflect the market priorities within the development project is clearly an important aspect of any organisational structure. Both these criteria need to be incorporated in the organisational structure that is built to support a development project.

### Project-based organisation structures

The total process of developing concepts through to market will almost certainly involve personnel from several different areas of the organisation. Most functions will have some part to play in making the decisions that will shape a final design. Yet any development project will also have an existence of its own. It will have a project name, an individual manager or group of staff who are championing the project, a budget and, hopefully, a clear strategic purpose in the organisation. The organisational question is which of these two ideas – the various organisational functions that contribute to development, or the development project itself – should dominate the way in which the development activity is managed? The matrix form of organisation is a compromise between two (or more) approaches to clustering resources. It is an ideal model to examine the debates over an appropriate organisational form for development projects. Here the two conflicting approaches are the functional (specialist) dominated structure and the project (or programme) dominated structure.

**Figure 8.10 Organisation structures for design processes**

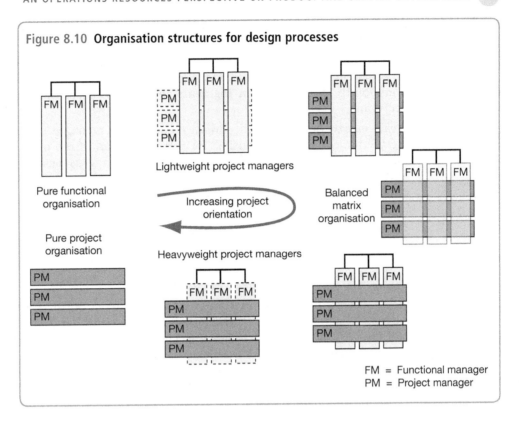

In a purely functional organisation, all staff associated with the design project are based unambiguously in their functional groups. There is no project-based group at all. They may be working full-time on the project but all communication and liaison is carried out through their functional manager. The project exists only because of agreement between these functional managers. At the other extreme, all the individual members of staff from each function who are involved in the project could be moved out of their functions and perhaps even physically relocated to a 'task force' dedicated solely to the project. A project manager, who probably holds the entire budget allocated to the design project, could lead the task force. Not all members of the task force necessarily have to stay in the team throughout the development period, but a substantial core might see the project through from start to finish. Some members of a design team may even be from other companies. In between these two extremes there are various types of 'matrix' organisation, with varying emphasis on these two aspects of the organisation (see Figure 8.10). And, although there are, in practice, an infinite number of structures, five stereotypical positions on the continuum are often discussed:

- *Functional organisation* – The project is divided into segments and assigned to relevant functional areas and/or groups within functional areas. Functional and senior management coordinate the project.
- *Functional matrix* (or lightweight project manager) – A person is formally designated to oversee the project across different functional areas. This person has limited authority over functional people involved and serves primarily to plan and

coordinate the project. The functional managers retain primary responsibility for their specific segments of the project.

- *Balanced matrix* – A person is assigned to oversee the project and interacts on an equal basis with functional managers. This person and the functional managers jointly direct workflow segments and approve technical and operational decisions.

- *Project matrix* (or heavyweight project manager) – A manager is assigned to oversee the project and is responsible for the completion of the project. Functional managers' involvement is limited to assigning personnel as needed and providing advisory expertise.

- *Project team* (or tiger team) – A manager is given responsibility for a project team composed of a core group of personnel from several functional areas and/or groups, assigned in a full-time basis. The functional managers have no formal involvement.

### Effectiveness of the alternative structures

Although there is no clear 'winner' amongst the alternative organisational structures, there is wide support for structures towards the project rather than the functional end of the continuum. In one widely respected study, Professors Clark and Fujimoto argued that heavyweight project manager structures and dedicated project teams are the most efficient forms of organisation for product competitiveness, shorter lead-times and technical efficiency.[18] Other studies, although sometimes more equivocal, have shown that, in terms of the best total outcome from the development process, structures from balanced matrix through to project teams can all give high success rates. Perhaps of more interest is the suitability of the alternative structures for different types of product or service development project. Matrix structures are generally deemed to be appropriate for both simple and highly complex projects. Dedicated project teams, on the other hand, are seen as coming into their own, especially in highly complex projects.

Yet again, there are advantages in functionally based development structures. In Chapter 10 we discuss how clustering resources around a functional specialism helps the development of technical knowledge. Some organisations do manage to capture the deep technological and skills development advantages of functional structures, while at the same time coordinating between the functions so as to ensure satisfactory delivery of new product and service ideas. Perhaps the best known of these organisations is Toyota, the Japanese car giant. They have a strong, functionally-based organisation to develop their products. It adopts highly formalised development procedures to communicate between functions, and places strict limits on the use of cross-functional teams. But what is really different is its approach to devising an organisational structure for product development that is appropriate for the company. The argument which most companies have adopted to justify cross-functional project teams goes something like this:

> *'Problems with communication between traditional functions have been the main reasons for, in the past, failing to deliver new product and service ideas to specification, on time and to budget. Therefore let us break down the walls between the functions and organise resources around the individual development projects. This will ensure good communication and a market-oriented culture.'*

Toyota and similar companies, on the other hand, have taken a different approach. Their argument goes something like this:

> '*The problem with cross-functional teams is that they can dissipate the carefully nurtured knowledge that exists within specialist functions. The real problem is how to retain this knowledge on which our future product development depends, while overcoming some of the traditional functional barriers that have inhibited communication between the functions. The solution is not to destroy the function but to devise the organisational mechanisms to ensure close control and integrative leadership that will make the functional organisation work.*'[19]

## SUMMARY ANSWERS TO KEY QUESTIONS

### Why is the way in which companies develop their products and services so important?

Competitive markets and demanding customers require updated and 'refreshed' products and services. Even small changes to products and services can have an impact on competitiveness. Markets are also becoming more fragmented, requiring product and service variants developed specifically for their needs. At the same time, technologies are offering increased opportunities for their exploitation within new products and services. Nor can one always separate the development of products and services on the one hand from the development of the processes that produce them on the other. Thus, product and service development influences and is influenced by almost all other decisions and activities within the operations function.

### What process do companies use to develop products and services?

There is no single product and service development process, as such. However, there are many stage models that attempt to define and describe the various stages that a process should include. Typical of these stages are such activities as concept generation, concept screening, preliminary design, design evaluation and improvement, prototyping and final design and developing the operations process. It is important to remember, though, that although these stages are often included (either formally or informally) within an organisation's product or service development process, they do not always follow each other sequentially. In reality, the process may recycle through stages and even miss some out altogether. A common metaphor to illustrate the process is that of the 'funnel of development'. Again, though, the idea of many ideas passing through a funnel, being periodically screened and a single product or service design emerging from the end, is itself a simplification.

### How should the effectiveness of the product and service development process be judged in terms of fulfilling market requirements?

The market effectiveness of any product or service development process can be judged in the same way as the day-to-day operations processes that produce the products and services themselves. That is, the development process can be judged in terms of its quality, speed, availability, flexibility and cost. Development projects must be error free, fast to market, deliver on time, retain sufficient flexibility to change as late as possible in the process and not consume excessive development resources.

▶

*What operations resource-based decisions define a company's product and service development strategy?*

Again, we can classify the decisions around the product or service development process in the same way as we can classify the decisions that specify the resources for day-to-day operations process. The overall development capacity of an organisation needs to be managed to reflect fluctuating demand for development activities, decisions must be made regarding the outsourcing of some, or all, of the development activity as well as the nature of the relationships with development 'suppliers', technologies such as computer-aided design and simulation may be required to aid the development process, and the resources used for development need to be clustered into some form of organisational structure.

## Further reading

Bettencourt, L. (2010) *Service Innovation: How to Go from Customer Needs to Breakthrough Services*. New York: McGraw-Hill Professional.

Cross, R. and Baird, L. (2000) 'Technology is not enough: improving performance by building organisational memory', *Sloan Management Review*, Spring.

Goffin, K. and Mitchell, R. (2010) *Innovation Management, Strategy and Implementation Using the Pentathlon Framework*, 2nd edition. Basingstoke, UK: Palgrave Macmillan.

Jurgens-Kowal, T. (2013) *Product Development Innovation Teams: Organizing for Success in New Product Development*. Dallas, TX: Get to the Point Books.

Steiber, A. (2014) *The Google Model: Managing Continuous Innovation in a Rapidly Changing World*. New York: Springer.

Tidd, J. and Bessant, J. (2013) *Managing Innovation: Integrating Technological, Market and Organizational Change*, 5th edition. New York: John Wiley & Sons.

Trott, P. (2011) *Innovation Management and New Product Development*, 5th edition. Harlow, UK: Financial Times/Prentice Hall.

Ulrich, K. and Eppinger, S. (2007) *Product Design and Development*, 4th edition. New York: McGraw-Hill.

Voudouris, C., Owusu, G., Dorne, R. and Lesaint, D. (2007) *Service Chain Management: Technology Innovation for the Service Business*. New York: Springer.

## Notes on the chapter

1 *Sources* include: *The Times* (2006) 'Timeline – Airbus A380 superjumbo', 26 October; BBC News website (2006) 'Q&A: A380 delays', 30 October; BBC News website (2007) 'Q&A: Airbus job cuts', 28 February; Hollinger, P. and Wiesmann, G. (2008) 'Airbus is hampered by cultural differences', *Financial Times*; *The Economist* (2008) 'Airbus Marathon man', 17 July; *The Economist* (2008) 'Boeing and Airbus – Swings and roundabouts', 27 November.

2 Baldwin, C.Y. and Clark, K.B. (1997) 'Managing in an age of modularity', *Harvard Business Review*, Sept-Oct.

3 Mass customisation was first fully articulated in Pine, B.J. (1993) *Mass Customisation: The new frontier in business competition*. Boston, MA: Harvard Business School Press. Also see Hart, C.W.L. (1995) 'Mass customisation: conceptual underpinnings, opportunities and threats', *International Journal of Service Industry Management*, 6(2).

4 Ahlström, P. and Westbrook, R. (1999) 'Implications of mass customisation for operations management', *International Journal of Operations and Production Management*, 19(3).

5 Lehnerd, A.P. quoted in Pine, B.J. (1993), op. cit.

6 *Sources* include: *The Economist* (2012) 'The last Kodak moment?' 14 January; Wright, M. (2010) 'Kodak develops: A film giant's self-reinvention', *Wired Magazine*, 15 February.

7 *Sources* include, Doran, J. (2006) 'Hoover heading for sell-off as Dyson sweeps up in America', *The Times*, 4 February.

8 *Sources* include: Ahmed, M. (2012) 'Apple nearly ditched the iPhone, designer admits', *The Times*, 31 July; Breillatt, A. (2012) 'You Can't Innovate Like Apple', http://www .pragmaticmarketing.com

9 von Hippel, E. (1988) *The Sources of Innovation*. New York: Oxford University Press.

10 Thomke, S. and Reinertsen, D. (1998) 'Agile product development', *California Management Review*, 41(1).

11 Ibid.

12 *Sources* include: Jervell, E. (2013) 'The Long, Slow Process of IKEA Design', *Wall Street Journal*, 14 October.

13 *Sources* include: Robert Lea, R. (2011) 'BMW and Toyota team up to develop sports car', *Financial Times*, 13 January; Foy, H. (2014) 'BMW and Toyota link up to crack electric car challenge', *The Times*, 2 December.

14 Haywood-Farmer, J. and Nollet, J. (1991) *Serviced Plus: Effective service management*. Quebec: Marin Boucherville.

15 von Hippel, E., Churchill, J. and Sonnack, M. (1998) *Breakthrough products and services with lead user research*. New York: Oxford University Press.

16 Ibid.

17 Iansiti, M. and MacCormack, A. (1997) 'Developing products on internet time', *Harvard Business Review*, Sept-Oct.

18 Clark, K.B. and Fujimoto, T. (1991) *Product Development Performance*. Boston, MA: Harvard Business School Press.

19 Sobek, D.K. II, Licker, J.K. and Ward, A.C. (1998) 'Another look at how Toyota integrates product development', *Harvard Business Review*, July-August.

# The process of operations strategy – formulation and implementation

## Introduction

The process of operations strategy formulation is concerned with 'how' to reconcile market requirements with operations resources over the long term. The reason for these final two chapters is simple: in practice, achieving this alignment is much more difficult than it sounds, and although any simple step-by-step model of how to 'do' operations strategy will inevitably be a simplification of a messy reality, we shall use a four-stage model to illustrate some of the elements of 'process'. This stage model is shown in Figure 9.1. It divides the process of operations strategy into: formulation, implementation, monitoring and control. In this chapter we examine the first two of these stages: formulation and implementation. The following chapter looks at the final two stages: monitoring and control.

### KEY QUESTIONS

- *What is the 'formulation' of operations strategy?*
- *What analysis is needed for formulation?*
- *What is operations strategy implementation?*

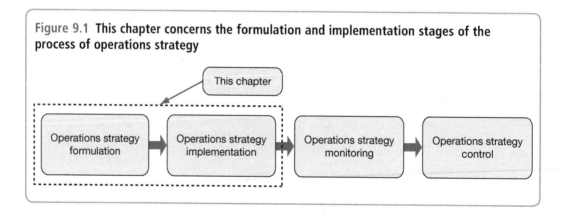

Figure 9.1 **This chapter concerns the formulation and implementation stages of the process of operations strategy**

## Formulating operations strategy

Formulation of operations strategy is the practical process of articulating the various objectives and decisions that make up the strategy. Unlike day-to-day operations management, formulating an operations strategy is likely to be only an occasional activity. Some firms will have a regular (e.g. annual) planning cycle, and operations strategy consideration may form part of this, but the extent of any changes made in each annual cycle is likely to be limited. In other words, the 'complete' process of formulating an entirely new operations strategy will be a relatively infrequent event. This often results in firms looking to consultancies for guidance with the process and as a consequence many detailed 'how to formulate' procedures – typically multi-stage models involving some type of performance 'gap' analysis – have been developed. Some of these models often share a number of common elements, for example:

- A process that formally aligns the total organisation strategic objectives (usually a business strategy) to resource-level objectives.
- Using operations performance objectives as a translation device for alignment between market positioning objectives and operations strategy.
- Judging alignment via assessment of the relative importance of operations performance objectives (in terms of customer preference) and achieved performance (usually compared against competitor performance levels).

In other words, formulating an operations strategy is essentially about different ways of aligning plans, activities and objectives.

## What is the role of alignment?

In the opening chapters of the book we discussed the process of reconciling operational resources with market requirements so that there is an approximate degree of 'fit' or alignment between them. When alignment is achieved, the firms' customers do not need, or expect, levels of operations performance that it is unable to supply. Nor does the firm have operations strengths that are either inappropriate for market needs or remain unexploited in the market. Figure 9.2 provides a diagrammatic illustration. Note that this diagram is not intended as a practical tool, but it does illustrate the nature of what is meant by alignment.

The position on the vertical dimension of Figure 9.2 (e.g. position Y) represents the nature and level of market requirements: reflecting both intrinsic customer needs and/or expectations that have been shaped by the firm's marketing activity. Movement up this axis is meant to indicate a broadly enhanced level of market performance or market capabilities, reflecting factors such as strength of brand/reputation, degree of differentiation, extent of plausible market promises, etc. The horizontal scale represents the level and nature of the firm's capabilities. The position on this axis (e.g. position X) will be determined by factors such as resource efficiency, process control,

**Figure 9.2 In operations strategy, 'fit' is the alignment between market and operations capability**

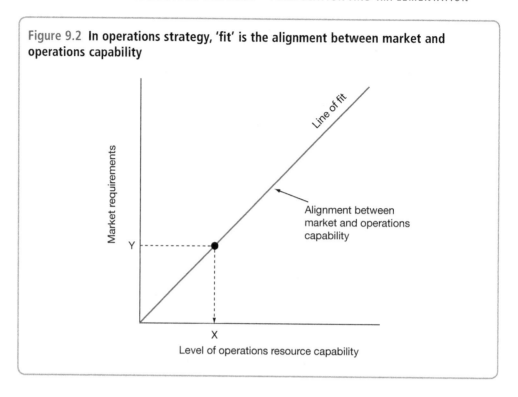

innovation and so on. Here, again, movement along the axis indicates a broadly enhanced level of operations capabilities and performance.

## The direction of alignment

The process of formulating an operations strategy to achieve alignment can be completed in two different 'directions'. Most commonly, firms start with their market requirements and then align resources to match them. That is, on Figure 9.2, they start by analysing point Y and then determine what point X should be. Such an approach has a number of intrinsic advantages, not least of which is the sheer availability of practical tools and techniques for classifying and identifying market requirements. This direction of alignment also corresponds with the traditional top-down hierarchy of strategies (discussed in Chapter 1), whereby operations' role is to support predetermined market decisions. The alternative approach is for the operation to analyse its resources and then seek market opportunities that align well with it. That is, again referring to Figure 9.2, they start by analysing point X and then determine what point Y could be. However, in practice this is difficult to do. All businesses have markets; they may not always be well understood and the business may not be good at identifying which part of a market it is trying to serve but nevertheless, all businesses have some idea of the requirements of their market. But, not every business understands its operations capabilities and many may not have any 'distinctive' capabilities. And while we have continually stressed the importance of leveraging operations capabilities into the marketplace, this does presuppose that a business has some operations capabilities worth leveraging. The logic of these alternative formulation processes is shown in Figure 9.3.

**Figure 9.3** **Align operations resources with market requirements, or align market positioning with operations resources capabilities**

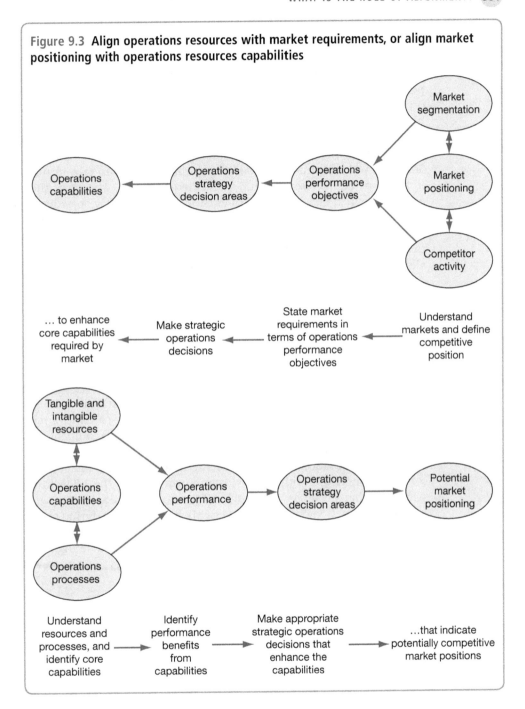

## Maintaining alignment over time

Most organisations are as mortal as the people who create and run them. So why are those firms that last for many years the exception rather than the rule? Most new business ventures fail to make it past their first year. The obvious explanation is that firms fail to reconcile market requirements and operations resources because it is all too easy either to misinterpret customer requirements or fail to develop the requisite operational capabilities. At the same time, history is littered with companies that had their moment of competitive glory but then faded or disappeared for ever. They may have effectively reconciled operational resources and market requirements to achieve alignment at one point in time. Yet, subsequently, they failed to sustain this position. And while many other factors, such as macroeconomic shifts and exchange rate fluctuations, have a huge influence on the success of organisations, the ongoing battle to reconcile resources and requirements to achieve sustainable alignment is clearly of great importance. This emphasises the idea that operations strategy formulation should not be a one-off event. Strategies will be formed repeatedly over time in order to take into account changes in both operations resources and market requirements. At each of these 'formulation episodes' (which may be both frequent and informal), a key objective is likely to be the retention of 'alignment'. Sometimes this will mean maintaining alignment during an increase in both operations resource capabilities and market requirements. More realistically, even the most successful long-running firms will experience differing degrees of alignment between market requirements and their operational resources.

## Time and timing

Firms such as Intel and Dell in the computer industry might, at any point in time, possess a significant design and manufacturing performance advantage over their competitors. Unfortunately, in their hyper-competitive markets the danger is that their advantage will be quickly 'competed away', with sustainability sometimes measured in months rather than years. Jeffrey Williams published a study of sustainability patterns in a range of industries.[1] He proposed a model that classifies capability-based advantages according to how fast they can be duplicated. Nothing lasts forever, and competitive success inevitably attracts imitators who offer superior product features or lower prices. Yet it is also clear that some organisations are able to sustain the advantages of their products and services for much longer than others. For instance, throughout the 1990s in the PC industry, why was it that certain products such as Microsoft's Office Suite of programs were highly stable, with functionality and prices essentially unchanged during more than ten years, whereas physical products sold by Hewlett Packard, Toshiba, Apple, etc. could last less than one year? In attempting to explain these and other differing patterns of sustainability, the following typology of resource life cycles offers some interesting insights:[2]

### Slow cycle

Products and services in this class (Microsoft Word, British Airways flights through Heathrow) reflect resource positions that are strongly shielded from competitive pressures by mechanisms that are durable and enduring. In economic terms, such resources exploit scarcity characteristics that are derived from factors that are impossible (or at least extremely difficult) to imitate, such as unique geographical locations, long-standing brand reputations, personal client relationships, etc. Although being the first mover into a resource/market position is not a guarantee of advantage, in certain markets it can lead to incredibly sustainable positions.

### Standard cycle

Products and services in this class (Toyota's cars, McDonald's fast food, Visa credit card services) exploit less specialised resources and therefore face higher levels of resource imitation pressure. Firms in this position often face direct competition over extended periods of time and this encourages a kind of trench warfare between established rivals (automobiles, banking, branded food, soft drinks, etc.). As a result, successful companies tend to emphasise discipline (control and coordination) in operations, and products tend to be standardised for production at high volumes (product/service line rationalisations are common in this type of firm) and are strongly market-share orientated. The huge financial and organisational commitments that derive from such strategies mean that firms tend to tread very carefully over their competitive territory. Indeed, efforts to streamline these operations and make them more lean can, if duplicated by rivals (and this is what normally happens!), bring on even more intense resource-imitation pressures – creating fast-cycle markets that they are poorly equipped to deal with.

### Fast cycle

Products and services in this class (iPods, Intel microprocessors, mobile phones, corporate financial instruments) face the highest levels of resource imitation pressure. Such products/services are often idea-driven and their economic half-life (the rate of product profit margin reduction minus reinvestment expenditure) is typically less than two years. Once established, these products do not require complex operations to support them and are increasingly outsourced to low-cost, focused producers. To maintain sustainable alignment, these firms must master competitive routines associated with innovation and time to market. In his article, Williams asks *'How is a 1 Mbyte DRAM chip like a Cabbage Patch doll?'* The answer: both products derive their value from the idea that information content is (unless protected by patents) inherently unsustainable.

The implications for management could seem counter-intuitive for operations managers used to emphasising speed and efficiency as key strategic goals. They include:

- *Determining the correct speed for innovation* – Too much innovation can become distracting for both the operation and its customers. The correct speed of innovation should depend upon the sustainability of the firm's resources. Williams cites the example of the Campbell Soup Company, which during the 1980s launched 300 products in a five-year period. Only a few were successful and the firm had to, according to CEO David Johnson, 'fight the motherhood of innovation'.

- *Resource cycles should influence diversification* – Business history is littered with examples of firms, such as many defence contractors, who attempt to shift from their own 'slow cycle' markets into seemingly attractive 'medium cycle' or even 'fast cycle' markets. Their lack of understanding and capabilities in dealing with faster resource/requirement dynamics leaves them with over-engineered products, missed development lead-times and exorbitant production costs, etc. The key lesson becomes, 'beware of hidden barriers to entry'.

- *Look out for cycle-time shifts* – Not all changes necessarily drive markets towards higher rates of imitation. For instance, the advent of hub and spoke control in airports gave less dominant regional airlines an invaluable source of competitive advantage over the major carriers. However, regardless of the direction of change, such shifts can be difficult to adjust to and therefore need to be actively sought out and analysed. At the same time, as in the airline example, they also represent major opportunities.

Clean and Green (CAG) recycling services

With the widespread adoption of copying and printing technologies, paper usage for most firms exploded, leaving them with vast quantities of paper to dispose of. Recognising this requirement as a potential opportunity for a new business, Clean and Green began operating in late 1990 as a venture in and around the town of Maastricht – initially targeting medium-sized businesses with a confidential paper removal and recycling service. The idea was to allow businesses to dispose of their paper without worrying about negative environmental impact (in effect, CAG was also offering intangible enhancement to their clients' reputation for citizenship) while also preventing confidential information leaks. As a support to its relatively focused operations, its marketing effort emphasised the quality and dependability of the service. Initially, the operation consisted of dedicated collection receptacles and a number of vehicles (capacity and process technology decisions). Additionally, the firm made special contractual arrangements with paper producers (a supply network decision).

The firm entered the next phase of its development when 'green' politics were increasingly influential at the national and local level and many publicly provided recycling services were developed. Having built up a reputation with local businesses, the firm was invited by a consortium of local authorities to tender for a domestic paper collection contract. This was not just an increase in requirements but also a very different kind of market. It required the company to collect and recycle a wider range of paper from more sites and without any value being placed upon the confidentiality of its service. It needed to add capacity and enhance its process technology in order to both increase flexibility and reduce costs. After negotiating with the consortium (who were keen to assist in the development of a range of potential contractors), CAG was awarded a contract with an understanding that it would take almost 12 months to acquire and develop the requisite operational capability.

After the award of this first very large contract, CAG won more public and private work and over time both added extra capacity and introduced other types (different materials etc.) of recycling process. This was an essentially incremental process over a period of about four years – leveraging and developing existing capability while introducing new relationships with other physical recycling plants.

The firm's next significant strategic decision was to gamble on future recycling legislation in The Netherlands and the rest of Europe. Over an 18-month period it invested heavily in a 'complete recycling' capability that allowed it to collect a large percentage of all recyclable household waste. This meant extra collection capacity (vehicles and staff), different collection and sorting systems and new external relationships (including political lobbying). In particular, growth of the firm and the nature of the work meant that significantly more temporary staff were employed. This necessitated the introduction of new control and training systems.

Future legislation was likely to 'require' much higher levels of domestic waste to be recycled, which would introduce a step change in market requirements. Unlike CAG's previous experience, in trying to achieve a sustainable advantage for this new market it deliberately developed capability before the market required it.

## CAG over time

The operations strategy matrix to describe CAG's changing issues over time allows us to see how different resource and requirement issues become more or less important as the company developed and allows us to discuss the complexity, coherence and

Figure 9.4 **Alignment over time at CAG Recycling Services**

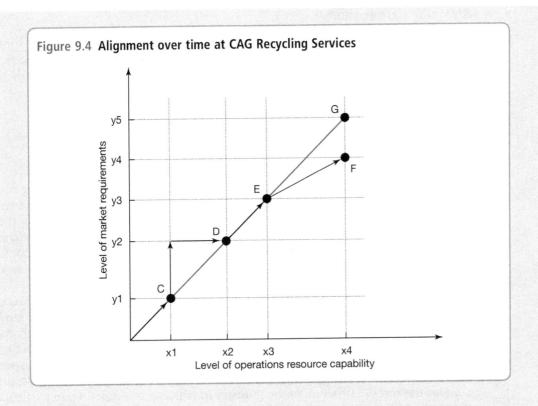

comprehensiveness of the overall strategy. However, it does not fully capture the balancing act of reconciliation over time. Figure 9.4 represents this dynamic process.

CAG was the first in its area to offer a confidential and environmentally friendly paper disposal service, and therefore the initial level of market requirement (shown as level y1 on Figure 9.4) exactly matched the operation's capability to deliver (x1). This 'start-up' phase is represented on the Figure 9.4 by the transition to position C. Having built up a reputation with local businesses over a three-year period, the firm was invited by a consortium of local authorities to tender for the much larger single contract (market requirement, y2). It was awarded the contract with an understanding that it would take the firm a number of months to acquire and develop the requisite operational capability (x2). This transition from points C to D on the diagram is shown as a shift to the left of the 'line of alignment' – indicating that initially it had insufficient capability for the market requirements. After the award of this first large contract, the firm won more and more similar public and private work and, over time (requirements shifting from y2 to y3), added gradually to its underlying capabilities. This incremental growth phase is represented by the transition from point D to E. The strategic decision to invest heavily in a 'complete recycling' capability (x3) allowed CAG to present a more extensive market offering (y3). It was then its strategic strategy to anticipate the introduction of new legislation introducing a step change in market requirements (y5). On the diagram, position F is to the right of the 'line of alignment' (this indicates that it only currently needs to meet y4 requirements) but it anticipates rapidly leveraging (i.e. moving to position G) these capabilities once the new market requirements are introduced.

## Strategic sustainability

The CAG example reinforces the point that even the most successful and apparently problem-free development paths include times of mismatch between resources and requirements. More specifically, it illustrates the two basic models for assuring sustainability:

- the use of 'static' mechanisms that defend a given position;
- the use of 'dynamic' mechanisms that encourage innovation and change.

### 'Static' or defensive approaches to sustainability

'Static' mechanisms for achieving sustainability are concerned with preventing competitors from attacking existing market and resource positions, rather than trying to move to an entirely new position. So, to some extent, it is a defensive rather than offensive approach. An operation can seek to identify the market-isolating (barriers to entry) and resource-isolating (barriers to imitation) mechanisms that minimise change and act to keep a lock on a specific resource/requirement position. It can do this by using internal and external approaches.

Internal approaches exploit the idea that we have used before – that operations resources can be considered particularly valuable if they are scarce, difficult to move, difficult to copy or difficult to find substitutes for. Because they are difficult to replicate, such resources act to sustain competitive advantage by preventing competitors replicating their advantage. External mechanisms are based on the idea that the overall performance of a firm will depend on how well its strategy and its actions take into account the specific structure of the industry in which it is competing. In particular, the work of Michael Porter has been hugely influential in understanding this view. The forces Porter refers to can be summarised as: (a) the bargaining power of suppliers and buyers; (b) the threat of potential market entrants; (c) the threat of substitute products/services; and (d) the challenge from existing competitive rivals. Table 9.1 offers some illustrations of how operations strategy can exploit both internal and external strategic attributes of sustainability.

### 'Dynamic' or offensive approaches to sustainability

Ultimately, even in the most isolated of market niches, customer requirements evolve and, as a result, operational capabilities also need to evolve. So, in addition to exploiting existing barriers to entry and imitation, operations can raise their game through innovation and change in order to achieve sustainability. Doing this involves the operation actively moving up the line of alignment and achieving a balance between market requirements and operations resources at a higher level. For instance, prior to the launch of the Federal Express 'next day' delivery service ('for when it absolutely, positively has to be there overnight'), market analyses suggested that few organisations needed such a fast and dependable service.[3] Once launched, however, early adopters of the service, such as global industrial firms and professional and financial services, obtained competitive advantage from the speed and dependability benefits of overnight mail. As a result, increasing numbers of firms began to use the service. Although rivals eventually began to imitate the services, for a number of years this radical operating innovation proved to be hugely profitable for Federal Express, who in effect had gone to market with an entirely new set of capabilities delivering significantly improved speed and dependability performance.

Table 9.1 Internal and external 'defensive' static mechanisms of sustainability

| 'Defensive' static mechanisms of sustainability | | | |
|---|---|---|---|
| *Internal* | *Notes* | *External* | *Notes* |
| Scarcity | Scarce operational resources might include customised production facilities, or experienced operational staff embodying tacit knowledge developed over time, etc. | Bargaining power of buyers and suppliers. | If an operation can control access to the market then other firms are effectively compelled to supply. Suppliers are able to exploit similar strategies if their products/services are seen as vital. The 'Intel Inside' marketing campaign was an example of such a strategy. |
| Difficult to move | Any operational resource (i.e. process technology) developed in-house cannot be accessed without purchasing the entire company. Because of greater labour mobility, critical skills and experiences can move to rivals quite easily. The resources that are the most difficult to move are, therefore, those that 'don't walk on legs' and are tied somehow into the operation. | The threat of potential market entrants. | The threat posed by new entrants can be dramatically reduced if firms have an effective 'barrier to entry' (e.g. economies of scale in steel production, installed networks in telecommunications). |
| Difficult to copy | Although similar to the idea of mobility, the relative imitability of a resource is an important defensive characteristic. Any 'learning curve' effects that might exist in operations can make capabilities difficult to copy. | The threat of substitute product and/or services. | Reducing the threat from substitute products/services is an extension of the mechanisms associated with barriers to entry (see above), but specifically related to products and services. If the operation has established a dominant technological standard (e.g. Microsoft operating systems), this can be a major barrier to entry. |
| Difficult to create a substitute | No operation wants its operational resources to become irrelevant through the introduction of a substitute (or alternative).Yet it can happen – the open protocols of the internet make switching and hence substitution far easier. | The challenge from existing competitive rivals. | The challenge from existing rivals is strongly influenced by all of the categories discussed above. Additionally, because operations guard their process secrets, most firms 'reverse engineer' rival products/ services to try to establish the nature of the process. |

**Example** **Dell – things change, OK?[4]**

What is right at one time may become a liability later on. For 20 years Dell had exhibited remarkable growth in the PC market. Yet by the mid-2000s, although still the largest seller of PCs in the world, growth had started to slow down and the company's stock market value had been downgraded. The irony of this is that what had been some of the company's main advantages,

▶

its direct sales model using the internet and its market power to squeeze price reductions from suppliers, were starting to be seen as disadvantages. Some commentators claimed that, although the market had changed, Dell's operating model had not. Over the 20 years Dell had developed a radically different and very successful set of operations based on an extremely efficient supply chain, low inventories, modular product designs that allowed it to customise to its individual customer requirements and a direct link to customers. All of this allowed it to sell robust computers at low prices. Some of the questions raised by commentators focused on Dell's size. Perhaps it had grown so big that its lean supply model was no longer appropriate? How could a $56-billion company remain lean, sharp and alert? Other commentators pointed out that Dell's rivals had also now learnt to run efficient supply chains (*'getting a 20-year competitive advantage from your knowledge of how to run supply chains isn't too bad'*). However, one of the main factors was seen as the shift in the nature of the market itself. Sales of PCs to business users had become largely a commodity business, with wafer-thin margins, and this part of the market was growing slowly compared to the sale of computers to individuals. Selling computers to individuals provided slightly better margins than the corporate market, but they increasingly wanted up-to-date computers with a high design value and, most significantly, they wanted to see, touch and feel the products before buying them. This was clearly a problem for a company such as Dell, who had spent 20 years investing in its telephone and, later, internet-based sales channels. Also, Dell's early attempts to move into products other than PCs, such as televisions, were also hindered by its lack of physical stores. What all commentators agreed on was that in the fast-moving and cut-throat computer business, where market requirements could change overnight, operations resources must constantly develop appropriate new capabilities.

## What analysis is needed for formulation?

However formulation is approached, it is likely to require some significant analysis. As one would expect in a process that reconciles market requirements with operations resource capabilities, the two chief areas of analysis concern markets and resources. The practical reason for emphasising the problems with this analysis is to help reinforce the balanced nature of the reconciliation between resources and requirements. Although analysis of the marketplace is generally characterised by better tools and techniques, in reality both are characterised by ambiguity and uncertainty.

### Analysing market requirements

It is beyond the scope of an operations strategy book to explore the many practical models that exist to help practitioners assess the requirements of the marketplace. There is a rich and sophisticated literature on marketing stretching back over the history of modern business. However, simply because there are many highly structured, rational models for analysing the external environment, this does not imply that these analyses are foolproof. No matter how complex and detailed the model, regardless of how much time and effort is invested in the data collection, it is still an ambiguous and unreliable process.

### Analysing operational resource capabilities

It can be difficult to analyse the external environment, despite the widespread availability of practical tools and techniques designed to help in this process. But it can be even more difficult to analyse the 'inside' of the organisation. This aspect of

Table 9.2 **Some possible operations-related factors in a SWOT analysis**

| Strengths | Weaknesses |
|---|---|
| Economies of scale | Uneconomic volume |
| Ability to adjust capacity | Under-utilisation of capacity |
| Reserve capacity | Insufficient capacity |
| Appropriate locations | Inappropriate locations |
| Long-term supplier relationships | Lack of power in supply market |
| Supply market knowledge | No long-term supply relationships |
| Supply chain control | Old process technology with poor performance |
| Advanced process technology knowledge | No capability to improve 'off-the-shelf' process technology |
| In-house process technology development capability | Rigid organisation or decision-making structure |
| Flexible organisational structure | No in-house operations expertise |
| In-house operations expertise | Static levels of operations performance |
| Continuous improvement culture | Poor product and service development skills |
| Effective product and service development processes | |

strategy formulation is not supported by many practical frameworks. In fact, Birger Wernerfelt, one of the first academics to advocate a resource-based view of the firm, argued that conceptually we tend to treat organisational resources as an 'amorphous heap'.[5] In fact, the widely applied strategy management tool SWOT analysis is a good starting point for the analysis of operations resources. This mechanism explicitly links internal (strengths and weaknesses) and external (opportunities and threats) factors. And although SWOT analysis is extremely difficult to incorporate into an effective planning process, the 'strengths and weaknesses' part of SWOT is particularly useful. Table 9.2 lists some possible operations factors that might be included in such an analysis.

Although only a selection of general strengths and weaknesses, many weaknesses (in Table 9.2) are simply a lack of a particular strength – for example, having 'in-house operations expertise' is a strength, while not having it is a weakness. But other strengths may conflict with each other. So, achieving good 'economies of scale' can leave the operation open to 'under-utilisation of capacity' if demand drops. Similarly, 'resource capability' is only a strength if there are greater benefits of capturing extra demand than there are costs of providing the excess capacity. What are strengths in one set of circumstances could be weaknesses in another. It is important, therefore, to clarify the assumptions under which such lists are derived.

Although every SWOT analysis will be unique to the operation for which it is being devised, some general hints have been suggested that will enhance the quality of the analysis:[6]

- Keep it brief: pages of analysis are usually not required.
- Relate strengths and weaknesses, wherever possible, to key factors for success.

- Strengths and weaknesses should also be stated in competitive terms, if possible. It is reassuring to be 'good' at something, but it is more relevant to be 'better than the competition'.

- Statements should be specific and avoid blandness: there is little point in stating ideas that everyone believes in.

- Analysis should distinguish between where the company wishes to be and where it is now; the gap should be realistic.

- It is important to be realistic about the strengths and weaknesses of one's own and competitive organisations.

## Capabilities

Analysing strengths and weaknesses is the starting point for understanding resources; the next challenge is to understand the capabilities that they (may) represent. The idea of core capabilities is central to understanding how operations strategy can be sustained over time. But the idea of operations capabilities is not a straightforward one. Capabilities derive from strategically important assets – those that are scarce, difficult to move, difficult to copy and difficult to substitute for. But these types of assets are, by definition, more difficult to manage than those assets that are well understood, widely available and easy to copy. Practical analysis and implementation that is based upon a concept that is so ambiguous is therefore not always easy. However, it is possible to highlight a number of critical issues:

- Definitions (such as, What is capability?) can be important. As one confused engineer once exclaimed to one of the authors, '*This is very difficult you know, you don't walk around the factory and bang your head on the core capabilities of the firm!*' Yet they do exist, and identifying them is an obvious first step in nurturing them. While complex definitions of different types of capability can be used, the more abstract the definition, the less likely it is that managers will find it useful. This drastically reduces the legitimacy of any decisions based upon the analysis and makes it harder for the dynamics of capability development to be incorporated on an ongoing basis. Therefore, if possible, keep definitions of capability as simple as is practical.

- The level of aggregation in how capabilities are defined is also critical. For instance, while one might reasonably assert that Sony's core capability is 'miniaturisation', this may be too generic for Sony's managers to act upon. Collis and Montgomery[7] illustrate this challenge with the example of a manufacturer of medical diagnostics test equipment that had defined its core capability as 'instrumentation'. Such an intuitively obvious definition was too broad for managers to act upon. Analysing to greater levels of disaggregation, however, revealed that the company's strength was mainly the result of competitive advantage in designing the human/machine interface. In order to exploit and deepen this competence, the firm hired ergonomists and set out to design a product for the fast-growing general practitioner market, where the equipment would not be operated by skilled technicians.

- Articulating capabilities in very abstract terms may capture their essence but can make them difficult to use. Some degree of operationalisation is usually necessary. Collis and Montgomery[8] argue that '*evaluating whether Kraft General Foods or Unilever has better consumer marketing skills may be impossible, but analysing which is more successful at launching product-line extensions is feasible*'. In many ways, such analyses are essentially forms of internal benchmarking and, as with that process, the greater the level of detail, the greater the cost and time necessary to perform the analysis.

- Much of the competence and capability literature regularly uses the words 'core' or 'distinctive' to add extra emphasis to those capabilities that are most important to the business. Indeed, the most celebrated of these authors, Prahalad and Hamel,[9] only use the phrase 'core competence'. Their implicit warning is to focus on the very few capabilities that really are 'core' to the sustainability of the operation.

- The practical consequences of identifying the 'core' capabilities within an operation are usually that additional resources will be acquired and deployed. This is clearly a political issue within the organisation. It can alter power balances – bolstering one set of managers, perhaps at the expense of others. It is important, therefore, to understand that asking managers to judge core capabilities is inevitably a political process. In one workshop, for example, a senior information technology (IT) manager was asked to rate the importance of 'managerial IT skills, knowledge and experience'. The answer was an unsurprising 'absolutely critical!'.

## The challenges to operations strategy formulation

There are limits to the ability of any organisation to align itself to changing environmental requirements. This is because in any complex system there are certain resources and processes that tend to prevent adaptation/innovation rather than enable it, or, in other words, organisations are subject to a wide range of inertial forces. The dictionaries tend to define inertia as 'the tendency to continue in the same state [or] to resist change', and as we discuss the practical challenges of achieving operational alignment, it is important to explore the sources of inertia. One of the most infamous examples of an operation that was unable to overcome inertia and adapt itself to a new set of market requirements is IBM between 1980 and the mid-1990s, when it struggled to adapt to the world of the PC. It is easy to forget that in 1980 Microsoft was a start-up with fewer than 50 staff (IBM had 300,000 employees), and that despite phenomenal growth, by 1982 the combined market capitalisation of both Intel and Microsoft was only about one-tenth of IBM's. But many successful organisations contain the seeds of their own downfall – a phenomenon that has been explored by a number of authors, including Dorothy Leonard.[10] When discussing the relationship between what she calls core capabilities and core rigidities. Leonard offers the following quote from John F. McDonnell of the McDonnell Douglas Corporation to illustrate the phenomenon of success-enabled inertia:

> *'While it is difficult to change a company that is struggling, it is next to impossible to change a company that is showing all the outward signs of success. Without the spur of a crisis or a period of great stress, most organizations – like most people – are incapable of changing the habits and attitudes of a lifetime.'*

But why should this be so? Surely success generates revenue and profits that in turn can be invested in the future of the firm? Inertial forces need to be understood if their negative impact is to be overcome. If we explore the impact of high levels of success we can discern a number of specific structural issues that can increase the potential level of inertia. For instance:

- *Operations' resource profile* – Once an investment has been made in either tangible or intangible assets, this inevitably influences subsequent decision making. It is fairly obvious how certain assets are dedicated to specific tasks and not readily transferable, but more broadly the whole profile of an organisation's operations strategy can create inertial forces. For instance, IBM's vertically integrated production system made it the largest chip manufacturer in the world. This technological independence had an inevitable influence upon its delayed decision to purchase Intel's market-leading 80386 chip. Similarly, the agreement with Microsoft that overlooked Windows was internally justifiable because at that time the software was just a prototype and it had its own system in development.

- *Investment bias* – Operations will tend to invest further in those resource/requirement intersections that have proved successful. Regardless of whether this takes the form of extra capacity, additional R&D expenditure or staff recruitment, etc., investment here appears to offer a more reliable return. Given a finite resource base to draw upon, other aspects of the operation can easily suffer comparative neglect.

- *History* – Organisations become constrained by their own history. Once systems and procedures and 'ways of working' are established, it becomes difficult and expensive to change them. So, for example, even though IBM invented both floppy disk and hard drive technology, the firm saw itself as 'a supplier of integrated systems' and therefore it did not sell these components – effectively leaving other firms to make a fortune from their invention.

- *Organisational structures/political forces* – Often overlooked in rational discussions of operations management, political forces have an enormous influence. In all operations there are individual managers and influential groups who compete for resources with their different priorities, opinions and values. In an organisation the size of IBM (in the mid-1980s), the combination of a cumbersome organisational structure (a single hierarchy for the whole business) and political machinations effectively killed off its entry into the PC market. Its first model, in 1981, had been very successful but the supposedly mass-market PC Jr. model (intended for launch in July 1983) was delayed by senior management interference. The company introduced an inferior keyboard, scrapped plans to sell it in department stores, missed the crucial Christmas sales period and gave it too high a price. A year later, IBM dropped the price, sold through different outlets and realised it was too late – its competitors had developed new, more appealing models.

## How do we know when the formulation process is complete?

Back in Chapter 1 we introduced the idea of the operations strategy matrix. We suggested that, because it emphasised the intersections between what is required from operations (in terms of the relative priority that should be given to each performance objective) and how the operation tries to achieve this through the choices made in each decision area, it was a useful device to describe any organisation's operations strategy. At least, it could act as a checklist to ensure that the organisation had been reasonably comprehensive in considering different aspects of its operations strategy. In fact, we can use the matrix to go further than merely describe an operations strategy. We can use it to question, develop and even formulate strategies. Indeed, using the matrix to check for comprehensiveness could be considered the first step in a

**Figure 9.5** 'Fit' is concerned with ensuring comprehensiveness, correspondence, coherence and criticality

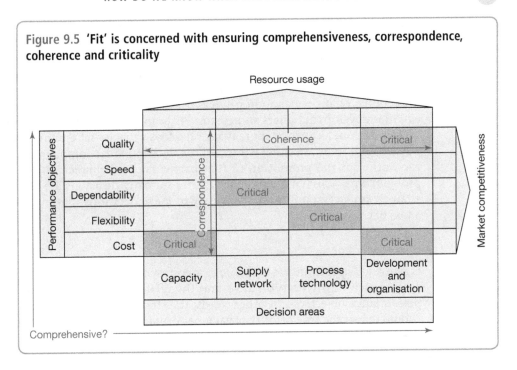

formulation process. Here we will use the matrix to explore some of the most basic aspects of operations strategy formulation (see Figure 9.5):

- exploring what it means for an operations strategy to be comprehensive;
- ensuring there is internal coherence between the different decision areas;
- ensuring that decisions taken as part of the operations strategy process correspond to the appropriate priority for each performance objective;
- highlighting which resource/requirement intersections are the most critical with respect to the broader financial and competitive priorities of the organisation.

### Comprehensiveness

The notion of 'comprehensiveness' is a critical first step in seeking to achieve operations alignment. Business history is littered with world-class companies that simply failed to notice the potential impact of, for instance, new process technology, or emerging changes in their supply network. Also, many attempts to achieve alignment have failed because operations have paid undue attention to only one of the key decision areas.

### Coherence

As a comprehensive strategy evolves over time, different tensions will emerge that threaten to pull the overall strategy in different directions. This can result in a loss of coherence. Coherence is when the choices made in each decision area do not pull the operation in different directions. For example, if new flexible technology is introduced that allows products or services to be customised to individual clients' needs, it would be 'incoherent' to devise an organisation structure that did not enable the relevant staff to exploit the technology because it would limit the effective flexibility of the operation. For the investment in flexible technology to be effective, it must be accompanied by an organisational structure that deploys the organisation's skills appropriately, a performance measurement system that acknowledges that flexibility must be promoted, a new product/service development policy that stresses appropriate types of customisation, a supply network strategy that develops suppliers and customers to understand the needs of high-variety customisation, a capacity strategy that deploys capacity where the customisation is needed, and so on. In other words, all the decision areas complement and reinforce each other in the promotion of that particular performance objective. The main problem with achieving coherence is that so many decisions are made that have a strategic impact that it is relatively easy to make decisions that inadvertently cause a loss of coherence.

### Correspondence

Equally, an operation has to achieve a correspondence between the choices made against each of the decision areas and the relative priority attached to each of the performance objectives. In other words, the strategies pursued in each decision area should reflect the true priority of each performance objective. So, for example, if cost reduction is the main organisational objective for an operation, then its process technology investment decisions might err towards the purchase of 'off-the-shelf' equipment from a third-party supplier. This would reduce the capital cost of the technology and may also imply lower maintenance and running costs. Remember, however, that making such a decision will also have an impact on other performance objectives. An off-the-shelf piece of equipment may not, for example, have the flexibility of more 'made-to-order' equipment. Also, the other decision areas must correspond with the same prioritisation of objectives. If low cost is really important, then one would expect to see capacity strategies that exploit natural economies of scale, supply network strategies that reduce purchasing costs, performance measurement systems that stress efficiency and productivity, continuous improvement strategies that emphasise continual cost reduction, and so on.

### Criticality

In addition to the difficulties of ensuring coherence between decision areas, there is also a need to include financial and competitive priorities. Although all decisions are important and a comprehensive perspective should be maintained, in practical terms some resource/requirement intersections will be more critical than others. The judgment over exactly which intersections are particularly critical is very much a pragmatic one that must be based on the particular circumstances of an individual firm's operations strategy. It is therefore difficult to generalise as to the likelihood of any particular intersections being critical. However, in practice, one can ask revealing questions such as, 'If flexibility is important, of all the decisions we make in terms of our capacity – supply networks, process technology, or development and organisation – which will have the most impact on flexibility?' This can be done for all performance objectives, with more emphasis being placed on those having the highest priority. Generally, when presented with a framework such as the operations strategy matrix, executives can identify those intersections that are particularly significant in achieving alignment.

## What is operations strategy implementation?

Operations strategy implementation is the way that strategies are operationalised or executed. It involves the processes that attempt to ensure that strategies are achieved. It is important, because no matter how sophisticated the intellectual and analytical underpinnings of a strategy, it remains only a document until it has been implemented. So implementation is an important part of operations strategy, even if it does come at the end of the operations strategy process. Yet it is not always straightforward to make general points about the implementation process because it is very context-dependent. That is, the way one implements any strategy will very much depend on the specific nature of the changes implied by that strategy and the organisational and environmental conditions that apply during its implementation.

**Example** | **Nokia – a failure to change[11]**

Back in the early 2000s, Nokia was the king of the mobile phone business – and it was a good business to be in, with double-digit growth year on year. Nokia was omnipresent and omnipowerful – a pioneer that had supplied the first mass wave of the expanding mobile phone industry. It dominated the market in many parts of the world and the easily recognisable Nokia ring-tone echoed everywhere, from boardrooms to shopping malls. So why did this once-dominant company eventually sink to the point where it was forced to sell its mobile communications business to Microsoft in 2013? The former Nokia CEO, Jormal Ollila, admitted that Nokia made several mistakes, but the exact nature of those mistakes is a point of debate amongst business commentators. Julian Birkinshaw, a Professor at London Business School, dismisses some of the most commonly cited reasons. Did it lose touch with its customers? Well, yes, but by definition that must hold for any company whose sales drop so drastically in the face of thriving competitors. And, anyway, Nokia had been praised for its customer-centric marketing and design capabilities. Did it fail to develop the necessary technologies? No. Nokia had a prototype touchscreen before the iPhone was launched, and its smartphones were technologically superior to anything Apple, Samsung, or Google had to offer for many years. Did it not recognise that the basis of competition was shifting from the hardware to the ecosystem? (A technology ecosystem in this case is a term used to describe the complex system of interdependent components that work together to enable mobile technology to operate successfully.) Again, this is not really true. The 'ecosystem' battle began in the early 2000s, with Nokia joining forces with Ericsson, Motorola and Psion to create Symbian as a platform technology that would keep Microsoft at bay.

While it was losing its dominance, Nokia was well aware of most of the changes occurring in the mobile communications market and the technology developments being actively pursued by competitors. Where it struggled was in implementation of the changes that were necessary. Arguably, Nokia was not short of awareness, but it did lack the capacity to convert awareness into action. The failure of big companies to adapt to changing circumstances is one of the fundamental puzzles in the world of business, says Professor Birkinshaw. Occasionally, a genuinely 'disruptive' technology (such as digital imaging – see the Kodak example in Chapter 8) can wipe out an entire industry. But usually the sources of failure are less dramatic. Often it is a failure to implement strategies or technologies that have already been developed, an arrogant disregard for changing customer demands, or a complacent attitude towards new competitors.

## What is implementation?

One way of thinking about the underlying purpose of an operations strategy implementation is to use the 'line of fit', or alignment, concept introduced earlier. To recap, the idea is that operations strategy can be diagrammatically illustrated by its position relative to its operations resource capabilities, the requirements of its markets and the degree of 'fit' or alignment between them. We focused on the idea of achieving sustainable alignment between operations resource capabilities and market requirements. We also stressed the difficulty of achieving alignment because of uncertain markets and operations resource capabilities. In Figure 9.6, moving along the market requirements dimension indicates a change in intended market performance. Moving along the operations resource capabilities dimension indicates changes in operations capabilities.

Using this model gives us a starting point for understanding the purpose of the operation's degree of change involved in the strategy implementation. It is important to be clear regarding how much change is intended. So, if, on Figure 9.6, point A is the current operations strategy and point B is the intended operations strategy, it is necessary to develop an understanding of current and intended market requirements

**Figure 9.6 Implementing an operations strategy that involves moving from A to B means understanding current and intended market requirements and operations resource capabilities so that the extent and nature of the change can be assessed**

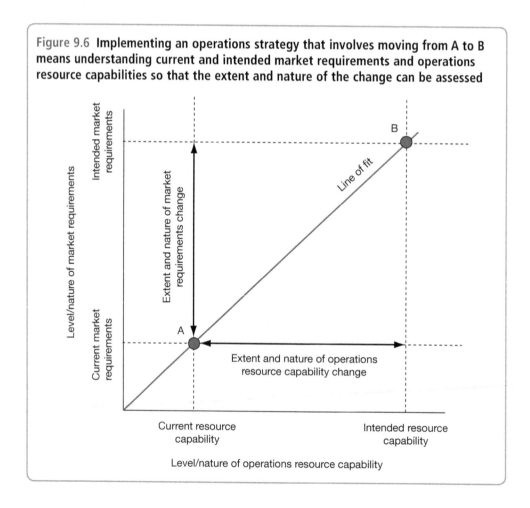

and operations resource capabilities. Certainly, without such an understanding, it is exceedingly difficult to expect the whole organisation to comprehend why, how and how much things are going to change when the new strategy is implemented. Yet, providing guidance to those who will be carrying out the implementation is not a straightforward task. We are again confronted with the tensions between seeing strategy as a plan that provides a 'grand design' for the operation on one hand, and seeing strategy as an emergent process that takes full account of the experiences that are derived from the day-to-day running of the operation and the day-to-day implementation of the new strategy. This means that any statement that articulates an intended change must be specific enough to provide useful guidance and yet broad enough to allow for adaptation of the implementation plan within an overall strategic direction.

But there is a problem. During the implementation from A to B in Figure 9.6, the balance between market requirements and operations resource capabilities may not always be maintained. Sometimes, the market may expect something that the operation cannot (temporarily) deliver. Sometimes, operations may have capabilities that cannot be exploited in the market. At a strategic level, there are risks deriving from a failure to achieve fit between operations resources and market requirements. And how to understand, and cope with, these risks during implementation should be part of any implementation plan.

## Who is responsible for implementation?

A particularly important organisational relationship that can have a profound impact on strategy implementation is that between those in the operations function who have responsibility for formulating strategy and those who run the day-to-day operations tasks. Of course, these two sets of people may be one and the same. Particularly in small organisations, there is simply not enough 'organisational slack' to resource a separate 'operations strategy formulation' function. However, in larger organisations it is now common to have a function or department devoted to the broader aspects of formulating the way in which operations should be managed and resources allocated. We shall call this group of people 'central operations'. This distinction between central operations and day-to-day operations managers is often termed 'staff' and 'line' roles.

### 'Staff' and 'line' in operations

People occupying classic 'staff' positions have a monitoring, planning and shaping role. They are the ones who are charged with building up the company's operations capability. They may look forward to the way markets are likely to be moving, judge the best way to develop each part of the operation and keep an eye on competitor behaviour. All of which are tasks that need close liaison with marketing planners, product and service development and finance. They are also tasks that need some organisational 'space' to be performed effectively. They are certainly not tasks that coexist readily with the hectic and immediate concerns of running an operation. These people constitute what could be termed 'central operations'. People occupying 'line' roles are those who run the day-to-day operations. Theirs is partly a reactive role, one that involves finding ways round unexpected problems: reallocating labour, adjusting processes, solving quality problems, and so on. They need to look ahead only enough to make sure that resources are available to meet targets. Theirs is the necessary routine. Knowing where the operation is heading, keeping it on budget and pulling it back on course when the unexpected occurs: no less valuable a task than the developer's but very different.

While these descriptions are clearly stereotypes, they do represent two types of operations task. The issue, for organisational design, is whether it is wise to separate them organisationally. It may cause more problems than it solves. Although it allows each to concentrate on their different jobs, it also can keep apart the two sets of people who have most to gain by working together. Here is the paradox: the development function does need freedom from the immediate pressures of day-to-day management but it is crucial that it understands the exact nature of these pressures. What makes the operation distinctive? Where do the problems occur? What improvements would make most difference to the performance of the operation? These are questions answered only by living with the operation, not cloistered away from it. Similarly, the day-to-day operations manager has to interpret the workings of the operation, collect data, explain constraints and educate developers. Without the trust and cooperation of each, neither set of managers can be effective.

### Four types of central operations function

Here we are particularly concerned with how headquarters *operations* staff can act to create value for their company and its individual operations. Central operations could be involved in any of the four headquarters parenting responsibilities. Particularly, though, they tend to become involved in the provision of central functional services, in their broadest sense. This includes the provision of central resources that could provide technical advice, information systems capabilities, laboratory testing services, improvement teams, quality procedures, environmental services, and so on. It also could be taken to mean the general coordination of all operations activity in the different parts of the company. This may include the compilation of performance statistics, the encouragement of inter-operations learning and the development of broad operations strategies.

Within this, how central operations exercises its responsibilities very much depends on the view it has of operations strategy and development. For example, we can use the dimensions that define the perspectives on operations strategy as described in Chapter 1:

● *Top-down or bottom-up?* – If central operations has a predominantly top-down view of the world, it is likely to take a programmatic approach to its activities, emphasising the implementation of overall company strategy. Conversely, if it takes a bottom-up view, it is more likely to favour an emergent model of operations development where individual business operations together contribute to the overall building of operations expertise.

● *Market requirements or operations resource focus?* – If central operations takes a market requirements view of operations development, it is likely to focus on the explicit performance achieved by each business operation and how far that performance serves to satisfy the operation's customers. An operations resource focus, on the other hand, emphasises the way in which each business operation develops its competences and successfully deploys them in its marketplaces.

We can use these two dimensions to define a typology of the central operations function, as shown in Figure 9.7. It classifies central operations into four pure types called governors, curators, trainers and facilitators – a typology based on Merali and McGee's

### Figure 9.7 A typology of the 'central operations' function

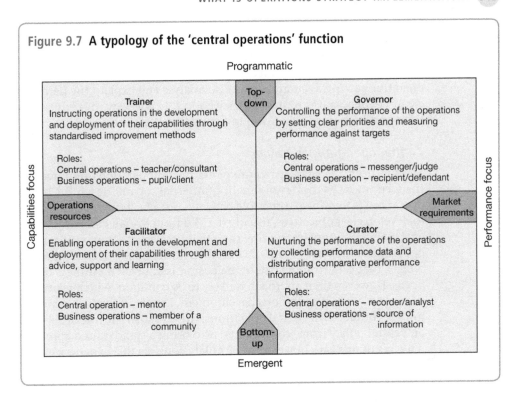

work.[12] Although, in practice, the central operations function of most businesses is a combination of these pure types, usually one type predominates.

### Central operations as governor

Here we use the term 'governor' to describe the role of central operations in its imperial sense. The ancient Roman Empire ruled its provinces by appointing governors whose job it was to impose the will of the Emperor and Senate on its possessions. They acted as the agent of a central authority, interpreting the Imperial will and arbitrating over any disputes within the framework of central rule. The word governor, however, is also used in mechanics to denote the mechanism that prevents an engine running out of control and damaging itself. Central operations of this type interpret strategy in terms of market performance, set clear goals for each business operation, judge their performance and, if performance is not to target, want to know the reason why. They are likely to have a set of predetermined responses to 'fix' operations that do not perform up to requirements and tend to expect results to improve in the short term.

### Central operations as curator

Central operations can be concerned primarily with performance against market requirements without being top-down. They may take a more emergent view by acting as the repository of performance data and ideas regarding operations practice for the company as a whole. We use the term 'curator' to capture this idea. Curators collect information and examples so that all can be educated by examining them. Central operations therefore will be concerned with collecting performance information, examples of best practice, and so on. They will also be concerned with disseminating this information so that operations managers in different parts of the business can benchmark themselves against their colleagues and, where appropriate, adopt best practice from elsewhere. The term curator can also be taken to mean more than a collector; it can also imply someone who nurtures and cares for the exhibits. So, central operations acting as curators may also analyse and explain the performance data and examples of operations practice they collect. In this way they educate business operations and encourage debate around operations practice.

### Central operations as trainer

Moving from the market requirements to the operations resources emphasis shifts the focus more to the development of internal capabilities. If the mind-set of central operations is top-down, their role becomes one of a 'trainer'. Trainers go to some effort to develop clear objectives, usually derived from overall company strategy, and devise effectual methods of instructing their 'pupils'. Because the specific needs of individual operations may differ, 'trainer' central operations may devise improvement methodologies that can, to some extent, be customised to each business operation's specific needs. However, their approach is likely to be common, with a relatively coherent and centralised view of operations development. Even if individual business operations do initiate contact with central operations, they do so in the role of clients seeking advice on central policy from 'consultants' who bring a standardised approach. These internal consultants can, however, accumulate considerable experience and knowledge.

### Central operations as facilitator

In some ways this final type of central operations is the most difficult to operate effectively. Central operations are again concerned with the development of operations capabilities but do so by acting as facilitators of change rather than instructors. Their role is to advise, support and generally aid the development and deployment of capabilities through a process of mentoring business operations. They share responsibility with the business operations in forming a community of operations practice. The development of the relationships between central operations and business operations is crucial in encouraging shared learning. The value placed on these relationships themselves becomes the prime, though somewhat diffused, mechanism for control of the improvement process. Implicit in this type of central operations is the acceptance of a relatively long-term approach to operations development.

### Central operations and information networks

The different types of central operations will play different roles within the information network that connects business operations to central operations and to each other. Figure 9.8 illustrates the likely nature of these information networks. In both the governor and trainer types, central operations is the dominant power player. Their vision of what the individual business operations should be doing dominates the rest of the network. When the emphasis is on individual business operations performance, as in the governor type, there is relatively little, if any, communication between the businesses. Because operations resource competences are more diffuse than hard performance measures, the trainer type will have to accommodate the needs and views of business operations to some extent and also rely on individual business operations having some, albeit weak, sharing of operations practice. Central operations that adopt a more emergent approach implicitly accept a two-way relationship between

**Figure 9.8** Information relationships for the four types of central operations functions

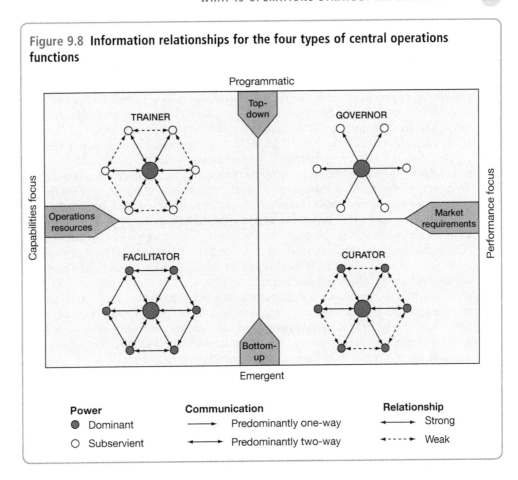

themselves and the business operations; only in this way can central operations be aware of emergent practice. The curator type, by publishing comparative performance data, is, to some extent, encouraging some communication between the individual business operations. The facilitator type of central operations, however, is entirely dependent on regular, strong and two-way communication between themselves and the community of business operations that they guide.

---

**Example** Implementing Renault's Romanian strategy[13]

One of Louis Schweitzer's ambitions before he retired as Chairman of the French carmaker Renault was to produce the '€5,000 car'. His goal was to produce a low-cost vehicle targeted at developing countries (80 per cent of consumers who have never owned a car live in developing countries). However, there also seems to be surprisingly buoyant demand in the West for utilitarian cars. Schweitrer succeeded when Renault started producing the Logan in Romania in its Dacia operation. But when Renault bought the Dacia plant in Pitesti, about 100 miles southwest of Bucharest, in 1999 it was described by one industry commentator as, '*one of the scruffiest car assembly operations I had seen in years. Dark, dismal and more like hell's kitchen than a manufacturing operation, it was hardly conducive to producing quality products.*' Now, having implemented a €500-million turnaround strategy, it is turning out a car that is thoroughly modern in terms of fit and finish, but without the frills.

But, in achieving its strategy, Renault/Dacia has needed to implement it in a manner that fits the particular conditions of the product and where it is being made. In a region where the public perception of privatisation is tainted by images of cowboy capitalists enriching themselves, Francois Fourmont, Dacia general manager, points out that *'you have to make it clear that you are very serious about running a business that benefits both shareholders and Romania. When Renault comes to a country, it does not come for only a few years.'* Yet Renault had to make some harsh decisions. It cut Dacia's workforce from more than 27,000 to 12,500. *'We had no choice',* said Fourmont. *'Our first responsibility is to make money, because that is the only way we can survive as a business',* he explains. *'Once we have that basis, we can start to think about other factors. And many of the fired workers were retrained and subsequently found jobs with the suppliers that had moved their production to the area.'*

In Romania, given the turbulence of the move from a centrally planned economy towards a market economy, it was also particularly important to work closely with state and local governments, especially over social issues. The company has had to address environmental concerns and develop a network of local suppliers that can produce to an international standard of quality. Many of the firms, including multinationals such as Valeo, are now based on-site. Renault also put continuous training at the heart of Dacia's business, although at first it was a challenge. But, argues Fourmont, *'the more efficient and better trained the workforce is, the more likely they are to withstand competition from abroad, allowing the company to reward staff better for their good performance and quality product'.* One worker, who had been with Dacia for more than a decade, remembered what life was like before Renault took over:

> *'It was hard work, with a lot of effort and very little satisfaction. People were suspicious (of the changes) at first, especially when the job cuts came. But then they saw the company was serious and they began to trust Renault.'*

The design of the car was critical to its low cost. Renault designed a car that was modern but without costly design elements and superfluous technology. Production costs for the Logan were estimated at $1,089 per car – less than half the $2,468 estimate for an equivalent Western auto. *'The Logan is the McDonald's of cars',* says Kenneth Melville, who headed the Logan design team. *'The concept was simple: reliable engineering without a lot of electronics, cheap to build and easy to maintain and repair.'* To keep costs low, Renault adapted the platform used for its other small cars and then slashed the number of components by more than 50 per cent. The dashboard is one continuous injection-moulded part, vs. up to 30 pieces for a top-of-the-line Renault. The rear-view mirrors are symmetrical, so they can be used on both the left and right side of the car. Renault also opted for a flat windshield as curves result in more defects and higher costs.

Sourcing from local suppliers was another critical factor, as was encouraging Renault's existing suppliers to set up shop on a new supplier park within the Dacia factory complex. This was not easy, because many suppliers were sceptical about the whole project. But they were won over, and now 65 per cent of parts bought in from suppliers are produced locally, with 26 of Renault's existing suppliers having agreed to set up nearby – 7 of them inside the supplier park.

Partly as a result of the Logan's low-cost objectives and simple design, assembly at the Romanian plant was implemented almost entirely without robots. This overcame some of the problems of using state-of-the-art technologies in a region where support services are relatively underdeveloped, and it let Renault capitalise on the country's low labour costs. Now, Renault is ramping up production of the Logan from Russia to Morocco. *'The investment in manufacturing is relatively low, so you can have factories that don't have to produce huge volumes to finance themselves',* says Christoph Stürmer, senior analyst at researcher Global Insight in Frankfurt. Renault has already expanded its output in Romania and is creating the world's largest logistical project that will ship Logan cars in bits so that they can be assembled in Russia, Morocco, India, Iran and Columbia.

## Participation in operations strategy implementation

More than 60 years ago Coch and French[14] argued that a key mechanism for overcoming resistance to change was to include the people to whom the change would happen in the process, and allow them to influence what changes would take place. After all, by including people in the decision process, they are more likely to 'buy in' to the change. Also, involving users in the design of the processes affected by implementation allows designers to access their detailed knowledge and experience. This is especially important because external contractors and consultants may develop some elements of strategy, at least partially. Although they may understand the details of the strategy, they often lack sufficient practical understanding of the organisational context of its implementation.

Professor Dorothy Leonard of Harvard Business School argues that the often-used term 'user involvement' is insufficiently precise because it covers a multitude of different approaches to interaction, each with its own advantages and disadvantages. She proposes a model of four different modes of user involvement, each of which offers a progressively greater degree of descriptive and prescriptive value. (She was referring to implementation involving new process technology, but her ideas have wider applicability.)

- *Delivery mode* – When users (and managers, for that matter) have very little knowledge of any new resources needed for the strategy, it is relatively easy for external vendors or internal developers to treat the implementation project like a product to be finished and then delivered to the client. This 'over-the-wall' mode of development requires almost no interaction with users and, where interaction exists, the feedback may have little impact beyond possibly improving the next generation of technology. The critical strategic question is whether such a one-way flow of information is sufficient to help develop underlying operational resources and capabilities.

- *Consultancy mode* – The next mode, requiring slightly more user interaction, is closer to a classic consultancy implementation project. Designers/vendors recognise that there are established patterns of work (routines, etc.) in the processes that they are helping to change, and invest time asking questions of experienced users. Again, although this accesses more of the firm's operational resources, it does not necessarily contribute to their development because the flow of information remains largely one way.

- *Co-development mode* – This mode is much closer to a form of partnership. This approach can be very effective when levels of uncertainty are high (either the developers' uncertainty about the existing system or users' uncertainty about any new resources). This is because there is relatively little pre-existing knowledge to be captured and exploited.

- *Apprenticeship mode* – Users wanting a greater degree of independence from developers often seek a mode of implementation whereby lead users are almost 'apprenticed' to the developer. This radically changes the nature of the implementation process, moving it much closer to what we described in an earlier section as 'learning'. Such an approach is normally more time- and money-intensive, but from a capability-building perspective it is very attractive.

Dorothy Leonard suggests three useful dimensions for thinking about different types of users:

1 *Form of expertise* – Certain users might be the best operatives in the organisation but this does not guarantee that they are capable of articulating what it is they do. Equally, they may well lack the critical skills to question a system development process.

2 *Representativeness* – Earlier we discussed the value of adopting a pilot approach to implementation. Doing so poses a problem common in all scientific experiments – namely, 'Is it representative of a broader sample or did something atypical occur during the experiment?' This is an issue that needs to be considered when selecting user participants for any implementation project. Are their skills and experience representative of the rest of the organisation?

3 *Willingness* – A basic question perhaps, but some studies[15] have shown that levels of user satisfaction amongst implementation participants are related to the level of involvement they originally wanted in the process, compared with the involvement they actually had. Anyone who is forced to spend more time than they believe reasonable on an implementation project may resent it, regardless of the outcome.

Increasing the level of user involvement is, of course, not unambiguously positive. Truly radical solutions do not always emerge from discussions limited to current experience. Such a limited range of experience can also lead to the development of processes that address today's rather than tomorrow's difficulties. Despite such concerns, the benefits of increased user involvement in overcoming process 'distance' are usually regarded as significant.

### Prerequisites for effective involvement

Although there is no simple formula that will ensure everyone's commitment to making strategic implementation a success, there are some key elements of basic human resource practice that can facilitate successful involvement. Here we group these elements in a structure known as the 'CEO Principle'. This means, simply, that for people to be involved effectively in an implementation they must:

● have the confidence that involvement will be a positive experience;
● have the education that will allow them to contribute intelligently;
● be allowed the opportunity to participate in the implementation process.

### Confidence that involvement will be a positive experience

One of the most important elements affecting peoples' confidence in their ability to contribute is an organisational culture that makes it clear that its people are an important strategic resource that can directly affect its success. If, through its actions and its communications, an organisation makes it clear that everyone's individual efforts can have an impact on what happens in the organisation, most people will feel that their contributions are worthwhile. Just as importantly, the opposite is also true. If people feel that they cannot influence what happens, why should they bother participating? The same argument applies to how people regard their security within the organisation. By security we mean both the obvious issues such as job security or salary security and more subtle types of security, such as security that their reputation will not suffer by making suggestions that are not supported by others in the organisation. Unless one has a future in the organisation, why become fully involved?

A factor that can negatively affect confidence is confusion over what a strategy is trying to achieve. An unambiguous and shared vision of the overall purpose of the implementation is clearly a help in moving everyone towards the same goal.

Charismatic leadership can sometimes achieve this, but even where this exists effective communication is equally important. Remember, though, that for people to have the confidence to participate, communication should be a two-way street. That is, individuals should feel that they can, without any threat to their own security, communicate their views honestly upwards in the organisation. Certainly, the ability to communicate upwards can be enhanced by support from colleagues and team members, as well as through more formal statements of individual empowerment.

### Education in the necessary skills

Experience at a job is not always sufficient to ensure effective participation. Experience must be structured and contextualised through education, training and development. Education allows individuals to generalise their experience so that it can be used in different contexts. It also provides a shared language and body of knowledge that helps in the generation of innovative ideas, as we discussed earlier. But education in the basics of (in this case) operations management and operations strategy must also be complemented by education about what the strategy implementation is trying to achieve. The general term for this is 'policy deployment'. This is the way in which high-level strategic objectives are translated into more specific objectives and measurements appropriate for each individual group within the organisation. Of course, this presupposes two things: first, that a clearly articulated and coherent implementation plan exists; and second, that there is an appropriate process in place to 'cascade' and communicate the purpose of the strategy and its implementation down the organisation.

For education to thrive there must be learning. For learning to be an important element in an organisation's culture, both individuals and the organisation in general must learn how to learn. Amongst other things, this means never wasting an opportunity to learn. And many of the best opportunities to learn come from the mistakes that one makes. It may be something of a cliché, but mistakes really are one of the most valuable sources of learning. They provide an opportunity to discuss and debate exactly why things went wrong and what can be done about it in the future. Of course, this will not happen if an organisation routinely punishes its employees for every mistake they make. And many organisations do claim that they punish mistakes only when there has been a clear dereliction of duty or when individuals refuse to learn from their mistakes. Yet relatively few organisations have managed to build a culture that genuinely exploits the full potential of being able to learn from mistakes. Those that have come close to it (including the much-quoted example of Toyota) have, over the years, developed a culture of continuous improvement based on a problem-solving methodology that emphasises the importance of learning.

### Opportunity to participate in the implementation process

Individuals may be supremely confident and soundly educated, yet unless they are provided with the opportunity to participate, their contribution will remain untapped. Those organisations who see implementation simply as a set of tasks, devised by senior management and communicated 'down the line', which people simply have to carry out, are not providing the opportunity for individuals to participate. The most obvious way to provide opportunities for participation is to expect employees to participate in planning the implementation itself. But organisational space must be provided to allow this. It cannot simply be expected that employees will participate in implementation planning in addition to an already excessive workload. Some organisations programme formal workshops or team meetings to provide opportunities for participation. Some also include implementation planning as part of their appraisal process. Whatever mechanisms are used, the overall intention is to foster a feeling of ownership of the implementation process. Devolving decision making downwards in the organisation, perhaps using self-managed teams, may facilitate this. However, especially in large organisations, this may work against other attempts to coordinate activities across the organisation, as well as conflicting with any attempt to promote a single and unambiguous vision for the organisation. Such devolved decision making, however, may be appropriate where the implementation climate has a high level of uncertainty, individual staff members' technical expertise is important and the organisation is relatively small.

## SUMMARY ANSWERS TO KEY QUESTIONS

### What is 'formulation' of operations strategy?

Formulation of operations strategy is the practical process of articulating the various objectives and decisions that make up the strategy. It is essentially about different ways of aligning plans, activities and objectives. It will be a relatively occasional activity, although operations strategy consideration may form part of an annual planning cycle. Many detailed formulation models have been developed. Alignment is the state where an operation's capabilities match the requirements of its market. Most organisations try to make their operations resources fit the requirements of their market, but at higher levels of alignment they may look at their unique capabilities and then attempt to leverage these into appropriate market positioning. Sustainability is the achievement of alignment over time. Maintaining an existing market requirements and operations capability balance is a 'static' approach to sustainability. Attempting to raise both operations capabilities and market requirements through a process of innovation is called a 'dynamic' approach to sustainability. There is really no alternative to considering sustainability if an organisation wishes to survive. Even if an operation's ambitions are not to raise its level of alignment to higher levels of market requirements and operations capabilities, it needs to ensure that its position is not eroded.

### What analysis is needed for formulation?

Although most frameworks start with the requirement to understand markets, this is not always straightforward. Markets are, by their nature, dynamic, and companies frequently mistake market reaction. Similarly, understanding operations resources is not straightforward. In particular, understanding the nature and value of intangible assets can be problematic. Also, the sheer inertia of organisations makes implementing strategic decisions difficult. In large companies, especially, radical new changes in markets or internal technologies can often be underestimated.

In terms of the operations strategy matrix, the formulation process is trying to make sure that the operations strategy:

- is comprehensive, covering all the important aspects of strategy;
- has internal coherence between the different decision areas;

- ensures that decisions correspond to the appropriate priority for each performance objective;
- highlights which resource/requirement intersections are the most critical with respect to the broader financial and competitive priorities of the organisation.

### What is operations strategy implementation?

Operations strategy implementation is the way that strategies are operationalised or executed. It involves the processes that attempt to ensure that strategies are achieved. It is important, because no matter how sophisticated the intellectual and analytical underpinnings of a strategy, it remains only a document until it has been implemented. Although operational line managers are important in operations strategy implementation, it is those managers occupying 'staff' positions who usually have a strategic monitoring, planning and shaping role. The role needs close liaison with marketing planners, product and service development and finance. They also need some organisational 'space'. There are four types of 'staff' central operations roles called governors, curators, trainers and facilitators.

A key aspect of overcoming resistance to the changes implied by any implementation is to include the people to whom the change would happen in the process, and allow them to influence what changes would take place. Doing so improves the likelihood of them 'buying in' to the change. Also, involving users in the design allows those managing the implementation to access their detailed knowledge and experience. This is especially important because external contractors and consultants may develop some elements of strategy, at least partially. Although there is no simple formula to ensure commitment to an implementation, there are some basic human resource practices than can facilitate successful involvement. For people to be involved effectively in an implementation they must have the confidence that involvement will be a positive experience, have the education that will allow them to contribute intelligently and be allowed the opportunity to participate in the implementation process.

### Further reading

Alkhafaji, A.F. (2003) *Strategic Management: Formulation, Implementation, and Control in a Dynamic Environment*. Philadelphia: Haworth Press Inc.

Beckman, S.L. and Rosenfield, D.B. (2007) *Operations Strategy: Competing in the 21st Century* (Operations Series). New York: McGraw-Hill.

Bettley, A., Mayle, D. and Tantoush, T. (eds) (2005) *Operations Management: A Strategic Approach*. London: SAGE Publications.

Carlopio, J. (2003) *Changing Gears: The Strategic Implementation of Technology*. Basingstoke, UK: Palgrave Macmillan.

Fitzsimmons, J.A. and Fitzsimmons, M.J. (2010) *Service Management: Operations, Strategy, Information Technology*. New York: McGraw-Hill Higher Education.

Hill, A. and Hill, T. (2009) *Manufacturing Operations Strategy: Texts and Cases*. Basingstoke, UK: Palgrave Macmillan.

Jessen, M., Holm, P.J. and Junghagen, S. (2007) *Strategy execution: passion & profit*. Copenhagen: Copenhagen Business School Press.

Kaplan, R.S. and Norton, D.P. (2004) *Strategy Maps: Converting Intangible Assets into Tangible Outcomes*. Boston, MA: Harvard Business School Publishing.

▶

Kaplan, R.S. and Norton, D.P. (2008) *Execution Premium. Linking Strategy to Operations for Competitive Advantage*. Boston, MA: Harvard Business School Press.

MacLennon, A. (2010) *Strategy Execution: Translating strategy into action in complex organisations*. London: Routledge.

Mintzberg, H., Ahlstrand, B. and Lampel, J.B. (2008) *Strategy Safari: The Complete Guide Through the Wilds of Strategic Management*. Harlow, UK: Financial Times/Prentice Hall.

Pearce, J.A. (2006) *Formulation, Implementation and Control of Competitive Strategy*. New York: McGraw-Hill.

Verweire, K. (2014) *Strategy Implementation*. London: Routledge.

## Notes on the chapter

1  Williams, J. (1992) 'How sustainable is your competitive advantage?', *California Management Review*, 34(3).

2  Ibid.

3  See James Gleick's fascinating book, *Faster* (Little Brown, 1999), for an exploration of the societal issues raised by the speed revolution.

4  *Source*: 'For whom the Dell tolls', *The Economist*, 13 May 2006.

5  Wernerfelt, B. (1984) 'A Resource-based Theory of the Firm', *Strategic Management Journal*, Vol. 13, pp. 111–125.

6  Lynch, R. (1997) *Corporate Strategy*, Harlow, UK: Financial Times/Prentice Hall.

7  Collis, D.J. and Montgomery, C.A. (1998) *Corporate Strategy: Resources and scope of the firm*, Boston, MA: Irwin.

8  Ibid.

9  Prahalad, C.K. and Hamel, G. (1990) 'The core competencies of the corporation', *Harvard Business Review*, May-June.

10 Leonard-Barton, D. (1992) 'Core capabilities and core rigidities: a paradox in managing new product development, *Strategic Management Journal*, Vol. 13, pp. 111–125.

11 *Sources* include: Birkinshaw, J. (2013) 'Why corporate giants fail to change', *CNN Money*, 8 May; Magazine, A. (2013) 'Two Lessons Learned from Nokia's Downfall', Techwell.com, 24 October; Hessman, T. (2013) 'The Road to Failure: Nokia, Blackberry and...Apple', *Industry Week*, 6 September.

12 Merali, Y. and McGee, J. (1998) 'Information competences and knowledge creation at the corporate centre', in Hamel, G., Prahalad, C.K., Thomas, H. and O'Neal, D. (1998) *Strategic Flexibility*. New York: Wiley. Here we use somewhat different terminology.

13 *Sources*: Lewis, A. (2005) 'Renault's Romanian route: Renault's Dacia plant gears up to build a quality, $5,000 car for Eastern Europe', *Automotive Industries*, February; Richardson, B. (2006) 'Renault tunes up Romania's top carmaker', BBC News website.

14 Coch, L. and French, J.P.R. Jr. (1948) 'Overcoming resistance to change', *Human Relations*, No. 1, pp. 512–532.

15 Doll, W.J. and Torkzaden, G. (1989) 'A discrepancy model of end-user computing involvement', *Management Science*, 35(10), pp. 1151–1171.

# The process of operations strategy – monitoring and control

## Introduction

In the previous chapter we explained how, although it is a simplification, the process of operations strategy can be divided into four stages: formulation, implementation, monitoring and control. The previous chapter examined the first two of these stages – formulation and implementation. This chapter looks at the final two stages – monitoring and control. Figure 10.1 illustrates how these two stages fit into the simple stage model, although more accurately the four stages could be seen as a cycle, in the same way that the DMAIC cycle (see Chapter 3) implies a continuous set of activities that create strategic intent, attempt to execute it, judge the progress towards implied or explicit objectives and replan if necessary.

### KEY QUESTIONS

- *What are the differences between operational and strategic monitoring and control?*
- *How is progress towards strategic objectives tracked?*
- *How can the monitoring and control process attempt to control risks?*
- *How does learning contribute to strategic control?*

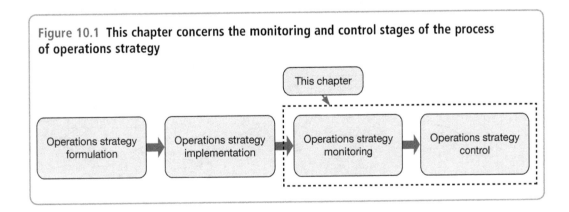

Figure 10.1 **This chapter concerns the monitoring and control stages of the process of operations strategy**

## What are the differences between operational and strategic monitoring and control?

Strategic monitoring and control involves the monitoring and evaluation of activities, plans and performance with the intention of corrective future action if required. The procedure should be capable of providing early indications (or a 'warning bell', as some call it) by diagnosing data and triggering appropriate changes in how the operations strategy is being implemented. In some ways this strategic view of monitoring and control is similar to how it works operationally. But at a strategic level there are differences. At an operational level, monitoring and controlling an operation's activities seems a straightforward issue. Having created a plan for the operation, each part of it has to be monitored to ensure that planned activities are indeed happening. Any deviation from what should be happening (that is, its plans) can then be rectified through some kind of intervention in the operation. Hopefully this will bring the operation back on course, which itself will probably involve some replanning. Eventually, however, some further deviation from planned activity will be detected and the cycle is repeated. Figure 10.2a illustrates this simple view of control.

At a more strategic level, control is less clear cut. Figure 10.2b shows just some of the many objections to its use in an operations strategy context. For example, are strategic objectives clear and unambiguous? Ask any experienced managers and they will acknowledge that it is not always possible (or necessarily desirable) to articulate every aspect of a strategic decision in detail. Many strategies are just too complex for that. Nor does every senior manager always agree on what the strategy *should* be trying to achieve. Often the lack of a clear objective is because individual managers have different and conflicting interests. For example, if two parts of an organisation are to be reorganised so that their activities are combined, the managers of each part are likely to have different views of how the merger is to be accomplished (presumably wanting less disruption to the resources for which they are responsible); even if they are agreed on the need for, and broad outline of, the new merged unit, at the margin they may favour different ways of bringing it about. In some public-sector organisations there

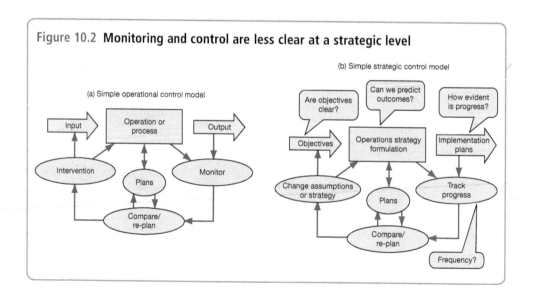

Figure 10.2 **Monitoring and control are less clear at a strategic level**

may be explicit and well-accepted differences of interests. In social-care organisations, for example, some managers are charged with protecting vulnerable members of society, others with ensuring that public money is not wasted, and yet others may be required to protect the independence of professional staff. At other times objectives are ambiguous because the strategy has to cope with unpredictable changes in the environment, making the original objectives redundant.

A further assumption in the simplified control model is that there is some reasonable knowledge of how to bring about the desired outcome. That is, when a decision is made one can predict its effects with a reasonable degree of confidence. In other words, operational control assumes that any interventions that are intended to bring a process back under control will indeed have the intended effect. Yet, this implies that the relationships between the intervention and the resulting consequence within the process are predictable, which in turn assumes that the degree of process knowledge is high (see Chapter 7). However, at the strategic level this is rarely totally true. For example, if an organisation decides to relocate in order to be more convenient for its customers, it may or may not prove to be correct. Customers may react in a manner that was not predicted. Even if customers seem initially to respond well to the new location, there may be a lag before negative reactions become evident. In fact, many strategic decisions are taken about activities about which the cause–effect relationship is only partly understood. There is a degree of uncertainty in most strategic decisions, which cannot be entirely eliminated.

A further difference between operational and strategic control is the frequency with which control interventions are made. Operational control interventions are often repetitive and occur frequently (for example, checking on progress hourly, daily, or even weekly). This means that the organisation has the opportunity to learn how its interventions affect the implementation process, which considerably facilitates control. By contrast, strategic control can be non-repetitive, with each implementation task involving unique projects or investments. So, because the intervention, or the deviation from plan that caused it, may not be repeated exactly, there is little learning.

How do these differences between operational and strategic control impact on the process of operations strategy? Professor Geert Hofstede, an academic better known for his work on the international characteristics of strategic decision making, has incorporated these, and other, differences into a typology of control, a modified version of which is shown in Figure 10.3.[1] Hofstede's typology identifies a number of types of control that are a function of the differences between operational and strategic control, discussed above.

Operational control, he concludes, is relatively straightforward: objectives are unambiguous, the effects of interventions are known and activities are repetitive. This type of control can be codified using predetermined conventions and rules. There are, however, still some challenges to successful routine control. It needs operational discipline to make sure that control procedures are systematically implemented. The main point, though, is that any divergence from the conditions necessary for routine control implies a different type of control.

### Expert control

If objectives are unambiguous, yet the effects of interventions relatively well understood, but the activity is not repetitive (for example, installing a 'new-to-the-company' piece of technology, such as an ERP system), control can be delegated to an 'expert' – someone for whom such activities are repetitive because they have built

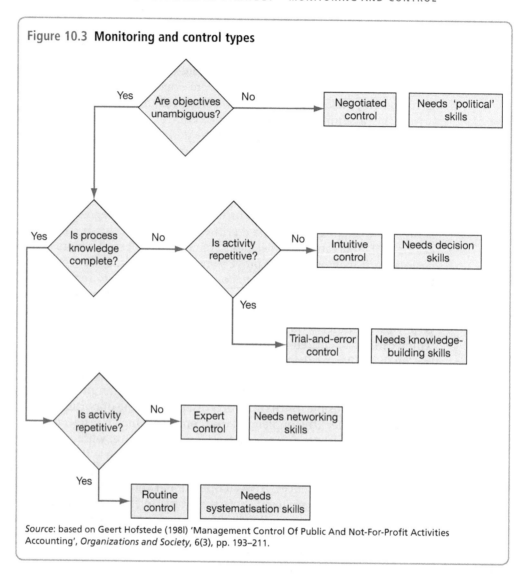

Figure 10.3 **Monitoring and control types**

*Source*: based on Geert Hofstede (1981) 'Management Control Of Public And Not-For-Profit Activities Accounting', *Organizations and Society*, 6(3), pp. 193–211.

their knowledge on previous experience elsewhere. Making a success of expert control requires that such experts exist and can be 'acquired' by the firm. It also requires that the expert takes advantage of the control knowledge already present in the firm and integrates his or her 'expert' knowledge with the support that potentially exists internally. Both of these place a stress on the need to 'network', both in terms of acquiring expertise and then integrating that expertise into the organisation.

### Trial-and-error control

If strategic objectives are relatively unambiguous but effects of interventions not known, while, however, the activity is repetitive, the organisation can gain knowledge of how to control successfully through its own failures. In other words, although simple prescriptions may not be available in the early stages of making control interventions, the organisation can learn how to do it through experience. It is the cause–effect 'knowledge gap' that defines this type of control that must become the target of the firm's knowledge-building activities. For example, if a firm is introducing a new product or service into a new market, it may not be sure how best to arrange the launch. But if the launch is the first of several, the strategic objective must be not only to make as good a success of the launch as possible, but equally (or more) important, it must learn from the experience. The organisation must put in mechanisms to gain knowledge and embed the learning into its decision making. It is these knowledge-building skills that will ultimately determine the effectiveness of trial-and-error control.

### Intuitive control

If strategic objectives are relatively unambiguous but effects of interventions not known, nor is strategic decision making repetitive, learning by trial and error is not possible. Therefore, says Hofstede, the organisation has to view strategic control as more of an art than as a science. And in these circumstances, control must be based on the management team using its innate intuition to make strategic control decisions. Many competition-based strategic decisions fall into this category. Objectives are clear (survive in the long term, make an acceptable return, and so on), but not only are control interventions not repetitive and their effects not fully understood, there are competitors whose interests are in conflict with yours. Yet, simply stating that 'intuition' is needed in these circumstances is not particularly helpful. Instinct and feelings are, of course, valuable attributes in any management team, but they are the result, at least partly, of understanding how best to organise their shared understanding, knowledge and decision-making skills. It requires thorough decision analysis not to 'mechanistically' make the decision, but to frame it so that connections can be made, consequences understood and insights gained. Put another way, instinct may thrive best when used in the context of refined decision-making skills.

### Negotiated control

The most difficult circumstance for strategic control is when objectives are ambiguous. This type of control involves reducing ambiguity in some way by making objectives less uncertain. Or, as Hofstede (who calls it 'political' control) puts it, *'resolving ambiguities so that external uncertainties become internal certainties'*. Sometimes this is done simply by senior managers 'pronouncing' or arbitrarily deciding what objectives *should* be irrespective of opposing views. More consensually, a negotiated settlement may be sought that then can become an unambiguous objective. Alternatively, outside experts (for example, consultants) could be used, either to help with the negotiations or to remove control decisions from those with conflicting views. The success of this method will depend partly on whether the 'expert' has credibility within the organisation as someone who can resolve ambiguity. Yet, even within the framework of negotiation, there is almost always a political element when ambiguities in objectives exist. Negotiation processes will be, to some extent, dependent on power structures.

## How is progress towards strategic objectives tracked?

Especially in times when their environment is changing rapidly, organisations feel the need to detect change by tracking performance, scanning the environment, interpreting the information that it detects and responding appropriately. Monitoring, in our terms, involves the first three of these activities. If the information resulting from this monitoring activity is to be useful for control purposes it should collect useful data and interpret its meaning through comparison to pre-existing standards or objectives, and then respond in some way. At a strategic level, this interpretation process should involve more than simple data analysis; it should be an exercise that tries to make sense of what is really happening with the implementation. To do this successfully, any operations strategy process should:

- be tracking the appropriate elements so that progress can be assessed;
- compare progress against some aspiration or target;
- have some idea as to what risks the implementation faces.

## Tracking the appropriate elements

*'Performance measurement is a hugely important but difficult area for organizations of all kinds. Accurately calibrating performance of activities and their outcomes has many advantages – as well as some risks. Performance measurement is therefore central to successful strategy execution.'*[2]

Which aspects of implantation performance are appropriate to track will obviously depend on the implementation itself. Implementations with different strategic objectives will focus on different operations objectives. Because of this, it is difficult to generalise. However, it is important to draw a distinction between two types of implementation objective:

- *'Project' objectives* – those that indicate the progress of the implementation towards its end point. In other words, is the strategy being implemented as planned?
- *'Process' objectives* – those that indicate the consequences that the implementation has on the operations processes that it is intended to affect. In other words, are the results produced by the strategy as they were intended?

### Project objectives

Project objectives help to provide a definition of the end point, which can be used to monitor progress and identify when success has been achieved. This can be judged in terms of what are usually called the 'three objectives of project management' – cost, time and 'quality'.

Any implementation will normally be allocated a budget to 'make things happen'. This should include the resources that will execute the implementation, as well as any disruption to the ongoing operation during the implementation. Similarly, no implementation would be planned without some idea of how long it will take. Sometimes the deadline for the implementation is set by external events (for example, competitors entering your market), sometimes the deadline is governed by internal views on what is appropriate. 'Quality' (the quotation marks are deliberate) is how well the 'project' meets its objectives – does the implementation do what it is supposed to do? In an operations strategy context one could argue that the best way to assess the 'quality' of the implementation project is by judging the consequences it has on the operations processes that it is intended to affect; in other words, 'quality' here means the process objectives of the implementation.

The relative importance of each project objective will differ for different types of implementation. Some implementations in the aerospace sector, such as the development of a new aircraft manufacturing technology, that impact on passenger safety, will place a very high emphasis on 'quality' objectives. With other implementations – for example, where cash availability is limited – cost might predominate. Other implementations emphasise time: for example, bringing new capacity online in time to honour a supply contract. In each of these implementation projects, although one objective might be particularly important the other objectives can never be totally forgotten.

## Process objectives

These objectives are so called because, when monitored, they measure the impact that the implementation has on the process within the operation (and therefore the operation as a whole). In Chapters 2 and 7 we introduced the core 'performance objectives' of operations strategy – quality, speed, dependability, flexibility and cost. So, at a minimum, the effect an implementation has on these five basic objectives should be assessed. But, in addition, broader measures such as return on assets, or more specific measures such as capacity utilisation could also be used. For example, a global oil exploration company is reorganising its technical support function and, over time, is centralising its risk assessment resources (they were previously organised on a regional basis). In this case, the 'process' objectives are shown in Figure 10.4. Each objective has its performance under the original organisational structure marked together with the performance of each objective that the new, centralised structure should achieve. Over the three-month implementation period the performance of each objective is measured and marked to indicate the progress of the implementation.

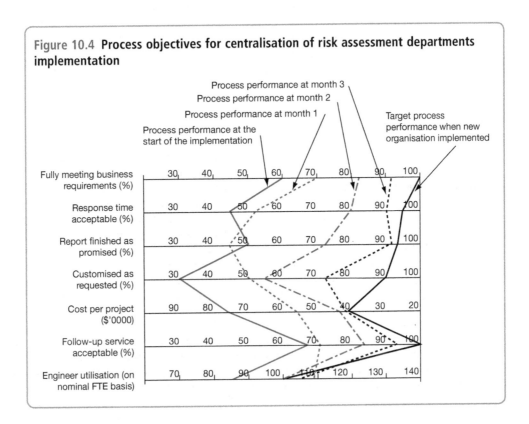

Figure 10.4 **Process objectives for centralisation of risk assessment departments implementation**

### The 'Red Queen' effect

For longer-term implementations, target levels of process objectives will not necessarily remain constant. They could shift during the implementation itself, especially in highly competitive or dynamic environments. For example, if competitors increase their performance during implementation, one's own performance will need to increase proportionately simply to stay (relatively) still. This is sometimes called the 'Red Queen' effect. In 1973, Leigh Van Valen was searching for a way to describe the discovery that he had made while studying marine fossils. He had established that no matter how long a family of animals had already existed, the probability that the family will become extinct is unaffected. In other words, the struggle for survival never gets easier. However well a species fits with its environment, it can never relax. The analogy that Van Valen drew has a strong resonance with business realities. He recalled that in Lewis Carroll's *Through The Looking Glass* (1871), Alice had encountered living chess pieces and, in particular, the Red Queen:

> 'Well, in our country', said Alice, still panting a little, 'you'd generally get to somewhere else – if you ran very fast for a long time, as we've been doing'. 'A slow sort of country!' said the Queen. 'Now, here, you see, it takes all the running you can do, to keep in the same place. If you want to get somewhere else, you must run at least twice as fast as that!'

In many respects this is like business. The strategy that proves the most effective is the one that people will try to block or imitate. Innovations are soon countered in response by others that are stronger. The quality revolution in manufacturing industry, for example, is widely accepted, but most firms that have survived the past 15 years (in the automotive sector, for example) now achieve much higher levels of quality performance, reflecting greater depth of operational capability. Yet their relative position has in many cases not changed. Their competitors who have survived have only done so by achieving similar levels of quality themselves.

---

**Example** ## Tesco changes its strategy[3]

The announcement of Tesco's trading figures in June 2014 brought a barrage of criticism from retail industry commentators. Although it was still comfortably Britain's market leader in grocery sales, its lead over its rivals, which had been narrowing for some time, had worsened. Like-for-like sales (sales in its stores and online stripping out the effect of new stores opening) were down nearly 4 per cent, and in the retail world that is significant. Tesco has not seen numbers this bad for 20 years. Why, asked its detractors, had the company not realised that its strategy was failing and made a change? One critic described Tesco as being 'like a juggernaut with a puncture and a worrying rattle in the engine'. But, partly, Tesco's problems at this time were, to some extent, beyond its control and a result of competitor activity. Waitrose (an up-market supermarket, with a good reputation for quality) was serving the top end of the market in the UK, while German discount stores Aldi and Lidl were attracting more cost-conscious customers. Yet the problem was also the result of Tesco failing to respond fast enough to an operations strategy that had become inappropriate. The strategy of building large, out-of-town superstores was continued, even though a sharper monitoring of consumer behaviour might have revealed that such large-capacity units had lost their attraction as families cut down on weekly trips to the supermarket and opted instead for home deliveries, topping up their groceries with trips to local stores. In fact, Philip Clarke, then Tesco's chief executive, admitted that he ought to have moved faster to cut back on planned superstore openings in response to clear radical changes in shopping habits. He expressed regret at taking time to halt expansion of its struggling network of superstores in favour of investment in online deliveries and smaller, neighbourhood stores. *'Hindsight is a wonderful thing. It's never really there when you need it'*, said Mr Clarke. *'I probably should have stopped more quickly that [superstore] expansion, I probably should have made the reallocation faster.'*

## The balanced scorecard approach

Generally, operations performance measures have been broadening in their scope. It is now generally accepted that the scope of measurement should, at some level, include external as well as internal, long-term as well as short-term and 'soft' as well as 'hard' measures. The best-known manifestation of this trend is the 'balanced score-card' approach taken by Kaplan and Norton:

> 'The balanced scorecard retains traditional financial measures. But financial measures tell the story of past events, an adequate story for industrial age companies for which investments in long-term capabilities are customer relationships were not critical for success. These financial measures are inadequate, however, for guiding and evaluating the journey that information age companies must make to create future value through investment in customers, suppliers, employees, processes, technology, and innovation.'[4]

As well as including financial measures of performance, in the same way as traditional performance measurement systems, the balanced scorecard approach also attempts to provide the important information that is required to allow the overall strategy of an organisation to be reflected adequately in specific performance measures. In addition to financial measures of performance, it also includes more operational measures of customer satisfaction, internal processes, innovation and other improvement activities. In doing so it measures the factors behind financial performance that are seen as the key drivers of future financial success. In particular, it is argued that a balanced range of measures enables managers to address the following questions (see Figure 10.5):

- How do we look to our shareholders (financial perspective)?
- What must we excel at (internal process perspective)?
- How do our customers see us (the customer perspective)?
- How can we continue to improve and build capabilities (the learning and growth perspective)?

The balanced scorecard attempts to bring together the elements that reflect a business's strategic position, including product or service quality measures, product and service development times, customer complaints, labour productivity, and so on. At the same time it attempts to avoid performance reporting becoming unwieldy by restricting the number of measures and focusing especially on those seen to be essential. The advantages of the approach are that it presents an overall picture of the organisation's performance in a single report and, by being comprehensive in

Figure 10.5 **The measures used in the balanced scorecard**

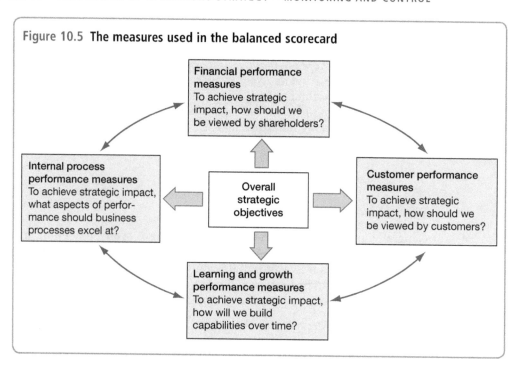

the measures of performance it uses, encourages companies to take decisions in the interests of the whole organisation rather than sub-optimising around narrow measures. Developing a balanced scorecard is a complex process and is now the subject of considerable debate. One of the key questions that has to be considered is how specific measures of performance should be designed. Inadequately designed performance measures can result in dysfunctional behaviour, so teams of managers are often used to develop a scorecard that reflects their organisation's specific needs.

Writing about how to create a strategic control system, and making use of balanced scorecard principles, Stephen Bungay and Michael Goold[5] say that there are a few important lessons about how to make strategic control really work effectively. Their prescriptions are as follows:

- Invest in the necessary training and adopt an appropriate style in reviewing plans, especially in the early stages.
- Invest in careful preparation before review sessions, as good questions are vital.
- Set stretching targets, but only a limited number.
- Follow through, take it seriously and make actions and words consistent.
- Create an explicit link with financial targets and budgets, integrating the two processes (or none of it will be taken seriously at all).
- Show that the operating company benefits from the process (e.g. through the business becoming easier to manage) and give strong support for success so that another real benefit becomes the approval of senior management, or a better relationship with the centre.

# How can the monitoring and control process attempt to control risks?

A key duty for any manager tasked with implementing an operations strategy is to think through the potential risks that might throw the implementation off track. The basic motivation for including consideration of risk in the monitoring and control phase of the operations strategy process is simply to 'be prepared' for the events that could cause implementation to deviate from its intended course. Of course, risk is an ongoing issue for all firms; this is why they have internal audit experts and departments. Internal auditing is supposed to be an independent, objective assurance activity that is designed to add value and improve an organisation's operations by bringing a systematic and disciplined approach to evaluating and improving the effectiveness of risk management.[6] Risk management is a huge topic in its own right, and one that is largely outside the scope of this book. But it is important to think in terms of how the practical issues of strategy implementation can incorporate some consideration of risk. Here we will look at six aspects of risk that are particularly relevant to operations strategy:

- the dynamics of monitoring and control;
- the risk of market and operations performance becoming out of balance;
- the distinction between pure and speculative risk;
- controlling risk through prevention, mitigation and recovery;
- Adjustment cost risk;
- Intervention risk.

## The dynamics of monitoring and control

As implementation proceeds and monitoring indicates its progress, the trajectory of the implementation may have to be changed. Competitive activity or more general environmental change could affect the level of performance required, as in the Red Queen effect previously described, or the change may need to be more fundamental with changes in the direction of strategy as well as extent. How easy an operation finds a change of direction will depend on its agility, which, in turn, will depend partly on how tightly its operations resources are aligned with its market requirements.

### *Tight alignment and loose alignment*

In the diagrammatic representation of alignment, explained previously in Figures 9.2 and 9.6, we represented alignment as being a single point between market requirements and operations resource capability. The implication of this is that there is a single, 'tight' and well-defined statement of market requirements together with a relatively narrow set of operations capabilities that correspond exactly with market requirements. Remember, though, that both market requirements and operations resource capabilities can change over time. Markets are dynamic and exhibit sometimes unexpected changes. Operations resource capabilities may change at a slower pace but are still subject to sometimes unexpected movements. Therefore, on our diagrammatic representation, the origin of the requirements and resources diagram can shift over time. This means that if the alignment between operations capabilities

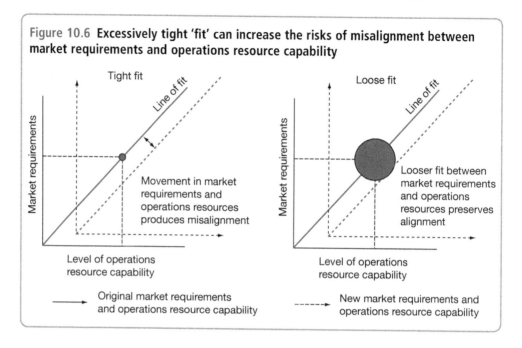

Figure 10.6 Excessively tight 'fit' can increase the risks of misalignment between market requirements and operations resource capability

and market requirements is too 'tight' or 'narrow' this could mean that what was previously alignment between the two can (relatively) move off the line of it. A looser or broader set of capabilities and market relationships, however, can provide some insurance against these unexpected shifts. This difference between tight and loose alignment is illustrated in Figure 10.6.

## Market and operations performance becoming out of balance

Particularly during implementation, when changes in both market positioning and operations resources are likely, the possibility of deviating from the 'line of fit' (see Figure 9.2 in Chapter 9) is very real. This may be because some part of the implementation is not going to plan – for example, delays in the implementation of a new website means that customers do not receive the level of service they were promised; or, it may be an inevitable and expected part of the implementation plan – for example, a firm may plan to install and de-bug a new IT system before it starts to use its potential to make promises to its market. Either way, the deviation from alignment between market requirements and operations resources is exposing the firm to risk, and while there is no widely accepted definition for operations-related risk, our working definition of operations-related risk is:

> 'Operations risk is the potential for unwanted negative consequences from an operations-related event.'

Many risks can be related to the uncertainty associated with both the development of an operational resource base and shifting market requirements. Any operations strategy implementation, therefore, must accommodate these risks. Figure 10.7 illustrates this idea. Moving above the diagonal implies that market performance (that is, the requirements and/or the expectations of the market) are in advance of the operation's

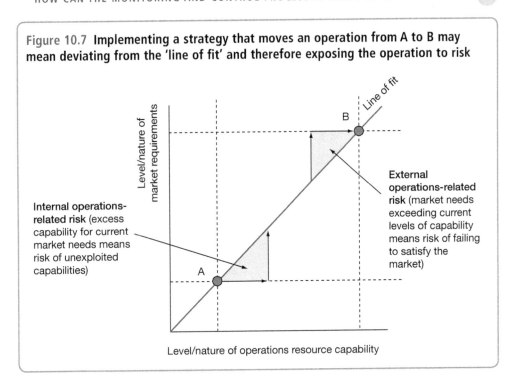

Figure 10.7 **Implementing a strategy that moves an operation from A to B may mean deviating from the 'line of fit' and therefore exposing the operation to risk**

capability to satisfy it. This is called external operations-related risk. The area below the diagonal implies that a firm has levels of competence or potential performance that are not being exploited in the marketplace. This is called internal operations-related risk.

## Pure and speculative risk

A useful distinction is that between pure risks (involving events that will produce the possibility only of loss, or negative outcomes) and speculative risks (which emerge from competitive scenarios and hold the potential for loss or gain – positive outcomes). A pure risk might be the risk that, while implementing a new blood-testing strategy for HIV, a technician at a medical laboratory is involved in an accident that leads to possible infection. A speculative risk might be the risk associated with developing a new computer-based diagnostics and information infrastructure to enable the laboratory to offer a range of profitable new services. The risk here is that the technology may not work (or not work on time or in budget), or that the market will not want to pay for the new services. This is illustrated in Figure 10.8. The pure-risk type of 'accident' involves a reduction in effective operations resource capability of the type represented by the movement between A and C. Speculative risk of the type represented by the new information infrastructure is represented by the possible outcomes B, D and E. Movement from A to B is positive in the sense that it represents a fulfilment of the intended outcome. Negative consequences are represented by point D, where market requirements have increased as intended but operations capabilities have failed to match them, and E, where operations capabilities have been increased but have not been fully exploited in the market.

**Figure 10.8** Pure risk has only negative consequences (A to C); speculative risk can have both positive (A to B) and negative (A to D or A to E) consequences

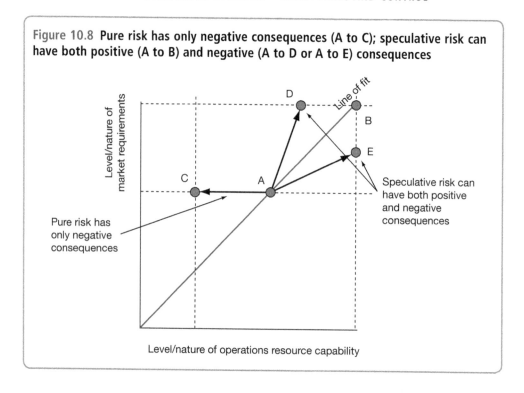

## Controlling risk

Operations strategy practitioners are understandably interested in how an operation can avoid failure in the first place or, if it does happen, how they can survive any adverse conditions that might follow. In other words, how they can control risk. A simple structure for describing generic mechanisms for controlling risk uses three approaches:

1 *Prevention strategies* – are where an operation seeks to completely prevent (or reduce the frequency of) an event occurring.

2 *Mitigating strategies* – are where an operation seeks to isolate an event from any possible negative consequences.

3 *Recovery strategies* – are where an operation analyses and accepts the consequences from an event but undertakes to minimise or alleviate or compensate for them.

### Prevention strategies

It is almost always better to avoid negative consequences than have to recover from them. The classic approach is to audit plans to try and identify causes of risk. For instance, by emphasising its use of 'fair trading' principles, the high-street retailer The Body Shop was able to develop its 'ethical' brand identity as a powerful advantage, but it also became a potential source of vulnerability. When a journalist accused one of the firm's suppliers of using animal-product testing, the rest of the media eagerly took up the story. To prevent this kind of accusation from resurfacing, the firm introduced a detailed auditing method to prevent any suspicion of unethical behaviour in its entire supply chain.

## Mitigation strategies

Not all events can be avoided, but an operation can try to separate an event from its negative consequences. This is called mitigation. For example, look at the way that an operation deals with exposure to currency fluctuations. After the collapse of communism in the early 1990s, a multinational consumer goods firm began to invest in the former Soviet Union. Its Russian subsidiary sourced nearly all products from its parents' factories in Germany. Conscious of the potential volatility of the rouble, the firm needed to minimise its exposure to a devaluation of the currency. Any such devaluation would leave the firm's cost structure at a serious disadvantage and without any real option but to increase its prices. Financial tools were available to mitigate currency exposure. Most of these allowed the operation to reduce the risk of currency fluctuations but involved an 'up front' cost. Alternatively, the company could restructure its operations strategy in order to mitigate its currency risk, developing its own production facilities within Russia. This may reduce, or even eliminate, the currency risk, although it would probably introduce other risks. A further option was to form supply partnerships with other Russian companies. Again, this would not eliminate risks but could shift them to ones that the company feels more able to control.

## Recovery strategies

Recovery strategies can involve a wide range of activities. They include the (micro) recovery steps necessary to minimise an individual customer's dissatisfaction. This might include apologising, refunding monies, reworking a product or service, or providing compensation. At the same time, operations have to be prepared for the (macro) major crises that might necessitate a complete product recall or abandonment of service. The question that an operations strategy needs to consider is, 'At what point do we reach the limit of avoidance and mitigation strategies before we start to rely on recovery strategies?'

---

**Example** | **Planning for recovery[7]**

It was a product recall that attracted more-than-usual negative media coverage. Cadbury's, the confectionary manufacturer, recalled seven product lines accounting for more than a million chocolate bars. This was the result of potential salmonella contamination caused by a leaking pipe in a production factory. Initially a decision was taken not to recall any products, but this was reversed later. According to Chris Woodcock, managing director of Razor, a risk assessment firm:

> '... this is a classic case of a business needing to consider all the reputational and brand-protection aspects of a possible food safety, technical problem before deciding whether or not to recall. The logical, technical facts are often not enough on their own to influence a decision on recall or no-recall. It is also vital to assess emotional and brand associations.'

Where a brand is trusted to the extent of Cadbury's, recovery planning is vital. In this case the scientific justification for a recall was considered when it was first discovered that the pipe leaking had caused the low levels of salmonella. *'There was possibly still a good case for reconsidering the longer-term brand damage should the no-recall decision subsequently escape into the public domain. It was the apparent lack of transparency that attracted most criticism in media and expert*

▶

*commentary.'* But the Cadbury's incident is far from being an isolated case. The number of product recalls is increasing as firms try to protect their reputations from the harm caused by faulty goods, according to Reynolds Porter Chamberlain a London law firm.

*'Corporate reputations have become more fragile as consumers increasingly use the internet and other media to share and publicise information about faulty products. The Sony laptop battery debacle, which saw nearly 10m battery packs recalled, is a perfect example. The growth of sites such as YouTube meant millions of consumers saw videos of a computer spontaneously catching fire due to the fault. The legal costs and compensation paid out can be colossal, so the need to recall quickly is vital, and so is insurance cover. With consumers becoming ever more litigious, companies are playing it safe and recalling even where the risk of a liability is slight. They know the courts and the press will punish them if they are seen as dragging their feet.'*

## Adjustment cost risk

It is worth emphasising that any implementation methodology will need to account for the costs of implementation. These costs include both the direct and/or investment costs of providing whatever additional resources the strategy requires, and also what could be termed the adjustment cost of making any changes. By adjustment costs we mean the losses that could be incurred before the new strategy is functioning as intended.

Calculating the true costs of implementing any strategy is notoriously difficult. This is particularly true because, more often than not, Murphy's Law seems to prevail. This law is usually stated as, 'if anything can go wrong, it will'. This means that most implementations will incur 'adjustment costs' before the strategy works as expected. This effect has been identified empirically in a range of operations, especially when new types of process technology are involved. Specifically discussing technology-related implementation (although the ideas apply to almost any implementation), Bruce Chew of Massachusetts Institute of Technology argues that adjustment costs stem from unforeseen mismatches between the new technology's capabilities and needs and the existing operation. New technology rarely behaves as planned and as changes are made, their impact ripples throughout the organisation. Figure 10.9 is an example of what Chew calls a 'Murphy Curve'.[8] It shows a typical pattern of performance reduction (in this case, quality) as a new process technology is introduced. It is recognised that implementation may take some time; therefore allowances are made for the length and cost of a 'ramp-up' period. However, as the operation prepares for the implementation, the distraction causes performance to deteriorate. Even after the start of the implementation, this downward trend continues and it is only weeks, indeed maybe months, later that the old performance level is reached. The area of the dip indicates the magnitude of the adjustment costs, and therefore the level of vulnerability faced by the operation.

## Intervention risk – getting performance back on track

Monitoring involves tracking how an implementation is progressing and interpreting the tracking data. Control requires decision and intervention. Decisions are needed as to whether to intervene or not, as well as how to intervene. Intervention means not only doing something to bring the implementation closer towards its

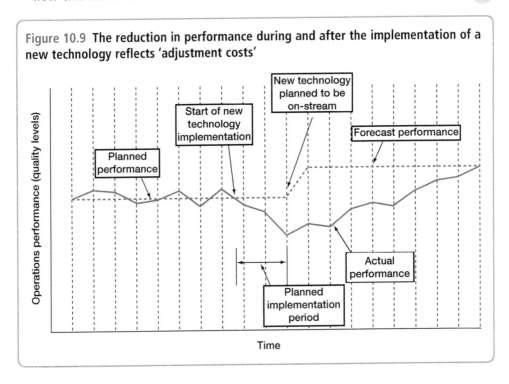

Figure 10.9 **The reduction in performance during and after the implementation of a new technology reflects 'adjustment costs'**

objectives but also learning from the intervention, so that future interventions will be better targeted.

## Type I and type II errors in control

The concept of type I and type II errors is commonly used in operational control and it is also useful in understanding strategic control. It concerns the possibility of getting the decision of whether to intervene wrong, although one can apply the idea to any decision. Take the example of a pedestrian waiting to cross a street. He or she has two main decisions: whether to continue waiting or to cross. If there is a satisfactory break in the traffic and the pedestrian crosses then a correct decision has been made. Similarly, if that person continues to wait because the traffic is too dense then he or she has again made a correct decision. There are two types of incorrect decisions or errors, however. One incorrect decision would be if he or she decides to cross when there is not an adequate break in the traffic, resulting in an accident – this is referred to as a type I error, taking action when one should not. Another incorrect decision would occur if he or she decides not to cross even though there was an adequate gap in the traffic – this is called a type II error, not taking action when one should. So type I errors are those that occur when a decision was made to do something and the situation did not warrant it. Type II errors are those that occur when nothing was done, yet a decision to do something should have been taken as the situation did indeed warrant it. Applied to strategic control, a type I error is when an intervention is made to the implementation when it was not necessary; a type II error is when there is a failure to intervene in an implementation even though an intervention is necessary. This is summarised in Table 10.1.

**Table 10.1 Type I and type II errors for the control of an operations strategy implementation**

| | Was the intervention necessary? | |
|---|---|---|
| Decision | No | Yes |
| Intervene to 'correct' the implementation | Type I error | Correct decision |
| Do not intervene to 'correct' the implementation | Correct decision | Type II error |

Managers identifying and interpreting monitoring data face the risk of both type I and type II errors. Effective operations strategy control prompts the appropriate response at the appropriate time, avoiding both types of errors. Type I errors can occur when managers are 'over-active', with a bias towards being more intervention-ist than is necessary. Type II errors may occur when the managers are too inert, failing to recognise the need for intervention where it actually exists. It has been argued that in uncertain and dynamic business environments, type II errors are more likely to occur.

## How does learning contribute to strategic control?

Both type I and type II errors will be reduced as an organisation and its managers increase their situational knowledge through learning. Over time, the smooth implementation of operations strategy changes needs to address four important issues:

1 How can an operations strategy encourage the learning necessary to make sure that operations knowledge is carried forward over time?

2 How can an operations strategy ensure that the organisation appropriates (captures the value of) the competitive benefits that are derived from the build-up of operations knowledge?

3 How can an operations strategy take into account the fact that the innovations that derive from the build-up of operations knowledge have a momentum of their own and are strongly path dependent (they are influenced by what has happened before)?

4 How can an operation take into account the interaction between the extent of resource and process change?

### Organisational learning

In uncertain environments, any organisation's ability to pre-plan or make decisions in advance is limited. So, rather than adhering dogmatically to a predetermined plan, it may be better to adapt as circumstances change. And, the more uncertain the environment, the more an operation needs to emphasise this form of strategic flexibility and develop its ability to learn from events. Generally this strategic flexibility depends on a learning process that concerns the development of insights and knowledge, and establishes the connections between past actions, the results of those actions and future intentions. The crucial issue here is an essentially pragmatic and practical one – 'How does an operations strategy encourage, facilitate and exploit learning, in order to develop strategic sustainability?' Initially this requires recognition that there is a distinction between single- and double-loop learning.[9]

### Single- and double-loop learning

Single-loop learning is a phenomenon that is widely understood in operations management. It occurs when there is repetitive association between input and output factors. Statistical process control, for instance, measures output characteristics from a process, such as product weight, telephone response time, etc. These can then be used to alter input conditions, such as supplier quality, manufacturing consistency and staff training, with the intention of 'improving' the output. In Chapter 7 we indicated how such forms of control provide the learning that can form the basis for strategic improvement. Every time an operational error or problem is detected, it is corrected or solved and more is learned about the process, but without questioning or altering the underlying values and objectives of the process.

Single-loop learning is of great importance to the ongoing management of operations. The underlying operational resources can become proficient at examining their processes and monitoring general performance against generic performance objectives (cost, quality, speed, etc.), thereby providing essential process knowledge and stability. Unfortunately, the kind of 'deep' system-specific process knowledge that is so crucial to effective single-loop learning can, over time, help to create the kind of inertia that proves so difficult to overcome when an operation has to adapt to a changing environment. All effective operations are better at doing what they have done before and this is a crucial source of advantage. But while an operation develops its distinctive capability only on the basis of single-loop learning, it is exposing itself to risks associated with the things that it does not do well (see Figure 10.10).

Sustainable operations strategies therefore also need to emphasise learning mechanisms that prevent the operation from becoming too conservative and thereby effectively introducing delays and inappropriate responses to major change decisions. Double-loop learning, by contrast, questions fundamental objectives, service or market positions or even the underlying culture of the operation. This kind of learning implies an ability to challenge existing operating assumptions in a fundamental way, seeking to re-frame competitive questions and remain open to any changes in the competitive environment. But being receptive to new opportunities sometimes

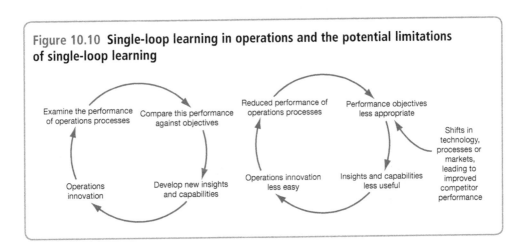

**Figure 10.10** **Single-loop learning in operations and the potential limitations of single-loop learning**

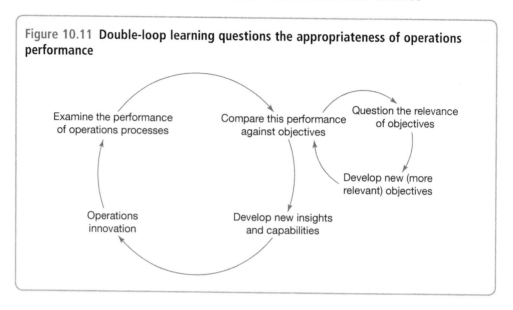

Figure 10.11 **Double-loop learning questions the appropriateness of operations performance**

requires the abandonment of existing operating routines at certain points in time – sometimes without any specific replacement in mind. This is difficult to achieve in practice, especially as most operations tend to reward experience and past achievement (rather than potential) at both an individual and group level. Figure 10.11 illustrates double-loop learning.

An operation needs both the limited single-loop learning, so it can develop specific capabilities, and the more expanded experience of double-loop learning. Single-loop learning is needed to create consistency and stability. At the same time, operations need double-loop learning for continual reflection upon their internal and external objectives and context. There has to be a continual balancing act if a sustainable position is to be developed. An operation may even have distinct phases or locations where it emphasises single- or double-loop learning, where companies will periodically engage in double-loop learning, searching to challenge accepted values and objectives, while at the same time maintaining some (single-loop) operational routines. Inevitably, perhaps, this means a degree of tension between preservation and change. For an operations strategy this tension is particularly keenly felt. The need for managers to question and challenge what is currently practised is clearly important but, at the same time, operations are largely responsible for delivering the already established organisational mission.

## Appropriating competitive benefits

One of the most surprising aspects of innovation is that, even if change works, and even if a market is created for a new product or service, there is no guarantee that the innovating operation will benefit commercially from the results. A critical question to ask in all strategic decisions is, 'Who actually captures the profits?' Powerfully innovative firms, such as Xerox in the US (who invented many of the core personal computer and interface application concepts) and EMI in the UK (who developed one of the most widespread medical revolutions – magnetic resonance imaging), have failed to gain full competitive benefit from their efforts. The issues of appropriation (i.e. getting the benefit from innovation) are particularly significant for operations strategy because, as we discussed in Chapter 5, 'partnership' relationships have become more important. Products and services are often developed jointly with customers,[10] and companies are increasingly actively sharing knowledge with suppliers. For example, firms such as Bose have adopted particularly close relationships with suppliers, often involving exchanges of key staff. It is argued that the benefit for the customer is instant access to 'rich' supplier expertise on a range of current and future product issues. The main benefit for the supplier is the 'opportunity' to learn of 'potential' new contracts.[11] Issues of long-term intellectual property rights can become very difficult to manage in such circumstances.

## Path dependencies and development trajectories

History matters when it comes to operations strategy. Very few operations have a completely blank sheet (or 'green field' scenario) when it comes to options and choices. Current resource and requirement positions act to constrain the future development paths, or trajectories, of the operation. In other words, operations capabilities are path dependent. For example, when chemical giant Monsanto first embarked upon its strategy to develop a biotechnology business, it had great difficulties in hiring new staff because it had no pre-existing capabilities for new staff to join – hence no visible career path, no guarantee of appropriate facilities, rewards and recognition, and so on.

The influence of path dependency on sustainability is best summed up by the idea of capability and market trajectories. An operation may have been pursuing a particular strategy in each of its decision areas over a period of time. The pattern of these decisions will have become well established within the decision-making culture of the operation to the extent that the pattern of decisions may have established its own momentum. The organisation may have developed particular skills at making decisions to support its strategies and may be building upon the learning that it acquired from previous similar decisions. The decision area has developed its own trajectory; this may have both positive and negative effects. For example, a clothing retailer may have an operations strategy that includes aggressive capacity expansion. The result is that the company succeeds in capturing significant and profitable market share. For one or two years its skills at identifying, acquiring and commissioning new stores is a major factor in its ongoing success. However, its competitors soon start to adopt a similar expansion strategy and the company finds it increasingly difficult to maintain its market share. Yet the policy of capacity expansion is so entrenched within the company's decision making that it continues to increase its floor space beyond the time when it should have been consolidating, or even reducing, its overall capacity. The trajectory of its capacity strategy, which was once a significant advantage, is now in danger of undermining the whole company's financial viability. What was once a core capability of the company has become a core rigidity.[12]

The same idea applies to the performance objectives that reflect market requirements. If an operation is used to thinking about quality, or speed, etc. in a particular way, it will find it difficult to reconsider how it thinks about them internally and how it communicates them to its customers. Again, there is a momentum based on the trajectory of previous decisions. And, again, this can have both positive and negative effects. Strong market-based trajectories can both lead to market success and expose companies to market vulnerability when challenged by radically new products and services. For example, Digital Equipment Corporation once dominated the mini-computer market. It was renowned for understanding its customers' requirements, translating these into products that matched its customers' requirements and developing operations to support its product/market strategy. But eventually it was its very expertise at following its existing customers' requirements that caused it to ignore the threat from smaller and cheaper personal computers. Clayton Christensen, of Harvard Business School, has studied companies who found themselves in this position precisely because these firms listened to their customers, invested aggressively in new technologies that would provide their customers more and better products of the sort they wanted, and because they carefully studied market trends they lost their positions of leadership; there are times at which it is right not to listen to customers.[13]

## The innovator's dilemma[14]

Both market and capability trajectories are brought together in what Christensen calls the innovator's dilemma – the dilemma being that, especially when faced by radical shifts in the technological or operating model of a product or service, meeting long-established customer needs can become an obstacle, rather than an enabler, of change. Christensen divides technologies into sustaining and disruptive technologies. Sustaining technologies are those that improve the performance of established products and services along the same trajectory of performance that the majority of customers have historically valued. Disruptive technologies are those that, in the short term, cannot match the performance that customers expect from products and services. They are typically simpler, cheaper, smaller and sometimes more convenient, but they do not often provide conventionally enhanced product or service characteristics. However, all technologies, sustaining or disruptive, will improve over time. Christensen's main point is that, because technology can progress faster than the requirements of the market, disruptive technologies will eventually enter the zone of performance that is acceptable to the markets (see Figure 10.12).

One example Christensen uses is that of the electric car. At the moment, no electric car can come close to the performance characteristics of internal combustion engines. In that sense, this technology is not an immediate threat to existing car or engine manufacturers. However, the electric car is a disruptive technology in so much as its performance will eventually improve to the extent that it enters the lower end of the acceptable zone of performance. Perhaps initially, only customers with relatively undemanding requirements will adopt motor vehicles using this technology. Eventually, however, it could prove to be the dominant technology for all types of vehicle. The dilemma facing all organisations is how to simultaneously improve product or service performance based on sustaining technologies, while deciding whether and how to incorporate disruptive technologies.

## Resource and process 'distance'

The degree of learning, and the degree of difficulty in the implementation process, will depend on the degree of novelty of any new resources and the changes required in the operation's processes. The less the new resources are understood (influenced perhaps by the degree of innovation), the greater their 'distance' from the current resource base of the operation. Similarly, the extent to which an implementation requires

Figure 10.12 'Disruptive' technological change

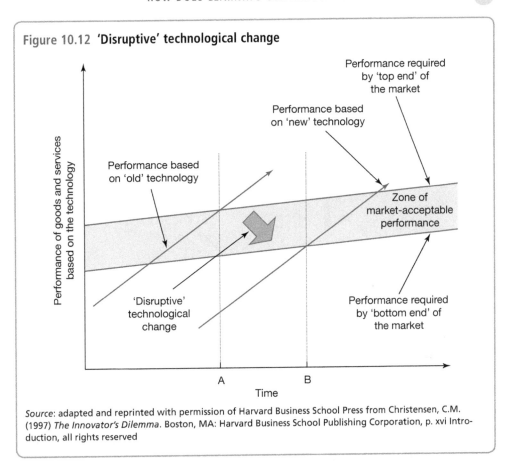

an operation to modify its existing processes, the greater the 'process distance'. The greater the resource and process distance, the more difficult any implementation is likely to be. This is because such distance makes it difficult to adopt a systematic approach to analysing change and learning from mistakes. Those implementations that involve relatively little process or resource 'distance' provide an ideal opportunity for organisational learning. As in any classic scientific experiment, the more variables that are held constant, the more confidence you have in determining cause and effect. Conversely, in an implementation where the resource and process 'distance' means that nearly everything is 'up for grabs', it becomes difficult to know what has worked and what has not. More importantly, it becomes difficult to know *why* something has or has not worked (see Figure 10.13).

## Stakeholders

All implementation projects have stakeholders who must be included in their planning and execution. By stakeholders we mean the individuals and groups who have an interest in the project process or outcome. Individual stakeholders are likely to have different views on a project's objectives that may conflict with other stakeholders. At the very least, different stakeholders are likely to stress different aspects of a project. So, as well any ethical imperative to include as many stakeholders as possible in an

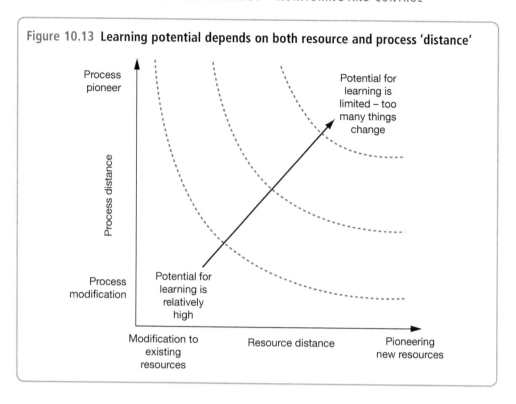

Figure 10.13 **Learning potential depends on both resource and process 'distance'**

implementation, it also can prevent problems later in the implementation. There may also be more direct benefits from a stakeholder-based approach. Powerful stakeholders may shape the implementation at an early stage, making it more likely that they will support the project.

### The power–interest grid

Managing stakeholders can be a subtle and delicate task, requiring significant social and, sometimes, political skills. It is based on three activities: identifying, prioritising, and understanding the stakeholder group. One approach to discriminating between different stakeholders and, more importantly, how they should be managed, is to distinguish between their power to influence the project and their interest in doing so. Stakeholders who have the power to exercise a major influence over the project should never be ignored. At the very least, the nature of their interest, and their motivation, should be well understood. But not all stakeholders who have the power to exercise influence over a project will be interested in doing so, and not everyone who is interested in the project has the power to influence it. The power–interest grid, shown in Figure 10.14, classifies stakeholders simply in terms of these two dimensions. Although there will be graduations between them, the two dimensions are useful in providing an indication of how stakeholders can be managed in terms of four categories:

1  *Manage closely* – High-power, interested groups must be fully engaged, with the greatest efforts made to satisfy them.

2  *Keep satisfied* – High-power, less interested groups require enough effort to keep them satisfied, but not so much that they become bored or irritated with the message.

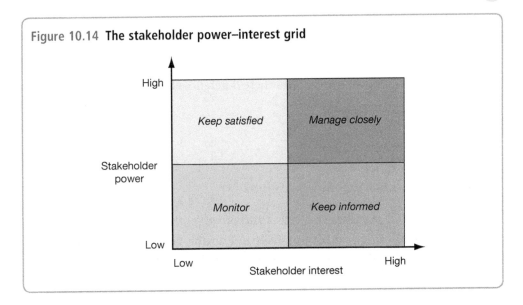

Figure 10.14 **The stakeholder power–interest grid**

3 *Keep informed* – Low-power, interested groups need to be kept adequately informed, with checks to ensure that no major issues are arising. These groups may be very helpful with the detail of the project.

4 *Monitor* – Low-power, but less interested groups need monitoring, but without excessive communication.

Some key questions that can help to understand high-priority stakeholders include the following:

- What financial or emotional interest do they have in the outcome of the implementation? Is it positive or negative?
- What motivates them most of all?
- What information do they need?
- What is the best way of communicating with them?
- What is their current opinion of the implementation project?
- Who influences their opinions? Do some of these influencers therefore become important stakeholders in their own right?
- If they are not likely to be positive, what will win them around to support the implementation?
- If you don't think you will be able to win them around, how will you manage their opposition?

## SUMMARY ANSWERS TO KEY QUESTIONS

### *What are the differences between operational and strategic monitoring and control?*

Strategic monitoring and control involves the monitoring and evaluation of activities, plans and performance with the intention of corrective future action if required. The strategic view of monitoring and control is similar to the operational view, but there ▶

are differences. At a strategic level, objectives are often less clear. There may also be less knowledge of how to bring about the desired outcome. Similarly, the frequency with which control interventions are made is different. Strategic control can be non-repetitive, with each implementation task involving unique projects or investments. One model of control uses these differences to distinguish between:

● expert control;

● trial-and-error control;

● intuitive control;

● negotiated control;

● routine (operational) control.

### How is progress towards strategic objectives tracked?

Monitoring and control involves tracking performance, scanning the environment, interpreting the information that it detects and responding appropriately. Monitoring includes the first three of these activities. To do this successfully any operations strategy process should:

● Be tracking progress against two types of implementation objective – 'project' objectives that indicate the progress of the implementation towards its end point, and 'process' objectives that indicate the consequences that the implementation has on the operations processes that it is intended to affect.

● Compare progress against some aspiration or target, preferably involving a broad range of measures – as is the intention of the balanced scorecard, which retains traditional financial measures but also includes measures of customer satisfaction, internal processes, innovation and other improvement activities.

### How can the monitoring and control process attempt to control risks?

A key task in the operations strategy process is the consideration of potential risks, because understanding risks can help to cope with them should they occur.

There are six aspects of risk that are particularly relevant to operations strategy:

1 The dynamics of monitoring and control, including the concept of loose and tight fit or alignment.

2 The risk of market and operations performance becoming out of balance, which can lead to 'external' and 'internal' operations-related risk.

3 The distinction between pure risks, involving events that will produce the possibility only of loss (or negative outcomes), and speculative risks, which emerge from competitive scenarios and hold the potential for loss or gain (positive outcomes).

4 Controlling risk through prevention strategies (where an operation seeks to prevent an event occurring), mitigating strategies (where an operation seeks to isolate an event from possible negative consequences) and recovery strategies (where an operation analyses and accepts the consequences from an event but undertakes to minimise or alleviate or compensate for them).

5 Adjustment cost risk – these are the losses that could be incurred before the new strategy is functioning as intended.

6 Intervention risk, which is incurring 'type I' and 'type II' errors. Type I errors occur when managers intervene when it is not necessary. Type II errors occur when the managers fail to recognise the need for intervention where it actually exists.

### How does learning contribute to strategic control?

Implementation risk is reduced as an organisation learns over time. Four issues are important in understanding how learning affects implementation:

1 How can an operations strategy encourage the learning necessary to make sure that operations knowledge is carried forward over time? Here the distinction between single-loop and double-loop learning is important.

2 How can an operations strategy ensure that the organisation appropriates (captures the value of) the competitive benefits that are derived from the build-up of operations knowledge?

3 How can an operations strategy take into account the fact that the innovations that derive from the build-up of operations knowledge have a momentum of their own and are strongly path dependent (they are influenced by what has happened before)?

4 How can an operation take into account the interaction between the extent of resource and process change?

All implementation projects have stakeholders, who are the individuals and groups who have an interest in the project process or outcome and who should be included in its planning and executions. One approach to discriminating between different stakeholders, and how they should be managed, is to distinguish between their power to influence the project and their interest in doing so. This results in the power–interest grid. Stakeholders' position on the grid gives an indication of how they might be managed.

### Further reading

Alkhafaji, A.F. (2003) *Strategic Management: Formulation, Implementation, and Control in a Dynamic Environment*. Philadelphia, PA: Haworth Press Inc.

Carlopio, J. (2003) *Changing Gears: The Strategic Implementation of Technology*. Basingstoke, UK: Palgrave Macmillan.

Jessen, M., Holm, P.J. and Junghagen, S. (2007) *Strategy execution: passion & profit*. Copenhagen, Denmark: Copenhagen Business School Press.

Kaplan, R.S. and Norton, D.P. (2004) *Strategy Maps: Converting Intangible Assets into Tangible Outcomes*. Boston, MA: Harvard Business School Publishing.

Kaplan, R.S. and Norton, D.P. (2008) *Execution Premium: Linking Strategy to Operations for Competitive Advantage*. Boston, MA: Harvard Business School Press.

Ketokivi, M. and Castaner, X. (2004) 'Strategic planning as an integrative device', *Administrative Science Quarterly*, 49(2), pp. 337–365.

MacLennan, A. (2010) *Strategy Execution: Translating strategy into action in complex organisations*. London: Routledge.

Menda, R. and Dilts, D. (1997) 'The manufacturing strategy formulation process: linking multifunctional viewpoints', *Journal of Operations Management*, 15(4), pp. 223–241.

Verweire, K. (2014) *Strategy Implementation*. London: Routledge.

## Notes on the chapter

1 Hofstede, G. (1981) 'Management Control Of Public And Not-For-Profit Activities Accounting', *Organizations and Society*, 6(3), pp. 193–211.

2 MacLennon, A. (2010) *Strategy Execution: Translating strategy into action in complex organisations*. London: Routledge.

3 *Sources* include: Clark, A. and Ralph, A. (2014) 'Tesco boss defiant amid 4% plunge in sales', *The Times*, 4 June.

4 Kaplan, R.S. and Norton, D.P. (1993) *The Balanced Scorecard*. Boston, MA: Harvard Business School Press.

5 Bungay, S. and Goold, M. (1991) 'Creating a Strategic Control System', *Long Range Planning*, 24(3), pp. 32–39.

6 Based on the definition issued by the Institute of Internal Auditors.

7 *Sources:* Moynihan, T. (2007) 'Product recalls up 20% as firms act quickly to shore up reputations', *The Guardian*, 19 February; Woodcock, C. (2007) 'Comment on Cadbury's recall', on http://www.continuitycentral.com

8 Chew, W.B., Leonard-Barton, D. and Bohnm, R.E. (1991) 'Beating Murphy's Law', *Sloan Management Review*, Spring.

9 Argyris, C. and Schon, D. (1978) *Organizational Learning*. Reading, MA: Addison-Wesley.

10 Lewis, M. (2000) 'Lean Production and Sustainable Competitive Advantage', *International Journal of Operations and Production Management*, 20(8).

11 Dixon, L. and Porter, A.M. (1994) *JITII: A revolution in buying and selling*. Newton, MA: Cahners Publishing.

12 This idea is pursued in the context of product development by Dorothy Leonard in Leonard-Barton, D. (1992) 'Core Capabilities and Core Rigidities: A paradox in managing new product development', *Strategic Management Journal*, Vol. 13, pp. 111–125.

13 Christensen, C.M. (1997) *The Innovator's Dilemma: When new technologies cause great firms to fail*. Boston, MA: Harvard Business School Press.

14 This discussion is based on Slack, N., Chambers, S. and Johnston, R. (2007) *Operations Management*, 5th edition. Harlow, UK: Financial Times/Prentice Hall.

# CASE STUDIES

# 1

# MCDONALD'S: HALF A CENTURY OF GROWTH[1]

## Nigel Slack

It's loved and it's hated. It is a shining example of how good-value food can be brought to a mass market. It is a symbol of everything that is wrong with 'industrialised', capitalist, bland, high-calorie and environmentally unfriendly commercialism. It is the best-known and most-loved fast-food brand in the world, with more than 32,000 restaurants in 117 countries, providing jobs for 1.7 million staff and feeding 60 million customers per day (yes, per day!). It is part of the homogenisation of individual national cultures, filling the world with bland, identical, 'cookie-cutter', Americanised and soulless operations that dehumanise their staff by forcing them to follow rigid and over-defined procedures. But whether you see it as friend, foe, or a bit of both, McDonald's has revolutionised the food industry, affecting the lives both of the people who produce food and the people who eat it. It has also had its ups (mainly) and downs (occasionally). Yet, even in the toughest times, it has always displayed remarkable resilience. Even after the economic turbulence of 2008, McDonald's reported an exceptional year of growth in 2009 – posting sales increases and higher market share around the world; it was the sixth consecutive year of positive sales in every geographic region of the business.

## Starting small

Central to the development of McDonald's is Ray Kroc, who by 1954, and at the age of 52, had been variously a piano player, a paper-cup salesman and a multi-mixer salesman. He was surprised by a big order for eight multi-mixers from a restaurant in San Bernardino, California. When he visited the customer he found a small but successful restaurant run by two brothers, Dick and Mac McDonald. They had opened their 'Bar-B-Que' restaurant 14 years earlier, adopting the usual format at that time: customers would drive-in, choose from a large menu and be served by a 'car hop'. However, by the time Ray Kroc visited the brothers' operation it had changed to a self-service drive-in format, with a limited menu of nine items. He was amazed by the effectiveness of their operation. Focusing on a limited menu, including burgers, fries and beverages, had allowed them to analyse every step of the process of producing and serving their food. Ray Kroc was so overwhelmed by what he saw that he persuaded the brothers to adopt his vision of creating McDonald's restaurants all over the USA, the first of which opened in Des Plaines, Illinois in June 1955. However, later, Kroc and the McDonald brothers quarrelled and Kroc bought the brothers out. Now with exclusive rights to the McDonald's name the restaurants spread, and in five years there were 200 restaurants throughout the USA. After 10 years the company went public – the share price doubling in the first month. But through this, and later, expansion Kroc insisted on maintaining the same principles that he had seen in the original operation: *'If I had a brick for every time I've repeated the phrase "quality, service, cleanliness and value", I think I'd probably be able to bridge the Atlantic Ocean with them.'*

## Priority to the process

Ray Kroc had been attracted by the cleanliness, simplicity, efficiency and profitability of the McDonald brothers' operation. They had stripped fast-food delivery down to its essence and eliminated needless effort to make a swift assembly line for a meal at reasonable prices. Kroc wanted to build a process that would become famous for food of consistently high quality using uniform methods of preparation. His burgers, buns, fries and beverages should taste just the same in Alaska as they did in Alabama. The answer was the 'Speedee Service System' – a standardised process that prescribed exact preparation methods, specially designed equipment and strict product specifications. The emphasis on process standardisation meant that customers could be assured of identical levels of food and service quality every time they visited any store, anywhere. Operating procedures were specified in minute detail. In its first operations manual, which by 1991 had reached 750 pages, it prescribed specific cooking instructions, such as temperatures, cooking times and portions, to be followed rigorously. Similarly, operating procedures were defined to ensure the required customer experience; for example, no food items were to be held for more than 10 minutes in the transfer bin between being cooked and being served. Technology was also automated. Specially designed equipment helped to guarantee consistency using 'fool-proof' devices. For example: the ketchup was dispensed through a metered pump; specially designed 'clam shell' grills cooked both sides of each meat patty simultaneously for a pre-set time; and when it became clear that the metal tongs used by staff to fill French-fry containers were awkward to use efficiently, McDonald's engineers devised a simple v-shaped aluminium scoop that made the job faster and easier, as well as presenting the fries in a more attractive alignment with their container.

For Kroc, the operating process was both his passion and the company's central philosophy; it was also the foundation of learning and improvement. The company's almost compulsive focus on process detail was not an end in itself. Rather, it was to learn what contributed to consistent high-quality service in practice and what did not. Learning was always seen as important by McDonald's. In 1961 it founded 'Hamburger University', initially in the basement of a restaurant in Elk Grove Village, Illinois. It had a research and development laboratory to develop new cooking, freezing, storing and serving methods. Also, franchisees and operators were trained in the analytical techniques necessary to run a successful McDonald's. It awarded degrees in 'Hamburgerology'. But learning was not just for headquarters. The company also formed a 'field service' unit to appraise and help its restaurants by sending field service consultants to review their performance on a number of 'dimensions', including cleanliness, queuing, food quality and customer service. As Ray Kroc said, '*We take the hamburger business more seriously than anyone else. What sets McDonald's apart is the passion that we and our suppliers share around producing and delivering the highest-quality beef patties. Rigorous food safety and quality standards and practices are in place and executed at the highest levels every day.*'

No story illustrates the company's philosophy of learning and improvement better than its adoption of frozen fries. French-fried potatoes had always been important for the company. Initially, it tried observing the temperature levels and cooking methods that produced the best fries. The problem was that the temperature during the cooking process was very much influenced by the temperature of the potatoes when they were placed into the cooking vat. So, unless the temperature of the potatoes before they were cooked was also controlled (not very practical) it was difficult to specify the exact time and temperature that would produce the perfect fries. But McDonald's researchers have perseverance. They discovered that, irrespective of the temperature of the raw potatoes, fries were always at their best when the oil temperature in the cooking vat increased by three degrees above the low temperature point after they were put in the vat. So, by monitoring the temperature of the vat, perfect fries could be produced every time. But that was not the end of the story. The ideal potato for fries was the Idaho Russet, which was seasonal and not available in the summer months, when an alternative (inferior) potato was used. One grower, who at the time supplied a fifth of McDonald's potatoes, suggested that he could put Idaho Russets into cold storage for supplying during the summer period. Notwithstanding investment in cold storage facilities, all the stored potatoes rotted. Not to be beaten, he offered another suggestion. Why don't McDonald's consider switching to frozen potatoes? This was no trivial decision and the company was initially cautious about meddling with such an important menu item. However, there were other advantages in using frozen potatoes. Supplying fresh potatoes in perfect condition to McDonald's rapidly expanding chain was increasingly difficult. Frozen potatoes could actually increase the quality of the company's fries if a method of satisfactorily cooking them could be found. Once again McDonald's developers came to the rescue. They developed a method of air-drying the raw fries and quick-frying and then freezing them. The supplier, who was a relatively small and local supplier when he first suggested storing Idaho Russets, grew his business to supply around half of McDonald's US business.

Throughout its rapid expansion, a significant danger facing McDonald's was that of losing control of its operating system. It avoided this, partly by always focusing on four areas – improving the product, establishing strong supplier relationships, creating (largely customised) equipment and developing franchise holders. But, also, it was the strict control of the menu that provided a platform of stability. Although its competitors offered a relatively wide variety of menu items, McDonald's limited its menu to 10 items. This allowed uniform standards to be established, which in turn encouraged specialisation. As one of McDonald's senior managers at the time stressed, '*It wasn't because we were smarter. The fact that we were selling just 10 items [and] had a facility that was small, and used a limited number of suppliers created an ideal environment.*' Capacity growth (through additional stores) was also managed carefully. Well-utilised stores were important to franchise holders, so franchise opportunities were located only where they would not seriously undercut existing stores. Ray Kroc used the company plane to spot from the air the best locations and road junctions for new restaurant branches.

## Securing supply

McDonald's says that it has been the strength of the alignment between the company, its franchisees and its suppliers (collectively referred to as the 'System') that has been the explanation for its success. Expanding the McDonald's chain, especially in the early years, meant persuading both franchisees and suppliers to buy into the company's vision. 'Working', as Ray Kroc put it, 'not for McDonald's, but for themselves, together with McDonald's'. He promoted the slogan 'In business for yourself, but not by yourself.' But when the company started out, suppliers proved problematic. McDonald's approached the major food suppliers, such as Kraft and Heinz, but without much success. Large and established suppliers were reluctant to conform to

McDonald's requirements, preferring to focus on retail sales. It was the relatively small companies who were willing to risk supplying what seemed then to be a risky venture. Yet, as McDonald's grew, so did its suppliers. Also, McDonald's relationship with its suppliers was seen as less adversarial than with some other customers. One supplier is quoted as saying: '*Other chains would walk away from you for half a cent. McDonald's was more concerned with getting quality. McDonald's always treated me with respect even when they became much bigger and didn't have to.*' Furthermore, suppliers were always seen as a source of innovation. For example, one of McDonald's meat suppliers, Keystone Foods, developed a novel quick-freezing process that captured the fresh taste and texture of beef patties. This meant that every patty could retain its consistent quality until it hit the grill. Keystone shared its technology with other McDonald's meat suppliers for McDonald's, and today the process is an industry standard. Yet, although innovative and close, supplier relationships are also rigorously controlled. Unlike some competitors, who simply accepted what suppliers provided, complaining only when supplies were not up to standard, McDonald's routinely analysed its suppliers' products.

## Fostering franchisees

McDonald's revenues consist of sales by company-operated restaurants and fees from restaurants operated by franchisees. McDonald's views itself primarily as a franchisor and believes franchising is ... 'important to delivering great, locally-relevant customer experiences and driving profitability'. However, it also believes that directly operating restaurants is essential to providing the company with real operations experience. In 2009, of the 32,478 restaurants in 117 countries, 26,216 were operated by franchisees and 6,262 were operated by the company. Where McDonald's was different to other franchise operations was in its relationships. Some restaurant chains concentrated on recruiting franchisees that may then be ignored. McDonald's, on the other hand, expected its franchisees to contribute their experiences for the benefit of all. Ray Kroc's original concept was that franchisees would make money before the company did, so he made sure that the revenues that went to McDonald's came from the success of the restaurants themselves rather than from initial franchise fees.

## Initiating innovation

Ideas for new menu items have often come from franchisees. For example, Lou Groen, a Cincinnati franchise holder, had noticed that in Lent (a 40-day period when some Christians give up eating red meat on Fridays and instead eat only fish or no meat at all) some customers avoided the traditional hamburger. He went to Ray Kroc with his idea for a 'Filet-o-Fish' – a steamed bun with a shot of tartar sauce, a fish fillet and cheese on the bottom bun. But Kroc wanted to push his own meatless sandwich, called the 'hula burger' – a cold bun with a piece of pineapple and cheese. Groen and Kroc competed on a Lenten Friday to see whose sandwich would sell more. Kroc's 'hula burger' failed, selling only six burgers all day, while Groen sold 350 of his 'Filet-o-Fish'. Similarly, the Egg McMuffin was introduced by franchisee Herb Peterson, who wanted to attract customers into his McDonald's stores all through the day, not just at lunch and dinner. He came up with the idea for the signature McDonald's breakfast item because he was reputedly 'very partial to eggs Benedict and wanted to create something similar'.

Other innovations came from the company itself. By the beginning of the 1980s poultry was becoming more fashionable to eat and sales of beef were sagging. Fred Turner, then the chairman of McDonald's, had an idea for a new meal: a chicken finger-food without bones, about the size of a thumb. After six months of research, the food technicians and scientists managed to reconstitute shreds of white chicken meat into small portions that could be breaded, fried, frozen and then reheated. Test-marketing the new product was positive, and in 1983 they were launched under the name 'Chicken McNuggets'. These were so successful that within a month McDonald's became the second largest purchaser of chicken in the USA. By 1992, Americans were eating more chicken than beef.

Other innovations came as a reaction to market conditions. Criticised by nutritionists, who worried about calorie-rich burgers, and shareholders who were alarmed by flattening sales, McDonald's launched its biggest menu revolution in 30 years in 2003 when it entered the prepared salad market. It offered a choice of dressings for its grilled chicken salad, with Caesar dressing (and croutons) or the lighter option of a drizzle of balsamic dressing. Likewise, recent moves towards coffee sales were prompted by the ever-growing trend set by big coffee shops such as Starbucks. McCafé, a coffee-house-style food and drink chain, owned by McDonald's, had expanded to about 1,300 stores worldwide by 2011.

## Problematic periods

The period from the early 1990s to the mid 2000s was difficult for parts of the McDonald's empire. Although growth in many parts of the world continued, in some developed markets the company's hitherto rapid growth stalled. This was due in part to changes in food fashion, nutritional concerns and demographic changes and partly because competitors were learning to either emulate McDonald's operating system, or focus on one aspect of the traditional 'quick service' offering, such as speed of service, range of menu items, (perceived) quality of food, or price. Burger King promoted itself on its 'flame-grilled' quality. Wendy's offered a fuller service level. Taco Bell undercut McDonald's prices with their 'value pricing' promotions. Drive-through specialists such as Sonic sped up service times. But it was not only competitors that were a threat to McDonald's growth. So-called 'fast food' was developing a poor reputation in some quarters, and as its iconic brand, McDonald's was taking much of the heat. Similarly the company became a lightning rod for other questionable aspects of modern life that it was held to promote, from cultural imperialism, low-skilled jobs, abuse of animals and the use of hormone-enhanced beef, to an attack on traditional (French) values (in France). A French farmer called Jose Bové (who was briefly imprisoned) got other farmers to drive their tractors through, and wreck, a half-built McDonald's. When he was tried, 40,000 people rallied outside the courthouse.

The chief executive of McDonald's in the UK, Jill McDonald (yes, really!), said that some past difficulties were self-induced. They included a refusal to face criticisms and a reluctance to acknowledge the need for change. '*I think by the end of the 1990s we were just not as close to the customer as we needed to be, we were given a hard time in the press and we lost our confidence. We needed to reconnect, and make changes that would disrupt people's view of McDonald's.*' Investing in its people also needed to be re-emphasised.

*'We invest about £35m a year in training people. We have become much more of an educator than an employer of people.'* Nor does she accept the idea of 'McJobs' (meaning boring, poorly paid, often temporary jobs with few prospects). *'That whole McJob thing makes me so angry. It's snobbish. We are the biggest employer of young people in Britain. Many join us without qualifications. They want a better life, and getting qualifications is something they genuinely value.'*

## Surviving strategies

Yet, in spite of its difficult period, the company has not only survived but through the late 2000s has thrived. In 2009 McDonald's results showed that, in the USA, sales and market share both grew for the seventh consecutive year, with new products such as McCafé premium coffees, the premium Angus Third Pounder, smoothies and frappes, together with more convenient locations, extended hours, efficient 'drive thru' service and value-orientated promotions. In the UK, changes to the stores' décor and adapting menus have also helped stimulate growth. Jill McDonald's views are not untypical of other regions:

*'We have probably changed more in the past four years than the past 30: more chicken, 100% breast meat, snack wraps, more coffee – lattes and cappuccinos, ethically sourced, not at rip-off prices. That really connected with customers. We sold 100 million cups last year.'*

Senior managers have put McDonald's recent growth down to the decision in 2003 to reinvent the company by becoming 'better, not just bigger' and by implementing its 'Plan to Win'. This focused on 'restaurant execution', with the goal of '... improving the overall experience for our customers'. It provided a common framework for its global business, yet allowed for local adaptation. Multiple improvement initiatives were based on its 'five key drivers of exceptional customer experiences' (people, products, place, price and promotion). But what of McDonald's famous standardisation? During its early growth no franchise holder could deviate from the 700+-page McDonald's operations manual, known as 'the bible'. Now things are different, at least partly because different regions have developed their own products. In India, the 'Maharaja Mac' is made of mutton, and the vegetarian options contain no meat or eggs. Similarly, McDonald's in Pakistan offers three spicy 'McMaza meals'. Even in the USA things have changed. In at least one location, in Indiana, there's now a McDonald's with a full service 'diner' inside, where waitresses serve 100 combinations of food, on china – a far cry from Ray Kroc's vision of stripping out choice to save time and money.

## Note on the case

1   This case originally appeared in Slack, N., Brandon-Jones, A., Johnston, R. and Betts, A. (2012) *Operations and Process Management*, 3rd edition. Harlow, UK: Pearson Education.

# 2

# DISNEYLAND RESORT PARIS

## Nigel Slack

In August 2006, the company behind Disneyland Resort Paris reported a 13 per cent rise in revenues, saying that it was making encouraging progress with new rides aimed at getting more visitors. *'I am pleased with year-to-date revenues and especially with third quarter's, as well as with the success of the opening of Buzz Lightyear Laser Blast, the first step of our multi-year investment programme. These results reflect the group's strategy of increasing growth through innovative marketing and sales efforts as well as a multi-year investment programme. This performance is encouraging as we enter into the important summer months'*, said Chairman and Chief Executive Karl L. Holz. Revenue for the quarter ending 30 June rose to €286.6 million ($362 million) from €254 million a year earlier. The results helped to boost overall profits at Disney Company, and the company's stock price soared.

Yet, it hadn't always been like that. The fourteen-year history of Disneyland Paris had more ups and downs than any of its rollercoasters. The company had hauled itself back from what some commentators had claimed was the brink of bankruptcy in 2005. In fact, from 12 April 1992 when Euro Disney opened through to this more optimistic report, the resort had been subject simultaneously to both wildly optimistic forecasts and widespread criticism and ridicule. An essay on one critical internet site (called 'An Ugly American in Paris') summarised the whole venture in this way:

> *'When Disney decided to expand its hugely successful theme park operations to Europe, it brought American management styles, American cultural tastes, American labor practices, and American marketing pizzazz to Europe. Then, when the French stayed away in droves, it accused them of cultural snobbery.'*

## The 'magic' of Disney

Since its founding in 1923, the Walt Disney Company had striven to remain faithful in its commitment to *'producing unparalleled entertainment experiences based on its rich legacy of quality creative content and exceptional storytelling'*. It did this through four major business divisions: Studio Entertainment, Parks and Resorts, Consumer Products and Media Networks. Each segment consists of integrated businesses that worked together to *'maximise exposure and growth worldwide'*.

---

*Source:* This case was prepared by Nigel Slack of Warwick Business School, Warwick University, United Kingdom, using published sources of information. It does not reflect the views of the Walt Disney Company, who should not be held responsible for the accuracy or interpretation of the information or views contained in this case. It is not intended to illustrate either good or bad management practice. Copyright © 2006 Nigel Slack.

In the Parks and Resorts division, according to the company's description, customers could experience the *'magic of Disney's beloved characters'*. It was founded in 1952, when Walt Disney formed what is now known as 'Walt Disney Imagineering' to build Disneyland in Anaheim, California. By 2006, Walt Disney Parks and Resorts operated or licensed 11 theme parks at five Disney destinations around the world. They were Disneyland Resort, California, Walt Disney World Resort, Florida, Tokyo Disney Resort, Disneyland Resort Paris and their latest park, Hong Kong Disneyland. In addition, the division operated 35 resort hotels, two luxury cruise ships and a wide variety of other entertainment offerings. But in the history of the Walt Disney Company, perhaps none of its ventures had proved to be as challenging as its Paris resort.

## Service delivery at Disney resorts and parks

The core values of the Disney Company and, arguably, the reason for its success, originated in the views and personality of Walt Disney, the company's founder. He had what some called an obsessive focus on creating images, products and experiences for customers that epitomised fun, imagination and service. Through the 'magic' of legendary fairytale and story characters, customers could escape the cares of the real world. Different areas of each Disney Park are themed, often around various 'lands' such as Frontierland, Fantasyland, Tomorrowland and Adventureland. Each land contains attractions and rides, most of which are designed to be acceptable to a wide range of ages. Very few rides are 'scary' when compared to many other entertainment parks. The architectural styles, decor, food, souvenirs and cast costumes are all designed to reflect the theme of the 'land', as are the films and shows.

Although there were some regional differences, all the theme parks followed the same basic setup. Over the years, Disney had built up a reputation for imaginative rides. Its 'imagineers' had years of experience in using 'auto animatronics' to help recreate and reinforce the essence of the theme. The terminology used by the company reinforced its philosophy of consistent entertainment. Employees, even those working 'back stage', were called cast members. They did not wear uniforms but 'costumes', and rather than being given a job they were 'cast in a role'. All park visitors were called 'guests'.

Disney employees were generally relatively young, often of school or college age. Most were paid hourly on tasks that could be repetitive even though they usually involved constant contact with customers. Yet, employees were still expected to maintain a high level of courtesy and work performance. All cast members were expected to conform to strict dress and grooming standards. Applicants to become cast members were screened for qualities such as how well they responded to questions, how well they listened to their peers, how they smiled and used body language and whether they had an 'appropriate attitude'.

All Disney parks had gained a reputation for their focus (some would say obsession) with delivering a high level of service and experience through attention to operations detail. To ensure that their strict service standards were met they had developed a number of specific operations policies.

- All parks employed effective queue management techniques such as providing information and entertainment for visitors.

- Visitors (guests) were seen as having a role within the park. They were not merely spectators or passengers on the rides, they were considered to be participants in a play. Their needs and desires were analysed and met through frequent interactions with staff (cast members). In this way they could be drawn into the illusion that they were actually part of the fantasy.

- Disney's stated goal was to exceed its customers' expectations every day.

- Service delivery was mapped and continuously refined in the light of customer feedback.

- The staff induction programme emphasised the company's quality assurance procedures and service standards. These were based on the four principles of safety, courtesy, show and efficiency.

- Parks were kept fanatically clean.

- The same Disney character never appears twice within sight – how could there be two Mickeys?

- Staff were taught that customer perceptions are both the key to customer delight, but also are extremely fragile. Negative perceptions can be established after only one negative experience.

- Disney University was the company's in-house development and learning facility with departments in each of the company's sites. The university trained Disney's employees in its strict service standards as well as providing the skills to operate new rides as they were developed.

- Staff recognition programmes attempted to identify outstanding service delivery performance as well as *'energy, enthusiasm, commitment, and pride'*.

- All parks contained phones connected to a central question hot-line for employees to find the answer to any question posed by customers.

## Tokyo Disneyland

Tokyo Disneyland was owned and operated by the Oriental Land Company. Disney had designed the park and advised on how it should be run. In return, they received 10 per cent of all admissions revenues, and 5 per cent of food and souvenir revenues. The Tokyo project was considered a great success. Japanese customers revealed a significant appetite for American themes and American brands, and already had a good knowledge of Disney characters. Feedback from visitors at the Tokyo park was extremely positive. Visitors commented on the cleanliness of the park, the efficiency of staff members and the courtesy with which they were treated. Visitors also appreciated the Disney souvenirs (a wider range than in the American parks) because giving gifts is deeply embedded in the Japanese culture. Although the Tokyo park was almost identical to Disney's Californian park, there had been no complaints about the dilution of Japanese culture by so strong an American-themed entertainment. The Japanese operators had added many new attractions since its opening. Many signs were written in English, as were cast members' name badges. Similarly, many of the live shows and attractions were conducted in English and although almost all visitors to the park were Japanese, only one out of its thirty restaurants sold Japanese food.

The success of the Tokyo park was explained by one American living in Japan:

*'Young Japanese are very clean-cut. They respond well to Disney's clean-cut image, and I am sure they had no trouble filling positions. Also, young Japanese are generally comfortable wearing uniforms, obeying their bosses, and being part of a team. These are part of the Disney formula. Also, Tokyo is very crowded and Japanese here are used to crowds and waiting in line. They are very patient. And above all, Japanese are always very polite to strangers.'*

Disneyland Tokyo had opened in 1982. Because Disney was wary of losing money on the Japanese venture it decided not to own the Tokyo site – a decision it came to regret. Disney also regretted allowing hotels owned by other companies to be built at its earlier US Disneyland parks, to the extent that Disney only owned about 25 per cent of hotels in the vicinity. It decided that it would take full control of Euro Disney and all its hotels.

## Disneyland Paris

By 2006 Disneyland Paris consisted of three parks: the Disney village, Disneyland Paris itself and the Disney Studio Park. The village was comprised of stores and restaurants; Disneyland Paris was the main theme park; and Disney Studio Park had a more general moviemaking theme. Yet, the idea of a European park was not new. Because many of Walt Disney's most successful animations were taken from European literature, he had always wanted to build a park in Europe. In the event, his wish wasn't completed until 25 years after his death. But when the Walt Disney Company planned its European venture, its reputation was riding high and it was confident of success. At the time of the European park's opening, more than two million Europeans visited the US Disney parks, accounting for 5 per cent of the total visitors. The company's brand was strong and it had over half a century of translating the Disney brand into reality. The name 'Disney' had become synonymous with wholesome family entertainment that combined childhood innocence with hightech 'imagineering'.

### Alternative locations

Formal plans to build a European Disney Park were first considered as early as 1975. Initially, as well as France, Germany, Britain, Italy and Spain were all considered as possible locations, though Germany, Britain and Italy were soon discarded from the list of potential sites. The decision soon came to a straight contest between the Alicante area of Spain, which had a similar climate to Florida for a large part of the year, and the Marne-la-Vallée area just outside Paris. Certainly, winning the contest to host the new park was important for all the potential host countries. The new park promised to generate more than 30,000 jobs.

It was the French location that eventually won out, partly because of the close proximity to the large population of the Paris conurbation and the city's attraction as a tourist centre. Also, its central positioning within Western Europe was thought to be crucial too if it was to attract sufficient visitors. Early concerns that the park would not have the same sunny, happy feel in a cooler climate than Florida were allayed by the spectacular success of Disneyland Tokyo in a location with a similar climate to Paris. The first letter of agreement was signed with the French government in December 1985, and financial contracts started to be drawn up during the following spring. Robert Fitzpatrick, a key organiser of the 1984 Los Angeles Olympics, was appointed as the Euro Disney President, and construction started on the 2,000 hectare site in August 1988. But from the announcement that the park would be built in France, it was subject to a wave of criticism. One critic called the project a *'cultural Chernobyl'* because of how it might affect French cultural values. Another described it as *'a horror made of cardboard, plastic, and appalling colours; a construction of hardened chewing-gum and idiot folk lore taken straight out of comic books written for obese Americans'*. However, as some commentators noted, the cultural arguments and anti-Americanism of the French intellectual elite did not seem to reflect the behaviour of most French people, who *'eat at McDonald's, wear Gap clothing, and flock to American movies'*.

The major advantage of locating in Spain was the weather. However, the eventual decision to locate near Paris was thought to have been driven by a number of factors that weighed more heavily with Disney executives. These included the following:

- There was a site available just outside Paris that was both large enough and flat enough to accommodate the park.

- The proposed location put the park within a two-hour drive for 17 million people, a four-hour drive for 68 million people, a six-hour drive for 110 million people and a two-hour flight for a further 310 million or so.

- The site also had potentially good transport links. The Euro Tunnel that was to connect England with France was due to open in 1994. In addition, the French autoroutes network and the high-speed TGV network could both be extended to connect the site with the rest of Europe.

- Paris was already a highly attractive vacation destination and France generally attracted around 50,000,000 tourists each year.

- Europeans generally take significantly more holidays each year than Americans (five weeks of vacation as opposed to two or three weeks).

- Market research indicated that 85 per cent of people in France would welcome a Disney park in their country.

- Both national and local government in France were prepared to give significant financial incentives (as were the Spanish authorities), including an offer to invest in local infrastructure, reduce the rate of value added tax on goods sold in the park, provide subsidised loans and value the land artificially low to help reduce taxes. Moreover, the French government were prepared to expropriate land from local farmers to smooth the planning and construction process.

The resort was to be 49 per cent owned by the Walt Disney Company and 51 per cent owned by a company called Euro Disney SCA, which was quoted on the French stock exchange. Initially all shares were offered to European investors. The Walt Disney Company was to receive management fees and royalty fees based on the park's revenues as well as an incentive-based management fee calculated on the park's cash flow.

## Designing Disneyland Resort Paris

Phase 1 of the Euro Disney Park was designed to have 29 rides and attractions as well as six hotels with over 5,000 rooms in total. In addition, the park had a championship golf course together with many restaurants, shops, live shows and parades. Although the park was designed to fit in with Disney's traditional appearance and values, a number of changes were made to accommodate what was thought to be the preferences of European visitors. For example, market research indicated that Europeans would respond to a 'wild west' image of America. Therefore, both rides and hotel designs were made to emphasise this theme. Disney was also keen to diffuse criticism, especially from French left-wing intellectuals and politicians, that the design of the park would be too 'Americanised' and would become a vehicle for American 'cultural imperialism'. To counter charges of American imperialism, Disney gave the park a flavour that stressed the European heritage of many of the Disney characters, and increased the sense of beauty and fantasy. They were, after all, competing against Paris's exuberant architecture and sights. For example, Discoveryland featured storylines from Jules Verne, the French author. Snow White (and her dwarfs) was located in a Bavarian village. Cinderella was located in a French inn. Even Peter Pan was made to appear more 'English Edwardian' than in the original US designs.

Disney conceded to the pressure for French to be the language of the park with English taking second place. The American actor Vincent Price's voice-over for the Phantom Manor, that was used initially, was replaced by a French actor. Only Price's maniacal laugh remained. In keeping with their desire to make this park more 'European', even the story behind the Disneyland Paris Phantom Manor (named The Haunted Mansion in the US versions), although open to interpretation, was changed to include bits of *The Phantom of the Opera* and *Great Expectations*. Main Street USA, built in the idealised style of America at the beginning of the twentieth century, contained ornate shopping arcades one of which (diplomatically!) contained an exhibition telling the history behind the presentation of the Statue of Liberty by France to the USA in a spirit of friendship.

Because of concerns about the popularity of American 'fast-food', Euro Disney introduced more variety into its restaurants and snack bars, featuring foods from around the world. In a bold publicity move, Disney invited a number of top Paris chefs to visit and taste the food. Some anxiety was also expressed concerning the different 'eating behaviour' between Americans and Europeans. Whereas Americans preferred to 'graze', eating snacks and fast meals throughout the day, Europeans generally preferred to sit down and eat at traditional meal times. This would have a very significant impact on peak demand levels on dining facilities. A further concern was that in Europe, (especially French) visitors would be intolerant of long queues. To overcome this, extra diversions such as films and entertainments were planned for visitors as they waited in line for a ride.

Discoveryland was new for a Disney park; it was based on the concept of the future based on past European visionaries. Fantasyland was also new in that it had its own new 'European' attractions, along with a newly created castle especially for Euro Disney. Adventureland gained some extra new areas, again with a more authentic 'European' look than in previous parks.

Before the opening of the park, Euro Disney had to recruit and train between 12,000 and 14,000 permanent and around 5,000 temporary employees. All these new employees were required to undergo extensive training in order to prepare them to achieve Disney's high standard of customer service as well as understand operational routines and safety procedures. Originally, the company's objective was to hire 45 per cent of its employees from France, 30 per cent from other European countries and 15 per cent from outside of Europe. However, this proved difficult and when the park opened around 70 per cent of employees were French. Most 'cast members' were paid around 15 per cent above the French minimum wage.

Espace Euro Disney (an information centre) was opened in December 1990 to show the public what Disney was constructing. The 'casting centre' was opened on 1 September 1991 to recruit the cast members needed to staff the park's attractions. But the hiring process did not go smoothly. In particular, Disney's grooming requirements that insisted on a 'neat' dress code, a ban on facial hair, set standards for hair and fingernails and an insistence on 'appropriate undergarments' proved controversial. Both the French press and trade unions strongly objected to the grooming requirements, claiming they were excessive and much stricter than was generally held to be reasonable in France. Nevertheless, the company refused to modify its grooming standards.

Accommodating staff also proved to be a problem, when the large influx of employees swamped the available housing in the area. Disney had to build its own apartments as well as rent rooms in local homes just to accommodate its employees. Notwithstanding all the difficulties, Disney did succeed in recruiting and training all its cast members before the opening.

## The park opens

The park opened to employees for testing during late March 1992, during which time the main sponsors and their families were invited to visit the new park. The formal press preview day was held on 11 April 1992, and the park finally opened to visitors on 12 April 1992. When opening the new resort, Roy Disney, nephew of Walt Disney, spoke of his *'emotional homecoming for the Disney family, which traced its roots to the French town of Isigny-sur-Mer'*. The opening was not helped by strikes on the commuter trains leading to the park, staff unrest, threatened security problems (a terrorist bomb had exploded the night before the opening) and protests in surrounding villages who demonstrated against the noise and disruption from the park. The opening-day crowds, expected to be 500,000, failed to materialise, and at close of the first day only 50,000 people had passed through the gates.

Disney had expected the French to make up a larger proportion of visiting guests than they did in the early days. This may have been partly due to protests from French locals who feared that their culture would be damaged by Euro Disney. Also all Disney parks had traditionally been alcohol-free. To begin with Euro Disney was no different. However, this was extremely unpopular, particularly with French visitors who like to have a glass of wine or beer with their food. But whatever the cause, the low initial attendance was very disappointing for the Disney Company.

It was reported that, in the first nine weeks of operation, approximately 1,000 employees left Euro Disney, about one half of whom 'left voluntarily'. The reasons cited for leaving Disney's employment varied. Some blamed the hectic pace of work and the long hours that Disney expected. Others mentioned the 'chaotic' conditions in the first few weeks. Even Disney conceded that conditions had been tough immediately after the park opened. Some leavers blamed Disney's apparent difficulty in understanding 'how Europeans work'. *'We can't just be told what to do, we ask questions and don't all think the same.'* Some visitors who had experience of the American parks commented that the standards of service were noticeably below what would be acceptable in America. There were reports that some cast members were failing to meet Disney's normal service standard:

> *'... even on opening weekend some clearly couldn't care less ... My overwhelming impression ... was that they were out of their depth. There is much more to being a cast member than endlessly saying "Bonjour". Apart from having a detailed knowledge of the site, Euro Disney staff have the anxiety of not knowing in what language they are going to be addressed ... Many were struggling.'*

It was also noticeable that different nationalities exhibited different types of behaviour when visiting the park. Some nationalities always used the waste bins while others were more likely to drop litter. Most noticeable were differences in queueing behaviour. Northern Europeans tend to be disciplined and content to wait for rides in an orderly manner. By contrast, some southern European visitors *'seem to have made an Olympic event out of getting to the ticket taker first'.*

The press in a number of countries debated whether Euro Disney really knew what it was trying to be. Is it an American theme park in Europe? Is it a theme park that exploits the European heritage of Disney characters? Had the park any connection at all with France, its host country? Is there a fundamental difference between Europeans and Americans in the type of entertainment that they appreciate? Is it even possible to devise a theme park that can please so many different nationalities and cultures? Others claimed that the nature of the European work force was such that they could never achieve the US standards of Disney service:

> *'The Disney style of service is one with which Americans have grown up. There are several styles of service (or lack of it) in Europe; unbridled enthusiasm is not a marked feature of them.'*

Nevertheless, not all reactions were negative. European newspapers also quoted plenty of positive reaction from visitors, especially children. Euro Disney was so different from the existing European theme parks, with immediately recognisable characters and a wide variety of attractions. Families who could not afford to travel to the United States could now interact with Disney characters and *'sample the experience at far less cost'.*

The first phase of development (the theme park, hotel complex and golf course) had gone massively over budget. And attendance figures failed to improve much (by May the park was only attracting around 25,000 visitors a day instead of the predicted 60,000). Moreover it appeared that only three in every 10 visitors were native French. Seven weeks after the opening of the park, visitor attendance was reported at 1.5 million, a disappointment for the park which had expected 11 million visitors in its first year, and when Euro Disney announced its first quarter revenues of $489,000,000, it also said that it would make a loss in its first financial year. Again, the loss was blamed on disappointing attendance figures. Nevertheless, the company pointed out that Disney's other theme parks had made comparable losses in their first year of operation, and anyway, it was foolish to try to predict future attendance so early in the park's history. However, the Euro Disney company stock price started a slow downward spiral, rapidly losing almost a third of its value.

## The next 15 years

By August 1992 estimates of annual attendance figures were being drastically cut from 11 million to just over 9 million. Euro Disney's misfortunes were further compounded in late 1992 when a European recession caused property prices to drop sharply, and interest payments on the large start-up loans taken out by Euro Disney forced the company to admit serious financial difficulties. Also, the cheap dollar resulted in more people taking their holidays in Florida at Walt Disney World.

At the first anniversary of the park's opening, in April 1993, Sleeping Beauty's Castle was decorated as a giant birthday cake to celebrate the occasion, however, further problems were approaching. Criticised for having too few rides, the roller coaster Indiana Jones and the Temple of Peril was opened in July. This was the first Disney roller coaster that included a 360-degree loop, but just a few weeks after opening emergency brakes locked during a ride, causing injuries to some guests. The ride was temporarily shut down for investigations. Also in 1993 the proposed Euro Disney phase 2 was shelved due to financial problems. Which meant Disney MGM Studios Europe and 13,000 hotel rooms would not be built to the original 1995 deadline originally agreed upon by The Walt Disney Company. However, Discovery Mountain, one of the planned phase 2 attractions, did get approval.

By the start of 1994, rumours were circulating that the park was on the verge of bankruptcy. Emergency crisis talks were held between the banks and backers, with things coming to a head during March when Disney offered the banks an ultimatum. It would provide sufficient capital for the park to continue to operate until the end of the month, but unless the banks agreed to restructure the park's $1 billion debt, the Walt Disney company would close the park and walk away from the whole European venture, leaving the banks with a bankrupt theme park and a massive expanse of virtually worthless real estate. Disney then forced the bank's hand by calling the annual stockholder meeting for 15 March. Shortly before the stockholder meeting, Michael Eisner, Disney's CEO, announced that Disney was planning to pull the plug on the venture at the end of March 1994 unless the banks were prepared to restructure the loans. Faced with no alternative other than to announce that the park was about to close, just before the annual meeting the banks agreed to Disney's demands. This effectively wrote off virtually all of the next two years' worth of interest payments, and granted a three-year postponement of further loan repayments. In return, the Walt Disney Company wrote off $210 million in unpaid bills for services, and paid $540 million for a 49 per cent stake in the estimated value of the park, as well as restructuring its own loan arrangements for the $210 million worth of rides at the new park.

In May 1994, the train connection between London and Marne-la-Vallée was completed, along with a TGV link, providing a connection between several major European cities. By August the park was starting to find its feet at last, and all of the park's hotels were fully booked during the peak holiday season. Also, in October, the park's name was officially changed from Euro Disney to 'Disneyland Paris', in order to, *'show that the resort now was named much more like its counterparts in California and Tokyo'* and to link the park more closely with the romantic city of Paris. Some commentators noted that the name change would disassociate the resort in people's minds with controversy, debts and politics. The end-of-year figures for 1994 showed encouraging signs despite a 10 per cent fall in attendance caused by the bad publicity over the earlier financial problems. And by the end of March 1995 Disney executives were predicting that Disneyland Paris might break even by the end of 1995.

1995 saw the opening of the new roller coaster, not after all to be called 'Discovery Mountain' but 'Space Mountain de la Terre à la lune', because it was decided that the new name was more exciting. Unlike its counterparts in Tokyo, Florida and California, it was not housed in a big white dome, but in a very ornate Victorian futuristic style dome. Intensive marketing of Space Mountain on television channels all over Europe and the release of the popular movie *Pocahontas* contributed to an improvement in the resort's financial results. In fact, the Euro Disney resort complex did announce its first annual operating profit in November 1995, helped by the opening of Space Mountain in June.

In 1997 the five-year celebrations included a new parade with Quasimodo and all the characters from the latest Disney blockbusting classic, *The Hunchback of Notre Dame*, the *'Year To Be Here'* marketing campaign, the resort's first Hallowe'en celebration and a new Christmas parade.

A new attraction was added in 1999, 'Honey I Shrunk The Audience', making the audience the size of a bug while being invited to Inventor of the Year Award Ceremony. This was the more modern replacement to the ageing 3D movie Captain EO. However, the planned Christmas and New Year celebrations were disrupted when a freak storm caused havoc, destroying the Mickey Mouse glass statue that had just been installed for the Lighting Ceremony and many other attractions. Also damaged were trees next to the castle, the top of which developed a pronounced lean, as did many street signs and lamp posts.

Disney's 'Fastpass' system was introduced in 2000. This was a new service that allowed guests to use their entry passes to gain a ticket at certain attractions and return at the time stated and gain direct entry to the attraction without queueing. Two new attractions were opened, 'Indians Jones et le temple du péril' and 'Tarzan le recontre' starring a cast of acrobats along with Tarzan, Jane and all their jungle friends with music from the movie in different European languages.

In 2001 the 'ImagiNations Parade' was replaced by the 'Wonderful World of Disney Parade', which received some criticism for being 'less than spectacular' with only eight parade floats. Also Disney's 'California Adventure' was opened in California.

The resort's tenth Anniversary saw the opening of the new Walt Disney Studios Park attraction. The Disney-MGM Studios at the Walt Disney World Resort, Florida, had already proved to be a major success and the original concept for the Paris studios had first been studied in 1992, shortly before the park opened. The concept, which was based on the world of cinema, seemed perfectly adaptable to the expectations of a European audience so development for the new park was started in 1997 when a small team of Disney Imagineers were asked to design it. In parallel to this, opinion leaders from the worlds of French and European cinema, culture and media were consulted about the project. R. Julienne, the famous French stunt designer, was among the first Europeans to work with Disney on the new theme park's concept. Also in this year, Disneyland Paris was renamed Disneyland Resort Paris and the original park was also renamed Disneyland Park to accommodate the new Walt Disney Studios.

André Lacroix from Burger King was appointed as CEO of Disneyland Resort Paris in 2003, to *'take on the challenge of a failing Disney park in Europe and turn it around'*. Increasing investment, he refurbished whole sections of the park, increased the numbers of dancers to the ageing 'Wonderful World of Disney Parade' and introduced the Jungle Book Carnival in February to increase attendance during the slow months.

By 2004, attendance had increased but the company announced that it was still losing money. It again renegotiated its €2.4 billion debt to the Walt Disney Company and French financial institutions. Losses were attributed partly to the costs of opening Walt Disney Studios two years earlier, just as the world theme park business slumped in the wake of the American terrorist attacks. New hotels were opened (not owned by Disney) close to the park, which meant increased competition for the park's own hotels.

The positive news of 2006 was well received. As one commentator put it:

> '[W]ould Disney, the stockholders, the banks, or even the French government make the same decision to go ahead if they could wind the clock back to 1987? Is this a story of a fundamentally flawed concept, or was it just mishandled?'

### Questions

1 What markets are the Disney resorts and parks aiming for?

2 Was Disney's choice of the Paris site a mistake?

3 What aspects of its parks' design did Disney change when it constructed Euro Disney?

4 What did Disney *not* change when it constructed Euro Disney?

5 What were Disney's main mistakes from the conception of the Paris resort through to 2006?

### some events in overview of the history of Disneyland Resort Paris

| | |
|---|---|
| 1955 | Disneyland, California opens |
| 1971 | Walt Disney World opens in Orlando, Florida |
| 1982 | Epcot Center opens in Orlando, Florida |
| 1984 | Tokyo Disney opens |
| 1987 | The announcement that the resort on Marne-la-Vallée had been chosen as the place to build the newest Magic Kingdom (called Euro Disney then). Construction starts with a plan to complete in five years |
| 1989 | Disney-MGM Studios Theme Park opens in Orlando |
| 1992 | The grand opening of Euro Disney resort with a cast of thousands there to meet the demand that did not materialise |
| 1993 | The second year of Euro Disney's operations. On the 12 April the castle was renamed from Le château de la belle au Bois dormant to the Le château du Gâteau |
| 1994 | Stand-off with French banks over taking away some of Euro Disney's debt that had accumulated because of lower-than-expected revenues and the project going over budget. On 14 March agreement is reached with the French banks and Euro Disney stays open. The company would pay fewer royalties to the Walt Disney Company and more money from the Walt Disney Company would be invested into the resort |
| 1995 | Opening of the new roller coaster proves a great success |
| 1996 | Planet Hollywood was opened within the resort |
| 1997 | The Park open for five years |
| 1998 | Disney's Animal Kingdom opened in Orlando |
| 1999 | Storm disrupts the Park's operations |
| 2000 | Disney's 'Fastpass' introduced |
| 2001 | Disney's California Adventure opened in California |
| 2002 | The tenth anniversary and Walt Disney Studio opened in Paris |
| 2003 | André Lacroix from Burger King is appointed as CEO of Disneyland Resort Paris |
| 2004 | The company announces that it is still losing money and again renegotiates its €2.4 billion debt to the Walt Disney Company and French financial institutions |
| 2006 | Rise in revenues reported |

# 3

# CARGLASS®: BUILDING AND SUSTAINING A CUSTOMER-CENTRIC ORGANISATION

## Kurt Verweire

## Wim Buekens

Hasselt (Belgium), end of January 2010. Jean-Paul Teyssen was surprised to find out that his colleagues of the executive team had organised a little party to celebrate his 10th anniversary as CEO of Carglass® Belgium/Luxembourg (Carglass® Belux). During the party, they presented the major achievements of the company over the last ten years. Everyone agreed they were impressive. Carglass® Belux had by far exceeded the goals set by the corporate parent, Belron® Corporation. Customer and employee satisfaction scores were at an all-time high. Revenues almost tripled over the period 2000–09, while operational profits had quadrupled.

Nevertheless, as Jean-Paul Teyssen contemplated the future, he foresaw some significant challenges for his company. He had built a very successful organisation on the basis of continuous improvement and had achieved performance that nobody thought was possible. His motto was always: *'Dream big – even in more difficult times.'* But with employee- and customer-satisfaction scores of 96 per cent and more, what was there to be improved? And, more importantly, how should he fight a culture of complacency?

## Company background

Carglass® Belux is a subsidiary of Belron®, the world's largest automotive glass repair and replacement corporation. Belron® operates in over 30 countries and more than 25,000 employees serve approximately 11 million customers per year. Founded in 1897 in Cape Town, South Africa, it has since grown into a global company specialising in fixing damaged vehicle glass across the world. At the heart of the service is the company's repair story: *'If we can repair a windscreen before replacing it, we will.'* Consisting of multiple business units operating under different names, such as Carglass®, Autoglass®, Safelite® and O'Brien®, among others, each responds to the local needs, with the support of operations standardised across the group. The corporation focuses on achieving a high level of customer service in all the countries in which it is present. (For more information on Belron® refer to Exhibit 1.)

---

This case was written by Kurt Verweire and Wim Buekens at Vlerick Business School. It is intended to be used as a basis for class discussion rather than to illustrate either effective or ineffective handling of an administrative situation. The case was compiled from field research.

**Exhibit 1** **Presentation of the Belron® Group (Figures 2009)**

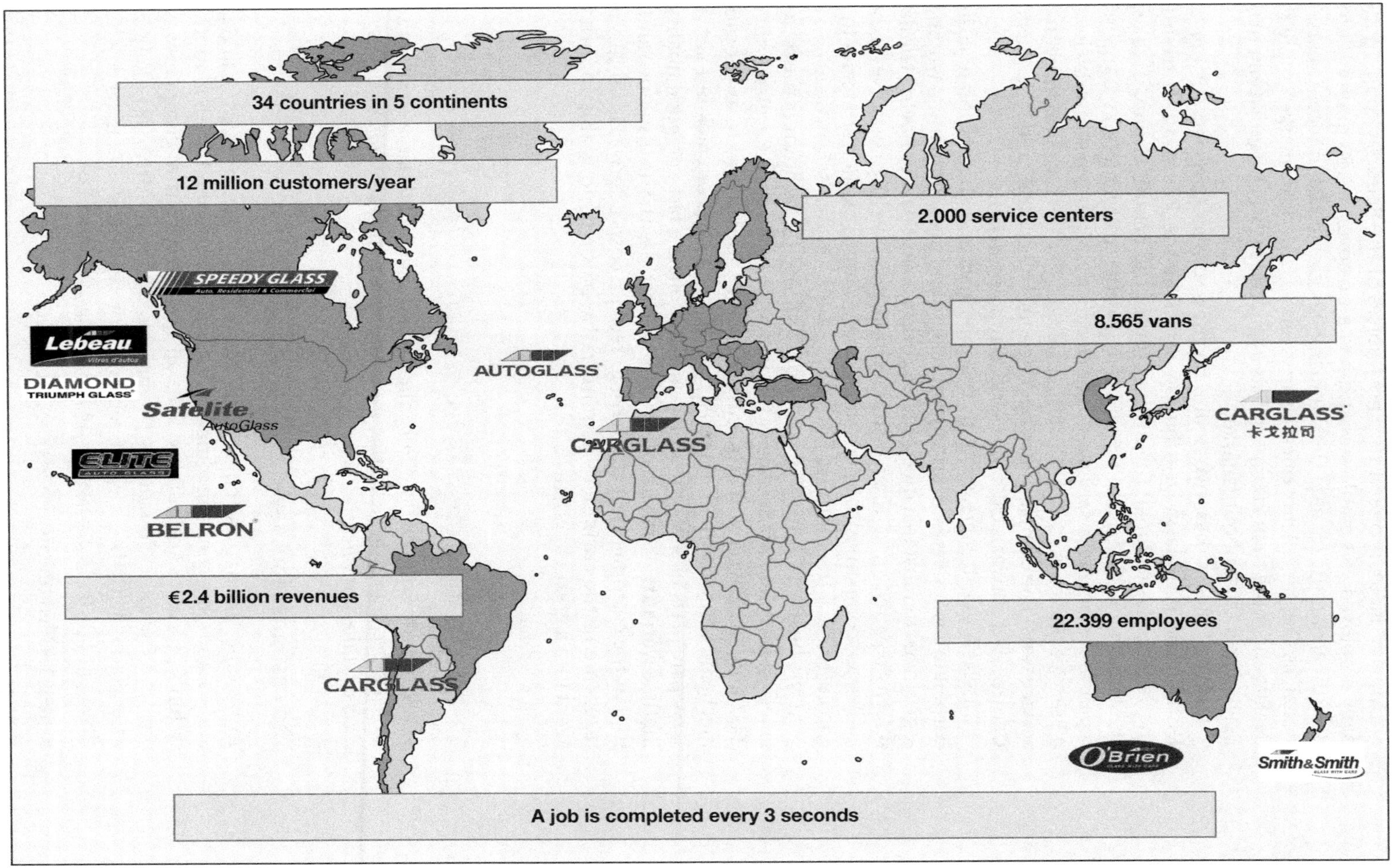
34 countries in 5 continents
12 million customers/year
SPEEDY GLASS
Auto, Residential & Commercial
Lebeau
Vitres d'autos
DIAMOND
TRIUMPH GLASS
Safelite
AutoGlass
ELITE
AUTO GLASS
BELRON
AUTOGLASS
CARGLASS
2.000 service centers
8.565 vans
CARGLASS
卡戈拉司
€2.4 billion revenues
CARGLASS
22.399 employees
O'Brien
Smith&Smith
A job is completed every 3 seconds

*Source*: Company information

Carglass® Belux is one of the show horses of the Belron® Group. In 2009, the company employed 754 employees and had a turnover of 168 million Euro. Despite the difficult economic climate the company has grown fast in recent years. This is exceptional, as Carglass® Belux operates in a very competitive market: more than 3,000 car dealers and more than 200 specialists offer glass repair and replacement services in the Belgian and Luxembourg market.

Carglass® Belux has two main business units: Carglass® Fitting and Carglass® Distribution. Carglass® Distribution serves as the European distribution centre of the vehicle glasses for all the fitting units of the Belron® Group. Carglass® Fitting – in the remainder of the text we will refer to this unit simply as Carglass® – offers the repair or replacement services of damaged glass in all types of vehicles. This unit has 43 service branches, called 'Customer Delight Centres', and has more than 100 mobile service vans. The company also operates one call centre, called the 'Customer Contact Centre', that converts calls into service appointments.

Carglass®'s customers are both the motorists and the corporate customers. These corporate customers are the insurance, lease and fleet companies, whom Carglass® sees as partners. In most instances, the motorists do not pay for having the damaged windscreens repaired since their insurance policies cover the costs. Nevertheless, as with all Belron® companies, Carglass® also has developed explicit strategies to deal with the end customer – the motorist.

At the heart of Carglass®'s exceptional service proposition is the idea that convenience and world-class service is fundamental to success. Carglass® offers its services 24/7 and 365 days a year. The customer can choose to go to any location or have a mechanic come to them. Carglass® can repair a chip or crack but also has all necessary spare parts in stock for replacement. It offers a fast and good quality service with lifetime warranty. Furthermore, it liaises directly with the insurance and leasing firms so that the customer does not have to reclaim costs afterwards. In this way, Carglass® takes care of the customer's administrative burden and is able to turn a hasslesome event into a great experience.

## Carglass®'s core operations

The vision of Carglass® is: *'To be the natural choice and the reference in service, we will exceed expectations, by delivering a caring, unforgettable, automotive glass service experience; anytime, anywhere.'*

### The customer journey

To become the natural choice and reference in the industry, Carglass® sought to understand how their customers interacted with them, before mapping the organisation's processes accordingly. Like all the other Belron® companies, they mapped out 'The Customer Journey' – the process that a motorist was likely to go through when faced with the task of repairing or replacing a damaged windscreen. The customer journey consists of the following 10 steps:

- Step 1: Glass on customer's car is damaged
- Step 2: Customer looks for information about possible suppliers that can fix this

- Step 3: Customer contacts Carglass® via mail or phone or visits a Customer Delight Centre
- Step 4: Customer schedules an appointment to fix the problem
- Step 5: Carglass® technician arrives at previously agreed time and place
- Step 6: Technician greets the customer upon arrival and explains what will be done
- Step 7: Technician completes the repair or replacement, cleans up after the job and explains what has been done
- Step 8: Customer pays (if applicable)
- Step 9: Follow-up with customer satisfaction survey
- Step 10: Carglass® follows up with customers that have had a poor experience.[1]

Subsequently, Carglass® built its internal organisation along those different steps.

## The creation of a strong brand

Carglass® understood that the creation of a strong brand for a low-involvement and somewhat unattractive product would be a huge challenge. Since every driver is only confronted with glass damage once every seven years, a motorist's involvement with car glass repair is very limited. For this reason, Carglass® decided to investigate all the possible means of advertising in order to educate customers about its offering. Caroline Ameloot, sales and marketing director, explains:

> 'We sell a service that is only occasionally needed. That is why we want to be top of mind in the heads of our (potential) clients. Whenever someone has a damaged screen, he or she should immediately think about us, and not about the local dealer or garage keeper. That is our challenge.'

Over the years, the company has succeeded in fulfilling this challenge and has created a strong brand that has consistently been able to achieve a top-of-mind brand awareness in Belgium of more than 90 per cent. The main communication instruments used in order to make customers aware of the brand have been radio and television advertising. Since 1999, Carglass® has advertised that repair is much cheaper and better than replacement. Each advertisement always finished with the same tag line: 'Carglass® repair, Carglass® replace!'

It has been a very simple, but effective advertisement and the same basic message is still used by the company today. One of the best-recognised advertisements in Belgium, it is also used by more than 20 other subsidiaries of the Belron® Group. Furthermore, all of the people involved in the production of the television ads are all Carglass® employees and not actors! This has not only been motivating for the people but has also improved the credibility of Carglass® amongst motorists. Carglass® analyses extensively when to run the ad and follows up on the effects of the ads on the number of incoming calls and customer visits.

## From opportunity to a job

Brand-awareness creation is the responsibility of the sales and marketing department. Once a customer gets in touch with Carglass® – either by calling the Customer Contact Centre, or via the website or by going to a Customer Delight Centre directly – the

**Exhibit 2 From opportunity to job: the 'Waterfall' concept (Figure 2009)**

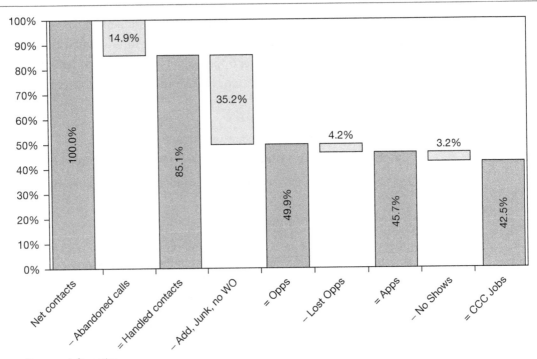

*Source*: Company information

stick is handed to the operations department. The goal of the operations department is to ensure that contacts with customers lead to a delighted service job. A lot of care is taken to collect the right information (including information to assess the damage and to identify the right glass as well as the process required) and to give the customers an appointment where and when they want it.

The company registers all incoming calls, email messages and visits, and identifies how many of them represent new service opportunities (see Exhibit 2). This is the 'Waterfall' concept. First, the Customer Contact Centre monitors the percentage of abandoned calls (these are calls that are abandoned due to a false connection or a too-long waiting time). Then it measures how many of the handled contacts represent true service opportunities. Some of the calls deal with previous appointments, e.g. a customer that asks for information or confirmation about an appointment. These calls are not considered new opportunities. New opportunities emerge when customers try to make an appointment for a repair or replacement. In 2009, 50 per cent of the calls represented new opportunities. Stefaan Hermans comments:

*'The Customer Contact Centre is actively stimulated to reduce the number of abandoned calls and junk calls so that every net contact is a new opportunity. We are constantly asking ourselves how we can do a better job at Carglass® so that the customer does not have to call us for extra information or confirmations. The goal is to provide the customer with all the right and necessary information the first time he gets in touch with us. In that way, we can significantly increase the efficiency in the Customer Contact Centre.'*

Once an appointment is made, the customer goes to the Customer Delight Centre or is served by one of the 100 mobile vans. Carglass® pays a lot of attention to train its technicians to deliver a high-quality job. Service technicians even receive special training on how to greet customers when arriving at the location of a job and on the information they are to provide to customers.[2] Carglass® records quality figures and measures the productive time in the Customer Delight Centres. Productive time is the time spent on driving to the customer and repairing or replacing the customer's damaged car glass. Training time is also considered as productive time. Doing rework, dealing with complaints and 'no shows' are considered to be unproductive time. The company reports the productivity figures of the Customer Delight Centres, and even links the team bonus to the achievement of productivity targets.

## Service recovery

Upon completion of the job, the customer is asked to pay any outstanding amounts, when necessary, and to complete a customer satisfaction survey. Special attention is paid to unsatisfied customers, by means of a service recovery programme, to ensure that these customers' problems are quickly resolved. Complaints are called 'actions to improve'.

## Dealing with partners

For the corporate customers of Carglass® – the insurance, lease or fleet companies – long-term relationships are developed in order to provide an even better service for the end customer. One of those corporate partners in Belgium, for example, is LeasePlan – a leading international leasing company with activities in more than 30 countries. Luc Norga, director of operations and procurement at LeasePlan Belgium, comments on the relationship they have with Carglass®:

> 'We work with Carglass® because they are the specialists in car glass repair. In view of the high standard of services and optimised repair ratio versus other channels, Carglass® is our dominant supplier and a majority of our customers go to Carglass® in case of glass damage.
>
> But there is more than that: we have a very open relationship with Carglass®. We learn from them and they learn from us. Carglass® is always eager to jump on new opportunities that will further strengthen the relationship. For example, we decided to set up an 'Integrated Services' concept that includes oil checks, air pressure control checks for pneumatic tyres and so on. We asked the key account manager whether Carglass® would participate in this initiative, and they immediately agreed. Now we receive monthly reports of the tyre controls, the oil controls, that they conducted. They even report the savings we make by having those controls. We can provide this information to our customers. This is typical for Carglass®: whenever you ask for something, you always receive something more.
>
> Another example is the integration of our back offices. When we asked for electronic invoicing, Carglass® was very open to link their back office to ours. Today, we have integrated back offices and for car glass repair we do not need to input anything in our systems.'

## The Carglass® 'Circle of Success'

Providing an unforgettable automotive glass service experience and continuously exceeding customers' expectations requires that the organisation also has a special culture. A key element of the Carglass® organisation is the Carglass® 'Circle of Success' (see Exhibit 3). While the concept is simple – satisfied employees lead to satisfied internal and external customers, which in turn leads to satisfied shareholders – executing all this is less straightforward.

### Organisational climate

According to CEO Jean-Paul Teyssen, the creation of the right organisational climate is key to the creation of a high-performance organisation. Key elements of a stimulating organisational climate are clarity on the organisational strategy, an organisation that mobilises individual initiative, and a strong emphasis on team commitment. In turn, the right organisational climate is shaped by appropriate management behaviour. Jean-Paul Teyssen comments:

> 'At Carglass® we work on both the leadership styles of our managers and on our organisational climate. Like other companies from the Belron® Group, we use the international consulting firm Hay Group to measure leadership styles and organisational climate across the organisation. The leadership style survey measures the extent to which leaders draw upon six core leadership behaviours. This leadership survey compares managers' intentions with their team members' perceptions. The organisational climate survey (OCS) measures the impact that leaders have on the work climate in their teams. It measures the extent to which they engage and motivate their team members to give extra effort. The results of the OCS provide a gap analysis of employees' ideal working climate and the climate they actually experience day to day. Based on the extent of the gaps, Hay distinguishes between four types of organisational climate: high-performance, energising, neutral and demotivating.[3] We have significantly improved our organisational climate. Our initial measurement in 2004 showed that none of our managers were high-performance leaders, more than half were demotivating. In 2008, we had 54 per cent high performance leaders and only 15 per cent demotivating leaders.'

**Exhibit 3 The Carglass® 'Circle of Success'**

*Source*: Company information

Exhibit 4 **Carglass®'s leadership effectiveness**

| | 2004 | 2008 | Hay benchmark |
|---|---|---|---|
| High-performance | – | 52% | 26% |
| Energising | 27% | 17% | 18% |
| Neutral | 25% | 15% | 15% |
| Demotivating | 58% | 16% | 41% |

*Source*: Company information

All members of the executive team, the management team and the middle-management team have to go through the assessment. For Carglass®, 35 people have participated in a 360-degree feedback programme. These assessments are very confrontational as they show – black on white – where the managers' leadership strengths and weaknesses lie. Managers are coached to improve their leadership skills by means of the 'Together for Better' programme, a programme that started in 2005. The results of the programme have been impressive, with Carglass® outperforming the companies of the Hay benchmark (see Exhibit 4 for an evolution of Carglass® Belux's OCS results).

## Employee satisfaction

A stimulating organisational climate creates the conditions that motivate and align employees to do their best work. Jean-Paul Teyssen confirms:

> *'If the strategy of our organisation is to continuously raise the bar and to exceed customers' expectations, we have to take care of our people. Nobody will deny that you have to work hard in Carglass®, but in return we give a lot to our employees.'*

Carglass® pays enormous attention to increase overall employee satisfaction. To start, Carglass® ensures that employees are heard: the company measures employee satisfaction every two years. Every other year, the company participates in the 'Great Place to Work' competition. The company participated in 2009 for the first time in this competition and was ranked eighth in the list of companies with more than 500 employees. In 2009, the employee satisfaction survey indicated that 96 per cent of the employees were 'satisfied' with the company, of which 56 per cent were 'extremely satisfied' (see Exhibits 5a and 5b).

Carglass® uses the employee surveys to improve operational and managerial processes within the company. When the employee satisfaction survey revealed that the Customer Contact Centre employees felt excluded and less committed to the organisation, Carglass® organised trips to the Customer Delight Centres. These

### Exhibit 5a Carglass®'s overall employee-satisfaction scores

| Year | General satisfaction | Satisfied | Very satisfied |
|------|----------------------|-----------|----------------|
| 2003 | 89% | 50% | 39% |
| 2005 | 94% | 56% | 38% |
| 2007 | 96% | 53% | 43% |
| 2009 | 96% | 40% | 56% |

*Source*: Company information

### Exhibit 5b Detailed employee-satisfaction scores

| | 2007 | 2008 | 2009 |
|---|------|------|------|
| Overall opinion/general satisfaction | 89% | 94% | 96% |
| Tools & equipment | 84% | 90% | 90% |
| Clarity of mission/strategy/goals | 89% | 90% | 94% |
| Health & Safety | 75% | 82% | 96% |
| Clear personal objectives | 90% | 88% | 91% |
| Recognition | 59% | 61% | 73% |
| Development | 72% | 72% | 76% |
| Relationship with manager | 79% | 73% | 84% |
| Teamwork | 93% | 90% | 95% |
| Pride | 77% | 87% | 94% |
| Customer service | — | 92% | 96% |

Overall opinion/general satisfaction: 'On the whole, I am satisfied to work for Carglass®'
Tools & equipment: 'The needed suitable work material is available to do my work properly'
Clarity of mission/strategy/goals: 'On the whole, I find myself in the Carglass® strategy'
Health & Safety: 'The safety of the staff is a priority for the organisation'
Clear personal objectives: 'I have clear objectives and targets'
Recognition: 'Thanks and recognition received'
Development: 'Enough training possibilities, enough means to improve quality, possibilities to grow within the organisation'
Relationship with manager: 'On the whole, I am satisfied with the cooperation with managers'
Teamwork: 'On the whole I am satisfied with the cooperation with colleagues'
Pride: 'I am proud to work for Carglass®'
Customer Service: 'Carglass® does the maximum to improve customer service'

*Source* : Company information

trips provided more clarity to these employees on the organisational strategy and overall direction of the company, which helped to increase employee satisfaction in this unit.

Each quarter, employees also have individual meetings with their team leaders to discuss their performance as well as the translation of team goals into individual goals.

All vacancies are open to the employees. This explains why 80 to 90 per cent of the team leaders of the Customer Delight Centres are recruited internally and why employee turnover is low. In 2008, employee turnover was only 6 per cent.[4]

Carglass® also invests in employer branding by sponsoring KRC Genk, one of the major Belgian soccer teams with its home base in Limburg (the province where the head office of Carglass® is located). Through employer branding, Carglass® hopes to reach out to qualified technicians. When recruiting, Carglass® not only pays attention to the technical skills of the applicant but also screens whether a candidate has the right service attitude.

## Customer satisfaction

A second element of the Carglass® 'Circle of Success' is customer satisfaction. The company uses mystery shoppers to check whether the service that is provided is in line with what is promised. In addition, research company GfK Significant has done more than 23,000 interviews with Carglass® customers in Belgium in 2009. GfK Significant not only measures the general satisfaction of Carglass® customers, but also customers' satisfaction for nine different dimensions of the service experience, such as ease of contact, friendliness, punctuality, quality and so on. (Exhibits 6a and 6b provide an overview of the customer satisfaction scores of Carglass® over the period 2007–09 and a more detailed overview of the customer satisfaction survey.)

Carglass® measures customer satisfaction in the Customer Contact Centre, in the Customer Delight Centres, and in the Customer Solution Centre (where the company deals with complaints). The company also measures the customer satisfaction of its insurance, lease and fleet partners. And it extends its customer satisfaction programme to its internal departments. Support departments are measured on how well they perform on their commitments.

Furthermore, the company has built a data warehouse and knowledge centre that analyses all the data and provides the departments with information on how to improve their operations. By gathering all the information in one integrated system, standardisation is possible throughout the Customer Contact Centre and the various Customer Delight Centres. All core processes are carefully described and documented, which allows for more learning and continuous improvement. It also allows for more flexibility as employees can move around the company more easily.

## Shareholder satisfaction

Shareholder satisfaction is the last block of the Carglass® 'Circle of Success'. So far, the financial results of Carglass® have been extraordinary. Revenues increased from 69.5 million Euro in 2000 to 168 million Euro in 2009. During this entire period,

**Exhibit 6a Carglass®'s overall customer-satisfaction scores**

| Year | % Overall Excellent | % Overall Good | % Overall Average | % Overall Poor |
|------|---------------------|----------------|-------------------|----------------|
| 2007 | 60.3 | 36.3 | 2.6 | 0.8 |
| 2008 | 63.3 | 33.5 | 2.3 | 0.8 |
| 2009 | 66.6 | 30.6 | 2.0 | 0.7 |

*Source*: Company information

Exhibit 6b **Detailed customer-satisfaction scores (Figures 2009)**

| | Overall | | | | Quality | | | | Information | | | | Maximum effort | | | | Appointment time | | | |
|---|---|---|---|---|---|---|---|---|---|---|---|---|---|---|---|---|---|---|---|---|
| | Exc% | Good% | Avg% | Poor% | Exc% | Good% | Avg% | Poor% | Exc% | Good% | Avg% | Poor% | Exc% | Good% | Avg% | Poor% | Exc% | Good% | Avg% | Poor% |
| Regio Noord-West | 64,3% | 33,5% | 1,4% | 0,7% | 63,8% | 30,9% | 4,0% | 1,3% | 58,0% | 40,1% | 1,7% | 0,2% | 62,6% | 35,9% | 1,3% | 0,1% | 71,6% | 26,3% | 1,9% | 0,2% |
| Regio Noord-Oost | 64,7% | 33,3% | 1,4% | 0,6% | 63,7% | 31,6% | 3,5% | 1,1% | 55,7% | 42,5% | 1,6% | 0,2% | 62,8% | 35,8% | 1,2% | 0,2% | 69,3% | 28,8% | 1,5% | 0,3% |
| Regio Centre | 68,5% | 28,4% | 2,5% | 0,6% | 65,9% | 27,8% | 4,7% | 1,6% | 60,7% | 36,3% | 2,5% | 0,5% | 65,3% | 32,1% | 2,1% | 0,5% | 76,2% | 21,8% | 1,6% | 0,4% |
| Regio Sud | 67,2% | 29,4% | 2,7% | 0,8% | 69,3% | 24,8% | 4,4% | 1,5% | 65,2% | 32,3% | 2,1% | 0,3% | 70,2% | 27,4% | 2,2% | 0,1% | 77,7% | 20,4% | 1,7% | 0,2% |
| Regio 24uur | 76,3% | 22,0% | 1,2% | 0,5% | 73,6% | 22,9% | 2,8% | 0,6% | 60,9% | 35,2% | 3,8% | 0,2% | 71,4% | 26,7% | 1,9% | 0,0% | 72,6% | 23,4% | 2,5% | 1,4% |

| | Friendly | | | | Punctual | | | | Professionalism | | | | Ease of contact | | | | Appointment location | | | |
|---|---|---|---|---|---|---|---|---|---|---|---|---|---|---|---|---|---|---|---|---|
| | Exc% | Good% | Avg% | Poor% | Exc% | Good% | Avg% | Poor% | Exc% | Good% | Avg% | Poor% | Exc% | Good% | Avg% | Poor% | Exc% | Good% | Avg% | Poor% |
| Regio Noord-West | 76,6% | 23,0% | 0,4% | 0,0% | 80,3% | 18,4% | 0,9% | 0,4% | 65,5% | 32,8% | 1,2% | 0,5% | 59,3% | 36,2% | 3,4% | 1,1% | 58,8% | 38,0% | 2,9% | 0,3% |
| Regio Noord-Oost | 75,5% | 23,8% | 0,5% | 0,1% | 78,3% | 20,1% | 1,1% | 0,4% | 64,8% | 33,6% | 1,3% | 0,3% | 59,3% | 36,2% | 3,2% | 1,3% | 58,6% | 38,2% | 2,7% | 0,5% |
| Regio Centre | 76,8% | 21,8% | 1,2% | 0,2% | 80,5% | 17,1% | 1,8% | 0,6% | 68,0% | 29,3% | 2,0% | 0,7% | 65,1% | 30,5% | 3,5% | 0,9% | 62,0% | 33,6% | 4,0% | 0,5% |
| Regio Sud | 79,9% | 18,7% | 1,1% | 0,2% | 80,3% | 17,6% | 1,5% | 0,5% | 72,7% | 25,2% | 1,6% | 0,5% | 67,6% | 27,7% | 3,7% | 0,9% | 60,6% | 32,3% | 5,8% | 1,3% |
| Regio 24uur | 82,1% | 16,3% | 1,4% | 0,2% | 77,1% | 19,9% | 2,5% | 0,5% | 77,0% | 21,5% | 1,1% | 0,3% | 65,9% | 28,6% | 3,8% | 1,7% | 56,9% | 35,4% | 6,2% | 1,6% |

Source: Company information

Exhibit 7 **Carglass®'s financial information**

|                              | *2000*  | *2004*  | *2007*   | *2009*   |
|------------------------------|---------|---------|----------|----------|
| Revenues (000 Euro)          | 69.507  | 92.839  | 132.632  | 168.006  |
| Operating profit (000 Euro)  | 3.241   | 4.860   | 6.607    | 12.455   |
| Profit after tax (000 Euro)  | 1.384   | 1.728   | 4.547    | 29.395*  |
| Profit margin (%)            | 4.66%   | 5.23%   | 4.98%    | 7.41%    |
| Return on equity (ROEat) (%) | 14.51%  | 13.58%  | 1.88%    | 11.58%   |

*In 2009, the company had exceptional revenues of more than 21 million Euro.
*Source:* Company information

revenues more than doubled! Operating profits have increased from 3.2 million Euro in 2000 to 12.5 million Euro in 2009. For more details on Carglass®'s financial figures, we refer to Exhibit 7.

## From measurement to motivation

### Performance measurement and incentives

Carglass® is very serious about measuring its performance towards its customers, employees and shareholders and has invested significantly to realise this. The company continuously measures all dimensions of its performance for these different stakeholders in line with the company's philosophy: *'From belief to knowledge. From knowledge to improvement.'*

Equally impressive is how the surveys and figures are utilised. The employees in the Customer Delight Centres receive a weekly report of the past results every Monday at 12 o'clock. These results are then discussed with their manager. Carglass® is very transparent about the scores of all Customer Delight Centres and managers see how well their centre has performed relative to the other Customer Delight Centres. Not only does the company report a weekly ranking, the scores are also used to calculate the team bonus of the Customer Delight Centres' employees.

The teams at the Customer Delight Centres are incentivised based on customer satisfaction scores and quality scores, and not on financial results. Quality is measured by looking at the number of jobs done in a particular time period and by subtracting the costs of complaint handling and reworks. Customer Delight Centres also measure resource utilisation; the resource utilisation index measures how much of the available time is productive and unproductive time. Employees are encouraged to find ways to increase the productive time. All this is graphically represented to make it clear for the employees how well they are doing and where there is room for improvement. Carglass® can also benefit from initiatives launched in Belron® as there is a dedicated corporate team of innovators, thinkers and doers who are all focused on driving technical standards and developing ground-breaking innovations in vehicle glass repair and replacement. An example is the group's development of cutting and lifting tools that do the job better, safer and more efficiently.

Carglass® also provides its Customer Delight Centres with all the complaints of the past week. The manager discusses these complaints and together with employees looks for ways to solve particular problems.

The other departments within Carglass® measure their performance as extensively as the Customer Delight Centres. Customer satisfaction and quality are the key components of the performance measurement system and the bonus system in all departments.

## Recognition and communication

Carglass® uses its performance measurement system not only to give bonuses but to identify best practices. The company recognises its best performers. COO Stefaan Hermans brings an energy box to the best-performing Customer Delight Centre every month. The energy box is a box full of candies and sweets. The best-performing team at the end of the year gets a VIP arrangement to one of the Formula 1 Grand Prix races. But it is the recognition of a top manager that makes people enthusiastic about this initiative.

Every department can also nominate a 'local hero', someone who has provided an exceptional service for a customer. That is how Carglass® recognises and stimulates service-orientated behaviour in the company.

Carglass® sets high standards for quality and customer satisfaction, but provides its employees with help. 'Get it right the first time' is part of the Carglass® culture, and this is made possible thanks to the use of well-thought out standards and efficient operating procedures. Best practices from one part of the company are transferred to other units in the organisation. Managers are responsible to 'take the rest to the best'. The company has set up cross-functional teams and organises cross trainings to ensure that team members have the knowledge and skills of the work of others. For example, the Customer Delight Centres that do not meet customer satisfaction or quality targets can ask for help from field coaches. Field coaches are former Customer Delight Centre managers that provide training on communication, sales, service orientation and quality to the entire Customer Delight Centre team. The company has set up a nine-week 'Smile on Tour' programme where the field coaches observe why the service is not up to standard. Together with the teams they then come up with a concrete action plan to improve their customer satisfaction scores. Carglass® has also organised a summer school programme to further develop the people from various departments in the organisation. The 'Business Plan Implementation Team', which consists of the managers of the executive committee and department heads, plans and discusses activities that span the entire organisation.

In addition, Carglass® organises several national and international competitions. The 'Best of Carglass® Belux' is a competition organised every two years between the service technicians of the 43 Customer Delight Centres. Jury members include Carglass® and Belron® employees; delegates of the insurance and leasing partners are invited to watch the competition. More than 50 per cent of the technicians participate in this competition. The best technician then represents Carglass® Belux in the international 'Best of Belron®' competition, a competition that is also organised every two years. (It is worth mentioning that four out of the six winners of the 'Best of Belron®' competition were from Carglass® Belux.) There are significant financial rewards for the winner. For Carglass®, this competition shows that the company is very serious about delivering a top-quality service. And for the participating technicians, it is a fantastic occasion to learn.

During the yearly roadshows, the top management communicates the results of the past year as well as the goals for the following year. It introduces the new strategy projects, and features some of the best Carglass® performers of the last year. This event is important to create momentum to celebrate the successes and to inspire employees to push even harder the next year.

## Raising the bar

But with all those fantastic results, Jean-Paul Teyssen wondered whether he could push the organisation much further in customer satisfaction and employee satisfaction. With customer-satisfaction scores of 97 per cent and employee-satisfaction scores of 96 per cent, what was there to improve? Did it really make sense to try to achieve satisfaction scores of 100 per cent? And, more importantly, if there was nothing to improve, would that mark the end of the company's exceptional culture?

## Notes on the case

1   Rangarajan, D. and Lubner, G. (2011) 'Delivering exceptional service: The Belron® experience', Vlerick Leuven Gent Management School Case Study, VLGMS-1105-C, p. 3–4.

2   Ibid., p. 4.

3   Coleman, M. (2011) 'Growing leaders grows profits', Blog posted on 15 March: http://www.hrneurope.com/blog/?author=2%2Fpage%2F2&paged=3 (website accessed 6 August, 2012).

4   Hermans, H. (2009) 'Scherven brengen Carglass® geluk', *Bizz*, May, pp. 38–41.

**4**

# HARTFORD BUILDING SOCIETY: TO MEASURE, OR NOT TO MEASURE?[1]

### Pietro Micheli and Haley Beer

## Jane's dilemma

It was 6pm and Jane Gardner, Director of Strategy at Hartford Building Society, was ready to leave the office. She had spent the afternoon preparing for the quarterly performance meeting with all the Society's directors tomorrow. These meetings, which should be central to guiding the Society's strategic direction, to Jane often felt like a formulaic rehearsal of what everybody already knew. Yet, in the last two to three years, there had been a serious attempt to match the organisation's performance management system (PMS) with its strategic ambitions. Over several months, the Society had progressively removed all performance league tables, personal incentives and numerical targets from its branches. The Society's performance mantra had become 'sales through service' and rather than basing 'performance' on the achievement of quantitative figures, the 'success' of all parts of the organisation, all teams and all individuals, was now judged on the basis of how decisions and behaviours were aligned with Hartford's core values. In fact, most traditional data (e.g. number of mortgages sold, number of new savings accounts opened, footfall traffic in branches, etc.) was still collected, but it was not made visible to employees in order to avoid potential distortions in their performance. As a method of managing performance, it had been a radical change and a rare move for a relatively conservative financial services business.

As Jane was leaving, Adam Davies, a branch manager, put his head round her door, obviously eager to speak.

*'Jane, I know you have the performance meeting with the senior team tomorrow. I'm not sure whether this will come up, but for us working in the branches – and I heard in the call centre it's the same – there's a feeling that we're losing focus on the company objectives. We say we are a 'members come first' organisation that needs to make decisions and promote behaviours that are 'in accordance with our values', yet, when my people question me on how to do their job better, or how well the Hartford is performing, I struggle to know what to tell them. We give the employees plenty of time by being on the floor with them and hosting monthly group discussions. But, to be honest, without visibility of any performance information I myself don't know what I'm meant to be changing on a day-to-day basis.'*

Jane was taken aback by what seemed to be this strategic confusion from an experienced branch manager. Would it be worthwhile to address this point tomorrow? Or would the CEO reply with his usual statement: *'other businesses may have numbers, we have things to do first'*? Yet Adam's confusion had raised some important points. Is the 'soft-touch' PMS approach being used at Hartford really working? Also, are all employee voices captured? And is this lack of formal systems really a good thing?

## Financial services industry

The financial services industry was heavily regulated and bound by many risk and compliance standards due to the sensitive nature of guarding people's money. However, the recent media coverage over such things as the mis-selling of payment protection insurance (PPI), the extravagance of large corporate bonuses for bank executives and the global financial recession, has led to increased public distrust for players in the field. Financial institutions had to put considerable effort into meeting government regulatory standards and maintaining a favourable image with the public. However, the landscape of service delivery within the industry was changing alongside technological advancements and capabilities such as internet and mobile banking. People increasingly did not want to handle cash and visit a bank branch to the same extent; instead, they would prefer banking processes to occur quickly, efficiently and securely from behind an online device of choice. In the UK, approximately 36 million people were using the internet daily – up to 50 per cent of those individuals for the purpose of online banking.[2] Furthermore, entirely new markets such as social enterprise and social impact investing were emerging that required tailored financial services.[3] Such impending changes meant that most financial services firms, including the Hartford, were considering how its services would fit in to the potentially new market, and how best to capitalise on the evolving technological interfaces for service delivery. In addition, how should they attract new and younger customers and employees?

## Hartford Building Society – where 'members come first'

Hartford Building Society had been a 'mutual', or member-owned, financial institution specialising in mortgages and savings accounts since it was founded 80 years ago. With more than 2.2 million members, 2,300 employees and 120 branches across the country, the Hartford had a significant presence in the UK's financial services industry and had worked hard to gain the respect and trust of its client base. Members' preferences and interests drove strategy, decisions and actions within the organisation. The Hartford culture had been built on five core values: care, kindness, integrity, fairness and transparency. Its aim was to provide all members with a great experience and continuously refine its internal processes so that it could offer competitive mortgage rates and higher savings account interest rates. In the words of one senior manager, 'we stick to the things we know how to do', and 'we feel right not doing anything too exciting'. This strategy had proved successful for the Society during the 2007–2010 financial recession when, by focusing its energies on improving service delivery, it had managed to sustain steady levels of business. During that period, numerous building societies that 'demutualised' (converted their status to that of a regular joint stock company) for the sake of a cash infusion failed operationally in their transition to a regular bank.[4]

After the financial turbulence of 2007–10, Hartford had retained its simple strategy based on straightforward mortgage and savings products, and a good physical 'high street' presence thanks to its vast network of branches. However, the Society was also aware that the landscape of the financial industry was shifting. Footfall traffic to the branches was decreasing rapidly, and the Society's customer service-based strategy had done little to prevent further decline. Its image of a solid and reliable organisation also risked turning into a 'stale' and 'boring' one (as recent customer feedback demonstrated). Also, the internal growth in the number of employees had made it increasingly difficult to embed, communicate and deliver its mission of 'members come first'. Besides this change to the PMS, the Society's strategy had changed little, but the top management team was conscious that major decisions over strategic direction and innovation could not be delayed for long.

## Better with or without the 'Golden Thread'?

Up until the changes to the PMS the Hartford had worked with what they called the 'Golden Thread'. This was a process by which objectives, targets and measures were consistently cascaded to the different organisational levels. The 'Golden Thread' procedure had started as a mainly top-down process, where directors would articulate a strategy and then implement it throughout the organisation. However, once the system was up and running, a more bottom-up approach was promoted: employees could give feedback, make suggestions and even change aspects of the system. On the whole, the 'Golden Thread' seemed to function fairly well. It was clear and it worked on a day-to-day level because there was a clear line from directors to frontline staff, and employees could link their performance to the organisation's results. But it did have problems. It could be overly formal and detailed. More seriously, it could promote dysfunctional behaviours such as 'gaming' the system and 'managing the system not the business'. In branches people were getting obsessed with personal targets, to the detriment of both customer satisfaction and collaboration between employees.

So, it was decided to change the PMS, scrapping the formal elements of the 'Golden Thread' system, at least at lower levels of the organisation. As the Director of Product and Proposition told Jane: '*weak managers use numbers, because they're not prepared to have conversations*'. Overall strategic achievement and direction at the Hartford was monitored, evaluated and reported at the quarterly performance meetings, as well as through team discussion meetings, employee observations, individual performance appraisals and regular one-to-one discussions. Formal measures were still being used to some extent but, as one manager put it, '*Who has got the time to go through 100-page reports?*' At these performance meetings, directors discussed the performance of their departments to check that all departments were contributing to the organisation's performance objectives (see the Appendix). However, there was a feeling that performance meetings were mostly a routine check, and beyond the quarterly meetings it did not seem that the documents and key high-level figures were ever shared with lower-level employees. There was also some evidence that employees had stopped wanting to approach managers with ideas. It was claimed that most were turned down on the spot due to their 'lack of fit' with the simple business model. Samantha, a junior branch colleague, told Jane:

> '*I approached my branch manager about an idea I had for mobile product development but all he said was "that is not something the organisation does". I had only brought it up as a suggestion as some friends of mine and I were discussing how we would like to see the banking industry evolve to better meet our needs. If the Hartford is truly all about its members, should it not be considering the up-and-coming generation of customers?*'

Jane wondered whether the executive team was receiving enough bottom-up feedback. Maybe they were making decisions too heavily based on their top-down perspective. Somehow, paradoxically, although a lighter formal system seems to have reduced certain negative behaviours, it had also reduced employees' capacity to provide feedback and suggestions. This was crucial. How could the Hartford retain its 'members come first' ethos if the members began to have different needs that the company was unaware of? Furthermore, was the company alienating the younger generation of workers with its 'slow and steady' culture? Speaking to several colleagues in the organisation, Jane found that directors and senior managers seemed to have clarity around the corporate strategy and objectives, and were proud of the behaviours in their respective departments. However, lower-level employees were complaining that irregular feedback sessions and lack of more structured targets and information hindered them seeing how to advance within the organisation. As one junior colleague from the call centre said to Jane: *'I think the management should make more time for us, because they can't expect us to consistently achieve these goals unless we're being encouraged and they're being monitored. Otherwise, you don't know where you've fallen behind, do you?'*

## 'Sales through service'?

Through her investigations, Jane uncovered several odd patterns, which further highlighted that the Hartford may need to reconsider its performance management system. In the call centre, for example, profitability and employee satisfaction were seemingly negatively correlated. When call volume was high and savings account-openings and mortgage sales were therefore high, motivation and morale within the centre actually decreased, attendance rates dropped and higher amounts of attrition occurred. The head of the call centre explained to Jane:

> *'The issue stems from the intangible nature of the performance management system. During periods of escalated workloads managers have less time to hold one-on-one meetings with staff. And although we attempt to allocate four hours of training development to each member of staff each month, throughout busy periods this time is also often reduced. At these points where there is not as much time for passing encouragement or informal discussion about progress and areas of weakness, employees start to feel lost as to what to aim for next.'*

Within the branches, this year only 3 per cent of new mortgage sales occurred in-store, with the remainder coming in through intermediaries and telephone or online sales. In the previous year there had been 350,000 new member-contacts, but 170,000 of those occurred via the telephone and another 150,000 were online contacts. Given this, the extent of the branch operation was considered to be in jeopardy by some managers. Other banks, such as IG Direct, were increasingly managing to deliver service with less person-to-person contact, yet within the Hartford there was not much energy being focused on exploring alternatives to traditional branch services. Instead, the focus was on improving branch service. From the point the customer walked through the door until they left, there were specific procedures in place to ensure they received the best possible service and the most robust information with which to make decisions. When Jane asked the director of branch network what he intended to do about the diminishing foot traffic numbers he was pessimistic about change: *'People know what they need to do and will just keep on ploughing on. Trying to introduce innovations here is like pushing porridge uphill.'*

## Back to Jane's dilemma

Jane's role was to monitor how well the PMS was helping Hartford communicate and achieve company objectives and goals, and whether the system could support future changes in strategy. The Society's conservative, yet safe, business model that had been in place for years at the Hartford was maybe appropriate during a time of market instability, but now the financial industry was changing and Jane was concerned that the Hartford would not be in a position to adapt with it. Overall, letting go of targets, personal rewards and league tables in branches had led to a decrease of dysfunctional behaviours and an increase in teamwork. However, it had also left the executive team in a position where 'routine processes are in the dark'. In other words, the informal nature of monitoring and reporting performance based on 'values' had left the 'business' side of banking overlooked at the lower levels. Whilst the top management teams collected data and sat comfortably in their position of strategic 'knowing', lower level employees struggled to see where they fitted in to the corporate strategy and had little opportunity to contribute to strategic developments. Jane increasingly believed that this was a major weakness that would need to be addressed. If top management was not aware what was happening on the frontline they would not be able to respond adequately to the changing demands of a younger workforce and of new target markets. How could they both retain current customers and attract new ones? As the head of product and propositions had said to Jane, they did not want to be *selling typewriters when everyone else is selling laptops and tablets*.

Jane looked again at the bulky performance report that all directors received two days before the quarterly meetings. Was it really useful? And what could the organisation do to its performance management system that would balance the need to drive its 'members come first' culture with the need to provide strategic direction and understand the health of the business?

## Appendix

### Hartford's performance review document

Hartford has identified the following 5 strategic goals. Each department underpins these strategic goals with key performance objectives.

| Strategic goals | Functional performance objectives |
|---|---|
| **1. Members come first** | – Listen to the members<br>– Focus on each customer's particular situation<br>– Collect customer feedback |
| **2. Sales through service** | – Focus on service delivery (instead of product delivery)<br>– Influence behaviours aligned with core values<br>– Employee engagement |
| **3. Do what we do best** | – Improve current process efficiencies<br>– Offer competitive mortgage rates and high savings accounts rates |
| **4. Fairness** | – No personal incentives<br>– Standard procedures in place for product delivery<br>– Standard performance appraisals |
| **5. Transparency** | – Adhere to risk and regulatory standards<br>– Advise clients appropriately on risks associated to products |

Managers should insert business, unit or functional objectives prior to cascading to employees.

## Questions

1 Do you agree with the executive team's decision to scrap league tables, personal targets and incentives in branches?

2 How can the Hartford keep an informal approach to performance management while providing greater clarity to employees?

3 Could the Hartford benefit from introducing a strategy map? What would it look like?

4 Which performance measures should the Hartford focus on?

5 Provide feedback and recommendations on how the Hartford can strengthen its performance review (see Appendix) – that is, the clarity of strategic goals and validity of objectives.

6 What can the Hartford do from a performance management point of view to keep being true to its values while becoming more explicitly business-focused?

## Notes on the case

1 Pietro Micheli and Haley Beer of Warwick Business School prepared this case. It is based on a real enterprise and is intended for the purposes of class discussion, but is not necessarily intended to illustrate either good or bad management practice.

2 'Internet Access Households and Individuals 2013 – Internet activities by year 2007-2013', Office for National Statistics: https://docs.google.com/a/mail.wbs.ac.uk/spreadsheet /ccc?key=0At6CC4x_yBnMdHdsRWhkQld3dms5U1pHMzlWUW03a1E#gid=1, retrieved 10 August 2013.

3 'Banks and Social Enterprise': http://www.theguardian.com/social-enterprise-network/2013 /jul/22/banks-and-social-enterprise, retrieved 8 August 2013.

4 'The History of Building Societies': http://www.bsa.org.uk/consumer/factsheets/100009.htm, retrieved 9 August 2013.

# 5 OCADO VERSUS TESCO.COM

Valérie Keller-Birrer

By 2009 online retailing had become an important channel for many product categories. However, it still represented only a relatively small part of the grocery business. Brick-and-mortar grocery retailers found it challenging to run a successful online business: despite category knowledge, they had to develop a completely new business model. Still, a few grocery retailers such as Albertson's in the US, Auchan and Carrefour in France, and Tesco and Sainsbury's in the UK managed to successfully operate an online service in parallel with their physical stores. Tesco, in particular, was often cited as an example of a retailer running a profitable online business and was the biggest online grocery retailer in the world.[1]

Several purely online start-up grocers were also launched around the world during the internet boom. However, few succeeded. Exceptions were LeShop in Switzerland and Ocado in the UK. Ocado was an internet grocery retailer headquartered in Hatfield, Hertfordshire. The company was founded by three former investment bankers in early 2000 and rolled out in early 2002. By 2009 Ocado had grown from its original three founders to over 3,000 employees and was just about to become profitable.

The challenge online grocers faced was in developing a business model that would allow them to sell groceries over the internet in significant volumes, at reasonable prices and still make a profit. The brick-and-mortar supermarkets and the start-up grocers competed with one another, but each had a different business model for their online operations. The general opinion was that the brick-and-mortar grocers had a more sustainable model than start-ups; however, Ocado was challenging that assumption. Had Ocado found a new way of making pure online retailing a profitable business? Or was Tesco CEO Terry Leahy right in saying that Ocado's business was not sustainable as food retailing had such low margins, and established supermarkets' online businesses were a more profitable way of selling and delivering groceries?

## The UK online grocery market

The UK online grocery market was estimated to be about £2.4 billion* in 2007, growing by nearly one-third that year.[2] Though it could still be characterised as a niche of the retail grocery market, accounting for at most 2 per cent to 3 per cent of total UK grocery sales, it was growing over six times as fast as the market as a whole. The market was forecast to more than double over the next couple of years to reach £6.9 billion in 2014.[3]

---

*£1 = US$1.94, €1.50

Source: Case Study CS.8 from Ocado Versus Tesco, IMD, 3-0323 (Keller-Birrer, V. and Tsikriktsis, N.), Copyright ©2010 by IMD International Institute for Management Development, Lausanne, Switzerland. Not to be used or reproduced without prior written permission directly from IMD.

The online grocery market was dominated by four of the UK's leading supermarket chains – Tesco, Sainsbury's, Asda and Waitrose – and by a fifth supplier, Ocado. Tesco was the market leader, with an estimated share of 49 per cent of the online grocery market, followed by Ocado which captured about 14 per cent of the market, in line with Asda and Sainsbury's.[4]

Demand for online groceries had been explosive, driven by increased service accessibility, thanks to increased broadband penetration and the steady expansion of online grocers' geographical coverage. Nevertheless, few consumers purchased their groceries online. A consumer research study conducted in 2009 showed that less than 18 per cent of customers ordered groceries online at least once a year, while the proportion of regular users was about 6 per cent.[5]

## Ocado

### Background

Ocado's annual turnover in 2008 was £338.5[6] million. It was growing, but was still relatively small. While the company was EBITDA* positive – generating cash on top of its £35 million fixed costs – it still had a net loss of £33 million in 2007. Although Ocado was an independent business, the three founders retained a 22 per cent share of the firm and 24.1 per cent was held by the John Lewis Partnership pension fund, which also owned the upmarket Waitrose supermarket chain that operated mainly in the Greater London area. Interestingly, Waitrose had its own delivery operation in London, where it competed with Ocado.[7]

### Operations

Ocado used what was known in the industry as a centralised distribution model. The company was based in a purpose-built 11.5 hectare Customer Fulfilment Centre (CFC). The four-story warehouse, which cost £80 million, housed the world's largest order storage and retrieval system.

All of the orders were received via the website www.ocado.com and processed in the computerised warehouse. Ocado believed that it could pick customers' orders at the rate of 300 items per hour (roughly three times the rate achieved by in-store pickers at Tesco or Safeway).[8] At its maximum capacity, it was capable of handling the same order volume as 25 supermarkets. A network of five regional trans-shipment points and a fleet of 70 double-decker trucks supported the CFC. Ocado operated a fleet of over 500 specially designed Mercedes delivery vans, equipped with satellite navigation systems.

Figure 1 **Key facts about Ocado operations**

| |
|---|
| 12,000 orders processed and delivered every day |
| 12 million items processed each day by the computer |
| 60 per cent of British households serviced |

---

*EBITDA = earnings before interest, taxes, depreciation, and amortisation

The whole picking process was computerised. Groceries were put in colour-coded boxes and routed to the delivery trucks over a maze of conveyor belts. The trucks then either went directly to home delivery or to one of the trans-shipment points, where the customer service team took over and delivered the goods in smaller trucks.

### Value

Ocado's selling proposition was *'to deliver world-class groceries and award-winning service straight into your kitchen'*.

Its product offer was focused on quality and included own-brand groceries from the Waitrose supermarket chain, renowned for its high-quality products, as well as a selection of name-brand groceries and other items including flowers, toys and magazines.

Ocado promised a one-hour delivery slot, a substantial improvement over the two-hour slot offered by competitors. It saw home delivery as an opportunity to further differentiate itself from competitors by offering a state-of-the-art service. There was a delivery charge of £1.49 to £6.49 on small orders (minimum order was £40), but delivery was free for orders over £75 during time slots with lower demand.

The prices of branded goods at Ocado were comparable with those of brick-and-mortar supermarkets. Waitrose own-label products were sold at an internet-only price, which was lower than the retail price in Waitrose shops. On 12 March 2008, Ocado announced a Tesco price match and guaranteed to match the prices of over 5,000 branded goods with Tesco's cheapest pricing format.[9]

### Marketing

Marketing efforts were focused on the company's target customer: a woman with one or more children under 15 in a household in which both spouses work. A key benefit for these customers was avoiding crowded stores at rush hour and the resultant 'trolley rage'.[10]

The grocer rolled out its service by focusing on its target group in fairly dense geographic areas in order to facilitate delivery. Initially, in order to best reach its target group and build its user base, Ocado preferred direct marketing over mass media.

Once Ocado was better established, it also focused on mass media, in particular TV and radio ads, to further build awareness and usage. Ocado's communication strategy was to tell customers that '... *they can have the best of everything – superior and convenient service, premium quality, accuracy that rivals shopping in a store and really competitive prices*'.

The company was active on the environmental front and had managed to lower its carbon emissions to the point where it could claim that shopping with Ocado was greener than walking to the supermarket. It used this as a selling point in its ad campaigns and the claim was endorsed by Greenstone, the carbon management consultancy.[11]

## Tesco

### Background

Founded in 1919, Tesco was the UK's biggest retailer and the third-largest retailer in the world. In 2009 the group's turnover rose to £59.4 billion, with £2.9 billion profits.

Tesco had more than 470,000 employees and owned 4,331 stores in 14 different countries – 2,306 of them in the UK.[12]

Tesco started its online grocery delivery service in 1996 and Tesco.com was launched in 2000. It was the first retailer to go online in the UK and the first retail grocer in the world to offer a robust home shopping service. Tesco managed to develop a successful and profitable online business with a relatively small investment of €30 million. With a turnover estimated at about £1.2 million, sales growth of 30 per cent, an operating margin of 5 per cent and a profit of £131 million, Tesco.com was well established as the UK's leading online grocer by 2009.[13]

## Operations

Tesco chose to keep its home delivery operation simple by using existing stores as distribution centres rather than building a new warehouse dedicated to its online business. Customer orders were sent to the server computer of the store nearest the customer's home and assigned to a van that would make the delivery. Then the orders were sent on to a 'picking trolley' manned by a Tesco employee or 'picker'. Each trolley was equipped with a touch-pad computer with shelf-identifier software that planned efficient routes through the store and scanned each item to verify that it was the one that had been ordered. Orders were then assembled in the back of the store and delivered by van. Tesco's pickers prepared around 250,000 orders per week from 300 stores in the UK.

## Value proposition

Tesco.com offered a wide range of food and non-food products, including books, CDs, DVDs, home appliances and clothing. Like Ocado, it used various web functions to make online shopping easier.

The prices of goods ordered from the website were the same as those in the physical stores, and in-store discounts, promotions and special offers were also available to online shoppers. Home delivery of groceries, seven days a week, was seen as a value-added service and Tesco charged between £3 and £6 for each delivery, depending on the day of the week and the two-hour time slot selected by the customer.

The company's fleet of delivery trucks consisted only of electric vans. In order to cut down on pollution and waste, Tesco tried to reduce its use of plastic bags for home deliveries, and customers could choose a 'no bag option', in which groceries were delivered in stackable, reusable plastic trays.

## Case discussion questions

1 As a customer, what do you want from an online grocery store? How do Ocado and Tesco.com perform on these dimensions?

2 Ocado delivers from a central, dedicated warehouse straight to the customer, while Tesco uses existing stores to deliver to nearby customers. What are the pros and cons of each model?

3 Does consumers' behaviour differ when shopping for groceries online vs. offline? If yes, how?

4 Should Tesco worry about Ocado? If, yes, what should Tesco do?

Exhibit 1 **Key data overview Ocado vs. Tesco.com**

|  | *OCADO* | *Tesco.com* |
|---|---|---|
| **Financial information** | | |
| Turnover | £338 million | £1.2 billion |
| Sales growth | 17% | 30% |
| Market share | 14% (50% in London) | 49% |
| Profit (Loss) (2009) | (£32.6 million) | £131 million |
| Operating margin | n.a. | 5.7% |
| **Operations data** | | |
| No. of sites used for picking | 1 | 300 |
| No. of employees | 3,000 | Tesco.com n.a. Tesco UK: 286,394 |
| No. of items picked per hour | 300 | 120 |
| Delivery price | £1.49 to £6.49 Free for orders > £75 | £3 to £6 |
| No. of deliveries per week | 56,500 | 250,000 |
| No. of delivery vans | 500 | 1,800 |
| Delivery coverage | 60% of UK households | 95% of UK households |
| Areas covered | South England, Midlands, North West England, South Coast and most of Yorkshire | 95% of UK |
| **Customer data** | | |
| Registered users | 1 million | n.a. |
| Active users | 150,000 | n.a. |
| Average amount spent per order | £117 | £90 |

*Sources:*

Davidson, A. 'The MT Interview: The Ocado Boys', *Management Today*, 8 June 2008. Tesco's Financial Report 2009.

Authors' estimates: Tesco.com sales are estimated based on number deliveries per week times average amount spent.

## Notes on the case

1  Enders, A. and Jelassi, T. (2009) 'Leveraging Multi-channel Retailing: The Experience of Tesco.com.' *MIS Quarterly Executive.*

2  www.ocado.com; media information: http://www.ocado.com/content/miscellany/pdfs/media_pack.pdf (accessed 11 January 2010).

3  Palmer, D. (2009) 'Online Grocery Still Treading Water', *Australian Food News – Thought for Food.* 30 September: www.ausfoodnews.com (accessed 16 October 2009).

4  Research and Markets, 'E-Commerce: The Internet Grocery Market Assessment 2009'.

5  Research and Markets, 'E-Commerce: The Internet Grocery Market Assessment 2009'.

6  'Ocado Delivers "First Ever" Profit for Year', Just-food.com, 7 October 2009.

7  Davidson, A. (2008) 'The MT Interview: The Ocado Boys.' *Management Today*, 8 June.

8  Delaney-Klinger, K., Boyer, K.K. and Frohlich, M. (2003) 'The Return of Online Grocery Shopping: A Comparative Analysis of Webvan and Tesco's Operational Methods', *The TQP Magazine*, 15(2).

9 www.ocado.com; media information: http://www.ocado.com/content/miscellany/pdfs/media_pack.pdf (accessed 11 January 2010).

10 Boyer, K.K. and Frohlich, M. (2002). 'Ocado: An Alternative Way to Bridge the Last Mile in Grocery Home Delivery'. Michigan State University, MI.

11 www.ocado.com

12 Tesco 2009 Financial Report. Tesco's fiscal year 2008/2009 ended on 28 February 2009.

13 Tesco 2009 Financial Report.

# 6  ZARA'S OPERATING MODEL[1]

## Michael Lewis and Nigel Slack

A Coruña in northern Spain was once renowned mainly for its food, beaches and surfing. But it then became famous for another reason. It was there that Amancio Ortega Gaona, now the world's third-richest man, founded the wildly successful fashion company, Inditex, which became more commonly known by its oldest and biggest brand, Zara. Back in 1963, Amancio Ortega started his company to manufacture women's pyjamas and lingerie products for garment wholesalers. In 1975, after one customer cancelled a large order, the firm opened a retail outlet in A Coruña. This Zara store was popular, and during the next 10 years others opened in all major Spanish cities. The Inditex corporate structure was created in 1985, and in December 1988 the first overseas Zara store opened in Porto, Portugal, followed shortly by New York in 1989 and Paris in 1990. By September 2013, Inditex had eight different business formats (including brands such as Zara Homes, Massimo Dutti, Bershka, Stradivarius, Oysho, Pull & Bear and Uterqüe), 6,104 stores in 86 countries (including 1,751 Zara stores) and employed 128,000 people. Each of these brands was responsible for its own stores, ordering system, designers, factories, subcontractors, suppliers, distribution centres and systems, sharing only core corporate services such as legal and finance. But they all followed a similar operating model that focused on speed to market. There was even some degree of competition between them. Zara, the largest Inditex division, accounted for around two thirds of total Inditex sales. In 2012 the group had a consolidated turnover of €2.3 billion.

Although initially a Zara store was simply intended to be an outlet for cancelled orders, a more fundamental lesson was also learnt: there were benefits of having, in the words of one Inditex executive, *'five fingers touching the factory and five touching the customer'*. This 'virtual' vertical integration gave significant control over the production/supply process – all the way from loom to shop floor without owning all of the production assets. Today, Zara is able to offer cutting-edge fashion at affordable prices because its operating model exerts control over almost the entire garment supply chain (retailing, design, purchasing and logistics).

## Retailing

At the heart of the Zara operating model, the stores (almost all of which were owned and operated by Zara) were located in expensive prime-retail locations, selected after extensive market research. Inside, much of the selling space was left empty in order to create a pleasant, spacious and uncluttered shopping environment. The layout of the stores, the furniture, and even the window displays were all designed at A Coruña, and a 'flying team' from headquarters was usually dispatched to a new site to set up the store. Location, traffic and layout were crucial for Zara because it spent relatively little on advertising. A typical Zara store had women, men's and children's sections, with a manager in charge of each. Women's wear accounted for more than half of sales, with the rest equally divided between men's wear and children's wear. The store manager was usually also the head of the women's section. Zara placed a great deal of emphasis on training its sales force and strongly emphasised internal promotion. Store employee remuneration was based on a combination of salary and a bonus derived from overall store sales. Although store managers were responsible for the 'profit and loss' of their respective stores, A Coruña controlled prices, transfer costs and even a certain amount of merchandising and product ordering. In practice, the critical performance measures for the store managers related to the precision of their sales forecasts (communicated through the ordering process) and sales growth. A simple yet key measure followed by senior managers was the rate of improvement of daily sales from year to year – for example, sales on the third Wednesday of June 2014 compared to the third Wednesday of June 2013.

To its customers, Zara offered fashionably exclusive (yet low-cost) products. Individual stores held very low levels of inventory – typically only a few pieces of each item – and this could mean that a store's entire stock was on display. Indeed, it was not unusual to find empty racks by the end of a day's trading. This created an additional incentive for customers to buy on the spot (because if a customer chose to wait, the item might be sold out and may never be made again). This allowed Zara both to carry less overall inventory and to have fewer unsold items that had to be discounted in end-of-season sales. Items that remained on the shelves for more than two or three weeks were normally taken out of the store and shipped either to other stores in the same country or (rarely) back to Spain. In an industry where discounting meant that the average product fetched only around 60 per cent of its full price, Zara often managed to collect almost 90 per cent. However, this approach meant that stores were completely reliant on regular and rapid replenishment of new designs. Stores were required to place their orders at pre-designated times and received shipments twice per week. If a store missed its ordering deadline, it had to wait for the next scheduled delivery. Zara also minimised the risk of oversupply by keeping production volumes low at the beginning of the season, reacting quickly to the orders and new trends that emerged during the season. The industry average pre-season inventory commitment – the level of production and procurement in the supply chain in, say, late July for the autumn/winter season – ranged from 45 per cent to 60 per cent of anticipated sales. At Zara it was only 15–20 per cent. The 'in-season commitments' at Zara were 40–50 per cent, whereas the industry average ranged from almost nothing to a maximum of 20 per cent.

## Design

Zara designed all its own products. It took its design inspiration from the prevailing global trends in the fashion market, trade fairs, discotheques, catwalks, magazines and, particularly important, its customers by using extensive information received from its stores. At its headquarters, the 'commercial team' comprised designers, market specialists (also known as 'country managers') and buyers. Together they produced designs for approximately 180,000 items per year, from which about 10,000 were selected for production. Unlike their industry peers, these teams worked both on next season's designs and, simultaneously and continuously, also updated the current season's designs. Women's wear, men's wear and children's wear designers sat in different halls. In each of these big open spaces designers, organised by products (e.g. dresses, T-shirts and denim, etc.), worked in the perimeter areas of the room. Country managers and the 'buyers', who sourced and planned production, sat around a long table in the middle area. This layout was designed to encourage spontaneous meetings and an air of informality and openness. The firm tried hard to encourage a collegial and dynamic atmosphere among its young team, with no design 'prima donnas'. Designers produced sketches by hand and discussed them with colleagues. The sketches were then redrawn using CAD, where further changes and adjustments for better matching of weaves, textures and colours, etc. were made. Before moving further through the process, it was necessary to determine whether the design could be produced and sold at a profit. The next step was to make a sample – often completed in the sample-making shop in one corner of each hall.

Market specialists had responsibility for dealing with specific stores. As experienced employees, who had often been store managers themselves, they emphasised establishing personal relationships with the managers of 'their' stores. They were in constant contact, especially by phone or Skype, discussing sales, orders, new lines and other matters. Equally, stores relied heavily on these discussions with market specialists before finalising orders. Augmenting their extensive phone conversations, store managers were supplied with hand-held tablet devices to facilitate the rapid and accurate exchange of market data. Final decisions concerning what products to make, when and in what volumes were normally made collectively by the relevant groups of designers, market specialists and buyers, and after the decision was taken the buyers oversaw the total order fulfilment process: planning procurement and production requirements, monitoring warehouse inventories, allocating production to various factories and third-party suppliers and keeping track of shortages and oversupplies.

## Production/sourcing

Unlike most competitors, Zara sourced around half of its products – mainly the most fashionable – from its own network of 22 factories in Spain, Portugal and Morocco. Ten of its own factories were located around the company's headquarters near Arteixo. These factories generally worked a single shift and were managed as independent profit centres. The rest of its products were procured from outside suppliers. Around a third of this volume came from Eastern Europe and Turkey. The more 'basic' products were sourced from Asia. With its relatively large and stable base of orders, Zara was a preferred customer for almost all its suppliers. The make or buy decisions were usually made by the procurement and production planners. The key criteria for making this decision were the required levels of speed and expertise, cost-effectiveness and the availability of sufficient capacity. If the buyers could not obtain desired prices, delivery terms and quality from Zara factories, they were free to look elsewhere. For its in-house production, Zara obtained much of its fabric supply from another Inditex-owned subsidiary, Comditel. Over half of these fabrics were purchased undyed to allow faster response to mid-season colour changes.

After in-house CAD-controlled piece cutting, Zara used subcontractors for all sewing operations. The subcontractors themselves often collected the bagged cut pieces, together with the appropriate components (such as buttons and zips) in small trucks. There were some 200 sewing subcontractors in very close proximity to A Coruña (in the Galicia region). Many worked exclusively for Zara, which closely monitored their operations to ensure quality, compliance with labour laws and, above all else, adherence to the production schedule. Subcontractors then brought back the sewn items to the same factory, where each piece was inspected during ironing (by machine and by hand). Finished products were then placed in plastic bags with proper labels and sent to the distribution centre. A system of automated rails carrying garments through tunnels connected the 10 factories in A Coruña to the distribution centre. Completed products procured from outside suppliers were also sent directly to the distribution centre.

## Distribution

Speed was clearly an overriding concern for Zara logistics. As one senior manager put it, '*For us, distance is not measured in kilometres, but in time.*' Contractors, using trucks bearing Zara's name, picked up the merchandise at, for example, A Coruña and delivered it either directly to Zara's stores in Europe or, for items to be shipped by air, to the airport at A Coruña (10 kilometres away) or a larger airport in Santiago (70 kilometres away). The trucks ran to published schedules (like a bus timetable), which made it easy to plan shipments without making special demands for transportation. Typically, stores in Europe received their orders in 24 hours, in the United States in 48 hours and in Japan in 48 to 72 hours. Compared to similar companies in the industry, shipments were almost flawless – 98.9 per cent accurate. Zara's first large distribution centre was located near A Coruña and had 400,000 square metres of storage space and about 1,000 permanent staff, who worked there on four shifts, five days a week. During peak-demand periods it added additional temporary workers and more shifts. This distribution centre used some of the most sophisticated and up-to-date automated systems available. Up until 2003, almost all Zara products passed through this distribution centre. However, continued expansion of the company necessitated the addition of new distribution centres. When Zara announced that it would build an additional distribution centre in Zaragoza (Spain) it caused some comments because the existing distribution centre was working at only 50 per cent capacity. Costing €120 million, the 390,000-square metre Zaragoza distribution centre was completed in October 2003. It was allocated the distribution of selected women garments for the entire world market. In 2011, Zara opened a third major distribution centre, also with 390,000 square metres of storage space, in Meco, near Madrid. This one specialised in children's garments and online sales. Zara also had three other small distribution centres – in Brazil, Argentina and Mexico – as well as engaged even smaller ones that operated like 'docking stations' for trans-shipping deliveries in some of the Asian and North and South American regions. Although all these centres were not running at full capacity, a new one had been planned to open in Guadalajara (Spain). This one would be shared with other Inditex brands.

## Zara online and in the future

Compared with some of its competitors, Zara was relatively late in establishing its online offering. But in 2008 Amancio Ortega decided, after five years' careful consideration, that it was time to launch an online offering. Zara's online store officially opened in September 2010 for customers in France, Germany, Spain, Italy, Portugal and the UK, after which it quickly built an online presence in 18 European markets, the USA, Japan, China, Canada and Russia. Talking to analysts in March 2013, a company spokesperson said '*Inditex's online operations have seen a very rapid rollout in recent years. Our business model allows a swift expansion of our online sales platform globally. We will continue to roll out online sales progressively in all the markets in which we are present with stores.*' Analysts at Citigroup concluded in 2013 that the results indicated that Inditex was '*one of the few beneficiaries of the ongoing, rapid channel shift to online from store-based apparel sales*'. In effect, Zara's online operations acted like macro stores (1 per country) and followed the standard ordering procedure. Products were sent to the distribution centre at Meco and then shipped to a specific warehouse in the corresponding country. From there, the orders were sent according to customers' preferences: pick up in a physical store for free (delivery in 3–5 days), standard delivery at home (2–3 days) or express shipment (48 hours) with some additional cost. In line with Zara's high-end image, there was a distinctive emphasis on attractive and exclusive packaging (i.e., boxes not plastic bags) and a great deal of focus on client service, both during and after sales.

During the last decade, Zara has repeatedly defied the predictions of those who had suggested that it had reached the limit of its business model. In 2014 it seemed to be continuing its phenomenal growth into the future. Nevertheless, some observers still wondered whether it needed to modify its business model and operating systems to account for its increasing size and global footprint. For example, would its current system of design, production and order fulfilment help or hinder serving the growing markets in Asia? Would it facilitate growth of online sales? Did it require a major overhaul of its well-organised operating processes?

A more intriguing question was why, after many years of people observing the phenomenal growth of Zara and learning about its model, competitors did not seem to be following its operating practices as much as one would expect. Was it because they believed these practices did not fit their business strategy? Or did they find it difficult to implement them?

## Note on the case

1   This case is based on public sources including: Ferdows, K., Machuca, J. and Lewis, M. (2002) 'Zara, Case Clearing House'; Jarrow, L. (2013) 'Inditex: Spain's fashion powerhouse you've probably never heard of', *The Observer*, 15 December; Hansen, S. (2012) 'How Zara Grew Into the World's Largest Fashion Retailer', *New York Times*, 9 November; Leroux, M. and Griffiths, K. (2013) 'Zara owner to open nine stores a week as it takes on world', *The Times*, 14 March.

# 7

# DELTA SYNTHETIC FIBRES (DSF)

Nigel Slack

*'When you are a small player in this business you really do need to develop your own approach to doing business. We are not in the same game as BASF or DuPont. Our key objectives have always been based on three things – niche markets, focused production and innovative products.'*

(Paul Mayer – CEO, Delta Synthetic Fibres)

By the standards of the synthetic fibre industry, DSF was a very small, but international and technically successful company. For over eight years the company had been heavily dependent on one range of products based on the polymer 'Britlene', which it had developed itself in the late 1990s. By 2004, Britlene products accounted for 97 per cent of total revenue (the other 3 per cent came from the sale of licences). In fact, since it was founded in the 1970s, the company had always limited itself to a single product range at one time. The original product range 'Teklon' had been replaced by 'Deklon', which had in turn been replaced by 'Britlene'. None of these product changes had required substantial changes to the company's processes.

*'I guess that, until now, we have been lucky in only having one product range to concentrate on. This means that the early parts of our manufacturing process have to cope with relatively little variety. There are different grades and variants of the basic Britlene polymer but only five or six main varieties, with around 10 or 12 "specials", which we make for specific customers. The real variety comes later on in the process, in the extrusion stage and especially in the finishing and packing stages. We have 35 extrusion "patterns" which, together with 17 "finishes" and 10 to 12 pack types, means that we have potentially around seven thousand ways of producing each polymer grade. Of course, as usual, 20 per cent of possible end product codes account for 80 per cent of our output. However, I feel it is important that we should try and control this variety. Not only does it add complexity to the process, it will become an even greater problem if we do not tackle it before we start producing Britlon as well as Britlene.'*

(Paul Mayer, CEO)

The Britlene range was used mainly as a 'blend fibre' in heavy-duty clothing, although smaller quantities were used to produce industrial goods such as tyre cord, flexible industrial drives and insulating sleeves. Its main properties were very high wear resistance, together with high thermal and electrical insulation. Sales of Britlene products, especially in the United States, had started to fall off in 2004 as competitor products eroded DSF's traditional markets. These products rarely matched the technical specification of the Britlene products but were significantly less expensive.

## From Britlene to Britlon

In 2004 the company had developed a new product range built around a new polymer to be known as Britlon. Britlon polymers had all the properties of Britlene but were superior in their strength, heat-resistant qualities and electrical insulation. It was hoped that these additional properties would open up new clothing uses (for example, as a substitute for mineral wool) as well as allowing entry into the far larger markets associated with thermal and electrical insulation. By late 2004, after some delays, the major technical and engineering problems associated with bulk production of the Britlon range seemed to have been solved.

> 'Britlon has come later than we hoped. Partly this is because it is a genuine advance in product formulation and we had some difficult technical problems to overcome. I have to admit though that partly the delay was due to not starting Britlon development early enough. Our marketing colleagues have been telling us for some time that an enhanced product range could have a significant impact on the market around this time. Yet now, because of construction lead-times, we are in the position of not being able to introduce the Britlon range into the market until early 2006.'

(Paul Mayer, CEO)

The basic production method for both the Britlene and Britlon ranges was similar to that of most synthetic fibres. An oil-based organic chemical is polymerised (a process of joining several molecules into a long chain) in conditions of intense pressure and heat, often by the addition of a suitable catalyst. This polymerisation takes place in large autoclaves (like an industrial pressure cooker). The polymer is then extruded (forced through a nozzle like the rose of a garden watering can), rapidly cooled and then finished in a variety of ways, for example, spun on to cones or collected in bales. After this, a variety of different conversion processes were used to add value before the product was shipped to the customer.

The later stages of the production processes were relatively flexible. With some 'change-over' losses in productivity, the equipment could be used to process most types of fibre with little modification. However, the early stages in the process, particularly the polymerisation stage, were usually designed for one range of polymer and might need substantial modification before a different polymer range could be made. For this reason a new Britlon line, or a Britlene line converted to produce the Britlon range, could only produce Britlon products, just as a Britlene line could only produce Britlene products.

## Current facilities

Currently the Britlene range was produced at the company's three factories: Teesside in the UK, Hamburg in Germany and Chicago in the USA. The largest site was Teesside with three lines. There was one line at each of the other two sites. All five production lines had a nominal design capacity of 5.5 million kg per year of Britlene. However, after allowing for change-over losses, maintenance and holidays, expected output was around 5 million kg per year. Each plant operated on a 24-hours-per-day, seven-days-per-week basis.

The cost of raw materials was more or less the same at each location, but labour costs, general employment costs, local taxation and energy costs did vary. The Hamburg plant had the highest production costs followed by the Chicago plant, with the Teesside plant having the lowest cost per kg produced (at full utilisation). However, the cost differences between the plants were less than the differences in the input costs. Partly this was because of higher productivity at both the Hamburg and Chicago plants, and partly because all three Teesside lines were relatively old and prone to breakdown.

## DSF's markets

The largest single market for the Britlene range was still the UK, although the percentage of sales to UK customers had declined from over 60 per cent in 1998 to around 41 per cent in 2004. The potential for volume growth was greatest in the Far East markets, especially South East Asia, and least in the UK. Earnings growth potential, however, was likely to be greatest in continental Europe and the USA. In terms of market sector sales, both industrial and domestic clothing were growing only slowly for DSF, while the company's sales into general industrial markets had grown from practically nothing in 1990 to around 13 per cent of sales in 2004 and were likely to grow further in the next five years, especially in the USA. Thermal and electrical insulation markets, after fast growth in the early 2000s, had grown only slowly over the last two years.

> 'We are trading in two quite different types of market. Clothing, both industrial and domestic, is relatively predictable, and we are established suppliers with a relatively large share of a very small market. The industrial and insulation markets, however, are far larger in themselves and we have only a tiny share. In the clothing markets we are competing, usually on price, against very similar products. In the other markets we are competing against a whole range of different materials, usually on product performance and supply flexibility.'

(Tim Williams, Vice-President Marketing)

Exhibit 1 shows market volumes for 2004.

Tim Williams also saw the new Britlon product range changing the sales profile of the company.

> 'Britlon products will be based on a technically superior material which is also likely to be marginally less expensive to produce. We should be able to, at least, maintain our share of the clothing market and possibly stop the margin erosion we have suffered in this sector over the last few years. But the real benefits are going to show in the insulation and, to only a slightly less extent, in the industrial markets. The improved strength and insulation properties of the Britlon range should let us capture a greater share of a larger and more profitable market. Also, because we will have two product ranges, we can differentiate between different market needs in different parts of the world. The future will be one where we will have far more choice as to how we position ourselves in our markets. But it will also be one where we will face increased level of market uncertainty.'

Exhibit 2 shows the aggregated volume and price forecasts for both products for 2005 through to 2010.

## Creating a Britlon capability

The production process needed to manufacture the Britlon range was very similar to that used for the Britlene range; however, a totally new type of polymerisation unit would be needed prior to the extrusion stage. Also the technologies for polymerisation were mutually exclusive. Britlon and Britlene products could not be produced on the same line. Early in the development of Britlon, DSF had approached Alpen GmbH, an international chemical plant construction company, for help on a largescale plant design of the new unit. Together they produced and tested an acceptable design for the new line and had explored different construction methods. Essentially there were two ways of acquiring Britlon capacity: DSF could convert the old Britlene-based lines, or it could construct entirely new lines.

For a conversion a new polymer unit would need to be constructed alongside the old line (without interfering with production). When complete it would be connected to the extrusion unit, which would itself require only minor conversion. Alpen were quoting a lead-time of two years for both the construction of a new Britlon line or to convert an old Britlene plant to Britlon production.

> 'The long lead-times which are being quoted for constructing this type of process are partly a result of a high level of demand for Alpen's services because of their reputation for providing sound technical solutions in process design. Also, I guess they are a bit cautious because of the technical novelty of the Britlon process.'
>
> (Liam Flaherty, Vice-President Operations)

Although the lead-time for building a new line was the same as for a conversion, the capital cost of the latter was lower. Exhibit 3 shows the capital estimates for both conversion and new lines. Economies of scale were such that, whether converted or built new, the capacity of Britlon plants would be around 5 million kg per year.

## Focus or flexibility?

Liam Flaherty, the Vice-President of Operations, based at Teesside, was keen to take advantage of the opportunities provided by the introduction of the Britlon range. In particular, he wanted to avoid concentrating exclusively on the problems posed in the short term by the introduction of new Britlon capacity.

> 'I know that getting the capacity expansion strategy right must be a priority. It is a major investment programme for the company and we must keep tight control of how the new capacity is installed. However, we are also laying down the structure of the company's operations for the long term. In effect we are moving, for the first time, into being a "two product range" company. This presents us with a whole range of issues which either we have not faced before or we have avoided confronting.'
>
> (Liam Flaherty, Vice-President Operations)

Liam had already identified what he regarded as some of the key questions in a report to Paul Mayer. These were as follows.

● Should every site produce both product ranges, or should we try and develop 'Centres of Expertise' for the two product ranges?

- Even if all three sites do produce both product ranges, should each site specialise in one part of each product range?

- How can we make sure that all sites understand their contribution to the company's overall operations capability? In other words, should strategic operations decisions still be made at the centre or should we allow each site some degree of autonomy in developing their own strategies for their markets or their product ranges?

- In the longer term should we give different sites different roles in developing our overall operations capability? For example, Chicago has shown particular enthusiasm (and enjoyed some success) in improving both productivity and flexibility on its line. It has done this mainly through a series of incremental technology improvements to the process. Because of this, should it be given responsibility for process improvement, even though traditionally this responsibility has been seen as belonging to the central technical resource at Teesside?

- Following from this last point, what should be the role of our central technology resource? In the past it has been good at understanding the practicalities of implementing modifications to our existing technology in a 'top-down' way. However, it has been less good at motivating and training factory-level operations people in the three sites to take responsibility on themselves for improvement.

- How can we link our technology/operations capabilities with sales and marketing? So far we have prospered through pushing our new technologies out into the market, but this is unlikely to be successful in the future. Although Britlon's enhanced performance will give a major boost to sales, increasingly it will be small product modifications that will win us extra business. I'm sure there will be some big technology breakthroughs in the future. But we can't wait for these to come through every few years. The future is more likely to be one of fast development and response to specific customer needs in a wider variety of markets.

## The capacity working group

In the autumn of 2004 Paul Mayer set up the capacity working group to consider the introduction of the new product range and all its implications. However, he did place some limits on what the company would do.

*'Liam is right, we have to consider the underlying issues and assumptions behind the reconfiguration of our operations, but for the time being we need to confine ourselves to existing sites. In the short term the creation of an entirely new site would increase the complexities of multi-site operation to an unacceptable level. Conversely, the complete closure of one of the three existing sites is, I consider, a waste of the manpower and physical resources that we have invested in that location. I believe expansion could take place at one, two or all of the existing sites. In the future, however, all things are possible. For example, it may make sense to develop a new site in Asia both to service the growing Eastern markets and to take advantage of lower costs.'*

(Paul Mayer, CEO)

Exhibit 1 **Current market volumes by product and region, 2004 (millions of kg)**

| Market sectors | UK | Continental Europe | USA | Far East |
|---|---|---|---|---|
| Clothing – industrial | 8.04 | 3.74 | 1.69 | 1.84 |
| Clothing – domestic | 1.22 | 0.09 | N.A. | N.A. |
| Clothing – general | 0.52 | 1.02 | 1.10 | 0.73 |
| Thermal insulation | 0.41 | 0.39 | 1.01 | N.A. |
| Electrical insulation | 0.18 | 0.64 | 1.10 | 0.98 |
| Total | 10.37 | 5.88 | 4.90 | 3.55 |

Exhibit 2 **Forecasts Britlene and Britlon ranges**

| | Potential sales | |
|---|---|---|
| | Britlene (all products) millions of kg p.a. | Britlon (all products) millions of kg p.a. |
| 2004 (actual) | 24.7 | |
| 2005 | 22 | |
| 2006 | 20 | |
| 2007 | 17 | 3 (assuming availability) |
| 2008 | 13 | 16 |
| 2009 | 11 | 27 |
| 2010 | 10 | 29 |
| | Average price forecast (p. per kg) | |
| | Britlene (across all products) | Britlon (across all products) |
| 2005 | 98 | – |
| 2006 | 98 | – |
| 2007 | 95 | 125 |
| 2008 | 90 | 120 |
| 2009 | 85 | 120 |
| 2010 | 85 | 120 |

Exhibit 3 **Estimated Britlon capital costs**

The table below gives estimated costs and stage payments required by Alpen for Britlon polymer line and extrusion unit construction.

| Type of order | Cost (£ million) | Timing | |
|---|---|---|---|
| Whole *new* 'Britlon' line including polymer and extrusion units | 4.8 | Begin<br>Onstream | 6 months from order<br>2 years from order |
| Conversion of 'Britlene' line to 'Britlon' line | 3.0 | Begin<br>Onstream | 6 months from order<br>2 years from order |

The cost of a new plant is payable in three six-monthly instalments – £1,000,000 being due one year after ordering, £1,000,000 due six months later and the balance on completion.

The cost of a conversion is payable in three six-monthly instalments of £1,000,000 at one year, at 18 months and on completion.

# 8 TURNROUND AT THE PRESTON PLANT

Nigel Slack

*'Before the crisis the quality department was just for looks, we certainly weren't used much for problem solving, the most we did was inspection. Data from the quality department was brought to the production meeting and they would all look at it, but no one was looking behind it.'*

(Quality Manager, Preston Plant)

The Preston plant of Rendall Graphics was located in Preston, Vancouver, across the continent from its headquarters in Massachusetts. The plant had been bought from the Georgetown Corporation by Rendall in March 2000. Precision-coated papers for ink-jet printers accounted for the majority of the plant's output, especially paper for specialist uses. The plant used coating machines that allowed precise coatings to be applied. After coating, the conversion department cut the coated rolls to the final size and packed the sheets in small cartons.

## The curl problem

In late 1998 Hewlett-Packard (HP), the plant's main customer for ink-jet paper, informed the plant of some problems it had encountered with paper curling under conditions of low humidity. There had been no customer complaints to HP, but its own personnel had noticed the problem, and they wanted it fixed. Over the next seven or eight months a team at the plant tried to solve the problem. Finally, in October of 1999, the team made recommendations for a revised and considerably improved coating formulation. By January 2000 the process was producing acceptably. However, 1999 had not been a good year for the plant. Although sales were reasonably buoyant the plant was making a loss of around $2 million for the year. In October 1999, Tom Branton, previously accountant for the business, was appointed as managing director.

## Slipping out of control

In the spring of 2000, productivity, scrap and re-work levels continued to be poor. In response to this, the operations management team increased the speed of the line and made a number of changes to operating practice in order to raise productivity.

*'Looking back, changes were made without any proper discipline, and there was no real concept of control. We were always meeting specification, yet we didn't fully understand how close we really were to not being able to make it. The culture here said, "If it's within specification then it's OK" and we were very diligent in making sure that the product which was shipped was in specification. However, Hewlett-Packard gets*

"process charts" that enables them to see more or less exactly what is happening right inside your operation. We were also getting all the reports but none of them were being internalised, we were using them just to satisfy the customer. By contrast, HP have a statistically-based analytical mentality that says to itself, "You might be capable of making this product but we are thinking two or three product generations forward and asking ourselves, will you have the capability then, and do we want to invest in this relationship for the future?".'

(Tom Branton)

The spring of 2000 also saw two significant events. First, Hewlett-Packard asked the plant to bid for the contract to supply a new ink-jet platform, known as the Vector project, a contract that would secure healthy orders for several years. The second event was that the plant was acquired by Rendall.

'What did Rendall see when they bought us? They saw a small plant on the Pacific coast losing lots of money.'

(Finance Manager, Preston Plant)

Rendall was not impressed by what it found at the Preston plant, which was making a loss and had only just escaped from incurring a major customer's disapproval over the curl issue. If the plant did not get the Vector contract, its future looked bleak. Meanwhile, the chief concern continued to be productivity, but also, once again, there were occasional complaints about quality levels. However, HP's attitude caused some bewilderment to the operations management team.

'When HP asked questions about our process the operations guys would say, "Look we're making roll after roll of paper, it's within specification. What's the problem?".'

(Quality Manager, Preston Plant)

But it was not until summer that the full extent of HP's disquiet was made:

'I will never forget June of 2000. I was at a meeting with HP in Chicago. It was not even about quality. But during the meeting one of their engineers handed me a control chart, one that we supplied with every batch of product. He said "Here's your latest control chart. We think you're out of control and you don't know that you're out of control and we think that we are looking at this data more than you are." He was absolutely right, and I fully understood how serious the position was. We had our most important customer telling us we couldn't run our processes just at the time we were trying to persuade them to give us the Vector contract.'

(Tom Branton)

## The crisis

Tom immediately set about the task of bringing the plant back under control. They first of all decided to go back to the conditions that prevailed in the January, when the curl team's recommendations had been implemented. This was the state before productivity pressures had caused the process to be adjusted. At the same time the team worked on ways of implementing unambiguous 'shut-down rules' that would allow operators to decide under what conditions a line should be halted if they were in doubt about the quality of the product they were making.

*'At one point in May of 2000 we had to throw away 64 jumbo rolls of out-of-specification product. That's over $100,000 of product scrapped in one run. Basically that was because they had been afraid to shut the line down. Either that or they had tried to tweak the line while it was running to get rid of the defect. The shut-down guidelines in effect say, "We are not going to operate when we are not in a state of control". Until then our operators just couldn't win. If they failed to keep the machines running we would say, "You've got to keep productivity up". If they kept the machines running but had quality problems as a result, we criticised them for making garbage. Now you get into far more trouble for violating process procedures than you do for not meeting productivity targets.'*

(Engineer, Preston Plant)

This new approach needed to be matched by changes in the way the communications were managed in the plant.

*'We did two things that we had never done before. First, each production team started holding daily reviews of control chart data. Second, one day a month we took people away from production and debated the control chart data. Several people got nervous because we were not producing anything. But it was necessary. For the first time you got operators from the three shifts meeting together and talking about the control chart data and other quality issues. Just as significantly we invited HP up to attend these meetings. Remember these weren't staged meetings, it was the first time these guys had met together and there was plenty of heated discussion, all of which the Hewlett-Packard representatives witnessed.'*

(Engineer, Preston Plant)

At last something positive was happening in the plant and morale on the shop floor was buoyant. By September 2000 the results of the plant's teams' efforts were starting to show results. Processes were coming under control, quality levels were improving and, most importantly, personnel both on the shop floor and in the management team were beginning to get into the 'quality mode' of thinking. Paradoxically, in spite of stopping the line periodically, the efficiency of the plant was also improving.

Yet, the Preston team did not have time to enjoy its emerging success. In September of 2000 the plant learned that it would not get the Vector project because of the recent quality problems. Then Rendall decided to close the plant:

*'We were losing millions, we had lost the Vector project, and it was really no surprise. I told the senior management team and said that we would announce it probably in April of 2001. The real irony was that we knew that we had actually already turned the corner.'*

(Tom Branton)

## Convincing the rest of the world

Notwithstanding the closure decision, and convinced that their overall performance could be substantially improved, the management team in Preston set about the task of convincing both HP and Rendall that the plant could be viable. The team figured it would take three things. First, it was vital to continue to improve quality. Second, costs had to be brought down so as to lower the break-even volume of the plant substantially. Third, the plant had to create a portfolio of new product ideas that could establish a greater confidence in future sales.

## First – quality

Progressing with the quality initiative involved establishing full statistical process control (SPC) and increasingly capable processes. (Exhibits 1 and 2 show how process variation reduced through this period and how process capability improved.) It also meant establishing quality consciousness and problem-solving tools throughout the plant.

*'We had people out there, professional engineers and operators, who saw themselves as concerned with the project rather than the processes that made it. But taking time out for quality meetings and discussing process performance and improvement, we got used to discussing the basic capabilities that we needed to improve.'*

(Quality Manager, Preston Plant)

## Second – get costs down

Working on cost reduction was inevitably going to be painful. The first task was to get an understanding of what should be an appropriate level of operating costs.

*'We went through a zero-based assessment to decide what an ideal plant would look like, and the minimum number of people needed to run it. By the way, in hindsight, cutting numbers had a greater impact on cost than the payroll saving figures seems to suggest. If you really understand your process, when you cut people it cuts complexity and makes things clearer to understand.'*

(Tom Branton)

Although most staff had not been informed of Rendall's closure decision, they were left in no doubt that the plant had its back to the wall.

*'We were careful to be very transparent. We made sure that everyone knew whether they would be affected or not. I did lots of walking around explaining the company's position. There were tensions and some negative reactions from the people who had to leave. Yet most accepted the business logic of what we were doing.'*

(Tom Branton)

By December of 2000 there were 40 per cent fewer people in the plant than two months earlier. All departments were affected. Surprisingly the quality department shrank more than most, moving from 22 people down to nine.

*'When the plant was considering down-sizing they asked me, "How can we run a lab with six technicians?". Remember that at this time we had 22 technicians. I said, "Easy. We get production to make good paper in the first place, and then we don't have to control all the garbage. That alone would save an immense amount of time. Also, having someone working with the suppliers so that we can guarantee to give production good material and take that problem out of the equation saves people as well."'*

(Quality Manager, Preston Plant)

## Third – work on new products

Several new ideas were investigated, including some that were only possible because of the plant's enhanced capability. The most important of these became known as 'Greenwrap', a product aimed particularly at the Japanese market. Short of landfill space, newsprint companies wanted their suppliers to ship newsprint in a wrap that could be repulped. Producing a protective wrap that was recyclable, an effective barrier against moisture, and could keep the newsprint free of welts and buckles was technically difficult. However, the plant's newly acquired capabilities allowed it to develop appropriate coatings at a cost that made the product attractive.

## Out of the crisis

In spite of their trauma in the autumn, the plant's management team faced Christmas of 2000 with increasing satisfaction, if not optimism for the plant's future. In December it made an operational profit for the first time for over two years. By spring of 2001 even HP, at a corporate level, was starting to look more favourably on the Preston plant. It was becoming obvious to HP that the plant really had made a major change. More significantly, HP had asked the plant to start work on trials for a new product – 'heavyweight' paper.

April 2001 was a good month for the plant. It had chalked up three months of profitability (which was to be the start of routine double-digit return on sales). HP formally gave the heavyweight ink-jet paper contract to Preston, and were generally more up-beat about the future.

At the end of April, Rendall reversed its decision to close the plant.

## The future

Both 2001 and 2002 were profitable years for the Preston plant. By the end of 2002 the plant had also captured the majority of Hewlett-Packard's Canadian business and was being asked to work on several other large projects.

*'Hewlett-Packard now seems particularly keen to work with us. I'm sure that one reason is that we have been obliged to understand their way of doing business. It has helped us with our own suppliers also. We have already given considerable assistance to our main paper supplier with improving their own internal process control procedures. Recently we were in a meeting with people from all different parts of HP. There was all kinds of confidential information going around. But you could never tell that there was an outsider (us) in the room. They were having arguments amongst themselves about certain issues and no one could have been there without feeling that basically we were a part of that company. In the past they've always been very close with some information. Basically the change is all down to their new-found trust in our capabilities.'*

(Tom Branton)

**Exhibit 1 Typical process control charts (May 1998)**

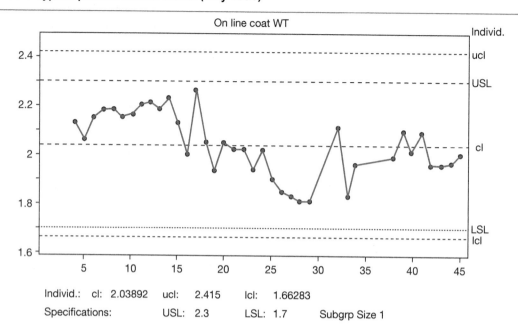

Individ.:    cl: 2.03892    ucl:    2.415    lcl:    1.66283

Specifications:            USL:    2.3      LSL:    1.7        Subgrp Size 1

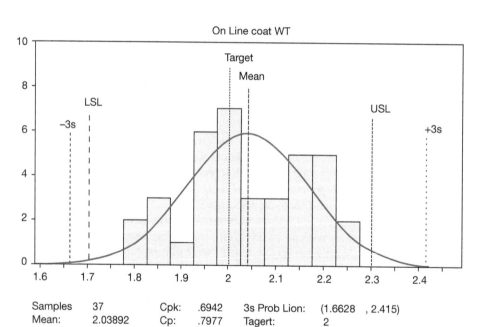

| | | | |
|---|---|---|---|
| Samples | 37 | Cpk: .6942 | 3s Prob Lion: (1.6628 , 2.415) |
| Mean: | 2.03892 | Cp: .7977 | Tagert: 2 |
| Std. Dev.: | .12536 | | Spec. Limits: (1.7 , 2.3) |
| Skewness: | −.19322 | | Est % outside: ( .343 , 1.864) |

Exhibit 2 **Typical process control charts (January 1999)**

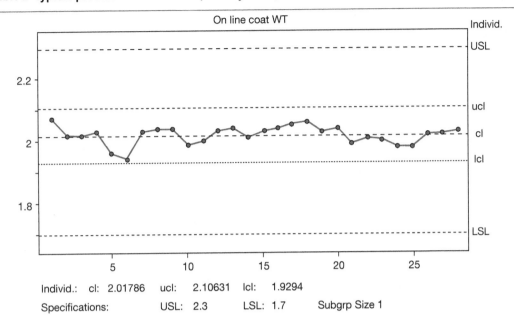

On line coat WT

| | | |
|---|---|---|
| Individ.: | cl: 2.01786 | ucl: 2.10631 | lcl: 1.9294 |
| Specifications: | | USL: 2.3 | LSL: 1.7 | Subgrp Size 1 |

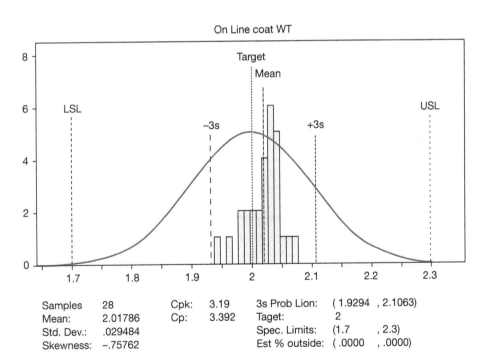

On Line coat WT

| | | | |
|---|---|---|---|
| Samples | 28 | Cpk: | 3.19 | 3s Prob Lion: | ( 1.9294 , 2.1063) |
| Mean: | 2.01786 | Cp: | 3.392 | Taget: | 2 |
| Std. Dev.: | .029484 | | | Spec. Limits: | (1.7 , 2.3) |
| Skewness: | −.75762 | | | Est % outside: | ( .0000 , .0000) |

# 9 IDEO: SERVICE DESIGN

## Ritesh Bhavnani and Manuel Sosa

'I should have had the café latte', thought Peter Coughlan as he sipped his strong decaf double no-fat soya latte macchiato at Peet's Coffeehouse, just around the corner from his office. Designers and engineers from his company, IDEO, one of the world's largest and arguably most successful design firms, often gathered here and talked. He looked up to see Dennis Boyle, another IDEO employee, glaring at his own coffee nearby. Boyle had been the project leader on the Palm V and Handspring Visor handheld computer projects, and Coughlan briefly wondered if Boyle had ever had to wrestle with the same kind of problem that he was facing now. The coffee he'd created was just terrible.

Coughlan had just come out of a four-hour meeting with David Becker, president and CEO of Portland General Health Center. Becker had chanced to see the famous *Nightline* documentary about IDEO's design process and had been suitably impressed. Ted Koppel, the host of *Nightline*, had challenged IDEO to completely redesign the traditional shopping cart in five days, and *Nightline* had filmed the entire process. In the end, IDEO delivered a sleek and streamlined shopping cart, with modular detachable shopping baskets, a baby chair, a do-it-yourself barcode scanner and a host of other innovations. More importantly, the report had given public exposure to the famed IDEO design process, a process that had elevated the firm to near-legendary status in the design world, enabling it to win more design awards than any other company year after year.[1]

Becker had come to IDEO looking for new ideas on how to improve healthcare service in his hospital. American healthcare had never been known for its design. When Tom Kelley, the general manager of IDEO and brother of David Kelley, one of the company founders, was interviewed on the radio programme *Fresh Air*, he had described a handful of things whose design 'had been bad so long that you don't even really think about them'. He mentioned irons ('The state-of-the-art method for deciding whether your steam iron is hot or not is to put your tender fingers onto the metal'), and airline tickets ('There's all sorts of codes and 17 digits on there').[2] When he came to hospital waiting rooms, no anecdotal evidence was required; everyone could picture the painfully bright fluorescent lighting, out-of-date magazines and stiff uncomfortable chairs.

Hospitals had to deal with severe financial pressures, escalating costs and staff shortages, yet, perversely, were expected to continue to deliver state-of-the-art medical care and keep up to date with rapidly evolving medical technology. 'Design' had never really been thought of as an important factor in delivering better patient treatment. The challenge that Becker put to IDEO wasn't easy: how do you redesign a healthcare service and improve patient care in the face of limited budgets and constrained resources?

## The history of IDEO

*'Good design is good business.'*

(Thomas Watson, CEO, IBM)

IDEO was a company born of two histories. The first part of the history began in 1969, when a British industrial designer, Bill Moggridge, set up Moggridge Associates in London. In 1979 he expanded his business by opening up an office in San Francisco called ID Two, which focused on industrial design.

The second part of the history took place in the early boom days of Silicon Valley, when David Kelley, a doctorate student at Stanford University, realised that most technology companies lacked access to general product-development skills. Accordingly, in 1978 he gave up writing his Ph.D. thesis and went on to form his own company, David Kelley Design, to address the engineering design requirements of firms in the Valley.

The two individuals met in 1979 and started cooperating on joint projects. They realised early on that the field of design was evolving to such a point that an inter-disciplinary, multifunctional approach was required to provide effective service to companies.

IDEO was formed in 1991 when David Kelly Design, Moggridge Associates, ID Two and Matrix Product Design (another design company) merged. The merger brought under one roof professionals with experience in the hitherto diverse fields of mechanical and electrical engineering, industrial design, ergonomics, information technology, cognitive psychology and prototyping – practice areas that rapidly came to be considered integral to product design. Another important advantage that IDEO had was the fact that it was a transcontinental firm from its very inception.

Both founders are still closely associated with IDEO, although Kelley, formerly CEO, became chairman in March 2000, relinquishing the reins of the organisation to Tim Brown, who used to be in charge of IDEO London. By January 2005 IDEO spanned two continents with six locations (Palo Alto, San Francisco, Chicago, Boston, London and Munich) and had a staff of 350 people and annual revenues of about $70 million. IDEO encourages the continual flow of people across locations and projects to enable the cross-fertilisation of new ideas and ensure knowledge sharing. The company also believes that multiple locations gives it access not just to local business and local space, but also local talent – an important necessity for a firm that prides itself on its ability to harness the differences in people to generate creative ideas.

## IDEO in 2005

The pace of technological change and ever-changing conditions in the broader business world have had the effect of radically transforming IDEO's business as well. Given the ever-increasing complexity of the assignments it undertakes today, most of its projects involve collaborating extremely closely, not just with clients but with external partners on behalf of its clients. These range from advertising and branding firms to contract manufacturers.

Another important change at IDEO has been its transformation from an organisational structure based primarily around geographies, to one where there is more emphasis on practice areas. According to Alan South, Service Design and Innovation principal and also head of IDEO Europe, *'IDEO used to be able to be considered a loose federation of independent studios, each with their own profit and loss'*, united by a strong shared culture. Today, IDEO is organised around seven practice areas (see Exhibit 1 for details), with a stronger sense of 'one firm'.

The organisation of the firm around practice areas is similar to the organisational structure of more traditional consulting firms. *'With practices you can talk to clients with one voice. It allows us to focus on their broader needs and serve them more effectively'*, says Tim Brown, CEO.[3]

## The IDEO innovation process

*As such, everything is now subject to innovation – not just physical objects, but also political systems, economic policy, ways in which medical research is conducted, and even complete 'user experiences'.*

(Laura Weiss, IDEO)[4]

IDEO's core competence is primarily in the process of design and innovation, followed by an understanding of specific domain knowledge. According to Laura Weiss, a principal of the Service Design and Innovation practice at IDEO, clients *'hire us to think about things in ways that [they] don't think about every day. [They] hire us to bring in a sense of wonder.'*[5]

On projects, IDEO views itself as a cross between a movie producer and a director – bringing together and coordinating the various 'stars' (some of whom may be external) and then determining what has to be done and how. Key to its creative process is 'radical collaboration', the intense, all-encompassing way that IDEO works with the client and external partners. Unlike mainstream consulting firms who tend to camp out at the client site, IDEO usually brings the client into its own working environment. By working closely and continuously with clients and external partners, IDEO ensures that the client is intimately involved in the creative process and, more importantly, that there are no last-minute surprises or costly mistakes on its part. IDEO goes as far as actually sharing its innovation process with clients, advising them on how they themselves can become more innovative (through its Transformation practice).

Another critical factor in IDEO's recipe for innovation is the use of interdisciplinary teams. On any project, an IDEO team is usually composed of people from disciplines ranging from cognitive psychology to industrial design. IDEO employees oftentimes find themselves working with employees from other offices or on projects staffed at different office locations. This fluidity ensures that ideas have a chance to propagate through the organisation, and that the creativity within the organisation is stimulated through the continual injection of new influences.

Although the IDEO innovation process is constantly evolving (see Exhibit 2), there is an underlying 'project journey' or set of steps:

---

### IDEO project journey
*Observe → Synthesise → Generate ideas → Refine → Implement*

---

*Observe:* IDEO functions not just through market surveys and aggregate user data, but spends a great deal of time observing and empathising with the user to truly understand their needs and requirements. This user-centric form of design is a big part of what has enabled IDEO to be so successful for so many years.

*Synthesise:* After generating a large number of observations and data points, IDEO steps back and synthesises all the data, distilling the information collected into cogent and succinct guiding principles for the solution to be designed.

*Generate ideas:* Based on the synthesised understanding of its observations, IDEO will work to cast a wide net for possible opportunities. A commonly-used process is that of brainstorming. There are strict rules that govern the brainstorming process and they have been well codified.[6]

*Refine:* An oft-quoted maxim at IDEO, espoused by its chairman David Kelley, is: *'Fail early and fail often.'* This 'culture of failure' is one of the foundation stones of the IDEO creative process: quick and dirty prototypes are created to refine ideas and ensure that they can be fleshed out early so that costly wrong decisions are avoided. Additionally, IDEO solutions are iterative loops, with each iteration being further refined and brought closer to the final solution.

*Implement:* Implementation is an important step of the design process. Often, design projects are carried out for commercial gain in the market, so if a design cannot be effectively implemented all the work has been wasted. Yet if IDEO's process is followed, implementation is the natural outcome of an evolution of iterative, increasingly refined prototypes.

A typical IDEO client assignment or 'project journey' follows the five basic steps described above. While the project evolution itself may be standardised, the specific tools used for a particular project will vary depending on the project.

IDEO's approaches to gathering insights that lead to design opportunities are recorded on 'IDEO method cards', which list some of its most popular research methods and detail how and when they are to be used (see Exhibit 3 for some examples). They are one of the mechanisms of sharing knowledge used by the company. Another mechanism for knowledge transfer is its 'Tech Box', a veritable treasure chest of gadgets, materials and mechanisms that are meant to spark creativity and aid in the communication of new concepts. Each office has a 'Tech Box' and there is a 'curator' who ensures that the collection is refreshed and continually growing.

Unlike traditional large companies, IDEO's knowledge sharing is more organic and less structured, with a greater reliance on informal, even social, mechanisms. *'Some organisations rely on big databases to disseminate information'*, says CEO Brown. *'We disseminate our knowledge through stories.'*[7] In Monday-morning meetings held across the firm, regular leadership meetings, lunchtime show-and-tell sessions and other meetings, the sharing and communication of ideas and best practices is done through stories. *'People hold stories in their heads better than other forms of information'*, says Brown.

*'Knowledge management at IDEO is largely organic and, by definition, chaotic. It's a Darwinian process'*, says Alan South. *'Only the fittest – that is the strongest ideas – survive.'* However it is done, the sharing of knowledge across its people and offices is critical to a company like IDEO. The company prides itself on its ability to leverage its process across any industry; indeed, it sees as one of its core strengths its ability to be a

'knowledge broker', leveraging information gleaned in one industry and applying it effectively to another.

## Service design

*'... the design of intangible experiences that reach people through many different touch-points, and that happen over time.'*

(live|work website)[8]

Service design is a relatively young field that has come into the spotlight due to the increasing and continuing importance of the service sector in most developed economies. Additionally, even traditional product companies are realising that by designing not just the product, but also the process and the service interface, they can add value and maximise profit through the entire value chain. This places a greater degree of emphasis on the service end of the entire cycle and, as a result, more emphasis is being placed on service design.

According to G. Lynn Shostack, who has chaired the task force on service marketing of the American Marketing Association, *'Traditionally, service design had been characterised by the lack of systematic method for design and control.'* As a result, new services were usually developed by trial and error: in the absence of a detailed design there was no metric to gauge whether the service was complete, rational and fulfilled the original need.

Service suppliers must be prepared to cope with the unexpected. While it is possible to blueprint the process through which the customer passes, the blueprints are rarely able to take account of the variability inherent in people-related processes. Richard Eisermann, formerly of IDEO and now director of Design & Innovation at the Design Council in the UK, agrees: *'The trick in service design is its subjective nature: that's difficult to codify and capture. The best you can do is give guidelines for people to follow. You can make millions of identical razors, and the four hundredth razor will be identical to the four hundred thousandth razor. It's easy to make a deliberate controlled experience for users. But if you are a service company, how can you attempt to brand that experience, make it standardised, make it consistent?'* Today, in addition to in-house departments within large firms, several companies are focused on serving the increasing demands of clients for service design. Companies like live|work in London, Design Continuum near Boston and Ziba Design in Portland all compete with IDEO for service design work.

## IDEO and service design

Whilst IDEO had been thinking of entering the service design field for strategic reasons to broaden its practice offerings, its actual entry into service design was opportunistic. In 1997 Amtrak approached IDEO to do an assessment of the designs for the train cars that it was building for Acela, its new high-speed rail service that was to run from Washington D.C. to Boston. IDEO realised that in order for the service to be successful Amtrak needed to be thinking about the entire customer experience, of which the train car was but one part. In other words, to design the train cars they first had to design the service. Recalls Eisermann, who was the IDEO project manager for the Amtrak project:

> *'There was considerable nervousness amongst the engineers in Palo Alto when we undertook this project. I remember pulling David Kelley (CEO of IDEO) aside and asking him for advice. He said that all we have to do is focus on the users, get the story out of them and build a solution out of it – that if we stick to what we know best, it'll be fine.'*

The design of both services and products is based on the same fundamental principles outlined earlier in the IDEO process section. Projects follow the basic steps of observation, synthesis, idea generation, refinement and implementation. *'Service design is not fundamentally different from product design. The fundamental methods we use in service design don't differ, they're just tailored'*, says Laura Weiss.

Service design projects also tend to have different staffing requirements due to the difference in the nature of the projects. Whilst service design is inherently usercentred, it also requires a systems-oriented approach and 'big picture' thinking due to the large number of implications that a service has across an organisation.

## Amtrak (1998)

When Amtrak was doing market research for the launch of its new Acela high-speed trains service serving the North-East corridor in the United States (Boston–New York–Washington D.C.), it discovered that people still loved trains but were sick of them being treated like a commodity. According to Barbara Richardon, Executive Vice President of Amtrak: *'People love the notion of travelling a long distance, relaxing, looking out of the window'*, but *'what was discouraging to us was that none of that translated to Amtrak. We were viewed like a utility.'*[9] Looking to provide a better passenger experience, Amtrak turned to IDEO to work on what would be one of its first service design projects.

IDEO's initial mandate was to design only the armchairs for the trains, which in itself was no trivial project given that most people view journey comfort as the most important criteria when they travel on trains. IDEO quickly realised that the seat was but one component in the overall customer experience; if Amtrak's new service was to be successful the entire consumer experience would have to be tackled.

As part of its research, IDEO embarked on several different strategies during its empathic observation phase. First, IDEO human factors experts[10] 'shadowed' a broad range of rail travellers: retired grandparents visiting their grandchildren, a businessman on a business trip, a young couple with kids going on vacation. For each group, IDEO tried to understand where the existing service was substandard, and which aspects of the service could be improved. They even shadowed a person in a wheelchair through the station and during the journey to get a feel for what he went through to get on the train and use it. But the observations didn't just stop at the customers. IDEO also surveyed train employees – everyone from conductors and train drivers to senior managers and station operators – to get more information not just about customer usage patterns and complaints, but also about what the train staff required to do their job better.

IDEO discovered that, in the customer's mind, a train journey started long before they actually boarded the train, and extended for a period of time after they had disembarked. To better understand the different stages of travel, IDEO created a 'customer journey' map which articulated the 10 steps that people went through on an Amtrak train ride, as follows:

| | |
|---|---|
| 1 Learning (about routes, times etc.) | 6 Waiting |
| 2 Planning | 7 Boarding |
| 3 Starting | 8 Riding |
| 4 Entering | 9 Arriving |
| 5 Ticketing | 10 Continuing (on their journey) |

IDEO realised that in order to provide customers with the service they were seeking it would have to design all 10 steps in the customer's journey, not just the train ride. *'We wanted to create a seamless journey'*, says Richard Eiserman, IDEO's project leader on Acela. *'Riding on the train was actually the eighth step. The 10 points became the core of what we tried to do. We wanted to look at design implications across the board.'*[11]

The customer journey framework has proved to be an enormously successful tool within the IDEO repertoire of service design methods. Essentially, a customer journey map is a blueprint for all the steps a user must go through in a service. The act of documenting the service is one that is highly useful, though not widespread. Observes Dr. Hollins: *'Unlike manufacturing organisations, in the service design field specifications . . . tend not to be written.'*[12] The customer journey framework enables a service designer to think about every step the user will take through a service, and also to account for all the different service 'touch-points', i.e., the points within the service environment when the user interacts with particular service components. Concurs Fran Samalionis, another London-based principal of the Service Design Practice within IDEO: *'A large component of service design is trying to make tangible the interactions that occur during the provision of a service.'*

The customer journey framework is useful because it enables service designers to make the invisible visible. The information gleaned through the processes used above guided the development of IDEO's three main deliverables:

- Train layout and design
- A set of station concepts (to deal with the other aspects of the customer journey)
- A brand strategy and image platform (done in coordination with a branding strategy firm)

IDEO subsequently worked closely with Amtrak on the implementation of the train layout and design, overhauling everything from the bathroom experience to the system for luggage handling. To appropriately prototype the various components of the service, IDEO built half a train car within its studio in Boston. They used the train car to mock up the passenger section, the service car and even the bathroom. All the prototyping was 'quick and dirty' using foam core[13] to represent virtually everything. As part of the prototyping, IDEO got actual service personnel from Amtrak and potential passengers to walk through the mocked-up cars and make comments and suggestions.

Recalls Ilya Prokopoff, an IDEO designer involved on the project:

*'For Amtrak, this was not just business as usual. They really needed to understand what their customer needs were, and organise the disparate elements of their system in a way*

*that hadn't been done before in order to meet those customer needs. We had to take a wider view and think about systems design and not just at the object level. We had to understand how everything connected together and focus on linkages, as the service straddled many intermediate steps captured in the customer journey framework.*

*We did a great job on building the hardware, because that's what we know how to do well. We didn't really focus on enabling the people who were delivering the service and training them to do so. That's something that has changed in IDEO over the past few years.'*

## Juniper financial (1999)

When a group of former employees of Wingspan, one of the first online banks, left to start Juniper Financial, they called on IDEO to help them define and establish their strategy, determine the suite of product offerings with a consistent service proposition and create the interface for the company's website.

IDEO realised that the founders of Juniper needed to decide who their customers would be, what those customers wanted and how they currently managed their finances. According to Fran Samalionis, the IDEO project leader: *'The founders of Juniper ... wanted to solve everything that was wrong with banking.'*

The IDEO team was composed of a mix of people specialising in human factors, business factors, environments design and more traditional product and industrial designers. Says Samalionis:

*'Even though most of the people were experts in one particular area, most of them had developed significant exposure and experience in another field. That's true about service design in general: you need to turn up the volume on the T-shapedness of the people – people who have both a breadth of experience and a depth of expertise . . . For most service design projects it's useful to bring "systems" thinking people into the team – physicists rather than engineers. They need to understand how systems are designed, how they interact, how one component will affect the others.'*

The first step was to understand the customer and the customer experience. IDEO and Juniper could then translate the customer experience into the value proposition for the customer, and use that to determine the specific service offerings.

To understand customers and their needs, IDEO conducted interviews in cities across the US. In contrast to traditional methods of market research such as focus groups and surveys, IDEO used techniques that were more in line with empathic research. Members of the IDEO project team acted like 'flies on the wall', watching how people used online banking, closely noting how they navigated through the interface, which functions and offers were used and how frequently. IDEO also walked through their homes and got people to show them what items they associated with money.

Another method used in this project was an empathic exercise known as 'Be a bill'. IDEO team members examined how bills would move through people's homes to try and understand the rituals around finance based on these patterns. The 'Be a . . .' method enables IDEO designers to get a perspective on an entire system by choosing an inanimate object within the system and observing the path it takes and the interactions that occur through the system. According to Samalionis: *'It was amazing to see how defined these patterns were. Bills would enter in the mailbox, then get passed into the kitchen and on to the bedroom or the study where they would get stacked until they reached a certain height before they got paid.'*

Another method IDEO used was to ask people to 'draw their money' to get a better understanding of what emotional ties people had to their money and finances. Says Samalionis:

*'The "draw your money" had face validity. It wasn't statistically significant in terms of market research, but the exercise proved to be enormously useful in segmenting the customer base. People are amazingly articulate when it comes to drawing stuff. And if nothing else, the technique stimulates conversation. The "draw your < whatever >" method is just a different way of tapping into the emotional aspects of a service. When it came to Juniper, we realised that people had very different emotional responses to money. Some weren't very engaged with their money – they viewed money as a means to an end . . . Others were very engaged with the management of their money, and what money meant . . . People's perspectives on money also varied over time: some had a very long-term outlook on money, and others had a much shorter-term view on money.'*

**Figure 1  Draw your money segments**

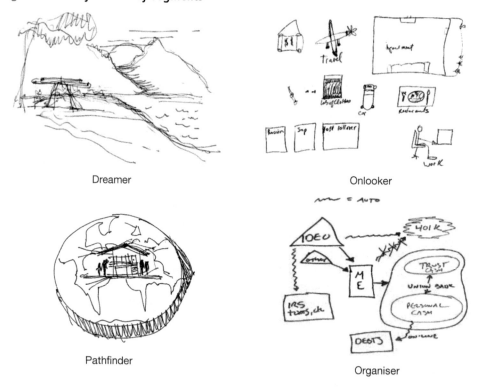

Dreamer

Onlooker

Pathfinder

Organiser

Based on the 'draw your money' exercise and the other empathic research, IDEO came up with four customer segments for Juniper. They divided up the potential customer base according to the level of engagement people had with their money, and the time horizon for their involvement with money.

Figure 2 **Juniper's customer segments**

```
┌──────────────────────────────────────────────────────────────────────┐
│  USER GROUPS                        long-term view                      │
│                                                                          │
│  DREAMER                            PATHFINDER                           │
│                                                                          │
│  ● achieving ultimate personal      ● have a holistic view of finances   │
│    goals/satisfaction is              that provides security and is a    │
│    facilitated by the vehicle         goal in and of itself              │
│    of finances                      ● sophisticated consumer of          │
│  ● should be more proactive           financial services                │
│    with finances (guilt)            ● inherent knowledge they are        │
│  ● optimistic/idyllic                 willing to share                   │
│  ● confident                        ● strong point of view               │
│  ● focused on possibilities         ● focused on the big picture         │
│                                                                          │
│  low engagement ────────────────────────────── high engagement          │
│                                                                          │
│  ONLOOKER                           ORGANISER                            │
│                                                                          │
│  ● focused on immediate wants       ● characterised by a need to know    │
│    and needs rather than              exactly what is going on, in       │
│    longer-term financial goals        detail, beyond the bottom line     │
│  ● low expectations for             ● mistrust of financial institutions │
│    financial services               ● maximise efficiency                │
│  ● pays for convenience             ● make the most from money           │
│  ● cash flows out                   ● controlling their money is part    │
│  ● focused on what money buys         of controlling their lives         │
│                                                                          │
│                         short-term view                                  │
└──────────────────────────────────────────────────────────────────────┘
```

Juniper then had to decide which customer segment they would target first. IDEO created giant posters of people representing each of the different customer segments. In a meeting in Wilmington (Delaware), IDEO got all the Juniper employees together in one room (at the time there were about 25 of them) and went through each of the segments to identify which ones Juniper would chase after. In the end it was decided that Jupiter would target the Onlookers: they needed the most help with their finances and were most likely to be loyal to services that they liked, attitudes that resonated well with the ethos at Juniper.

The service definition flowed from the customer segment decision. According to Samalionis: *'The customer segment decision then drove all our subsequent decisions: it determined what features we would offer as part of the service, what the interface would look like – everything.'* For example, IDEO realised that Onlookers were least likely to pay their credit card bills on time. Thus, they would appreciate and depend on message alerts to remind them when payments were due.

Based on the customer segments, IDEO came up with an 'experience architecture' schematic for the company and the service offering. This was a visual representation of the customer's online experience at the Juniper website. Similar to a customer journey, the experience architecture enabled service designers to map out and visualise all the major service 'touchpoints' during a customer's interaction with the service. The experience architecture dictated the specific nature of the service offerings, and how they interacted with each other.

Figure 3 **Experience architecture**

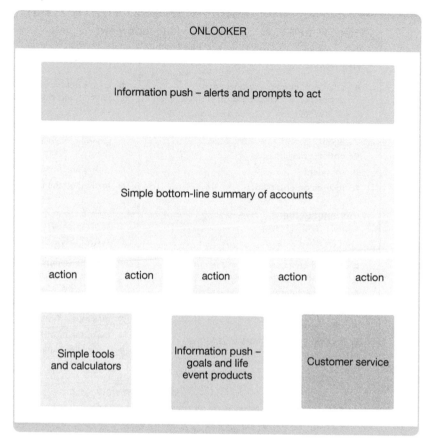

Another method that IDEO utilised for the Juniper project was the 'path to participation'. While an experience architecture prototyped one single interaction between the user and the service, the path to participation was meant to chart the evolution of the repeated interactions between the user and the service over time.

Figure 4 **Path to participation**

The subsequent design of the website, both in terms of functionality and form, was largely driven by the customer segmentation and experience architectures developed.

Recalls Samalionis about the service design process:

*'Having had four more years of experience with service design, would we do things differently? Probably. A couple of basic steps that we do these days are experience and information audits right at the beginning of a project. An experience audit is when we look at the various touch-points for a particular service and audit them, both from the perspective of the user and the organisation, to get a better idea of what's working and what's not. An information audit is used to figure out where the information in an organisation resides and how it moves through the organisation. After all, at the end of the day it is information that enables the provision of a service.'*

## AT&T mMode (2003)

In January 2003, AT&T Wireless asked IDEO to assist it in designing a new, easier-to-use interface for its mMode service. mMode was the GPRS service[14] launched in 2002 to enable users to surf the web, conduct transactions, send and receive messages and carry out a host of other data-driven functions. Says Sam Hall, a vice-president at AT&T Wireless: *'It was clear that we had reached beyond the classic 35-year-old early adopter. We saw our customers are now moms and teens and older folks.'*[15] The new design was supposed to help AT&T Wireless make the service appealing to the wider mainstream market.

IDEO was tasked with providing a new user interface for the mMode service and a style guide that would be passed to content partners to guide them in the development of third-party content for the service.

IDEO usually hosts a project kick-off prior to the start of the actual project itself in order to get the client to buy in to 'the IDEO way' and get an understanding of its innovation process. For this project, IDEO took the AT&T Wireless managers on a scavenger hunt in San Francisco. Executives were shuttled around San Francisco in cars, and asked to conduct basic errands such as finding a book or buying an aspirin. Whilst everything they were asked to do was theoretically possible using mMode, they were allowed to use any means they wanted to accomplish the tasks.

The executives quickly found out that it wasn't as easy as they thought it would be. For starters, the mMode service went down midway through the game. Eventually, frustrated by their inability to use the mMode service effectively, they resorted to traditional methods like looking up a phone directory, or asking someone on the street.

Says Laura Weiss, one of the leads on the AT&T project: *'The aim of the scavenger hunt was to get the AT&T people to start thinking from the user's perspective. The scavenger hunt was very effective in showing them just how difficult the service was: they got a first hand view of what worked and what didn't.'*

The problem was that whereas the mMode service, much like other mobile data services at the time, had been designed as a portable web browser, the cell-phone was a vastly different medium from the computer and needed to be designed for accordingly.

In designing the user interface for the phone, IDEO needed to understand exactly what a mobile was meant to do – from the users' perspective, naturally. Says Weiss: *'When we're doing the research for a particular project we try and look for "extreme users" – i.e.*

*people who fit a particular profile, use (or are likely to use) a particular service fairly often and hence will be able to give interesting results fairly quickly.'* In the case of mMode, IDEO talked to a range of extreme phone users from teenagers in school to business people on the go. In addition, IDEO had to consider a whole other set of stakeholders as well, says Weiss:

> 'We had to talk to the third-party content developers and ensure that the newly designed user interface would meet their requirements as well as those of end users. In service design projects you end up dealing with an ecosystem and not just the end users. And if you don't deal with all the stakeholders, you don't have a great service solution. The business element in a service design project is probably more important than in product design projects. Designing a service is as close to designing a business as you can get. Thus, it's more critical to introduce the business factors into the design process as early on as possible.'

The third-party content developers were critical to the success of mMode: if they were not happy with the new service design, or their requirements were not accommodated, then they wouldn't develop services for mMode, and users wouldn't use their phones as much.

The insight gained from the interviews and observations allowed IDEO to create a set of unified design principles that would act as a platform for the development of the new user interface and the accompanying style guide for the mMode service. The three guiding design principles were:

*Social:* This was based on the notion that data services needed to provide connectivity between people, the way voice is able to, but also go beyond and create rich communities and social networks.

**Figure 5 'Social' design principle (note the phone display as well)**

*TimeSlice:* Interacting with data on a mobile phone is fundamentally different from surfing the Web on a PC. On a mobile phone, people are more task-orientated and stay online for small slices of time instead of surfing for long, sustained periods. Thus, the interface needs to be able to support services that can be done in 20 or 30 seconds, with a greater focus on immediacy and access.

Figure 6 'TimeSlice' design principle (note the phone display as well)

*Relevance:* The mMode services needed to be relevant, not just from a geographical and contextual perspective, but also relevant to the individual. A person's phone is as personal as their wallet. The relevance of the service could be best expressed through two main tenets:

● *Customisation* (e.g. the four most frequently used functions were organised together for faster and easier navigation)

● *Personalisation* (e.g. a personal storage space on the service to store ring-tones and screensavers for the phone)

Based on the three design principles listed above, IDEO created a style guide, the codified set of design rules that third-party developers were expected to adhere to when developing content for the mMode service. The user interface developed by IDEO for the mMode service was based around the design principles and style guide it had itself created.

For every screen IDEO would mock up several variations using a cardboard cutout phone and printed pieces of paper depicting the screen. The IDEO team would storyboard the navigation and user interface through the use of these screens, quickly and cheaply, without the need for expensive programming. IDEO would create several variations for each screen and test the variations with users to see which ones worked best. The final user interface implementation was based on the selected prototypes.

In the two months after the launch of the new and improved mMode service, AT&T Wireless realised initial success around three critical measures: an increase in page-views-per-visit (a good indicator of the time users are spending online), an increase in m-commerce (a good indicator of the overall sales of premium content for content partners), and compliance by an overwhelming majority of third-party developers with the newly-issued style guide, a testament to the quality of work done by IDEO, especially considering that the developers themselves had to bear the costs of changing their existing designs to conform.

## The Portland General Health Center project

Coughlan ruminated about the Portland General Health Center project. The health-care industry was not completely unknown to IDEO though: a significant number of its projects and a large share of its revenues came from the design and engineering of medical devices – products such as Lilly's insulin pens, the Heartstream ForeRunner defibrillator and the Oral-B Gripper toothbrush. Even so, IDEO had no direct experience in the design of healthcare services, and that made the project even more challenging. Coughlan was confident that the IDEO process could be easily transposed to healthcare services, just as it had to the other service design projects in the past. Besides, IDEO was always eager to expand into new practice areas and expand its design process by exposure to new industries.

Coughlan had been asked by Becker to focus on the patient experience at the hospital and suggest steps for improving the quality of the healthcare service. Additionally, the project's budget constraints meant that IDEO would have to work within the existing hospital parameters: quick and cheap incremental innovation would be required.

IDEO had come a long way in the five years it had been involved in service design. It had a fairly robust process and had developed a full suite of methods to be used in the design of a service. As Coughlan drained the dregs of his coffee, he wondered how best to approach this particular project. What process would he follow? Which of the established IDEO methods would he use, and at which stages? Wrestling with these thoughts as he finished up his strong decaf double no-fat soya latte macchiato, he went back upstairs to meet with Tim Brown.

Exhibit 1 **IDEO practice areas as of January 2005**

| Practice Area | Description |
|---|---|
| CxD | Consumer Experience Design, focused on creating emotional connections between people and companies, applying IDEO's 'from think to build' concept to experiences. |
| SX | Experiences revolving around the design of software experiences based on PC, internet, mobile and emerging platforms. |
| Health | Healthcare-related projects. |
| Transformation | A change consultancy practice, teaching clients how to foster innovation within their own companies. |
| Zero20 | Focused on designing products and services for children. |
| Smart Space | Focused on the emerging field of environment design. |
| Service Design | Centred on service design and innovation. |

**Exhibit 2** **IDEO's product development process**

**This is the IDEO Way**

Five steps in the process of designing a better consumer experience

**1. OBSERVATION**

IDEO's cognitive psychologists, anthropologists, and sociologists team up with corporate clients to understand the consumer experience. Some of IDEO's techniques:

**Shadowing** Observing people using products, shopping, going to hospitals, taking the train, using their cell phone.

**Behavioural mapping** Photographing people within a space, such as a hospital waiting room, over two or three days.

**Consumer journey** Keeping track of all the interactions a consumer has with a product, service, or space.

**Camera journals** Asking consumers to keep visual diaries of their activities and impressions relating to a product.

**Extreme user interviews** Talking to people who really know – or know nothing – about a product or service, and evaluating their experience using it.

**Storytelling** Prompting people to tell personal stories about their consumer experiences.

**Unfocus groups** Interviewing a diverse group of people. To explore ideas about sandals, IDEO gathered an artist, a bodybuilder, a podiatrist, and a shoe fetishist.

**2. BRAINSTORMING**

An intense, idea-generating session analysing data gathered by observing people. Each lasts no more than an hour. Rules of brainstorming are strict and are stencilled on the walls:

**Defer judgement** Don't dismiss any ideas.

**Build on the ideas of others** No 'buts', only 'ands'.

**Encourage wild ideas** Embrace the most out-of-the-box notions because they can be the key to solutions.

**Go for quantity** Aim for as many new ideas as possible. In a good session, up to 100 ideas are generated in 60 minutes.

**Be visual** Use yellow, red, and blue markers to write on big 30 × 25-inch Post-its that are put on a wall.

**Stay focused on the topic** Always keep the discussion on-target.

**One conversation at a time** No interrupting, no dismissing, no disrespect, no rudeness.

Exhibit 2 **Continued**

---

### 3. RAPID PROTOTYPING

Mocking up working models helps everyone visualise possible solutions and speeds up decision-making and innovation. Some guidelines:

**Mock up everything** It is possible to create models not only of products but also of services such as healthcare and spaces such as museum lobbies.

**Use videography** Make short movies to depict the consumer experience.

**Go fast** Build mock-ups quickly and cheaply. Never waste time on complicated concepts.

**No frills** Make prototypes that demonstrate a design idea without sweating over the details.

**Create scenarios** Show how a variety of people use a service in different ways and how various designs can meet their individual needs.

**Bodystorm** Delineate different types of consumers and act out their roles.

---

### 4. REFINING

At this stage, **IDEO** narrows down the choices to a few possibilities. Here's how it's done:

**Brainstorm** in rapid fashion to weed out ideas and focus on the remaining best options.

**Focus prototyping** on a few key ideas to arrive at an optimal solution to a problem.

**Engage the client** actively in the process of narrowing the choices.

**Be disciplined** and ruthless in making selections.

**Focus** on the outcome of the process – reaching the best possible solution.

**Get agreement** from all stakeholders. The more top-level executives who sign off on the solution, the better the chances of success.

---

### 5. IMPLEMENTATION

Bring **IDEO**'s strong engineering, design, and social-science capabilities to bear when actually creating a product or service.

**Tap all resources** Involve **IDEO**'s diverse workforce from 40 countries to carry out the plans.

**The workforce** Employees have advanced degrees in different kinds of engineering: mechanical, electrical, biomedical, software, aerospace, and manufacturing. Many are experts in materials science, computer-aided design, robotics, computer science, movie special effects, moulding, industrial interaction, graphic and Web information, fashion and automotive design, business, communications, linguistics, sociology, ergonomics, cognitive psychology, biomechanics, art therapy, ethnology, management consulting, statistics, medicine, and zoology.

---

*Source*: Bruce Nussbaum. (2004) 'The Power of Design', *BusinessWeek*, 17 May, p. 71.

**Exhibit 3 IDEO method cards**

IDEO Method Cards show some of the ways that IDEO puts people at the centre of the design process. These methods are typically used at the earliest stages of the design process to support observation-based research and learning consistent with the firm's user-centred design process. The techniques are not proprietary and have been adapted from various established human and social research methods. Initially compiled to inspire and inform IDEO's own design teams, the cards are now available publicly to inspire creative teams in almost any context.

---

*Shadowing*

*How:* Tag along with people to observe and understand their day-to-day routines, interactions and contexts.
*Why:* This is a valuable way to reveal design opportunities and show how a product might affect or complement users' behaviour.

---

*Extreme User Interviews*

*How:* Identify individuals who are extremely familiar or completely unfamiliar with the product and ask them to evaluate their experience using it.
*Why:* These individuals are often able to highlight key issues of the design problem and provide insights for design improvements.

---

*Draw the Experience*

*How:* Ask the participants to visualise an experience through drawings and diagrams.
*Why:* This can be a good way to debunk assumptions and reveal how people conceive of and order their experiences or activities.

---

*Fly on the Wall*

*How:* Observe and record behaviour within its context, without interfering with people's activities.
*Why:* It is useful to see what people actually do within real contexts and time frames, rather than accept what they say they did after the fact.

---

*Role Playing*

*How:* Identify stakeholders involved in the design problem and assign those roles to members of the team.
*Why:* By enacting the activities within a real or imagined context, the team can trigger empathy for actual users and raise other relevant issues.

Exhibit 3 **Continued**

---

### Character Profiles

*How:* Based on the observations of real people, develop character profiles to represent archetypes and the details of their behaviour or lifestyles.

*Why:* This is a useful way to bring a typical customer to life and to communicate the value of different concepts to various target groups.

---

### Bodystorming

*How:* Set up a scenario and act out roles, with or without props, focusing on the intuitive responses prompted by the physical enactment.

*Why:* This method helps to quickly generate and test out many context and behaviour-based concepts.

---

### Camera Journal

*How:* Ask potential users to keep a written and visual diary of their impressions, circumstances, and activities related to the product.

*Why:* This rich, self-conducted notation technique is useful for prompting users to reveal points of view and patterns of behaviour.

---

### Narration

*How:* As they perform a process or execute a specific task, ask participants to describe aloud what they are thinking.

*Why:* This is a useful way to reach users' motivations, concerns, perceptions and reasoning.

---

### Quick-and-Dirty Prototyping

*How:* Using any materials available, quickly assemble possible forms or interactions for evaluation.

*Why:* This is a good way to communicate a concept to the team and evaluate how to refine the design.

---

*Source*: IDEO Method Cards deck.

This case was written by Ritesh Bhavnani, Research Associate and INSEAD MBA (July 2004), and Manuel Sosa, Assistant Professor of Technology and Operations Management at INSEAD, as a basis for class discussion rather than to illustrate either effective or ineffective handling of an administrative situation. The information in this case has been obtained from both public sources and company interviews. © 2006 INSEAD

## Notes on the case

1. In 2004, the company won 10 Industrial Design Excellence Awards (IDEA), double the number of the next two firms, Smart Design and fuseproject, each of which won five.
2. Christopher Hawthorne. (2002) 'The IDEO Cure', *Metropolis Magazine*, October, pp. 3–7.
3. Bruce Nussbaum. (2004) 'The Power of Design', *Business Week*, 17 May, p. 75.
4. Laura Weiss. (2002) 'Developing Tangible Strategies', *Design Management Journal*, Winter, p. 34.
5. Harold Greenberg. (2004) 'Building a Better mMode', *mMode Magazine*, Fall, p. 34.
6. For details on IDEO's brainstorming refer to Kelley, T., *The Art of Innovation* (chapter 4), 2002.
7. Catherine Fredman. (2002) 'The IDEO Difference', *Hemispheres Magazine*, August, p. 56.
8. http://www.livework.co.uk/home/research0/glossary.html
9. 'Acela', @ Amtrak Magazine, p. 25
10. Human factors specialists, according to IDEO's website, employ a range of observational and empathic techniques to understand the issues people face and are an integral part of interdisciplinary design teams.
11. 'Acela', @ Amtrak Magazine, p. 27.
12. Dr. Bill Hollins, 'About: Service Design', www.designcouncil.org.uk, p. 11.
13. Foam core is also a sheet material, like cardboard, and is used extensively in art and design projects.
14. GPRS stands for General Packet Radio Service, and is traditionally considered as 2.5G, enabling data to be transferred wirelessly at speeds of up to approximately 500 Kbps.
15. Harold Greenberg. (2003) 'Building a Better mMode', *mMode Magazine*, Fall, p. 34.

# 10 SLAGELSE INDUSTRIAL SERVICES (SIS)[1]

## Nigel Slack and Michael Lewis

Slagelse Industrial Services (SIS) had become one of Europe's most respected zinc, aluminium and magnesium die-cast parts suppliers, serving hundreds of companies in many industries, especially automotive and defence. The company cast and engineered precision components by combining the most modern production technologies with precise tooling and craftsmanship. Slagelse Industrial Services (SIS) began life as a classic family firm when Erik Paulsen opened a small manufacturing and die-casting business in his hometown of Slagelse – a town in east Denmark, about 100 km southwest of Copenhagen. He had successfully leveraged his skills and passion for craftsmanship over many years, whilst serving a variety of different industrial and agricultural customers. His son, Anders, had spent nearly 10 years working as a production engineer for a large automotive parts supplier in the UK, but eventually returned to Slagelse to take over the family firm. Exploiting his experience in mass manufacturing, Anders spent years building the firm into a larger-scale industrial component manufacturer, but retained his father's commitment to quality and customer service. After 20 years he sold the firm to a UK-owned industrial conglomerate, and within 10 years it had doubled in size again and employed in the region of 600 people, with a turnover approaching £200 million. Throughout this period the firm had continued to target its products into niche industrial markets where its emphasis upon product quality and dependability meant it was less vulnerable to price and cost pressures. However, in 2009, in the midst of difficult economic times and widespread industrial restructuring, the company had been encouraged to bid for higher-volume, lower-margin work. This process was not very successful but eventually culminated in a tender for the design and production of a core metallic element of a child's toy (a 'transforming' robot).

Interestingly, the client firm, Alden Toys, was also a major customer for other businesses owned by SIS's corporate parent. It was adopting a preferred-supplier policy and intended to have only one or two purchase points for specific elements in its global toy business. Alden Toys had a high degree of trust in the parent organisation, and on visiting the SIS site was impressed by the firm's depth of experience and commitment to quality. In 2010, Alden Toys selected SIS to complete the design and begin trial production:

> 'Some of us were really excited by the prospect . . . but you have to be a little worried when volumes are much greater than anything you've done before. I guess the risk seemed okay because in the basic process steps, in the type of product if you like, we were making something that felt very similar to what we'd been doing for many years.'

(SIS Operations Manager)

> 'Well obviously we didn't know anything about the toy market but then again we didn't really know all that much about the auto industry or the defence sector or any of our

*traditional customers before we started serving them. Our key competitive advantage, our capabilities, call it what you will, they are all about keeping the customer happy, about meeting and sometimes exceeding specification.'*

(SIS Marketing Director)

The designers had received an outline product specification from Alden Toys during the bid process and some further technical detail afterwards. Upon receipt of this final brief, a team of engineers and managers confirmed that the product could and would be manufactured using an up-scaled version of current production processes. The key operational challenge appeared to be accessing sufficient (but not too much) capacity. Fortunately, for a variety of reasons, the parent company was very supportive of the project and promised to underwrite any sensible capital expenditure plans. Although this opinion of the nature of the production challenge was widely accepted throughout the firm (and shared by Alden Toys and SIS's parent group), it was left to one specific senior engineer to actually sign both the final bid and technical completion documentation. By early 2011, the firm had begun a trial period of full-volume production. Unfortunately, as would become clear later, during this design validation process SIS had effectively sanctioned a production method that would prove to be entirely inappropriate for the toy market, but it was not until 12 months later that any indication of problems began to emerge.

Throughout both North America and Europe, individual customers began to claim that their children had been 'poisoned' whilst playing with the end product. The threat of litigation was quickly levelled at Alden Toys and the whole issue rapidly became a 'full-blown' child health scare. A range of pressure groups and legal damage specialists supported and acted to aggregate the individual claims. Although similar accusations had been made before, the litigants and their supporters focused in on the recent changes made to the production process at SIS and, in particular, the role of Alden Toys in managing its suppliers.

*'... it's all very well claiming that you trust your suppliers but you simply cannot have the same level of control over another firm in another country. I am afraid that this all comes down to simple economics, that Alden Toys put its profits before children's health. Talk about trust ... parents trusted this firm to look out for them and their families and have every right to be angry that boardroom greed was more important!'*

(Legal spokesperson for US litigants when being interviewed on UK TV consumer rights show)

Under intense media pressure, Alden Toys rapidly convened a high-profile investigation into the source of the contamination. It quickly revealed that an 'unauthorised' chemical had been employed in an apparently trivial metal cleaning and preparation element of the SIS production process. Although when interviewed by the US media, the parent firm's legal director emphasised there was '*no causal link established or any admission of liability by either party*', Alden Toys immediately withdrew its order and began to signal an intent to bring legal action against SIS and its parent. This action brought an immediate end to production in this part of the operation and the inspection (and subsequent official and legal visits) had a crippling impact upon the productivity of the whole site. The competitive impact of the failure was extremely significant. After over a year of production, the new product accounted for more than a third (39 per cent) of the factory's output. In addition to major cash-flow implications, the various investigations took up lots of managerial time and the reputation of the firm was seriously affected. As the site operations manager explained, even their traditional customers expressed concerns:

*'It's amazing but people we had been supplying for thirty or forty years were calling me up and asking "[Manager's name] what's going on?" and that they were worried about what all this might mean for them . . . these are completely different markets!'*

## Note on the case

1   This case originally appeared in Slack, N., Brandon-Jones, A., Johnston, R. and Betts, A. (2012) *Operations and Process Management*, 3rd edition. Harlow, UK: Pearson Education.

# Index